The Hamlyn CHILDREN'S ENCYCLOPEDIA in colour

The Hamlyn CHILDREN'S ENCYCLOPEDIA in colour

Revised Edition

DEAN

Edited by Kenneth Bailey

The publishers wish to thank the following contributors:

Writers

Kenneth Bailey
Alan Blackwood
Joan Fisher
Janet Haffner
A. P. Harvey
Robin Kerrod
Alfred Leutscher
Brenda Lewis
Moira Maclean
Brian Mathew
Robin May
Elizabeth Palmer
E. A. Walsh
David Young

Artists

Martin Aitcheson
Barrington Barber
Norman Barber
Henry Barnet
John Beswick
Hugh Chevins
Ralph Coventry
Gordon Davies
Gerry Embleton
Ron Embleton
Dan Escott
Gay John Galsworthy
Ian Garrard
Bill Geldart
Gwen Green
Harry Green
Roger Hall
John Keay
Ken Kirkland
Ivan Lapper
Barry Linklater
Gary Long
Angus McBride
Malcolm McGregor
Bob Mathias
Max Studios
James Nichols
David Nockels
Richard Orr
Outline
Bill Robertshaw
John Robinson
Meg Rutherford
Michael Shoebridge
Sally Slight
John Smith
Bill Stallion
George Thompson
Peter Thornley
Carlo Tora
George Tuckwell
Leo Walmsley
Ross Wardle
David Warner
Peter Warner
Brian Watson
Whitecroft Designs Limited
Michael Whittlesea
John W. Wood
Walter Wright

This edition published 1994 by Dean,
an imprint of Reed Children's Book's Limited,
Michelin House, 81 Fulham Road, London SW3 6RB,
and Auckland, Melbourne, Singapore and Toronto.

ISBN 0 603 55429 6

British Library Cataloguing-in-Publication Data
A catalogue record for this book is available from the British Library.

Printed in the Czech Republic

Contents

6 Introduction
7 The country we live in
49 The world we live in
145 The world of plants and animals
241 The world of science and invention
337 The world of ideas and beliefs
433 The world of art and music
529 Index
544 Acknowledgements

Introduction

The Hamlyn Children's Encyclopedia in Colour tells in one volume the exciting story of human thought and achievement. Everyone has a natural instinct to explore and this encyclopedia will help you to look further and deeper into the wonderful world of today. The book covers a vast range of knowledge and will capture your interest with words and pictures. Each chapter may be read as a continuous story, showing how things are related to each other and have developed historically. The encyclopedia is presented in six sections and the following outline gives a general idea of how the subjects are arranged.

The country we live in
Britain's history and traditions – The British people – Social customs
Language – King and Parliament – The Industrial Revolution
Social and economic history – Great events in British history

The world we live in
The earth's age and structure – Rocks and minerals – Precious stones, ores and natural products – Shaping the land – The oceans – Currents and tides – Exploration and discovery – Maps and charts – The solar system – The galaxies – Nature and origin of the universe – Astronomy – Space travel

The world of plants and animals
The balance of nature – Classification of plants – Reproduction
Bacteria and viruses – Plants for food and raw materials – Animal characteristics – Food chains – Animal classification – Evolution and the coming of man – Fossils – Prehistoric animals – Survey of all forms of animal life

The world of science and invention
The microscopic world – The elements – Time, motion and energy
Gravity – Transport – Aeronautics – Space flight – Sound waves
Radio and television – Movement of forces – The electron
Electricity in nature – X-rays and lasers – Atomic energy – Medical science – Inventors and inventions

The world of ideas and beliefs
Early literature – Systems of writing – Greek and Roman literature
The Renaissance – The novel – Drama – Mass communication
The theatre and popular entertainment – Religions of prehistory – The living religions – Myths and legends – Philosophy and philosophers

The world of art and music
Form and structure – Light and colour – Drawing and painting
Sculpture – Metal work and ceramics – Textiles – Architecture
Photography – Early music – Greek music – History of western music and composers – The world of the dance

Each section contains its own list of contents with page references and there is a detailed index at the back of the book. There are facts enough to answer your most demanding questions, but this is not simply a book to look things up in – it is a book to read and enjoy.

The country we live in

CONTENTS

9 The country we live in
The United Kingdom – The people of Britain – The English language – William the Conqueror – Systems of government – Parliamentary democracy – Simon de Montfort – Henry VIII and Parliament – Divine right of kings – The Civil War – Restoration of the monarchy – The Bill of Rights – The House of Lords – Freedom of speech – The Industrial Revolution – The Poor Laws – The Chartists – The suffragettes – Commons versus Lords – The People's Budget – The Law – Trial by Jury – Protection for the poor – Insurance and welfare – Working conditions – Peterloo – Trade Unions – Rise of the Labour Party – The General Strike – Education, health and housing – Religious toleration – The British Empire – Immigrants to Britain – Roads and canals – The railways – Growth of cities – Agriculture – Town planning – Britain and its European partners – Britain in the 1980s

44 Great events in British history

48 Facts about Britain

The country we live in

Britain is a country teeming with history. In almost every part of her islands, history stands like a sentinel of the past: the magnificent and ancient cathedral at Canterbury, or the Norman keep of the Tower of London, or the mysterious lonely blocks of Stonehenge on Salisbury Plain.

Workmen laying the foundations of new buildings dig up history by the spadeful: it can be dredged from rivers or washed up on shores, and it can even turn up in back gardens.

In 1954, when the Temple of Mithras was uncovered during building work in the City of London, the discovery made newspaper headlines for days. Spectators flocked to this silent relic of Britain's Roman past.

One hundred and twenty years or so earlier, the banks of the Thames were thick with crowds when the building of the new London Bridge revealed hundreds of Roman coins buried deep in the river bed.

These people, and millions of others both before and since, came to see what they thought of as history; to try to imagine the time when the Temple of Mithras was a scene of worship, or when Roman coins were actually spent in shops.

However, history is found not only in such remnants of the past. The people themselves, more than all the historic old houses, ancient temples, coins and other objects which are left behind, are the history of a country.

This is found in the way people look, the way they live, the way they are governed, the way they work, and the way they think. History lies in the privileges that people enjoy, in the traditions they observe and in the duties they are called upon to perform as citizens.

The United Kingdom

The proper title of Britain is the United Kingdom of Great Britain and Northern Ireland. Great Britain consists of England, Scotland and Wales.

Not belonging to the United Kingdom, but existing as dependencies of the English Crown, are the Channel Islands, which lie to the south-west

Above Stonehenge on Salisbury Plain in Wiltshire is a prehistoric monument dating from about 1500 BC. The main structure consisted of thirty upright stones erected in a circle and linked by lintel stones across their tops. Within the circle other stones were set up, including an 'altar' stone. The structure's purpose is not known but it was probably to do with a religious cult linked with worship of the sun. Certain stones are seen to act as pointers to sunrises and sunsets and could have been used for astronomical calculations.

REGIONS OF SCOTLAND
1 SHETLAND (Islands Area)
2 ORKNEY (Islands Area)
3 WESTERN ISLES (Islands Area)
4 HIGHLAND
5 GRAMPIAN
6 TAYSIDE
7 STRATHCLYDE
8 CENTRAL
9 FIFE
10 LOTHIAN
11 BORDERS
12 DUMFRIES & GALLOWAY
COUNTIES OF WALES
1 CLWYD
2 GWYNEDD
3 POWYS
4 DYFED
5 WEST GLAMORGAN
6 GWENT
7 MID GLAMORGAN
8 SOUTH GLAMORGAN
COUNTIES OF ENGLAND
1 NORTHUMBERLAND
2 TYNE & WEAR
3 CUMBRIA
4 DURHAM
5 CLEVELAND
6 NORTH YORKSHIRE
7 LANCASHIRE
8 HUMBERSIDE
9 WEST YORKSHIRE
10 MERSEYSIDE
11 GREATER MANCHESTER
12 SOUTH YORKSHIRE
13 CHESHIRE
14 DERBYSHIRE
15 NOTTINGHAMSHIRE
16 LINCOLNSHIRE
17 STAFFORDSHIRE
18 SALOP (SHROPSHIRE)
19 LEICESTERSHIRE
20 NORFOLK
21 SUFFOLK
22 WEST MIDLANDS
23 HEREFORD & WORCESTER
24 WARWICKSHIRE
25 NORTHAMPTONSHIRE
26 CAMBRIDGESHIRE
27 GLOUCESTERSHIRE
28 OXFORDSHIRE
29 BUCKINGHAMSHIRE
30 BEDFORDSHIRE
31 HERTFORDSHIRE
32 ESSEX
33 AVON
34 WILTSHIRE
35 BERKSHIRE
36 GREATER LONDON
37 SOMSERSET
38 HAMPSHIRE
39 SURREY
40 KENT
41 EAST SUSSEX
42 WEST SUSSEX
43 DORSET
44 DEVON
45 CORNWALL
46 ISLE OF WIGHT
DISTRICTS OF NORTHERN IRELAND
1 LONDONDERRY
2 LIMAVADY
3 COLERAINE
4 BALLYMONEY
5 MOYLE
6 LARNE
7 BALLYMENA
8 MAGHERAFELT
9 COOKSTOWN
10 STRABANE
11 OMAGH
12 FERMANAGH
13 DUNGANNON
14 CRAIGAVON
15 ARMAGH
16 NEWRY & MOURNE
17 BANBRIDGE
18 DOWN
19 LISBURN
20 ANTRIM
21 NEWTOWNABBEY
22 CARRICKFERGUS
23 NORTH DOWN
24 ARDS
25 CASTLEREAGH
26 BELFAST
BRITISH ISLES
UNITED KINGDOM
GREAT BRITAIN
Scale
0 Miles 50
0 Kilometres 80
SCOTLAND
NORTHERN IRELAND
IRELAND
ENGLAND
WALES
NORTH SEA
IRISH SEA
ENGLISH CHANNEL
ATLANTIC OCEAN
FRANCE
Isle of Man
Scilly Isles
Channel Islands
Guernsey
Jersey
Isle of Wight
Lerwick
Kirkwall
Wick
Stornoway
Tarbert
Golspie
Dornoch
Dingwall
Nairn
Elgin
Banff
Portree
Inverness
Aberdeen
Stonehaven
Tobermory
Forfar
Dundee
Perth
Kinross
Cupar
Inveraray
Lochgilphead
Alloa
Stirling
Linlithgow
Dumbarton
Edinburgh
Haddington
Rothesay
Paisley
Glasgow
Duns
Hamilton
Peebles
Selkirk
Jedburgh
Ayr
Dumfries
Stranraer
Wigtown
Kirkcudbright
Londonderry
Omagh
Belfast
Enniskillen
Armagh
Downpatrick
Douglas
Newcastle upon Tyne
Carlisle
Durham
Appleby
Kendal
Northallerton
Lancaster
Preston
York
Beverley
Wakefield
Beaumaris
Llangefni
Mold
Caernarvon
Ruthin
Harlech
Dolgellau
Welshpool
Aberystwyth
Llandrindod Wells
Aberayron
Cardigan
Brecon
Haverfordwest
Carmarthen
Monmouth
Cardiff
Newport
Chester
Matlock
Lincoln
Nottingham
Boston
Derby
W. Bridgford
Sleaford
Stafford
Oakham
Norwich
Shrewsbury
Leicester
Presteigne
Huntingdon
Warwick
Northampton
Bury St. Edmunds
Worcester
Cambridge
Bedford
Ipswich
Hereford
Buckingham
Aylesbury
Hertford
Gloucester
Oxford
Chelmsford
Trowbridge
Reading
London
Kingston upon Thames
Guildford
Maidstone
Salisbury
Winchester
Taunton
Lewes
Chichester
Exeter
Dorchester
Newport
Bodmin
Truro

across the English Channel off the coast of France, and the Isle of Man, which is in the Irish Sea.

At least two parts of the United Kingdom became joined to England through conquest.

The first was Wales, a country in which Edward I of England (1239-1307) waged a long war during the 13th century. In 1301, he 'gave' to Wales his eldest son (later to become Edward II) as Prince of Wales, as all the native Welsh princes had been killed in the war. Twenty-one sons of English monarchs have been Princes of Wales, though only twice, in 1911 and 1969, has the dignified and solemn ceremony of investiture been performed at Caernarvon Castle. It was in this castle that, as legend has it, the baby Prince Edward was presented formally to the Welsh chieftains by Edward I.

The second conquered country was Ireland, a tragic land, where for centuries the people were cruelly treated by their English masters. Ireland became part of the United Kingdom in 1801. Over a century later, in 1922, after years of fighting by Irish patriots, twenty-six counties in the south became a separate country called the Irish Free State: this name has now been changed to the Republic of Ireland.

The other six counties in the north-east remained within the United Kingdom. These counties are called Northern Ireland, or sometimes Ulster – the name of the ancient kingdom which existed some two thousand years ago in much the same area as Northern Ireland now occupies.

Scotland became joined to England in 1603, when James VI (1566-1625), King of Scotland, also became James I of England. However, for nearly a century afterwards, the two countries were separate as far as government was concerned. They had separate government departments and also separate laws and churches. Even when, in 1707, England and Scotland were officially joined in 'The United Kingdom of Great Britain', Scotland kept her own church and her own laws, which she still has to this day.

All four parts of the United Kingdom send members to Parliament in London.

Above Caernarvon Castle was built in the 13th and 14th centuries and although little more than the walls remain it is one of the finest fortresses in Wales. The town itself retains almost the entire circuit of its medieval walls.

The Channel Islands and the Isle of Man also have their own Parliaments, as well as their own systems of taxation.

The people of Britain

In the years before the Norman Conquest of 1066, Wales, Scotland and Ireland were inhabited by some of the same immigrants from continental Europe as England. A glance at people's appearance today could reveal just who some of these immigrants were.

If the eyes and hair are brown, then somewhere far back in that person's family there may have been one of the Roman soldiers who invaded Britain in AD 43 or helped rule it until the early 5th century, when the Roman armies were recalled to Rome.

A tall person with a broad head suggests ancestry that may go even further back, to the invasions of a tribe which crossed the Channel from the Low Countries some time between 1900 and 1800 BC.

Black hair may reveal descent from the Celts, who came to Britain in two great invasions, in about 600 and 400 BC. It was the Celts who brought with them the foot plough, a farming implement which can still be seen in use in parts of north-west Scotland.

When the skin is dark-toned, there may be some connection with the Phoenicians from North Africa, who are thought to have settled in Cornwall. And in some Britons today, the tall, blond, blue-eyed characteristics still exist of Viking warriors from Scandinavia who crossed the North Sea to Britain in the 9th and 10th centuries.

Other invaders were the Angles and Jutes (from Denmark), Saxons (from north Germany and Holland), Belgae

Robert Bruce (1274–1329) Scottish patriot, whose seal is seen above. He joined William Wallace in his uprising against the English king, Edward I. After Wallace had been executed, Bruce became the chief hero in Scotland's struggle for independence. He was crowned king in 1306. Defeated the English in 1314 at Bannockburn. This led to the treaty of Northampton in 1328 which recognised Scotland's independence.

Above Celtic design and craftsmanship are shown in these examples of a brooch (top) and the head of a Celtic stone cross with its elaborately carved decoration of patterns and scenes.

(from France) and the short, dark settlers from the Mediterranean who came by sea to Wales and western England.

The original presence of these different peoples is revealed by the names of such towns as Colchester, Manchester or Leicester. These began as Roman camps: *castra* (anglicised to *-cester* or *-chester*) was the Latin word for camp.

The names of towns like Hastings and Worthing suggest Anglo-Saxon origin; and in the eastern half of England, the area closest to the original Viking homeland of Scandinavia, place names which come from these brave seafarers are plentiful. The ending *-by*, as in Grimsby, indicates a township; *-toft* in Norse meant homestead – hence the name Lowestoft; *-thorpe* (an offshoot from the original settlement) appears in such names as Scunthorpe or Cleethorpes; while the Viking word-ending for a creek or bay – *wick* – appears in such a name as Berwick.

Of the four countries in the United Kingdom, England was the easiest to invade from Europe. That part of the English coast which faces Europe is relatively flat and offers many natural landing places and harbours. Also, flowing back from the coast are a number of rivers which made it easier for immigrants to enter the country and set up communities.

In contrast, the Scottish Highlands, or the craggy hill country of Wales, as well as the Welsh marshes, presented a less attractive prospect to would-be settlers. The Romans, for example, never established any permanent settlements in Scotland and the Anglo-Saxons settled only in a small part of that country. And the Normans never made much headway in Wales or Ireland, and, as a result, left little of their influence behind.

Ireland, of course, was even less inviting, because settlers from the mainland had to brave the Irish Sea crossing. Its treacherous coastal waters and violent gales made Ireland difficult to reach safely and few, apart from the Vikings, were brave enough to attempt it.

So it is in Wales, Ireland and Scotland that the characteristics of the Celts, the people who reached Britain before any of the others, are most clearly seen today.

Left Two scenes from the Bayeux Tapestry, made in the 11th century, which describes the conquest of England by William the Conqueror. On the far left is depicted the moment when, in the heat of the battle, William lifts his visor to show that he has not fallen. Near left is seen King Harold pulling an arrow from his face during the last stand of his army. The tapestry is embroidered on linen in wool of different colours and is about 70 metres long. It was made for the cathedral at Bayeux in France, where it is now preserved.

The English language

Though modern English is spoken all over the United Kingdom, there are also the 'native' languages of Scotland, Ireland, Wales and the Isle of Man, all of which are Celtic in origin.

The English language, on the other hand, is a mixture of tongues. It retains some traces of Celtic, but it also contains words which come from old German, Latin and old Norse. In addition, English contains a lot of French words, because for nearly three hundred years after the Norman Conquest French was the language of the royal court and nobility. In fact, until late in the 14th century, proceedings in Parliament were conducted in French.

Norman French is still the local language of the Channel Islands, which became joined to England at the time of the Norman Conquest.

William the Conqueror

The Celts, Anglo-Saxons, Vikings and other immigrants to Britain were the 'raw material' which formed the British people. The final wave of invaders – the Norman French – shaped that 'raw material' into the kind of nation we know today.

The England of which William the Conqueror (1027-87) became king after the Battle of Hastings in 1066 was mainly a land of forests, dotted with tracts of bleak moorland and uninhabitable marshes. Less than one and a half million people lived in it.

In general, these people were more conscious of being men and women of Sussex, Wessex or Mercia than of being 'English'. This was not really surprising because most people lived in villages, many of which were very isolated. Some were so remote that it is possible that by the time William was crowned king on Christmas Day 1066, two months after the invasion, many people had not even heard that he had landed.

William's coronation ceremony was just like an Anglo-Saxon one. Although he had taken the country by force, he did not want to alter its customs. William tried to organise a government in which Normans and English could take an equal part. Unfortunately, this did not work. There were many armed rebellions which William was forced to crush, and

Alfred the Great (849–99) King of Wessex. He reigned for thirty years and fought many battles against the Danes who were eventually forced to submit to his rule. Alfred formed a strong army and navy for the defence of his country and did much to help the establishment of law and order. He also encouraged ordinary people to read and educate themselves.

Above The flags seen here are (from top to bottom) St George's Cross (left), St Andrew's Cross (right), St Patrick's Cross (left), and the Union Jack of 1630. Below them is seen the Union Jack of 1801 and the Royal Standard.

harsh military rule had to be imposed.

As time went on, the laws that governed England became as mixed in origin as the people themselves. Some were Norman and French, some were Danish, some Anglo-Saxon, some Celtic. The result was a melting pot of customs, many of which seemed quite opposed to each other.

For example, the feudal system, which made peasants the property of their lords, also bound the lords in their turn to perform duties for the king. At the same time, there was the Anglo-Saxon belief that the powers of kings should be limited, that they should not govern alone, but with the advice of their nobles.

Four hundred years before William the Conqueror became king, it was already well established that no man, however low his position in life, should be without the protection of the law.

Many of these ancient principles still exist today. As such, they are part of a solid framework of tradition within which many changes have taken place.

This is one of Britain's great strengths, which has made it possible for the country to survive many upheavals. You could compare it to the walls of a house which, because they are built on firm foundations, do not collapse when builders start making drastic alterations to the rooms inside.

Systems of government

Parliament in Britain consists of the House of Commons, whose members are chosen by the adult population; the House of Lords, composed chiefly of people who have either inherited their right to sit there or who have been appointed members for life; and the sovereign (the reigning king or queen).

The system of government works in this way.

A member of the House of Commons, usually a minister of the Crown, introduces a 'bill' which the government wishes to make into a law.

The title of the bill is read out and the Speaker of the House, who acts as a sort of chairman, asks the minister to name a date in the future when the bill can be discussed. The bill is then printed, so that members of Parliament can get to know what it contains.

Although no actual discussion has taken place so far, this is known as a 'First Reading'.

The 'Second Reading' takes place when the main points of the bill are debated in the House of Commons.

After this Second Reading, the bill goes to one of the Parliamentary Standing Committees whose task it is to discuss the bill in detail. Every part of the bill is examined separately and is either accepted as it stands, or is altered if the committee members think it necessary.

After this, the bill is handed back to the House of Commons together with the committee's report.

The House discusses the bill a third and last time, and it is then sent to the House of Lords, whose turn it now is to consider it.

In the House of Lords, the bill goes through exactly the same stages as it did in the House of Commons. If, after discussion, the House of Lords accepts the bill as it stands and makes no alteration to it, then it becomes an Act of Parliament.

If, however, the House of Lords *does* make alterations the bill has to go back to the House of Commons where these alterations are discussed. Once agreement is reached, the new Act is sent to the Royal Commission which, on behalf of the sovereign, gives its agreement: this is known as the 'Royal Assent'.

You may think this is a very long-winded way of going about things. Perhaps it is, but by the time a bill has gone through all these various stages, what remains is a law which has been very fully considered and is most likely to be acceptable to the majority of people in the country.

This is the most important thing about the way in which the government of the country operates: that everyone whom the law will affect should, either in person (as in the House of Lords), or through elected representatives (as in the House of Commons), be allowed to have a say in what that law contains.

Winston Churchill (1874–1965) British statesman. Entered Parliament in 1900. Became prime minister in 1940 when his inspired leadership led Britain to victory. In the background is seen the debating chamber of the House of Commons in which Sir Winston earned the title of the 'great parliamentarian'.

Parliamentary democracy

This system is what democracy is all about. It has not been easy to achieve in Britain. In fact, the process has been extremely difficult and sometimes tragic.

Until as recently as 1928, there was always some section of the adult population that found itself without a chance to give opinions on the law it had to live by.

The story of how each of these sections managed to get the right to vote representatives into the House of Commons is the story of how Britain came to be what she is today. A very important part of it is the way in which the power of the monarch and the lords was gradually reduced to fit into a modern democracy.

Originally, the word *parliamentum* meant a 'parley' or a 'talking together' which took place when the king met in the Great Council with his bishops and barons to discuss matters affecting the government of the country. Bishops and barons at one time were

Henry VIII
(1491–1547) king of England from 1509. A very gifted young man, who inherited great wealth from his father, Henry VII. His need for a son and heir caused him to divorce his first wife, Catherine of Aragon. In so doing he broke away from the Roman Catholic church, making himself head of the church in England. He married six times, but left only three children. Loved by the people, he was often ruthless and faithless to his friends.

the most powerful subjects in the kingdom and their support was of great importance to the king.

Simon de Montfort

In this Great Council you can clearly see the core of Parliament as it exists today. What was missing, of course, was a House of Commons.

This entered the Council in 1265 when Simon de Montfort (1208?-65), who was then ruling England by military dictatorship, summoned to the Council representatives of the shires (divisions of the country we would now call counties) and of the boroughs or towns. For this reason, Simon de Montfort has been called 'Father of the English Parliament', even though he summoned these representatives only in the hope that their support would outweigh the influence of the other barons, who were opposed to his rule.

Thirty years later, in 1295, Edward I copied Simon de Montfort's idea, though for a rather different reason. He summoned representatives to a Great Council, known as the 'Model Parliament', because he needed money to finance his wars in Wales, and these were the men who could give it to him.

Gradually, as time went on, such men came to be regarded as people who spoke on behalf of the communities or communes from which they came. There was no doubt, though, that they were still much less important than the powerful nobles and clergy: in the Great Council, the representatives stood at the back of the hall, while the king and other great men did most of the talking.

By the end of the 14th century, the representatives were known as the House of Commons, though it was nothing like the Commons as we know it today. Its members included small property owners, squires, lawyers and merchants, who were far richer than the ordinary people.

As businessmen they were careful with money, and because of this sometimes made life very difficult for the king, particularly if they thought he was extravagant. As a result, there were constant financial tussles between king and Parliament. These tussles went on for many years until the first Tudor king, Henry VII (1457-1509), came to the throne in 1485.

The great weakness of former kings had been their financial dependence on Parliament, so Henry VII proceeded to make himself rich, and therefore independent of Parliament. When he died he left his son a fortune of £1½ million, a huge sum indeed for those days.

Henry VIII and Parliament

Kings were not financially independent of Parliament for long. Within a few years of succeeding his father, Henry VIII (1491-1547) had squandered his fortune and found that, as before, he had to ask Parliament for money when he needed it.

It seemed that the old quarrels over money would start again, but Henry,

a cunning, ruthless man, found another use for Parliament in 1529 which gave it something even more important than control of the country's purse-strings.

Even before that year Henry had decided to divorce his wife Catherine of Aragon and marry her lady-in-waiting, Anne Boleyn. He applied to the pope in Rome for a divorce, but the pope refused to grant it. Determined to get what he wanted, Henry VIII then proceeded to abolish the pope's power in England, and himself became head of the Church of England with power to appoint bishops. In this powerful position, Henry pronounced himself divorced, and in 1533 he married Anne Boleyn.

To make this revolutionary change Henry VIII used Parliament, and in doing so he gave Parliament more power than it had ever had before.

By passing the various laws which made the Church of England independent of the pope, Parliament had transformed the organisation of the country. As a result, Parliament started to realise its importance as an instrument of government. Individual members looked on themselves as special people. They began to claim privileges not open to ordinary citizens, such as freedom of speech and freedom from arrest.

The king kept the 'Reformation Parliament', as it was called, in existence for eight separate sessions spread over seven years. Thus its members became extremely experienced in parliamentary business and formal procedure.

In this way, Parliament began to grow into a power in its own right.

As long as the sovereign agreed with Parliament, or was strong enough to control it, there was little or no trouble. Queen Elizabeth I (1533-1603) was a very strong ruler and controlled Parliament by placing her best councillors in the House of Commons where they sat close to the Speaker's chair and worked out tactics to ensure victory in debates. Since the Speaker was also one of the Queen's officials, she could hardly fail to be successful.

Divine right of kings

Unfortunately for himself and his family, Elizabeth's successor was not so clever.

When James I became king in 1603, one of the first things he did was to

Above Queen Elizabeth about to board the royal barge on the River Thames.

Mary, Queen of Scots (1542–87) Married to the dauphin of France in 1558, she returned to Scotland a widow in 1560. She remarried unwisely, first to Lord Darnley (1565) and, when he was killed, to the Earl of Bothwell (1567). She became unpopular with the nobles and was forced to abdicate. She sought protection from Queen Elizabeth I but was imprisoned. As a Catholic she was a constant threat to the English throne and was executed for her supposed part in plots against Elizabeth.

Above During the Civil War in England between the Royalists (Cavaliers) and the Parliamentarians (Roundheads) the most important battles were at Edgehill, Marston Moor and Naseby, the last two being great victories for the Parliamentarians.

Below Old London Bridge as it was about 1600. This drawing is based on what is considered the earliest genuine view of the bridge, that is an engraving in the Pepys' Collection in Magdalen College, Cambridge.

remove from the Commons Elizabeth's most brilliant councillor, Robert Cecil, and send him to the House of Lords. In Cecil's place, James appointed two second-rate men who proved totally unable to get Parliament to agree to his wishes.

This was not surprising because James's most frequent wish was for money to support a lavish court and an extravagant wife. What was more, the Parliament of James I's day became convinced that the king's duty was to ask for its advice and take it, and not to expect automatic agreement to his policies whether Parliament approved of them or not.

Within this idea of the king's role in government lay the germ of constitutional monarchy, where a king or queen, while not completely powerless, has no power to oppose Parliament's will.

However, neither James I nor his son Charles I (1600-49) was willing to hand over to Parliament the right it was now claiming – the right to rule the country. In the end, this right had to be taken from the Stuart Royal Family by force.

King and Parliament each had one important weapon. Only the king had the right to summon Parliament and he could dissolve it when he wished. Only Parliament, on the other hand, could grant the king money. If the king wished to rule without Parliament – and both James and Charles did for several years – he had to raise money by other means.

These 'other means' included forced loans, the revival of half-forgotten taxes, as well as fines for breaking ancient laws. All of this angered Parliament deeply and made the members determined on revenge. When, as he eventually had to, James I was forced to summon Parliament in 1621, the members lost no time in attacking the king's ministers, accusing them of bribery and corruption, fining them heavily and taking away their positions.

Charles I, who succeeded his father in 1625, learned nothing from this dramatic show of parliamentary power and angered Parliament even more by his continued belief in the 'divine right of kings'.

This meant that Charles considered his royal powers came directly from God, and that he was therefore not accountable to anyone, least of all his subjects. This was a completely opposite view to the principle established in 1215 by Magna Carta: that the king was not above the law and had a duty to rule with the advice of his nobles.

Like his father, Charles ruled without Parliament, and also like his father he raised money by all sorts of underhand means. In 1640, when the king was finally forced to summon

Above Charles I was beheaded upon a scaffold erected before the Banqueting House of Whitehall Palace in London in 1649.

Parliament to grant him money, he found that a very sinister development had taken place: Parliament was angry, as he had no doubt expected, but its anger was directed not only against the king's ministers – it was also aimed at the king himself and at his powers.

The Civil War

It was through this that the tragic Civil War came about. The king's enemies were intent on drastically reducing his royal powers, including taking away from him control of the army. Others, who did not agree with these ideas, rallied round the king.

The Civil War, which began in 1642, ended in 1649 with Charles's execution. The House of Commons, victors in the war, did away with the monarchy and the House of Lords and declared England a republic: this, its members thought, would be a better arrangement.

They quickly found out that they were wrong.

The three-part system of king, Lords and Commons was already too strongly rooted in English tradition to be done away with.

Oliver Cromwell (1599-1658), who was elected Lord Protector in 1653, came up against exactly the same problems as the king: lack of money and a hostile Parliament. And he found himself acting in just the same way: dissolving Parliament when it would not co-operate, raising money by forced loans and heavy taxes. The trouble was that he did not have a king's traditional authority behind him.

The dead king had not been completely wrong when he believed that kingship had a certain divinity about it. Even today the monarchy retains a glamour which people regard as a natural focus for their loyalty. Oliver Cromwell, a country gentleman and member of Parliament, simply did not have that glamour. For the first and only time, the basis of government in England was knocked off balance.

While Cromwell was alive, some sort of order was maintained. Despite royalist plots and constant threats to his life, he did much that was good for England. When Cromwell died in 1658, to be succeeded by his weak son Richard, nothing stood in the way of rule by armed force. In 1659, Richard Cromwell was made to retire, Parliament was dissolved and two army generals tried to take control.

Oliver Cromwell (1599–1658) Became Lord Protector of England in 1653. First returned to Parliament in 1628, his reputation was as a soldier rather than as a politician. Was a cavalry officer at the start of the Civil War. Founded New Model Army, which gained many victories over the Royalists.

Above Kings and queens of England since the time of William I.

Normans
1 William I 1066–87
2 William II 1087–1100
3 Henry I 1100–35
4 Stephen 1135–54
Plantagenets
5 Henry II 1154–89
6 Richard I 1189–99
7 John 1199–1216
8 Henry III 1216–72
9 Edward I 1272–1307
10 Edward II 1307–27
11 Edward III 1327–77
12 Richard II 1377–99
House of Lancaster
13 Henry IV 1399–1413
14 Henry V 1413–22
15 Henry VI 1422–61
House of York
16 Edward IV 1461–83
17 Edward V 1483
18 Richard III 1483–5
Tudors
19 Henry VII 1485–1509
20 Henry VIII 1509–47

Restoration of the monarchy

By this time, Britain was heartily sick of the situation and many people longed for a return of the monarchy. This wish was clearly expressed in March 1660 when an election was held for a new Parliament: an overwhelming number of royalist members were returned.

Two months later, on 8th May 1660, Charles I's son was declared king as Charles II (1630-85), and on 25th May he returned to England from the Continent where he had spent the years since his father's death. There was no doubt at all that the British people were delighted to have a king once more.

'The ways were strewn with flowers', wrote John Evelyn, the diarist, describing the day on which Charles entered London, 'the bells ringing, the streets hung with tapestry, the fountains running with wine . . .'

As for Charles, he was just as glad to see his kingdom as his subjects were to see him. He was very careful not to do anything which might upset Parliament, because he was determined never to go into exile again. Parliament and the people, for their part, were equally afraid of another civil war.

This produced what appeared to be a period of peace between them. It did not mean that the king and Parliament agreed about everything: far from it, some of Charles's policies were strongly opposed, although in the end Charles usually won. Parliament had learned a hard lesson from the years without a king: the British people could not be ruled successfully by Parliament alone.

Parliament even agreed, though with some fears, when Charles insisted that his Catholic brother James (1633-1701) should succeed him as king.

Ever since the time of the Catholic Queen Mary in the 16th century, when several hundred people were burned at the stake for their religious beliefs, Catholicism had been feared and disliked in Britain.

Charles II died in 1685 and immediately it became clear that it had been a great mistake to allow James to succeed him. The new king was stubborn and would not listen to advice.

11 12 13 14 15 16 17 18 19 20

His one aim in life was to restore Roman Catholicism to Britain. James even began to act like his father Charles, not only dissolving Parliament when it suited him, but claiming the right to suspend laws he did not like.

Memories of the Civil War were still painful, and Parliament was at first willing to let James keep his throne: it was thought that he would eventually be succeeded by the Protestant daughters of his first marriage, Mary and Anne. However, when James II's second wife, also a Roman Catholic, gave birth to a son in 1688, Parliament saw before the country an endless line of Catholic monarchs.

Some of the members sent a secret invitation to Mary's husband William of Orange, asking him to come to England with an army. William arrived in November 1688 and landed at Torbay in Devon. In December, James, fearing that he would lose his head like his father, fled to France.

On 13th February 1689, William III (1650-1702) and Mary II (1662-94) were proclaimed joint sovereigns of England. William later became king of Scotland as well.

The Bill of Rights

After its disputes with Charles I and James II, Parliament decided once and for all to limit the powers of the monarchy, and so protect what it regarded as its rightful liberties.

The Bill of Rights became law in 1689. It was declared illegal for a monarch to tamper with any law, or to collect taxes or keep a standing army without the consent of Parliament. Roman Catholics were barred for ever from the throne. Parliament claimed the right to complete freedom of speech: no monarch would ever again be able to tell them what they might or might not discuss. And they also claimed the right to approve or disapprove of the ministers the king chose. If Parliament disapproved, the king could do nothing about it.

This did not mean that a king or queen had no say at all in the government of the country. Both William III and his successor Queen Anne (1665-1714) took charge of meetings of the

Below
Tudors
21 Edward VI 1547–53
22 Mary I 1553–8
23 Elizabeth I 1558–1603
Stuarts
24 James I 1603–25
25 Charles I 1625–49
26 Charles II 1660–85
27 James II 1685–9
28 William III 1689–1702 and
29 Mary II 1689–94
30 Anne 1702–14
Hanoverians
31 George I 1714–27
32 George II 1727–60
33 George III 1760–1820
34 George IV 1820–30
35 William IV 1830–7
36 Victoria 1837–1901
House of Saxe-Coburg
37 Edward VII 1901–10
Windsor
38 George V 1910–36
39 Edward VIII 1936
40 George VI 1936–52
41 Elizabeth II 1952–
Not included in this gallery of sovereigns are Lady Jane Grey, who reigned as queen for nine days in 1553, and Oliver Cromwell who ruled England during the time of the Commonwealth.

1 32 33 34 35 36 37 38 39 40 41

Above The Royal Pavilion at Brighton was built between 1787 and 1821 for the Prince of Wales, later King George IV.

Horatio Nelson (1758–1805) Greatest English naval commander in wars against the French. He won many sea victories, most famous of which was at Trafalgar in 1805, when Nelson was killed.

cabinet, which consisted of a small group of important advisers chosen from members of Parliament. It was only when the first Hanoverian kings came to the throne that this practice changed: the reason was that George I and George II spoke only German and so they handed over chairmanship of the cabinet to a 'prime minister'.

This, more or less, is the situation that has existed in Britain ever since. Today, it appears that the Queen has a great deal of political power. It is the Queen who opens Parliament, the Queen who reads the speech from the throne, in which she informs both Houses of the bills that are to be presented for their consideration, and it is the Queen who officially chooses a prime minister.

In reality the Queen by herself has no political power at all. A prime minister, when he is appointed, is not really her personal choice: he is the choice of the voters of the country, because it is they who choose members to represent them in the House of Commons, and the leader of the party that gets the most seats in the House automatically becomes prime minister. And it is the prime minister and his government who put forward the bills contained in the Queen's speech.

She regularly summons the prime minister and other ministers to Buckingham Palace or one of the other royal residences, and there discusses with them the country's affairs. Even here the Queen's power is strictly limited. She may express her opinion on any subject under discussion, but it is always the views of her ministers that are acted upon.

The House of Lords

Another point of view on public matters is given by the House of Lords. As with the Queen, the powers of the House of Lords are limited because, in a modern democratic country like Britain, it is unacceptable for anyone who is *not* elected by the people to have a more important say in government than those who *are* elected.

But many of the people who sit in the House of Lords are men and women of considerable experience from various walks of life and their advice is well worth listening to. The House of Lords debates in a calm atmosphere, and acts rather like a wise and cautious father towards the

Above Coronets are small crowns worn by peers attending coronations and the state openings of Parliament. From top to bottom are shown the coronets of a duke, an earl and a baron.

Above left The Queen's speech, read at the state opening of Parliament, outlines the policies which the government intends to introduce in the House of Commons in the next session.

House of Commons, where discussions can become rather heated and where, possibly, hasty decisions may be made.

As with the position of the Queen in Britain today, the present role of the House of Lords is the product of centuries of struggle.

Freedom of speech

In the 17th century, when both Houses of Parliament were trying to reduce the power of the king, there was very little difference between their members: both Houses contained men of property and wealth. These men, whether they had aristocratic titles or not, were the most powerful people in the country.

It was when the ordinary people, those without much money and little or no property, began to demand that they, too, should be represented in the House of Commons that arguments began to arise between that House and the House of Lords.

Two hundred years or so ago, when these arguments first began in earnest, it was very fortunate that Parliament was already well established as the central authority in Britain. Because of this, people did not aim simply at taking power away from those who already had it: they wanted instead to join them and share in that power.

This is still a distinctive characteristic of the British people. It means that, in general, they do not want to achieve their aims by violent revolution, but by trying to influence those people who are already in authority – the people who can best help them.

It is important that people with a grievance should have a chance to air their views. The history of many countries has shown that the scene may be set for violent revolution when this right is suppressed.

In just the same way as today, those people in the past who wanted to obtain for themselves a say in the way their country was governed held meetings, staged demonstrations or presented petitions to Parliament.

At the time of the French Revolution in 1789, only about five in every hundred people in Britain had the right to vote in elections. Even half a century later, seven years after Parliament passed the Great Reform Bill in 1832, this number had risen to only thirty-four in every hundred.

Above Freedom of speech is one of the characteristics of a democracy and nowhere is it more freely practised than in Britain.

Above Hargreaves's 'spinning jenny', invented in 1767, made it possible for one person to turn a handle and spin 16 threads at a time.

Right Steam tractors were used in farming in the 19th century.

Below Three pioneers of the Industrial Revolution whose inventions improved the efficiency of the textile industry. From left to right they are Edmund Cartwright (1743–1823), who perfected the power loom; Samuel Crompton (1753–1827), who invented the spinning mule; and Richard Arkwright (1732–92) who is remembered chiefly for his spinning frame.

The Industrial Revolution

Between the two dates of 1789 and 1832 a remarkable and very fundamental change took place in British life. It was the coming of the Industrial Revolution, which introduced more and more machines to do work which had formerly been done by hand.

Such machines were the 'flying shuttle', first devised in 1733 by John Kay (1704-64?), a Lancashire weaver; and the 'spinning jenny', perfected in 1767 by James Hargreaves (d.1778), an inventor who also came from Lancashire. These machines, and others which were developed later, were able to do a vastly increased amount of work. The spinning jenny, for example, enabled one person to spin sixteen threads at a time.

Probably the most important machine invented around this time was the steam engine. The type of steam engine that really revolutionised factory practice was the one patented by James Watt in 1769. Steam engines were soon producing enough power to drive the machines in cotton mills, or to operate bellows and hammers in iron works.

Naturally, weavers, spinners and other workers grew suspicious. They feared that machines were going to put them out of work and their first reaction was to wreck them. However they gradually came to realise that as machinery increased production it might also help them increase their small wages. As the 19th century opened, so more and more workers were leaving the countryside and flocking to the towns in the hope of earning more money.

Eventually, thinly populated country areas, which became known as 'Rotten Boroughs', were represented by members in the House of Commons while the now heavily populated new industrial towns were not.

In September 1831, a bill was introduced into the House of Commons which sought to put right this unfair situation. It never became law because it was rejected by the House of Lords. This was one of the first signs of trouble between the two Houses of Parliament.

The solution was a drastic one. The Lords were told that, if they continued to oppose the bill, the king would raise to the peerage so many men who were known to favour it that the bill would be passed.

The threat was sufficient. In June 1832, the Lords passed the First Reform Act under which seats in the Commons were redistributed so as to create new constituencies (as the parliamentary divisions of the country are called) in the towns.

The effect of this bill, and of other similar ones which were passed separately for Scotland and Ireland, was to give the vote to those people who had recently become wealthy through the growth of the factories. Thus for the first time since the 13th century a new section of the community had representatives in Parliament to challenge the economic and social interests of the Lords, who were concerned with ownership of land.

There were still vast numbers of workers who did not have the right to vote simply because they were too poor: their pay was below the minimum amount which qualified men to vote.

Tragically, a vote was not all these people lacked. Today, when most people in Britain live in clean, well ventilated houses and have enough to eat, it is terrible to realise that poor people a century or more ago lived in filthy, overcrowded homes, worked very long hours for very little money and often went hungry because they were too poor to buy food. Under these conditions, disease and early death were all too common.

Above Although the Industrial Revolution brought many benefits to man, it also brought bad working conditions to many men, women and children in ill-lit, overcrowded and dangerous factories. Such conditions led to the formation of the first trade unions, as workers banded together to demand greater consideration from their employers.

The Poor Laws

Members of Parliament – the only group of people in Britain with power to do anything to relieve this poverty – cared very little about it. They seemed determined to heap extra suffering on the poor. This is what many people thought when the Poor Law Amendment Act was passed in 1834.

Ever since 1601, when the Elizabethan Poor Law was passed, it had been recognised that the State had a duty to help the poor. The new Poor Law of 1834 did not alter this principle, but it did make people suffer for what was regarded as the 'crime' of being poor.

Under the law, no man could receive help from the State unless he entered a workhouse. Discipline was brutal; so brutal that many were called 'houses of terror'. The conditions of work, the living quarters and the food were deliberately made as bad as possible, because the whole idea was to put people off from coming to the workhouse at all. It was thought that if the workhouse was made too attractive some poor people might not bother to go out and find work and would simply get the State to support them and their families.

The Chartists

The 1834 Poor Law caused a great deal of bad feeling, particularly in the northern counties, where there was a lot of poverty. Out of this grew the

Above William Gladstone (1809–98) was probably the greatest of all 19th century political figures in Britain. He entered the House of Commons in 1832 and left it in 1894. During this time he became prime minister on four separate occasions. A man of high principles, he was a scholar and a great orator.

Above right The spirit of the British soldier in the First World War was expressed by Bruce Bairnsfather in a series of celebrated cartoons. The caption to this one reads, *The Young and Talkative One: 'Who made that 'ole?' The Fed-up One: 'Mice!'*

belief that the only solution was representation in Parliament for the ordinary working man.

In 1839, the Peoples' Charter, which bore over a million and a quarter signatures gathered in 214 villages and towns throughout Britain, was presented in Parliament by the radical MP Thomas Attwood.

Its requests were simple: it asked for universal male suffrage (a vote for every adult male); voting by ballot, which meant that votes should be recorded on paper and in secret so that no voter could be bullied, assaulted or bribed at elections – something which was quite common at the time; the payment of members of Parliament; and the right to stand for election whether or not one owned any property. The last two demands aimed to allow men who were not wealthy to sit in Parliament: at that time the cost of being an MP was so great that only rich people could afford it.

Not surprisingly, Parliament rejected the Charter. There were violent reactions. In November 1839, there was a rising by miners at Newport in Monmouthshire, but its leaders were arrested and many were imprisoned. Three years later, another petition containing three and a quarter million signatures was presented to Parliament and this time it was even more strongly worded than the first.

This second petition was also rejected by Parliament. So was a third, presented in 1858.

Weakened by lack of co-operation within its own ranks, the Chartist Movement eventually collapsed. But the ideals that had inspired it survived, and in 1867 there came the first move towards fulfilling the main demand of the Chartists: a vote for every man in Britain.

In that year, the Conservative government headed by Benjamin Disraeli (1804-81) introduced the Second Reform Act. When this became law, it gave the vote to one million working men in the towns.

Seventeen years later, in 1884, the Liberal government under William Gladstone (1809-98) passed the Third Reform Act, which gave the right to vote to about two million agricultural workers.

These reforms did not come about simply because Parliament had had a sudden change of heart. Both Disraeli and Gladstone certainly had some sympathy with the idea that it was not right for people to be ruled by a Parliament they had not helped to choose. But a far more important reason was that by giving more people the vote, both Disraeli and Gladstone hoped to enlist more support for their parties.

It was the disaster of the First World War (1914-18) that helped achieve a vote for every adult man in Britain.

Above A suffragette being carried away by a policeman after a demonstration.

Above left The second People's Charter was signed by three and a quarter million people and was carried through the streets to Parliament amid scenes of great enthusiasm.

At the end of the war, in which nearly a million British soldiers were killed, the prime minister, David Lloyd George (1863-1945), promised to make Britain 'a land fit for heroes to live in'. To keep at least part of that promise, the Representation of the People Act was passed in 1918. This granted the right to vote to all men over the age of twenty-one, and also to married women, women who owned houses and women university graduates over the age of thirty.

The suffragettes

This right for women to vote was not given easily. Women had to fight for it, many had to suffer and some had to die.

Like the Chartist Movement, the movement to gain votes for women started quite calmly. During the 19th century, many petitions had been presented to Parliament, while sympathetic MPs had fought within Parliament for the right of women to vote, and also for their right to own property and to receive similar education to men.

The idea that women were too fragile for the rough and tumble of everyday life was still widely believed at the beginning of the 20th century. Then a group of women called suffragettes proved that some women could be even more violent and determined than men.

In 1903, Mrs Emmeline Pankhurst (1858-1928), already an experienced fighter for women's rights, formed the Women's Social and Political Union in Manchester. In this, she was joined by her two daughters, Sylvia and Christabel.

For a period of eight years from 1905, the suffragettes brought attention to their demands by setting fire to pillar boxes and public buildings, cutting telephone wires, and tying themselves to railings outside the Houses of Parliament. When they were sent to prison as punishment, they refused to eat and had to be forcibly fed. And in 1913, one suffragette, Emily Davison, threw herself under the king's horse as it ran in the Derby race. She died from her injuries.

Public sympathy for the suffragettes rapidly increased and many hundreds of thousands of pounds were contributed to help them in their fight.

This activity came to an end at the outbreak of the First World War. The

David Lloyd George (1863–1945) Welsh politician. Entered Parliament as a Liberal in 1890. As Chancellor of the Exchequer (1908–15) he introduced social reforms with the Old Age Pensions and National Insurance Acts. Coalition prime minister (1916–22), and led Britain to victory in the First World War.

Above James Keir Hardie, the first Labour MP, speaks at a meeting in Trafalgar Square in London.

Below During the First World War women took over various public service duties from men and the first 'clippies' appeared on London buses in 1917.

suffragettes used their energies in helping Britain's war effort and when men went off to fight, took over many of their jobs. Women delivered the post and the milk, worked in factories, drove buses and swept the streets.

They did this work so well that by the time the war ended, it was realised at last that women deserved the right to vote. This they were granted, according to the Act of 1918, together with the right to sit in Parliament. Ten years afterwards, in 1928, women between the ages of twenty-one and thirty were also given the vote.

So, at last, just over 660 years after the first representatives of the people were summoned by Simon de Montfort to join the lords in the Great Council, a true parliamentary democracy was achieved.

Commons versus Lords

In those 660 years, a basic change had taken place in the power of the lords. In Simon de Montfort's Parliament of 1265, they were the most powerful men in the land. By 1928, their power was so greatly reduced that the House of Lords was not as important as the House of Commons.

The struggle for power between the Lords and the Commons reached its climax in the early years of the 20th century.

The House of Lords was largely Conservative; that is, its members wished to conserve, or keep, not only their political rights, but also their privileges of wealth and position as landowners. Some of these had already been lost because of the various reforms of the 19th century. The Liberal government of 1906 threatened to take away even more of their power.

The Lords still possessed the right to delay or reject bills which had already passed through the Commons. But since the 17th century they had no power to interfere with laws about taxation. It was this point that was used against them as a political weapon by the Liberals.

The People's Budget

A bill was presented to the Lords in 1909 which concerned taxation *and* contained some of the measures to which the Lords were opposed. This bill was popularly called the People's Budget and contained ideas which laid the foundations of what we now call the Welfare State. It proposed the payment of old age pensions, and new taxes on landowners and those with high incomes.

These last two proposals hit very hard at the Lords, whose members nearly all enjoyed high incomes from their ownership of land and property. The Lords immediately rejected the People's Budget and, of course, found they had put themselves in the wrong.

The Commons claimed that because the bill was partly about taxation, the Lords had no right to reject it.

The following year, 1910, the Lords found themselves faced with the Parliament Act, under which their powers were to be greatly reduced: they could not hold up for more than two years bills which had already passed through the House of Commons, and they were to lose completely the right to reject any bills which concerned money.

When they opposed the bill the king, George V, agreed to create enough new peers to enable the Parliament Act to be passed by the House of Lords. It was 1832 all over again, and again the threat worked.

Rather than risk being permanently outnumbered by up to 250 specially-created Liberal peers, the Lords gave in, and in 1911 the Parliament Act became law. Thirty-eight years later, another Parliament Act was passed

which reduced to one year the period during which the House of Lords could delay any bill presented to it by the Commons.

The Law

As well as their part in Parliament, the House of Lords also acts as the highest court of appeal in Britain. This means that people convicted of some crime in the law courts can, in the last instance, appeal to the Lords to have that conviction quashed, or cancelled.

The power to do this goes directly back to the days before Parliament began to develop out of the Great Council of the Norman kings.

The Great Council, where king and nobles met together to make decisions affecting the government of the country, was also the place where people could come for justice. Judgement would be given by judges who had been specially summoned for that purpose.

As time passed, the business of ruling the country grew more complicated, and to reduce the amount of work the Great Council had to do, separate royal courts were set up for the judges to do their work in.

These courts were not always at fixed places. The judges, who were regarded as representatives of the king, travelled all over the country on planned routes known as 'circuits'. They set up courts in the towns and villages at which they stopped.

Some of the ways in which they dealt out justice seem barbarous today. People suspected of crimes might have to undergo an ordeal by water. They were flung into a pond and if they sank to the bottom they were pronounced innocent. If, on the other hand, they floated, they were regarded as guilty. Magic and superstition played a large part in this practice.

Another method of deciding disputes was trial by battle: whichever of the opponents killed the other or forced him to yield was judged to be in the right.

There was also trial by ordeal. Here, an accused person had to undergo certain tortures. If that person managed to endure them, then he was judged innocent.

Above At the start of the legal year the Lord Chancellor and the justices walk in procession from Westminster Abbey to the House of Lords.

Above left Trial by combat in the Middle Ages was one method of settling disputes. The accused and his accuser fought each other and the winner was judged to be in the right.

Above One of the earliest drawings of the martyrdom of St Thomas Becket is shown in this copy from the 13th-century Harleian manuscript in the British Museum. He clashed with Henry II and was murdered in 1170. In 1172 he was canonised and his shrine became the object of pilgrimages.

Above right The Knight from the Ellesmere manuscript of *Canterbury Tales*.

The principle that an accused person is considered innocent until proved guilty – a very important one in a democratic society – had its beginnings during the reign of Henry II (1133-89). In 1166, Henry II set up a court known as the Assize of Clarendon. At this court, people came for justice if their land had been stolen from them. In this and other royal courts set up in the years that followed, decisions were given by judges who heard evidence from a panel of twelve local men who had taken a solemn oath to tell the truth.

Trial by jury

In this twelve-man panel lay the origins of the modern trial by jury. Today, the duty of a jury is to judge the case being tried before it with complete fairness. This means the members of the jury must not favour or condemn an accused person before all the evidence on both sides has been heard.

The modern jury is completely free to make whatever decision it considers to be the right one, but this was not always the case. For a very long time, juries were little more than the obedient mouthpiece of kings and judges. If juries tried to give verdicts that a king or judge did not approve of, they were often punished.

In 1670 the courage of a jury which refused to be bullied made people realise how wrong this was. This jury had found two Quakers not guilty of taking part in an unlawful assembly.

In an effort to make the members of the jury change their minds, they were locked up for three days, then fined and finally imprisoned. The widespread public sympathy they received on their release from prison helped to establish the principle that juries should be free to reach whatever verdict they chose. Since then, the right of juries to give independent verdicts has been a vital part of trials in British law courts.

The members of modern juries are men and women chosen at random from the list of those entitled to vote.

Sitting on a jury, and so taking part in the working of the law, is a very important duty in a democratic country. The right to vote gives men and women a say in the making of laws, and jury service requires them to take an active part in seeing that those laws are both properly applied and obeyed.

The right to appeal against a verdict is a protection for the individual citizen against the danger of injustice. Persons convicted of crimes can appeal first to the Court of Criminal Appeal and then, if necessary, to the House of Lords. If both the Court of Criminal Appeal and the House of Lords agree with the original verdict then it must stand.

Protection for the poor

Besides injustice there are many other things people need to be protected against: things over which they sometimes have no control, such as unemployment, poverty and ill health. These three conditions often go together and not until this century were people suffering from any or all of them regarded with any sympathy.

In the days of Henry VIII, in the early-16th century, vagabonds and tramps were whipped when caught. It was the custom to brand vagabonds with the letter 'V' on their shoulders. They were often forced to wander the roads, begging for food and money simply because they were unable to live by any other means. There was a shortage of work, food cost a lot of money, and religious charities, which for centuries had made it their business to help the poor, had almost ceased to exist.

In 1572, an Act of Parliament was passed under which every parish in the country had to collect a tax called the poor rate. This poor rate was to be used to set up the grimly-named Houses of Correction which were worse places even than the workhouses of the 19th century.

As time went on, there were changes in the way the poor rate was distributed, but there was little or no change in the unsympathetic way poor people were regarded.

There were some private charities and also the Friendly Societies which did much the same job as the National Insurance Scheme does now. Members of Friendly Societies got together and contributed money to a fund which, in the event of a member's unemployment or illness, was to be used to help support him and his family. The Friendly Societies also provided money to help members with such things as the expenses of travelling to find work, and insurance against loss or damage to their tools. This was not enough to deal with all the problems of poverty. Private charities and Friendly Societies were able to help only a small number of those people in Britain who were in need.

Fortunately there were many social reformers in the mid-19th century who insisted both in and out of Parliament on more help for the poor. It was the feeling that the community as a whole, headed by the government, should look after *all* its citizens that led to the eventual creation of the Welfare State.

Insurance and welfare

The foundations of the Welfare State were laid by the Liberal government in 1906.

First, in 1909, they introduced old age pensions. Under this scheme, people over seventy received pensions of five shillings per week if their incomes were too small for them to live decently.

Then, in 1911, the National Insurance Scheme was introduced,

Above The modern trial by jury before a judge and a panel of twelve men or women whose job it is to reach an impartial verdict originated in the 12th century when Henry II set up the Assize of Clarendon.

William Beveridge (1879–1963) British economist. Taught law and was a journalist. Became an authority on unemployment insurance and compiled a report in 1909. After serving on a number of commissions produced the 'Beveridge' report in 1942 which formed the basis for much post-war social insurance legislation.

Above The threat of transportation as a punishment for even minor crimes was very real in the 19th century. Offenders were sentenced to serve terms in the convict colonies in Australia and their treatment on the voyage from England was very harsh. Even trespass and damage to the railways was met with such sentences, as can be seen from this reproduction (below) of a railway notice of the period.

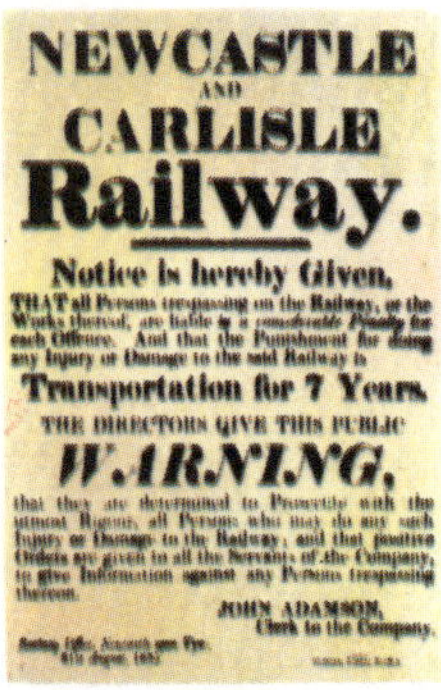

NEWCASTLE
AND
CARLISLE
Railway.

Notice is hereby Given,

Transportation for 7 Years.

THE DIRECTORS GIVE THIS PUBLIC

WARNING,

JOHN ADAMSON,
Clerk to the Company.

Above right In the early 19th century small children were sent up chimneys to work as sweeps.

under which both employers and workers contributed small weekly amounts to a central government fund. Then if workers were ill or out of work, they could get money from this fund to live on.

The Welfare State as we know it today was planned during the Second World War (1939-45). In 1942, William Beveridge (1879-1963) published a report called *Social Insurance and Allied Services*, which was known as the Beveridge Report. Among its recommendations were plans for children's allowances and health services, and for steps to be taken by the government to prevent mass unemployment.

When the war ended these proposals and many others became law.

The National Health Service was set up, providing free medical attention for everyone in Britain; the Industrial Injuries Act was passed to help factory workers and others who were injured as a result of accidents at work; and family allowances were granted to help poor people bring up their children.

The years between the Poor Law of 1834 and the Welfare State of 1945 had seen a great change in the public attitude towards poverty and the responsibility for its relief. These years also saw other very drastic changes.

Working conditions

In the 19th century, life was certainly difficult for the unemployed, but it was not much better when people did have work.

In one Manchester cotton mill, men, women and children worked for fourteen hours every day without a break. The door of the mill was locked during working hours, and the workers inside were not even allowed to send for water to drink, although it was always very hot in the mill.

The wages were small – only a few shillings a week – and life was made even harder by penalties for misbehaviour: a cotton spinner who opened a window was fined one shilling! And if a worker fell ill and could not find anybody to take his place, he had to pay the mill owner six shillings a day until he returned to work.

As for small children, they had no chance of going to school or enjoying themselves. Children of four or five worked in coal mines opening and shutting doors. Older, stronger children hauled trucks full of coal, crawling on all fours with belts round their waists and chains passing between their legs.

Small children were also sent up chimneys to work as sweeps and were employed in factories to clean the moving parts of the machinery or tie up loose threads in cotton spinners. Here, they were in constant danger of getting caught in the machines, for none of them was protected. Many a

man, woman and child lost a hand or an arm when they got too close to a machine or stumbled against it.

Factory workers protested strongly against their conditions. They staged demonstrations, smashed machinery or refused to work. But they were met with even greater violence from the authorities.

Very harsh prison sentences were imposed even for minor crimes. Many offenders were transported to Australia to serve sentences in convict colonies. Some Manchester weavers, who set out on a march to London taking nothing with them but blankets to sleep in, were arrested and imprisoned.

The government considered this kind of protest a danger to law and order and increased the number of offences punishable by death to as many as 200. So severe were some of the penalties that juries refused to convict many prisoners who were tried before them.

Peterloo

In Manchester in August 1819, a large crowd gathered to hear speeches demanding a change in the government's attitude. Soldiers were ordered to break up the meeting and in the panic which followed six people were killed and some four hundred injured.

This tragic event happened in a large open space called St Peter's Fields, and came to be known as 'Peterloo', a sarcastic reference to the battle of Waterloo which had been fought four years earlier. At least it shocked people into taking notice of the dreadful conditions of workers in particular, and the poor in general. During the next ten years people who were determined to improve those conditions – the social reformers – attracted more and more attention.

These were people like Elizabeth Fry (1780-1845) who devoted herself to improving prison conditions, and the Earl of Shaftesbury (1801-85) who worked to have the employment of children in factories banned.

There were also members of Parliament who had the same ideals, such as Sir Robert Peel (1788-1850) who created the 'peelers' or 'bobbies' (the first Metropolitan Police Force) and

Above When a large crowd assembled in St Peter's Fields in Manchester to demand parliamentary reforms, soldiers were called out to disperse it. In the conflict several people were killed and many injured.

Elizabeth Fry (1780–1845) English prison reformer and Quaker. In 1813 she visited Newgate prison, and was so horrified by the conditions there that she devoted the rest of her life to prison reform.

Above The Crystal Palace, a building of glass and iron designed by Joseph Paxton to house the Great Exhibition of 1851, a great display of the Victorian belief in progress.

Above right Victoria became queen at 18 years old and her reign (1837–1901) was the longest in British history.

Albert, Prince Consort of England (1819–61). Born in Germany, married Queen Victoria in 1840. Responsible for many social reforms and his encouragement of arts and industry promoted the Great Exhibition.

William Wilberforce (1759-1833), the man who fought to outlaw slavery.

In 1833, the Factory Act was passed which prohibited the employment of children under the age of nine in textile mills, and limited the amount of work older children should do to nine or twelve hours a day, depending on their ages.

Most important, the Act appointed factory inspectors to see that the law was obeyed. It was also part of this law that children working in factories should receive at least two hours' education a day.

It took another eleven years of protest before the Factory Act of 1844 was passed. This prohibited altogether the employment of children, made it necessary for dangerous machinery to be fenced in to prevent accidents, and laid down certain regulations about cleanliness in factories.

Having attacked conditions in the factories, the reformers in Parliament turned their attention to the mines. The result was the Collieries Act of 1842 which forbade the employment of women and children in the mines.

It was in the textile factories and mines that the worst conditions existed, and although the laws of the 1830s and 1840s improved those conditions for women and children, there were still millions of men who suffered long hours, low wages and filthy surroundings.

Trade unions

As early as 1720, a group of tailors in London, followed by another group in Sheffield, got together to persuade their employers to agree to better wages and conditions of work.

These were followed by other similar 'unions', as they were called, and the employers became suspicious. They were afraid that if workers organised themselves in this fashion, it could only mean trouble for them.

In 1833, the Grand National Consolidated Trades Union was formed, and half a million workers joined it within a few weeks. The Union planned to cause a general strike throughout the country and compel the government and employers to hand over control of Britain to the workers.

The employers used their influence in Parliament to fight these unions and such revolutionary ideas. They scored a victory in 1834, when six farmworkers from Tolpuddle in Dorset were convicted of 'administering illegal oaths'.

The oaths or promises had been taken when the workers were forming a farmworkers' union to try to obtain higher wages and better conditions.

The men were sentenced to transportation to Australia where they were to work in convict colonies for seven years.

This harsh sentence showed how determined government and employers were not to allow workers to have a say in how much – or rather, how little – they were paid and how long they worked.

The more intelligent workers then realised that there was a far greater chance of success if, instead of opposing their employers, they started to work for co-operation with them.

During the 1850s and 1860s, the strength of the trade unions grew, and in 1868 the first Trades Union Congress was called. That year thirty-four trade union delegates met at the Mechanics Institute in Manchester to discuss the 'present aspect of trade unions'.

Since that day, the Trades Union Congress, an organisation which has been called the 'Parliament of the Workers', has met almost every year.

Above A sense of pride in belonging to trade unions was expressed in the colourful banners paraded at meetings in the early 20th century. This is the banner of a branch of the National Union of General Workers in the 1920s.

Rise of the Labour Party

It soon became clear to the unions that they would be in a far more secure position if they formed their own political party and got their own members elected to Parliament. In this way the Labour Party was created.

A few men of working-class origin had been elected to Parliament during the 1870s, but the real breakthrough came with the election, in 1891, of James Keir Hardie (1856-1915) as the first Labour MP. In the General Election of 1906 the Labour Party won twenty-nine seats.

Although their numbers were growing, it was difficult for Labour members in Parliament. Unlike most other MPs they were not rich men and, since at that time they were not paid for their services, they had to be supported by the trade unions.

However, the situation brightened in 1911 when it was decided that MPs should receive a salary.

At last the Labour Party was on a reasonably firm basis and its strength increased after 1917, when its leader, Arthur Henderson (1863-1935), organised it into a truly national party with a definite policy of its own.

By 1924, the Party was strong enough to form, with some help from the Liberals, the first Labour government in Britain. Although this party of the working class was now a powerful force inside Parliament, it still did not mean that the sufferings of working people were over.

The General Strike

Effective power in the land remained in the hands of the employers, rather than the employed, and the attitude of some employers towards the workers was still very harsh. This was made clear in the events that led up to the General Strike in 1926.

At this time, relations between mine owners and coal miners were extremely bad. A crisis was reached when the

Above During the General Strike of 1926 many people came forward as volunteers to drive buses and trains and man other essential services.

mine owners decided to reduce miners' wages and lengthen their hours of work. On 3rd May 1926 the miners went on strike, using a slogan 'not a penny off the pay, not an hour on the day.'

They were quickly followed by workers in other trades and industries, and the result was that public services in Britain came to a complete standstill: no railways or buses ran, no food was distributed, no newspapers were printed, and the docks of Britain's great ports were silent and deserted.

The government called out soldiers and appeals were made for volunteers to keep essential services running. Thousands of professional people and university undergraduates came forward to drive buses and trains, to distribute food supplies, unload ships and act as policemen. They did these jobs so effectively that the trade unions realised that to stay out on strike was useless. Except for the miners, most of Britain's workers were back at work by 12th May.

The miners, however, stayed on strike for seven more months, but by December they were unable to support themselves and their families any longer. Cold, hungry and resentful, they were forced to return to work.

The bitterness caused by the General Strike grew more intense during the years that followed. In the early 1930s, more and more men found themselves unable to find work and having to live on the 'dole' – as the state pay to unemployed was called.

It was a hard and difficult time which was only beginning to improve when the international crisis of 1938 and the coming of world war in 1939 plunged the nation into yet another fight for survival.

Education, health and housing

The Factory Act of 1833, which made it illegal to employ children under the age of nine in textile mills, also made it compulsory for children to receive at least two hours' education a day. This education was paid for by the state, and it was with this Act that compulsory education in Britain began.

Before, poor families had been unable to pay for their children's education, and, in any case, they badly needed the money the children could earn working in the factories and mines.

Later in the 19th century several Education acts were passed by Parliament. One made it compulsory for all

Below In 1907 Lord Baden-Powell (as he later became) founded the Boy Scouts, an international movement for boys. It was an immediate success and Scout patrols were eventually formed in over 120 different countries.

Above There have been great improvements in the conditions in schools since the early 19th century. Contrasted here are a London charity school, 1819 (left) and a modern primary school (right) with landscaped gardens and built of prefabricated materials.

children up to the age of ten to go to school (1880) and another made education in elementary schools entirely free (1891). By 1921, the school leaving age had been raised to fourteen. In 1944 this was again raised to fifteen and a system introduced in which children took an examination at the age of eleven to decide what sort of secondary school they should go to – a grammar school or a secondary modern. In the 1960s people began to feel this system was unfair as children in secondary modern schools had little chance to reach high standards. A new comprehensive scheme was introduced in which schools taught a wide range of subjects to all the children in their area. This scheme was however strongly resisted in some areas. Some grammar schools became independent, like the fee-paying 'public' schools. Then the Conservative government elected in 1979 gave more support to traditional schools.

The National Health Service (1948) has enabled the sick to receive treatment and drugs they could not have afforded to pay for themselves. In this way, the health of Britain's citizens has improved and, just as important, some of the *fear* of illness has been taken away.

Then there was the question of housing. In 1851 the principle was first established that local councils had a duty to provide houses for poor people. Today, many people in Britain live in council houses and flats at subsidised rents. This means that they do not have to pay the full rent for their homes, only part of it. The rest is provided by the local council through rates and government grants.

Religious toleration

Britain today is not a secular state, like the United States or India. This means that Britain has an established state church: in England, this is the Church of England, and in Scotland, the Presbyterian Church of Scotland.

The Church of England, as we have read, came into being in the 16th century, when Henry VIII made himself head of the English church in place of the pope.

After the time of Henry VIII, there were several attempts to make the English church Roman Catholic again but none succeeded. In fact, there was a hatred of Roman Catholicism which lasted until well into the 19th century.

It was this hatred that led to the passing of the Test Act in 1673, which made it impossible for Catholics to hold any political or military positions in the country.

However, by the early 19th century, there were many who believed it was wrong to make laws against anyone just because he or she belonged to a different religion.

But it was not until 1890 that Catholics and Jews were allowed to hold public office, to sit in Parliament, or to go to university and enjoy the same rights as those people who belonged to the Church of England.

Today there is, officially, complete religious toleration in Britain. So long as it harms no one else, people are free to follow what religion they please.

Hugh Latimer
(1485?–1555) English Protestant martyr. Appointed a university preacher he soon became a reformist and took the side of Henry VIII in his divorce dispute with the pope. Became Bishop of Worcester, 1535. Fell out of favour and retired from court. When Mary became queen he was tried and executed for heresy.

Above The Menai suspension bridge across the Menai Strait, a channel between Caernarvon and Anglesey. It was built by Thomas Telford in 1826. The Strait is also crossed by the Britannia tubular bridge built by George Stephenson in 1850.

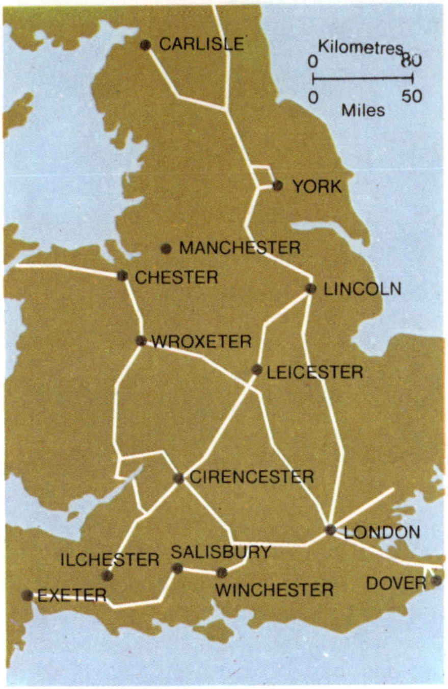

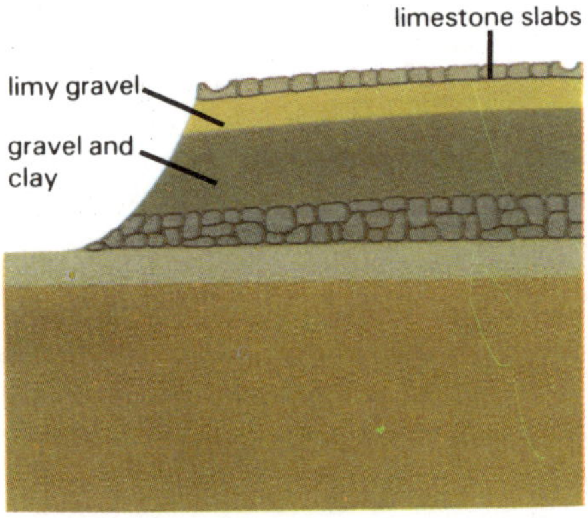

Above right Map of the principal Roman roads in Britain and a cross-section of a Roman road.

Thomas Telford (1757–1834) Scottish engineer. One of the greatest builders of roads and bridges of all time. Constructed the Caledonian canal in Scotland (1803–23), and is said to have built over 1,500 kilometres of roads and 1,200 bridges.

The British Empire

In the 19th century Britain took control of large areas of land in every part of the world. That empire, the largest the world had ever seen, was a reflection of the enormous power that Britain possessed through its command of trade, finance and manufacturing.

The colonies looked impressive on the map because they covered large areas, but they were less important than they looked. The colonies, such as Canada, Australia, South Africa and the British West Indies were scattered around the world. Each one was different from the others and was governed differently. The British did not care much for colonies in the early 19th century, but by the last quarter of the century they began to change their attitude. Within a few years, almost the whole of the continent of Africa was divided up among the powers of Europe. Britain also added part of New Guinea and Burma to its growing Asian empire.

However, the Second World War encouraged the growth of nationalism and independence. By 1945 it was obvious that the British Empire would have to be abolished or turned into something else. India and Pakistan became dominions within the British Commonwealth like Canada and Australia. Later they became republics, no longer recognizing the British monarch as head of state. The Commonwealth then became an association of independent states, with the monarch as head of the Commonwealth but not necessarily head of any member state.

Most ex-colonies, became independent, and chose to remain inside the Commonwealth of Nations. Links remained, and these helped to keep the Commonwealth – an organization without political or economic significance – in existence.

Immigrants to Britain

Many people from places like India, Pakistan and the West Indies have emigrated from their own countries to Britain because if offers better opportunities for work. Also, Britain offers a high degree of social justice and political freedom to people who become its citizens. No matter what their country of origin, their colour or their religion, all British citizens enjoy the same civic rights: the right to vote, full protection under the law, and proper entitlement to such social benefits as education, national insurance and free medical care.

About 100,000 people, most of them from the Commonwealth, entered the country each year in the 1950s, and early 1960s. Being black, the Commonwealth immigrants were easily noticeable, and they naturally tended to stick together. This put extra strain on the social services of the areas concerned: housing, hospitals, welfare and so on.

In 1962 the government introduced the first of a series of acts, each limiting immigration more closely. The 1971 act made immigration almost impossible for anyone without family connections in Britain. These sad, if necessary laws put an end to the old tradition of hospitality to people of other races and nations, of which the British had once been justifiably proud.

In 1981 serious riots broke out in several cities where there was a high proportion of poor people of West Indian or Asian origin. Unemployment was a major cause of the riots, but so was the general resentment felt by many blacks in a white-dominated society.

Above The canal built by James Brindley for the Duke of Bridgewater crossed the River Irwell by means of a three-arched stone aqueduct.

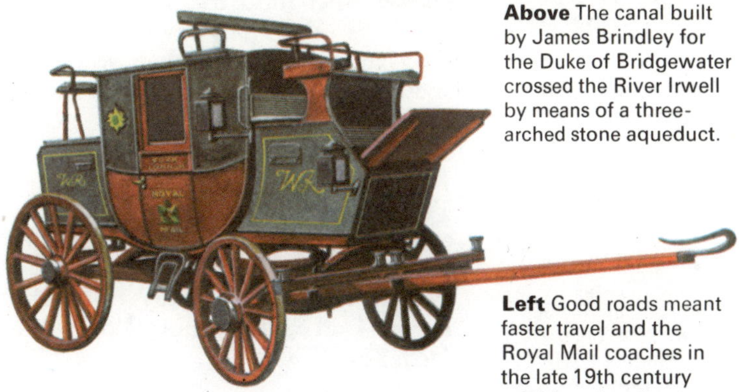

Left Good roads meant faster travel and the Royal Mail coaches in the late 19th century sped from London to Bristol in sixteen hours.

Roads and canals

When the Romans occupied Britain, they set about building a road system, and the place where London now stands was ideal for the hub of that system. It was the place nearest the sea where the River Thames could be forded and where a bridge could be built across it. As the same spot was also the tidal limit of the river, seagoing ships could reach it.

The sort of roads the Romans built were superb examples of civil engineering. Instead of wandering all round the hills, they cut through them and ran straight from town to town.

The actual network of main roads in Britain has remained much the same as it was when the Romans planned and built it.

It was just as well that Roman roads were solidly built, because for about 1,500 years very little was done to them beyond a few minor repairs.

Not until the start of the 19th century did a Scotsman, John McAdam (1756-1836), invent a system for hard road surfacing. But the new factories' owners could not wait for such an enormous task as the rebuilding of Britain's roads to be completed. Instead they found other means of transport.

Goods were frequently sent by sea round the coast, and, by the end of the 18th century, through a network of canals.

Britain's first important canal was opened in 1761 and connected the Duke of Bridgewater's coal mine at Worsley with Manchester, about sixteen kilometres away.

When it was realised that canals, built to run just where man wanted,

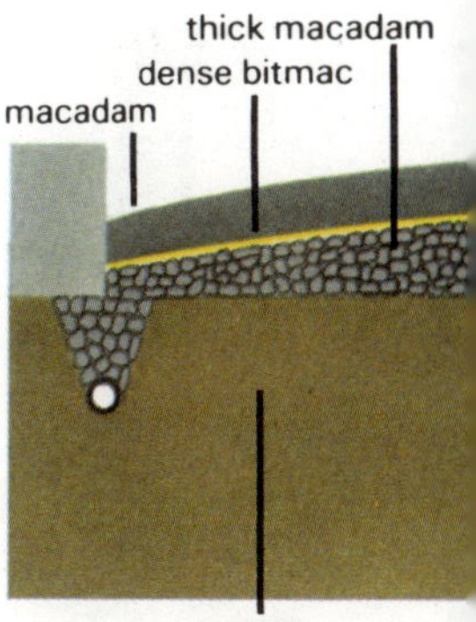

Above A section of a road built by John McAdam.

Isambard Kingdom Brunel (1806–59) English engineer. Designed Clifton suspension bridge (completed 1864) and Royal Albert bridge at Saltash. Built *Great Western,* first steamship to cross the Atlantic, and *Great Britain,* first ocean screw steamer. Appointed engineer to the Great Western Railway in 1833 and built tunnels, bridges and viaducts on that line. The *Great Eastern* (above right) which he built in 1853–8 was then the largest vessel afloat.

Below The *Planet,* built by George Stephenson in 1830 for the Liverpool and Manchester railway, with one of its first class carriages.

could save time and money, there was a mania for building them.

By the end of the 18th century, canals connected Leeds and Liverpool, Merthyr Tydfil and Cardiff, and several other industrial centres.

It was also industry's need for good communications that produced another alternative to road transport – the railways.

The railways

The first public railway in Britain, connecting Wandsworth on the Thames with Croydon, was opened in 1803. Along this railway, called the Surrey Iron Railway, horses drew the carriages.

Railways as we now know them began twenty-two years later. On 27th September 1825, an engine called *Locomotion* No. 1 built by George Stephenson (1781-1848) drew a train of wagons filled with people along a thirty-three kilometre railway which ran from Darlington to Stockton.

There was a great deal of opposition to the railways which, not unfairly, were described as noisy and smelly. 'Who would consent to be hurried along through the air at the rate of twenty miles per hour, all their lives being at the mercy of a tin pipe or a copper boiler?' wrote a journalist in 1835. Landowners, too, often did not want to sell their land to the railway companies, despite the handsome profit they might make.

However, as with the canals, so there was a railway building mania, and by 1845 the major English cities and towns were served by rail.

Among the engineers of this period, none was more remarkable than Isambard Kingdom Brunel (1806-59). As engineer to the Great Western Railway Company he designed and constructed the line from London (Paddington) to Bristol, with all its bridges, tunnels and cuttings. He saw this line to the west as the first section of a regular route between London and New York,

and went on to design ships for the Atlantic crossing. One of these, the *Great Eastern*, was the largest ship ever built at the time of its launching in 1858.

Railways had a great influence on life in Britain. By the turn of the century all parts of the country were linked by rail. With railways carrying newspapers, mail and food all over Britain, the differences between local areas were reduced, places were no longer isolated and the country as a whole became much closer together.

Growth of cities

Another effect of the railways has been to produce so-called 'dormitory' towns – towns where people live, but do not work.

All round London and other large cities, thousands of people travel in every day from outlying areas. During the day the population of the big cities and towns can 'grow' several times over. For many years only about 4,500 people actually lived in the City of London, while the working population was in the region of half a million.

Inevitably, the dormitory towns have become part of the cities. One example is Highbury, which is now in north London. In every direction, you can see row upon row of houses and streets full of traffic. Yet in 1811, Jane Austen (1775-1817), the novelist, could still describe Highbury as 'a large and populous village'.

Harrow in Middlesex was once an isolated country village. Today, it is part of Greater London, and a quarter or more or its inhabitants travel into the capital every day to work.

Agriculture

The move of workers away from the countryside, which was well under way by 1800 and has continued ever since, has meant a great reduction in the number of farmworkers.

In 1871, for example, there were still one and a half million people working on the land. By 1951, there were less than a million, and by 1960 this figure had dropped almost to half a million.

This has not been the only difficulty which British farmers have faced. Ever since the 1880s, they have had to compete with competition from cheap imported food. The vast prairies of Canada could produce greater quantities of wheat more cheaply than the fields of Britain, and the invention of refrigerated ships meant that meat from Argentina and New Zealand could be shipped to Britain in huge quantities.

By the turn of the 20th century, this situation was proving disastrous to British farmers. The British government did not protect British farm products by imposing a tax on imported food, which was done by most other European countries. This was because Britain was obliged to accept produce from the Commonwealth and Empire.

In order to protect themselves, some British farmers turned to specialising in fruit, milk or poultry production, while others tried to attract customers away from imported food by emphasising the 'quality' of their products.

During the 1930s the British government at last began to help the farmers. From 1929, rates were no longer charged for farm land, and, two years later, government organisations were set up to help farmers sell their potatoes, bacon, milk and other products.

During the Second World War this government help increased, because Britain was suddenly dependent on the food British farmers could grow. And when the war was over, the government continued to give farmers loans, grants and subsidies. Prices for livestock, milk, eggs, wool, potatoes,

Richard Trevithick (1771–1833) English engineer and inventor. Invented pumps and water pressure engines for use in mines. Developed a steam road carriage in 1801. Built the first steam locomotive for use on rails in 1804.

Above Two engines are shown, the one at the top being a GWR locomotive on the broad gauge favoured by Brunel and the one below on the narrower standard gauge.

Right Greenwich Hospital, built by Christopher Wren in 1705, was begun in the reign of Charles II to designs by Inigo Jones and Webb, and was added to in both the 18th and 19th centuries. Since 1873 it has housed the Royal Naval College.

Christopher Wren (1632–1723) English architect. Educated at Oxford and notable for work in mathematics and physics. Became a professor of astronomy. Designed buildings for Oxford and Cambridge universities. After the Great Fire of London, (1666) he drew plans for the rebuilding of London which were not followed. He did however design the new St Paul's cathedral and about fifty other new churches in London. Many other famous buildings were designed by him, including Greenwich Hospital and the Royal Exchange.

wheat, barley and other cereals were guaranteed and grants were made for farm improvements.

Town planning

Quite apart from the food needs of this increased population, it is vital for the future towns of Britain to be carefully planned. Most of our present towns were not planned at all: they simply grew to their present size as more people came to live in them and so they are now overcrowded and congested with traffic.

Britain's first planned garden city, Letchworth in Hertfordshire, was founded as long ago as 1903. As in Welwyn Garden City, founded seventeen years later, the plans included separate living areas and working areas, within easy reach of each other. These two towns were in the nature of experiments.

The planned town became particularly important after the Second World War, because millions of people were without homes, many of which had been destroyed in air raids.

In 1946, the New Towns Act was passed by Parliament. Twelve new towns were 'designated' in England and Wales, and three in Scotland. The first new town, Harlow in Essex, was created in 1955.

Britain and its European Partners

The acts restricting Commonwealth immigration were a sign of Britain's changing interests in the world during the 1960s. Britain had ceased to be a world power and was becoming a medium sized European power. Trade with Commonwealth countries fell steadily after 1945, while trade with European countries increased.

In 1957 the EEC – European Economic Community (now the EC) was founded. Britain, cautious about the decision, was not to join until January 1 1973, under the Conservative government of Edward Heath. However, despite the 'economic miracle' which the original EEC members had enjoyed in the 1960s, Britain found itself on the edge of disaster in the 1970s.

The Labour government of 1964-70 had achievements in education and other social affairs, but the industrial difficulties remained. In 1971 a Conservative

Industrial Relations Act and a freeze on wages provoked furious opposition from the unions. Heath had to call a general election in 1974, which Labour won, gaining co-operation from the TUC in a 'social contract' to regulate wages.

The Conservative government of Margaret Thatcher was elected in 1979 and became the longest serving government in the history of Britain, winning three consecutive general elections. Amongst its most significant changes has been the selling of nationalized industries to the public. Margaret Thatcher resigned in 1991, partly because of her reluctance over closer ties with the European Community (EC), and John Major replaced her as the new Prime Minister. However, by 1992 it was generally considered that Britain's future lay in Europe, but there was continuing discussion about such matters as a common currency and agricultural policy.

Above An area of the City of London known as the Barbican. This area was heavily bombed during the Second World War and plans were made to redevelop the site into a 'living city' for the future. The residential area provides homes, shops, offices, a school and recreational areas. In the Barbican arts centre there are theatres, a concert hall, cinema, conference facilities and restaurants.

Britain in the 1980s

In Britain, the Welsh and the Scots have naturally been anxious to preserve their own cultural identity, and there have been movements towards political independence in both countries. However, in Northern Ireland the Protestant majority have clung fiercely to their right to remain part of the United Kingdom. In 1922 Ireland had gained its independence, but Britain kept the six counties of Northern Ireland. Most of the large minority of Roman Catholics would have preferred union with the Republic in the South. They were therefore distrusted and kept out of the top jobs and politics. A peaceful rights campaign in the 1960s failed to get the reforms the Catholics wanted. In 1969 rioting broke out and British troops were sent to keep the peace. Secret revolutionary organisations, both Catholic and Protestant carried out murders, tortures and bombings. Internment (imprisonment without trial) was resented and imprisoned terrorists went on hunger strike, several deaths resulting.

Britain during the 1990s

Britain's political system is dominated by two parties - Conservative and Labour, with a Liberal Democrat party strong in local government. Although there are many critics, the social services are good. Care of the increasingly elderly population and of the sick causes much emotion. Defence spending is curtailed, but Britain's forces were successful in the Falkland Islands conflict in 1982, and in the Gulf War in 1991. The tragedy of Northern Ireland is still not resolved.

Inflation is down to a new low, but unemployment continues at around 3 million in 1993. Britain's standing as a major trading nation depends on its influence as a partner in the various Trade agreements. Its relationship with the United States is less cordial, as America turns its face to Asia. The position of the Monarchy as a stabilizing factor is increasingly doubted.

Despite all this, the country remains green and pleasant over vast tracts. Most people care about the environment, and about others' welfare. Supermarkets are full if the Churches are empty. There is less danger of complacency. And perhaps it is the ability to question the rightness of things that will ensure the nation continues for another thousand years.

Great events in British history

Coins of the emperor Hadrian

A crusader

Axe and block from the Tower of London

BC
750 Beginning of migration of Celtic people to Britain
55-54 Invasions of Britain by Julius Caesar
AD
43 Roman invasion of Britain under Aulus Plautius
61 Unsuccessful rebellion of Boadicea, British warrior-queen, against Roman invaders
78 Julius Agricola becomes Roman governor of Britain
120 Visit of the emperor Hadrian
122 Building of Hadrian's Wall to keep out northern tribes from Roman-occupied Britain
211 Visit of the emperor Severus
270 First attacks on England by Saxon pirates
345 Cult of Mithras at its height in Britain
410 Roman soldiers withdraw from Britain, which ceases to be part of the Roman Empire. Raids and settlements from about this time by the Jutes, Angles and Saxons
449 Landing in Kent of Jutish chiefs, known traditionally as Hengist and Horsa
519 Saxon kingdom of Wessex founded
530 At about this time the Romano-British leader 'King' Arthur leads resistance to invaders of Britain
563 Landing of St Columba in Iona and beginning of conversion of Picts
597 St Augustine lands in Kent, sent by Pope Gregory to spread Christianity in Britain
664 Synod of Whitby, which allies the English church to Rome
758 Mercia established as the strongest state in Britain
760-80 Offa, king of Mercia, builds his dyke as a defence against the Welsh
825 Wessex defeats Mercia at Ellandun
828 King Egbert of Wessex is recognised as overlord of all England
844 Kenneth MacAlpine first king of a united Scotland
850-80 Danish invasions on a large scale
854 Norsemen from Denmark and Norway settle for the first time in England
871 Alfred becomes king of Wessex and fights the Danish invaders. He builds a navy
878 Treaty of Wedmore between Alfred and Guthrum, the Danish leader, which divides England between them
883 Winchester becomes capital town in Alfred's England
900 Edward the Elder succeeds Alfred and recaptures most of England from the Danes
980-1000 Further Danish invasions of England
1013 England submits to Sweyn, the Danish king, who is acknowledged as king of England
1017 Sweyn's son, Canute, becomes king of England and Denmark
1040 Duncan, king of the Scots, murdered by Macbeth, who takes the crown
1042 Edward the Confessor succeeds to the throne of England and, by tradition, names William of Normandy as his successor
1053 Harold becomes earl of Wessex
1064 Harold of Wessex is shipwrecked in Normandy and held captive by William, to whom he does homage
1066 Harold becomes king of England. William of Normandy invades England to claim the throne. He defeats the English at the battle of Hastings, at which Harold is killed
1069 Feudal system begins in England
1072 Rebellion of Hereward the Wake against the Normans is defeated
1086 Domesday Book, a survey of all land and buildings in England for tax purposes, is compiled
1096 Beginning of the Crusades
1135 Succession to the English throne is disputed between Stephen and Matilda. Stephen is eventually crowned king.
1138 Scots invade England on the side of Matilda but are defeated at battle of the Standard
1154 Henry of Anjou, ruler of most of France, becomes Henry II of England. Nicholas Breakspear becomes Pope Adrian IV, the only Englishman ever to be elected
1162 Becket becomes archbishop of Canterbury and refuses to submit to Henry
1166 Assize of Clarendon sets up jury system. The beginning of 'Common Law'
1170 Thomas Becket murdered in Canterbury Cathedral
1171 Ireland partly conquered. Henry II becomes lord of Ireland
1190 Richard I sets out on third Crusade
1215 Barons rebel against King John. Signing of Magna Carta, which lessens the power of the king
1258 Great Council of Oxford. Simon de Montfort compels Henry III to rule with council of Barons. Civil war follows
1265 Simon de Montfort's Parliament sits. He is later killed at battle of Evesham by Henry III's son, Prince Edward
1284 Edward I conquers Wales. The first prince of Wales is born at Caernarvon
1290 Expulsion of the Jews from England
1295 The Model Parliament is summoned by Edward I
1296 Stone of Destiny, on which Scottish kings were crowned, captured by Edward I at battle of Dunbar
1297 Scottish war of independence. Battle of Stirling Bridge at which William Wallace defeats the English
1298 Wallace defeated at battle of Falkirk
1303 Execution of William Wallace
1306 Robert Bruce crowned king of Scotland
1314 Robert Bruce defeats Edward II at battle of Bannockburn
1337 Beginning of the 'Hundred Years' War' between England and France
1346 Siege of Calais. Battle of Crécy won by the English
1348 Black Death reaches England from the Continent
1356 English defeat the French at battle of Poitiers
1381 The Peasants' Revolt led by Wat Tyler
1382 John Wyclif, the religious reformer, condemned as a traitor
1400 Owen Glendower leads Welsh revolt against the English

1403 Henry IV's victory at Shrewsbury ends the rebellion of the Percys
1415 Henry V defeats the French at battle of Agincourt
1431 Joan of Arc is burned as a witch by the English at Rouen
1450 Jack Cade's rebellion, demanding reforms in government, is defeated
1455 Wars of the Roses begins between Yorkists (white rose) and Lancastrians (red rose)
1476 William Caxton's first printing press set up in England
1483 Murder of the boy king, Edward V and his brother in the Tower of London
1485 Battle of Bosworth Field. Richard III is defeated and Henry VII becomes the first Tudor king
1486 Henry VII marries Elizabeth, the daughter of Edward IV and unites the Houses of York and Lancaster
1487 Rebellion of Lambert Simnel, Yorkist claimant to the throne, defeated
1497 Rebellion headed by Perkin Warbeck defeated
1513 Scots invade England and are defeated at battle of Flodden Field. James IV of Scotland killed
1515 Wolsey becomes Lord Chancellor of England
1520 Henry VIII attends conference with Francis I of France at the 'Field of the Cloth of Gold'
1521 Pope Leo X grants Henry VIII title of Defender of the Faith
1525 William Tyndale's translation of the New Testament of the Bible is published
1534 Henry VIII denies the authority of the pope in England and becomes head of the English church
1536 The Pilgrimage of Grace, a Catholic revolt against religious changes. Dissolution of the monasteries begins. Union of England and Wales
1549 The first Book of Common Prayer
1553 Edward VI dies and Lady Jane Grey is proclaimed queen. Country rallies to Mary and plot fails
1554 Execution of Lady Jane Grey
1555 Protestant martyrs Ridley and Latimer burned at the stake
1558 Calais, the last English possession in France, is lost. Elizabeth I becomes queen of England and Protestantism is restored as the national religion
1570 Elizabeth I is excommunicated by the pope
1580 Francis Drake returns to England after his voyage around the world
1587 Babington's plot to assassinate Elizabeth is discovered. Mary, Queen of Scots, is executed.
1588 The Spanish Armada, sent by Philip of Spain to invade England, is defeated
1592 Presbyterian Church founded in Scotland
1600 East India Company is formed
1601 Rebellion and execution of the Earl of Essex
1603 James VI of Scotland becomes James I of England and the two kingdoms are united
1605 The Gunpowder Plot to blow up the House of Commons is discovered
1607 First British colony founded in Virginia

449 Hengist and Horsa land in Kent

1215 King John accepts the Magna Carta
1605 The Gunpowder Plot is discovered

Cromwellian soldier

African slave

Broadcasting House in London

1611 Authorised Version of the Bible completed
1618 Sir Walter Raleigh executed for treason
1620 Pilgrim Fathers sail in the *Mayflower* for America
1629 Charles I dissolves Parliament
1629-40 Personal government by Charles assisted by Strafford and Laud
1640 Charles I recalls Parliament
1641 Trial and execution of Strafford
1642 Civil war between Royalists and Parliamentarians begins
1644 Battle of Marston Moor in which the Royalists are defeated
1645 Formation of the New Model Army by Cromwell which wins an overwhelming battle at Naseby
1646 Charles I gives himself up to the Scots who surrender him to the Parliamentarians
1648 The House of Commons is cleared of Royalist sympathisers and the House of Lords abolished
1649 Trial and execution of Charles I
1653 Blake's victory over the Dutch brings to an end the war with Holland. Cromwell becomes Lord Protector of England
1656 Cromwell is offered the crown but refuses
1658 Death of Cromwell. He is succeeded by his son Richard
1660 Restoration of the monarchy under Charles II
1665 Great Plague in London
1666 Great Fire of London
1678 Titus Oates reveals the existence of a great 'Popish Plot'. Many Roman Catholics put on trial
1679 *Habeas Corpus* Act passed, making it illegal to imprison anyone without trial
1683 Rye House Plot to murder Charles II discovered
1685 Monmouth's rebellion ends in his defeat at Sedgmoor. There follows the 'Bloody Assizes' of Chief Justice Jeffreys
1688 James II flees from England to France. William of Orange and Mary land in England and accept the throne
1689 Declaration of Rights establishes the rule of Parliament
1690 Battle of the Boyne
1692 Massacre of Glencoe
1694 Bank of England established
1704 Marlborough's victory against the French at Blenheim
1707 The Act of Union unites the Parliaments of England and Scotland in the United Kingdom of Great Britain
1708 Victory of Oudenarde against the French
1709 Victory of Malplaquet against the French
1711 The Duke of Marlborough is dismissed from all offices
1713 The Treaty of Utrecht ends war with France
1715 First Jacobite rebellion in Scotland
1720 The South Sea Bubble 'bursts' and causes a financial scandal
1721 Sir Robert Walpole becomes the prime minister
1739 Wesleys start Methodist religious revival
1743 The battle of Dettingen against the French won by George II, the last English monarch to lead his troops in battle
1745 Second Jacobite rebellion led by Prince Charles Edward Stuart
1746 The rebellion is crushed at the battle of Culloden and Prince Charles is forced to flee to France
1752 Reformation of the calendar so that New Year starts on 1 January and not 25 March
1753 War between English and French colonists in Canada
1756 The Black Hole of Calcutta
1757 Clive wins a brilliant victory in India at the battle of Plassey
1759 General Wolfe leads a British victory over the French at Quebec
1760 The conquest of Canada is completed
1773 Warren Hastings appointed first Governor-General of India
1775 Outbreak of the American War of Independence
1783 The Treaty of Versailles ends the American War and Britain recognises the United States
1793 Outbreak of war between Britain and Revolutionary France
1797 Naval mutinies at Spithead and the Nore
1798 Nelson destroys a French fleet at the battle of the Nile
1799 Income Tax introduced by the younger Pitt as a wartime measure
1800 Parliaments of England and Ireland united by Act of Union. British forces capture Malta from the French
1801 Union Jack becomes flag of United Kingdom. First census taken in Britain
1807 Slave trade abolished
1808 Beginning of Peninsular War against Spain
1809 Sir John Moore is killed in battle at Corunna
1811 The Prince of Wales becomes Regent because of George III's insanity
1812 Luddite riots by unemployed workers against use of machinery in factories
1815 Battle of Waterloo won by Wellington and abdication of Napoleon
1819 The 'Peterloo' massacre at Manchester
1820 The Cato Street conspiracy
1832 First Parliamentary Reform Act in England
1833 First of many Factory Acts forbids employment of children under nine
1834 Reform of the Poor Law
1839 The first Chartist petition, calling for Parliamentary reforms, is presented to Parliament and refused. The colonisation of New Zealand
1840 Penny post introduced by Rowland Hill and the first use of adhesive postage stamps on letters
1841 Hong Kong becomes British colony
1842 Income Tax reintroduced
1845 The Potato Famine in Ireland
1846 Act passed for the abolition of the Corn Laws. Free trade begins
1851 Great Exhibition opens in Hyde Park
1854–56 Crimean War. Battles of Alma and Balaclava
1857 The Indian Mutiny
1867 Canada becomes a self-governing Dominion. Second Reform Act passed
1870 First Elementary Education Act. The Irish Land Act
1875 Britain gains major interest in Suez Canal
1877 Queen Victoria proclaimed Empress of India

1879 Zulu War
1882 Britain occupies Egypt
1884 Third Reform Act passed
1885 Fall of Khartoum and murder of General Gordon
1886 Gladstone becomes prime minister for third time and introduces Home Rule Bill
1888 Local Government Act establishes county councils
1891 Education Act makes all elementary education free
1892 Gladstone becomes prime minister for fourth and last time
1894 Parish councils created by Act of Parliament
1897 Diamond Jubilee of Queen Victoria
1898 The Sudan is conquered by Kitchener's victory at Omdurman
1899–1902 War with Boer Republics in South Africa
1900 The Boxer rising in China is crushed. The relief of Mafeking
1900 Modern Labour Party founded
1908 Old Age Pensions Act
1910 Union of South Africa constituted under the South African Act
1914 Outbreak of First World War. Irish Home Rule Act restores Irish Parliament
1918 Armistice signed to end First World War
1919 Treaty of Versailles
1920 League of Nations established
1922 End of British Protectorate in Egypt. Irish Free State established in southern Ireland
1924 First Labour Government. Wembley British Empire Exhibition
1926 General Strike in Britain
1928 Women's Suffrage Act gives vote to women on same terms as men
1931 Statute of Westminster by which British Dominions become sovereign states
1936 Abdication of Edward VIII. He becomes the Duke of Windsor
1938 Meeting at Munich between Hitler and Neville Chamberlain
1939 Outbreak of Second World War
1944 Allied landings in Normandy and the invasion of Germany
1945 Surrender of Germany and, later, Japan ends Second World War
1947 India and Pakistan become self-governing
1952 Accession of Queen Elizabeth II
1956 Britain and France enter Suez Canal Zone but later withdraw
1965 Death of Sir Winston Churchill
1969 Investiture of Prince of Wales
1969 British troops sent to N. Ireland
1971 Decimal currency introduced
1973 Britain joins Common Market
1977 Silver Jubilee of Queen Elizabeth II
1979 Margaret Thatcher is first woman prime minister
1980 Rhodesia becomes The Republic of Zimbabwe
1980 Formation of Social Democratic Party
1981 Street riots break out in many cities
1981 Marriage of Prince of Wales to Lady Diana Spencer
1982 Falkland Islands War between Britain and Argentina
1987 Mrs Thatcher re-elected for third term
1991 John Major elected as Conservative PM
1991 Gulf War between Iraq and the U N

1704 Marlborough's victory at Blenheim

1820 Arrest of Cato Street conspirators
1914 'Over the top' in the First World War

Facts about Britain

Highland and Lowland Britain

Physical The British Isles form a group of islands off the north-west coast of Europe (total area about 315,000 square kilometres). These islands include Great Britain (England, Wales and Scotland) and Ireland (Northern Ireland and the Republic of Ireland); the Isle of Wight, the Isles of Scilly and Anglesey; and the Orkneys and Shetlands together with numerous islands off the west coast of Scotland. All these form administrative counties or parts of counties of the mainland, but the Isle of Man and the Channel Islands, also part of the British Isles, are largely self-administered and are not part of England, Wales, Scotland or Northern Ireland.

It is about 960 kilometres in a straight line from the south coast of Britain to the extreme north and a little over 480 kilometres across at the widest part. Because of the many bays and inlets no point in the British Isles is more than 120 kilometres from tidal waters.

A red deer

Geology Great Britain contains rocks from all the main geological periods. New rocks lie to the south and east and the island can be divided roughly into two main regions – Lowland Britain and Highland Britain. Lowland Britain, where land hardly ever reaches a height of 300 metres above sea level, runs from about the mouth of the Tyne in the north-east of England to the mouth of the Exe in the south-west. Highland Britain includes all of Scotland, the whole of Wales and, in England, the Lake District, the area of the Pennines and the south-western peninsula of Devon and Cornwall.

The highest peaks are: in Scotland, Ben Nevis, 1,342 metres; in Wales, Snowdon, 1,085 metres; and in England, Scafell Pike, 978 metres.

St Edward's Crown

Animals The types of animals in the British Isles are, in general, similar to other parts of north-western Europe. Some mammals, including the wolf, bear, boar and reindeer, have become extinct. Mammals that survive in the wild include the red deer, roe deer, fallow deer, badger, fox, otter and the common and grey seals. Smaller mammals include the mouse, rat, vole, shrew, hedgehog, mole, squirrel, hare, rabbit, coypu, weasel and stoat. There are about 430 species of birds, some 230 of which are resident, the rest being regular visitors. Reptiles and amphibians are few and include snakes, frogs and toads. River and lake fish include salmon, trout, sea-trout, perch, roach, dace, grayling and pike. There are more than 21,000 different kinds of insects in the British Isles.

Population It is believed that at the end of the 11th century the population of Britain was about two million. At the end of the 17th century the population of England and Wales was about five and a half million, and that of Scotland about one million.

Censuses of the people of Great Britain have been taken regularly every ten years since 1801, with the exception of 1941, because of the war. The census of 1981 showed a population in the United Kingdom of 55,506,131.

The Monarchy The continuity of the monarchy has been broken only once in over a thousand years, and the hereditary principle upon which it was founded has never been abandoned. Queen Elizabeth II is a descendant of the Saxon king, Egbert, who united all England in the year 829. The inheritance of the crown is governed by rules of descent, so that sons of the sovereign are in order of succession according to seniority. If there are no sons, the daughters inherit in order of their seniority, and a queen is invested with the full powers of the crown as effectively as if she were a king. By convention, the wife of a king becomes a queen but the husband of a queen who inherits the crown in her own right has no special rank or privileges in the eyes of the constitution.

Parliament The supreme legislative authority in the United Kingdom is the Queen in Parliament, that is, the Queen and the two Houses of Parliament – the House of Lords and the House of Commons. The three elements of Parliament meet in separate places and come together only on ceremonial occasions. By the passing of the Parliament Act of 1911 the life of a United Kingdom Parliament was fixed as five years. During its life it can make or unmake any law and it even has power to prolong its own life in a time of national emergency, such as a war. Although in theory the power of Parliament is absolute, in practice it always bears in mind the common law which has grown up in Britain over the centuries, and would be unlikely to pass an Act which it knew would receive no public support. Also the system of party government in Britain ensures that Parliament makes laws with its responsibilities to the public clearly in mind.

These facts are abstracted from *Britain: an official handbook*, published by Her Majesty's Stationery Office.

The world we live in

Contents

51 The world we live in
Origin of the earth and life – Time chart of life on earth – Origin of fossils – The uses of fossils – The structure of the earth – Land and sea – Building mountains – Earthquakes – Mohole project – Rocks and minerals – Gemstones – Mineral deposits – Igneous rocks – Sedimentary rocks – Metamorphic rocks – Soils – Uses of rocks and minerals – Shaping the earth – Movement of rivers – Lakes – Water beneath the ground – Water as ice – The work of the sea – Working wind – Land on fire – The oceans – Ocean islands – The moving oceans – Waves and winds – Oceanography – Food from the sea – Weather and climate – Life from the sun – The moving air – Air masses – Clouds – Rain, hail, snow and fog – Violent winds – Local winds – Thunder and lightning – Weather forecasting

81 Man explores his world
The Norsemen – Exploring for trade – Around the world – Australia and America – The African continent – First steps in Asia – The Australian interior – The north and south poles
Maps
Mercator's projection – Europe – Asia – Far East – Africa – North America – South America – Australia and New Zealand

99 The world in space
The first astronomers – The moving heavens – The laws of Newton

103 The solar system
The photosphere – How does the sun shine? – The planet earth – The seasons – Gravity and atmosphere – The moon – The origin of craters – The moon's phases – The planets – Mercury – Venus – Mars – Jupiter – Saturn – Uranus and Neptune – Pluto – Life on other planets – Asteroids – Meteors – Comets

116 The stars
Measuring distances – Star brightness – Composition of stars – Movement of stars – Doppler effect – Star maps – Star groups – Interstellar material – The moving galaxies – Star clusters – Binary stars – Variable stars – Radio sources – Mysterious objects in space – Life and death of a star – How the universe began

129 Space travel
Rocket engines – Artificial satellites – The Apollo programme – Man in space – Training astronauts – Life support system – Satellites into orbit – Multi-stage rockets – Staying in orbit – Communications satellites – Moon probes – Aiming at the moon – Probes to the planets – Space laboratories – Space shuttle

Above The great buttes in Arizona's Monument Valley in the United States rise in some cases to over 150 metres in height. These dramatic natural monuments are carved by wind and water, the process of erosion which has lowered the desert floor over a long period of possibly millions of years. This area of the United States is one of the country's main tourist attractions and has been the scene for many Western films.

The world we live in

Very few of us imagine that the earth ever had a birthday – but, of course, it did. Scientists today think it happened about 4,700 million years ago but it may be even older.

Throughout time man has investigated the age of the earth and various figures have been given. Possibly the most definite, if not the most accurate, was published by James Usher (1581-1656), archbishop of Armagh, who wrote that the beginning of time fell upon the night before the twenty-third day of October in the year 4004 BC. Gradually it was realised that the earth was certainly much older than this, and that such a short space of time could not have contained all the known geological events.

Time is the most important factor in the history of the earth's formation, for periods of mountain building, erosion (the wearing away of rock), continental drift and evolution all suppose vast spans of time: not hundreds or thousands of years but hundreds of millions.

At the end of the 18th century the Scottish geologist James Hutton (1726-97) published his famous work *Theory of the Earth*, in which the now well-known phrase 'the present is the key to the past' appeared. Charles Lyell (1797-1875) adopted the same idea in his *Principles of Geology*, and as more and more geologists studied rocks in the field it soon became evident that the surface of the earth must have taken millions of years to form.

The modern figures for the age of the earth are based on the dating of rocks by radioactivity. The constant decay of radioactive substances is the basis of this method. The element Uranium 238 is known to have a half-life of 4,500 million years. All this means is that a given quantity of the material will be reduced by one-half in 4,500 million years. Therefore the age of some rocks which contain Uranium 238 can be determined directly.

Promising results have also been obtained by other methods, and some rocks have been dated as 3,500 million years old.

Another interesting method was used by a Swedish geologist to try to find the time that had elapsed since

Right This scene is an imaginative reconstruction of what the surface of the earth may have looked like during its early life. The planet was covered with a red sea of fiery liquid and in places the molten rock has solidified into islands of granite which were eventually to form the land surface. After the violent upheavals of those very early years the surface would have cooled and the rains begun. In this way the oceans were formed in which all life probably started.

Sweden was covered by ice. During the summer the fast-running streams deposit quantities of coarse material in the lakes. In winter, because much of the land is frozen, only very fine particles of material are deposited. Thus there are alternating coarse and fine layers which, if a section is cut through them, can be counted rather like the rings of a tree.

Although useful at the time, such methods have been overtaken by the use of radio-carbon (Carbon 14), which is used in exactly the same way as Uranium 238.

Incidentally, the figure arrived at by the Swedish geologist for the passing of the ice was 8,500 years, while the figure given by the more accurate radio-carbon method was 11,000 years.

Origin of the earth and life

'Where did the earth come from?' 'How did the earth form?', 'How did life originate?' – these are the sort of questions that have been asked for hundreds of years. The subject of the origin of the earth and life has fascinated man in every age and there has been no shortage of theories to account for it. Even now, when we can go to the moon and know more than ever before about the earth's interior, we cannot tell the whole story of the earth's beginning. Scientists of all kinds are involved in trying to provide the missing details. Geologists, astronomers, mathematicians, chemists and biologists are all needed if we are ever to answer the questions beginning 'where?' and 'how?'

Any theory of the origin of the earth which is put forward must also apply to the other planets. Indeed the origin of the solar system is the true starting point for discovering the origin of the earth.

The bodies in the solar system are thought to have formed from the same cloud of gas and dust. Certain definite

principles have been established for the origin of the earth. It almost certainly started its life as small particles which may have been gaseous or solid. These gradually came together and, again, it is almost certain that heat was involved.

Perhaps the most acceptable chain of events started with a mass of hot gases in which the particles gradually came together. This primeval earth passed through a liquid stage until finally the first crust was formed. The original earth must have had a very thick atmosphere. There would have been much steam in it. Gradually the mass would have cooled, leading to the first rains and the first weathering and destruction of the rocks. These first rains most likely lasted for years and they would have been torrential. The make-up of the atmosphere was very different from that of today and probably resembled the atmosphere that would still be encountered on planets such as Jupiter. There was most likely no free oxygen and the atmosphere would consist mostly of ammonia, methane and water vapour.

The origin of life is still something of a mystery. The fossil record does little to help except to suggest a steady development from relatively simple animals to the more complex. Undoubtedly the first animals would not have had any hard parts, so that there was little or no chance of them becoming fossils. However, various fossils have been found in Pre-Cambrian rocks (a period much advanced from that of the origin of life), many of them with no known relatives.

Of the several theories about the origin of life, scientists usually discard a supernatural event as being unscientific, since it is not capable of being investigated. That living organisms came to earth from outer space or that they arose from inorganic matter such as carbon dioxide or water, also seems unlikely. This leaves the proposal that life began spontaneously from organic compounds, almost certainly in the oceans of the primitive earth. This theory is generally accepted by scientists today.

The evolution of the earliest animals and plants must be seen against the vast differences in the earth's atmosphere and general condition today compared with earliest times. Because of these differences it is believed that no spontaneous generation of life could happen at the present time.

It has been proved in the laboratory that by subjecting water vapour, methane and ammonia to an electrical discharge (in nature lightning would provide this) complex organic molecules are produced. This may well be how the first amino-acids and proteins were formed. Possibly they became concentrated in lagoons or sheltered areas of the sea. There are today one-celled plants which live in environments without free oxygen and, in fact, emit it themselves. This could well have been the case in those far distant days when life began. One thing is certain: in the history of the earth the early stage of 'preparation' for life took much longer than the actual development of life as we know it today.

Above Two typical fossils. At the top is a late Pre-Cambrian fossil of a worm – the oldest type of animal to be preserved. It comes from the Ediacara Hills, South Australia. At the bottom is an example of a group of fossils called *Turritella* which are slender spiral-shaped shells of gastropods from the Cretaceous period.

Eras	Age in millions of years	Periods
Azoic	4700	**Pre-Cambrian** Origin of the earth
Proterozoic	3000	
Palaeozoic ancient life	570	**Cambrian** After Cambria, the Roman name for Wales
	500	**Ordovician** After Ordovices, a Celtic tribe
	440	**Silurian** After Silures, a Celtic tribe
	395	**Devonian** After the English county of Devon
	345	**Carboniferous** From the existence of coal seams
	280	**Permian** After the Russian province of Perm
Mesozoic middle life	225	**Triassic** After three-fold division in Germany
	195	**Jurassic** After Jura mountains on French-Swiss frontier
	136	**Cretaceous** From the Latin word for chalk
Cainozoic recent life	65	**Palaeocene** Meaning the earliest of recent forms of life
	54	**Eocene** Meaning the dawn of recent life
	38	**Oligocene** Meaning few recent forms of life
	26	**Miocene** Meaning less recent forms of life
	7	**Pliocene** Meaning more recent life
	2	**Pleistocene** Meaning most recent life
	50000 BC	**Holocene** Meaning wholly recent life

Geographical conditions

From the formation of the earth: barren landscapes, torrential rain, several ice ages, the beginning of life.

Shallow seas, advancing and retreating. Volcanoes in Wales and Europe generally. Warm climate.

Seas advance and retreat. Volcanic activity, warm climate. First animals with backbones.

Fluctuations of sea level. First evidence of new mountains being formed. First land plants.

Mountain building in north west Europe and North America. Plants become abundant, as do fishes. First amphibians.

Shallow seas and swamps. Giant insects and first reptiles. Trees grew to thirty metres in height.

Lofty mountains formed, such as the Appalachians in the United States. Deserts in northern hemisphere.

Deserts, salt lakes and shallow seas. First ichthyosaurs and mammals.

Sea invades land. Continents possibly begin to divide. Reptiles evolve. Dinosaurs roam the land.

Swamps and deltas. Mountain building – Rocky Mountains and the Andes. Insects and flowering plants spread.

Advance of sea. Warm climate. Dinosaurs have become extinct along with many other reptiles.

Further mountain building. Lava outpourings in Scotland, Ireland and Arctic. Warm. Beginning of modern mammals.

Mountain building of Alps commenced. Warm. Grasslands. Spread of mammals.

Formation of Alps and Himalayas. Primitive anthropoid ape.

Present-day climate. Lands appear almost as today. Man-like apes continue to develop.

Ice sheets advance and retreat over Europe, North America and Antarctica. Development of primitive man.

Ice retreats. Sea level rises. Forests develop. Man becomes dominant over his environment.

Past geography

The dark areas show the probable land formation of each period.

Cambrian times

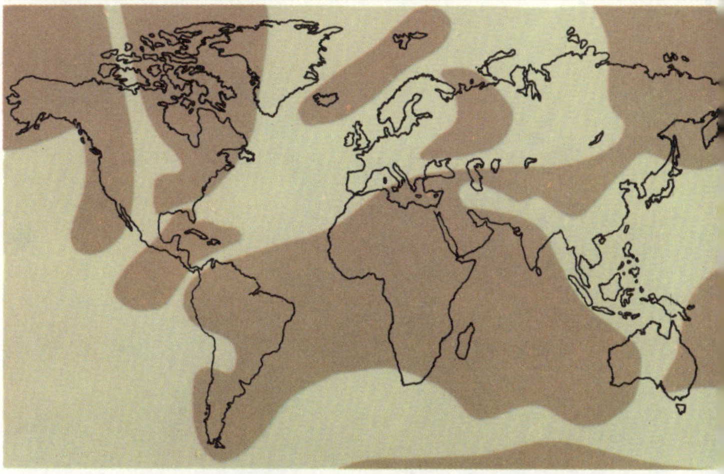

Jurassic times

Eocene times

Above Geology as a science is little more than a century and a half old, but it has provided us with a remarkably detailed record of the earth's past. This diagram illustrates how a geologist can tell the order in which the various periods of earth history came. Starting at the bottom strata with the fossil of a jellyfish of the Cambrian period and going on to a fossil flying reptile of the Jurassic period, and a mastodon of the Pleistocene, we are given clues as to how the lands and oceans gradually evolved. In mountain areas the strata often cracked and were pushed out of line. Since each strata contains fossils a geologist will be able to recognise and identify the period of history it represents.

Origin of fossils

The word fossil comes from the Latin word *fossilis*, which means dug up. In days gone by anything discovered in soil or rock was termed a fossil. The old books grouped together rocks, minerals and true fossils as the same things. Gradually, over the years, the word came to mean only animal and plant remains that were dug up. Later still the word was restricted only to those plants and animals which lived before historic times.

By no means all animals and plants that lived and died have become fossils. Those that lived on land or flew over it had really very little chance of being preserved. When they died their bodies were quickly attacked by the forces of the weather and by other creatures so that there was nothing left to become a fossil. Those which lived in the sea or along its shore had a much better chance of being quickly covered with mud or sand and hence of becoming a fossil. The burying of the body must happen soon after death for fossilisation to take place. Sand and mud have been mentioned but volcanic dust may have the same effect.

Rarely are entire animals preserved, although there are a few spectacular examples. Entire mammoths have been found in Siberia and Alaska completely refrigerated in frozen ground for some 25,000 years. It was even possible to examine the contents of their stomachs. Insects are often found preserved in the sticky resin of trees known as amber. The Baltic area of Europe is famous for such finds.

The natural tar-pits of Rancho La Brea in Los Angeles, California, claimed many victims and such has been their state of preservation that it has enabled scientists to say much about the otherwise unpreserved parts of the various prehistoric animals.

The dry climate of Patagonia in South America has led to the mummification of the skins of the giant ground sloths. Although not quite the same thing, for in this case it is really an impression, the skins of dinosaurs have been preserved as well.

One of the most startling fossil finds was that of nests of dinosaur eggs. In Mongolia eggs have been found with their fossilised embryos. Just as the soft parts are unlikely to have been preserved so, too, is there no evidence of the colour of prehistoric animals and plants.

The bones and teeth of mammals and birds, and the shells of molluscs, are the most frequent fossil finds. Very rarely a soft-bodied creature has left a trace or impression on very fine mud and this has been preserved. The hard parts themselves are changed. Often silica replaces the original calcium carbonate. It may be due to percolating waters that grain by grain such replacement takes place. In Arizona whole tree trunks have been replaced by silica and the cell structure of the plant faithfully reproduced.

Sometimes all that remains in the rock is a hollow mould or an internal cast after the original shell has been washed and dissolved away. These less spectacular finds form the bulk of the fossils in any collection, and it is due to such collections and the study of them that we are able to know so much about the past life of the earth and how man can use fossils.

The uses of fossils

Palaeontologists (people who study fossils) are often asked what use fossils have. Not an unreasonable question, really, considering how they are found and what they are. Perhaps the greatest use of fossils is in correlating rocks in different areas or countries. This is a method used by geologists to relate stratas or rock to each other by the comparison of the fossils they contain. The location of fossils can also prove that various land areas were once joined together.

The correlation of rocks throughout the world owes much to fossils. Various fossils are typical of certain former conditions and ages. A trilobite in rocks of Lower Cambrian age will not be found in Silurian rocks. Thus by the fossil content of any rock outcrop a good indication of its age and position relative to others may be evident. The correlation of rocks is important to all forms of mining.

Not all fossils are suitable for such work. The various zones of the Jurassic system (136-195 million years ago) are recognised by the different types of ammonite, while the divisions of the Ordovician (440-500 million years ago) are shown by means of graptolites.

Both coal and oil are fossil fuels and the tremendous importance of these to the modern world clearly shows what we owe to fossils. In some regions of the world fossils are so abundant that they are used for road metal.

Above The fossils shown in this drawing are **1** Tree fern, Eocene period (50 million years ago). **2** Leaf of a Platanus tree, Miocene period (11 million years ago). **3** Sea-urchin. **4, 6, 7, 8** Various ammonites up to 400 million years old. **5** Crab of Eocene period (40 million years ago). **9** Uintacyon, a tree-climbing carnivorous animal of the Eocene period (55 million years ago).

The study of fossils is the only way in which evolution can be practically demonstrated. But long before the science of geology and the study of fossils had been begun in any serious way, these remains of former worlds were used for various decorative and medicinal purposes. They have been used to make necklaces by primitive peoples all over the world. Medicinal use includes fossil oysters once used in England to cure cattle illnesses, and belemnites used in the treatment of eye infections in horses.

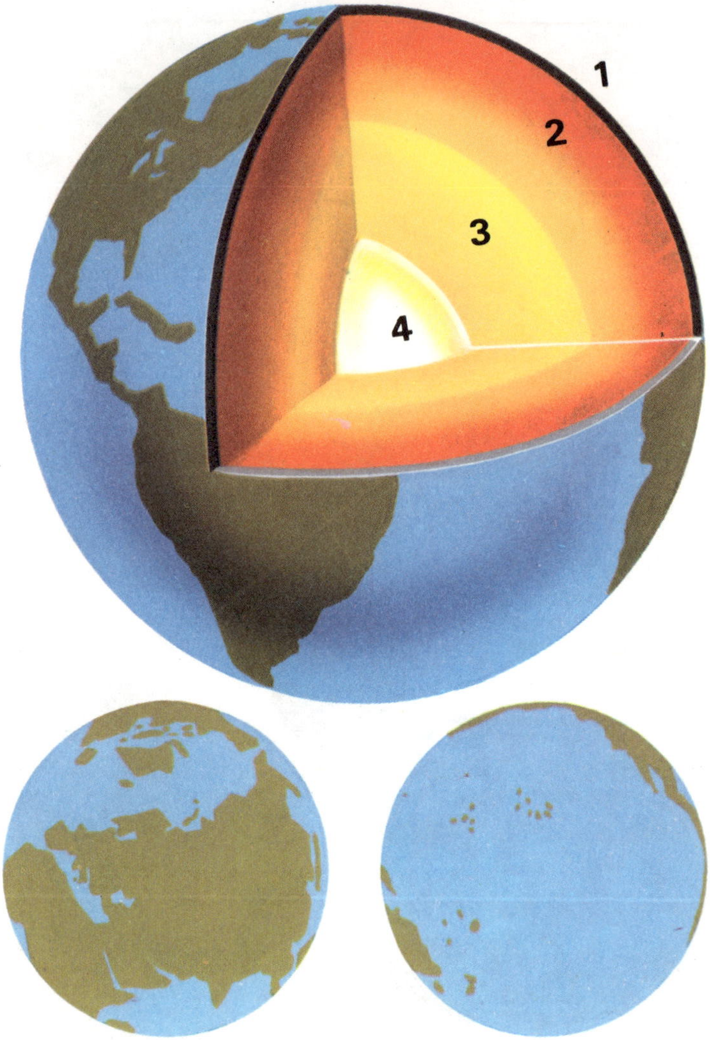

Above The cutaway drawing of the earth shows its supposed interior structure based on readings of earthquake waves. This diagram has been simplified but it indicates the four basic layers: **1** crust, **2** mantle, **3** outer core, **4** inner core. The other two spheres show how much of the land is crowded together on one side of the globe, whereas a view taken looking at the Pacific Ocean produces the impression of a world covered by water.

The structure of the earth

Most people think of the earth as a ball or sphere. This is the way it is always shown on globes or in an atlas. In reality it is an ellipsoid, meaning that it is slightly flattened at the north and south poles.

Wherever we may be on earth, there is solid rock somewhere beneath us. This rock may be covered by an ocean, or thick layers of ice, or a variety of sub-soils on dry land, but it is always there, as we should find if we could dig or drill deep enough. Such rock forms the first true layer of the earth, going towards the centre, and is known as the earth's crust. The crust of the earth is not constant in its depth, being thinner beneath the oceans than below the mountain ranges.

The upper portion of the crust is generally called sial because it is largely composed of rocks made of *si*lica and *al*umina. The lower portion is called sima because here the rocks contain *si*lica and *ma*gnesia. The average depth of the earth's crust is not greater than sixty-five kilometres, which, although it sounds quite a long way, is very thin and we think of the earth as a whole. And beneath some of the deep ocean trenches it may be no more than three kilometres.

Below the crust is the mantle, which is made up of more basic rocks and is about 2,900 kilometres thick. Beneath this is the central core. We still don't know a great deal about the core but it is thought to be made up of ferro-nickel, which is an alloy of iron and nickel. The outer core is in molten form and the inner core is solid. Intense pressures and great heat exist at the centre of the earth.

Thus we have a very definite layered structure to the earth, with density increasing towards the centre.

If you look at a world map you will see that the coastlines of the Americas fit roughly into those of Africa and southern Europe, which suggests that they might once have been joined together.

Other evidence is slowly coming to light. Fossils of certain animals and plants have been found in rocks now widely separated by oceans, and nowhere else. It has also been found that rock formations on the land on both sides of the Atlantic Ocean are related to each other. These facts are more easily explained if in fact the continents were once joined.

Geologists who study the magnetism of ancient rocks (called palaeomagnetism) have proved that at different times the poles have been located in different places. For example, the north pole was once sited in the Pacific Ocean. This too supports the theory of 'one' continent.

So there is a great deal of evidence to suggest that the continents have moved, and are doing so still.

A generally accepted theory which explains this movement, or continental drift, is plate tectonics. According to this theory, the top layer of the mantle, on which the crust rests, is rigid and is divided up into sections or 'plates'. Under this is a weaker layer of mantle which is able to flow. Material from this

layer sometimes wells up to the surface of the earth and spreads out. Material also sinks into the earth at the oceanic trenches.

We cannot usually see this flow because it takes place under the oceans, but we can see its effects. The flow of material moves the plates, pushing them together in some areas and pushing them apart in others. So, tremendous pressures build up at the boundaries of the plates. These may cause the surface of the earth to rise up slowly to form mountains, or sink to form, say, ocean trenches. Volcanic eruptions and earthquakes are more immediate effects. Most volcanoes and earthquakes occur along plate boundaries, as do recent mountains.

Land and sea

Ours is a world of sea. About 71 per cent of the surface of the earth is water, and only 29 per cent is land.

Most of the land is found north of the equator. The only large masses to the south are Africa (south of the Sahara), Australasia, and South America; but the vast block of Euro-Asia and North America in the north is far greater.

A great mountain chain, which includes the Rockies and the Andes, runs down the western side of the whole continent of the Americas. A similar range is found running through eastern Asia and eastern Australia, though it is by no means so high. The other great mountain mass stretches from the Pyrenees in southern Europe, through the Alps to the Balkan Peninsula and the lofty heights of the Himalayan range, and then onward through the East Indies.

The distribution of all these mountain ranges is due to the structure and past history of the earth. Many of the mountains are geologically young; in fact the Himalayas are still rising. On the other hand, some of the once great mountain chains, such as the Appalachians of North America and the Highlands of Scotland, now exhibit only a small part of their past glory.

Building mountains

The crust of the earth, whether on land or under water, is often covered by rocks which have their origin in the sediments of some ancient sea. The great thicknesses of sediment have slowly piled up over a long period. On land these sediments date back many hundreds of millions of years but on the sea bed they are no more than about a hundred million years old.

However unlikely it may seem, many mountains begun deep in the ocean. As mentioned earlier, the crust of the earth moves very slowly, carried on 'plates' of the mantle. Where an oceanic plate collides with a continental plate it is pushed beneath it, forming a

Above These three drawings illustrate the theory of Continental Drift, which suggests that all the existing continents were once part of the same land mass. There are many reasons for believing this to be true, chiefly the evidence of the land formations, the similarity of types of animals and plants which exist in different lands and, not least, the existing shapes of continents themselves. For example it is easy to see how South America and Africa fit together like pieces in a jigsaw puzzle.

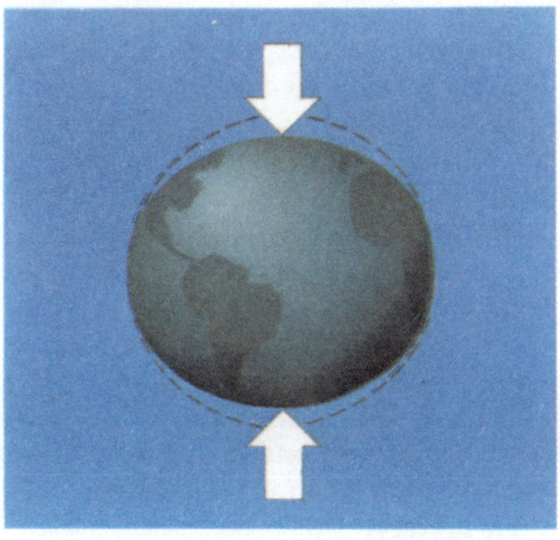

Left This simple diagram illustrates the fact that the earth is not a circle but an ellipsoid, that is it is flattened at the north and south poles.

Right The great forces which work upon the earth's surface move very slowly to produce the kind of rock folds seen in this drawing.

Below If the Mohole project had been successful it might have answered many of the scientists' questions about the nature of the earth's mantle. This drawing suggests the difficulty of trying to drill from a ship through the earth's crust, which is about five kilometres below the surface of the water.

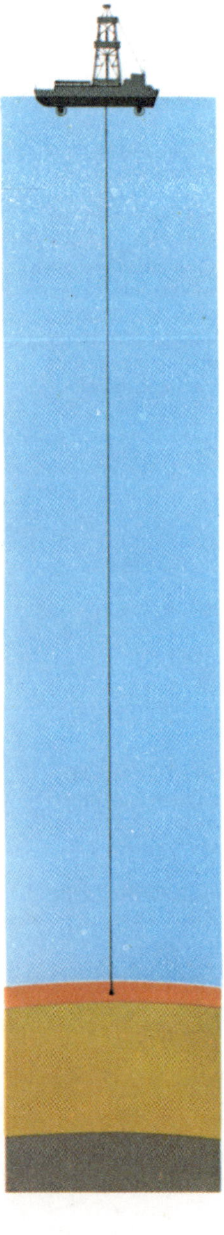

trough, known as an oceanic trench. As the oceanic plate is forced into the earth, huge pressures build up. Vast amounts of sediment accumulate in an oceanic trench. Gradually, over millions of years, the pressure folds and uplifts the material in the trench, creating mountain ranges, such as the Andes in South America.

Similarly, pressures can build up where continental plates collide. They 'crumple' along the boundary of the plates, and the rocks fold and are raised up. The Himalayan mountains are thought to have been formed in this way.

Sometimes mountains are not formed by folding but by what is called faulting. This happens when great blocks of the earth's crust are forced upwards. The Pennines in England, the great Sierra Nevada in the United States and the Little and Great Kharas of the Kalahari in Africa are all block mountains.

It sometimes happens that a great block will sink to form a rift valley, such as the famous Great Rift Valley stretching hundreds of kilometres from the Middle East area southwards down eastern Africa. The River Rhine, too, flows through a rift valley bounded by block mountains of the Vosges and the Black Forest.

Some other mountains are really volcanoes built high by vast outpourings of lava and heaps of ash and broken rock fragments ejected from their craters.

Earthquakes

Most of us have read about earthquakes, or seen pictures of the damage they can cause. Fortunately, few of us have actually experienced them. The study of earthquakes is called seismology (from the Greek *seismos* meaning a shaking) and the shock waves produced by them are recorded on an apparatus called a seismograph.

There are many centres throughout the world recording and studying earthquakes. The instruments used are able to detect many very small earthquakes which could not be felt by man. Such waves prove that our earth is not the solid and unmoving mass we might imagine.

Earthquakes originate where rock structures beneath the surface of the land break up and move along lines known as faults.

Earth tremors can occur anywhere, but real earthquakes, during which whole cities or towns may be shaken to pieces and thousands of people killed, are almost all limited to certain regions. These regions correspond to the major mountain ranges, volcanoes, and deep sea trenches where land is still being built up and where subterranean, or underground, activity is therefore most frequent.

The most immediate effects of an earthquake are landslides and the creation of large crevices in the surface of the earth. If earthquakes originate under the sea, they can also produce

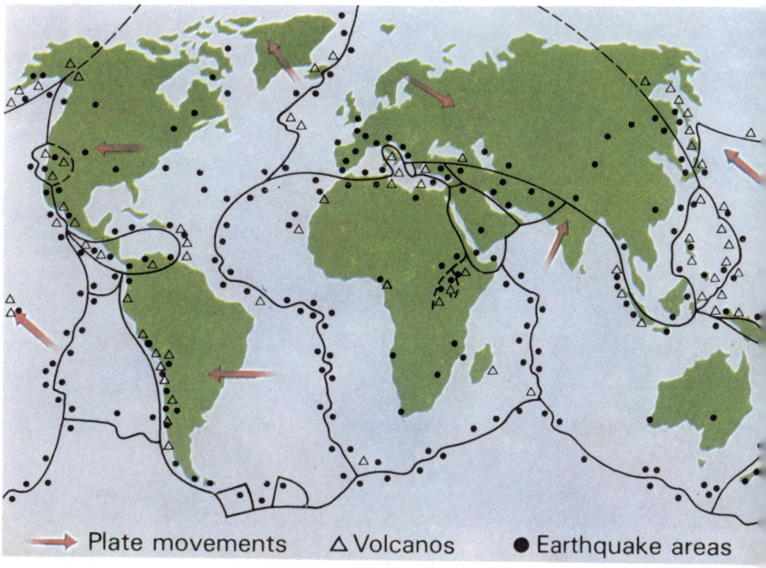

Above This map shows the principal earthquakes and volcanic zones, and plate boundaries. These correspond with areas of recent mountain building.

huge ocean waves, which may travel for thousands of kilometres. When such a wave reaches land it causes flooding and a great loss of life and property. Tidal wave is the name sometimes given to such a wave although, of course, it has nothing to do with the tides. Its correct name is a tsunami.

The intensity of the shock waves recorded on the seismograph are measured by the various earthquake stations. By studying these waves scientists can find out much about the interior of the earth. A comparison of the time taken for the waves to reach different stations, and their position in relation to each other, enables the exact location of an earthquake to be worked out wherever it may have occurred. This location is called the epicentre. The point directly beneath this where the earthquake originated in the earth's crust is called the focus.

The various layers of the earth's crust have all been determined from the study of shock waves. It has also led to the discovery of a definite boundary line between the crust and the mantle, called the Mohorovicic Discontinuity after the Yugoslav scientist Andrija Mohorovicic who first identified it in 1909.

Mohole project

American scientists once had the idea of drilling to the mantle layer of the earth to try to find out what it was really composed of. This project was called Mohole from the Mohorovicic Discontinuity (abbreviation Moho). The scientists decided the best place to drill would be at sea at a point where the crust of the earth was fairly thin.

The technical difficulties of drilling at sea, and lack of funds, caused the project to be abandoned. The greatest depth reached so far is 9.7 kilometres, on the Kola peninsula in Russia. As technical expertise increases, it is hoped that more of the earth's secrets will be revealed.

Rocks and minerals

The earth is made up of rocks, and rocks are made up of minerals. What is a mineral? It has a definite chemical make-up, and is classified according to this. A mineral is inorganic, which means that it is not like an animal or a plant and is found naturally in the earth's crust.

Each mineral has a particular set of properties which are used to identify it. Many of these can be examined by the amateur.

The form of a mineral is often expressed in terms which explain themselves, for example, columnar (shaped like a column). Other terms which are not so easy to interpret are amygdaloidal (which means almond-shaped); botryoidal (like a bunch of grapes); and dentritic (with tree-like markings).

The colour of a mineral is not very useful in identifying it, as many

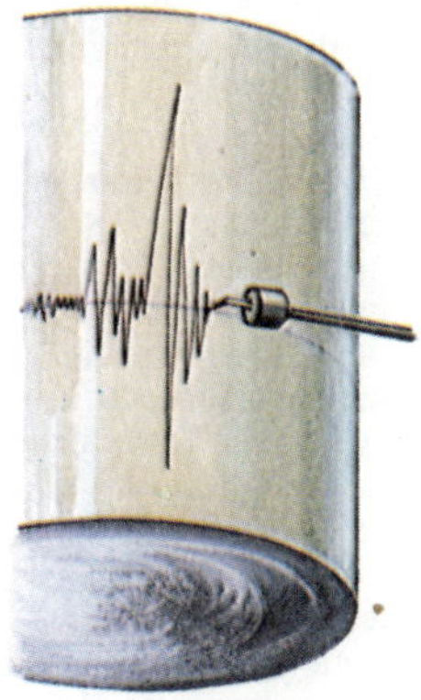

Above The basic principle of the seismograph is shown in this drawing. When an earth tremor occurs the needle and weight remain steady, as they are suspended like a pendulum from a frame. The cylinder, however, is fixed to the ground and moves with the earth tremor and causes the needle to trace its wavy line.

Above The earth is rich with minerals and all over the world man seeks precious raw materials to meet the demands of industry. This open-cast copper mine displays a vast geometric pattern as the galleries are driven deep into the earth in search of ore.

Mohs' scale
The relative hardness of minerals can be tested by scratching one against another, using the following list of minerals as standards. They range from the softest – talc, to the hardest – diamond.

1 talc
2 gypsum
3 calcite
4 fluorite
5 apatite
6 orthoclase
7 quartz
8 topaz
9 corundum
10 diamond

minerals can occur in one of several colours. However, as a simple starting point many guides to the identification of minerals use colour as the first feature.

The resistance a mineral offers to being scratched is called its hardness. Hardness is measured against a scale known as Mohs' Scale, named after the German mineralogist Friedrich Mohs (1773-1839). As a very rough guide a fingernail will scratch up to hardness 2, a penknife to hardness 6.

Another property of some minerals, called cleavage, is their tendency always to split in the same direction along a certain plane. Mica is a mineral which splits easily and is said to have good cleavage.

Other useful aids to identification are how a mineral feels (talc is soapy); how it tastes (rock salt); its lustre or brilliance; streak (this is the colour of the mineral when drawn along a piece of unglazed porcelain); how it fractures; and its specific gravity (this is the relative weight of a mineral compared to the weight of the same amount of water).

There are other more complicated tests including the examination of atomic structure, and the use of what are known as blow pipe and flame tests.

The crystal structure of a mineral is one of the most useful aids to its identification, and the science of crystallography (the study of the structure, form and property of crystals) is most important. It is however a very difficult subject to study.

There are six major crystal systems and they are given names which describe their shape: these are cubic, tetragonal, hexagonal, orthorhombic, monoclinic and triclinic.

Present-day knowledge of the mineral kingdom, like all other forms of learning, has been gained slowly. The Greek philosopher Aristotle (384-322 BC) taught that rocks were made from sunlight. People of later ages imagined that male and female minerals had families; or that minerals were formed from water or made in the bodies of animals. For many centuries rocks, fossils and minerals were regarded as one great kingdom.

The so-called 'father of mineralogy' is Georg Agricola (real surname Bauer) (1490-1555), a German mining expert. As such he was very concerned with minerals and learned about them from studying actual specimens in the field. He worked out a system of classification of minerals based on colour, texture and shape, but the chemical properties of such bodies remained a mystery to him.

The science of crystallography was founded by René Just Haüy (1743-1822), a French mineralogist, and the Swedish chemist Johan Jakob Berzelius (1779-1848) invented the system of chemical symbols now in use.

Gemstones

Those minerals which have a good lustre or brilliance, are capable of being cut and are reasonably rare, have been valued by man for centuries as

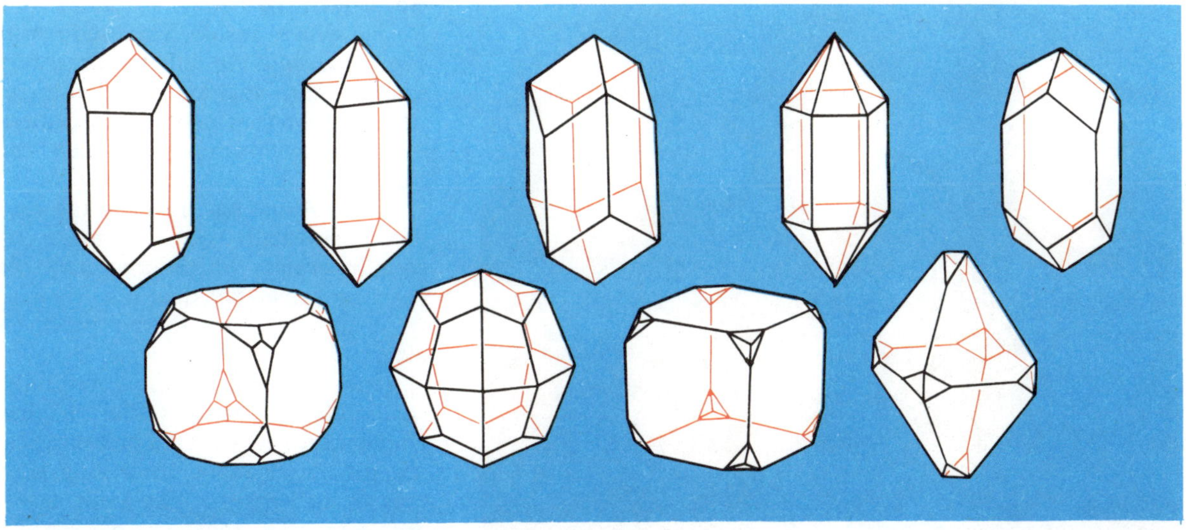

Above (top) All minerals have crystal structures and any crystal belongs to one of several systems which have been established based upon their geometric shape. Shown above are examples of the various forms.

Above Shown here are the minerals gold, silver and amethyst in their natural states. Alongside them are a Quimbaya gold mask in beaten gold made by the ancient peoples of Colombia in South America, and a modern ring with an amethyst set in silver.

gemstones. They are usually very hard as they receive a great deal of wear, for example in jewellery.

With the advance of modern science it has been possible to produce a number of gemstones artificially, and manufactured 'diamonds' are of great value to industry.

Mineral deposits

The collecting together of several substances makes up a mineral deposit. There may be only one mineral present but almost always there are several. They occur either as veins within ordinary rock or as very large masses.

The molten material which erupts from volcanoes is called lava. Magma is the name given to similar molten material which lies below the surface. Magma forces its way up from the depths of the earth and penetrates rocks. It contains large amounts of gases and liquids which, when they cool, form various minerals. It is rather like letting a very small quantity of sea-water evaporate from a saucer – the salt is left as a deposit.

Other mineral deposits may form around hot springs, or on the ocean floor, or as a result of metamorphism (this means the way in which the condition or shape of rocks is altered because of heat or pressure).

Sometimes a deposit on the surface of the earth weathers and breaks up. The debris is then carried by gravity and the flow of water to a lower level where a further accumulation may take place. The heavier minerals such as gold and silver tend to do this. The American gold rushes were based on such accumulations, which are called placer deposits.

Igneous rocks

Rocks are classified according to their origin. Those which result from the cooling of molten material, either deep within the earth as magma or flowing over it as lava, are called igneous rocks.

When magma cools slowly beneath the surface of the earth there is time for crystals to grow and the resulting rock is one in which the various crystals can be recognized with the

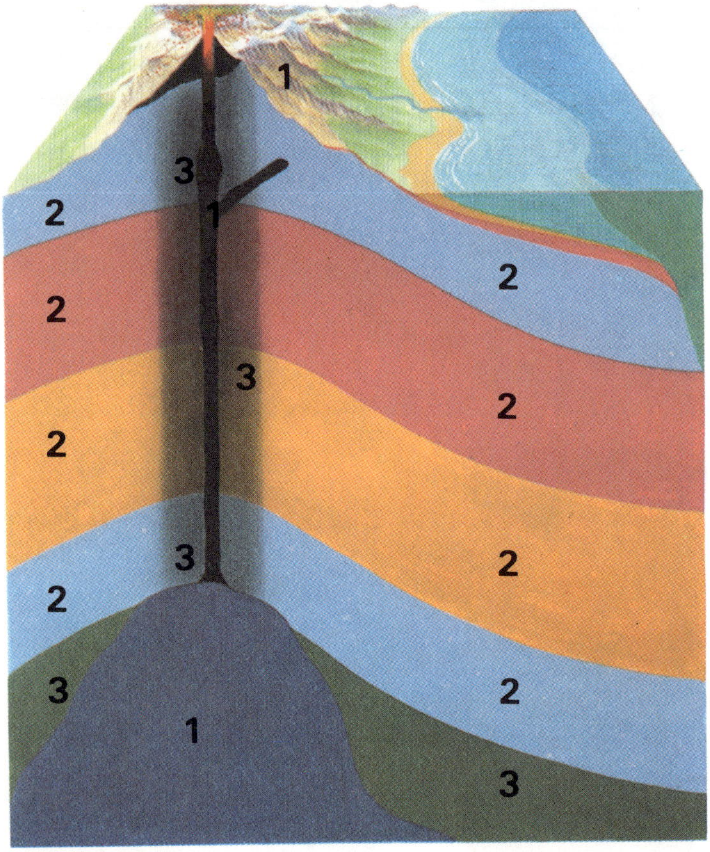

Above The earth's crust is made up of masses of rocks and these are classified into three groups. Illustrated in the drawing are **1** Igneous rocks, such as gabbro, which are formed from molten materials at very high temperatures. **2** Sedimentary rocks, including shale, slate and limestone, are formed chiefly by the action of water or wind. **3** Metamorphic rocks, which are those altered by heat, pressure or chemical action, including marble, quartzite and schist.

naked eye. Examples of this type of rock are granite, diorite and gabbro.

Of these, granite is well-known and is found in the United States, Canada, Scandinavia, Scotland and England – particularly in Devon and Cornwall where it forms hills known locally as tors. It varies greatly in colour, some varieties being white and others pink or deep red.

If molten material cools very quickly, as it does in the case of lava, a very fine-grained rock results. If there are any crystals they can be seen only with the aid of a microscope. A typical example of this type of rock is basalt, seen in the columnar pillars forming the Giant's Causeway in Ireland and on the island of Staffa. It is also widely distributed in India, Hawaii and Iceland.

Other similarly produced rocks are obsidian, which is black, and pumice. The latter is formed by the action of gases escaping from surface layers of lava, causing a fracturing of the lava which leaves many small holes. Lava flowing under the sea also gives rise to pumice.

Sedimentary rocks

Rocks which result from sediments becoming solid are called sedimentary rocks. They include conglomerates (that is, pebbles which become cemented together), sandstone, shale and clay.

Material that has travelled the least distance usually goes to make up conglomerates, which are really old beach and river-bed deposits. Material which has the longest journey produces clay.

Sand becomes, quite naturally, sandstone. Sometimes the original ripple marks on sand are preserved, as are pit marks made by a long-gone rain or hail-storm. The sand grains are cemented together by various substances and it is this which determines the strength of the rock.

Shale, sometimes called mudstone, is mainly clay that has hardened into rock, and it splits very easily. Clay itself is really sediment, which has not become solid, with very small grains.

Another type of sedimentary rock is limestone. Many limestones are formed organically, that is they contain both plant and animal life, and are the result of the accumulation of millions of shells of tiny organisms or the remains of corals.

Chalk deposits are limestones made up mostly of the remains of one-celled animals which can be seen only with the aid of a microscope. Chalk forms the famous white cliffs of Dover in England.

Other sedimentary deposits are very important to man, for example coal, iron and oil. Coal is in fact the compressed remains of plant life and the coal found in the British Isles dates from 310 million years ago. Often the remains of the plants can be seen in lumps of coal. There are various types of coal, some of which are not suitable for household use; the hardest is anthracite, which burns well and gives out a good heat.

The origin of oil has long been disputed but it most likely consists of the remains of vast numbers of microscopic animals and has accumulated in the sea. Oil is found in what are called 'traps' beneath the earth.

Natural gas is often found with oil and has a similar origin. Both can be used for heating and cooking, and are sources of many useful chemicals.

Large pockets of natural gas have been found under the sea. Pipelines transport it from the well to the coast. In Britain, it is then pumped into a national grid which carries it to homes and factories.

Metamorphic rocks

The final important group of rocks is the metamorphic one, which means rocks that have been changed in some way from their original state. This change may be very slight so that it is hardly noticeable, or very great so that it is difficult to distinguish the original rock.

All kinds of rocks can be changed, or metamorphosed, either by the action of heat or pressure, or by the influence of other substances, such as gases and liquids. Shales are changed into slates, limestones into marbles, sandstones into quartzites, and granite into gneiss (pronounced nice).

Soils

Soil is in fact a type of rock that has been worn down chemically and by weathering. Soil formation depends also on plants and animals, particularly microscopic ones. It takes many centuries for all these things to produce the surface layer of soil with which everyone is familiar. The original bed-rock is broken down into small particles and at first looks more like rock than soil, but it is gradually changed by climate and vegetation.

The depth of soil varies over the surface of the earth from a few centimetres to as much as thirty metres, but the average depth is only about thirty centimetres. Nearly all life depends on soil, and it is vital to man's existence that it is treated properly and conserved. Soils are classified according to their texture and colour, and also by area – such as tropical soils, forest soils and grassland soils.

Uses of rocks and minerals

Man has long used both rocks and minerals to make weapons and ornaments, and to build himself homes. Thousands of years ago the flint from chalk deposits was used by early man for axes and for arrow and spear heads.

Such things as oil, coal and iron ore are all valuable to man. Many of the minerals are used in the manufacture of substances which are in everyday use – copper, silver, tin and zinc. Many rocks, such as gabbro, diorite and basalt, are used as road metal; slate is used on roofs; marble for facings and statues; and granite and certain sandstones for building.

Above This cutaway drawing of a coalmine shows the lift shaft on the left and the ventilation shaft on the right. Running across the drawing are three coal seams at various depths.

Shaping the earth

The appearance of the land is constantly changing. Sometimes these changes can occur literally overnight, as when there is a volcanic eruption,

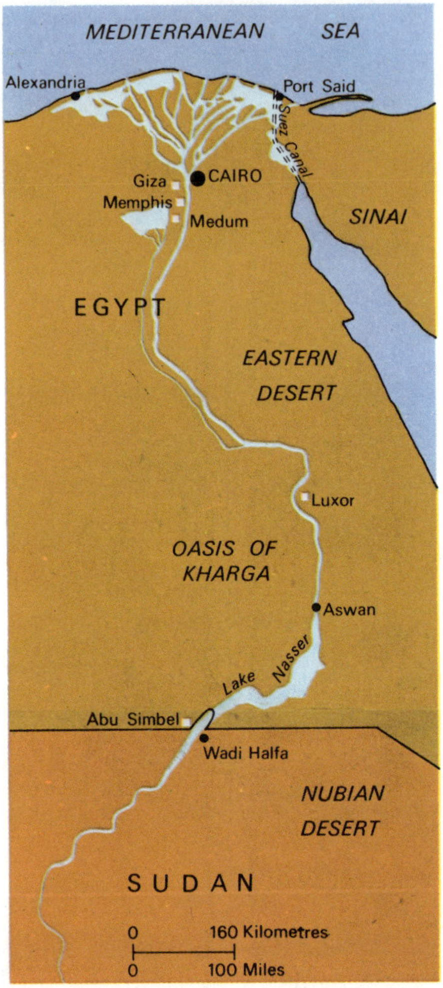

Right This map shows the area of the Nile delta in Egypt, which is an extension of the land built up from material deposited by rivers.

Below Rocks are split or worn away by the effects of wind and water. The reason for these strangely carved shapes is the different resistance of the rocks to the effect of weathering: the soft layers are destroyed more quickly than the hard ones.

an earthquake or a landslide. At other times the changes are so slow that no difference could be seen in the shape of a range of hills or the flatness of a long low plain for a period of thousands of years.

But, fast or slow, the land is changing all the time. The tendency is for all land to be reduced to sea-level. Indeed, the greatest single factor in this process is the sea itself. Apart from the fact that it erodes, or wears away, stretches of the coastline by the direct action of its waves, it is also the source of rain.

Water in the sea evaporates by action of the sun and is drawn up into the sky. This water eventually falls on the land as rain, forming streams, rivers and torrents as it runs back to the sea, and carrying with it large quantities of earth.

Rain can act on the land in other ways, too. In the form of ice (glaciers) it will scoop out vast quantities of rock as it slides very slowly down the sides of mountains. As frost it will penetrate cracks in rocks and stones and break them open through expansion, so gradually reducing them to sand.

Two forces are at action on the earth, one breaking and crumbling the rocks, the other removing the debris to lower levels and eventually to a lake or the sea.

Extremes of temperature, both very hot and very cold, cause rocks to crack and peel. Rain water also attacks rock, especially limestone. The joints in the limestone are widened by rain and should the water be concentrated into one particular spot this will become funnel-shaped and is known as a swallow hole. In Britain, Gaping Ghyll, near Ingleborough in Yorkshire, is a famous swallow hole.

The water often plunges below the surface in a limestone area, so we have rivers which suddenly disappear only to come into the open again at a much lower level. While in the limestone the water will continue to widen joints and may form great caves. Sometimes the roofs of these caves collapse and a gorge is formed. Cheddar Gorge in Britain may have been formed in this way.

Movement of rivers

Even a small river is capable of moving a lot of material and anyone who has seen such a stream in full flood will know that its size is no indication of its ability to transport boulders.

A river in the early stages of its journey to the sea (or a lake) has steep sides to its valley, and there may be potholes or waterfalls along its course. Waterfalls are formed where water meets a layer of resistant rock. The river plunges over the rock, often under-cutting the hard layer and causing it gradually to recede.

This is why waterfalls are so short-lived, geologically speaking. Even the Niagara Falls are not permanent, for if they go back another three kilometres the hard rock will be cut through, the falls will disappear, and only rapids will be left.

As the river flows on, the valley will become wider and towards the end of its journey it may well meander, or wander about, from side to side.

Above The face of the earth is always in a state of change. It is constantly being built up and broken down but change usually takes place too slowly for man even to be aware of it. According to the geologists the Colorado River has taken about two million years to carve out the deep gorge of the Grand Canyon in the United States, seen in this drawing.

When the river reaches the sea it will be forced to drop its load of material, first the larger particles, and then the very small ones.

At this stage the river is very liable to flood. If it does so regularly then it will build up natural banks called levees. Should these ever break the result can be disastrous flooding. However, regular flooding is often of great benefit to the land; without the regular flooding of the Nile the great Egyptian civilisations could not have existed.

Normally the movement of the sea gradually carries away the material deposited by a river, but where such movement is lacking, for example in sheltered areas such as the Gulf of Mexico and the Mediterranean, it gradually builds up into an extension of the land.

Such a formation is called a delta, after its resemblance to the shape of the fourth letter of the Greek alphabet. Famous deltas are the Mississippi, the Nile, the Po (Italy) and the Hwang Ho (China).

The effect that water has will depend on the resistance of the rocks. In the states of Dakota, Nebraska and Wyoming in the United States, water has created what is known as the badlands. The lack of vegetation causes the water to carry away vast quantities of soil leaving great barren scars across the landscape.

Sometimes, when water encounters a hard top layer, a steep-sided hill is left called a mesa or butte. Then there is the earth pillar, created in the same way. These are usually small, but in the Austrian Tyrol they have been known to attain a height of over twenty metres. Other examples, not so high, have been found in Scotland.

Rain water starts many a landslide. The coastal areas of England between

Above The Hoover Dam on the great Colorado River. It is on the border of the states of Arizona and Nevada, and forms part of the Boulder Canyon project. The Colorado's value for water power and irrigation is immense. This dam has made possible the irrigation of vast areas of land and has prevented serious flooding of the Colorado basin.

Folkestone and Dover are very prone to landslides. The rocks dip seawards, the chalk surface having clay beneath it. Rain causes the clay to act as a greased board and any loose chalk rolls towards the sea.

Landslides have been known to create lakes by blocking rivers and have on a number of occasions caused extensive damage in many parts of the world.

Lakes

Lakes are a beauty of nature and are much used for sport and recreation. They also provide a good source of water. Lakes have many different origins: sometimes a valley is blocked by lava flows or landslides; or the ice of a former age has gouged out a basin; or earth movements or extinct volcanic craters have provided the necessary foundation.

Finland is famous for its many lakes, all of which have originated because of the action of ice. The Great Lakes of North America began in the same way, although these occupy far older valleys.

In East Africa a number of lakes, Tanganyika and Malawi among them, occupy a rift in the earth's crust.

The famous Crater Lake in Oregon in the United States is the best-known example of a lake situated in the crater of a volcano (Mount Mazama).

Lakes gradually become filled in with sediment, or a change of climate may cause the death of a lake. Great Salt Lake in Utah in the United States is all that remains of the once enormous Lake Bonneville.

Water beneath the ground

There is water below the earth's surface almost everywhere, even beneath a desert. Rain water and snow penetrate the soil and become trapped in tiny spaces. Gradually the land is saturated, the upper layer of this being called the water-table. The depth of the water-table determines whether or not a spring or well will dry up.

Sometimes when wells are dug water comes to the surface unaided, due to internal pressure. These are called artesian wells and are so named from the region of Artois, in France, where the first such wells were drilled. In a true artesian well water does not need to be pumped up.

The principle of the artesian basin, important for water supply, is well illustrated by the London Basin. Originally the famous fountains in London's Trafalgar Square worked by artesian head, but nowadays they have to be pumped as the demand for water in the London area is so great. The largest known basin of this type is in Australia and covers parts of Queensland, New South Wales and South Australia.

The effects of rain water on limestone have been described. The caves produced in this way are a source of wonder to man, especially when they contain the fantastic shapes called stalactites and stalagmites.

These may take thousands of years to form, as they are built by water dripping from the ceilings of caves.

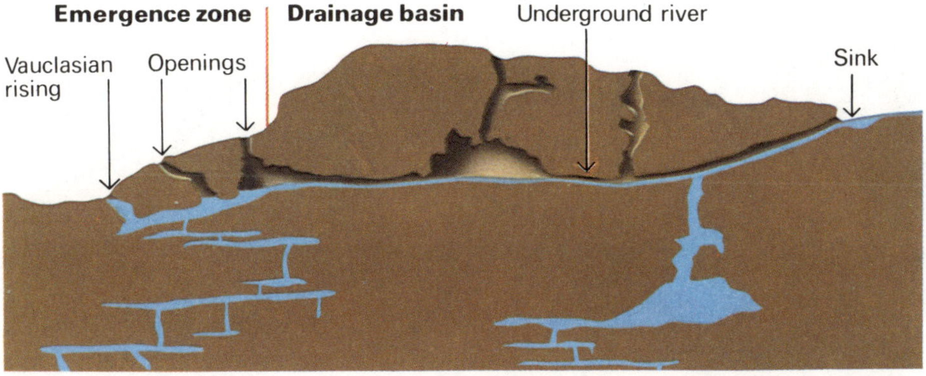

Left One of the chief hazards in the popular sport of pot-holing is underground water. The course of an underground river is shown here.

Stalactites grow downwards and stalagmites build up from ground level. Sometimes stalactites and stalagmites meet and a pillar is formed.

One of the largest cave systems in the world is that of Mammoth Cave in Kentucky in the United States, but smaller ones found in Europe are no less interesting.

Should the water-table remain near the surface all the time, swamps are formed. Should it be covered by a shallow layer of water the result is a marsh. A mass of decaying vegetation constitutes a bog. Ireland has many such swamps and bogs. The Ganges delta in India and Pakistan is swampland, but undoubtedly the most famous swamps in the world are the Everglades of Florida in the United States.

Water as ice

The great glaciers of the Alps are a well-known tourist attraction but there is a great deal going on below the surface which cannot be seen. Glaciers are born in hollows below the mountain peaks and from here the ice moves out and down until it is stopped by the warmer climate of the lower valley.

As the ice moves – for it does move, however slowly – it smooths the rocks and carries with it boulders and general debris. If the ice passes over large rocks, or the valley suddenly widens, the glacier cracks and great crevasses appear.

In many regions near the poles glaciers reach the edge of the sea. Here pieces gradually break off the end to form icebergs.

In the case of a valley glacier the point at which it ends is marked by a heap of material which it has pushed and carried. This is known as moraine. The work of former ice ages can be seen especially in the Highland areas of Scotland. Here there are U-shaped valleys, rocks which have been marked by the moving ice, and cirques (semi-circular mountain recesses). At lower altitudes there are boulders on the hillsides, perched blocks and drumlins (mountain ridges formed under the ice sheets). Boulder clay is also a glacier deposit.

The work of the sea

Waves are constantly pounding the shores, breaking up the land in one place and depositing new sediments somewhere else. The retreat of the shore may be rapid where rocks are soft. Parts of the coast of Britain have retreated up to five kilometres since Roman times. But however hard the rock, it is gradually worn down by the ceaseless waves.

Wherever the rock is hard, the action of the sea produces wonderful

Above The continual seepage of water down walls of underground limestone caves over thousands of years forms strange 'icicles' called stalactites (which grow downwards) and stalagmites (which build up from the ground). Sometimes these meet and weird and beautiful shapes and columns are formed.

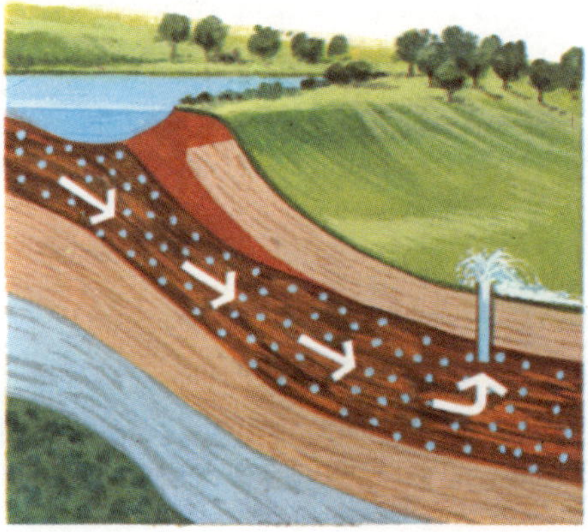

Left An artesian well. Water flows underground downhill beneath an impervious layer of rock until it reaches a well pipe. It then spouts up this pipe because the top of the pipe is lower than the source of the water. Such wells were first noted and used by monks in the Artois region of France in the 12th century.

Above This picture shows how lava is forced upwards to erupt finally from the cone of a volcano. We do not know exactly how magma, the name given to the lava when it is below the earth, is formed or how it moves. Nor do we know how deep is its origin. One of the ideas believed in ancient times to explain volcanic activity was that of a river of fire in the centre of the earth. We do know that magma contains large amounts of gases, and these produce the eruption.

coastal scenery, with stacks and arches and many small coves.

Currents in the oceans move vast quantities of material, building up all sorts of features along the coast, such as sandbars and spits.

Sandbars are built up parallel to the shoreline, and spits are formed from material attached to the land at one end and projecting into the sea at the other. Chesil Beach in Dorset runs for nearly twenty-six kilometres and is Britain's best example of a bar. The growth of a spit is clearly seen at Yarmouth where the river Yare is forced to enter the sea some distance south from where its normal outlet would be.

In other places currents transport material from one point on the coastline only to deposit it at another.

On the coasts of Norway and New Zealand are found very steep-sided valleys, some going inland for more than 150 kilometres. These are called fiords. They result from the action of glaciers when the sea stood at a much lower level than it does now. Some of them are as deep as 1,200 metres.

Where the land has been submerged, definite coastal features are produced, such as the drowned valleys in Cornwall and Devon, and the so-called submerged forests found around the coast of the United Kingdom.

Working wind

In lands where there is very little rainfall winds tend to remove a great deal of material. Sometimes small particles act as an abrasive and wear away the rocks on to which they are blown. Sand is swept into dunes which then build up across deserts or beaches. The dunes of the Sahara can be up to 200 metres high.

When sand dunes penetrate inland, as they have done in parts of Scotland, for example, they can cause great hardship to farmers and the loss of valuable land. Fences are erected, and various types of grass and Scots pine are planted in order to try to stop the advance. The very fine particles picked up by the wind cause dust storms. Some of those in the Sahara have even been swept north into Europe.

Land on fire

Some of the most spectacular scenery on earth must be that provided by volcanoes and their outpourings. Magma from the inner regions of the earth manages to find a weak spot in the crust and pours out to flow as lava over the land. Gradually it builds itself up into a cone made of fragments of rock, solidified lava and various other materials.

Sometimes a cone does not form but the lava just remains where it is in a great flow across the landscape. This often results in a rock called basalt, and a great plateau of it once covered an area from Greenland to Scotland, forming such features as the Giant's Causeway in Ireland and Fingal's Cave on the island of Staffa, famous for its columnar jointing. There are vast accumulations of a similar type in India and America.

Volcanoes have been the cause of much loss of life and destruction to property. There is usually very little warning of an impending volcanic eruption. Volcanoes that have not erupted for years may suddenly start to do so. An example is Tristan da Cunha, thought to be extinct, but which erupted violently in 1961. Some lavas flow for a long distance, others solidify quite quickly, resulting in a mass of jagged blocks.

Cone-shaped volcanoes such as Vesuvius, Etna, Cotopaxi and Popocatepetl are in strong contrast to the shield volcanoes (so called because they appear on the earth's surface like vast shields) such as Mauna Loa in the Hawaiian Islands. Mauna Loa is truly a great volcano, rising over 9,000 metres from the ocean floor, and therefore higher than the biggest land volcanoes.

Volcanoes often lie dormant for many years with no sign of activity at all. Some, like Stromboli (sometimes called the lighthouse of the Mediterranean), erupt regularly. Others die altogether and are gradually attacked by the elements, often all that remains is the plug which has solidified in the neck. Many examples of these plugs are found throughout the world: a region particularly famous for them is the Auvergne in France.

Magma does not always reach the surface of the earth but sometimes solidifies below it and is only exposed at a much later date. When it lies horizontally in rocks to form a sheet, it is called a sill. Hadrian's Wall is built partly on the Great Whin Sill which stretches over large areas of northern England.

When magma forms upright wall-like masses these are called dykes. They are very common on the west coast of Scotland, especially on the islands of Arran and Mull. The great dyke of southern Zimbabwe extends for over 480 kilometres while the Cleveland dyke in the north of England can be traced for over 160 kilometres.

Batholiths are very large underground masses of igneous rocks. Often they form the roots of mountain chains.

Where there are hot springs, geysers or fumaroles, this is a sign that activity is dying out. Hot springs are found in New Zealand, Japan, Iceland and the United States. Often they build terraces around themselves by depositing minerals. Geysers are distinct from hot springs in that they send

Above When Pompeii was excavated hundreds of years after the eruption of Vesuvius in AD 79, hollows were found formed by bodies, the shape of which had been preserved by the petrified cinders. As well as humans, animals had died under the ashes and this plaster cast was made of a dog on the spot where it had suffocated.

Above A monastery in Thessaly, Greece, built on a hardened plug – all that remains of an ancient volcano.

Right For more than five weeks Magellan battled through the strait that now bears his name at the tip of South America. Fierce gales battered his tiny fleet of ships before they finally reached the last rocky cape and sailed into the calm of the Pacific Ocean.

Ferdinand Magellan (1480?–1521) Portuguese seaman and navigator. Financed by Charles V of Spain, he sailed west from Seville in 1519 with five ships. Voyaged down east coast of South America and through the Strait named after him. Named the Pacific Ocean and sailed to Philippines where he was killed. One ship of his fleet survived, the first to circumnavigate the world, arriving back in Seville in Sept. 1522.

up enormous columns of hot water, sometimes at regular intervals: Old Faithful in the Yellowstone National Park in the United States is probably the most famous. Fumaroles are holes in a volcano through which gases escape.

The oceans

The oceans cover 71 per cent of the globe and meet each other on very broad fronts. They have a great effect on climate, provide vast quantities of food and are, as yet, little understood compared with many other natural things. The average depth of the oceans is 3,600 metres, against the average height of the land – 760 metres.

The study of oceanography (the science of the seas) brings together various other sciences, such as geology (which is the study of the earth's crust), botany (the study of plant life), zoology (the study of animal life) and meteorology (the study of weather and climate).

Oceanographers recognise only three oceans: Pacific, Atlantic and Indian. To get the seven major seas we have to divide both the Pacific and Atlantic into north and south and add the two polar oceans, Arctic and Antarctic.

The origin of the oceans is somewhat obscure. The movement of currents in the earth's mantle may have helped to sweep together the lighter material which formed the continents, leaving the heavier type of crust found under the oceans to sink a little and so gradually fill with water as soon as the first rain started.

These first downpours lasted for many years, possibly centuries. Originally, the water must have been fresh, but the minerals swept down by the rain coupled with the evaporation of the sea water gradually increased the

Right Few corals are used industrially, but ever since ancient times the precious red variety from the Mediterranean has been highly valued for jewellery and other decorative purposes.

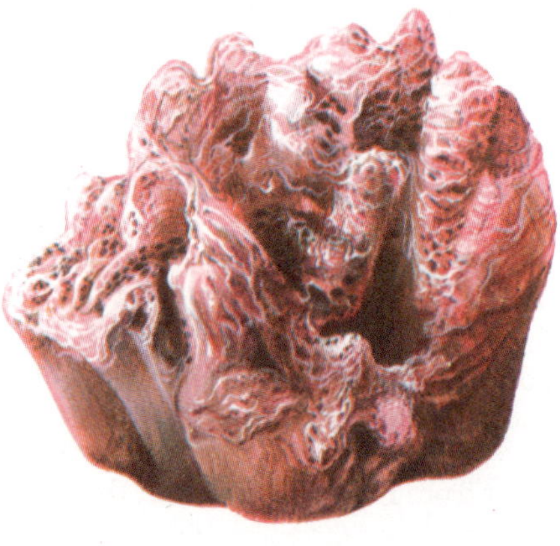

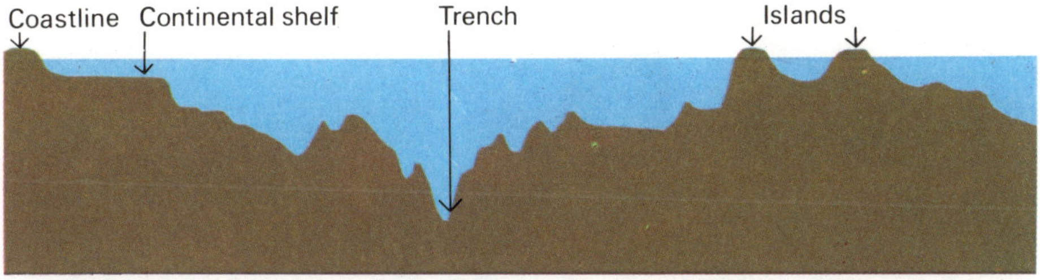

Left Only recently has man begun to explore the ocean depths. Although two-thirds of the earth's surface is covered by water we still know very little about the sea and what it contains. However, quite detailed maps of the sea-bed have been made showing the position of canyons, ridges and submarine mountains. Particularly well mapped is the area of the Atlantic Ocean. The diagram on the left shows a typical cross section of the rise and fall of the ocean bed with the continental shelf, deep trenches and mountain ranges which rise above the surface of the water to form ocean islands.

saltiness. The average salt content of the oceans is 3.5 per cent. Certain parts have a greater percentage, while inland lakes, such as the Great Salt Lake in the United States, reach 28 per cent.

The water, the temperature of which varies greatly, is in fact colourless. Any colour it may possess is due chiefly to reflection of the sky or, in the case of the Red Sea, to its animal content, or, with the Yellow Sea, the amount of mud it contains.

The general structure of the oceans consists of three parts: the continental shelf, which is really just an extension of the land mass, the continental slope, and the ocean floor. Scientists consider that the ocean commences where the continental slope begins.

At one time it was thought that the ocean floor was dull and monotonous but this is not the case at all. There are great mountain chains and deep trenches beneath the seas.

The oceanic ridges stretch throughout the oceans for a total length of about 65,000 kilometres, running down the mid-Atlantic and into the Pacific and Indian oceans. These ridges are areas where the crust is unstable, and are the centre of volcanic and earthquake activity.

In the Pacific, particularly, deep trenches run right alongside fairly tall mountains, so there is a great drop in height over a very short horizontal distance. There are other deep canyons like that off the Hudson River on the eastern coast of the United States which stretches for many kilometres. Another is found off the mouth of the Congo in Africa.

At least part of the canyons are the result of wearing away by rivers, but no one really knows how they were formed, although the suggestion has been made that they might be caused by sea-water charged with sediment. It is thought that underground cables have been broken by the movement of this sort of sediment.

Ocean islands

The oceans are not entirely without land as they contain many islands of various origins. Most islands near the land are in fact continuations of it and are on the continental shelf. Should the level of the sea be lowered slightly then they would once again be joined to the continents. The British Isles are an example.

Other islands, such as those of New Zealand, are a fair way from any land mass but are made up of continental-type rock. The true oceanic islands are found to be volcanic. Yet the Seychelles, which are unquestionably oceanic, are made up of continental rock. Such islands, are important in finding out about the past geography of the world.

The island arcs, really continuations of the mountains of the main continental masses, are particularly interesting as they form part of the belt which is frequently shaken by earthquakes and volcanic eruptions.

In the Pacific there are many so-called sea mounts, submerged flat-topped mountains often with dead coral attached to them. This proves they were once above sea level, although they are now many metres below the waves.

Coral islands have a charm all of their own. Many of the oceanic islands and edges of the continents are fringed with deposits of coral. These deposits are the hard, sharp remains of millions of little animals. The corals grow outwards and upwards, often keeping pace with a rising sea level so that a ring of coral remains visible although the original mountain is below the waves. This is called an atoll.

Certain conditions are necessary for the growth of coral, for the creatures whose remains form the coral cannot

Above The invention of the mariner's compass is attributed to many different nations, including the Chinese, Arabs, Greeks and Italians. The compass with a card floating on a needle in a bowl was very common in the 18th century. The *fleur-de-lys* which marks the north point (as shown here) was first chosen in honour of Charles of Anjou, king of Sicily and Naples.

Right The Swiss scientists Auguste Piccard and his son Jacques designed the bathyscaphe *Trieste* for exploration of the sea-bed. The occupants of the bathyscaphe ride in the sphere at the bottom of the craft. Jacques Piccard, in 1960, descended in it to a depth of some 11,000 metres in the Challenger Depth in the Pacific Ocean and found that life existed even at this depth in the near-freezing oceans.

Right During her voyage of oceanic research, which lasted over three years, HMS *Challenger* covered 69,000 nautical miles.

Charles Wyville Thomson (1830–82) Scottish zoologist. Studied in Edinburgh and became professor of natural history. Notable for deep-sea research he was made scientific head of the *Challenger* expedition (1872–6). His research showed that deep-sea temperatures vary and that animal life exists at much greater depths than was supposed.

live below 45 metres. In addition the mean temperature of the sea must not fall below 20 degrees C., and the water must be clear.

An excellent example of an off-shore coral reef is the Great Barrier Reef off eastern Australia, which is 1,900 kilometres long and anything between sixteen and one hundred and fifty kilometres wide.

The moving oceans

Most coasts experience two tides every twenty-four hours, having two periods of high and two of low water. The incoming tide is known as the flood tide and the outgoing as the ebb.

The tides are caused by the gravitational pull of the moon and to a lesser extent the sun. The earth's gravitational pull is overpowered by the moon's and the water is literally pulled away. Thus there are two great masses of water, one facing the moon and the other facing away from it, constantly in motion.

The range of the tide varies from place to place according to differences in the shape of the land – for example, the depth of the sea bed or the width of a bay. The greatest range from high to low tide is in the Bay of Fundy in Canada, while in the Gulf of Mexico the difference is only a few centimetres.

Tides are very important to shipping, much of which still docks and sails at high tide even in the larger ports of the world.

Ocean currents are really like large 'rivers' within the ocean itself. The Atlantic circulation is clockwise in the north and anti-clockwise in the south. The warmer water of the equatorial regions tends to move out and is helped by the prevailing winds. The colder currents coming from the north tend to sink towards the equator, with the warmer water moving over. The mingling of cold and warm currents often leads to fog.

The currents themselves have a great effect on the land masses which they pass. For example, Great Britain, and to a certain extent Norway, are kept much warmer during the winter

Left The science of mapping seas, lakes and rivers is called hydrography. In this sequence of three pictures a ship is shown 'sounding' the bottom of the sea-bed so that charts can be made of its contours. The distance from the surface of the water to the sea-bed is shown by the time it takes for sound waves to reach the bottom and then return to the sounding device on the ship.

months than they should be for their latitude because of the North Atlantic Drift sweeping along the shores.

The idea of a two-level ocean was put forward a long while ago but it is only recently that it has been proved to be the fact. What happens is that the surface currents tend to be balanced by deeper counter currents sinking from the Arctic and rising again in the Antarctic. Thus the Gulf Stream has a counter current moving in the opposite direction.

Waves and wind

Most waves are caused by the wind which pulls the water into walls. Waves are rarely more than twelve metres high in the Atlantic and fifteen metres in the Pacific. The height of a wave is determined by wind strength, how long the wind blows and how far it has come since it last passed over land. The water itself does not really move but the wave passes through it. On reaching the coast the drag on the bottom of the shallowing sea causes the wave to topple over so that it breaks on the shore.

The giant waves produced by earthquakes, called tsunami, have already been mentioned.

Oceanography

In recent years exploration of the oceans has greatly increased. The old idea of the weighted line to measure depth has given way to the use of sonic, or sound, waves. These sound waves are transmitted from a ship into the sea and are reflected back from the sea bed. The time taken for the sonic wave to travel from the ship and back again is recorded and from this it can be worked out how deep the water is.

By using two ships and creating very minor earthquakes it is possible to measure the thickness of sediments as well as their depth.

Most countries of the world have active departments concerned with oceanography and many have data centres. Research vessels plough the waves, while below them increasing use is being made of underwater craft such as the submarine and the bathyscaphe. In 1960, the bathyscaphe *Trieste* went down to a depth of nearly 11,000 metres in the Marianas Trench. On board was Jacques Piccard, son of the pioneer Swiss explorer of the ocean depths Auguste Piccard (1884-1962).

The first person to study the sea scientifically was the American Matthew Fontaine Maury (1806-73). He produced the first book on the subject in 1855, called *The Physical Geography of the Sea*.

The voyage of the British ship *Challenger* under its scientific head, Charles Wyville Thomson (1830-82), in 1872-6 covered all the oceans and collected thousands of specimens. It was the first scientific ocean-going expedition and its findings, published in a large number of volumes, began the proper study of life in the sea.

Food from the sea

The oceans hold a great store of wealth both in the way of food and minerals. We have learned very little yet about farming the sea, but we shall need to very soon if we are to feed the growing number of people in the world.

Care will also be needed in the matter of dumping such things as radioactive wastes in the oceans, for we know too little about deep-sea

Above Temperatures below the sea are measured by a reversing thermometer which is enclosed in thick glass to protect it from pressure. It is generally attached to a water sampling bottle and lowered on a heavy wire rope. Here a scientist aboard a research ship removes a bottle from the wire.

Right This map shows the areas of comparative wetness throughout the world. As can be seen, the areas of greatest rainfall often coincide with the hottest places.

currents to be sure that such wastes would be safely dispersed.

Undoubtedly in years to come much of our water supply will come from sea water that has had the salt removed from it.

Judging by the quantities of manganese and iron oxides found in parts of the oceans there is also a great deal of mineral wealth to be obtained. The ocean floor is already being drilled for oil and natural gas, and tunnelled into to mine coal.

One of the pioneer underwater explorers who has done so much to help man meet the challenge of what he has called 'the silent world' is Jacques Cousteau, a French naval officer. He invented the aqualung diving gear in 1943 and has also taken part in experiments to show that man can live underwater in special 'houses' for long periods.

Below Jacques Cousteau's underwater exploration has led to the construction of many curiously shaped buildings, such as the one seen here, which are adapted for living in beneath the sea. A French naval officer, Cousteau was born in 1910 and is celebrated not only for his invention of the aqualung, but for pioneering the use of television under water and for his underwater archaeology.

Weather and climate

When an Englishman meets a stranger his opening remarks are always supposed to be about the weather. He will probably comment on what he considers is a very poor climate. But the English climate is one which many regard as ideal, since it does not go to extremes and gives lush green pastures all the year round.

What is the difference between weather and climate? Weather may be defined as the immediate general meteorological conditions existing at any one time – for example, whether the day is sunny and fine or dull and wet. Climate is really long-term weather and refers to the meteorological conditions experienced in an area over a period of time, possibly a year.

The science of weather is called meteorology, and a person who studies the weather, a meteorologist. Most countries have a central meteorological office where various weather reports for that country are prepared and where research is carried out on the atmosphere and how to forecast changes.

Near the equator the weather is so similar from day to day that in these areas the term weather means almost the same thing as climate.

Temperature varies in different parts of the world, and it also changes from season to season. In general, the farther north we go, the less likely we are to meet high temperatures.

In summer, northern nights are much longer than they are in the south. Indeed, in the far north daylight persists for twenty-four hours, but in winter it is dark all day and everything

Left This map shows how hot it is in various parts of the world. The areas of greatest heat are around those places on the earth which receive the sun's rays from directly overhead.

has to be done with the help of strong artificial lights.

Land masses have a very marked effect on climate. Inland cities and towns will have greater extremes of both temperature and rainfall than those in coastal regions. Thus central Europe has hotter summers and colder winters than the British Isles.

The various ocean currents, both hot and cold, also have a definite effect on the overall climate of an area. Because of the North Atlantic Drift the British Isles enjoy mild winters compared with those on the east coast of North America at the same latitude. Altitude also affects climate, as people who live in mountainous regions know.

Life from the sun

The earth receives its heat from the sun even when it is hidden behind the clouds. Without heat from the sun there would be no life on earth.

The various waves coming from the sun have differing results. Ultra violet ones are absorbed by the ozone in the atmosphere, but others reach the earth and are of great importance to life, for they form the basis of the manufacture of vitamin D in animal bodies. Infra-red rays we feel as heat.

Visible rays are seen as what is known as 'white light', although this is not a true description, for if such light is passed through a prism it will be found to be made up of the colours of the spectrum (violet, indigo, blue, green, yellow, orange and red).

An example of the scattering of the sun's rays can be shown by the fact that from the top of a high mountain a climber will see the sky as rich violet-blue. By the time the rays reach earth the colours responsible for this – violet, indigo and blue – have been greatly diffused in the atmosphere.

The wonderful reds and yellows of the sunset are due to the fact that the light waves yellow, orange and red are scattered in the lower atmosphere, particularly by impurities in the air and water vapour.

The moving air

The various air movements caused by belts of pressure have a direct effect on climate. The constant winds, allied to the various wind systems, were very important to sailors in the days of the great sailing ships.

The equatorial regions have a uniform low pressure and the weather is similar from day to day. From these regions to points 30 degrees north and 30 degrees south the trade winds blow. Between areas called the sub-tropical high and the sub-polar low, winds called westerlies rage. The polar regions themselves are areas of high pressure.

Air masses

The weather at any one time will be decided by the type of air mass which is present. An area of high pressure is called an anticyclone and the result is clear skies and little wind. The area of

Below Man has been interested in exploring under water since the earliest times. Writers of Ancient Greece record the exploits of divers used to recover treasure from wrecked ships. It is important to remember that, in this sense, a diver was simply a man who could hold his breath under water for a long time. Not until some time in the 15th century is there a record of divers working with some sort of equipment which enabled them to breathe from an air-bag which floated on the surface of the water. Such a device is seen in the drawing below. On its left is seen a modern diver wearing an aqualung, which is a free-diving system invented by Cousteau.

Above Clouds give a useful indication of weather conditions. There are ten different types generally recognised all over the world. Those shown above are (from top to bottom) **1** cirro-cumulus, **2** cirro-stratus, **3** cirrus, **4** strato-cumulus, **5** cumulus and cumulo-nimbus.

low pressure called a cyclone or depression is responsible for most of the so-called bad weather.

Depressions which start in America cross the Atlantic to Britain and sweep over the seas to western Europe. The initial cause of these areas of low pressure is unknown.

With the depression there are 'fronts'. A front is really the line on the earth's surface where cold and warm masses of air meet. The cold front brings heavy rain, possibly thunder and, as its name suggests, the temperature drops after it has passed. The reverse is true as regards temperature in the passing of a warm front. In this case, the temperature rises, usually preceded by rain.

Another condition associated with this type of pressure mass is called an occulsion, in which a mass of warm air is lifted from the earth's surface by a mass of cold air.

The line marking the presence of such a front is often found on weather maps in newspapers, and many depressions have reached this stage in their life history by the time they have crossed the Atlantic to Europe.

Weather-men also refer to a trough of low pressure and its reverse a ridge of high pressure. These are really extensions of areas of low and high pressure, although a ridge of high pressure will sometimes occur between two areas of low pressure.

Clouds

These are literally masses of condensed water vapour, with possibly some ice particles. The various types are classified according to the height at which they are found. Different types of weather are associated with different clouds. Often they can be used as a guide to the sort of weather likely to occur in the near future.

Rain, hail, snow and fog

Water evaporates into the atmosphere from the sea and from the land. Warm air is able to pick up a great deal of moisture from large areas of water – for example, as it passes over the Atlantic Ocean. On reaching coastal areas the air is forced by mountains to rise and hence to cool. As the air cools so the vapour condenses and turns into water again, to fall either as rain or

snow, according to how cold it becomes. Cloudbursts are no more than very heavy downpours of rain, although they can do considerable damage.

On very cool, clear nights the air in contact with the ground may be cooled so as to form droplets of water which are left on the ground as dew.

Mists and valley fogs result in the same manner, especially when the process of cooling extends upwards from ground level or, for instance, up the sides of a valley. If the air contains a large number of specks of dirt and dust, fog will be the result. Fog also happens where warm air passes over cool surfaces, for example, off the coast of Newfoundland where warm air from the Gulf Stream passes over the cold Labrador current.

Hail consists of pellets of ice, and when it falls it is often associated with thunderstorms. It is caused by warm air rising suddenly, possibly by means of powerful up-draughts, causing the water drops to freeze. As the hailstone falls to the ground it may be subjected to several upward thrusts, resulting in a 'stone' of several layers before it finally reaches the earth.

Snow is often driven by the prevailing wind into great drifts which cause havoc to transport and are responsible for cutting off whole villages and even towns.

When the sun is shining and it rains at the same time a beautifully coloured arch is often seen in the sky, called a rainbow. This is the result of the reflection and bending of the sun's rays by the water droplets. The colours the rainbow displays are those of the spectrum, red on the outside, and shading through orange, yellow, green,

blue and indigo to violet. Sometimes two bows are seen, one inside the other, with the smaller one showing the colours in reverse.

Violent winds

A hurricane is the name given to a tropical depression that results in a violent storm. Hurricanes are found mainly in the Caribbean from June to October and to identify them are given girls' names. A lot of research has been done into how to spot hurricanes in advance and so give enough warning to inhabitants of the islands and the south and south-eastern coasts of the United States where they are most common. Scientists have also experimented with methods of dispersing or breaking up hurricanes, although they have met with little success.

In the Far East and the west Pacific Ocean, hurricanes are often called typhoons, whereas in the area of the Indian Ocean they are known as cyclones.

Tornadoes are violent whirlwinds which vary in their width from a few metres to 400 metres. They move at speeds of fifteen to fifty kilometres an hour. A water spout occurs when a typhoon passes over water and draws it up, sometimes to a height of 1,500 metres.

Local winds

Perhaps the most familiar local winds are sea breezes, which everyone experiences on a seaside holiday. They are due to the fact that land heats more quickly than water, causing air above the land to rise and draw in colder air from over the sea. This takes place during the early afternoon, but in

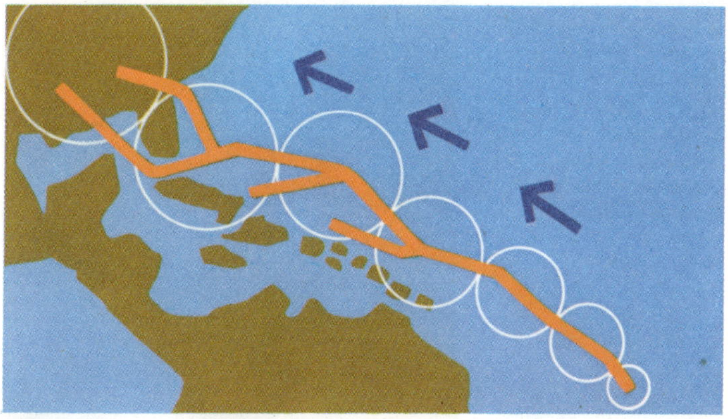

Above The drawing at the top of the page shows the effect of a hurricane. Below it is a hurricane chart showing how it builds up. Each circle on the map gets bigger as the hurricane extends its area from about 8 kilometres to about 1,200 kilometres.
Below In countries where heavy snowfall occurs regularly snowploughs are used to keep the railways open. This one is working on the line from Chur to Arosa in Switzerland.

Right Some of the instruments used to gain information about the weather. **1** A cup anemometer measures the speed and direction of wind. **2** Sunshine recorder (a card is placed at the focus of a spherical glass lens. As the sun shines it burns a thin line along the card which is marked with a scale of hours). **3** Rainfall recorder. **4** Radiosonde carried into the upper air by a weather balloon. **5** This box contains a series of thermometers behind a ventilated screen.

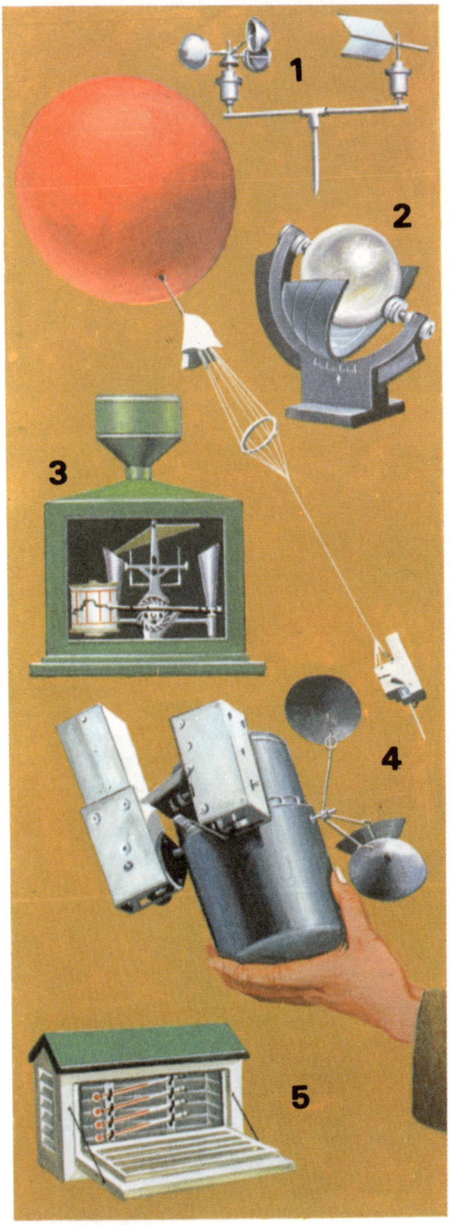

Below Benjamin Franklin's historic experiment with a kite proved that lightning in the sky was a form of electricity.

the evening when the land cools more quickly than the sea the reverse happens and so the air is drawn seawards.

Föhn winds are warm dry winds which have a considerable effect on the temperature and do a great deal of good in melting snow and drying the land. They are most common in the valleys of Switzerland. Similar types of wind are the chinook of the Rockies in Canada, the nor'-wester in New Zealand, and the samoon in Persia. A bitingly cold wind of a similar local type is the mistral of the Rhone Valley in France.

Thunder and lightning

A violent storm in which there are very strong up-currents of air produces thunder and lightning. During the storm static electricity develops which causes the flashes of lightning.

The speed of the lightning varies greatly and the length of a flash is determined by cloud height. Lightning is more likely to hit very tall buildings and this is why they are protected by what are called lightning conductors. These are strips of copper connecting the highest points of the building with the ground and acting as an earthing mechanism.

Two kinds of lightning are usually recognised, although to the experts there are many more. Fork lightning is the actual visible stroke we can see, while sheet lightning is produced by a hidden flash.

Weather forecasting

A vast number of people need accurate weather forecasts. Farmers, pilots, and river-board officials all want to know what is going to happen in the skies. Meteorological offices do produce special agricultural forecasts, river and flood warnings, marine, aviation and, of course, general forecasts. In the regions where they occur, hurricane warnings are prepared.

The weather is studied as it happens and the amount of such things as sunshine, cloud and rain is measured. Meteorology is truly an international science and many countries co-operate with each other in order that their forecasts may be more accurate.

To record surface conditions there is a network of weather stations both on land and at sea, while balloons carry equipment high into the atmosphere to record and measure. Vast amounts of equipment are involved, from the humble thermometer and barometer to highly developed instruments housed in weather satellites, which study cloud formations and heat loss and gain from high above the earth's surface.

Weather satellites have proved to be of major importance and are constantly opening up new fields of research. It may be that with their help we shall not have so many complaints in the future about the man who reads the weather forecast.

Above The earliest explorers came from the ancient world and they were often led to undertake perilous journeys to seek new areas for trading. This, and man's natural desire to see what lies beyond his own limited horizons, and the urge to conquer new lands, has taken him into every corner of the earth and now into space itself. In this picture can be seen Alexander the Great, who led his armies from Greece to India; Viking warriors; an Egyptian in Crete; and a Roman soldier.

Man explores his world

Man has always had an urgent desire to explore the world around him. Already his travels have taken him to the moon, although there are still some land areas on earth that remain unexplored, and certainly the whole of the ocean floor awaits investigation.

From the evidence of fossils it is apparent that from earliest times man has roamed, colonised and explored. The reasons for his actions have been many and varied; possibly it was the desire for trade, or war and conquest, but basically it is man's desire to explore the unknown that has driven him into the four corners of the earth and now into space itself.

The motive of trade spurred the Egyptians to explore the Mediterranean and the coast of east Africa many centuries before the birth of Christ. The Phoenicians and Greeks explored the same areas and travelled even farther. In 700 BC the Phoenicians sailed possibly as far as Britain to the Cornish coast in search of tin.

The great journeys of conquest made by Alexander the Great (356-323 BC), king of Macedonia, were mostly overland. He covered much of the Middle East and even reached India. Not only was he interested in conquest but also in recording and understanding all the new marvels he encountered on his travels. He sent a mission up the Nile to find out the causes of the floods and is responsible for this early scientific expedition.

During the rise and supremacy of the Roman Empire many regions of Europe were thoroughly explored and charted. New ways were opened for trade and travel. Eratosthenes (276-194 BC), the Greek mathematician and geographer, formed his great library in Alexandria – one of the cities founded by Alexander the Great – where he produced the first maps of importance.

After the collapse of the Roman Empire, explorers moved north and east. Eastward to the Arab countries, where many voyages were made in the Indian Ocean, and in the period AD 800-1000 to the Far East itself.

The Norsemen

The Norsemen (Vikings from Scandinavia) are known to all by their proud ships, with carved war-heads and shields along the sides. Too often they are thought of simply as warriors and not as explorers who colonised lands which were to remain unknown to the rest of the world for centuries.

From the 9th to the 11th centuries this hardy sea-going people reigned supreme. Their boats sailed up rivers

Above In this group of scenes from the history of exploration are, from left to right, Marco Polo, whose travels in Asia lasted for twenty-five years; Prince Henry of Portugal (Henry the Navigator), with two of the many great explorers from his country, Vasco da Gama and Ferdinand Magellan; Christopher Columbus landing in the Bahamas; the massacre of the Aztecs by the Spaniards under Cortes, who appears clad in black armour; Sir Francis Drake, the first Englishman to sail round the world; and Henry Hudson during his voyages in Newfoundland.

to the very heart of Europe and by the evidence of oriental coins found in their graves they undoubtedly traded with the East.

They swept across the northern seas to reach the Orkneys, Shetlands and Faroes in the 9th century. By 870 Iceland was reached, and the first republic of Iceland was founded in the year 930.

Onward they sailed, landing in Greenland in 982, and by the year 1000 they had actually set foot in the New World, in Labrador and Newfoundland. Here they stayed for three centuries, only to die out because of hostile natives and a climate which grew steadily worse.

Their presence in North America is supported by literary history and by archaeological remains, or the digging up of things they left behind them. If the recently discovered Vinland Map is genuine then this also is evidence of Viking settlements and their knowledge of the North Atlantic and North America.

Exploring for trade

The spread of Christianity brought new exploration in Europe and particularly in Asia. The famous Polo family from Venice first visited the great Mogul Empire as merchants and ambassadors from the Pope. The brothers Maffeo and Nicolo Polo took many years on their visit to Mongolia and China, and when Marco Polo (1254-1324), Nicolo's son, undertook his great journey he was away for twenty-five years. He came back to Venice by sea, like a true explorer going one way and coming back another.

At different times, different people and different countries have taken the lead and greatly added to man's knowledge of his world.

Such was the case in the 15th and 16th centuries, the great period of exploration by Portuguese and Spanish seamen. Prince Henry of Portugal (1394-1460), sometimes called Henry the Navigator because of his interest in the science of navigation, inspired and guided many voyages of discovery.

A vast Portuguese fleet explored the west coast of Africa, the Azores, Madeira, the Canaries and Cape Verde Islands, and all for a route to the east for purposes of trade.

But in spite of his devotion to the sea, it was not until after Prince Henry's death that the African continent was sailed around.

In 1488 the Portuguese navigator Bartholomew Diaz (1450?-1500) rounded the Cape of Good Hope and in 1497-8 his fellow countryman Vasco da Gama (1469?-1525) reached India.

Seeking a new trading route, Christopher Columbus (1451-1506) sailed

westwards from Europe in 1492, convinced that he could reach the fabulous East Indies. Instead he landed in the Bahama islands and the West Indies. On later voyages he visited South America and the Gulf of Mexico, trying to find a passage across Panama.

The new continent of America was to be named after the Florentine explorer, Amerigo Vespucci (1451-1512), after whom Venezuela is also named.

Further efforts to reach the east resulted in the discovery of the mainland of North America by John Cabot (1450?-98?), the Genoese pilot who settled in England and sailed from there in 1497 to reach Nova Scotia in the same year.

Around the world

In 1513 Vasco Nunez de Balboa (1475-1517), a Spanish explorer, first viewed the Pacific Ocean from a mountain in Panama, while several years later Ferdinand Magellan (1480?-1521), again from Portugal, sailed into the ocean on his attempted round-the-world voyage. After the terrible storms and rough seas off South America, the ocean Magellan sailed into was so calm that he named it the Pacific. The voyage, which started and finished at Seville in Spain, was successfully completed after three years (1519-22) by one of the five ships that had set out. Magellan himself was killed on the voyage in the Philippine Islands, but the *Victoria* under the command of Sebastian del Cano became the first ship to sail right round the world.

Half a century passed before it was sailed round again, this time by the English seaman and navigator Francis Drake (1540?-96).

With many of the seas crossed it was natural that attention should be turned to exploration of the land. The stories of fabulous wealth in gold and silver spurred on the Spanish in their conquests of South and Central America. Hernando Cortés (1485-1547) crushed the Aztecs in Mexico with an expeditionary force that consisted initially of less than 600 Spaniards, about 250 Indians, and 15 horses. Another Spanish soldier, Francisco Pizarro (1478?-1541) conquered the Incas and explored Peru in South America.

The idea of trade routes was always a driving force in exploration and several British sailors attempted to find new routes. Hugh Willoughby died in 1554 in the frozen north after reaching Novaya Zemlya in Russia during an expedition backed by London merchants. Richard Chancellor (died 1556) sought a north-east passage to India, reached Archangel and made treaties with the Russians in Moscow. In the west Henry Hudson (died 1611) reached Newfoundland and explored what is now the Hudson Bay. He was

Above An animal-headed post carved from wood and found in the wreck of the Oseberg ship, a Viking burial ship which dates from about AD 800.

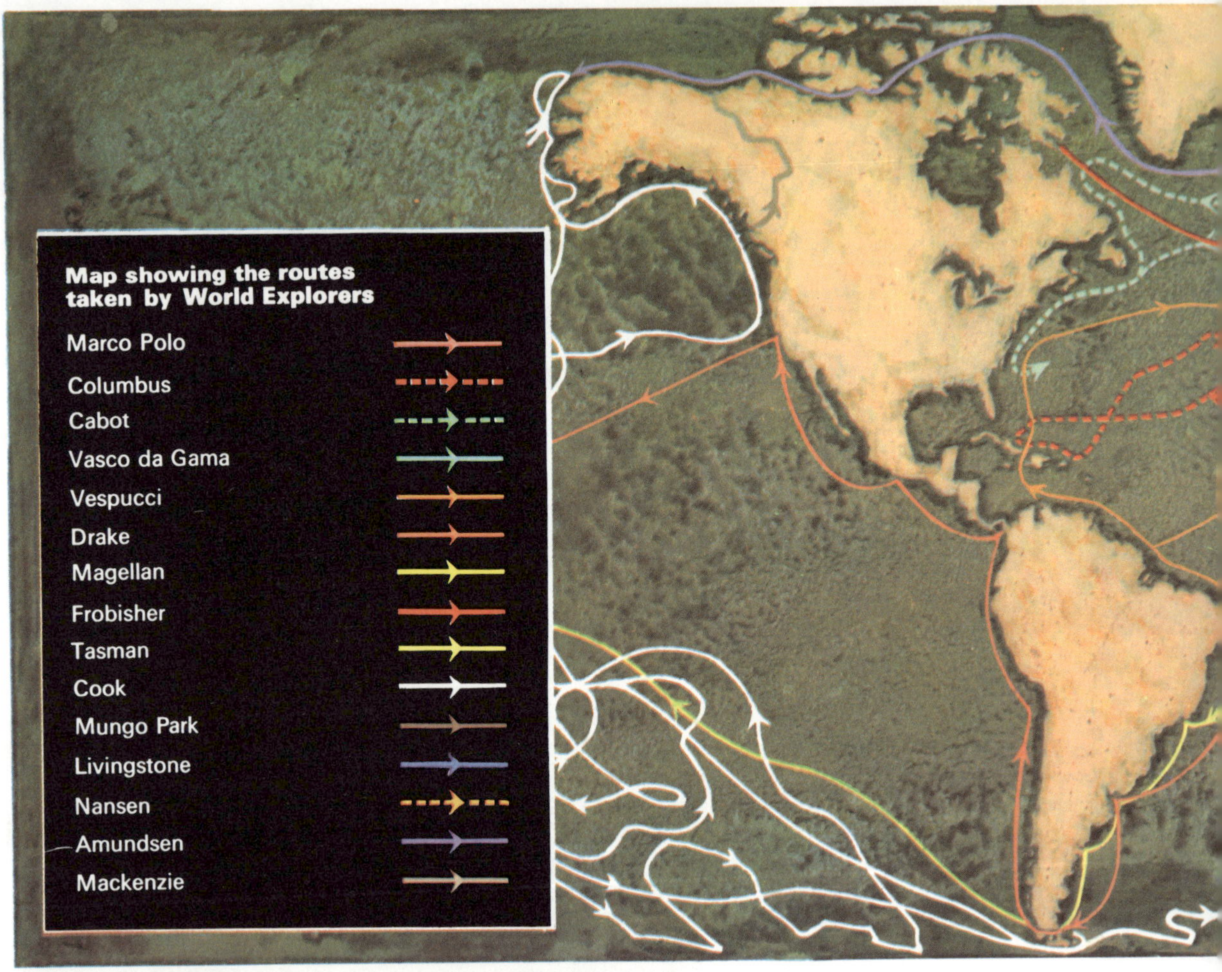

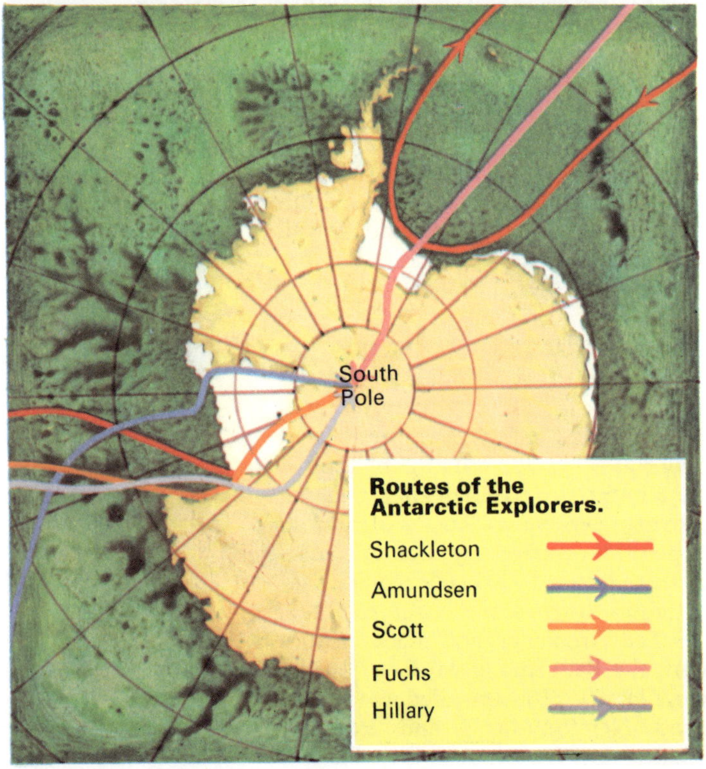

followed by William Baffin (1584?-1622) who discovered Baffin Bay.

These voyages were followed by even longer and more dangerous ones as the vast areas of the Pacific Ocean were explored. Pedro Fernandes de Quiros sailed to the New Hebrides in 1606 and another member of his expedition, Luis Vaez de Torres, passed through what is now the Torres Strait between New Guinea and Australia. Abel Tasman (1602-59), the Dutch navigator, discovered Tasmania in 1642 and explored the Australian coast.

Australia and America

In the 18th century came one of the greatest explorers and navigators, the Englishman James Cook (1728-79). In 1768-71 he was in command of the *Endeavour*, which was carrying scientists to the Pacific to observe the planet Venus. After the first object of the voyage had been achieved, Cook sailed

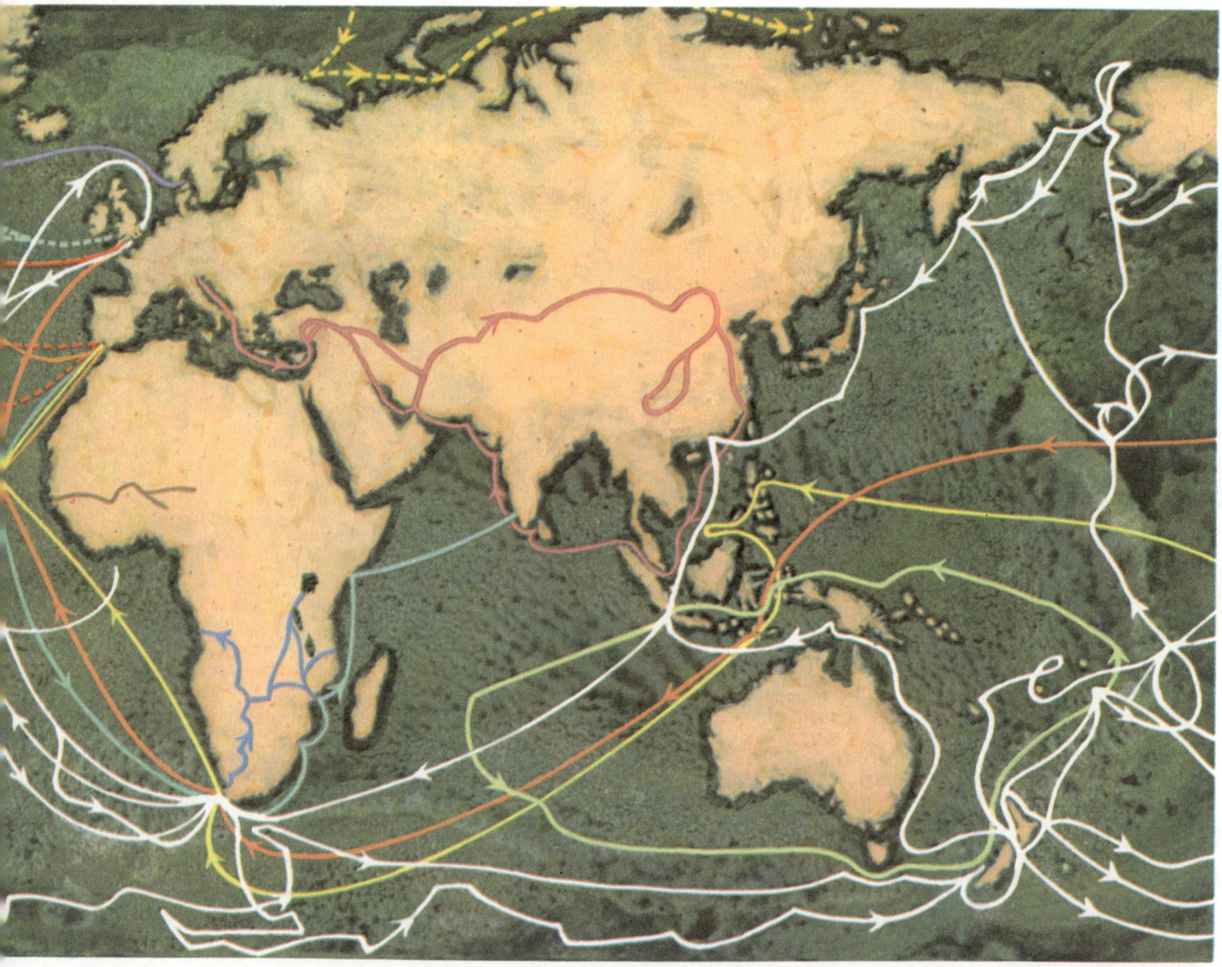

round New Zealand, visiting the Society Islands, founding Botany Bay and exploring Australia, of which he took possession for Great Britain.

Cook's second voyage in 1772-5 saw him in the South Pacific and the third (1776-9) in the North Pacific. He penetrated farther south than any other person was to do for many years. The scientific results of his voyages greatly increased man's knowledge of his world and brought many new discoveries in animals and plants.

Thus the major seas had at last yielded some of their secrets and attention was now firmly fixed on exploration of the land masses.

In North America Alexander Mackenzie (1755?-1820) discovered the great river which is now named after him and crossed the Rockies overland to the Pacific. Meriwether Lewis (1774-1809) and William Clark (1770-1838) approached the Pacific by way of the Missouri river and the Rockies.

The coastal areas of South America were visited by such famous naturalists as Charles Darwin (1809-82) and Alfred Russel Wallace (1823-1913), who together originated the theory of evolution by natural selection. Another naturalist from Germany, Alexander von Humboldt (1769-1859) explored the reaches of the Orinoco in Venezuela.

The African continent

The African continent offered a great challenge and one of the earliest explorers was the Scot, James Bruce (1730-94), who travelled in Ethiopia and found the source of the Blue Nile which he followed downstream to Cairo (1770-3).

The great Niger River attracted Mungo Park (1771-1806), another Scot who made two expeditions there and was killed on the second. He was author of *Travels in the Interior of Africa* published in 1799.

Above The two maps on these pages trace the routes taken by some of the explorers who braved the unknown, often under conditions of great physical hardship, in order to discover the exact boundaries of the world we live in.

Above The explorers seen in this picture are, from left to right, David Livingstone and H. M. Stanley on the occasion of their historic meeting in Africa; Burke and Wills, the two men who explored the heart of the Australian continent and died there; the English explorer and navigator Captain Cook; the airship *Norge* in which Amundsen made the first successful polar flight; Mungo Park; Burton and Speke, who discovered the source of the Nile; Scott on his way to the south pole; Fridtjof Nansen; and Edmund Hillary on the summit of Mount Everest.

The great English traveller and linguist Richard Burton (1821-90) reached Lake Tanganyika in Africa in 1858 with John Hanning Speke (1827-64). Speke later went on to discover the true source of the Nile and the area around Lake Victoria.

The area of the Zambesi and the Zaire was opened up by David Livingstone (1813-73), Scottish missionary and traveller, who went through Central Africa during the years 1849-56, discovered the Victoria Falls (1858-64) and Lake Nyasa (1866-73). On the last expedition, fears for his safety resulted in the British explorer and journalist, Henry Morton Stanley (1841-1904), setting out to look for him. This led to their historic meeting at Ujiji in 1871. Stanley was later responsible for following the Zaire River and discovering the Ruwenzori Mountains.

First steps in Asia

Interest in Asia had been aroused by the voyage of da Gama around the Cape of Good Hope, first by Portugal and later by the vast commercial concerns of England and France. In 1580 the Russians started across Siberia and within half a century had added a vast portion of Asia to their land. Missionaries were responsible for many trips to China and in the mid-19th century were active in Central Asia and finally reached Tibet. The Russian Nicholas Prjevalsky (1839-88) crossed the Gobi Desert and visited Peking and Tibet. Nils Nordenskjöld (1832-1901), the Swedish Arctic navigator, finally found the elusive north-east passage from the Atlantic to the Pacific along the northern coast of Asia in his ship *Vega*.

The Australian interior

In view of the pattern of settlement in Australia the south-eastern region was, not unnaturally, explored first. Thomas Mitchell (1792-1855), from Scotland, made several overland expeditions. The Englishman Edward John Eyre (1815-1901) suffered great hardship in his attempt to reach the centre of Australia and again during his journey from Adelaide westwards to Albany. Ludwig Leichhardt (1813-48), a German explorer, travelled from the Darling Downs up the eastern side of Australia and across the north to Port Essington. He also tried an east-west crossing of the continent but the expedition was lost.

The expedition of the Irishman Robert Burke (1820-61) and William Wills (1834-61), from Australia, to the heart of the continent in 1860-1 also ended in tragedy when both men perished. The first to reach the interior was another Scot, John McDouall Stuart (1815-66), in 1859; and later he

made the journey from south to north. The Australian brothers John (1847-1918) and Alexander Forrest (1849-1901) travelled widely in the region between Perth and Adelaide.

The north and south poles

The forbidding polar regions were the last areas of the earth to be explored by man. The idea of northern trade routes gave point to Arctic exploration and the first person to reach the north pole was the American admiral Robert E. Peary (1856-1920) on 6th April 1909. Before this Fridtjof Nansen (1861-1930) from Norway had first crossed Greenland in 1888, and in 1893 attempted to reach the pole from his ice-locked ship the *Fram*, but was forced back.

In 1926 there were flights over the north pole by an American, Richard E. Byrd (1888-1957), and by a Norwegian, Roald Amundsen (1872-1928).

The Antarctic continent is remote from other lands and therefore possibly even more difficult to explore. Captain Cook on his second voyage reached the pack ice but it was many years before anyone was to go there again.

John Biscoe of the firm of Enderby of London sailed the southern ocean in 1831-2 in search of seals, while in 1840-3 the Englishman James Clark Ross (1800-62) explored Victoria Land from the two ships *Erebus* and *Terror*.

Two other great Antarctic explorers from Britain were Robert Falcon Scott (1868-1912) and Ernest Shackleton (1874-1922). Both men sailed in the *Discovery* on the National Expedition (1900-4), and Shackleton made three further expeditions, in 1908, 1915 and 1920, on the last of which he died.

Scott made his famous attempt on the pole in his expedition of 1911-12 which resulted in his reaching the pole only to find that Amundsen had beaten him. He and his companions died on the return journey to base. Scott followed his route to the pole by means of the Beardmore Glacier while Amundsen had to make the ascent of the treacherous Axel Heiberg Glacier.

The first Australian expeditions of these regions were under the guidance of Douglas Mawson (1882-1958), who explored and mapped King George V Land and Queen Mary Land.

This icy wilderness is now an international continent and many countries have bases there. During the International Geophysical Year (1957-8) Vivian Fuchs made his 3,500 kilometre crossing of Antarctica with the help of Edmund Hillary. This trip, together with other recent polar expeditions, had proved that great courage and skill are still needed to explore such regions in spite of all the help given by modern aids.

Above A ship's compass designed to hang from the bulkhead of a ship during the days of sail.

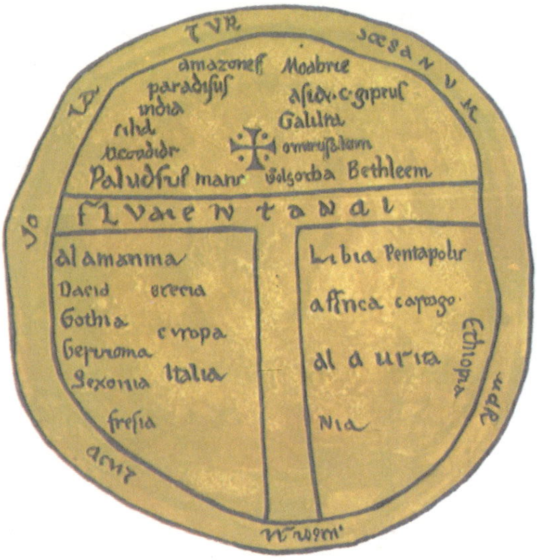

Above At the top of the page is seen Mercator's World Map of 1569, based on the projection which is now known by his name, together with a likeness of Mercator himself. Below on the left is an example of the so-called T-O maps of medieval times, while on the right is shown a clay tablet map of part of northern Mesopotamia which dates from 500 BC.

Maps

A map sets out to record where places and objects are and to be a guide to the traveller who wants to go from one place to another. Maps are very ancient and there is plenty of evidence that primitive people made and used them. The Eskimo drew his map on a piece of animal skin, the North American Indian on bark, and the Arab used a pointed stick to trace the outline of a map in the sand. The Marshall Islanders used charts made of bamboo cane and shells to help them on their long journeys by canoe between the hundreds of Pacific islands.

The greatest map-makers of the ancient world were the Greeks, the first people to make a science of map-making, or cartography as it is called. In the 2nd century AD the Alexandrian Greek Claudius Ptolemy (AD 90?-168?) published his famous writings on astronomy and geography. His ideas about map-making were lost to Europe for many years, although his books were translated into Arabic in the 9th century. Then his work was rediscovered at the time of the Renaissance in Europe in the early 15th century.

During the so-called 'dark ages' in Europe, religious beliefs dominated

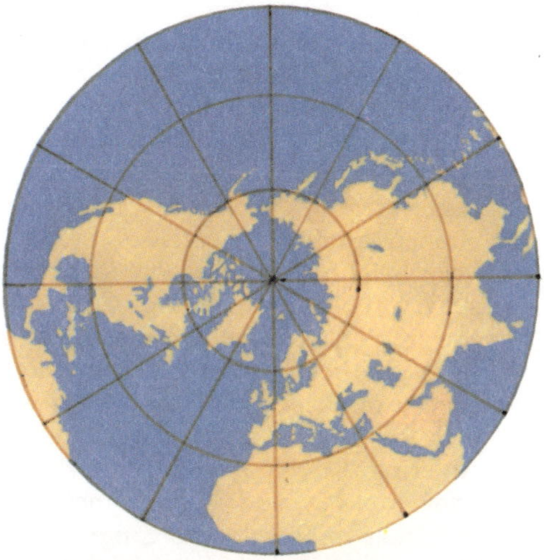

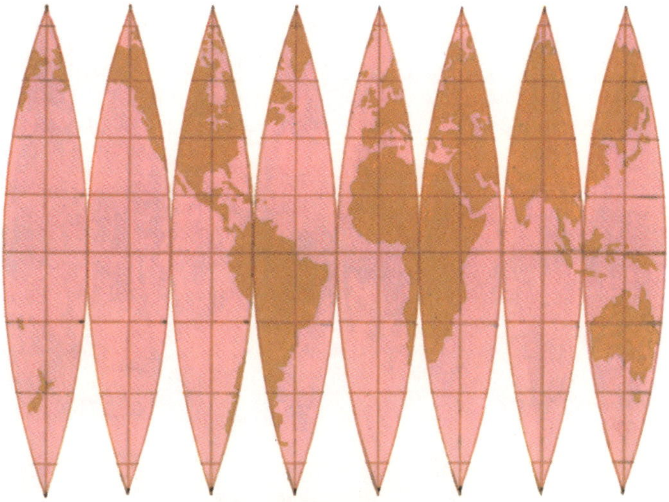

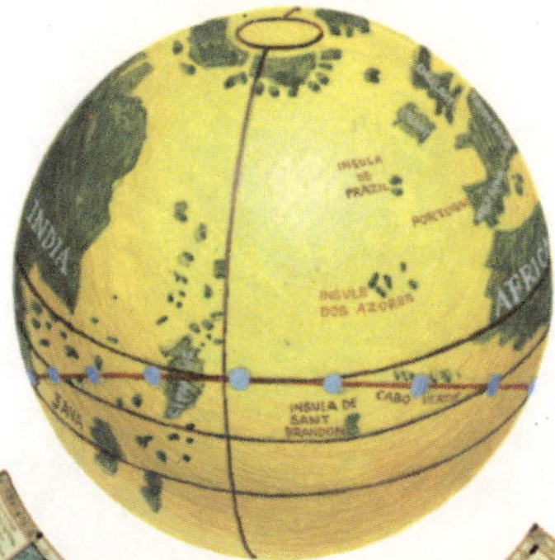

Above The globe at the top of the page illustrates the true relationship of Asia and North America. To construct a globe information is plotted on to shapes called gores (top right) which will fold into a sphere. On the left is seen a portolan chart of the 14th century with a network of lines which connect ports and coastal landmarks. On the right is a 15th-century globe and below it Ptolemy's World Outline from a book printed in Rome in 1490.

the map-makers' conception of the world, as is seen in the curious T-O maps of medieval times. The official view of the Church was that the earth was flat and Jerusalem was the centre of the world.

The Age of Discovery led to a great increase in the number of maps and charts as the sailors of the world explored across the seas. As man's knowledge advanced so his maps became more accurate. Such inventions as the mariner's compass, which came into use in the 13th century, made it possible to produce more exact drawings of the coastlines.

Mercator's projection

In the 16th century the Flemish map-maker and geographer, Gerhardus Mercator (1512-94) – this was the Latin form of his real name, Gerhard Kremer – published his collection of maps and called it an atlas, the first time the word had been used. It was the development of map engraving in the 16th century that made this possible and it led to large numbers of maps being printed and to the appearance of the first atlas.

During the 16th and 17th centuries progress in map-making was due mainly to cartographers in Portugal,

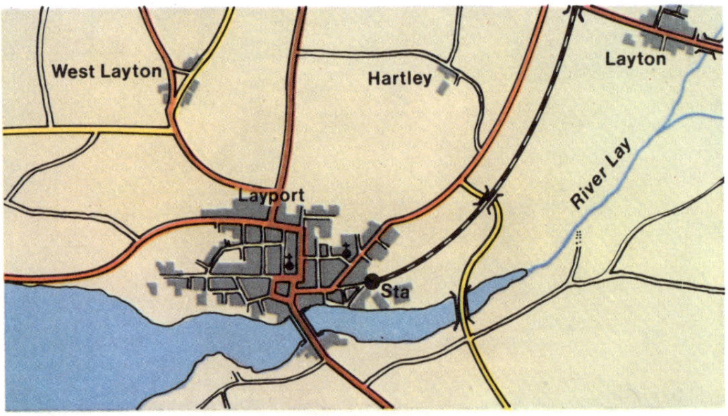

Above Three maps of the fictional town of Layport and surrounding areas, in greater and greater detail. The bottom picture shows the town itself. Notice how the roads and bridges correspond with their position on the map. On the right are seen some of the common symbols used on maps.

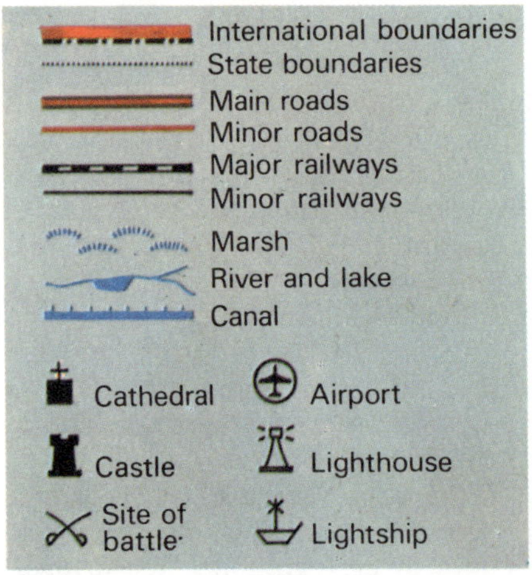

Italy, the Netherlands and France. The French Royal Academy of Sciences was instructed by Louis XIV to prepare new maps, not only of France, but of the whole world, and this enormous task was undertaken by four generations of the Cassinis, an Italian-French family of scientists.

In Britain the idea of a national land survey began when the Ordnance Survey was officially established in 1791. Its first aims were to complete a survey of Britain and produce a one inch to a mile map. The work of covering the whole country took from 1798 to 1853, and the one inch to a mile map of Britain was completed in 1870. Today Britain is one of the best-mapped countries in the world and the work of the Ordnance Survey has become a model which many other countries have followed in creating their own map systems.

Always there has been great difficulty in showing the round earth on a flat surface. The only true way to study the world is by means of a globe. Since Mercator, various projections have been devised in an attempt to produce more accurate maps. Some of these show direction correctly, others pay more attention to the correct presentation of areas and shapes. The best projection, of course, is the one that takes all the different factors into account. To make it easier to find and pinpoint any spot on a map, lines of latitude and longitude are drawn in an imaginary network over the world's surface.

When an area is to be mapped for the first time it is necessary to have a number of inter-related points, the location of which is known, and the production of such a 'base-map' is called a triangulation. The country is covered with imaginary evenly sized and shaped triangles. The base line from which all the work begins is measured with great accuracy in flat country, allowing a possible error of about one centimetre in fifteen kilometres. From this the triangles are built up.

Aerial photographs are now much used in mapping and these speed up the production of maps greatly, especially in the developing countries where the first surveys are only just taking place.

Scale
0
Kilometres
600
Miles
0
375
ICELAND
Reykjavik
a Slovenia
b Croatia
c Serbia
d Bosnia & Herzogovina
e Montenegro
f Macedonia
NORWAY
SWEDEN
FINLAND
Bergen
Stavanger
Oslo
Stockholm
Turku
Helsinki
Gothenburg
Gotland
UNITED KINGDOM
SCOTLAND
Glasgow
Edinburgh
N. IRELAND
Belfast
IRELAND
Dublin
Manchester
WALES
Birmingham
ENGLAND
Cardiff
London
NORTH SEA
DENMARK
Esbjerg
Copenhagen
Odense
Malmo
ATLANTIC OCEAN
Hamburg
Amsterdam
NETHERLANDS
Berlin
GERMANY
Brussels
BELGIUM
Bonn
Leipzig
LUXEMBOURG
Gdansk
Warsaw
Lodz
POLAND
Prague
Krakow
CZECH REP.
Brno
SLOVAKIA
Paris
FRANCE
Munich
Vienna
Berne
Innsbruck
AUSTRIA
SWITZERLAND
Budapest
HUNGARY
Cluj
ROMANIA
Bordeaux
Lyons
Venice
a
Zagreb
b
d
Belgrade
c
Marseilles
Genoa
ITALY
Porto
PORTUGAL
SPAIN
Barcelona
Madrid
CORSICA
Sofia
BULGARIA
e
Tirana
ALBANIA
f
Rome
Naples
Palma
MAJORCA
SARDINIA
Seville
GREECE
Gibraltar
MEDITERRANEAN SEA
SICILY
Athens

a Armenia (Yerevan)
b Azerbaijan (Baku)
c Belarus (Minsk)
d Estonia (Tallinn)
e Georgia (Tbilisi)
f Kazakhstan (Alma-Ata)
g Kyrgyzstan (Frunze)
h Latvia (Riga)
i Lithuania (Vilnius)
j Moldova (Kishinev)
k Russia (Moscow)
l Tajikastan (Dushanbe)
m Turkmenistan (Ashkhabad)
n Ukraine (Kiev)
o Uzbekistan (Tashkent)
Murmansk
Arkhangelsk
Leningrad
Riga
Kaliningrad
Minsk
Smolensk
Moscow
COMMONWEALTH OF
Gomel
Kiev
Tula
Kazan
Perm
Odessa
Kharkov
Saratov
Kuybyshev
Istanbul
BLACK SEA
Volgograd
Petropavlovsk
Omsk
Ankara
Astrakhan
Guryev
TURKEY
Adana
CASPIAN SEA
Karaganda
Nicosia
CYPRUS
Aleppo
Beirut
LEBANON
SYRIA
Tel Aviv
Damascus
Al Mawsil
Tabriz
Krasnovodsk
Khiva
ISRAEL
Jerusalem
Amman
JORDAN
IRAQ
Rasht
Aqaba
Baghdad
Tehran
Askhabad
Tashkent
Samarkand
Mary
Mashhad
Esfahan
Basra
Abadan
Herat
Neutral Territory
Yazd
KUWAIT
Medina
RED SEA
IRAN
AFGHANISTAN
Kabul
Persian Gulf
Islamabad
Jidda
Mecca
Hofuf
BAHRAIN
Kandahar
Quetta
Bandar Abbas
Lahore
SAUDI ARABIA
QATAR
UNITED ARAB EMIRATES
PAKISTAN
Delhi
Muscat
INDIA
Karachi
ARABIAN SEA
Sana
YEMEN
OMAN

RCTIC
OCEAN
BERING
SEA
Sredne Kolymsk
Nordvik
DEPENDENT STATES
Yakutsk
Kirensk
Tomsk
ovosibirsk
Novokuznetsk
Irkutsk
Khabarovsk
Harbin
Changchun
Ulan Bator
MONGOLIA
Mukden
NORTH KOREA
Pyongyang
SOUTH KOREA
Seoul
Pusan
JAPAN
Tokyo
Yokohama
Osaka
Hiroshima
Nagasaki
Peking
Tsinan
Changyeh
Lanchow
Suchow
Shanghai
CHINA
PACIFIC
OCEAN
Chengtu
Changsha
Nanchang
Chungking
Lhasa
Foochow
Taipei
TAIWAN
Tainan
Kanchow
Scale
0 Kilometres 800
0 Miles 500
Katmandu
BHUTAN
MYANMAR (BURMA)
Darjeeling
Patna
Shillong
Myitkyina
BANGLADESH
Canton
HONG KONG

Hyderabad
PAKISTAN
Delhi
Kanpur
Lucknow
NEPAL
BHUTAN
INDIA
BANGLADESH
Dacca
Calcutta
Bombay
Bangalore
Madras
SRI LANKA
Colombo
CHINA
Nanking
Shanghai
Chungking
Nanning
Canton
HONG KONG
TAIWAN
Mandalay
MYANMAR (BURMA)
Yangon
Luang Prabang
LAOS
SOCIALIST REPUBLIC OF VIETNAM
Hanoi
Da Nang
Ho Chi Minh City
Chiang Mai
THAILAND
Bangkok
CAMBODIA
Phnom Penh
PACIFIC OCEAN
PHILIPPINES
Manila
Davao
MALAYA
Kuala Lumpur
Singapore
MALAYSIA
BRUNEI
SABAH
SARAWAK
KALIMANTAN
BORNEO
Bandjarmasin
SUMATRA
Palembang
INDONESIA
Djakarta
Bandung
JAVA
Surabaja
SULAWESI
MOLUCCAS
IRIAN JAYA
TIMOR
INDIAN OCEAN
Scale
0 Kilometres 800
0 Miles 500

MEDITERRANEAN SEA
RED SEA
SOUTH ATLANTIC OCEAN
INDIAN OCEAN
Tangier
Rabat
Casablanca
Madeira
CANARY ISLANDS
MOROCCO
Aiun
WESTERN SAHARA
MAURITANIA
Ouahran
Algiers
ALGERIA
Tunis
TUNISIA
Tripoli
Beida
Benghazi
LIBYA
Alexandria
Cairo
Suez Canal
EGYPT
SENEGAL
MALI
NIGER
CHAD
SUDAN
Khartoum
ERITREA
DJIBOUTI
Djibouti
Addis Ababa
ETHIOPIA
Niamey
BURKINA FASO
Ouagadougou
Bamako
GUINEA
SIERRA LEONE
LIBERIA
Monrovia
IVORY COAST
Abidjan
GHANA
Accra
TOGO
BENIN
NIGERIA
Kano
Ibadan
Lagos
N'djamena
CAMEROON
Yaoundé
Douala
CENTRAL AFRICAN REPUBLIC
Bangui
EQUATORIAL GUINEA
Libreville
GABON
CONGO
Brazzaville
Kinshasa
CABINDA
ZAIRE
SOMALI REPUBLIC
UGANDA
Kampala
KENYA
Nairobi
RWANDA
BURUNDI
TANZANIA
Pemba
Zanzibar
Dar-es-Salaam
Luanda
ANGOLA
ZAMBIA
Lusaka
MALAWI
Lilongwe
MOZAMBIQUE
Mozambique
Harare
ZIMBABWE
NAMIBIA
Windhoek
BOTSWANA
Gaborone
Johannesburg
SWAZILAND
Māputo
REP. OF SOUTH AFRICA
LESOTHO
Cape Town
Antananarivo
MADAGASCAR
Scale
0 Kilometres 1000
0 Miles 630
Scale
0 Kms 70
0 Mls 44
Port Louis
MAURITIUS
St. Denis
RÉUNION

ARCTIC OCEAN
GREENLAND
ICELAND
Ellesmere I.
Sverdrup Islands
BEAUFORT SEA
Parry Islands
BAFFIN BAY
DAVIS STRAIT
Banks I.
Somerset I.
Prince of Wales I.
Baffin I.
ALASKA
Franklin Dist.
Victoria I.
King William I.
Boothia Pen.
Melville Pen.
Anchorage
YUKON
NORTHWEST TERRITORIES
Southampton I.
Whitehorse
Mackenzie Dist.
Keewatin Dist.
Yellowknife
Juneau
HUDSON BAY
CANADA
Alexander Arch.
BRITISH COLUMBIA
ALBERTA
SASKATCHEWAN
MANITOBA
ONTARIO
QUEBEC
NEWFOUNDLAND
Labrador
I. of Newfoundland
Queen Charlotte Islands
Edmonton
PRINCE EDWARD I.
NEW BRUNSWICK
NOVA SCOTIA
Halifax
St John
Quebec
Vancouver I.
Vancouver
Calgary
Saskatoon
Regina
Winnipeg
Port Arthur
Fort William
Montreal
Ottawa
Seattle
WASHINGTON
MONTANA
N. DAKOTA
MINN.
GREAT LAKES
Toronto
MAINE
VT.
N.H.
Boston
MASS.
R.I.
CT.
Portland
OREGON
Minneapolis
St Paul
WISC.
Hamilton
NEW YORK
New York City
IDAHO
S. DAKOTA
MICH.
Detroit
Windsor
PENN.
N.J.
Pittsburgh
Philadelphia
WYOMING
IOWA
Chicago
OHIO
MD.
DEL.
NEBRASKA
Omaha
Salt Lake City
IND.
Washington, D.C.
NEVADA
UTAH
Denver
COLORADO
Kansas City
KANSAS
ILLINOIS
Louisville
W. VA.
VIRGINIA
San Francisco
MISSOURI
St Louis
KENTUCKY
CALIFORNIA
UNITED STATES
N. CAROLINA
Las Vegas
OKLAHOMA
Memphis
TENNESSEE
S. CAROLINA
Los Angeles
Albuquerque
Oklahoma City
ARKANSAS
Birmingham
Atlanta
ATLANTIC OCEAN
ARIZONA
NEW MEXICO
ALA.
GEORGIA
Phoenix
MISS.
Fort Worth
Dallas
TEXAS
LOUISIANA
Cape Canaveral
Houston
New Orleans
FLORIDA
San Antonio
Miami
BAHAMA ISLANDS
GULF OF MEXICO
Monterrey
Havana
CUBA
PACIFIC OCEAN
Mexico
HAITI
DOMINICAN REP.
Merida
JAMAICA
Guadalajara
Mexico City
CARIBBEAN SEA
BELIZE
HONDURAS
GUATEMALA
EL SALVADOR
NICARAGUA
COSTA RICA
Scale
0 Kilometres 800
0 Miles 500

Barranquilla
Maracaibo
Caracas
TRINIDAD AND TOBAGO
Scale
0 Kilometres 800
0 Miles 500
PANAMA
Panama
VENEZUELA
Medellin
Georgetown
GUYANA
SURINAME
Paramaribo
Cayenne
FRENCH GUIANA
Bogota
Cali
COLOMBIA
Quito
ECUADOR
Guayaquil
Belém
Manaus
Fortaleza
PERU
BRAZIL
Recife
Salvador
Lima
Brasilia
La Paz
BOLIVIA
Belo Horizonte
PACIFIC OCEAN
PARAGUAY
São Paulo
Rio de Janeiro
Asuncion
Tucuman
CHILE
ARGENTINA
Porto Alegre
Cordoba
Mendoza
URUGUAY
Santiago
Rosario
Buenos Aires
Montevideo
Bahia Blanca
ATLANTIC OCEAN
Port Stanley
Falkland Is
Punta Arenas
Tierra del Fuego
Cape Horn
South Georgia

Darwin
TIMOR
SEA
CORAL
SEA
Cooktown
Cairns
NORTHERN
TERRITORY
Broome
Townsville
QUEENSLAND
Alice Springs
Rockhampton
WESTERN
AUSTRALIA
A U S T R A L I A
SOUTH
AUSTRALIA
Brisban
Geraldton
NEW SOUTH
WALES
Kalgoorlie
Boulder
Port Pirie
Newcastle
Perth
Fremantle
Great Australian Bight
Sydney
Adelaide
Canberra
VICTORIA
Bendigo
Geelong
Melbourne
TASMANIA
Hobart
Auckland
TASMAN
SEA
NORTH
ISLAND
Wellington
SOUTH
ISLAND
Christchurch
NEW
ZEALAND
Dunedin
Stewart Island
Scale
0 Kilometres 500
0 Miles 300
Scale
0 Kilometres 320
0 Miles 200

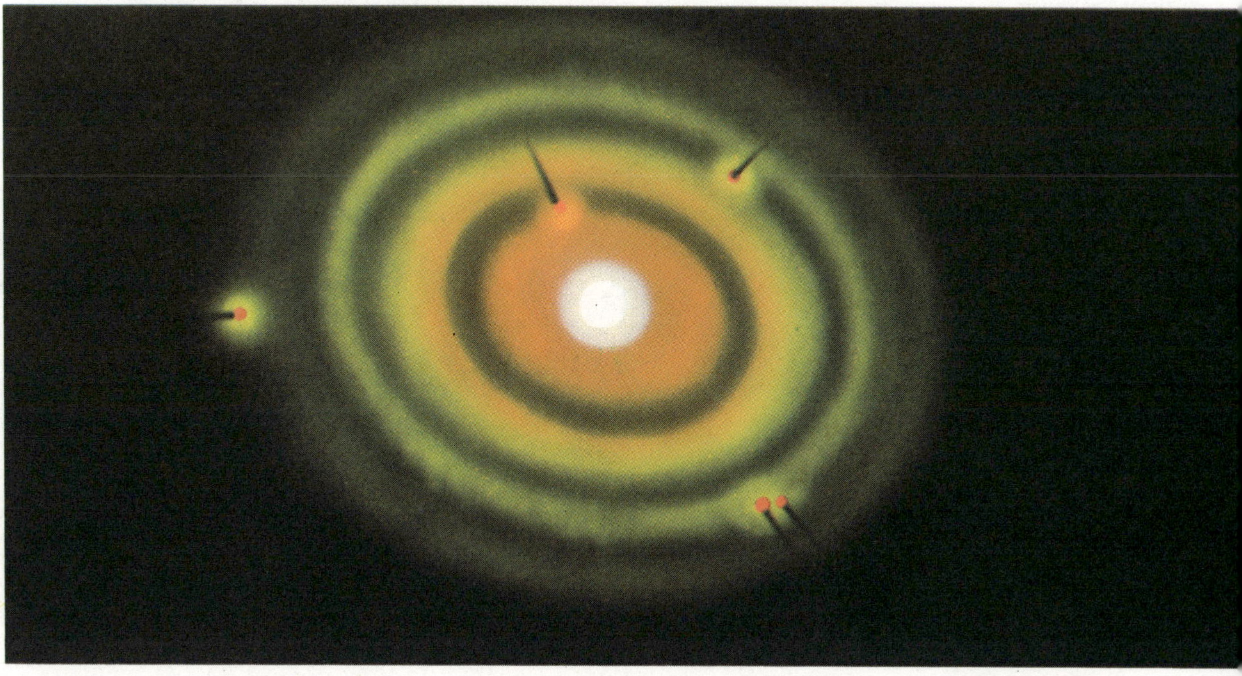

Above When the universe began it was probably filled with swirling clouds of gas and dust. The various particles were drawn towards each other by gravity and eventually formed themselves into stars. Our solar system is also thought to have been a great glowing disc of gases which centred itself around a nucleus that became the sun. Large and small pieces of matter became the planets and satellites which revolved around the nucleus and were attracted to it.

The world in space

Few of us have not spent some time 'star-gazing' – and for good reason too. The night sky is a truly magnificent sight. Unfortunately, those of us who live in or near towns never see the heavens in their true glory. The weather often obscures a clear view of the sky; the background glare of electric street lighting, the smoky waste from chimneys, and the haze of car exhaust fumes all help dim the pure light of the stars.

But for those who live in the country, and preferably high up, the heavens are often crystal clear. It is better to be high up, because you can then be above the thickest and dustiest part of the earth's atmosphere. This is the part that obscures our vision most. Seen from a high position, the stars do not 'twinkle' quite as much. The twinkling is caused, not by the stars themselves, but by the presence of dust and air currents in the atmosphere.

What picture did early man have of the world in space, this universe of sun, moon and stars? The earth, he knew, was flat. Why should he think otherwise? The countryside certainly looks flat. Without any form of transport he could not travel very far and, believing the earth was flat, did not want to. He might fall over the edge!

Above the earth was the great dome of the sky in which the stars were fixed for all time in their respective positions. This dome revolved steadily around the flat earth. The great golden ball of the sun moved slowly across the dome of the sky by day, giving light, colour and warmth to an otherwise cold and drab earth. The sun, man knew, brought life. It was a god, watching over man by day just as the silvery moon, another god, watched over man by night.

Sun-worship was common to most early peoples. The Sumerians, who founded the Babylonian civilisation in about 4000 BC, were ardent sun-worshippers. So were the people of ancient Egypt, where sun-worship reached its peak under the enlightened pharaoh Akhenaton in the 14th century BC. Great temples were built and dedicated to the sun-god, who Akhenaton decreed was supreme among the gods. The last great civilisations to

Right The Dutch spectacle-maker, Hans Lippershey, who lived in the early 17th century, is one of the people said to have discovered the principle of the telescope by focusing two lenses before him on to a distant object.

Nicolas Copernicus (1473–1543) Polish astronomer. Studied optics, mathematics, perspective and canon law. Appointed canon in 1497. Studied medicine and worked as medical attendant until 1512. Completed his book *De revolutionibus orbium coelestium*, his proof that the sun was at the centre of the solar system, in 1530.

practise sun-worship were the Incas of Peru and the Aztecs of Mexico. Both were wiped out by Spanish invaders in the 16th century.

The Sumerians, the Egyptians, and the Chinese, too, were content merely to observe the heavens. They did not try to explain what they saw there. Astronomy, the scientific study of the heavens, really began with the ancient Greeks, who completely changed man's outlook on the universe.

The first astronomers

The first notable Greek astronomer was Thales of Miletus who lived from about 624 to 565 BC. Although he still believed the earth was flat, he did try to interpret the changes in the heavens. And he caused a sensation by predicting an eclipse of the sun in 585 BC. Eclipses have always been regarded with awe. The light dims, birds cease their song and begin to roost. The eclipse is supposed to have taken place during a battle between the Lydians and Persians – so no wonder Thales's prediction startled the people.

Greek philosophers soon challenged the idea of a flat earth. The flatness could be explained, they said, if the earth was a gigantic sphere, which they regarded as the perfect shape. The round earth was the fixed centre of the universe, and around it circled the sun and the moon. The stars were tiny crystals in a great celestial sphere, with the earth at its centre. Moving across the celestial sphere were wandering stars which they called planets. The famous mathematician Pythagoras (580?-500? BC) and later the philosopher Aristotle (384-322 BC) supported this view of the heavens.

Then doubts began to creep in. Aristarchus of Samos, in the 3rd century BC, proposed the revolutionary theory that instead of the sun going round the earth, the earth moved round the sun. But the Greeks preferred the earth-centred view of the universe. This view was held by the last great astronomer of ancient times, Ptolemy of Alexandria (AD 90?-168?), who made his astronomical observations in about AD 150. Every heavenly body, he said – sun, moon, the planets, and the stars – moved in perfect circles around the fixed, round earth. Ptolemy's picture of the universe was accepted for almost 1,400 years.

Ptolemy handed down to us a list of constellations. A constellation is a group of bright stars which form recognisable patterns in the heavens. The ancients imagined that they could see all kinds of animals and people outlined in the patterns. They explained their presence in the sky by legends involving gods and heroes. Many of the constellations do not really look like the things they are meant to represent but some of them do. For instance, you can easily imagine Cygnus as a flying swan, or Scorpio as a scorpion with a curved, poisonous tail.

The moon and planets appear to travel in a broad belt across the sky. This imaginary belt is called the zodiac. The ancients divided the zodiac into twelve equal parts called signs of the zodiac and named each after the constellation that occupied its position. The position in the zodiac of the heavenly bodies at a person's birth was supposed to influence him for the rest of his life. This belief forms the basis of astrology. In the Middle Ages astrologers were held in high esteem. They became associated with the so-called alchemists, who tried in vain to find an 'elixir' to grant eternal life and a 'philosopher's stone' to turn base metals into gold.

The moving heavens

Such were the beliefs in the 1400s, when a Polish priest and astronomer, Nicolas Copernicus (1473-1543), challenged Ptolemy's view of the universe. He showed how the movements of the heavens were equally well, if not better, explained if the sun, not the earth, were the centre of a rotating solar system. Earth then became just another planet. But few supported the Copernican system; the Church considered it heretical to suggest that the earth was not the centre of the universe.

In about 1608 the telescope came into use. The Italian astronomer Galileo Galilei (1564-1642) built one the following year and made some astonishing discoveries. He found that the planet Jupiter was itself the centre of a miniature solar system, with four 'moons' revolving around it. (There are at least sixteen but Galileo's telescope was not strong enough to see the smaller ones.) He also discovered that the planet Venus showed phases like those of the moon. All of this pointed to Copernicus being right.

At about the same time the German astronomer Johann Kepler (1571-1630) was trying to account accurately for the motion of the planets, assuming a solar system. He based his work on the observations of the Danish astronomer Tycho Brahe (1546-1601), with whom he had worked for many years. At last he made the great breakthrough in astronomical thinking. He found that the planets move around the sun not in circles but in ellipses (which look somewhat like elongated circles). This means that the distance between a planet and the sun varies.

He published his findings in 1619 as his first law of planetary motion. At the same time he published his second law which states that a planet does not

Above The zodiac consists of twelve constellations in the apparent path of the sun across the sky. Representations of the zodiac are very ancient. This shows the zodiac ceiling of an Egyptian temple at Dendera dating from 100 BC.

Left There were many theories in the ancient world about the shape of the earth. This drawing is taken from an ancient Indian manuscript and shows an old Hindu belief that the earth was supported on four elephants which in turn rode upon a giant turtle as it swam in the sea.

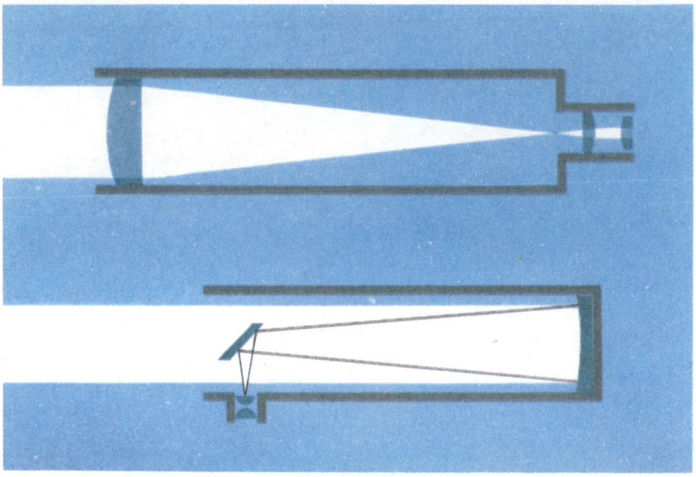

Above The diagrams at the top illustrate the principles of the refracting telescope (top) and reflecting telescope. On the right is Newton's original reflecting telescope. Immediately above is shown the way a prism splits a ray of light, showing the colours of the spectrum.

Johann Kepler (1571–1630) German astronomer. Professor of mathematics in 1593, later studied astronomy and worked with Tycho Brahe. First published his views on the universe in 1596.

move at the same speed along its path, or orbit, around the sun: it moves faster when it is closest to the sun than when it is farthest from the sun. Ten years later Kepler published his third law, which relates the time it takes a planet to circle the sun and the distance the planet is from the sun. With these fundamental laws, Kepler gained immortal fame. But he could not understand why the planets behaved in this way.

The laws of Newton

It was one of the greatest scientific thinkers of all time, Isaac Newton (1642-1727), who provided the answer. His law of universal gravitation (1666) states that every particle of matter attracts every other particle with a force which varies according to the masses of the particles and the distance between them. Doubling the mass doubles the attraction. Doubling the distance decreases the attraction four times.

Newton showed that it was the gravitational attraction of the sun which keeps the planets in their orbits, and which keeps the moon circling the earth. He was able to predict in advance where the heavenly bodies would be at any time, and he could estimate their comparative masses. With this one law Newton laid the foundations of modern astronomy. Myth and superstition gave way to scientific reasoning and so to accurate calculation.

Newton made other discoveries which greatly influenced the course of astronomy. His discovery that light could be split up into a band of colours (the spectrum) led much later to the development of the instrument called a spectroscope, which is a tiny telescope mounted on a turntable through which the colours of the spectrum can be examined one by one. He also invented a new kind of telescope called the reflecting telescope. Instead of having glass lenses like a normal refracting telescope, the reflecting telescope has a concave (bowl-shaped) mirror which gathers and focuses light falling upon it. The image in such a telescope is sharp and free from colour distortion. It was a great improvement on the refracting telescopes of the period.

Today the biggest and best telescopes are of the reflecting type. Dwarfing both kinds are the more recently invented radio telescopes, which are much larger in diameter. They collect radio waves, not light, from the heavens. As we shall see later, the use of radio telescopes has led to some of the most exciting discoveries in the long and fascinating history of astronomy.

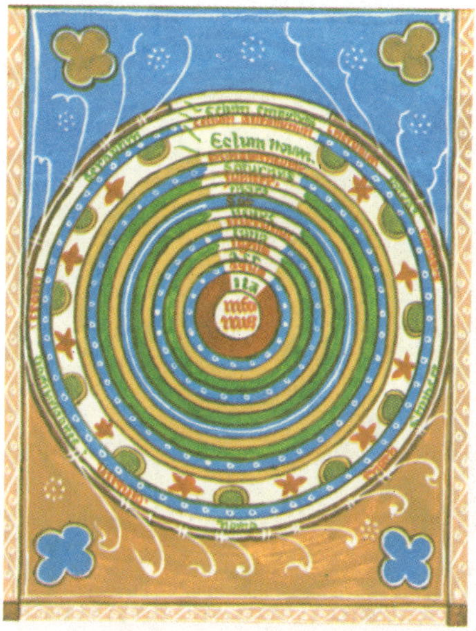

Far left Ptolemy of Alexandria thought the earth was fixed at the centre of the universe. The planets revolved round the earth and the fixed stars were in the outermost circle of the universe. This theory was accepted by men of science from the 2nd century AD until the 16th century and this drawing is a medieval interpretation of it. The picture on the right is taken from Copernicus's great work *De revolutionibus* and shows clearly his belief that the sun was the true centre of the solar system. The original of this drawing was made by his own hand and it is said that the mark of his compasses can be seen in the centre.

The solar system

Dominating our little corner of the universe is the mighty, glowing orb of the sun. Travelling around it at different distances in great elliptical (oval) orbits (paths) are the earth and the other planets. Some of the planets are themselves the centre of tiny, solar-type systems, with one or more moons – or satellites – revolving around them. The sun, the planets and their moons form the major part of the solar system. But there are a number of smaller, minor bodies which also belong to it and travel, like the planets, in orbit around the sun. These are the asteroids, meteors, and comets. The sun and all these bodies travel through space as a great physical unit, or 'family', held together by the sun's gravitational attraction.

The warmth and light of the sun are the most important things to us on earth, for without them there would be no life of any kind. The sky would be always inky black and the temperature would be deadly cold.

The fiery sun is a great globe of hot, glowing gases. We can call it our star, for that is what it is – just another star. As far as stars go, it is very ordinary, being neither particularly big nor particularly bright. There are stars very much bigger and brighter but there are also many that are much smaller and dimmer.

In terms of actual size, the diameter of the main 'ball' of the sun is about 1,390,000 kilometres or 109 times the diameter of the earth. The sun is over 333,000 times more massive than the earth, but it has only one-quarter of the density. The average distance from the sun to the earth is 150 million kilometres. Astronomers find that this is a quite convenient unit of distance in the solar system and call it one astronomical unit. To get a rough picture of the size and distance of the sun, think of the earth as the size of a pea. On this scale the sun would be the size of a beach ball about forty metres away.

After these essential facts and figures, let us look at the sun more closely. Don't take this too literally though! It is extremely dangerous to look at the sun directly by any means. You are sometimes told to look at it through a piece of smoked glass or a photographic negative, but don't. You could permanently damage your eyesight. The only safe way of looking at the sun is to project an image of it on to a screen or a sheet of paper. So be warned!

The photosphere

The visible surface of the sun, which we see as a bright disc, is known as the photosphere (light-sphere). Although it looks to the naked eye to be the same all over, through a telescope there is a definite darkening towards the edges. This is caused by absorption in the

Above An armillary sphere, which is a skeleton celestial globe made up of circular metal hoops representing the great circles of the equator, the tropics of Capricorn and Cancer and the Arctic and Antarctic circles. The whole instrument revolves on an axis. Such spheres are said to have originated in ancient China.

Right During a total eclipse of the sun by the moon, the corona, which is the sun's rarefied outer atmosphere, can best be studied. This drawing shows a solar flare shooting up from the surface of the sun.

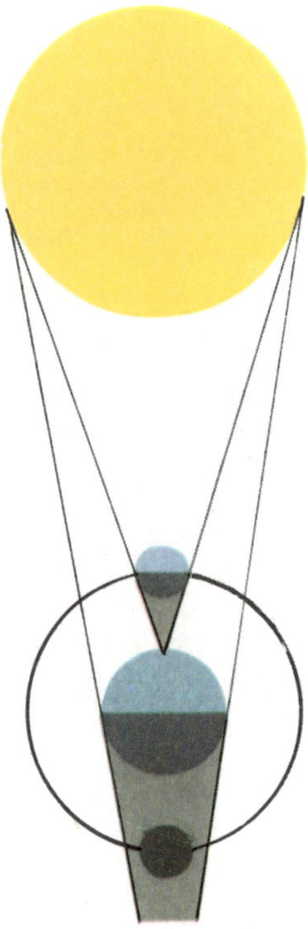

Above This diagram illustrates both a solar and a lunar eclipse. When the moon passes between the earth and the sun it blocks the sun from view and causes a solar eclipse. When the moon passes through the earth's shadow the sun's light is cut off from it and causes a lunar eclipse.

sun's 'atmosphere'. In powerful telescopes the photosphere is seen to be speckled with tiny, bright specks against a darker background. The specks, known as granules, are thought to be currents of hot gases bursting out of the sun's interior. The temperature of the photosphere is about 6,000 degrees C.

The most striking features of the photosphere are the dark markings, or spots, which often appear on it. These are, appropriately enough, called sunspots. They appear to be areas of madly whirling gases. The smallest, called pores, are only a few hundred kilometres in diameter. They may last for just a few hours, or a day or so. But the large ones, which grow rapidly to tens of thousands of kilometres across, may last for weeks or even months. Typical large sunspots have a dark centre, or umbra, surrounded by a lighter region, or penumbra. These spots are about 2,000 degrees C. cooler than the rest of the photosphere, which makes them show up against it.

Sunspots give rise in some way to magnetic disturbances which can be detected here on earth. Eruptions near sunspots, called solar flares, intensify the disturbances. At times of marked sunspot activity, magnetic and electrical instruments on earth are affected, and radio communications are disrupted. The interesting thing about sunspots is that they rise and fall in intensity in a regular cycle called the sunspot cycle. The cycle takes about eleven years to complete.

Around the photosphere there is an 'atmosphere' of cooler, less dense, or much 'thinner' gases. Normally this atmosphere cannot be seen because the photosphere is too dazzling. The only time it can be seen is at the time of a total eclipse of the sun. During an eclipse, the moon passes between us and the sun and for a short while covers the bright disc. Then you see a narrow, rose-red fringe around the dark body of the moon. This is the lower part of the sun's atmosphere, called the chromosphere (colour-sphere), which extends to several thousand kilometres. Shooting up hundreds of thousands of kilometres through the chromosphere are magnificent, flame-like streamers of hot gas. They are called prominences. The outer atmosphere of the sun is called the corona (crown). During a total eclipse it can be seen as a pearly white halo extending some millions of kilometres.

Whether the sun is 'quiet', with little sunspot activity, or 'noisy', with intense sunspot activity, it sends out a constant stream of electrified particles known as the solar wind. These particles become trapped in great 'belts' by the earth's magnetism. They also in some way give rise to luminous, shimmering arcs and streamers in northern and southern regions called *aurora borealis* (northern lights) and *aurora australis* (southern lights). The effect is increased at times of intense sunspot activity.

Above The *aurora borealis* or northern lights, is a luminous phenomenon seen in the sky at night in northern latitudes, generally only from polar regions. It is caused by charged particles from the sun entering the earth's magnetic field. In the Antarctic, a similar phenomenon can be observed, called *aurora australis* or southern lights.

How does the sun shine?

One problem we have still to consider is how the sun continues to shine year after year, century after century, without dimming. Scientists believe that the earth is at least 4,500 million years old so that the sun must have been shining for as long as that. Obviously it can burn no ordinary fuel like coal, oil or gas, otherwise it would have fizzled out after a thousand years or so.

In fact the sun burns nuclear fuel. It behaves like a giant atomic furnace 'consuming' atoms, the tiny, basic particles of matter. At the intensely hot centre of the sun, four atoms of hydrogen, the simplest of all atoms, combine together to form one atom of the next simplest element, helium. This process is known as nuclear fusion. During the fusion a small amount of matter is 'lost', because the mass of one helium atom is a fraction less than the combined mass of four hydrogen atoms.

It is this loss of mass which holds the key to the problem. The physicist Albert Einstein (1879-1955) showed that mass and energy are equivalent. And 'destroying' mass releases an unbelievable amount of energy. That is what happens during nuclear fusion inside the core of the sun, a core that is estimated to be at a temperature of at least some 14 million degrees C. The same energy-producing process must hold for all the other millions of stars in the universe.

As we all know, the sun rises in the east and sets in the west. But this is only an apparent movement caused by the rotation of the earth itself. It has nothing to do with the sun. The sun, nevertheless, does move. It moves in two ways: it rotates about its own axis and it moves in an orbit around the centre of one of the great star systems, or galaxies, of the universe. Its dual motion resembles that of the planets which rotate on their own axes as well as moving in orbit around the sun. What this dual motion means can be seen by looking at the most familiar of the planets – the earth.

The planet earth

We do not feel the earth's movement because we are travelling with it at the same speed. But it does move – in two ways. First of all it spins round on its axis just like a top. The axis is through the 'top' and 'bottom' of the earth – the north and south poles. The earth in twenty-four hours. To be precise, it makes one revolution relative to the position of the sun in twenty-four hours. Because the earth is moving around the sun at the same time as it is spinning on its axis, it takes a little more than one revolution to return to the same point relative to the sun each day. Therefore the true period of revolution of the earth is a little less than twenty-four hours – four minutes less, in fact. We call this period a sidereal day – a day measured in relation to the stars, which for all intents and purposes can be regarded as fixed points. In a similar way we speak of a sidereal year, which is the time it takes the earth to return to the same point in its orbit relative to the stars. The sidereal year is twenty minutes longer than the solar year.

The planets move through space in the same manner as the earth. They each have a 'day' and a 'year'. Naturally their days and years are different from the earth's, because they are of different sizes and lie at different distances from the sun.

Jean Foucault (1819–68) French physicist. He was noted mainly for his proof that light travels more slowly in water than in air, and his measurement of the speed of light. In 1851 he proved that the earth rotates by using a freely suspended pendulum and studying the way it swings from side to side. He also invented the gyroscope and other optical instruments. The scene of Foucault's pendulum demonstration in the Pantheon, Paris, is shown here.

makes one complete revolution in twenty-four hours. This spinning causes our days and nights. Day is when our part of the earth's globe is facing the sun. Night is when we spin out of reach of the sun's rays. Astronomers call the whole twenty-four hour period the solar day. The earth spins towards the east, which makes the sun appear to move in the opposite direction, from east to west.

The earth's second motion is in its orbit around the sun, which lies 150 million kilometres away. It takes the earth almost 365¼ days to travel once around its orbit so as to end up in the same position relative to the sun. This period we call a year, or more properly a solar year. You notice that this year is a quarter of a day longer than our calendar year. To keep in step therefore we add a day on to our calendar every four years to make a leap year of 366 days. An extra day is added to February to give it twenty-nine days.

It is not quite accurate to say that the earth makes one complete revolution

The seasons

We have explained the division of time into days and years. What about the seasons? How are they brought about? The answer is that the earth's axis is tilted at an angle (23½ degrees) with respect to the path it follows round the sun. This means that the northern and southern hemispheres receive more or less sunlight, and therefore heat, depending on whether they are tilted towards (summer) or away (winter) from the sun.

Because of this tilt the sun appears to be low in the sky in winter and high in the sky in summer. You can easily check this for yourself. In the northern hemisphere it reaches its highest point on about 21st June. This is called the summer solstice. It reaches its lowest point on 21st December, the winter solstice. The summer solstice is the longest period of daylight, the winter solstice the shortest. In the southern hemisphere the dates are reversed.

On about 21st March the sun is directly over the equator moving north. This is called the vernal, or spring equinox, and is the beginning of spring in the northern hemisphere

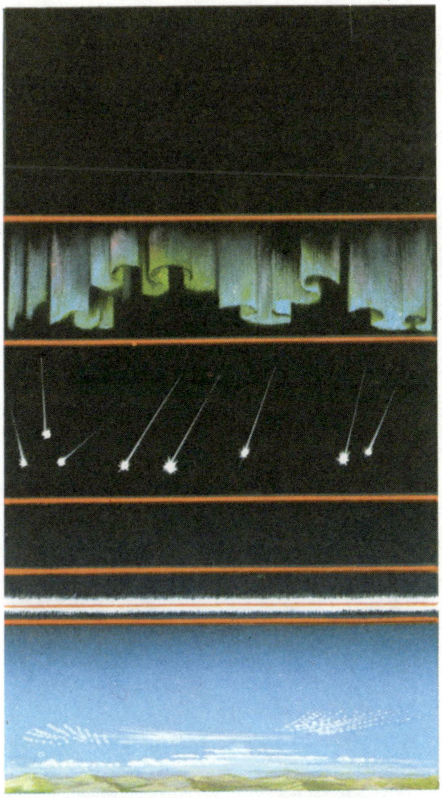

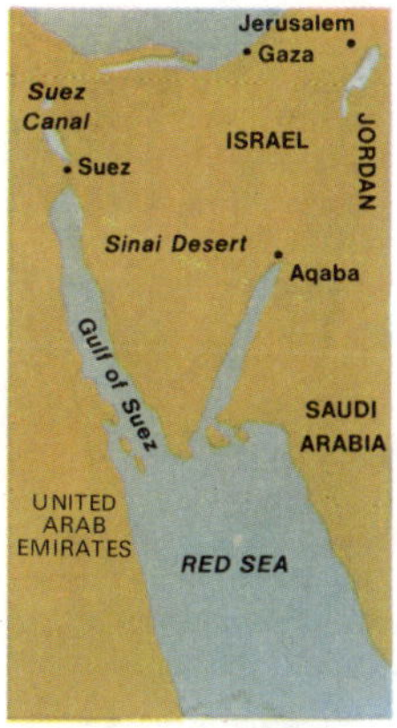

Above For thousands of years man has made maps by plotting the earth on which he stood. Now at last he is able to see what the earth looks like from above, thanks to the work of American and Russian space programmes. Compare the view of the Sinai Peninsula as seen by Gemini astronauts (left) with the conventional map of the same area.

Far left In this drawing of the earth's atmosphere are shown (from top to bottom) the exosphere, the upper and lower ionospheres, the chemosphere, the stratosphere, and the troposphere.

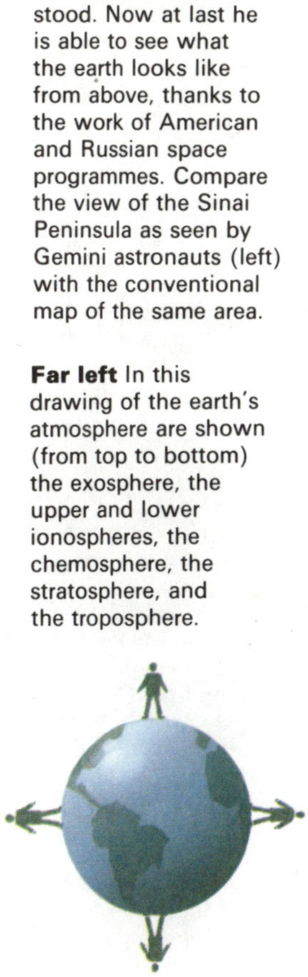

Above This picture illustrates in simple form the fact that the force of gravity acts equally on every part of the globe.

(autumn in the southern). On about 23rd September the sun is directly over the equator again moving south. This is known as the autumnal equinox: autumn begins in the northern hemisphere (and spring in the southern).

The inner core of the earth is thought to consist of iron and nickel. Both iron and nickel are magnetic, so this may be the explanation for the earth's magnetism. The earth acts as a huge magnet with one magnetic pole near the north pole and one near the south pole. This is why a compass needle points north and south.

The earth is like a big round ball but it is not completely spherical. Because of its rotation on its axis, it bulges slightly at the 'waist' – its equator. The polar regions are therefore correspondingly flatter. The earth's diameter at the equator is 12,754 kilometres; that at the poles is about 12,700. The bulge was first discovered from differences in measurements of the earth's gravity. Gravity is less at the equator than nearer the poles because the surface is farther away from the centre of the earth. More recently, observations of the orbits of artificial earth satellites have indicated that the earth is in fact slightly pear-shaped.

Gravity and atmosphere

Gravity holds down everything on earth and is what makes everything have a natural tendency to fall towards the ground. Particularly important is that it holds back the atmosphere of oxygen and other gases which we breathe to live. Were the earth much less massive than it is, the gravity would not be strong enough to retain an atmosphere, and earth would be a dead world. The atmosphere not only provides us with oxygen to live. It also forms an insulating 'blanket' around the earth which prevents us from scorching in the sunlight and freezing in the dark. It protects us from other dangerous particles and radiation coming from space, too.

Close to the ground the density, or pressure, of the atmosphere is such that no undue effort is needed to breathe. But the air becomes thinner and thinner as you go farther up. Even a thousand metres up you can become

Right A full view of the moon taken from the lunar module of Apollo 11, the spacecraft in which the first successful landing on the earth's satellite was made. In this photograph many craters can be seen as well as the dark shaded areas called seas. These are, in fact, enormous plains, which are sometimes bordered by mountains.

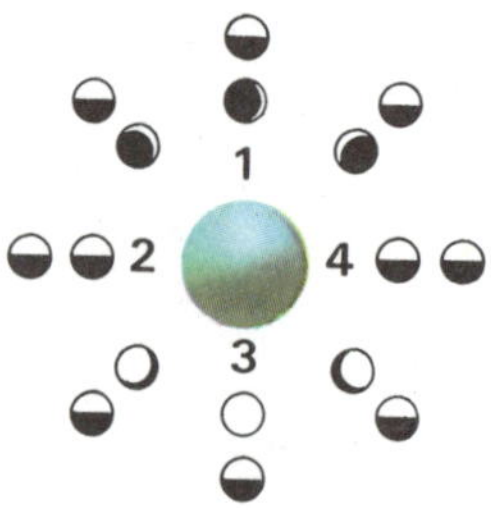

Above This diagram illustrates the phases of the moon as it orbits round the earth. The rays of the sun are assumed to be shining from the top of the drawing, so that figure **1** shows the position of the moon when it is new and almost totally in shadow. Figure **2** shows the first quarter, **3** the full moon and **4** the last quarter.

breathless quickly because there is less oxygen in the thinner air. At the top of Mount Everest it is practically impossible to breathe without assistance. The pressure is less than a third of what it is at sea level. That is why aircraft flying at such heights have to be pressurised to allow their passengers to breathe easily. They fly so high up in order to be above the weather. Our weather – winds, rain, snow, clouds, and so on – develops in the lower ten thousand metres of the atmosphere.

The moon

Just as the sun's gravity holds the earth in its orbit around the sun, so the earth's gravity holds the moon in its orbit around the earth. As far as the earth is concerned the moon is very special. It is our nearest neighbour in space; it is our only natural satellite; and it was the first heavenly body which man reached and set foot upon. We therefore know much more about it than about any other heavenly body.

The moon lies on average about 384,000 kilometres from the earth. It is only about a quarter the size of the earth, with a diameter of 3,475 kilometres. And it has less than one-eightieth of the earth's mass. The moon's gravity, therefore, is much less strong than the earth's, only one-sixth, in fact. Astronauts walking on the moon feel light on their feet because they weigh only one-sixth of what they do on earth.

Gravity on the moon is so weak that it has not been able to hold back any gases to form an atmosphere. This means that there can be no wind, no weather, no sound and no life. The moon is silent and barren. Because there is no insulating atmosphere, there is a wide variation in temperature between day and night. In the merciless heat of the lunar day the temperature of the surface reaches more than 100 degrees C., which is the temperature of boiling water. During lunar night the temperature falls to 150 degrees C. below zero.

What is the surface like? Photographs taken by the many probes and landing craft show its features to perfection. Covering half of the surface of the moon are enormous plains called *maria*, or seas. Early astronomers gave them delightful names such as Sea of Showers, Sea of Serenity, Sea of Tranquillity, and Sea of Fertility. You can see these with the naked eye from earth as dark patches against the brighter body. In places across the *maria* run long, low ridges and narrow, crooked clefts, or valleys, called rills. Some *marias* are bordered by jagged mountain ranges, some of which tower well over 6,000 metres.

The origin of craters

The most common lunar features, however, are the craters. The largest, Clavius, is about 240 kilometres in diameter. These large craters are often called ring mountains. Some of them have one or more mountain peaks rising from the crater floor, which is much lower than the general surrounding level. Several of the largest craters, such as Tycho and Copernicus, have conspicuous bright rays issuing from them.

At least 300,000 craters can be seen on the moon's face from earth. And of course there are thousands more which are too small to be seen. Some are little more than shallow pits. It is thought that many or most of the craters have been caused by the impact of meteorites – rocks from outer space. There is no atmosphere to protect the moon from such bombardment as there is on earth. Some authorities consider that the larger lunar craters may be volcanic in origin.

As for the actual surface material, it is a fine black dust. The first astronauts who set foot upon it, in the Sea of Tranquillity, described it as finely powdered charcoal. Fortunately they found that the dust covering was only thin. It tends to stick together like damp soil, as can be seen from photographs of the astronaut's footprints. Strewn all over the dusty surface are lumps of rocks, probably thrown up when meteorites crashed to the surface.

Back on earth, we say that the moon 'shines', just as we say the sun shines. But the moon gives off no light of its own. It is, as we have seen, a dead world. It merely reflects light from the sun, which is the only body in the solar system that gives off light of its own.

We only ever see one face of the moon. This is because it turns on its axis once while it travels once around the earth, a journey taking $27\frac{1}{3}$ days. Actually it 'nods' and wobbles slightly on its axis which means that we can see just a little more than half its surface. These irregularities in its motion are called librations.

The moon's phases

As the moon travels around the earth, it changes its position in relation to the sun. And the area of the moon's surface reflecting light back to earth varies. These changes in the appearance of the moon are called phases. When the moon is almost directly between us and the sun, the side facing us is unlit. This phase is the new moon. After a few hours a slim crescent appears. In a week the crescent has become a half circle. This phase is the first quarter. A week later the whole of the moon is illuminated, and we call it the full moon. From then on the area illuminated reduces to a half circle

Tycho Brahe (1546–1601) Danish astronomer. First studied law, but was more interested in astronomy. In 1563 he discovered serious mistakes in the astronomical tables, and a 'new' star in the constellation of Cassiopeia. Was given land for an observatory at Uraniborg (pictured in an old print left), where he worked for 20 years. He did much important work on the movement of the stars and moon, though he rejected the Copernican theory for a version of that of Ptolemy, which believed the earth to be the centre of the solar system and of the universe itself.

Above The *Surveyor* spacecraft launched by the United States transmitted photographs from the surface of the moon and even examined samples of the soil.

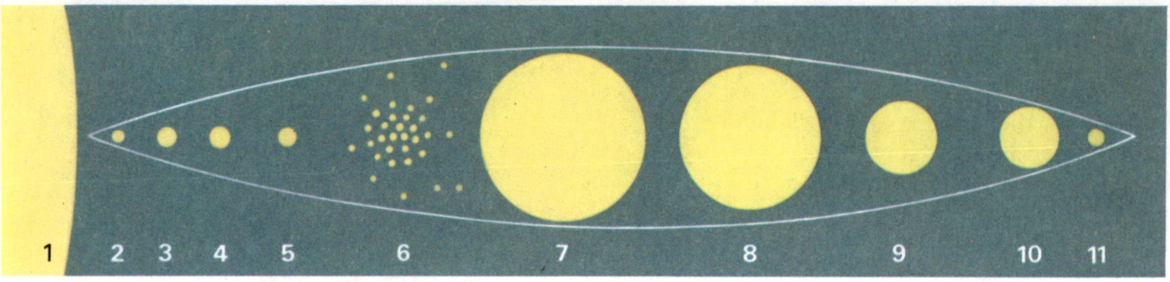

Above This diagram shows the sun (**1**) and the planets of our solar system:
2 Mercury, **3** Venus, **4** Earth, **5** Mars, **6** asteroids, **7** Jupiter, **8** Saturn, **9** Uranus, **10** Neptune, **11** Pluto.

(last quarter) and then back to new moon again. From new to full moon the moon is said to be waxing. From full to new, it is said to be waning.

The period between one new moon and another is $29\frac{1}{2}$ days. It is the time the moon takes to return to the same position relative to the sun. It differs from the orbital period of $27\frac{1}{3}$ days because the earth itself has moved relative to the sun while the moon has been completing one orbit.

The unending movement of the moon around the earth has an effect on the earth which we can observe ourselves. It causes the ceaseless rising and falling, ebbing and flowing of the ocean tides. The moon's gravity, although weak compared with that of earth, still attracts the earth. It causes tides by tending to pull the nearest water away from the earth, and also by pulling the earth itself away from the farthest water. Thus there is a double effect which results in two tides a day.

The sun, too, tends to produce tides, but its effect is slight because of its great distance away. However, when the sun is in line with the moon, the combined attraction causes exceptionally high and low tides called spring tides. When the attractions of the moon and sun oppose each other there are neap tides, with less difference than usual between high and low tide.

James Jeans (1877–1946) British mathematical physicist and astronomer. He was educated at Cambridge and, later, professor of Applied Mathematics at Princeton University, USA. Did much work on the application of mathematics to physics and astronomy. He wrote on the aspects of radiation. Showed that Laplace's theory of the evolution of the universe was incorrect, and studied the effect of gravity on the stars. He wrote many popular works on astronomy.

The planets

Five of the planets, the 'wandering' stars, were known to the ancient world because they can be seen with the naked eye. They are, going outwards from the sun: Mercury, Venus, Mars, Jupiter and Saturn. Beyond Saturn, in the depths of the solar system, lie three more planets which have been discovered comparatively recently: Uranus (1781), Neptune (1846) and Pluto (1930). Earth itself lies between Venus and Mars.

Venus, Mars, Jupiter and Saturn are among the brightest objects in the sky. Mercury, too, can occasionally be seen shining bright very low on the horizon. You can sometimes see Uranus if you have keen eyes and the night is exceptionally clear. In order to see Neptune, you need a telescope.

Right This table shows how the time taken to circle the sun by each planet, or its 'day', varies.

Name of planet	Average distance from sun (million kilometres)	Equatorial diameter kilometres	Average density (water=1)	Mass (Earth=1)	Circles the sun in*	Turns on axis in † (hours: mins)
Mercury	58	4,878	5·5	0·05	88 days	59 days
Venus	108	12,100	5·25	0·8	225 days	243 days‡
Earth	150	12,756	5·5	1	365 days	23:56
Mars	228	6,794	3·9	0·1	687 days	24:37
Jupiter	778	142,200	1·3	320	11·9 yrs	9:50
Saturn	1,427	120,000	0·7	95	29·5 yrs	10:14
Uranus	2,870	51,400	1·1	14	84 yrs	16 hrs?
Neptune	4,497	49,000	1·5	17	165 yrs	18:24?
Pluto	5,900	3000?	0·5?	0·0025?	248 yrs	153 hrs?

*i.e. its 'year' †i.e. its 'day' ‡retrograde

Name of planet	No. of moons
Mercury	0
Venus	0
Earth	1
Mars	2
Jupiter	16
Saturn	20+
Uranus	5
Neptune	2
Pluto	1

Pluto is beyond all but the most powerful telescopes.

The planets vary greatly in size, mass and distance from the sun. Mercury and Pluto are much smaller than the earth. Yet Jupiter is more than 1,300 times bigger than the earth. To get an idea of the comparative sizes of the planets, again think of earth as the size of a small pea. Mercury and Pluto would be pinheads, Mars a large pinhead, Venus a small pea, Neptune and Uranus marbles, Saturn a table-tennis ball, and Jupiter a golf ball. (Again on the same scale the sun would be a large beach ball!)

The distances of the planets from the sun are average distances because the path of a planet through the sky is an ellipse. Therefore at some times it is farther away than at others. The planets fall naturally into two groups – four inner planets and five outer planets. Between the two groups, that is, between Mars and Jupiter, there is a gap where it appears there should be another planet. This is where the belt of small bodies called asteroids are to be found. We shall look at them later with the other minor bodies of the solar system.

Like the earth, the planets have a dual motion, travelling in orbit around the sun to make their 'year' and turning on their own axes to make their 'day'. The farther the planets are from the sun, the longer is their orbit, and therefore their orbital period, or year. At a distance of 5,900 million kilometres Pluto's year is almost 248 earth-years.

The interesting thing about the orbits of the planets is that they are all more or less in the same plane. We call the plane of the earth's orbit the plane of the ecliptic. Only the orbit of Pluto is inclined at any appreciable angle (about 20 degrees) to this plane. Another significant feature is that all the planets are moving in the same direction around the sun, which is the same direction as the sun is turning on its own axis. If you imagine looking down on the solar system from above, or from the north side, the planets move in an anti-clockwise direction.

In general this holds for the rotation of the planets on their own axes. But it appears that Venus is the odd one out. Radar measurements have shown that it rotates in a clockwise direction, what is known as retrograde motion. It is also interesting to note that the biggest planets have the shortest days. The giant Jupiter revolves in less than ten hours.

All the planets except Mercury and Venus are the centre of a kind of planetary system of their own. They have rotating around them one or more moons, or satellites. Earth's satellite is our familiar moon. The systems of Jupiter and Saturn are particularly extensive. Most of the satellites rotate around the planets in the usual anti-clockwise direction. But a number of them do have retrograde motion, as Venus has.

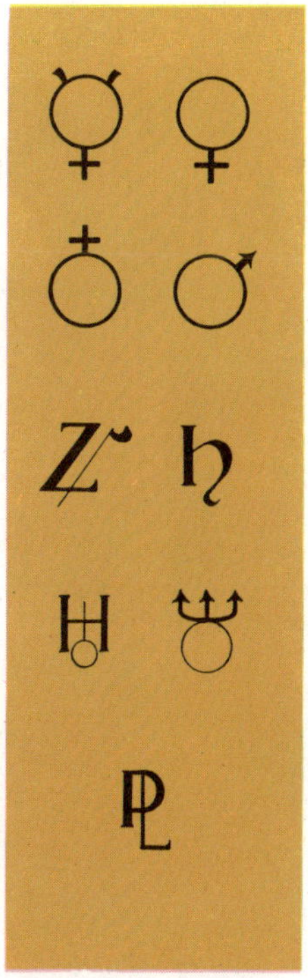

Above These symbols are used to designate the planets (reading from the top and left to right): Mercury, Venus, Earth, Mars, Jupiter, Saturn, Uranus, Neptune, and, lastly, Pluto.

Above left This table shows the satellites, or moons, of the various planets.

Left Mont Saint Michel is a fortified abbey off the coast of northern France. In this picture it is seen at low tide. When the tide floods in at speeds of over twelve kilometres an hour it very soon turns the abbey into an island, when only a narrow causeway connects it to the mainland.

Above The giant telescope built by the third Earl of Rosse at Parsonstown in Ireland in 1845. It was about sixteen metres long and the diameter of its mirror was about 180 centimetres. It was the largest telescope of the 19th century.

Pierre Laplace (1749-1827) French astronomer and mathematician. Famous chiefly for the way he applied mathematics to practical astronomy. He published his work *Mécanique céleste* in the years 1799–1825. It was an attempt to explain the mechanical problems presented by the solar system.

Mercury

The four inner planets – Mercury, Venus, Earth and Mars – are all solid and seem to be made up of similar materials.

Being so close to the sun, Mercury is very difficult to observe from earth and most information about it has come from the Mariner 10 probe. Like the moon, its surface is heavily cratered from meteorite bombardment, and it contains basins similar to the moon's *maria*, including the 1,400-kilometre-wide Caloris basin. The surface temperature can rise to over 400 degrees C. on the sunlit face and falls to minus 170 degrees C. on the opposite side. Since it also has no permanent atmosphere, it appears to be an inhospitable planet.

Mercury sometimes passes between the sun and the earth, when it appears as a blank dot against the brilliant solar disc. These passages are called transits and about fourteen occur every century.

Venus

This planet is sometimes the brightest object in the sky. When it is west of the sun, it may be seen before dawn as the morning 'star'. When east of the sun, it may be seen after sunset as the evening 'star'. Like Mercury, Venus transits the sun, but only very occasionally.

Venus approaches closer to the earth than any other planet. Despite this, little was known about it until recently because it is shrouded in dense cloud. This reflects much of the sunlight falling on it, making it appear bright, but also hiding its surface. However, the surface has now been mapped using radar and a number of probes have visited it. Its size and density are similar to earth's, and it seems to have a similar composition. The radar maps show many large craters, huge basins, mountain ranges, volcanoes and canyons, including one 1,500 kilometres long. The rocky surface is very hot, about 480 degrees C. This is due to the incredibly dense atmosphere of, mainly, carbon dioxide, which traps the sun's heat. It has a pressure ninety times that of the earth's atmosphere, and early probes were not strong enough to operate in it. In addition, the clouds seem to be mainly sulphuric acid and frequent lightning bolts rent the atmosphere.

Mars

Beyond earth lies our next nearest planet, Mars. Often called the Red Planet, it is much smaller than earth. It has only a thin atmosphere, and so its surface can be seen through a telescope. Its clouds, polar ice caps, the seasonal changes in the size of the ice caps and in some surface markings, led people years ago to compare it to earth and to imagine the existence of Martian civilisations. Some people even thought they could see canals criss-crossing the surface. Unfortunately, later observations and the results of space probes have dispelled this myth. Indeed, no trace of any kind of life has yet been found.

Apart from its core, which may be smaller and less dense, its composition seems to be similar to earth's. Its axis is tilted at an angle of nearly 25 degrees, producing the seasons. However, the seasonal changes in surface markings, which were thought to be caused by vegetation, seem to be due to dust storms. Iron oxide gives the dusty, rock-strewn surface its red colour. Again, the surface has craters and basins, and it includes spectacular features, such as Olympus Mons – at 26 kilometres high, the tallest volcano in the solar system – and vast canyons, including Vollis Marineris which is 4,000 kilometres long. Although no trace could be found of canals, other areas of Mars have markings caused by dust erosion, and channels similar to those made by rivers on earth. It is thought that water may have existed on the surface in the past. However, now the temperature may drop to minus 120 degrees C. and is always below 0 degrees C, the water is permanently frozen, forming the ice caps, clouds and fog. These also contain carbon dioxide and most of the atmosphere is carbon dioxide.

Jupiter

The four 'gas giants' – Jupiter, Saturn, Uranus and Neptune – all have a similar composition to the sun, being mainly hydrogen. Jupiter is by far the largest, bigger than all the other planets put together, and has a very strong magnetic field. It may have a small rocky core but is otherwise mainly liquid hydrogen.

From earth, all that can be seen are the swirling clouds, which form coloured bands around the planet. This dense atmosphere is made up of many substances, including water, methane and hydrogen. Jupiter emits more heat than it receives from the sun, but it is so far away from the sun that it is still very cold. This heat and the planet's spin produce the cloud patterns, which include spots and streaks. The most noticeable one, the Great Red Spot, has a surface area as big as the earth's, and is a vast whirling eddy of cloud.

Saturn

Its ring system makes this the most beautiful object in the solar system, when viewed through a telescope. There are three main rings, about 10 kilometres thick and stretching out to a radius of 137,000 kilometres. They are made up of numerous tiny ice-covered particles, which shine because they reflect sunlight. The planet also emits heat, and is similar in composition to Jupiter, although its rocky core may be surrounded by ice. Its yellow-coloured atmosphere forms thick bands. One of its moons, Titan, is the largest satellite known in the solar system, and at 5,800 kilometres wide, is bigger than Mercury.

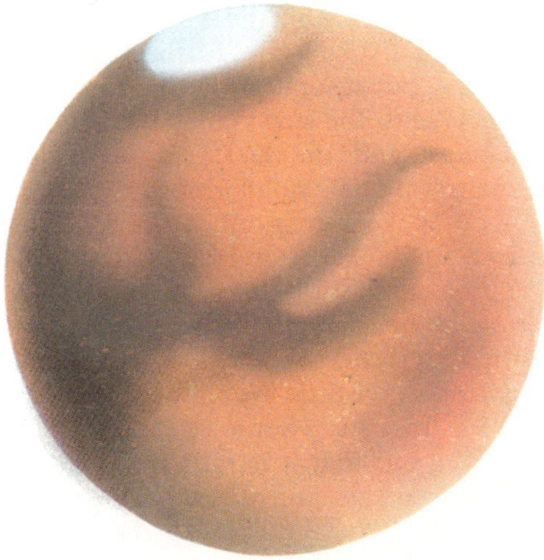

Left Mars is a small planet, about half the diameter of earth. Its surface has a reddish orange colour with dark patches and white polar ice caps.

Below Jupiter, the largest planet in the solar system. The Great Red Spot, which can be seen in this drawing, may be the site of a centuries-old hurricane.

Uranus and Neptune

These planets are very similar in size, and are much smaller than the other two 'gas giants'. Their composition is similar to that of Saturn. They both have surface temperatures below minus 200 degrees C., Neptune being further away from the sun and hence colder than Uranus. Their surfaces are hidden by clouds in their atmospheres, which are mainly methane and hydrogen. Uranus has up to nine rings circling it, although these are not bright like Saturn's and so were not observed until recently. Uranus is tilted at such an angle that its poles receive more sunlight than its equator.

Below Mercury is the planet nearest to the sun. The bright glare of the sun makes it difficult to observe from earth.

Above An illustration from one of the books by French novelist, Jules Verne (1828–1905), who wrote several books in which the adventures of the characters in a world of popular science included voyages into outer space.

Above Despite all the reports there have been of flying saucers seen hovering over the earth, it seems unlikely that there is any life as we known it on any of the other planets in our solar system.

Pluto

Pluto is usually the furthest of the planets, but at some points in its orbit it is nearer to the sun than Neptune. Its distance and the fact that it is the smallest planet, smaller even than our moon, make it very difficult to observe from earth. Little is known about its composition and it is probably too small to have an atmosphere. It is very different from the 'gas giants' and seems to have little in common with the inner planets. Some people have pointed out that it is rather similar to some asteroids, and others have speculated that it may be an escaped moon of Neptune.

Life on other planets

What are the prospects of life elsewhere in the solar system besides earth? Are there any Mercurians, Venusians, or Martians? From our present knowledge of the conditions on other planets, we can say that it is most unlikely that there is any other life *as we know it*. We must say 'as we know it' because it is just possible that some other form of life has evolved in conditions different from ours on earth.

Life as we know it definitely could not exist on Mercury because it is too hot. And Jupiter and the outer planets are much too cold. The only planets where life as we know it has been considered possible are Venus and Mars. But the available evidence from Russian and American space probes makes the possibility remote.

What about life outside the solar system? The sun is but one of millions of millions of stars in the heavens. It would be incredible if there were not other stars with planetary systems like ours. Some dark, planet-like bodies have indeed been identified, associated with some of the nearer stars. It is therefore likely that there are within the universe planets on which conditions are much like those on earth. Why then should there not be other life elsewhere similar to our own? Why not indeed? This is a mystery which we might one day solve, when we learn more about how life began and when, if ever, we can travel to the stars. We say 'if ever' advisedly. A spaceship travelling at 40,000 kilometres an hour, the speed at which man travels to the moon, would take more than 110,000 years to reach even the nearest star!

Asteroids

We have already mentioned that there appears to be a 'gap' between Mars and the inner planets and Jupiter and the outer planets. Within this gap, circling around the sun in orbit, is a belt of small bodies called asteroids, also known as minor planets and planetoids. More than 3,000 asteroids have been found, but it has been estimated that there may be hundreds of thousands. Many which have been identified are only a few kilometres in diameter, and the rest may be even smaller, which is why they have not yet been detected.

Some asteroids, however, are reasonably big. The largest and first to be discovered (1801) was Ceres, which has a diameter of about 1,000 kilometres. Within six years three more were discovered: Pallas (540 kilometres), Vesta (515 kilometres), and Juno (225 kilometres). One of the best-known asteroids is Eros, which is a cigar-shaped body about thirty kilometres long. It is interesting historically because earlier this century observations of it were used in estimating the distance of the earth from the sun. Eros approaches within 25 million kilometres of the earth. Some asteroids approach even closer.

Most asteroids are thought to be rocky fragments, some of which may be covered in ice or frozen gas. Originally it was thought that asteroids were the remains of a large planet, but this seems unlikely. Probably they were formed at the same time as the planets.

Meteorites and meteors

The majority of the particles entering the atmosphere are small and literally burn up when they are still eighty kilometres or more up. But occasionally larger lumps manage to survive the normally destructive passage through the atmosphere and reach the ground, reduced in size but whole. They are called meteorites. They are found to be of two main sorts – stony and metallic. The metallic ones contain mainly nickel and iron.

Two tremendous meteorite falls have occurred this century in Siberia,

Left Saturn is surrounded by rings of tiny particles which produce the characteristic image seen in this drawing.

in 1908 and 1947. The impact of the 1908 meteorite flattened over fifty square kilometres of forest. The blast was felt eighty kilometres away. Naturally enough many craters were formed. There are quite a number of recognisable meteorite craters in many parts of the world. The most famous one, in Arizona in the United States, is 1,280 metres in diameter and 174 metres deep.

Wandering through the solar system are particles and chunks of material called meteoroids. When you look up at the night sky you often see bright streaks as though a star were 'falling' from the sky or 'shooting' upwards. Those streaks are the result of meteoroids entering the earth's atmosphere at very high speed from outer space. The friction, or rubbing effect of the atmosphere, heats up the meteoroid until it begins to glow white hot. That is when we see the falling or shooting star, properly called a meteor.

From time to time meteors become more frequent and we talk of a meteor shower. This happens when the earth encounters a whole stream, or swarm, of meteoroids. These swarms travel around the sun in definite orbits and the earth meets them regularly. The most spectacular annual meteor shower (the Perseids) occurs in early August.

Comets

It is thought that these orbiting meteor swarms are the remains of the last members of the solar system we shall consider – the comets. Occasionally there is seen in the heavens what appears to be a very large bright star with a massive, luminous 'tail' streaming out behind it. Often the tail stretches right across the sky, extending millions of kilometres in space – an awe-inspiring sight that filled our ancestors with fear, believing it to be an evil omen and an indication of the wrath of God. At large distances from the sun, comets are very faint or completely invisible.

The main part, or nucleus, of a comet is composed of small, solid 'dust' particles and ice. When the comet approaches the sun, some of it is vapourised by the sun's heat. The pressure of the stream of particles from the sun, called the solar wind, forces the vaporised particles away from the nucleus in a great tail. This tail therefore does not stream out behind the comet, but away from the direction of the sun.

One of the most famous comets is Halley's Comet, named after the astronomer Edmund Halley (1656-1742), who accurately calculated its time of orbit (about seventy-six years) around the sun. It was this comet which appeared in 1066 just before the Battle of Hastings. Well might the English have blamed their defeat by William on the evil influence of the comet! It was last seen in 1986, the year of the world's greatest nuclear accident at Chernobyl.

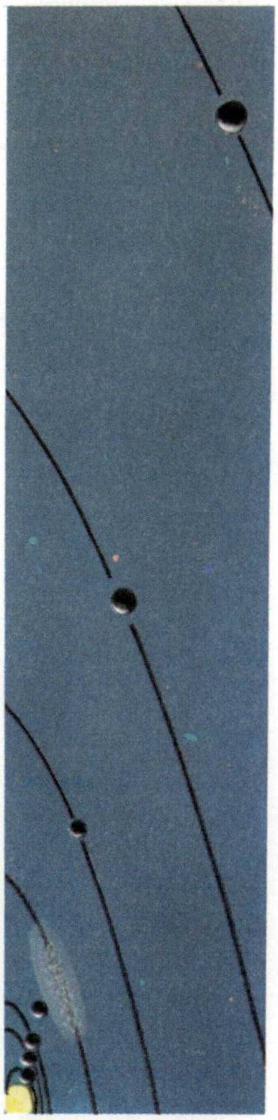

Above The German astronomer, Johann Bode (1747–1826), discovered a curious numerical relationship between the distances of the planets from the sun. Taking the numbers 3, 6, 12, 24, 48, 96, 192 and 384, where each number is double the preceding one, and then adding four to each of them, we get a series of numbers which is very close to the actual distances. This is known as Bode's Law.

Right The telescope at Mount Palomar observatory in San Diego, California, was, at the time of its erection, the largest in the world, its reflector having a diameter of about 500 centimetres. It was built by money given by the Rockefeller Foundation in 1948. The telescope can look into space some two billion light years away, but it covers so small a section of the sky at a time that it would take about 5,000 years to cover it all.

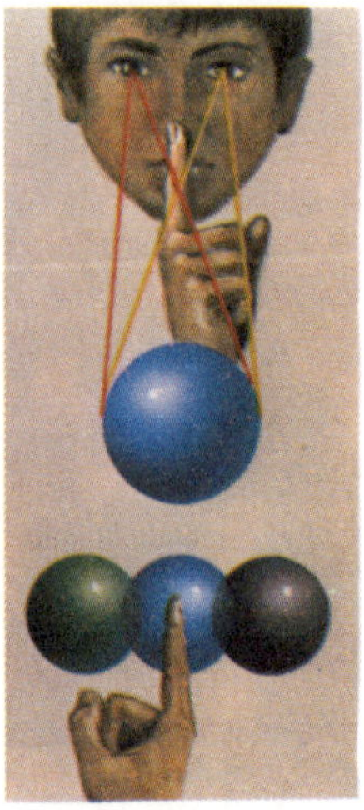

Above The principle of parallax is shown in this drawing. Close one eye, and line up one of your fingers with a distant object. Look at the finger with the other eye and you will find that your finger 'moves' relative to the object in the background.

The stars

The sun then is an ordinary kind of star. It appears big and bright only because of its closeness. Although 150 million kilometres may not seem very close to us on earth, in terms of distances in space it is. The other stars are so far away that it takes the starlight many years to reach us. And light travels at the incredible speed of 300,000 kilometres a second, or about $9\frac{1}{2}$ million million kilometres a year.

The nearest star (except the sun) is called Proxima Centauri and lies about 40 million million kilometres away. Expressing such distances in terms of kilometres is very inconvenient. It is like expressing the width of the Atlantic Ocean in millimetres! There is nothing wrong with it, but the unit of measurement is just too small for the length to be measured. To simplify matters, therefore, astronomers express distances in terms of the distance light travels in a year – about $9\frac{1}{2}$ million million kilometres. They call this unit a light-year. Things immediately appear a lot simpler. Proxima Centauri, for example, lies just over four light-years away. But even this unit is hardly adequate for the farthest objects in the sky, which are estimated to be over 10,000 million light-years away. (In terms of kilometres, this would be a rough figure of nine followed by twenty-two noughts!)

Measuring distances

One question that immediately springs to mind is how do astronomers measure such vast distances. For the nearest stars they use what is known as the parallax method. You can demonstrate the principle on which this works for yourself. Close one eye, and line up one of your fingers with a distant object. Then look at the finger with the other eye. You will find that your finger 'moves' relative to the object in the background. This apparent shift (parallax) occurs because each eye sees the finger from a slightly different angle. It would be possible to calculate how far your finger was away by measuring the distance between your eyes (the baseline) and the angle at which each eye looked at your finger, that is, the angle of parallax.

The principle of measuring distance by this method is, then, relatively simple. Astronomers can measure the distance to the moon in this way. They observe the position of the moon against the background of stars from two different points on earth, separated by, say, 6,500 kilometres. They find that the angle of parallax is about one degree, which is easily measurable. From this information they calculate that the distance to the moon is 384,000 kilometres. But 384,000 kilometres is a mere nothing in space. When it comes to the vast distances to the stars, the baseline of 6,500 kilometres, or any baseline on earth for that matter, is hopelessly inadequate. There is not the slightest trace of any parallax. The stars appear in exactly the same direction from all points on earth.

What astronomers do, therefore, is to use the diameter of the earth's orbit around the sun as a baseline. They observe the position of a star from one point in the earth's orbit, and six months later they observe it again. In that six months the earth has moved to the opposite end of its orbit. The baseline is therefore the diameter of the orbit, that is, 300 million kilometres. But even with such a baseline, the maximum parallax is still very slight, less than one two-thousandth of a degree.

The limit to which the parallax method can measure distances is between 100 and 150 light-years. At greater distances the stars show no measurable displacement, and astronomers have to use less direct methods of measurement for their calculations.

One method they use is to observe the periodic increase and decrease in brightness of certain stars. Most stars, of course, shine steadily. But some, the so-called variable stars, vary in brightness, and it is these that astronomers use as a guide. The period of its variation in brightness is compared to the star's actual brightness. By observing its apparent brightness from earth, astronomers can work out how far away it is. When such stars are in a group of stars, or galaxy, they know just how far away the galaxy is.

Astronomers come up against another distance 'barrier' at about 12 million light-years. Beyond that distance it is impossible to observe variable stars. Then astronomers use different distance indicators, but no one is quite sure how reliable these are.

Above The most famous refracting telescope is the one at Yerkes observatory in the University of Chicago in Wisconsin. It has a focal length of over nineteen metres and an aperture of about a hundred centimetres and was built in 1897.

Star brightness

When you look up at the night sky you can see possibly as many as 2,000 stars with the naked eye. Through a pair of binoculars, you can see almost ten times as many. And a large telescope can reveal several million.

One thing that strikes you immediately is that some stars are much brighter than others. This might mean either that the stars all have different brightnesses and are about the same distance away from us, or that they have similar brightnesses but are at

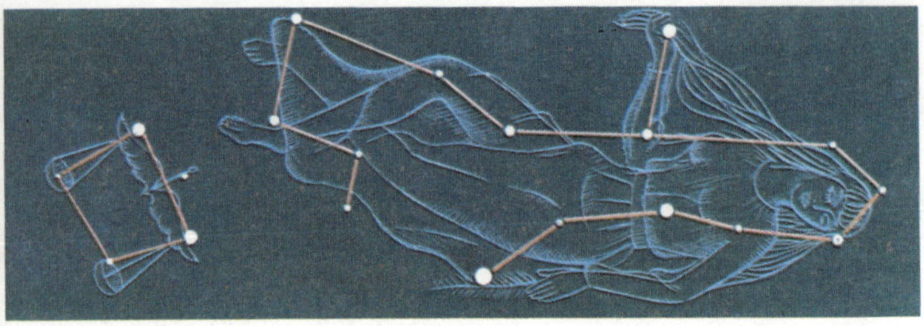

Above The symbols traditionally used in astrology to signify the signs of the zodiac are based on the classical names for different constellations. Seen here are two of them: Libra and Virgo.

different distances. The true explanation lies in between these two alternatives. The stars have both different brightnesses and are at different distances from us.

The brightness we see from earth, then, bears no real relation to the true brightness of the star. A truly dim star close to us may appear to be brighter than a truly bright star which is far away. We therefore call the brightness we observe on earth the apparent brightness. The famous ancient astronomer Ptolemy was one of the first to classify stars in terms of their apparent brightness. He called about twenty-five of the brightest stars in the sky 'stars of the first magnitude'. The stars which were just visible to the naked eye he called 'stars of the sixth magnitude'. And he grouped the other visible stars into second, third, fourth and fifth magnitudes.

Astronomers still use the same kind of scale, but they have improved on Ptolemy's original classification. In general they found that a star of the first magnitude was about 100 times brighter than a star of the sixth magnitude. Therefore they adjusted the scale so that a star of the first magnitude was exactly 100 times brighter than that of the sixth. Now that astronomers can see stars much fainter than the sixth magnitude the scale has been extended to describe their brightness.

Below The groups of stars that are so familiar to us today have not always looked the same. For example the Plough in the constellation Ursa Major (Great Bear) changes it shape because of the proper motions of the stars. The white dots in the drawing show its position today while the blue dots indicate its probable position about 100,000 years ago.

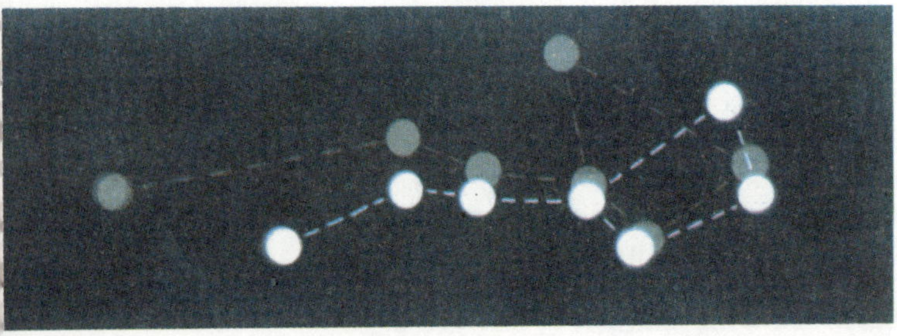

At the other end of the improved scale, a few of the brightest stars are now considered brighter than the first magnitude, and so the scale has been extended 'backwards' to give minus values. For example, Sirius, the brightest star in the night sky, is given a magnitude of minus 1.5: on the same scale, the sun is minus 27.

The magnitudes quoted so far are apparent magnitudes. To give a better idea of the true brightness of a star astronomers have devised a scale of absolute magnitudes. On this absolute scale the sun is 4.8 and Sirius is 1.3.

Another way of looking at the brightness of a star is to compare it with that of the sun. We then speak of a star's luminosity. Sirius has a luminosity of 26. Some stars have luminosities much smaller than the sun's, others have luminosities of several thousands.

Composition of stars

Stars are great globes of hot, glowing gas, just as the sun is. But what exactly are they made of? They contain a great deal of hydrogen and helium, for they shine by changing hydrogen into helium in the vast nuclear furnace of their central core. Astronomers have discovered that stars contain most of the other chemical elements – the basic 'building bricks' of matter – found on earth. They have identified more than sixty of the ninety-two natural elements found on earth. As you might expect, the elements do not occur in the same proportions in the stars as they do on earth. And the composition varies from star to star. But in general stars contain large amounts of the lighter elements such as hydrogen, helium, calcium, sodium and iron.

How, when the stars are so far away, can we be sure that these elements are present? The answer lies in the light they give off, which is the only thing that reaches us. White light is not a pure light but is made up of all the colours of the rainbow. And this means exactly what it says. In a rainbow, drops of rain in the atmosphere split up the white light from the sun into the seven main colours of the spectrum – violet, indigo, blue, green, yellow, orange and red. Astronomers use an instrument called a spectroscope to split up the starlight into a broad band of colour. At intervals along the band are a number of dark lines. The position, number and size of the lines tell astronomers an enormous amount about the star's outer 'atmosphere', including its gaseous chemical content, its density and temperature.

Movement of stars

If you remain star-gazing at night for any length of time you will notice that the stars appear to move across the sky. Like the sun, they rise in the east and set in the west. But this movement has nothing to do with the stars. It is caused by the earth rotating on its axis. Another apparent movement of the stars occurs because of the motion of the earth in its orbit around the sun.

Ignore this apparent movement and look at patterns of stars, and you will find they are the same night after night, and year after year. You can understand why the ancients considered them 'fixed' stars set in a celestial sphere. However, nothing in the universe is fixed. The moons move around their planets, the planets move around their sun, the sun moves around the centre of its galaxy. All these bodies move around their own axes. Everything is constantly in motion. And so are the stars.

The stars do not appear to move because they are incredibly far away. Remember that the closer you are to a moving object, the faster it appears to move. However, by painstaking measurement, astronomers can detect slight sideways movements of a few of the stars. This sideways movement of a star relative to the earth is known as its proper motion. For the vast majority of stars the proper motion is undetectable.

Of course, a detectable proper motion does not mean that the star is travelling completely sideways at the same distance from us. It is almost certainly travelling diagonally towards or away from us, but we cannot see this part of the motion. The star remains a tiny point of light, getting neither bigger as it approaches us nor smaller as it recedes.

Movement of a star towards or away from us is called its radial motion. Astronomers can detect and measure this motion by a fascinating method using that invaluable tool, the spectroscope. As we have already seen, the spectrum of light from a star shows dark lines characteristic of the chemical elements it contains. The interesting thing is that when a star is moving towards or away from us, the lines show a shift in position from where they would have been if the star were at rest. When the motion is towards us, the lines shift towards the blue end of the spectrum. When the motion is away from us, the lines shift towards the red end. The extent of the shift is a measure of the speed at which the star is travelling towards or away from us.

Doppler effect

These blue and red shifts can be explained in terms of what is called the Doppler effect, named after Christian Doppler (1803-53), the Austrian physicist who discovered it. The wavelength of light from a body coming towards us is effectively shortened. In other words, the light appears bluer, and the whole spectrum shifts towards the blue. On the other hand, the wavelength of light from a body travelling away from us is effectively lengthened, and the light appears redder.

This is not as mysterious as you may think. You have probably experienced the Doppler effect yourself – not with light waves but with sound

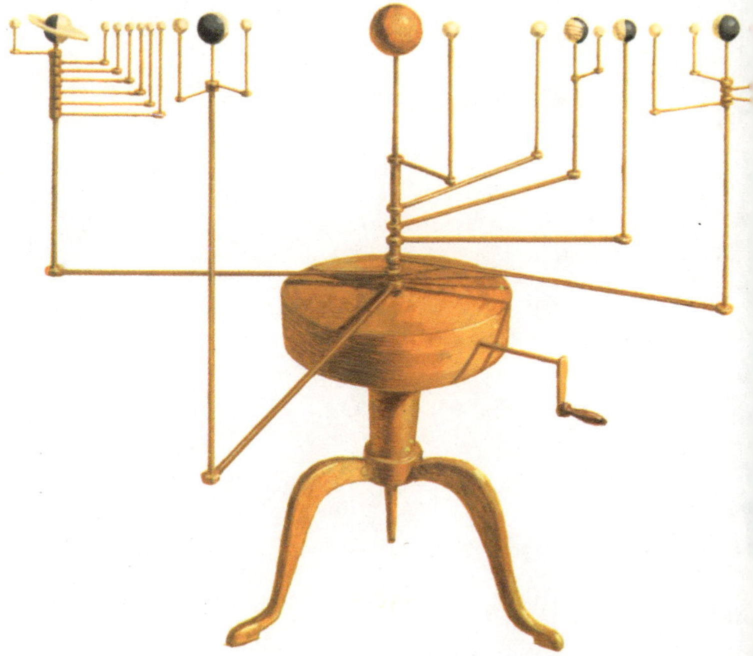

Above The orrery was the forerunner of the planetarium and was a mechanical device which demonstrated the movements of the planets and other bodies in the solar system and their positions relative to each other. These were made to revolve by a series of wheels and cogs operated by turning a handle. The orrery was so named in honour of the 4th Earl of Orrery (1676–1731) by its inventor, George Graham.

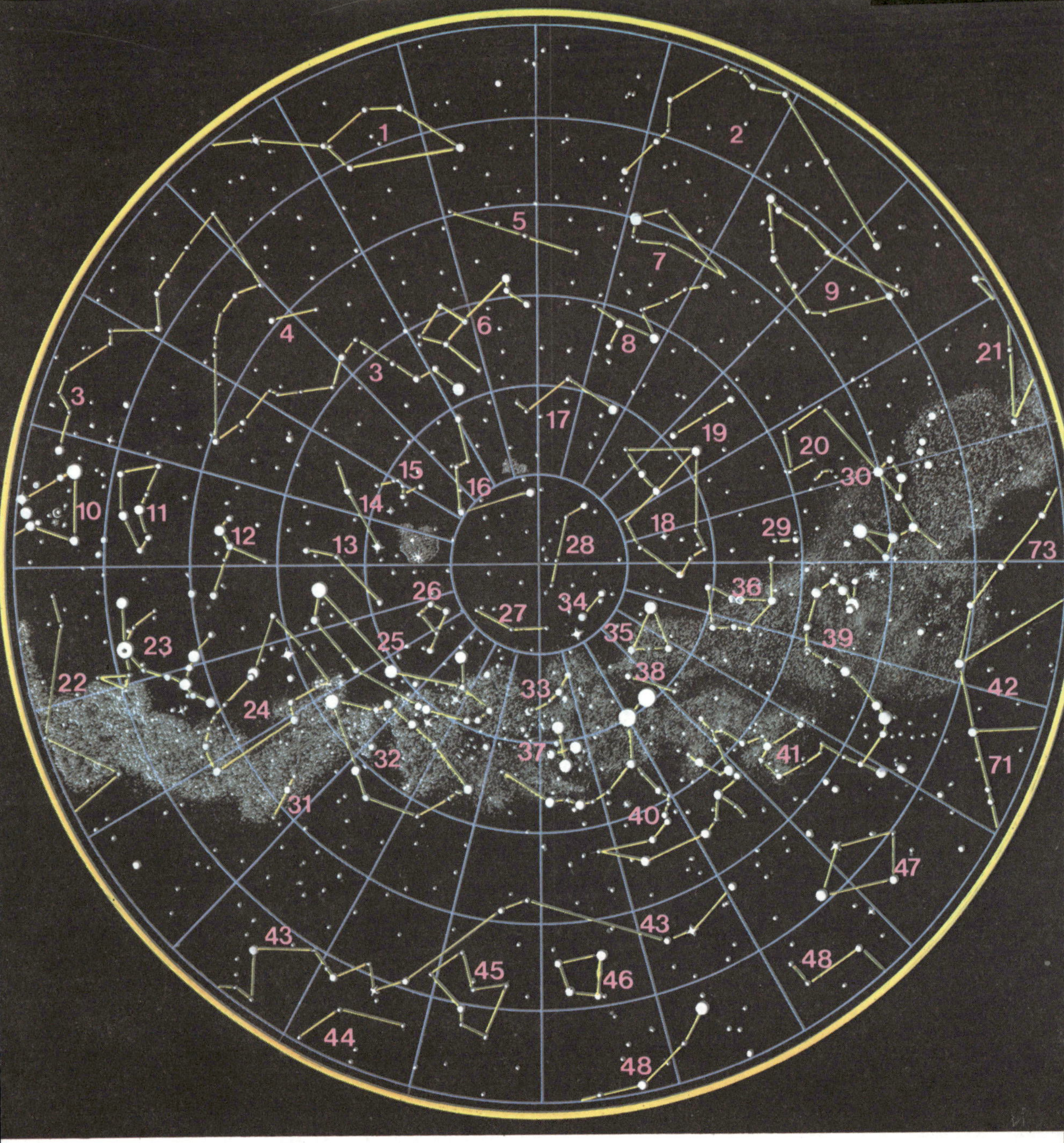

A map of the heavens

Constellations of the southern sky

1 Cetus
2 Aquarius
3 Eridanus
4 Fornax
5 Sculptor
6 Phoenix
7 Piscis Austrinus
8 Grus
9 Capricornus
10 Orion
11 Lepus
12 Columba
13 Pictor
14 Dorado
15 Reticulum
16 Hydrus
17 Tucana
18 Pavo
19 Indus
20 Sagittarius
21 Aquila
22 Monoceros
23 Canis Major
24 Puppis
25 Carina
26 Volans
27 Chamaeleon
28 Octans
29 Telescopium
30 Corona Australis
31 Pyxis
32 Vela
33 Musca
34 Apus
35 Triangulum Australe
36 Ara
37 Crux
38 Circinus
39 Scorpius
40 Centaurus
41 Lupus
42 Ophiuchus
43 Hydra
44 Sextans
45 Crater
46 Corvus
47 Libra
48 Virgo

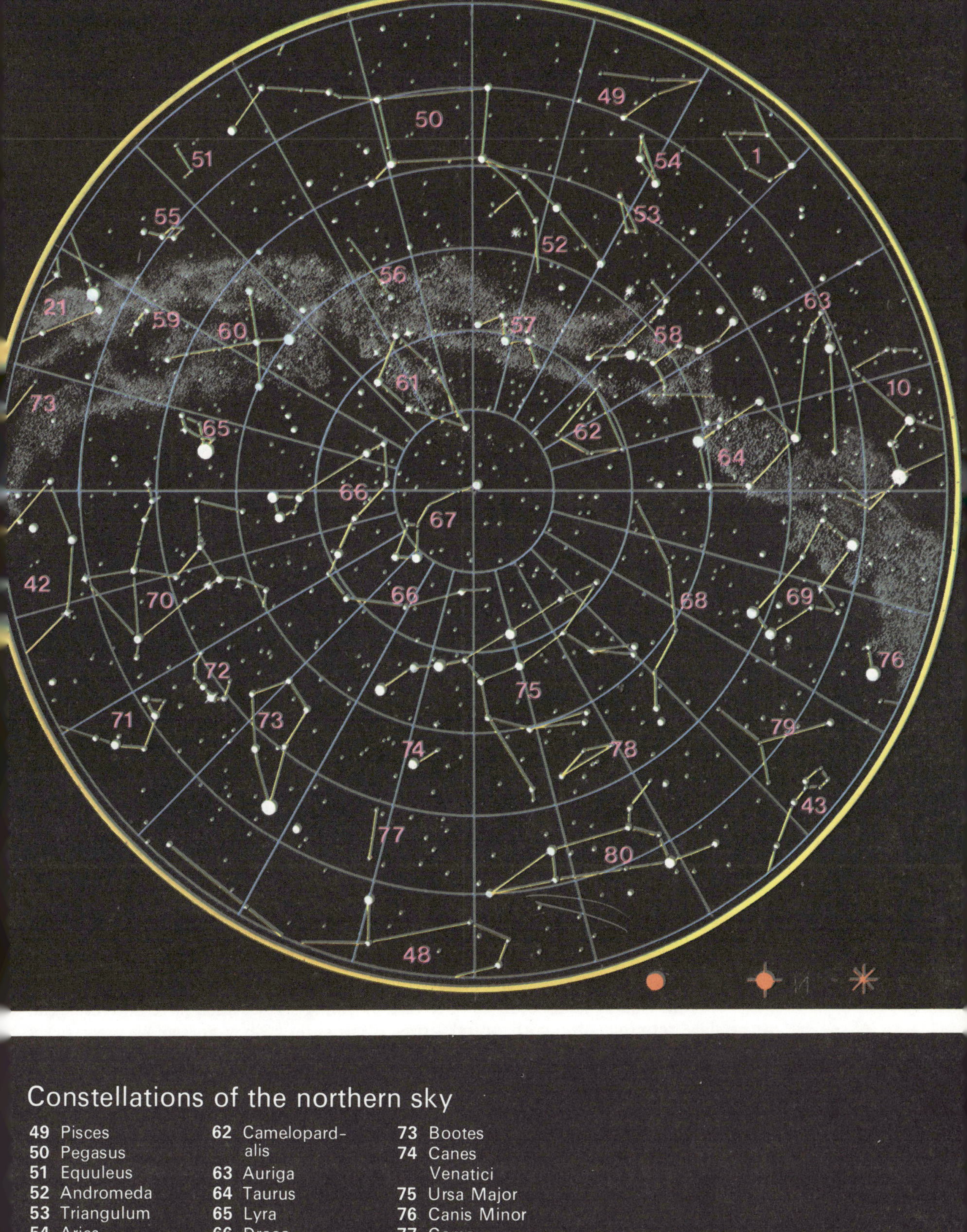

Constellations of the northern sky

49 Pisces
50 Pegasus
51 Equuleus
52 Andromeda
53 Triangulum
54 Aries
55 Delphinus
56 Lacerta
57 Cassiopeia
58 Perseus
59 Sagitta
60 Cygnus
61 Cepheus
62 Camelopardalis
63 Auriga
64 Taurus
65 Lyra
66 Draco
67 Ursa Minor
68 Lynx
69 Gemini
70 Hercules
71 Serpens
72 Corona Borealis
73 Bootes
74 Canes Venatici
75 Ursa Major
76 Canis Minor
77 Coma Berenices
78 Leo Minor
79 Cancer
80 Leo

Above Planetariums are buildings in which images of the stars, planets, sun and moon are projected on to a dome which represents the sky. A very complex projector is used which can show such things as the actual motions of heavenly bodies, eclipses and the movement of comets. The first planetarium was built at Jena in Germany using a Zeiss projector.

waves. When a police car blaring its siren drives past you, you notice that the note, or pitch, of the siren changes. As it approaches you, the sound waves are made shorter and the pitch is high. As it goes away, the sound waves are made longer, and the pitch is low. This change in pitch is equivalent to the shift of the lines in the spectrum of starlight.

Star groups

The stars are not distributed equally throughout the universe. They occur grouped together in great star systems called galaxies. The bright stars we see in the sky belong to the galaxy of which our sun is a part, the Milky Way galaxy, or simply the Galaxy.

The Galaxy is believed to be a vast flat, rotating disc with spiral arms, somewhat like an enormous Catherine-wheel. At the centre of the disc is a great spherical mass of stars forming what is called the nucleus (the appearance has been likened to that of two fried eggs placed back-to-back). The Galaxy is estimated to contain something like 100,000 million stars. Its diameter is believed to be 100,000 light-years, and its maximum thickness 20,000 light-years.

Stretching right across the sky is a fuzzy, glowing band of light which we call the Milky Way. Even a small telescope will show that it is made up of millions of faint stars.

Whereabouts is the sun in this huge disc? At first, astronomers assumed it was near the galactic centre. But we know now that it is a long way out from it, about 30,000 light-years in fact. The sun takes about 225 million years to make one revolution around the centre of the Galaxy.

Interstellar material

We cannot see as far as the centre of the Galaxy because between it and us there are obscuring 'clouds' of gas and 'dust', so-called interstellar material. These clouds are found in other parts of the sky too. They are called nebulae, the Latin word for clouds. There are bright nebulae and dark nebulae.

The so-called Sword of Orion in the constellation Orion is quite a conspicuous bright nebula. It is a shining cloud which glows because of the radiation from stars embedded within it. Other bright nebulae glow simply by reflecting starlight. Most bright nebulae are irregular in form, but a number have a generally rounded shape and contain at the centre one or more very hot stars. They are called planetary nebulae. The most distinctive of these look like a giant smoke ring. The Ring Nebula in the constellation Lyra is the brightest of them. One of the most remarkable planetary nebulae, however, is the Crab Nebula in the constellation Taurus. It is the remains of a gigantic stellar explosion, called a supernova, which Chinese astronomers observed and recorded in AD 1054.

Dark nebulae are thought to contain young stars, which have not yet begun to shine. They appear as great black thunderclouds, obscuring everything behind them. One of the most famous and aptly named of the dark nebulae is the Horsehead Nebula in Orion.

There are other misty, bright patches in the sky which appear at first sight to be nebulae. In the constellation Andromeda, for example, there is such a patch, which has long been called the Great Nebula in Andromeda. But large telescopes reveal that it is not a nebula at all but another great system of stars, that is, another galaxy. And like our own

Galaxy it is spiral in form and contains a central nucleus and nebulae, as well as all the other familiar kinds of stars. But it is twice as big as our own Galaxy, and naturally contains many more stars. It lies 2 million light-years away, yet is among the closest of the neighbouring galaxies. Sometimes these outer galaxies are called extra-galactic nebulae, which simply means nebulae outside the Galaxy.

The moving galaxies

Almost all the galaxies are regular in form, although a few are irregular. The only two other galaxies besides Andromeda which can be seen with the naked eye are of this nature. They are the Large and the Small Magellanic Clouds, named after the great Portuguese navigator Ferdinand Magellan.

On a somewhat larger scale, the galaxies tend to appear in clusters. Our own Galaxy and Andromeda form part of a cluster known for obvious reasons as the Local Group. It consists of nearly thirty members within a sphere about 6.5 million light-years across. Some of the remoter clusters contain thousands and thousands of galaxies.

As we have seen, the shift in the spectrum of light from a star tells us whether a star is approaching us or receding from us and how fast it is travelling. When the light from the fainter galaxies is analysed, it is found that they all show pronounced red shifts, no matter where they are situated in the heavens. In other words, all of the galaxies are racing away from us and from each other. In 1929 the American astronomer Edwin Hubble (1889-1953) found that the red shift increased with distance. The fainter and farther the galaxies are away, the faster they seem to be travelling. This suggests that the whole universe is *expanding*. By tracing the expansion back in time, astronomers have calculated that it must have started between 10 to 20 thousand million years ago.

One of the most distant galaxies photographed so far in the giant Palomar telescope is, according to its red shift, travelling away from us at two-fifths of the velocity of light. It is estimated to be some 5,000 million light-years away, which means in effect that we are seeing it as it was 5,000 million years ago, very early on in its evolution. As we shall see later, there are other objects in the sky, the mysterious quasars, that appear to be much further away!

Star clusters

After looking at the great star systems, let us consider the stars themselves. Most stars, like the sun, appear to be travelling round their galaxy on their own and shining steadily. But many have features that make them distinctive. Some cluster together in groups; some have just a few companions; some vary in their brightness; and some even explode.

Stars are sometimes found in closely knit groups, or clusters. Large numbers of globular clusters appear to surround the nucleus of a galaxy as a kind of shell. Those of our own Galaxy are too far away for us to appreciate with the naked eye their true magnificence. But in a powerful telescope they are fascinating. Thousands upon thousands of stars are clustered together into a distinctive globe shape, hence their name of globular clusters. The globe may be as much as 150 light-years across.

Less important on the astronomical scale, but more easily visible to us, are the so-called open star clusters. They

Left The galaxy of Andromeda is, like the galaxy to which our sun belongs, a vast rotating mass of millions of stars.

Below The signs of the zodiac, which was the name given to the then-known part of the heavens by the ancient Greeks. The stars in this were grouped into twelve constellations, each of which was given a symbol. They are (from top to bottom): Capricornus, Aquarius, Pisces, Aries, Taurus, Gemini, Cancer, Leo, Virgo, Libra, Scorpio and Sagittarius.

Above The Jodrell Bank radio-telescope in Cheshire, England, was completed in 1957 and was used to track the orbit of the first sputnik. Its reflecting bowl is about 76 metres in diameter and it can 'look' into the skies much farther than optical telescopes.

John Flamsteed (1646–1719) First astronomer-royal of England. In 1676, when Greenwich Observatory was built, he began observations which really began modern practical astronomy. The first reliable catalogue of fixed stars was compiled by him, and he wrote the great book *Historia Coelestis Britannica,* published 1725. His work supplied the background for some of Newton's theories. The picture (right) shows the interior of one of the rooms at Greenwich Observatory.

contain many fewer stars than the globular clusters – hundreds instead of thousands – and are much more widely spaced. Two of the most distinctive open clusters in the sky are the Pleiades, or Seven Sisters, and the Hyades, both in the constellation Taurus. Most people can see seven stars in the Pleiades with the naked eye, some people nine, but in fact it contains at least 200.

Binary stars

A great many stars, one out of every two or three, are in fact double stars, or binaries. The component stars revolve around each other. Some stars are triple stars and there are even multiple stars, but binaries are the most common. Some, called visual binaries, can be seen through telescopes to be double systems. There is one in the Hyades which can be resolved with the naked eye. Sirius is an interesting visual binary because one of its components is extremely faint compared with Sirius itself. Other binaries are too close together for the two components to be visible. They can be separated only with the help of a spectroscope. They are called spectroscopic binaries.

A third class of binaries is the eclipsing binaries. These are systems in which the components rotate in a plane level with our line of sight. This means that periodically one passes in front of the other and masks its light. Therefore the brightness of the system varies regularly. The star Algol in the constellation Perseus is a well-known eclipsing binary which fades noticeably every two and a half days for about five hours at a time while the bright component is being eclipsed.

Variable Stars

Some of these may vary in brightness because of processes which go on inside. Little is known about what these processes are. But it seems as if the change in brightness is caused by the stars contracting and expanding. They are therefore called pulsating stars. The most distinctive one is Betelgeuse, in the constellation Orion, which is one of the brightest stars in the sky.

Sometimes what seems to be a new star suddenly appears in the sky. It shines brightly for a few days or even weeks and then fades away, returning to its original state. What has happened, in fact, is that an existing, faint star has suddenly flared up, or exploded, and become noticeable. Such a star is called a nova. Novae are not uncommon, and already this century there have been five novae of the first magnitude, vying with the brightest stars in the sky. Some novae reappear after a lengthy interval, but they seem to be rare.

Very occasionally the disturbance inside a star is so fantastically violent that it tears the stars apart. The sudden flare-up so far outstrips a nova in intensity that we call it a supernova.

The first recorded supernova was that in AD 1054 which gave rise to the Crab Nebula. There were supernovae in 1572 (studied by Tycho Brahe) and in 1604 (studied by Johann Kepler), but there has been none since in our Galaxy. A supernova may leave a very dense remnant, called a neutron star. This is so dense that a neutron star only 20 kilometres wide would weigh as much as the sun.

Radio sources

In 1931 an American engineer, Karl Jansky, detected radio waves coming from space, somewhere in the Milky Way. From this has developed one of the most important and fastest-growing branches of astronomy – radio astronomy. Radio waves have now been found to come from many parts of the universe.

The instrument astronomers use to study them is called a radio telescope. It consists basically of an aerial, or antenna, and some kind of reflector, which may be bowl-shaped. The reflector of a radio telescope collects and focuses radio waves in much the same way as the mirror of a reflecting telescope collects and focuses light waves.

Light and radio waves are both forms of radiation, or energy release, as heat is, too. Radiation travels in the form of waves, and the difference between the various kinds of radiation lies in the length of the wave, that is, the distance between one crest and another. Light has a relatively short wavelength, heat waves are longer, and radio waves are longer still. The important thing about radio waves is that they have better penetration than light waves. They can, for example, pass through the light and dark nebulae which obscure parts of the heavens.

The sun sends out radio waves, but we cannot detect any coming from the stars. Presumably they are too weak to reach us. But several thousand intense 'point' sources of radio waves have been located. Some have been identified with visible objects in the heavens, but many have no equivalent that can be seen. There is also a kind of general background radio 'noise' coming from the nucleus of our Galaxy.

Some sources have been identified optically with the remains of supernovae. The Crab Nebula is a case in point. Several normal galaxies, such as Andromeda, and several abnormal ones, such as one in the constellation Cygnus, emit radio waves, too.

Above The radio telescope at the Arecibo Ionospheric Observatory in Puerto Rico has a reflecting mesh about 300 metres in diameter hung in a valley floor. Above it swings a platform which is held by cables from three towers.

Mysterious objects in space

Pulsars and quasars were first discovered by radio astronomy. Pulsars are so-called because they emit regular pulses of waves. They are thought to be rotating neutron stars, which give out bursts of radiation as they turn. Pulsars were first identified in 1967, a few years after quasars.

Quasar is a shortened form of quasi-stellar radio sources. They are called quasi-stellar because they appear on photographs as small, star-like objects. But that is where any resemblance to stars ends. From their red shifts, many appear to be travelling at speeds well over half the speed of light. The fastest and farthest ones are estimated to be between 7,000 and 10,000 million light-years away, almost back to when some astronomers consider the universe began. And yet for such great distances they are incredibly bright.

A typical quasar has a brightness more than 100 times greater than that of the brightest-known galaxy. Yet it is 10,000 times smaller than our own Galaxy, with a diameter of only a few light-years.

Quasars are so startlingly different from everything else in the universe that some authorities doubt whether they are in fact so far away as the limits of the universe. They suggest that the

Frederick (William) Herschel (1738–1822) German-British astronomer, born in Hanover. At first he was a musician, then took up astronomy and made a reflecting telescope in 1773/4. Discovered the planet Uranus, which he called 'Georgium Sidus'. In 1782 he was appointed astronomer to King George III. He also discovered 2 satellites of Saturn, the rotation of Saturn's rings and the motions of binary stars. In 1789 he erected a telescope twelve metres long.

Right The fact that Moslems are required by their religion to prostrate themselves in the direction of Mecca when they pray was one of the reasons why Islamic astronomy developed. Wherever a Moslem lived – in Arabia, Spain, Africa or India – he needed to know his position in relation to Mecca and the only accurate directions at that time were based on the position of the stars. The first Islamic observatories were built in Arabia and Africa, and these were later copied in India. This picture is based on the observatory at Jaipur, built in the 18th century.

Above The astrolabe is an instrument used for taking altitudes of the sun, moon or stars. The portable astrolabe of the type shown originated in the east about AD 700 and was introduced into Europe by the Arabs. The mariner's astrolabe was first used in the 15th century, notably by Christopher Columbus.

enormous red shifts may have some other meaning and that quasars are members of our own Galaxy.

Life and death of a star

When we look at the stars in the night sky we see them more or less as the ancients saw them thousands of years ago. The stars appear more or less in the same positions and are shining as brilliantly now as then. They seem eternal, unchanging. But we know now that they, like us, must some time cease to be. They shine, as we have seen, by 'burning' hydrogen as their fuel. And when their fuel is exhausted, they must die.

A star is formed from the whirling cloud of hydrogen gas and dust that is a nebula. Vast, cool pockets, or globules, of gas condense out of the nebula just like droplets of water condense out of a cloud of steam. Gravitational attraction gradually draws the gas globule into a denser, more compact mass. As the globule contracts, its temperature rises. Eventually its core is not enough to allow nuclear reaction to take place to change hydrogen into helium. And the star begins to shine. It glows red, orange and yellow in turn as its surface temperature increases.

There comes a time, after millions and millions of years, when most of the hydrogen in the star is used up. Some very large stars may then end their lives dramatically as supernova, leaving behind a very dense neutron star. More usually, the star suddenly swells up to a gigantic size and becomes what is called a red giant. It is much cooler than before, but is more luminous because it is two or three hundred times as big.

The core of the red giant is now hot enough for other nuclear processes to take place. The helium is converted into heavier elements. And the star rapidly begins to shrink in size and become hotter and whiter. At some point, all its helium fuel is exhausted, and it dies. Its white light becomes more feeble as it gradually cools down. It continues to shrink until it becomes really tiny compared with what it once was. For this reason we call it a white dwarf.

The matter inside a white dwarf is incredibly dense. One white dwarf, called Kuiper's Star, after a famous American astronomer, is particularly well-known. It is much smaller than the earth, with a diameter of only about 6,500 kilometres. Yet its mass is equal to that of the sun! It is so dense that just a thimbleful would weigh thousands of kilograms.

There are incredibly large stars known as supergiants. The size of some of these, for example Betelgeuse and Antares, is enormous. Betelgeuse is 400 million kilometres in diameter, and Antares is probably 150 million kilometres bigger still. If it were where the sun is, its globe would stretch beyond the orbit of Mars. And there is a star called Epsilon Aurigae whose diameter is over 3,000 million kilometres! You can understand now why we consider our sun, with a diameter of a mere 1,390 *thousand* kilometres, such an ordinary kind of star.

Eventually, in a few thousand million years' time, the sun will expand into a red giant. In so doing it will engulf the solar system up to and beyond the earth's orbit. Earth and the inner planets will disappear in the hot, luminous gaseous outer layers. Then the sun will contract and finally die as a white dwarf.

How the universe began

Planets, moons, suns, galaxies, nebulae, and above all – space: that is what the universe consists of. But just how did it come into being? What happened 'in the beginning'? Was there ever, in fact, a beginning? Will there ever be an end? These are questions astronomers have been trying to answer for years. The whole field of study relating to the origin of the universe is known as cosmology.

There have been many theories put forward to explain how the universe began, some fanciful and far-fetched, others reasonable and basically sound. Two of the main theories which have been put forward are very different. One is that the universe began at a certain time in the past and reached its present state as a result of a gigantic explosion. This is the 'Big-Bang', or evolutionary, theory. The other assumes that the universe is the same now as it always has been and always will be. This is the 'Steady-State' theory.

The renowned Belgian astronomer Abbé Georges Lemaître originally proposed the evolutionary theory in 1927, some thirteen years after it was found that the universe is expanding. The theory supposes that at one time all of the matter in the universe was concentrated in one enormous, very dense ball, or 'primeval atom'. Then, some thousands of millions of years ago, this atom exploded, scattering the material in it outwards in all directions. From this ejected cosmic gas and dust, the galaxies condensed and the stars formed, still expanding with the impetus of the original explosion. The theory implies that there was a single

Above The Jesuit Observatory at Peking in China, based on an engraving of the late 17th century. This was built by Jesuit missionaries on the lines of a European observatory by order of the Chinese emperor. The instruments used were copied from those of Tycho Brahe and were preserved until quite recently.

Right This 16th-century engraving may seem amusing to modern eyes but in the Middle Ages there were many fantastic ideas about the nature of the universe which were at the time found acceptable. In this drawing a man thrusts his head through the vault of the heavens to see the complicated mechanism of cogs and wheels which moves the stars.

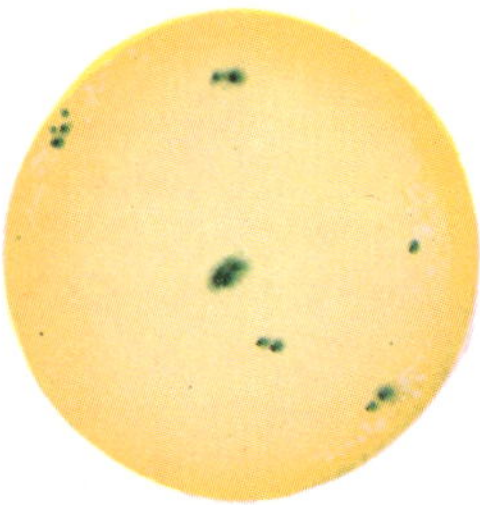

Above One of the most remarkable features of the sun's surface are sun-spots. These are dark areas which show up when the sun is examined with spectroscopic equipment. They are cooler areas of the sun and do not last for very long.

act of creation of all the matter in the universe, which the 'Big-Bang' scattered far and wide. Since no fresh matter is being created, the universe must surely die one day when all the stars have used up their nuclear fuel. Thus there was a beginning and there will be an end, according to this version of the evolutionary theory.

In 1948, Hermann Bondi, Thomas Gold and Fred Hoyle, then at Cambridge University, put forward the rival Steady-State theory. They maintained that the universe has always existed and will exist for evermore. For this to happen, matter is being continuously created in the form of the basic 'stuff' of the universe – hydrogen atoms. As the existing galaxies fly apart, new ones gradually condense from the newly created matter to take their place. The universe remains overall in a uniform state. In 1966, Hoyle modified the theory slightly by proposing that locally in the universe there may be evolution, but overall there is a steady state. Thus this theory supposes continuous creation as opposed to the single act of creation in the evolutionary theory. According to those who uphold the Steady-State theory there was no beginning and there will be no end.

However, it has been pointed out that the 'Big Bang' universe could go on for ever. When the expansion has slowed down, the universe may start to contract under the force of gravity. This could bring all the matter together again to be followed by another 'Big Bang'.

The 'Big Bang' theory is the one most favoured by astronomers today. One consequence of the theory is that distant galaxies should be more closely packed than near ones. And radio studies of remote galaxies tend to confirm that this is so. The Steady State theory on the other hand would indicate the same distribution of galaxies both near and far. Doubtless other theories will take the place of these two, be held for a time, and then be dropped for new ones. As our knowledge of the heavens increases, there is a better chance of improving on existing theories. Whether we shall ever really know what happened 'in the beginning', if indeed there was a beginning, is extremely unlikely. Here is one mystery which will continue to tax minds for many years to come.

Above Lift-off for the giant American Saturn V rocket as it begins the first stage of the historic Apollo 11 journey to the moon. In the photograph on the left, taken by Neil Armstrong after he had reached the moon's surface, Edwin Aldrin is seen as he steps out of the module.

Space travel

On 21st July 1969 there occurred the most awe-inspiring moment in the history of man's exploration of the universe. A human being from our planet earth set foot on another world. Neil Armstrong, an American astronaut, watched by countless millions of television viewers, stepped from part of an Apollo spacecraft on to the surface of the moon.

Thus, after years of dedicated preparation, man at last achieved what he had dreamed of doing for so long: he had travelled in space to another world.

It is astonishing to think that today man can fly 384,000 kilometres to the moon and back again in safety, yet before the year 1900 he could not really fly at all, except in fragile balloons and gliders which were at the mercy of the winds.

At that time few people thought seriously about travelling in space. It was difficult enough to believe that man could fly over the English Channel. Space travel was still very much in the realms of fantasy, although early science-fiction writers had suggested many original methods of reaching the moon.

Rocket engines

One of the first people to treat the matter seriously was Konstantin Tsiolkovsky (1857–1935), a Russian schoolteacher. In 1903 he suggested in a scientific paper the use of rockets for

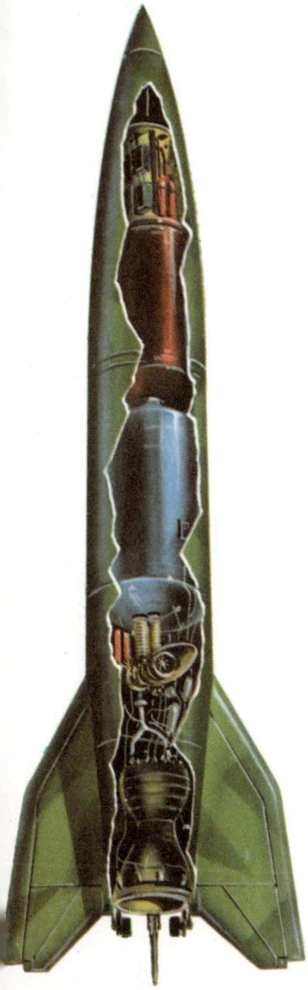

Above A cutaway drawing showing the internal mechanism of the V-2 rocket, with which Germany bombarded England in the Second World War.

Above right At the top is Sputnik 3, the Russian artificial satellite launched in May 1958, while below is seen an astronaut within the confines of his capsule.

space flight. This was one of the first principles of space flight because a rocket engine is the only one known so far that can work in the vacuum of space. The rocket itself is not a recent invention. The Chinese, for example, used rockets in 1232 in their war against the Mongols.

In 1923 Hermann Oberth in Germany developed the idea of rocket propulsion and space flight in great detail in his famous book *The Rocket into Interplanetary Space*. His theories were all basically sound, but there was at the time no rocket powerful enough to lift itself into space. The rockets of his day were much as they had been from the days of their earliest invention. They contained a solid fuel – gunpowder, which burned to produce gases to propel them along.

In 1926 Robert Hutchings Goddard (1882-1945) in the United States fired the first liquid-fuelled rocket. Using suitable liquid fuels, rockets can be propelled much more quickly than when using solid fuels.

Germany continued to be the main centre for rocket development and in 1927 a group of enthusiasts formed a society for space travel called *Verein für Raumschiffart (VfR)* to carry out research on rockets. When Hitler came to power in Germany he set up a rocket research centre at Peenemünde on an island in the Baltic Sea. The V-2 rocket used in the Second World War was developed there. The first successful launching of the V-2 (at first called A-4) took place in 1942. In 1944 it was fitted with an explosive warhead and used to bombard London.

Development of the V-2 was under the direction of Dr Wernher von Braun, an ex-member of the *VfR*. After the war von Braun and many of his colleagues continued their work in the United States. There he later became director of the American space programme. Other members of the German research team went to Russia. The United States and Russia thus shared the wealth of experience gained by the Germans. This, coupled with their vast natural resources, has made them leaders in space research.

It was soon realised that a single rocket could not by itself lift an object into space. Experiments were made with a 'step' rocket, an idea which had been put forward some time before. The first rocket thrusts the second high into the air and then falls away when its fuel is spent. Then the second rocket fires and rises higher still.

The United States launched its first two-stage rocket in 1949, using a captured V-2 as the first stage. The second stage, a *WAC Corporal*, reached an altitude of nearly 400 kilometres.

In 1955 the Americans announced that they would make attempts to launch small artificial satellites around the earth between July 1957 and December 1958. This was the period known as the International Geophysical Year, when scientists from all over the world co-operated in research projects to find out more about the earth and its atmosphere.

Artificial satellites

In the event the Russians beat the Americans to it. On 4th October 1957

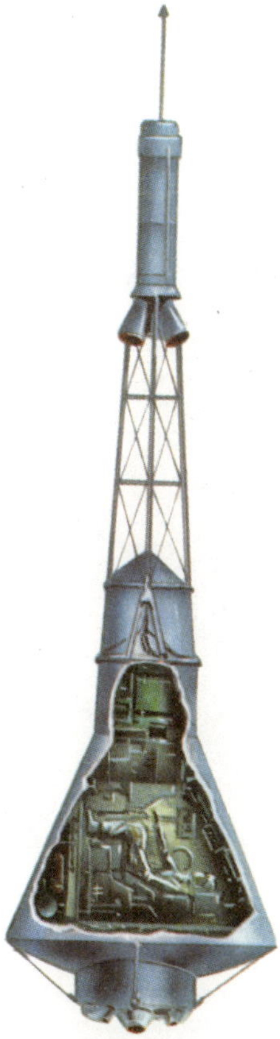

Above Friendship 7, the Mercury capsule used by John Glenn when he became the first American to go into orbit on 20th February, 1962.

Above left It was an historic occasion for the United States when Edward White became the first American astronaut to walk in space. He remained outside the Gemini 4 space capsule for twenty minutes.

they launched the world's first artificial satellite, *Sputnik 1*. It was a sphere about fifty-eight centimetres in diameter and weighed eighty-three kilograms. Projecting from it there were aerials for its radio transmitter. It sent out a steady 'bleep, bleep' of signals as it orbited the earth every ninety-six minutes. A month later the Russians launched *Sputnik 2*, weighing about 500 kilograms. It carried the very first space traveller, a dog named Laika. The sheer size of the satellite amazed the Americans. The Russians obviously had much more powerful launching rockets. When the Americans launched their first satellite, *Explorer 1*, on 31st January 1958, it weighed only fourteen kilograms.

Over the next three years both Russia and the United States launched several satellites and a number of so-called 'probes' to the moon. Then on 12th April 1961 man himself ventured in space for the first time and returned alive. Major Yuri Gagarin, a Russian pilot, became the world's first astronaut (the Russians say cosmonaut) when he made one orbit of the earth in his spacecraft *Vostok 1* (meaning East). Four months later another Russian cosmonaut, Herman Titov, circled the earth seventeen times in *Vostok 2* before returning safely. It was not until 20th February 1962 that the United States launched a man into orbit. He was Colonel John Glenn, who made three orbits in *Friendship 7*. This was the opening of the American *Mercury* series of one-man space shots. Russia continued with her one-man *Vostok* programme.

By the end of 1963 four American astronauts and six Russian cosmonauts had been sent into space. They included the first woman in space, Russian cosmonaut Valentina Tereshkova. The Russian cosmonauts had spent in all more than twelve days in space as compared with the American astronauts' two days. Russia appeared to be ahead in what was beginning to be called the 'space race'. This view was encouraged on 12th October 1964, when no less than three Russian cosmonauts orbited together in the same spacecraft, named *Voskhod 1* (meaning Sunrise). Four months later *Voskhod 2* was launched with two men on board. During the flight one of them, Alexei

Above If long-term space flights are to be possible spacecraft must be able to meet and link up in space. This docking procedure was first accomplished on 16th March, 1966.

John Glenn
(Born 1921) American astronaut. In 1962 he made a three-orbit flight in the Mercury capsule *Friendship 7*, the first American to encircle the earth in a satellite. Now a consultant to the US space programme and active in both business and politics.

Leonov, 'walked', or rather floated, for twenty minutes outside the spacecraft and astonished the world.

However, a few days after *Voskhod 2* returned to earth the United States launched its first two-man spacecraft, appropriately called *Gemini* (The Twins). With its ten *Gemini* launchings up until November 1966 the United States won back lost ground. Edward White in *Gemini 4* made the first American 'walk' in space. *Gemini 7* spent practically a fortnight in orbit. *Gemini 8* achieved the first successful 'docking', or link-up manoeuvre, which was essential for subsequent space flights.

The Apollo programme

After the resounding successes of the Gemini programme and of the *Voskhod* launchings, the next logical step seemed to be the moon, earth's nearest 'neighbour' in space. America's much-publicised *Apollo* programme aimed at putting a man on the moon by 1970. All seemed fine until January 1967 when disaster struck the *Apollo* project. Three astronauts, Virgil Grissom, Edward White and Roger Chaffee, were killed by a flash-fire inside their *Apollo* spacecraft on the ground. This caused a severe set-back to the project. Modifications had to be made in the design of the crew cabin, or capsule of the craft, to prevent a similar disaster happening again.

The Russians, too, had their troubles. Three months after the *Apollo* tragedy, cosmonaut Vladimir Komarov became the first in-flight space casualty when he was killed while returning to earth in *Soyuz 1* (meaning Union).

Despite these set-backs, the moon programme continued. In November 1967 an unmanned *Apollo 4* craft was launched on top of the incredibly powerful *Saturn 5* rocket designed to take astronauts to the moon. In September and November 1968, Russia recovered two *Zond* (meaning probe) spacecraft that had flown around the moon. In October a three-man American team in *Apollo 7* made a successful ten-day flight in an earth orbit rigorously testing the *Apollo* craft. This was a prelude to *Apollo 8's* pioneering trip to the moon and into orbit around it in December. Frank Borman, James Lovell and William Anders were the crew. Television viewers on earth saw live television pictures of the moon taken by *Apollo 8* as they orbited about 100 kilometres above the surface.

The year 1969 began with a successful link-up between two Russian *Soyuz* spacecraft, during which two cosmonauts transferred from one ship to another before returning to earth. March saw the launching of *Apollo 9* into an earth orbit to test the so-called Lunar Excursion Module designed for the actual moon landing. Two of the astronauts separated in the module over 150 kilometres from the main craft and returned successfully. In May, astronauts in *Apollo 10* repeated similar manoeuvres but this time while in orbit around the moon.

All went well and everything was set for an actual moon landing. The astronauts were ready; all parts of the spacecraft and launching rockets had been rigorously tested; and the manoeuvres to be performed appeared faultless. Then in July came the historic moment when Neil Armstrong and Edwin Aldrin stepped on to the moon from the lunar module of *Apollo 11*.

In all it cost the United States almost forty thousand million dollars, but the country achieved its goal of putting a man on the moon by 1970.

Left Some idea of the comparative sizes of these rockets can be seen when they are studied against the size of St Paul's Cathedral in London, which is about 110 metres high from the ground to the top of the cross on the dome. From left to right: Saturn 5, Saturn 1, Vostok and Mercury/Atlas.

Yuri Gagarin (1934–68) Russian cosmonaut. He joined the Soviet Air Force in 1957. Then on 12th April 1961 became the first man in space, making a 108 minute journey in a Vostok space satellite. He was killed in an air crash in 1968.

Valentina Tereshkova (b. 1937) Russian cosmonaut. She became the first woman in space when she made 48 orbital flights in Vostok VI from 14-19th June 1963. This craft was one of a dual launch with Vostok V.

Man in space

Before man goes on a voyage of discovery to Mars or Venus, he will explore near-space and the moon thoroughly first. In the years since Gagarin's first orbit of the earth in 1961, we have gradually increased our knowledge of the problems and dangers involved in manned space flight. And now we can send astronauts safely to the moon.

The astronauts start their journey into space in a spacecraft on top of a giant rocket. The fantastically powerful stages of the launching rocket thrust the spacecraft from rest to a speed of more than 27,000 kilometres an hour in only a few minutes. The acceleration is extremely fierce. You can experience the effects of acceleration in a motor car. When the driver accelerates hard, you are pressed back in your seat by an unseen force. The greater the acceleration, the greater is the force pressing you back. Yet the fiercest acceleration in a car is only one-twentieth of that which astronauts experience on launching. You can imagine, therefore, what kind of force they have to bear.

Such acceleration forces are called G-forces. G represents the force of gravity, which pulls everything towards the centre of the earth. A fast accelerating car produces a G-force of about $\frac{1}{2}$ G, but a rocket produces about 10 G. To withstand such forces, the astronauts have to be strapped flat on their backs on couches. If they stood up, or sat, they would black-out, or lose consciousness, and might suffer internal damage.

The same kind of problem, only in reverse, arises when the astronauts return from space. What happens then

Right Apollo astronauts wore this spacesuit on the moon.

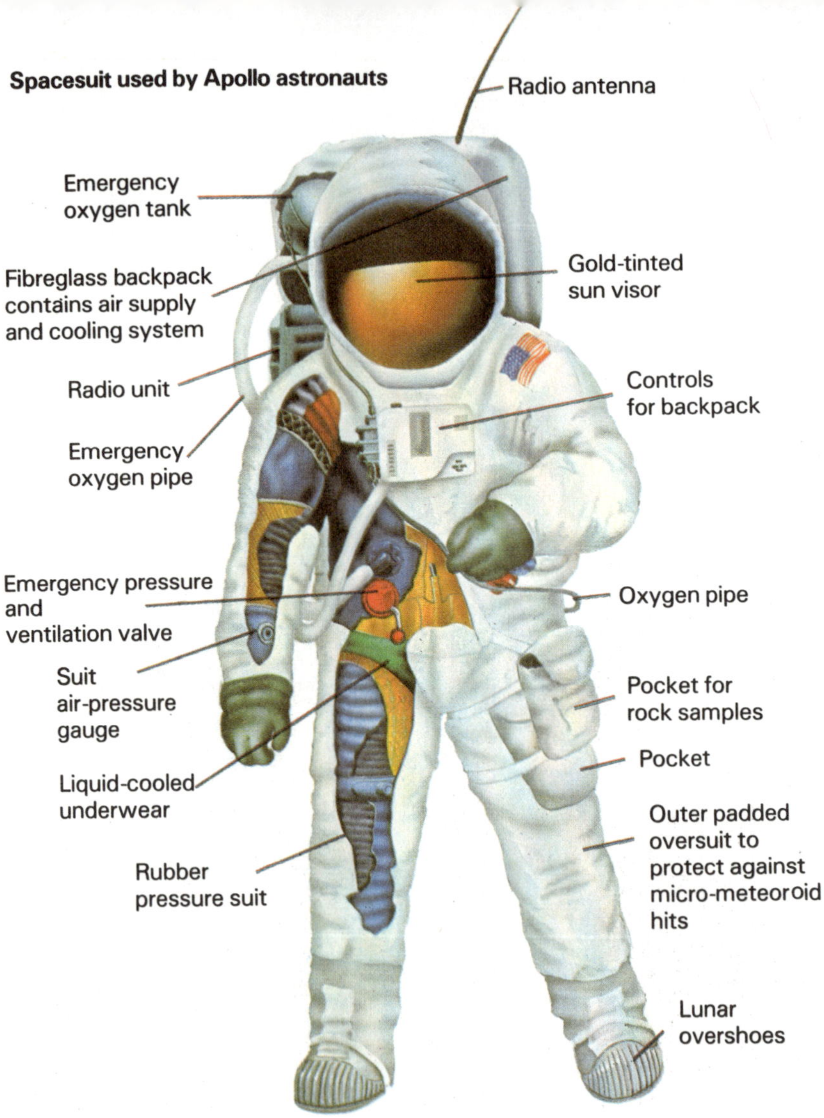

is that the spacecraft in which they are travelling is slowed down from 27,000 kilometres an hour to only a few kilometres an hour. The greater part of this deceleration is caused by the resistance, or drag, of the earth's atmosphere. The G-forces involved are again of the order of 10 G or thereabouts.

Training astronauts

The astronauts are prepared for such forces by training in a giant machine called a centrifuge, which whirls them around in a cabin at the end of a long arm. There they experience forces as high as 16 G, more than they should ever encounter in space. Another machine is designed to spin the astronauts in all directions to get them used to the tumbling they may experience in a spacecraft.

This is part of the very special and rigorous training which astronauts undergo before they are launched into space. Their training takes them as far as possible through all the conditions and problems they might encounter in a space flight. They spend an enormous amount of time inside a dummy of the capsule, or crew compartment of the spacecraft they will be flying in. The dummy capsule is identical in every respect to the real thing. It is coupled to a machine called a flight simulator which makes it react as though it were actually flying in various conditions. A picture of what would be seen out of the capsule's windows in space is projected inside the dummy. When the pilot moves the controls, the simulator makes the capsule respond in the same way as a real craft would.

One condition which is very difficult to simulate on earth is weightlessness. In space, a spacecraft travels in orbit. It may be a more or less circular orbit close to the earth or an elongated orbit which extends to the moon. As we have seen, in orbit the forces on the spacecraft are balanced. The outward force due to motion balances the inward pull of gravity. This means that there is no effective gravity acting on the craft or anything inside it. And when there is no gravity, there can be no weight. The astronauts in space, then, are weightless. They can float effortlessly in all directions. We cannot talk of them floating upside down, because in orbit there is no up or down. Everything floats, nothing falls.

The only way of simulating weightlessness on earth is to fly a plane at high speed up and over in a steep arc. For a short time people inside the plane are in an apparently weightless condition. What is actually happening, however, is that they are falling at the same time as the plane is. But the effect is more or less similar to weightlessness.

Life-support system

In space there is no atmosphere to provide air for the astronauts to breathe, to insulate them from the extreme heat or cold, and to protect them from harmful radiation. To survive in space, they must therefore take their 'atmosphere' with them. When they are inside their space capsule, they are supplied with air under pressure from the so-called life-support system. The air is changed constantly, filtered and treated to remove odours. The temperature and humidity are carefully controlled to make the astronauts as comfortable as possible.

Much of a space flight is carried out in this 'shirt-sleeve' environment. But when the astronauts leave their craft to 'walk' in space, or explore the moon, or if the pressure system fails, they must wear carefully designed spacesuits to give them the protection they require. In or near the spacecraft the suits may be connected to the spacecraft's life-support system. But for moon exploration, for example, the astronauts must carry a portable life-support pack on their back so that they can be mobile.

The spacesuit is made up of a number of separate layers. Cooling water circulates through the thin undergarment next to the astronaut's skin to keep the body temperature steady. Another layer is made airtight and supplied with air. Above this is a pressure 'skin' which keeps the air at more or less the same pressure as that on earth. Thick padding and a tough outer garment protect the inner layers. The outer garment is coated with a shiny material such as gold to help reflect the strong heat and radiation coming from the sun. On the head astronauts wear a helmet with a transparent visor in front. The visor has a fine gold coating, too. Inside the helmet are the earphones and microphones by which they can keep in contact with their fellow astronauts and base.

Above American astronaut, Gerald Carr, clowns in the weightless environment inside the Skylab space station.

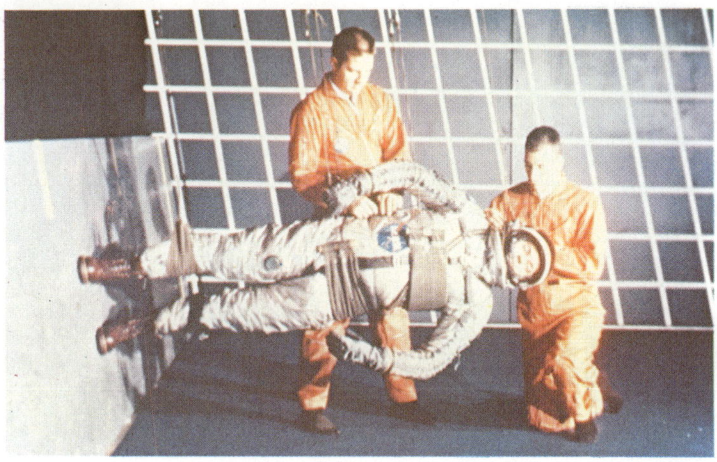

Below An astronaut is suspended horizontally in a special harness to simulate the feeling of walking on the moon's surface.

Satellites in orbit

First and foremost among the equipment of space flight there are the rockets which thrust spacecraft into orbit. The rocket works on the same principle as the jet engine used in aircraft. Burning a fuel inside the engine produces hot gases which shoot out backwards at high speed. Reaction to the escaping gases thrusts the engine forwards. This is the principle of jet propulsion.

To get an idea of how it works, blow up a balloon and pinch the neck. The pressure inside the balloon is the same in all directions, therefore the balloon does not move. Now release the neck so that the air rushes out. The forward pressure on the balloon will be the same, but there will be no backward pressure because the air is escaping. This means that there is a total forward pressure to propel the balloon forwards. And if you have ever blown up a balloon and let it go, you will know that it certainly shoots forwards!

Jets and rockets work on this same principle. The essential difference between them is that a jet engine obtains the oxygen to burn its fuel from the air, whereas a rocket carries its own oxygen. That is why a rocket can work in space where there is no air. The substance a rocket carries to provide oxygen is called an oxidant. Both the rocket fuel and the oxidant are known as propellants.

Powerful space rockets have liquid propellants and the oxidant normally used is oxygen in its very cold, liquid form. Many early rockets used alcohol or hydrogen peroxide as oxidants. The most powerful fuel in common use today is liquid hydrogen. The giant *Saturn 5* rocket which thrust man to the moon used liquid oxygen and liquid hydrogen as propellants for its upper stages. The massive first, or booster, stage used kerosene (paraffin) as fuel.

The engine of a liquid-propellant rocket is quite simple really. Fuel and oxidant from storage tanks are pumped through control valves into an open-ended combustion chamber where they are burned. They enter as a fine

Below Cape Canaveral, Florida, USA. This is the site where all American space flights begin. It is possible to trace the history of US space flight projects from this picture. On the left are smaller complexes where Mercury/Atlas, Atlas, Titan and Gemini/Titan depart, then the bigger Saturn complexes, and finally the sites of Apollo launching pads from which spacecraft were sent to the moon.

spray so that they mix easily with one another. The hot gases produced by the burning shoot out of the chamber through a nozzle at high speed and drive the rocket forwards. The propellants are circulated through the nozzle walls before entering the combustion chamber. This serves both to pre-heat the propellants and to cool the nozzle, which has to withstand the fierce heat of the burning gases.

Solid-propellant rockets are also sometimes used in spacecraft, although not for the main rocket engines because they are not powerful enough and they cannot be controlled very easily. They may, however, be used for the retro-rockets – the rockets which slow down an orbiting spacecraft so that it falls back to earth. The main use for solid-propellants, though, is for rocket missiles. The common firework rocket has solid propellants, too. The solid-propellant rocket is very simple in design, consisting of little more than a combustion chamber and an exhaust nozzle for the hot gases to shoot out through.

Multi-stage rockets

As we have seen earlier, no single rocket is powerful enough to launch an object into space. We must use a step rocket, also called a multi-stage rocket, consisting of a number of separate rockets linked together. The first, or booster, stage of the step rocket is enormous. The *Saturn 5* booster, for example, consists of five separate rockets clustered together and is about fifty-seven metres long. It is so huge because it must contain the vast amount of fuel it needs to burn to thrust itself and the other stages into the air. In fact the rocket consists mainly of fuel, which the engines then burn at the rate of several thousand kilograms *every second*.

The first stage does all the hard work of the launching. It lifts the maximum load through the densest part of the atmosphere, where the air resistance is highest. Close to the earth gravity is at its maximum, too. The booster fires for about two minutes and thrusts the rocket about sixty kilometres up above the thickest part of the atmosphere.

Below One of the major advantages of the site is that it opens directly on to the ocean, with its thousands of kilometres of open space to the east. The site was first called Canaveral, and was desert wasteland. The construction of the vast site began in May, 1950. The name was later altered to Cape Kennedy as a tribute to the late President Kennedy, but has since changed back to Cape Canaveral. The space centre itself is called the Kennedy Space Centre.

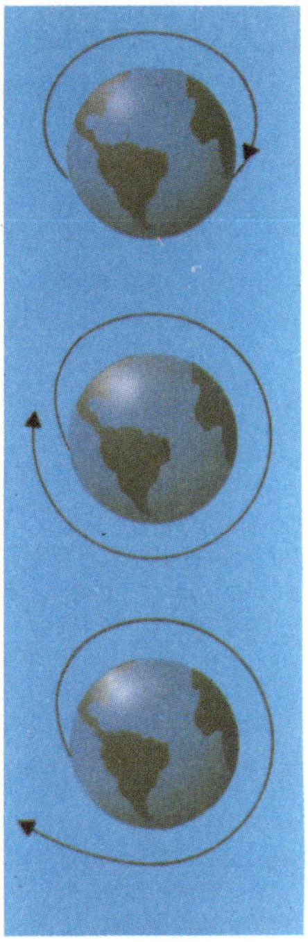

Above These three drawings illustrate spacecraft launchings at three different speeds. At the top the speed is insufficient for the spacecraft to maintain its orbit. The centre spacecraft has achieved the correct orbital velocity. At the bottom the speed of the launching has been such that the spacecraft has escaped from earth's gravity.

Above Man's efforts to fly have led him to adopt many strange methods, such as wings, rocket motors and even skis. Such attempts often ended in disaster.

Speed is about 9,600 kilometres an hour. There the booster burns out and falls away. The second stage fires for five or six minutes and boosts the speed of the now-lighter craft to about 24,000 kilometres an hour at an altitude of a hundred and fifty kilometres or so. Then the second stage falls away and the third stage fires to thrust what is left of the rocket into orbit at a speed of about 27,000 kilometres an hour. Then the third stage is usually jettisoned, leaving the spacecraft on its own circling around the earth.

'On its own' is not really quite accurate because the third stage is in orbit, too, though usually some distance away. In fact there is an enormous amount of such space 'junk' consisting of spent rocket stages floating uselessly in orbit. In time they could well become a safety hazard for orbiting astronauts.

Staying in orbit

Just how does an artificial satellite stay up in orbit? You know that if you throw a ball through the air it travels a certain distance and then falls to the ground. The earth's gravity pulls it back. The harder you throw the ball, the faster and further it goes before falling back to the ground. For a short while, you are overcoming gravity by speed.

This is more or less what we must do to keep a satellite in orbit. We give it such a high speed that it 'falls' only the same amount as the earth curves. This means in effect that the satellite remains travelling parallel to the earth, that is – in orbit. The outward force on the satellite due to its motion is equal and opposite to the inward pull on it due to gravity. This is exactly the same as natural satellites travelling around their parent planets, such as the moon travelling around the earth.

Gravity gets weaker the farther we go from earth. Therefore the force, and hence the speed, required to keep a satellite in orbit is less the higher up it is. The speed a satellite must achieve to stay in orbit is called the orbital velocity. At 160 kilometres above the earth, the orbital velocity is about 28,000 kilometres an hour. At 1,600 kilometres high it has dropped to about 25,400 kilometres an hour. At 384,000 kilometres it is only 3,650 kilometres an hour. This is the speed at which the moon circles the earth.

'Circles' is not really an accurate description of the moon's motion. As we have seen earlier, the moon travels around the earth, and the earth and planets travel around the sun, not in circles but in ellipses. The same goes for artificial satellites, too. Very few travel in circular orbits. Most orbits are elliptical. The closest point of the orbit to earth is called the perigee; the farthest the apogee.

For a satellite to remain in orbit indefinitely, it must be launched high enough up to be clear of the earth's atmosphere. Otherwise the air resistance, or drag, on it will gradually slow it down until its speed is below orbital velocity. Then it will fall back to earth. Even 160 kilometres up there is enough atmosphere, even though it is very thin, to slow down a satellite quite quickly – probably within a year. Over 320 kilometres, however, we can for practical purposes say that drag is negligible.

The time a satellite takes to travel once around the earth is called its period. The higher the orbit, the greater is the period. The satellite not only has farther to go but is also travelling slower. For an orbit 160 kilometres up, the period is almost $1\frac{1}{2}$ hours. At 1,600 kilometres up, it has increased to almost 2 hours. At 384,000 kilometres up, it is almost 28 days. And, as we know, that is the time the moon takes to wax and wane.

Another interesting period is that at 35,800 kilometres up, when it takes a satellite twenty-four hours to go round the earth. This means that a satellite in that orbit travels around the earth in the same time that the earth itself rotates. Therefore to an observer on earth the satellite appears not to move in the sky. We call this special orbit a twenty-four hour, or stationary, orbit. It is extremely important for communications satellites.

Communications satellites

Communications satellites have been the most immediately useful of all the spacecraft launched by man. They pass on, or relay, telephone and telegraph messages and television programmes from one ground station to another. Being so high up they can relay programmes over a much wider area than a normal transmitter can. A communications satellite over the Atlantic Ocean, for example, can relay to and from Europe and the United States. The latest satellites can handle a number of different television channels and hundreds of telephone calls all at the same time.

These satellites are in a stationary orbit above the equator, which simplifies the transmitting and receiving arrangements. The early communications satellites, such as *Telstar* (1962), were in orbits and could relay messages from one particular station to another only for the time they were passing overhead. Special movable aerials were also required.

The satellite's radio receiver, amplifier and transmitter need electricity to work. An ordinary chemical battery, like the one used to supply electricity to a car, would be no use in space because it would soon run down. And there would be no means of recharging it. Communications satellites, like all kinds of satellites, are powered by special batteries which get their power from sunlight. The sun is always shining in space, and therefore the batteries never run down.

These solar batteries consist of a very large number of cells of a chemical element called silicon. When sunlight falls on silicon a tiny electric current is produced. Joining hundreds of these solar cells together produces enough electricity to power a satellite's equipment. In some satellites, the cells form part of the outer surface of the satellite itself. In others, the cells are arranged in flat panels which stick out of the sides of the satellite like wings.

Another kind of satellite which has proved useful is the weather satellite. It is equipped with television cameras and a variety of instruments which transmit pictures of cloud formations and other information back to earth. It is launched a few hundred kilometres up and circles the earth a number of times every day. And, because the earth is rotating, too, it scans a different part of the earth on every orbit. In this way a comprehensive and up-to-date picture of the weather situation throughout the world is obtained.

Scientists also launch an enormous number of satellites that do not immediately benefit man but add to his fundamental scientific knowledge of earth and the universe in general. These scientific satellites contain a variety of instruments to measure such things as magnetism and radiation.

Moon probes

Spacecraft sent to the moon or to the planets are generally called probes. From 1959 onwards the moon has been the target for an enormous number of probes. They were sent to take measurements and photographs not only to further scientific knowledge but also to prepare the way for the manned landings of 1969.

Below The anatomy of a satellite. Although each satellite is different, they all have basic systems in common. They have a structural system, to which other systems are attached, an instrument system, that supports and links equipment from cameras and telescopes to x-ray sensors and magnetometers, and a communications and control unit. Also on board are canisters of gas that is used as propellant for the satellite's manoeuvring system. Electrical power for the satellite is obtained from panels of solar cells.

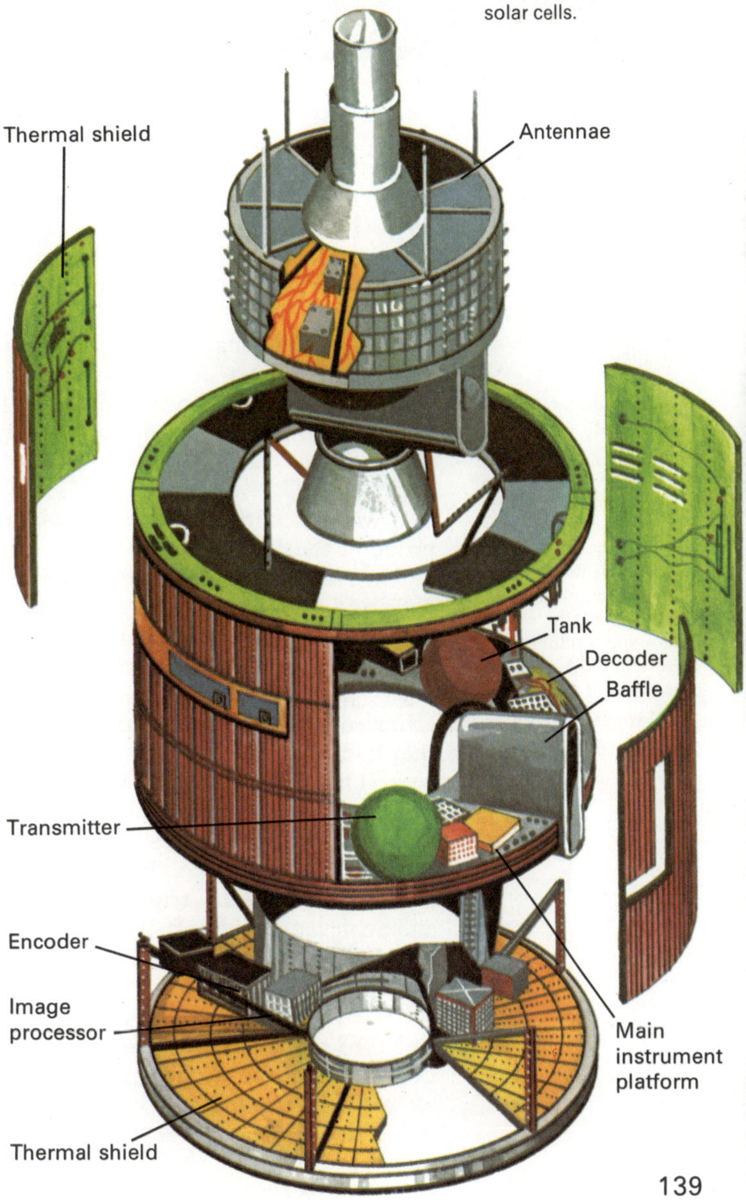

Above Landing on the moon by the Apollo spacecraft is illustrated in these four drawings. In the first is seen the spacecraft at the moment when the lunar module separates from the command module. The second shows the lunar module firing its retro-rocket for a soft touchdown on the moon's surface. Then the lunar module is shown taking off from the moon to blast itself back into orbit. Finally, the module joins up with the command module into which the crew transfer for the journey back to earth.

The first successful lunar probe was *Lunik 1* which flew past the moon, about 7,200 kilometres up, in January 1959. It then disappeared into space and became a tiny planet circling endlessly around the solar system. Eight months later *Lunik 2* actually crash-landed on the lunar surface, the first man-made object to reach another world. Less than a month later *Lunik 3* sent back to earth a picture of the far side of the moon that we do not normally see.

It was not until 1962 that a *Ranger* probe of the United States struck the moon. However, later *Ranger* craft, in 1964 and 1965, sent back spectacular television pictures of the moon's surface before crash-landing on it.

In January 1966 the Russians achieved with their probe *Luna 9* what they had twice failed to do the previous year. They soft-landed an instrument capsule on the moon which sent back the first close-up pictures of rocks and craters on the surface. Four months later the Americans triumphed, too, and achieved a true soft-landing of an entire *Surveyor* probe. This sent back thousands of television pictures of the surface. Later *Surveyor* probes in 1967 and 1968 made an on-the-spot chemical analysis of the surface material and scooped a furrow in it to test its texture. All of the evidence from these probes indicated that the surface was firm enough to permit a safe manned landing. It was apparent that the dust layer covering it was only very shallow and not deep as had been feared. Both Russia and the United States had meanwhile sent several probes into lunar orbit to make a comprehensive photographic survey of both the near and far sides of the moon, again with particular emphasis on possible manned landing sites.

Launching a probe to the moon requires a lot more power than launching a satellite into an earth orbit. The technique which uses least fuel is to launch a probe from the earth at a speed of 39,400 kilometres an hour and then let it coast the rest of the way in a long, curved path. When coasting, the probe is said to be in free fall. On its way to the moon, the probe is gradually slowed down by the pull of the earth's gravity until, at about 320,000 kilometres out, it is moving very slowly indeed. At this point the gravity of the moon becomes stronger than the gravity of the earth. And the probe begins to accelerate again, towards the moon. If the launching speed were much less than 39,400 kilometres an hour, the probe would not reach this point where the moon's gravity is stronger. Therefore the probe would be drawn back towards earth.

Aiming at the moon

Aiming a probe at the moon is not

simply a matter of pointing it and firing. Remember that the moon is a moving target. When you throw a ball to someone who is running, you do not throw it directly at him. If you did, you would miss him completely because while the ball you threw was travelling, he would be moving on, too. Therefore you aim your ball at a point in front of him so that he and the ball arrive at the same time. And this is what we must do to make sure a probe reaches the moving moon. A probe takes about 60 hours to reach the moon. During this time the moon travels about 220,000 kilometres through space. We must therefore aim the probe 220,000 kilometres in front of the moon at launch.

Of course, the whole thing is much more complicated than this. And the matter of being a few kilometres an hour out on the launching speed or a fraction of a degree off the precise course makes all the difference between success and failure. Usually, therefore, slight corrections have to be made once or twice during the flight to bring the probe back on to course. The probes are therefore equipped with small rocket motors which can be fired by remote control from the earth to manoeuvre the probe into the correct flight path.

As the probe nears the moon, it gets faster and faster under the attraction of the moon's gravity. If its flight were not checked it would smash to pieces on the surface at more than 8,000 kilometres an hour. For the probe to go into orbit around the moon, it must be slowed down and correctly positioned. The manoeuvres are carried out by using the probe's rocket motor again. To slow it down to a suitable orbital velocity, the motor is fired for a while against the direction of travel, as it were, backwards. This is known as retro-braking. If the intention is to make a 'soft' landing on the moon's surface, the speed is reduced so much by retro-braking that the probe drops down from orbit. Of course, as it drops from orbit, it accelerates once more due to gravity. To reduce the speed to a safe landing speed therefore, the retro-rocket is fired the whole way down. Remember, there is no atmosphere on the moon to aid the vehicle's braking.

Probes to the planets

The problems of sending probes to the planets are similar to sending moon probes, only much greater because of the enormous distances involved. Venus and Mars are planets 'closest' to earth. But the nearest Venus comes to us is about 38 million kilometres; Mars about 54 million kilometres. Most of the time, however, these planets are a lot further away. It is only at times of favourable opposition that they come as close as that. And

Above The first living creatures to leave the earth were a sheep, a cock, and a duck, in a Montgolfier hot-air balloon in 1783. The Russian dog Laika followed in this tradition when she became the first creature to travel in space.

Right *Pioneer 10*, a probe which flew past Jupiter in December 1973. It was followed by the near identical *Pioneer II*. They provided pictures of the turbulent clouds around the planet.

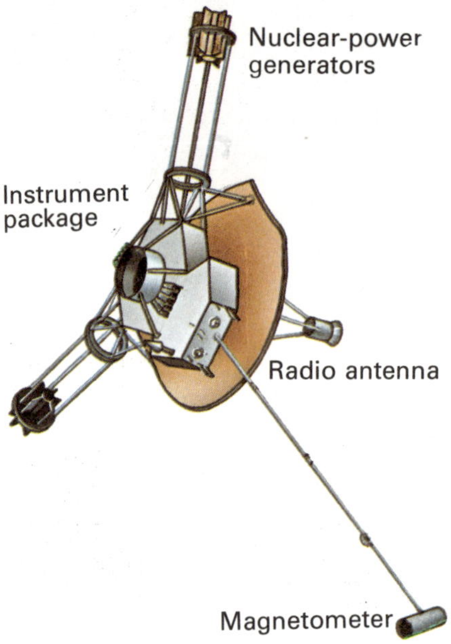

38 and 54 million kilometres is rather a different matter from the 384,000 kilometres to the moon.

Nevertheless, successful probes have been sent to both planets and much valuable knowledge has been gained about them. The Russians launched the first interplanetary probe, to Venus, in February 1961. But, although the flight path was accurate, the communication system failed. The United States scored the first success with their *Mariner 2* probe, launched in August 1962, which passed within about 34,000 kilometres of Venus four months later. They achieved an outstanding feat of communications with their *Mariner 4* probe to Mars, launched in October 1964. This success was followed by others by both the United States and Russia. The American *Mariner 10* in 1974 was the first probe to photograph the thick cloud layer around Venus, and further Russian probes in 1975 photographed its stony surface. In 1976 the American *Viking 1* and *Viking 2 Landers* conducted valuable life-seeking experiments on the soil from Mars and sent back some very enlightening pictures of the surface.

For a probe to travel to the planets, it must leave the vicinity of the earth and escape from the earth's gravitational pull. To be able to do this, the probe must be given an initial speed of at least 40,000 kilometres an hour, or 11 kilometres a second. This speed is known as the escape velocity. A probe launched with this velocity will travel away from earth until it is no longer influenced by gravity. At this point its speed relative to the earth will be zero because all of its speed has been used up in escaping. It therefore remains in an orbit close to that of the earth and becomes a tiny planet circling the sun at the same speed as the earth does.

If we increase the speed of the probe above escape velocity, the probe ends up with a different speed from that of the earth. Therefore it moves away from it in a different orbit around the sun. By carefully selecting the velocity and direction of launching we can arrange that the probe's new orbit takes it outwards towards Mars or inwards towards Venus. The new orbit is called a transfer orbit, because it transfers the probe from an earth orbit to the orbit of Mars or Venus.

In 1977, American space scientists at NASA launched the Voyager 1 and 2 space probes on journeys of exploration to the outer planets and moons of the Solar System. Some extremely interesting photographs have already been sent back from Jupiter and Saturn by the spacecraft, and much important new information has now been gained. Voyager 2 flew past Uranus in 1986, and is now on a journey to Sirius.

Below Saturn photographed by *Voyager 1* in November 1980. The lighted crescent of the planet is visible through the rings.

Space laboratories

Laboratories, placed in orbit around the earth, have been an important development in recent years. These have a number of uses. The atmosphere around the earth is essential for life but it has a disadvantage – it blankets out much of the information from space. Some electromagnetic radiation, such as X-rays and gamma rays, and cosmic rays cannot pass through the atmosphere. Satellites and laboratories orbiting above this blanket are greatly adding to our knowledge of space, as well as observing the earth.

Space laboratories are helping astronauts learn to live and work for long periods in space. In 1980, two Russians spent a record 185 days in space. However this record was broken again in 1984.

Out in space there is virtually no atmosphere nor force of gravity. Conditions of weightlessness and vacuum provide an opportunity for much important scientific research. In addition, materials for earth, such as new drugs, alloys and glass, can be manufactured in space, which would be difficult or impossible to produce on earth.

The first laboratory to be launched was the Russian Salyut 1 in April 1971. Unfortunately, the first few years of the Salyut programme were dogged with misfortune, including the deaths of three cosmonauts on board Soyuz 11, while it was returning them to earth after a 23-day stay on Salyut. But by 1975 it was going more smoothly, and since the launch of Salyut 6 in 1977, and Salyut 7 in 1982, crews have been staying on board for longer and longer periods.

The larger American Skylab was launched in May 1973 and was carried into space by Apollo craft. Three teams of astronauts stayed on Skylab, the last returning to earth in February 1974. Then, in 1975 the first joint space venture between the Russians and Americans took place – an Apollo-Soyuz link-up in space. The crews trained together first, and after the successful docking they entered each other's craft through the airlocks.

In 1983, the first Spacelab was taken into orbit by the Space Shuttle. Built by the European Space Agency, it is not left in space but remains on board the Shuttle in orbit for a week and is then returned to earth.

Space Shuttle

The huge rocket craft which carried people into space were very wasteful. As we have seen, only a small part of the craft, the command module, returned to earth while the rest was unusable debris. The American Space Shuttle, nearly all reusable, was launched in 1981, and followed in 1988 by the first Russian shuttle.

Below Spacelab. Inside the pressurized working areas, up to four scientists can conduct a wide variety of experiments.

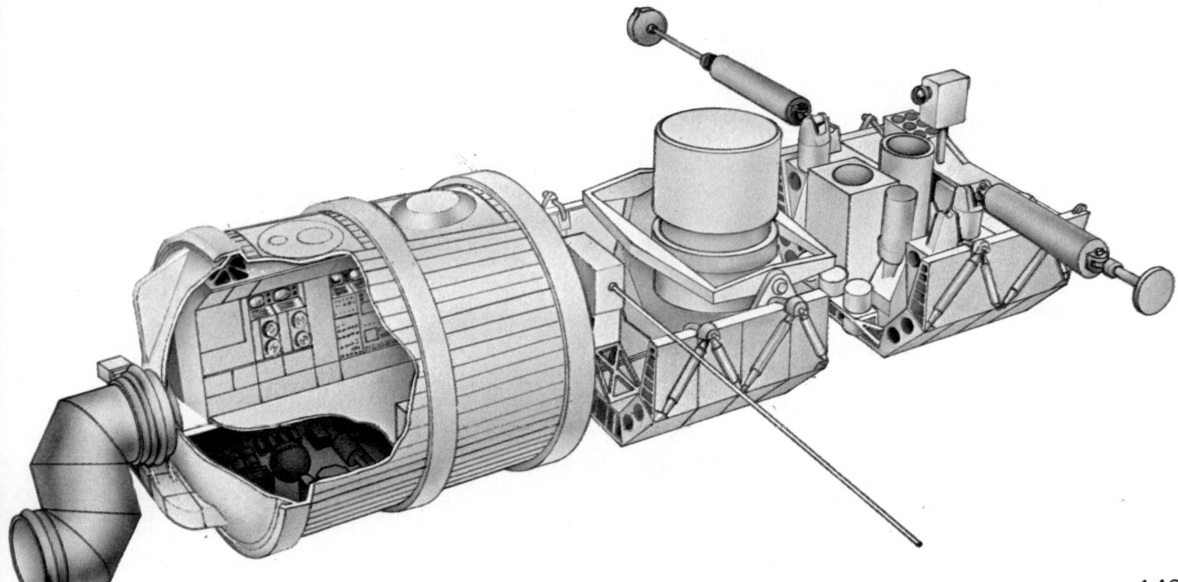

Above Astronaut Bruce McCandless participating in the historic extra-vehicular activity (EVA) which took place from the Space Shuttle, *Challenger*, in February 1984. For the spacewalk he used a nitrogen-propelled, hand-controlled device called the manned manoeuvring unit (MMU), which allows for much greater mobility than that given to previous spacewalkers who had to use restrictive tethers.

The Space Shuttle's first flight was launched on 12th April 1981. It is roughly the size of a jet airliner, about 37 metres long with a wingspan of nearly 24 metres. The body of the craft is made of light materials, mainly aluminium alloys, covered with heat-resistant tiles. It can house a crew of three, and up to four passengers. In addition, a massive 30 tonnes of equipment and parts can be carried into orbit.

The Shuttle is launched by three main rockets and two solid-fuel boosters. As it ascends, the boosters are released and float back to earth by parachute, to be recovered and used again. Once in orbit, the tank which fuels the main rockets is released, and this is the only part of the craft which is not reusable.

When it has delivered its cargo and passengers, it can bring back up to 15 tonnes of equipment for disposal or repair. On the return trip, rockets are fired to make it descend from orbit. It then glides down, slowed by the earth's atmosphere, and lands on a runway, just like an ordinary aircraft! Within a week it is ready for another flight.

The Space Shuttle can lift satellites, laboratories, spare parts and personnel into orbit. It is hoped that, in the future, this or a larger craft could carry parts for larger stations, to be assembled in space. Such stations would provide a range of exciting possibilities. They could be power stations, collecting the sun's energy, undiluted by the earth's atmosphere. This could be converted into electricity and then microwaves, and beamed down to earth. Larger factories could provide more useful materials for earth. And a station could form a stepping stone into space, bringing nearer the day when people will travel to other planets or even other stars.

The world of plants and animals

Contents

147 The world of plants
Life from the soil – Origin of plants – Plant cells – Plant reproduction – Cell tissues – Chlorophyll – Photosynthesis – How a plant breathes – The plant kingdom

155 Thallophytes
Algae – Fungi – Bacteria – Antibiotics and viruses

159 Bryophytes

159 Pteridophytes

160 Spermatophytes
Gymnosperms
Angiosperms
Seed dispersal – Classification of fruits – The root – How the root grows – Storing food – The stem – Shapes of stems – The leaf – Leaf classification – Stomata – Inflorescence and flowers – Petals and sepals – Pollination

173 Plant adaptations
Hydrophytes – Xerophytes – Insect-eating plants – Parasites and saprophytes – Epiphytes

176 The uses of plants
Foods – Fruits – Oil crops – Beverages – Wood – Fibres – Medicines and drugs – Sugar – Rubber – Dyes – Tobacco – Finding new plants

183 The world of animals
How animals live – Food chains – Classification of animals – The evolution theory

188 The story in the rocks
The first fossils – The age of shellfish – The early vertebrates – The walking fishes – The 'halfway' animals – The great invasion – Early reptiles – The age of dinosaurs – The chalk period – The dawn period – The rise of mammals – The beginnings of man – The ice age – Modern man

199 Animals of today
Coelenterates
Annelids
Parasitic worms
Molluscs
Arthropods
Insects – Arachnids – Millepedes and centipedes – Crustaceans
Echinoderms
Vertebrates
Fishes – Amphibians – Reptiles – Birds – Mammals

Above Beautiful flowers, such as these herbaceous paeonies, are not only pleasing to look at – they play a vital part in the scheme of nature giving nectar to bees and other insects.

The world of plants

Man's existence on earth depends on all the other living matter around him and a large part of this belongs to the plant kingdom. Without the extraordinary variety of living organisms that make up the world of plants animal life could not survive and our planet would be a barren and lifeless world of deserts.

Some plants are of more use than others. High on the list of plants upon which our lives depend are the food crops. The grass family is probably the most important of these, for it supplies the world with its wheat, rice, oats, barley and sugar cane. After a certain amount of processing, these are all eaten more or less as they are grown.

Other grasses provide the basic foodstuff for cattle and sheep, on which man depends for milk and meat. Then there are root crops such as potatoes and carrots, as well as the great variety of fruits. Some plants give us beverages like tea and coffee. Medicinal plants give us quinine and morphine, and microscopic plants belonging to the group known as fungi provide antibiotics such as penicillin and streptomycin to fight disease. We use plant materials to provide us with heat by the burning of coal and wood. Other sources of fuel are the underground deposits of oil formed about 300 million years ago. Other plants help to clothe us and provide wood for building.

When all these necessities have helped to make our lives more comfortable, we can then plant our gardens with flowers. Such flowers are not only pleasing to look at but are important in their turn in the huge cycle of natural events, for they give nectar to the bees and other insects which are an essential part of the balanced world of nature.

Life from the soil

Man sometimes upsets this balance and there are many spectacular examples of this in the world. A species of cactus called prickly pear was once introduced from America into Australia where it found conditions so favourable to its rate of growth that it

Above Small woodland plants flourish in rich soil shaded by the leaves of trees.

Above Prickly pear *(Opuntia vulgaris)*, the species of cactus that was introduced into Australia in the 19th century. It was finally destroyed by an insect called *Cactoblastis*.

quickly spread and took over vast areas of land which soon became an impenetrable and useless tract. In this case a cure was possible, for a caterpillar which ate nothing but this cactus was also introduced. With such a quantity of its food growing in one area the caterpillar too spread rapidly and the prickly pear was soon wiped out in much of the land it had once destroyed.

In the past, man has felled large forests to obtain wood for building and to create clear areas for cultivation. This was before he realised that the trees were the very reason for his land being fertile and well watered. Their roots, as we shall see later on, seek out moisture in the soil below, often at a considerable depth, and after using some of this for its life processes, the tree loses the excess through pores, called stomata, in its leaves.

This causes damper air in and above the forests and in consequence a more suitable atmosphere for the trees and other plants to grow in. Their leaves give shade to the ground beneath and prevent the hot sun from evaporating all the moisture from the surface layers of the soil, so that other smaller plants can develop in the rich woodland soil. In autumn the leaves fall and eventually rot down to give the leaf-mould and humus (organic matter which has decomposed in the soil) which is essential if soils are to support rich vegetation.

When forests were removed by man, the sun scorched the ground, the atmosphere was dry, the soil soon lost its fertility with the lack of rotting vegetable matter, and the area became barren. Without any trees to provide shelter or roots to bind the soil together the wind and rain removed the surface soil, in some cases down to the bare rocks beneath.

So we can see by these examples that the world of plants is not a haphazard arrangement but a balanced society, built up over hundreds of millions of years and much thought must be given to any activity which might upset this, for our lives depend on the vegetation around us.

Origin of plants

No one knows for sure how life began. It was certainly a long process and it is likely that plants began to evolve before animals. Life began in the seas during Pre-Cambrian times (that is during the period of about 4,000 million years which followed the estimated date of the origin of the earth) and the earliest living things were microscopically small, probably similar to one-celled plants which exist today. At some stage in evolution they would have progressed from being free swimming organisms and anchored themselves to rock under water. At a later stage land vegetation somehow began when plants 'migrated' to the land, possibly by being washed ashore as seaweed.

Biology is the science of living things and includes botany (the science of plants) and zoology (the science of animal life). In general terms a plant is distinguished from an animal by its ability to manufacture its own food supply. Many minute organisms are in fact a mixture of plant and animal and botanists and zoologists do not always agree as to the way they should be classified.

Plant cells

Plants are built up from units called cells. These cell units can be thought of as the bricks which are used to build houses. Although the bricks themselves are very similar to each other, they can be joined together in many ways to create buildings of different shapes and sizes. In much the same way all plants, ranging from daffodils to oak trees, are composed of different arrangements of cells. But unlike bricks used for building houses, individual cells do differ to some extent according to their purpose in the building of a plant.

Cells are far too small to be seen by the naked eye, and so are some plants which are composed of only two or three cells, or even just one single cell. In the ordinary way it is only when such tiny individual plants are grouped

Left Two plants of the Carboniferous period are shown with specimens of their barks. On the left is *Sigillaria* and on the right, *Lepidodendron*. Both these plants grew to a height of about thirty metres.
Below This chart shows the development of plant life through the prehistoric ages.

Development of plant life

Age in millions of years	Periods		
4700	Pre-Cambrian	Very little known about plant life. Seaweeds, fungi and bacteria may have existed.	
570	Cambrian	Seaweeds certainly existed. It is possible there may have been land plants.	Age of algae
500	Ordovician	Various kinds of sea-weeds (green and red).	
440	Silurian	The earliest land plants.	
395	Devonian	First true seed plants. Ferns, horsetails and seed-ferns.	Age of early land plants
345	Carboniferous	Evergreen plants grew in profusion, including giant club-mosses.	Age of fern like plants
280	Permian	Increase of coniferous trees.	
225	Triassic	Cycads, conifers (including ginkgo) and ferns.	Age of gymnosperms
195	Jurassic	Plant life abundant and varied but still coniferous.	
136	Cretaceous	Development of flowering plants and 'modern plants.	
54	Eocene	Vegetation of modern aspect. More trees than herbaceous plants.	
38	Oligocene	Grassland increased and forests dwindled.	
26	Miocene	Grassland now firmly established all over the world.	Age of flowering plants
7	Pliocene	Modern temperate plants existed, especially in Europe.	
2	Pleistocene	Many of the temperate plants driven south by increasing cold.	

Right The parts of a typical plant cell are shown in this drawing. They are **1** chloroplast, **2** grana, **3** ribosomes, **4** endoplasmic reticulum, **5** nucleolus, **6** nuclear membrane, **7** nucleus, **8** vacuole, **9** golgi complex, **10** mitochondrion, **11** cell wall, **12** cell membrane. Cells are the basic units of living matter, and all plants and animals are made up of cells.

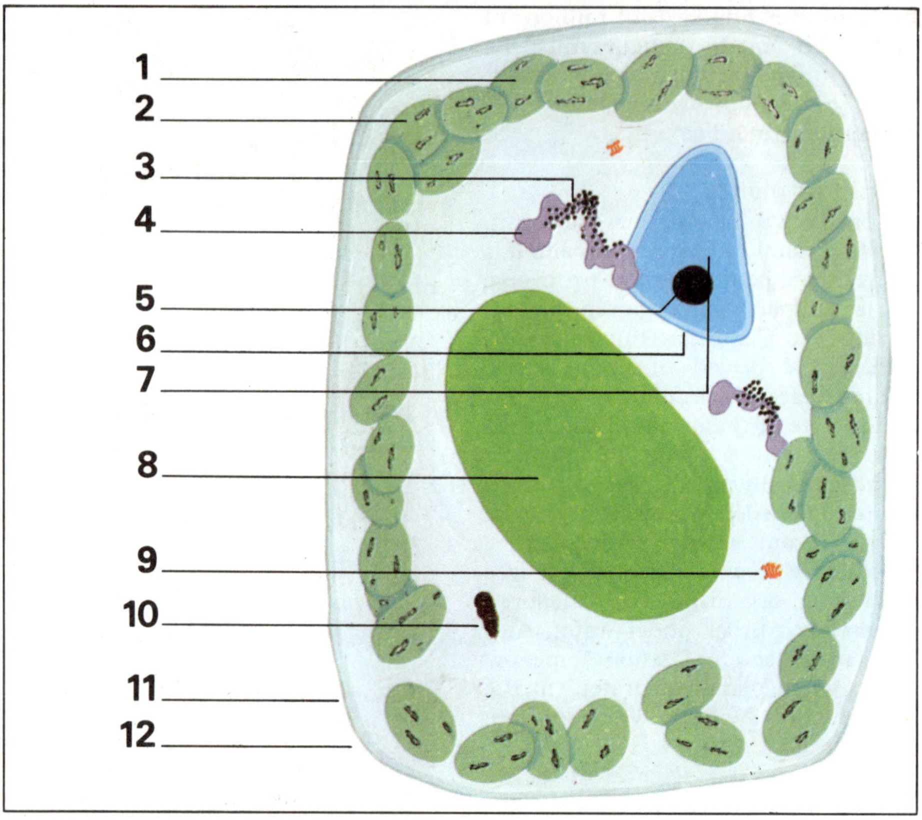

Below A model of the atomic structure of chlorophyll. It is made up of carbon (yellow), hydrogen (red), oxygen (green), nitrogen (blue) and a single atom of magnesium (black).

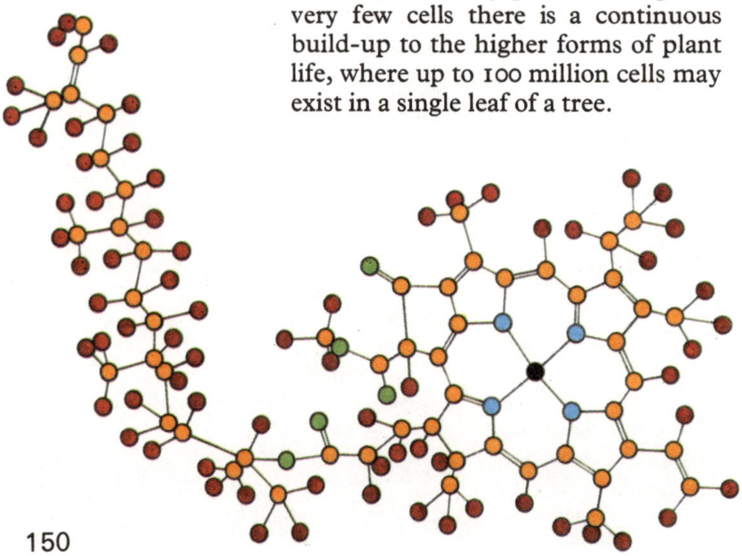

together in millions that we can see them. The green slime which collects in stagnant water is a good example. A more spectacular colony of individual plants exists in the Red Sea, so named because a primitive plant in its waters contains cells with a reddish pigment. Gathered together in millions, these plants give a definite red tinge to the water.

From these tiny plants of single or very few cells there is a continuous build-up to the higher forms of plant life, where up to 100 million cells may exist in a single leaf of a tree.

New cells can only be created by the division of an existing cell and even the largest tree, containing countless millions of cells, began life as a single cell. The process of cell division is confined to areas known as growing points. These are nearly all located at the tips of the roots and shoots. The entire life cycle of some primitive plants may last only one or two hours, while an advanced plant such as a yew tree can live for hundreds of years.

Plant reproduction

When a cell – also known as a spore – divides, first into equal parts to form two new cells, and then into four and eight, and so on, this is called asexual reproduction. Primitive plants and the growing points of higher forms of plant life depend on asexual reproduction. The other type of reproduction is called sexual. This is a much more complicated process and it results in the production of a seed.

Sexual reproduction in plants involves the formation of two special types of cell called gametes. Neither can increase without the other but when they are brought into contact they join together into a single cell which in time will develop into a new plant. This contact between the two types of gamete takes place in flowering plants after the pollen (the male gamete) has been transferred to the stigma, which is the female part of a plant.

Since the English chemist and physicist Robert Hooke (1635-1703) first identified plant cells through his microscope in 1665, botanists have gone on to discover that the cell itself is made up of several different parts. To start with, cells are composed of a living substance called protoplasm, which is encased in a non-living cell wall made of cellulose. This wall gives the cell its shape and strength and protects the protoplasm, which can, however, sometimes be kept alive without a cellulose wall around it.

Cell tissues

The simplest forms of plant life, like bacteria and algae, contain cells of only one basic type, but in higher plant forms the different types of cell are themselves grouped together to form tissues. Many different types of tissue go into the making of highly developed plant forms like trees and flowers. For example there has to be some way of getting water and food from a root in the ground to the leaves. To do this there are special types of cell joined together to form what is called vascular tissue. This can be seen clearly as veins on the large leaf of a horse-chestnut tree.

Substances need to be able to pass from one cell to the next quickly and easily. So the cells are elongated and joined end to end, with a hole at each end to provide a continuous passage from one cell to the next. Within the vascular tissues these long chains of cells are called vessels. These vessels can also develop thick sides which lend support to the stem of a flower or the trunk of a tree. Other types of cell tissue go into the production of leaves, flowers or such protective growths as thorns.

Protoplasm itself is an almost colourless jelly-like liquid composed mainly of water, together with various proteins and other solids. The most important part of the protoplasm in each cell is the nucleus, enclosed in a thin wall of its own called the nuclear membrane. It is the nucleus which holds the key to the cell's own development, and beyond this to the development and character of the entire plant. For within the nucleus are the genes, grouped together in thread-like bodies called chromosomes. It is these which determine, for example, the colour of a plant's flowers or whether it will grow upright and unsupported or develop into a creeper.

Above Using this compound microscope, Robert Hooke, the English physicist, made many detailed drawings of the structure of insects. Hooke was one of the most remarkable men of science during the 17th century. Apart from his experiments which established the science of microscopy, and his original thoughts on gravitation and the flying machine, he invented a balance spring for watches and experimented in optics, surgery, architecture, music, astronomy and engineering.

Chlorophyll

The green colouring of leaves is caused by substances in the cells which are of great importance to all green plants. These substances also cause other colours in plants, such as the red in carrots, but those called chloroplasts are the really important ones. They contain the chemical chlorophyll (from two Greek words meaning green and leaf), which gives the majority of plants their familiar green colour and enables them to manufacture their own food and so maintain an independent life.

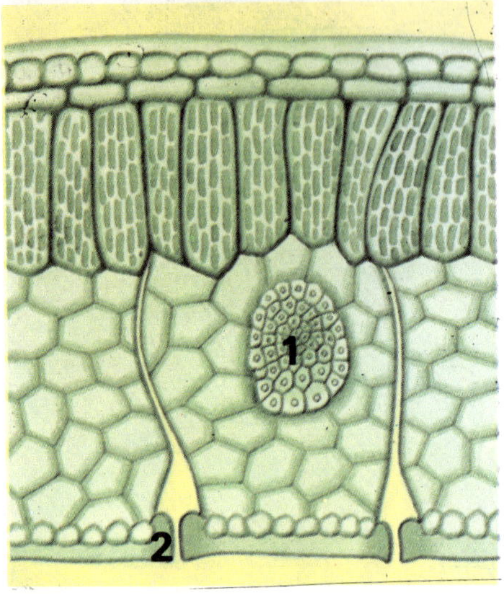

Right This cross section through a leaf shows **1** a vein and **2** the stomata. A leaf breathes in air through its stomata, which are openings on the leaf's surface formed by pairs of cells. One leaf may have hundreds of thousands of stomata on its surface.

Above Green plants need sunlight to grow properly. The two plants on the left have been in the shade and are weak, with few flowers or leaves. Those on the right have grown strongly, with many flowers.

Plants which have no chloroplasts, and hence no chlorophyll, must rely on some other source of food. Some are parasites and live entirely on other plants and others are partly self-supporting and partly parasitic.

Photosynthesis

Ordinary green plants, however, depend very much on chlorophyll, which will normally only appear if the plant is exposed to light. This can be seen in a potato, which is a whitish colour when dug up from the soil, but if left on the surface for some time will turn green. In an ordinary green leaf the chlorophyll is carrying on a process called photosynthesis (which means the building up by means of light) and to do this it gets its energy from sunlight.

Photosynthesis is a complicated process whereby the water and carbon dioxide (a gas) absorbed by plants from the air are converted into glucose sugar. Some of this food substance may be used right away by the plant to maintain its strength and help it to grow. What is left over will be converted into starch and stored in the leaves. At the same time as the sugar is being made, oxygen (the gas which forms part of the air and water and which all forms of life must breathe in order to live) is given off and this can easily be seen in a fish tank on a sunny day, when the green water weeds give off bubbles.

Other conditions such as the brightness of the light and the state of the temperature affect photosynthesis. In cold weather, in poor light, the rate of photosynthesis is very slow. Also, as carbon dioxide and water are involved in the process there must be an ample supply of both to keep the reaction supplied with raw material. If the light is removed altogether for a long time, say a period of weeks, the chlorophyll cannot do its work and the green colour disappears. The plant looks yellowish, cannot function properly and will eventually die.

In some plants far more food is produced than the plant needs and it can be put into long-term store as starch, such as in the tuber of a potato. Thus with the help of chlorophyll a potato can, by photosynthesis, store up the sun's energy in the form of starch, then when the plant requires materials and energy, convert the starch back to sugar and transport it to the area where it is needed most, that is the growing points.

How a plant breathes

In order that a plant may make use of this energy stored away as starch, the reverse of photosynthesis must take place. The starch is converted back to sugar which then has to be broken down again and the energy released. This process is known as respiration, or breathing. Unlike photosynthesis it does not need light or chlorophyll to work. In fact it goes on all the time through the life of the plant, although the speed may vary a lot according to its activity. For example, resting seeds are scarcely respiring at all, whereas young seedlings are doing so very actively. Very simply, the cells in this case take in oxygen and use this to break the sugar down into its original substances – carbon dioxide and water – and at the same time energy is released. This process is brought about by the action of chemicals known as enzymes.

The energy released by this process gives the protoplasm the necessary power to carry on its activities of growing and dividing. Not all the sugar is broken down in this way to provide energy. Some must be used to provide material for further building within the plant. But the proteins which are essential for the build-up of protoplasm itself are very complicated substances and cannot be made by the transformation of glucose sugar alone. Other elements from the soil, such as sulphur, phosphorus and nitrogen, must be added, and these are combined in living cells with glucose to form these proteins.

Some of the sugar is left untouched to remain in store for any difficult period ahead, such as during the winter period of inactivity when photosynthesis has practically stopped, when it can be called upon as a reserve. Glucose is easily transported through a plant because it is very soluble in water and will travel without hindrance, but it is not a suitable substance to put into store. For this purpose it must be converted back into starch again or, to a much smaller extent, into fats.

In primitive plants the starch must be stored more or less in the same place as it is manufactured, especially in single-celled plants, whereas in higher forms such as the potato it can be put away in special organs designed for this purpose. The sunflower is an example of a plant which stores its reserves, in the form of fats, in its seeds. Others, such as sugar cane, have reserves of food in their stems. Then there are plants which store their reserves in fruits or seeds in order to give the new seedling plant a good start in life before it has a sufficient root of its own.

Left This drawing illustrates the oxygen cycle. Oxygen is given off by green plants in daylight, thus constantly renewing the supply in the air. Animals breathe in oxygen and breathe out carbon dioxide (CO_2). In turn the carbon dioxide in the air is used by green plants in the process of photosynthesis. By removing the carbon dioxide this process also purifies the air.

Left The most important function of the roots is to absorb water from the soil. The water is carried up the stalk or trunk of the plant to the leaves where food for the whole plant is manufactured.

The plant kingdom

Man's first interest in plants must have been as a source of food and, later, as a source of drugs for the treatment of diseases. The first people to study plants scientifically were the ancient Greeks. Theophrastus (372?-286? BC), a pupil of Aristotle, wrote a *History of Plants*, and Dioscorides, another Greek writer of the 1st or 2nd century AD, compiled a *Materia Medica* listing the medicinal use of plants which remained the principal information on the subject until the 16th century.

Several attempts were made during the 16th and 17th centuries to classify plants into some ordered system. Then in the 18th century Linnaeus (Carl Linné) (1707-78), the Swedish botanist, began a system of naming plants which has continued in use more or less unchanged to this day. When

Right This chart illustrates the family tree of the creeping buttercup plant. The whole plant kingdom can be broken down in this way to show the position of each plant within its group.

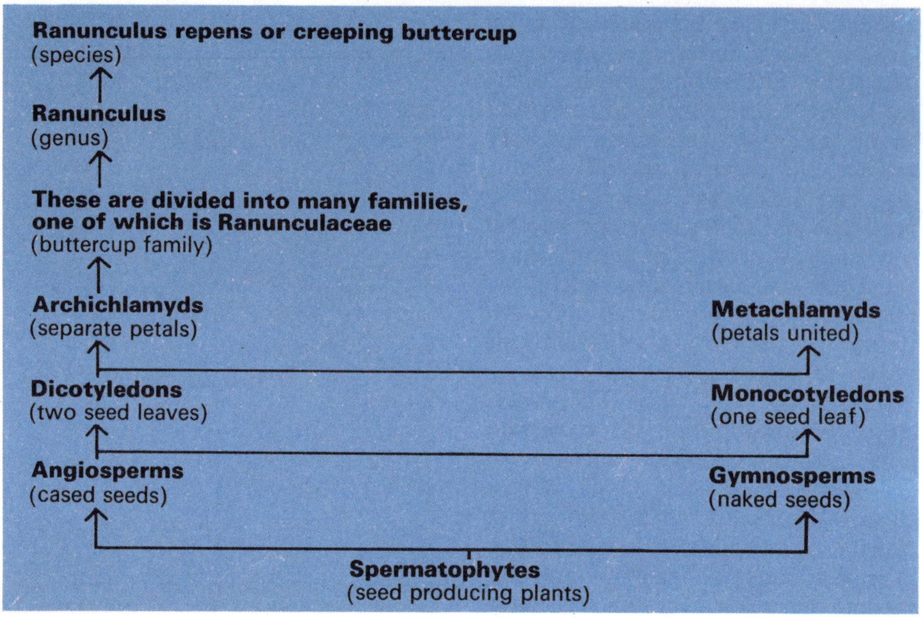

Right Two flowers commonly called bluebells. Left is the English *Scilla nonscripta*; and right, the Scottish *Campanula rotundifolia,* also called the harebell.

Linnaeus began to name and classify plants it was natural that he should use Latin, for this was the universal language spoken by all learned men of his time. Today, although Latin is a 'dead' language, it is still convenient to use it for the naming of plants because it can be understood all over the world. Since it is estimated that there are now about 350,000 different types of living plants the need for a universal system of classification is obvious.

Most plants have common names as well, but these are of much less value for they mean something only to the people of the country or district in which the names are used. There is a good example of this within the British Isles. The familiar bluebell of the English woods is not the same plant at all in the north, for the bluebell of Scotland belongs to another family altogether. Given their Latin names there could be no confusion over these two flowers, for the English bluebell is in the genus *Scilla* and the Scottish one in the genus *Campanula*.

Each species of plant belongs to a genus, which in turn belongs to a family. Thus the common creeping buttercup is in the family Ranunculaceae, the genus is *Ranunculus* and the species *Ranunculus repens* (*repens* meaning creeping).

The whole plant kingdom can be broken down this way into species, but first of all there are four major divisions. These are thallophytes (from two Greek words meaning a young shoot and a plant), which include algae (seaweeds), fungi and bacteria; bryophytes (from the Greek, a moss or liverwort) which include mosses; pteridophytes (from the Greek, a fern), which include ferns; and spermatophytes (from the Greek, a seed), which are seed-producing plants. Spermatophytes are divided into gymnosperms (naked seeds), which include fir trees, and angiosperms (cased seeds), the common flowering plants.

Most of the familiar plants around us are angiosperms and these can be further divided into monocotyledons (meaning one seed leaf) and dicotyledons (meaning two seed leaves), depending partly on whether the young seedling produces one leaf or two when it germinates.

Above Seaweeds show a great variety of form and colour. The types shown are **1** *Ulvą,* **2** *Nitophyllum,* **3** *Laminaria*, **4** *Laurencia*, and **5** *Draparnaldia.*

Thallophytes

This division is made up of algae (including seaweeds), fungi and bacteria. Of these, algae are probably the most primitive of all plants on earth at present.

Algae

Although there are freshwater species the majority of algae live in the sea, and the various seaweeds found at low tide are familiar examples. A lot of the most primitive of these plants are single-celled and invisible to the naked eye, whereas the large, more advanced seaweeds are made up of countless cells which may be divided into groups or tissues performing different tasks. Such plants may have primitive roots. These algae are very similar to other plants in the way they obtain their food, for they contain chlorophyll and photosynthesis takes place in the same way as it does in the advanced forms of plant life. Although many are green, quite a number have pigments in their cells which are stronger colours than green, giving the algae red, brown or even bluish colours.

Their method of increase can be either by simple division of the original plant or by sexual reproduction. There are thousands of different species of algae and it would be impossible here to describe even a small proportion of them, but one or two examples can be taken to show what life-forms exist in this group.

Some of the tiny single-celled species are capable of movement and such a plant is *Chlamydomonas*, which is found in ponds and ditches. It is roundish in shape and is built up in the same basic way as other cells. At one end are two thread-like 'arms' which project through the cell wall. These are called flagella, and by waving them around the cell can move in the water. The cell contains a nucleus and chloroplasts for manufacturing food, and in addition an orange-coloured object known as the 'eye-spot'. This helps the *Chlamydomonas* find its way towards brighter light, and in doing so gives the chloroplast a better chance to produce food.

Other single-celled algae do not go through life individually, but group themselves into a colony and hundreds or thousands together may just be visible without a microscope. These types are interesting in that they all use their flagella together and move as a whole colony towards light. Sometimes in bright weather the rate of reproduction is so fast that the water in ponds may be coloured green by their presence, and can easily be seen.

The hard green covering often seen on older wooden fences is formed by large numbers of a small land alga known as *Pleurococcus*. It can withstand long periods of drought but like those which live in water it only becomes very active when there is plenty of moisture and it is warm. Many of the other algae in water can

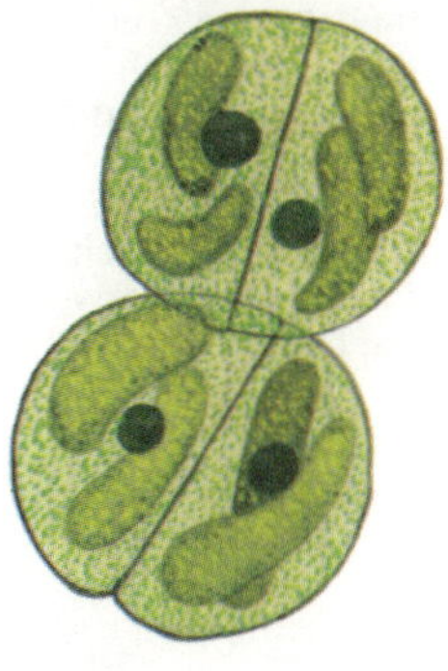

Above *Chlamydomonas* (top) a single-celled alga, and below it cells of *Pleurococcus*, one of the commonest forms of vegetable life. These drawings show close-up views of these microscopic plants.

Above Fungi have no chlorophyll, or green colouring matter, but they do display a wide range of colours and, sometimes, weird shapes. The types shown above are, from left to right, *Bovista, Amanita muscaria, Morchella esculenta, Psalliota campestris* (the common field mushroom), *Clavaria formosa, Boletus satanus* and *Lactarius rufus*. The fairy ring shown is caused by the fungal threads' outward growth and such rings are usually formed by poisonous toadstools. On the right of the picture can be seen a fungus which grows on the bark of trees.

also form what are called resting stages so they can withstand adverse conditions such as the drying out of the pond in which they live.

One of the commonest alga in ponds and slow streams is the plant which sometimes forms the slimy green masses familiar to all who spend some time near the water. This is called *Spirogyra* and is a long thread-like plant formed from short cylindrical cells joined end to end.

Among the most advanced of the algae are the common forms of seaweed called wracks which inhabit rocky coasts all over Europe. *Fucus vesiculosus,* commonly called bladder wrack, has a portion at its base which is adapted to clasp on to rocks and prevent the plant being washed away. This part of the plant has no powers of absorbing foods and is entirely an anchor. The 'stem' is cylindrical at first, then higher up it is flattened out and has built-in bladders of air which act like water-wings and keep the plant upright in the water. The whole plant is very slippery, being covered with a jelly-like substance, and it is rubbery to withstand the buffeting of waves.

Reproduction is either by the simple breaking off of sections of the 'stem', which in these plants is called the thallus, or by the formation of two kinds of special cells, one of which is capable of movement like *Chlamydomonas* plants. These special cells are set free when the tide is in and the mobile ones 'swim' to the others and they fuse together forming a spore. This can germinate and develop into another plant.

Fungi

Fungi represent a very important part of the thallophytes, and are separated from the rest by many definite characteristics. They have no chlorophyll and no starch is present in their cells, and it is easy to see from the example of a few familiar toadstools that they are quite different in actual make-up from all other plants. They do not live on their own manufactured food, but rely either on the decaying remains of other plant and animal life (these types are called saprophytes) or on living plants or animals (parasites).

The fungi may be single-celled plants such as yeast, which is used for baking bread and brewing beer, or multi-celled plants such as the mushroom. In these more advanced forms the main part of the plant is an intricate web of threads known as hyphae, the whole web being called the mycelium. This often lives underground or inside the host plant on which the fungus is living. The hyphae threads run about

either in or between the cells of the plant and have the power of dissolving the cellulose of the cell walls and living on the contents.

The saprophytic ones act in a similar way on dead organic material and are not generally harmful to plants or animals. The parasites on the other hand cause man a great deal of trouble and expense in trying to get rid of them. Some fungi attack animals, including man, an example being the fungal disease athlete's foot. With the larger fungi, the hyphae sometimes come above ground and form a special structure which can produce spores. This is the 'fruiting' stage of the plant and the mushroom and toadstool are examples of this.

The hyphae have another property which is important to the fungus, and this is the formation of a hard tuber-like body called a sclerotium (again a resting stage) which is capable of existing for a long time without actually growing, or doing damage in the case of harmful fungi. This stage makes it difficult to get rid of some fungal diseases for they can withstand a lot of adverse treatment, and then germinate when conditions are suitable.

As fungi lack chlorophyll they cannot make their own food by photosynthesis. They must therefore absorb carbohydrates from the plant or animal matter on which they live. Having got a source of supply of carbohydrates they can themselves convert these substances into the more complicated ones needed to make cellulose for cell walls, and for proteins and protoplasm. The last two can only be formed if the fungus has a source of nitrogen and other more complex chemicals from an outside source, so for this reason a lot of fungi are rather specialised in their choice of where to grow.

Like the animals, fungi are dependent upon green plants for their food and could not live without them. So it is that the first living matter to colonise a new piece of ground will be something which can manufacture its own food, without depending on any other life-form, and it must therefore be a green plant, whether one-celled or multi-celled. When this is established, fungi and animals will appear, either to grow on or eat the plant or live on the organic matter which occurs when it dies.

Bacteria

Bacteria also come within the division of thallophytes that are dependent on green plants, for they are a group of minute organisms without any chlorophyll. They are parasites or saprophytes and are usually single-celled, often with the power of movement in the

Above This rare orchid, the bird's nest orchid, grows in woodlands and is a plant which has no chlorophyll and cannot survive on its own. On its roots a species of fungus grows which lives on the rotting leaves of other trees. The orchid depends on the fungus to extract for it carbohydrates from the leaf mould.

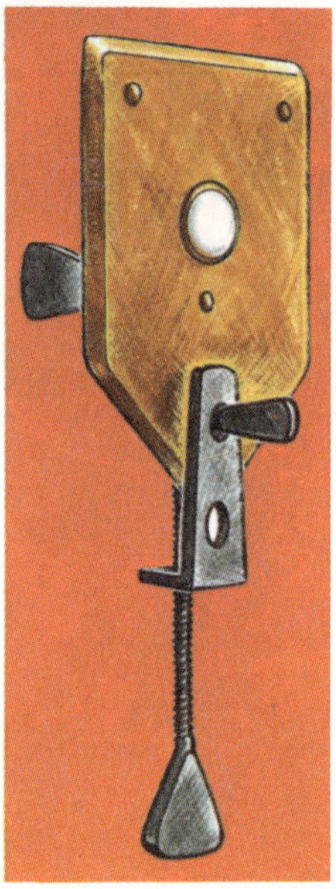

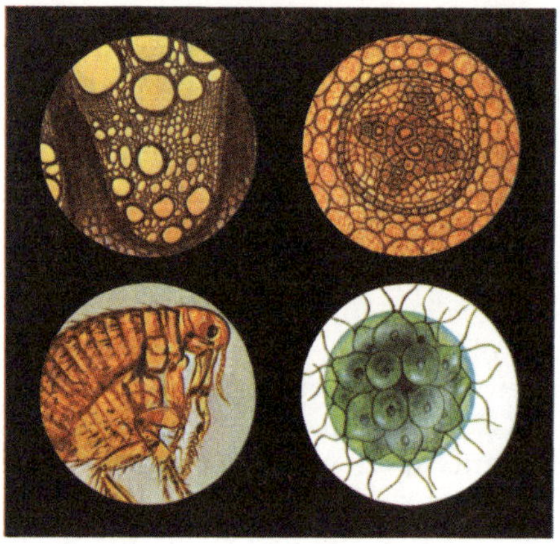

Above On the left is seen Leeuwenhoek's microscope, through which he made some of the first detailed observations of plants and animals. On the right is a modern electron microscope and some close-up views of plant and animal life as seen through a microscope.

Anton Leeuwenhoek (1632–1723) Dutch scientist. Famous as a microscopist, he used single lenses with a short focus to study animals and plants.

same way as *Chlamydomonas*. They increase by straightforward division of an old cell into two new ones, or they can also form 'resting spores'. These consist of cells which have specially tough cell walls, and in this stage the bacteria is very resistant, in some cases even to boiling water.

These spores are very numerous and are present in the soil, the air and water. In fact they are present virtually everywhere unless special precautions are taken to kill them. During the resting stage they are not increasing at all, but when conditions are suitable for their growth the cell wall breaks down and the bacteria become active again. Parasitic bacteria are often harmful, such as anthrax in animals, tetanus in man and soft rots in plants, but quite a number do exist on other living organisms without doing them any harm.

Saprophytic bacteria are often useful, for they help in rotting down dead material. They are very active in, for example, a compost heap. Some are used to convert alcohol into vinegar. One group of bacteria (nitrogen-fixing bacteria) are especially important as they live in swellings in the roots of plants of the legume family (peas and beans) and have the power of extracting nitrogen from the surrounding air in the soil and making it into a form that can be used by plants. This is why plants of this family, especially clover, are often grown in fields and then ploughed in to improve the soil.

Other bacteria in the soil (nitrifying bacteria) can convert plant and animal remains into a form that plants can use. So by the very valuable action of these tiny life-forms a continuous process is set up of turning waste and dead materials back into food for other plants. This is called the nitrogen cycle.

Antibiotics and viruses

Some tiny plant organisms produce substances which are capable of killing bacteria, and penicillin and streptomycin are two examples of these. The organisms producing these useful antibiotics are in fact fungi, and are 'cultivated' by man in order to obtain large quantities for treating diseases.

Viruses are organisms which are very much smaller even than bacteria and very little is known about them. They seem to be on the borderline between the living and non-living, although they do have the ability to increase and spread. They cause many diseases to plants and animals and in man are thought to be responsible for such things as colds, influenza and measles. In plants they produce disorders such as wrinkling and yellowing of leaves. They seldom kill plants, but completely upset their normal way of life, and because they can ruin crops are a problem to man. Unlike a lot of bacterial and fungal diseases in plants, they cannot be killed by chemical sprays.

Far left *Marchantia*, a common liverwort, produces stalked heads which are part of the plant's reproductive system. These heads are a roundish disc in the male and shaped like a star in the female.
Left The royal fern, (*Osmunda regalis*), has a mat of roots which can be cut out of the ground in large pieces, known as 'Osmunda fibre', and used for growing orchids in.

Bryophytes

These are the mosses and liverworts. Liverworts are plants requiring damp conditions and they are often found in shade by water or near ditches, where they make green growths on the surface of the soil or on rocks. The flattish visible part of the plant is called the thallus and from its underside are produced simple root-like growths which anchor it to the ground.

Most liverworts can increase by sending out branches which eventually become detached from the main plant. They can also reproduce sexually and after the fertilisation of the egg a stalk is produced from the upper surface of the thallus. At the top of the stalk is a capsule containing spores which, when released to fall on a suitable place for growth, will produce a new generation of liverworts.

Mosses are rather more advanced bryophytes and have stems with simple leaves on them. The rhizoids are more complicated but are still not nearly as advanced as roots of ordinary plants. Mosses too are plants of damp situations – in bogs, on trees and walls and near streams. They have a rather complicated life-cycle and reproduce by means of capsules which appear at the apex of the stems, and contain spores which are distributed by the wind when released.

There are very many different mosses, some of which – the sphagnum mosses – actually live in water. These hold a lot of water like sponges and are used by florists and nurserymen to provide a damp base for wreaths, and for packing plants to send through the post.

Above Horsetails, belonging to the genus *Equisetum*, are the only survivors of a very ancient group of plants.

Pteridophytes

The ferns form the great majority of the plants in this division. They are a group which grow mostly in shady or damp places, although some occur in drier areas. Others in the tropics grow on other plants without extracting food from them (they are not parasites but are given the name epiphytes). The fern plant usually has a rhizome (a root-stem which produces roots and leafy shoots), which grows either on the surface or just underground, but there are tree ferns which have upright stems of up to twenty metres in length. From the rhizome arise fibre-like roots, tough and interwoven.

The leaves are often made up of many small leaflets but sometimes they have an entire, or whole leaf. In the young stage the leaves are rolled, with the tip in the centre of the coil. The stems and leaf-stalks are often covered with thick brown hairs.

In many species the fern can increase itself by dividing off its rhizome into side branches which eventually give rise to separate plants. However, the main method of reproduction is by producing spores on the undersides of the leaves. If a fern leaf is inspected it will be seen to have small outgrowths from the veins. These contain small capsules full of spores and when the spores are ripe they are ejected in a catapult-like way. When these spores reach a suitable spot they germinate into a small flat growth, which develops on its underside primitive roots (rhizoids) plus reproductive organs able to produce a new fern plant.

The most familiar of the other plants in this division are the club mosses and horsetails. They are of interest principally because they are surviving representatives of plant life that existed in earlier geological periods.

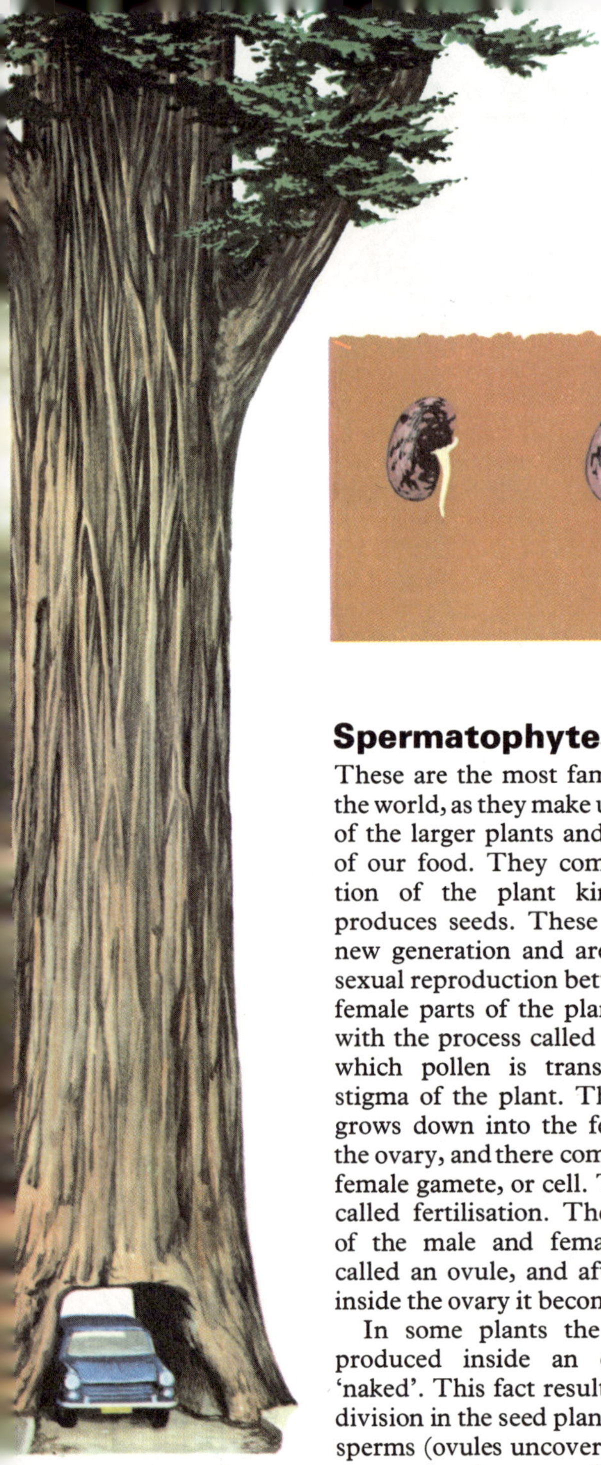

Spermatophytes

These are the most familiar plants in the world, as they make up the majority of the larger plants and provide most of our food. They comprise the section of the plant kingdom which produces seeds. These give rise to a new generation and are the result of sexual reproduction between male and female parts of the plant. This starts with the process called pollination, in which pollen is transferred to the stigma of the plant. The pollen then grows down into the female portion, the ovary, and there combines with the female gamete, or cell. This process is called fertilisation. The combination of the male and female gametes is called an ovule, and after developing inside the ovary it becomes the seed.

In some plants the ovule is not produced inside an ovary and is 'naked'. This fact results in the major division in the seed plants into gymnosperms (ovules uncovered) and angiosperms (ovules covered).

Gymnosperms

These are either trees or shrubs and represent a group which stands between the lower forms of plant life and the more highly developed flowering plants, the angiosperms. The most primitive ones, the cycads, are similar to some tree ferns. They are also like some fossil plants, as is the ginkgo tree (maidenhair), which is closely related to trees which grew in the Palaeozoic period.

The conifers are the highest forms in this group and often grow in mountain regions, higher up than other trees, being very tough and able to withstand extremes of cold. To adapt themselves to dry areas in mountain regions of low rainfall, or where the soil is poor, their leaves are often very small – like needles.

Another way in which gymnosperms differ from angiosperms is their method of producing seeds, these being found in cones in most of the gymnosperms. Taking the cones of a pine as an example, they are of two types – male and female – carried separately on the tree. The male cones are smaller than the female ones and produce the pollen, while the female 'flowers' consist of the more familiar scaly cones.

In May clouds of pollen are produced by the male cones and at the same time the scales of the female cones open up so that the wind-blown pollen enters the cone and settles on the ovules. After pollination, the scales close again and the ovule continues to grow into a seed, although this is a very slow process and seeds may take three years to mature. During this time the cone increases in size and changes from green to brown and becomes dry. In wet weather the cone

Above The giant redwood tree, *Sequoia gigantea*, is so large that a roadway big enough for a car to be driven through it can be cut out of the base of the tree.

Above right The development of growth of a runner bean seed, in which cotyledons come above ground.

scales remain closed but during dry spells they open up and allow the seeds, which have a wing attached to help them drift in the wind, to be released.

Not all gymnosperms have cones like this, and some, such as the yew, have seeds with a fleshy part attached, sometimes brightly coloured to attract birds who eat the 'berries' and distribute the seeds.

Many of the gymnosperms are very important timber trees, often being fast growing and with straight trunks that give planks with few knots in them.

Angiosperms

When the outer coat of a large seed such as a broad bean is removed, two equal halves are found, joined only for a short distance at one side: these are called cotyledons. Other groups of seeds such as those of a lily have only one cotyledon and belong to the group known as monocotyledons (*mono* meaning single); whereas the bean belongs to the other group known as dicotyledons (*di* meaning two).

Further study of the bean seed shows that there is a tiny plant situated between the two cotyledons, and this is the embryo which will develop when the seed starts to grow or germinate. The embryo is in two distinct parts. One, called the plumule, develops into the shoot and comes above ground level, and the other, the radicle, forms the root.

The seed coat bears a dark scar where the seed was joined to the pod before it ripened, and next to this, though very small and difficult to see, is a tiny hole called the micropyle which assists moisture to enter and trigger off the germination of the seed. The young root also emerges at this point.

The cotyledons are the store for starch and proteins to supply the young plant before it has leaves and roots to support itself. When the seed is given the right conditions in which to germinate – that is mainly warmth and water – it absorbs moisture and swells up and the embryo starts to develop. In the broad bean the cotyledons stay below ground level and as their food is gradually used up they shrink away. In other plants the cotyledons come above ground and turn green as soon as they are in the light and so, by photosynthesis, start manufacturing food for the young plant. In this way they act as leaves until the seedling can produce true leaves of its own. This type of germination occurs in mustard seedlings and the two cotyledons can easily be seen.

There are very many other ways in which different seeds may germinate. The seed may be produced singly or in groups, such as the cluster of seeds inside an apple, but whether singly or in a cluster, the seed, with coverings

Above There are about seventy species of coniferous trees, all of which are evergreen. Shown here are the Scots Pine *(Pinus sylvestris)*, much used for soft timber, and below it the Chilean Pine *(Araucaria imbricata)* known popularly as the monkey puzzle tree.

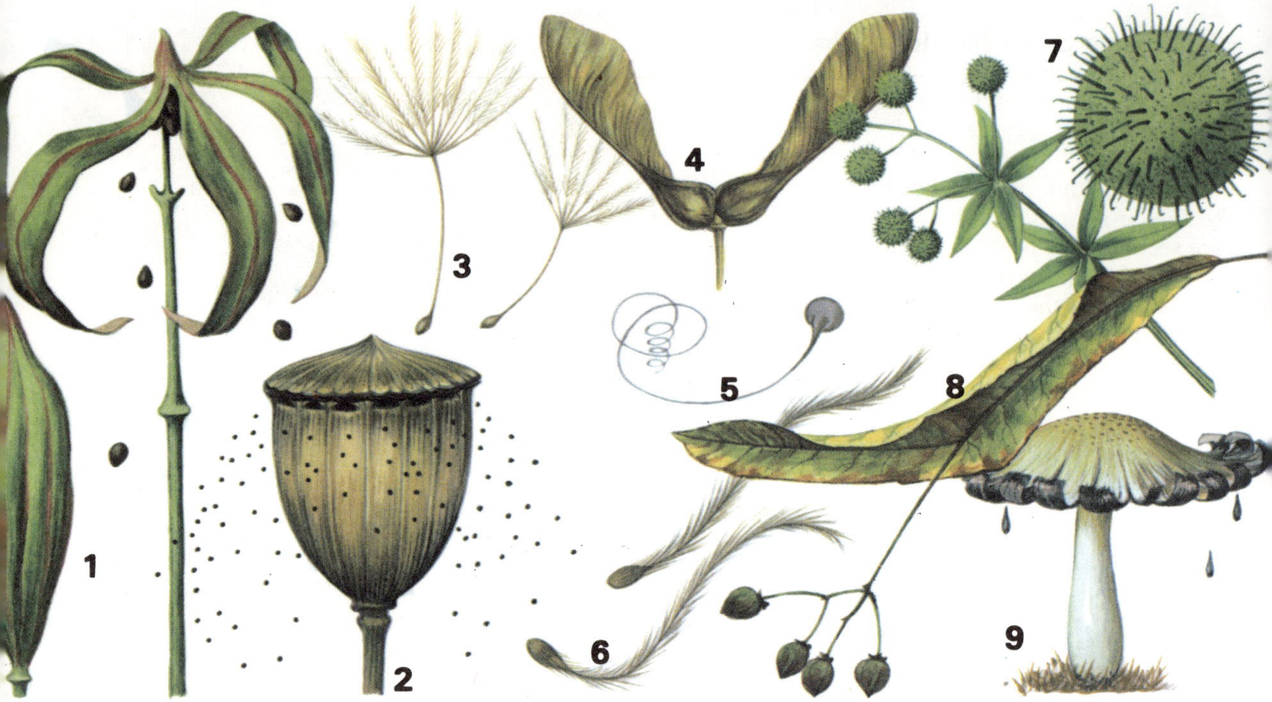

Above Examples of seed dispersal are shown in this drawing. **1** balsam (explosion), **2** poppy (shaking), **3** dandelion (wind), **4** sycamore (wings), **5** cyathus (springs), **6** old man's beard (wind), **7** goosegrass (sticking), **8** lime (sail), **9** inkcap (spore drop).

Gregor Mendel (1822–84) Austrian biologist. Trained in Augustinian monastery. Ordained priest 1847. Studied science at Vienna. Experimented on plant hybrids and established Mendelian Law of hereditary characteristics. His great work was not recognised until after his death.

and its attachments, is known as the fruit. For example, the acorn of an oak tree with its cup, or the cluster of winged seeds of a sycamore, are fruits.

Seed dispersal

The fruit is often adapted in such a way that it assists in the carrying away, or dispersal, of the seed. There would be little use in a plant dropping its seeds immediately beneath it where they would all germinate and compete with each other for food and light. There exist adaptations of the fruit, or the seed coat itself, with the purpose of getting the seeds away from the parent. For example in sycamore the wings of the seed allow it to drift in the wind.

The four commonest ways in which seeds can be distributed are by wind, by animals, by water, and by explosion of the fruit.

There are various ways in which seeds are dispersed by the wind. The seeds may be very small and easily blown about, as in most orchids, or they may be large and flattened or winged. Many of the lily family have flat seeds, while the ash tree produces a twisted wing on the end of its seed. Others have a parachute mechanism like the dandelion or the clematis.

Some plants such as the poppy have seed pods which are carried on long stems, and as the wind blows the stem about the seeds are jerked out. Usually great numbers of seeds have to be produced by a plant relying on this method of scattering them, because many seeds will fall in unsuitable places for germination.

Animals can play a great part in transporting seeds, either by eating them or by getting them stuck to their fur. Many plants produce fruits which have a juicy outer coat (for example blackberries and strawberries) which are attractive to animals. After the fruits have travelled through the animal's digestive system, the remains are passed out of the body and deposited some distance from the original plant. The seeds within the succulent coat are very resistant and undamaged by the digestive juices – in fact some seeds will not germinate unless the outer coat is removed by means such as this. Sometimes the seed is not swallowed but just dropped after the outside has been eaten.

Animals can also spread seeds by carrying them in their hair or fur. In this case it is usually the fruit which is adapted and it is often covered with hooked spines.

A few plants which grow in or near water do rely on it to spread their seeds. These float for a while after they are released from the capsule, and

eventually sink to germinate in the mud at the bottom of a pond. In tropical countries the coconut has been spread over considerable distances by the large nuts floating either in the sea or along rivers.

Some fruits have an explosive mechanism which throws the seeds for quite a distance. The balsams are examples of plants which do this. Their seed pods are rather fleshy and as they ripen a tension is set up in the cells until finally the whole thing bursts with some force and the seeds are scattered. In others, such as gorse and broom, the fruits or capsules are not fleshy and as they ripen they become hard and try to twist. Eventually the pressure is too great and the two halves open rapidly in a twisting motion, ejecting the seeds. They can often be heard cracking open on a hot sunny day in late summer.

Classification of fruits

Fruits can be classified into simple fruits, which are formed from a single flower such as the fruit of a cherry or a rose (rose hip); and the more complicated composite fruits, which are formed from a whole head of flowers such as the fig or pineapple. Each of these groups can be divided into dry (like a hazel nut) or fleshy (like a blackberry). All fruits can be further classified according to the way in which they are produced, their shape and structure, and their method of releasing seeds.

Although a great many fruits will not develop unless there has been fertilisation of the ovary, resulting in the formation of seeds, some – like the banana – will develop without this. Oranges and grapefruit can also be obtained in seedless varieties and it is to the advantage of man to have fruits without hard seeds in them.

The root

When a seed germinates, the portion which grows downwards is called the radicle, and it develops into the root system of the plant. This has two main purposes, to anchor the plant in the soil and to provide food materials such as water and salts for the rest of the plant. It is quite unlike the stem for it grows away from light, contains no chlorophyll, does not produce leaves and has a growing point which is covered by a protective tip – called the root cap.

The main root which is formed from the radicle of the young seedling is often large and remains obvious throughout the life of the plant. This is known as the tap root and exists in many dicotyledons such as the dandelion. It is sometimes swollen for food storage as in a carrot. The tap root usually grows straight downwards and produces smaller branches known as secondary roots, forming the whole root system.

In many plants, especially the monocotyledons, the main tap root never develops, but a group of roots is produced from the base of the stem. This can easily be seen if a hyacinth

Above Fruits are either fleshy or dry. Fleshy fruits are **1** apple, **2** blackberry, **3** cucumber, **4** tomato, **5** plum and **6** cherry (in these the seeds are enclosed in the fruit). The strawberry (**7**) bears its seeds on the outside of the fruit. The coconut (**8**) is an example of a dry fruit.

Above The seed of this plant develops along a cylinder only until the shoot and root can resume their natural tendency to grow up and down.

Above Various root forms are illustrated. From left to right: tap root (turnip and carrot), fibrous root system, adventitious root (swollen in the dahlia), and aerial roots. Some climbing plants, such as ivy, often produce roots to hang on to walls or trees and these are called clinging roots.

bulb is grown in a jar of water. Such roots which develop from any part of the plant except the radicle are called adventitious roots. They occur in many plants which creep along the ground, rooting from the stems as they travel along. The strawberry sends out runners at the end of which a small plant develops. This then grows adventitious roots from its base and takes root in the soil.

Blackberry bushes and other plants will also take root if a branch happens to touch the ground. The gardener takes advantage of this fact when he takes cuttings from his plants. He removes a small shoot from the plant, and if it is put in damp sand and kept from dying by spraying with water, it will eventually produce roots and make a new plant.

Above Monocarpic perennials are plants which live for a number of years before flowering, sometimes dying immediately afterwards. The drawing shows *Agave americana*, which can grow for up to sixty years before producing a flower, although it normally blooms after about ten years. It is found chiefly in Mexico.

How the root grows

To avoid damage to a root as it pushes its way through the soil, the root tip has been provided with a protective cap rather like a bandage on a finger. The actual root tip is a very active part of a plant where the cells are constantly dividing. The cells which are formed nearest the end of the root are then used to repair the root cap as it wears away. Those behind the tip grow and lengthen the root. Farther back still the root is older and larger and it is here that the root hairs develop. These are single-celled, very fine and usually very numerous, and are the means by which a plant absorbs its water and minerals from the soil.

On the oldest parts of the roots are the root branches, or lateral roots, which spread out through the soil, giving the plant better anchorage and providing a larger area for nutrients to be absorbed. In general the larger the plant, the larger the area needed for the roots to 'search' for food and water.

Most plants which produce a large tap root do not have a lot of lateral roots, but if the tap root does not develop, as in a great many plants, then there is usually an extensive root system known as a fibrous root system. This occurs in most of the grasses and an average grass plant could have several hundred kilometres of roots if they were placed end to end.

This is one of the reasons why grasses are used on sandy land which has been reclaimed from the sea, for they can bind it together with their mat of roots to prevent the sand blowing or washing away. Marram grass is often used for this purpose as it can withstand the dry conditions in sandy dunes, and also is unaffected by the salt from the sea which kills many plants.

Storing food

Tap roots vary a lot in their shape from being long and narrow, as in a dandelion, to short and rounded, as in a turnip. The larger swollen types are associated with the storage of food and many of these plants are biennials, which means they normally have a life of two years. In their first year of growth from seed these plants produce only leaves, whilst underground they form a food store in the tap root which may be quite large by the end of the season. This is the stage at which man makes use of them as vegetables, such as carrots and turnips. If the plant is left for another year, it has enough food stored away in this root to make the extra effort needed to flower and seed, after which it dies: thus the life of a biennial is only for two years.

Above Mangrove trees grow on tropical coasts and send down roots from their branches to form dense mangrove swamps. The timber does not rot in water.

Most annuals (one year of life) do not need this great store of food and therefore have only a rather small tap root, as in the common weed groundsel. Some perennials (plants which live for several years) also have tap roots. These may be fairly thick so that the plant can store food while it rests in the winter months, then grow rapidly in the spring when it calls on these reserve supplies. The thick tap root of a plant such as a dandelion serves this purpose.

Adventitious roots are perhaps even more varied in their structure and can serve many different purposes apart from their normal functions. They too can be swollen as in a dahlia, and form a cluster arising from the base of the stem just below ground level. Some plants produce aerial roots from their branches which grow down until they reach the soil and then act as 'props' for the plant. The banyan tree is the famous example of this, but the same thing can be seen in a smaller way in sweet corn which produces a ring of adventitious roots just above the soil level that prop up the top-heavy plant.

Mangrove trees which grow in tropical swamps produce roots which come up out of the water and can act as 'breathing' organs to supply the normal roots – which are down in the airless mud – with oxygen. Roots, like other parts of the plant, must have a supply of air to develop and work properly, and in ordinary soils this is in plentiful supply in the spaces between the soil particles.

The stem

This is the upper part of the plant which conducts water and dissolved minerals to the leaves and generally grows upwards towards the light. It is developed from the plumule, which is the upward-growing part of the original embryo in the seed, and is capable of producing branches, leaves and flowers. The growing point is called the stem apex and has immature leaves curled over it. The point where each leaf or branch arises from the stem is called a node and these are sometimes easy to see, like the joints of a bamboo cane.

If you examine a horse chestnut

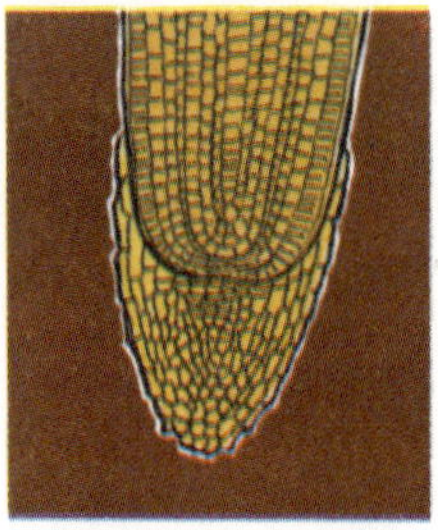

Above the root tip of a plant, showing its protective cap, as seen through the magnifying eye of a microscope.

Above Cacti are among the best known plants of the desert. Their flowers are often showy and colourful, as the drawing above of four different species illustrates.

Right The traveller's tree of Madagascar. It gets its name from the fact that the sheaths of the leaf stalks contain a quantity of water-like liquid which a passing traveller can tap by cutting the stem.

shoot you will see on the stem at the base of each leaf a small bud which later develops into another branch. The point at which the bud is formed is called the axil of the leaf, and the bud, an axillary or lateral bud. At the end of the shoot is a larger bud (the 'sticky bud' seen in spring) and this develops into the terminal shoot, which may produce a flower or continue to grow in length. To avoid damage to the young growth inside, buds are usually protected by overlapping scales like armour, or by dense hairs or a wax-like substance. Although buds are normally produced at nodes this is not always the case and they can be produced from most other parts of the plant in various species.

Stems are capable of producing other outgrowths apart from side shoots, leaves and flowers. These may be hairs, thorns, prickles or tendrils for climbing. Hairs can usually arise all over the surface of stems and may be concerned with protecting the stem by providing a felt-like layer, and may contain irritating substances to ward off animals which brush into them. Thorns and prickles are usually for protection, but may also assist a weak and floppy plant to scramble up through other vegetation. Spines which are hooked, such as those of the bramble, are usually meant for this. Some climbers produce tendrils which twine around other vegetation and help the plant support itself, as in the grape-vine, the cucumber or marrow.

Shapes of stems

The stems themselves may be various shapes or adapted for different purposes and can be upright, or creeping along the ground. If the plant is weak and hardly self-supporting it might have the power of twining around other plants, as bindweed (*Convolvulus*) does. The stem is often round, but can be square like a deadnettle (*Lamium*) or flattened like a lot of cacti, the stems looking like leaves and doing their work. The small flattened green 'leaves' of duckweed which float on ponds are really flattened stems, the true leaves having almost disappeared.

The stem might be very short and hardly noticeable and we can again use the dandelion as an example. The cluster of leaves, called a rosette, is right at ground level, and there is practically no stem between the root and leaves. This habit occurs in many alpine or rock plants which are dwarf because of the very hard conditions in which they live. The rosettes become covered with snow in winter and are protected from the cold winds and extremely low temperatures found on mountains.

Stems may be modified to act as storage organs, both above and below ground. The cactus stores a lot of water in its fleshy stems and in some species this is so plentiful that it can be useful to the traveller in the desert. Underground, the storage organs are often more familiar and more useful to us. The tubers of potatoes are actually stems and if we examine one carefully we can see buds known as eyes. These are portions we have to scoop out when peeling potatoes. If a potato is left in the spring to sprout these buds will start to grow and green shoots appear.

Some plants produce rhizomes, stems which have become thickened and creeping. Other underground stems are thinner but still act as storage organs. Some underground stems do not creep about but stay in one place and become swollen and rounded or bottle-shaped. These are known as corms and occur in such plants as gladiolus and crocus.

A few plants, of which the tiger lily (*Lilium tigrinum*) is an example, produce small swollen buds in the axils of the leaves. These fall off when fully grown and can take root in the soil, eventually forming new plants.

The runner of a strawberry is a stem which is produced by the plant in such a way that it grows along the ground, producing buds at intervals. These buds grow into young plants which then take root. Eventually the runner shrivels away when the new plant is self-supporting on its own roots. Mint forms 'suckers' which are underground runners that produce aerial shoots at intervals. Aerial shoots are also sometimes produced from buds formed on roots as in the suckers of a plum tree.

Stems vary greatly in size from the thin very soft ones of young seedlings to the large woody stems of trees.

Above The leaves of a plant are arranged on the stem in one of three general ways. The first (left) is called opposite, as in dead nettle; the second (centre), alternate, as in privet; the third, whorled, as in lilies.

Left Alpine plants are usually dwarf and grow close to the ground to help them survive the harsh winter weather in the areas where they live.

The leaf

Leaves are generally flattened outgrowths of the stem and represent the main part of the plant for food production. Where the leaf arises from the stem is the leaf-base and this in turn becomes a sheath which clasps the stem. In grasses the sheath is well-developed but it may not be very easy to see in many plants. The sheath often has other organs growing from it known as stipules, which may be spiny-like thorns for protection or tendrils for climbing.

After the sheath and stipules comes the stalk, or petiole, of the leaf. This supports the blade, or flattened portion of the leaf. If the blade expands directly from the sheath and there is no petiole, the leaf is said to be sessile. The petiole is like most other parts of the plant and is very variable in shape and function. Although usually rather

Joseph Priestley (1733–1804) English chemist and clergyman. Took up study of chemistry when he was a Presbyterian minister at Leeds. He was one of the discoverers of oxygen and a noted pioneer in chemical science. Controversial writing forced him to leave England and settle in the United States, where he died.

Above The leaves illustrated give some idea of the enormous variety of shape and colour that exists in nature. Botanists classify leaves into different types according to their appearance. Among the leaves above are **1** holly, **2** bamboo, **3** water plantain, **4** arrowhead, **5** croton, **6** maple, **7** grevillea, **8** dandelion, **9** clover, **10** horse chestnut, **11** violet, **12** pine.

slender and rounded in cross section it can also be flattened and green, assisting the blade in food production.

The leaf blade is the flattened green portion where all the food is manufactured and it is arranged to receive sunlight so that photosynthesis may take place. The petioles have the power of twisting so that all the leaves are turned to the light. The veins of a leaf are the tissues through which water and dissolved substances are taken to the cells, and by which manufactured foods are removed to other parts of the plant for use or storage. They are the continuation of the same conducting tissues in the stem and are the framework upon which the softer parts of the leaf are built.

The midrib is especially strong and forms the 'backbone' of the blade. From this arise lateral veins which in turn produce even thinner ones, forming a network within the leaf. A study of the underside of a large leaf such as the sycamore will show this network very well.

Leaves which last for several years on a plant are called evergreen. If they fall off annually they are called deciduous, which means to fall.

Leaf classification

There are many shapes and sizes of leaves and botanists concerned with the naming and classification of plants have terms to describe all the different types. The two major divisions of leaves are simple and compound. A simple leaf such as that of a beech tree consists of a single flattened blade. It may have a smooth edge or teeth along it giving a jagged appearance. In some cases, like a maple or sycamore, the leaf might have large indentations.

In compound leaves, the blade is actually divided up into separate portions, or leaflets, attached to the central rib. If they all arise from one point it is called palmate, or finger-veined (horse chestnut), or if they arise from the midrib along its length it is pinnate, or feather-veined (vetch). The separate leaflets of a compound leaf might also have teeth along their edge in the same way as the simple leaf.

Leaves can be modified to suit various purposes in addition to their basic function as food producers. For protection again, the plant might have spines on its leaves (holly) or the leaves themselves might be complete spines, leaving the flattened stems to carry on the photosynthesis (some cacti). In the sweet pea, part of the leaf is produced as a tendril to assist in climbing. In many plants of dry regions, or those growing on poor rocky soils, the leaves are swollen for water storage. The stonecrop can last for many months without any water, thanks to its fleshy leaves. Some plants have very

curious adaptations, especially those which catch insects.

Leaves may produce outgrowths from their edges or surfaces and these can take the form of hairs or spines, or sometimes a sticky substance is produced. The hairs may also contain an irritant which stings when touched (stinging nettles).

Leaves may also be concerned with food storage, and the commonest example of this is the bulb. The thick fleshy scales seen when a daffodil bulb is cut in half are really leaves built up on a very reduced stem – which can be seen as the core of hard tissue at the base of the bulb. Some bulbs are the swollen bases of the normal green leaves whilst others produce their green leaves separately from the swollen scale leaves.

Stomata

We have seen that the leaf cells contain chloroplasts which enable the leaf to photosynthesise and produce sugar by the combination of water and carbon dioxide. Water arrives by means of the vascular tissue of the stem and leaf, but air containing carbon dioxide must also be able to enter the leaf, and as oxygen is given off during photosynthesis it must be able to escape from the leaf. Similarly, during respiration gases must be interchanged with the outside air. Excess water absorbed by the roots must also be able to evaporate from the leaf surfaces.

All this takes place mainly through small openings in the surface of the leaf called stomata. These can be opened or closed according to the requirements of the plant by the aid of two cells called guard cells. These have the power of expanding or contracting and so making the actual opening larger or smaller. For example in very dry weather, the stomata on the leaf would be arranged so that the openings were all very small and would not allow very much water vapour to be lost from the plant. The stomata are normally open only during daylight and are closed at night.

Inflorescence and flowers

When a plant produces a head of flowers, the whole flowering stem, including the flowers themselves, is called an inflorescence. This may consist of only one flower, like the daffodil, but more generally there is a cluster of flowers arranged in various ways according to the method of branching of the flowering stem. There are terms to describe all of these various types of inflorescences but they can be divided mainly into two groups, the indefinite and definite inflorescenses.

The first group contains all those which have no obvious flower at the

Jean Lamarck (1744–1829) French naturalist. Became interested in plant life while serving with French army on the Riviera. In civilian life he studied botany and became keeper of the French royal garden. He was one of the first scientists to explain the principle of evolution in the animal world.

end of the main flowering stem, but continue to grow, throwing out flowers from the sides all the way up. A foxglove is like this and a close inspection of one in flower will show that flowers keep forming laterally all the way up the stem until it is difficult to see where they actually come to an end.

A definite inflorescence is one in which the central flowering stem comes to an obvious end with a terminal flower, like the chrysanthemum. More branches may arise below this, and they in turn produce a similar type of flower. The gardener often removes this terminal flower in the chrysanthemum to encourage buds lower down to come into growth and produce more flowers.

The flower itself is a special part of the plant concerned with the production of seeds for a new generation. Although flowers are extremely variable in form, they are basically all alike and we can compare various plants to illustrate this.

The simplest flower consists of four different parts, which grow from the stem and are arranged in circles (whorls), one inside the other. These are called the pistil (gynoecium), the stamens (androecium), the petals (corolla) and the sepals (calyx). The first two are concerned with reproduction and seed formation. The pistil is the female part in the centre of the flower and consists of an ovary which contains ovules (later becoming seeds), a style and, at its tip, a stigma. Growing around the outside of the pistil is the male group of parts which is the familiar cluster of stamens. Each stamen consists of an anther, the swollen part, supported on a stalk or filament. The anther contains pollen which can be seen as dust-like yellow powder if an open flower is touched. The anthers are very easy to see in lily flowers as the parts are all quite large.

Petals and sepals

Outside the two reproductive parts of a flower come the petals and the sepals, which are concerned only to assist in the process of reproduction.

The petals are often brightly coloured and larger than the rest of the parts. Their main purpose is to attract insects and give them somewhere to land on arrival at the flower, the insects being necessary to transfer pollen from one flower to another. There is often a sweet sticky substance called nectar at the base of the petals and this encourages the insect to crawl right into the flower and become dusted with pollen on the way. Plants which do not rely on insects to pollinate their flowers often have only small insignificant petals, such as in hazel catkins.

Finally, on the outside are the sepals and these are usually smaller than the petals, and green. They are concerned mainly with the protection of the inner parts of the flower until it opens out from a bud. In some cases however they can be large and coloured, also assisting in the attraction of insects. There are sometimes bracts below the flowers which are not a part of the actual flower. These can be large and showy for attraction purposes and are easily seen in the poinsettia.

The sepals are commonly small and green, capable of photosynthesis in the same way as leaves, but they can be enlarged and coloured as in the Christmas Rose (*Helleborus*), or converted into a silky tuft of hairs forming the 'parachute' (pappus) of many plants such as the dandelion. They can be scaly and used for protection, or occasionally swell up and become fleshy, enclosing the seeds like a fruit. Like the petals, the sepals are not always separate from each other but may be joined and form a tube. They can sometimes be leaf-like, and this shows the close relationship between flowers and the rest of the plant. Flowers are really only modified shoots, and sepals, petals, or even stamens can occasionally revert to being green and leaf-like.

The corolla, made up of several petals, varies a great deal in the way in which the petals are joined and arranged and this fact has largely determined the way in which flowering plants have been divided up into groups.

Pollination

Before seeds can be produced, pollen must be carried from the stamens to the stigma. Both male and female parts can be in the same flower, in which case the process is called self-pollination, or they can be on separate flowers so that pollen is transferred from the stamens of one to the stigma of another. This is cross-pollination. Both methods are very common in plants, and are brought about in various ways.

Self-pollination is simply a case of the plant having its pollen ripe at the same time that the stigma is ready to receive it. The pollen may just fall on to the stigma as the flower is moved or be knocked on by an insect. A few plants produce special flowers which are closed all the time, with anthers and stigma inside. These pollinate themselves and as they have no need for showy flowers to attract insects are often very small and insignificant (for example the viola produces two sets of flowers, one set showy and the other small and dingy). Some flowers are even produced underground.

Cross-pollination involves two separate plants of the same species although occasionally different species will cross, giving what are called hybrids. Cross-pollination is a more effective way for a plant to produce its seeds because the offspring are sometimes healthier than their parents, inheriting characters from both. Plants

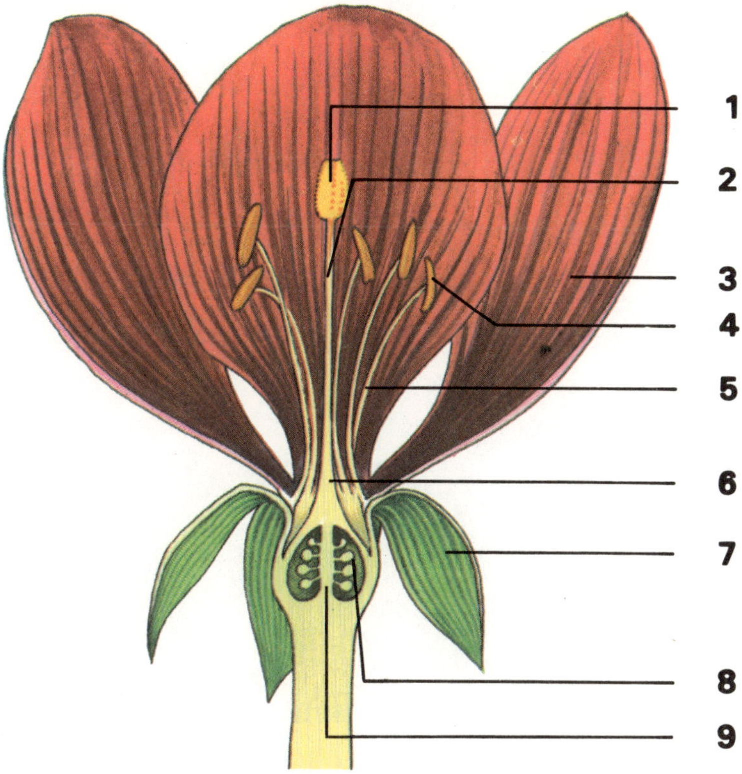

Left This drawing shows the various main parts of a flower. **1** stigma, **2** style, **3** petal, **4** anther, **5** filament, **6** pistil, **7** sepal, **8** ovule, **9** ovary.

Opposite page The drawings show four different types of inflorescence. The diagrams on the left reveal the basic structure of the flower head while those on the right show the complete flower.

Above At the top is *Stapelia grandiflora*, known as the carrion flower, which smells like rotting meat and attracts flies. It is pollinated by the flies, which lay their eggs in the flower.

Above The lower drawing shows a bee on a flower, to which it has been attracted either by colour or scent. Pollen from flowers is usually distributed by insects in this way.

often have elaborate devices to encourage cross-pollination. Man often uses cross-pollination to produce hybrids between species, perhaps to get larger flowers, or fruits which suit his needs.

The main ways in which pollen can be distributed are by insects, wind, water and animals. Insects are attracted to flowers by the bright colours, the scent or perhaps the sweet nectar at the base of the flower. It is quite often the night-flowering plants which resort to the use of scent, attracting such insects as night-flying moths.

Even with coloured flowers there is often an added attraction in the form of nectar when the insect arrives. This nectar is usually situated in such a way that the insect must push past the anthers to get at it, and in doing so becomes covered with pollen. On arrival at another flower, some of this pollen may fall off on to the stigma as it brushes past.

Not all plants which smell are sweet smelling. Some, like the *Stapelia* and certain arums, smell of bad meat and attract all sorts of flies which normally gather around rotting animal matter.

Wind-pollinated plants often have small dull flowers, as they do not need to attract insects; neither do they need to be scented nor produce nectar. As the pollen is carried by the wind, and it gets scattered over a wide area, it is usually very light and produced in large quantities. The stigmas are often very long and protruding so that they 'catch' the pollen more easily. Wind-pollinated plants often produce catkins which are easily shaken by the wind to release the pollen.

Some water plants have their pollen distributed by the current, especially those with submerged growth and flowers. *Vallisneria*, a tropical submerged water plant releases the male flowers which float to the female and pollinate them. Animals play a rather smaller part in pollination than insects, but some plants have their pollen carried by small birds, squirrels, snails and slugs.

Quite a number of plants have developed in such a way as to make cross-pollination, instead of self-pollination, almost certain. For example, in cucumbers separate male and female flowers are produced on the same plant so that neither flower can pollinate itself. This is carried to an extreme in some plants, for example holly, which produces all male flowers on one plant and all female on another. This is the reason why some holly trees never have berries.

After pollination of a flower, the pollen grain at the tip of the stigma begins to grow and sends out a tube (pollen tube) which travels down the style and into the ovary where it joins with an ovule and eventually produces a seed.

Above Water lilies are anchored to the ground beneath the water by their roots. Their flowers, which are often spectacular, come up on long stems. They close at night and open in the day, being attracted by the light of the sun.

Plant adaptations

Plant ecology is the study of plants in relation to their environment, or the way that plants adapt themselves to live in their surroundings. It includes the study of the climate (such things as temperature, rainfall, wind and sunshine), the type of soil conditions, and the animals which affect the soil (for example earthworms). Man also influences the conditions when he cultivates the land.

All these things must be studied together since each condition is dependent on the other. Thus in a tropical forest there are a very large number of trees because of the heat and the high rainfall and, in turn, because of the trees, there is a deep layer of leaf-mould in which smaller plants, fungi and small animals can live.

There are many different ecological groups of plants in the world. Mesophytes (or intermediate plants), for example, are the ordinary land plants which inhabit fields and woods, with an average supply of water and no very unusual conditions to cope with. The other important groups are hydrophytes (water plants) and xerophytes (dry plants).

Hydrophytes

These are plants which grow in or near water and are adapted according to whether they live on the surface, or are submerged, or grow in the mud at the edge of the water. Some are a combination of all these and have several different types of leaves. Some hydrophytes (for example water lily) are anchored to the bottom by roots, and send up leaves on long stems until they reach the surface, when they unfold and spread out. The giant water lily (*Victoria regia*) is an extreme example of this. The flowers too come up on a long stem and open out above the water.

Some water plants are not rooted to the bottom and merely float on the surface (for example duckweed) or under the surface (for example bladderwort). Such water plants can only live in still waters but some submerged plants are anchored to the bottom by roots and produce long growths with small leaves and these are better adapted to life in running water. The leaves of most water plants have large air cavities in them to act as 'water wings', and some produce large bladder-like swellings for the same purpose (for example water hyacinth).

The water crowfoot is amphibious, that is it can live both in water or at the edge in the damp mud. It has surface leaves which are flat and large compared to the submerged leaves which, when living in water, are finely divided with narrow lobes. These smaller leaves disappear if the water level drops and the plant is left at the edge.

Xerophytes

These are the plants of the deserts or other dry places. For this reason they must have some method of withstanding long periods of drought, very bright light, strong winds and, perhaps, very high temperatures – although not all deserts are hot.

There are various ways in which plants can overcome these conditions. With annual plants, the seeds often have a long life and will only germinate

Above Tumbleweed is a general botanical term for a plant which breaks loose from the ground when it is dry. It can then be blown long distances and scatter its seeds far and wide.

Above Desert areas are not totally without life. Although they appear barren, enough rain falls in most deserts for certain plants to grow.

Above When an insect lands on a leaf of the Venus fly trap *(Dionaea muscipula)* the two halves of the leaf, which are hinged close rapidly and trap the insect. The plant then digests its prey.

after rainfall. They then grow very rapidly and complete their life cycle before the drought occurs. On the other hand perennial plants have to exist through bad spells and usually have some method of storing up moisture to tide them over. Cacti are a good example of this with their swollen fleshy growth.

Large thin flat leaves would be of no use in the desert as they would evaporate too much moisture from their surfaces, so leaves are often very small or narrow, and usually have a very thick outer layer (cuticle), preventing water loss. They might even be reduced in size to hard spines as in many cacti and succulents. The *Yucca* has leaves which are narrow and with a very tough cuticle to withstand the desert conditions in America.

Roots may be adapted to store water, becoming thick and fleshy, and it is noticeable that in drier parts of the world, such as the Middle East, there are many plants which produce underground bulbs, corms or tubers. Leaves can also be thick and fleshy for water storage, or develop only during the rainy season, to drop off again when the dry summer comes.

Some grasses can roll their leaves inwards from the edges in dry spells, thus leaving a smaller surface exposed to the sun, while acacias in Australia can turn their leaves sideways on to the sun so that it does not scorch down on to the flat surfaces. Leaves sometimes have dense coverings of hairs to protect them from sun and drying winds.

Plants which grow in places where the soil is very salty, such as by the sea, in river mouths or salt lakes inland, and have adapted themselves to overcome the peculiar conditions, are called halophytes. Most normal land plants are killed by salt in the soil but these plants are so successful that they can be important to man when trying to reclaim new land from the sea.

Insect-eating plants

Although green plants are self-supporting as far as their food requirements go, some plants do rely to a certain extent on other living creatures. One group of these, known as insectivorous plants (plants which live on insects), gain part of their nourishment by trapping insects in various ways. The plants digest the insects' bodies and take the dissolved proteins into their systems. Several of these interesting plants occur in Europe, and there are many others in tropical countries, often large and with weird methods of trapping insects. Insectivores are usually plants of marshes and bogs where the soil is poor in the nitrogen compounds so necessary for

their continued healthy existence. Although they are mostly green plants, producing some of their own food, they do need the proteins of the insects to make up the lack of nitrogenous food.

Some plants produce hollow leaves containing liquid in which the insects drown, the *Sarracenia* being an example of this. The leaves are rather funnel-like with a lid to the opening at the top. The rim of the funnel has nectar to attract insects, and the whole plant is often brightly coloured. Inside the funnel is a slippery area, and downward pointing hairs, which prevent any insects crawling out again. *Nepenthes*, the pitcher plant, produces curious pitcher-shaped extensions to the leaves which act in the same way as *Sarracenia*. They are usually climbing plants rather than bog plants, and are widely grown in greenhouses in hanging baskets. In both of these plants, the insects' bodies are decomposed in the watery fluid at the base of the pitcher, which contains many bacteria, the plant then using the dissolved substances.

Parasites and saprophytes

These are plants which depend entirely or partly on other organisms. We have already dealt with the fungi, which are the largest group of parasites and saprophytes in the plant kingdom. But there are other plants which exist on living material (parasites) or make use of dead organic substances (saprophytes). Parasites may be 'total' or 'partial', that is they either get the whole of their food materials from the host plant on which they live, and have no green parts, or they have chlorophyll of their own and can manufacture a certain amount of their own food, but also need some from the host.

Dodder, in the Convolvulus family, is a total parasite and can be seen on the stems of plants such as gorse and heather. This is a stem parasite but other plants such as broomrape are root parasites and penetrate and live on the roots of a host plant.

Mistletoe is another good example of a parasite which occurs on the stems and trunks of trees, while several members of the foxglove family live on the roots of grasses in meadows.

Saprophytes make use of decaying matter and usually occur in woodlands where there is plenty of rotting vegetation. The bird's-nest orchid can be seen growing in woods and is a brownish plant which only appears above ground when it sends up a flowering stem. The roots actually live in association with a fungus which breaks down the rotting materials *it* lives on into soluble substances. The fungus also penetrates the roots of the orchid and gains some of its materials from the cells there, while the orchid gets its supplies of food materials through the fungus. Thus the two plants are living together and depending on each other for their existence, this being called symbiosis.

Epiphytes

Some plants which may be mistaken for stem parasites are the epiphytes which grow in trees usually in tropical areas, and many of the mosses come into this group. The difference is that epiphytes are normal green plants which have taken to a life of growing on the bark of trees but do not gain any of their nourishment from them. They live entirely on what food materials happen to be lodged in the crevices of the bark and a lot of orchids which live in this way send out thick white 'roots', capable of extracting water from the damp tropical atmosphere.

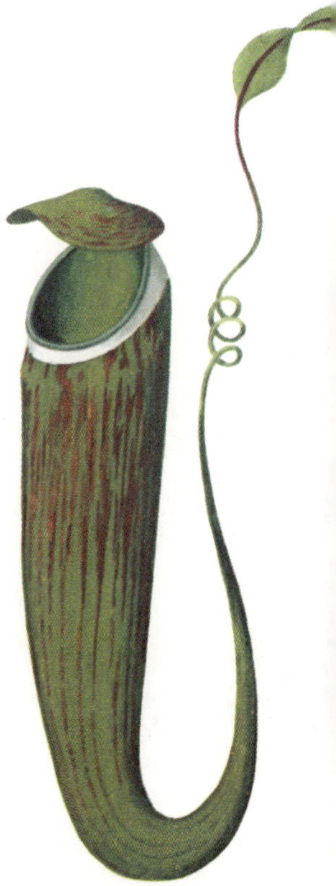

Above The pitcher of the insectivorous plant called *Nepenthes alba marginata* (pitcher plant), is a form of leaf, adapted to trap insects, which fall into it and drown in a watery fluid.

Joseph Banks (1744–1820) English naturalist and explorer. Went to Newfoundland in 1766. Accompanied Capt. Cook on his voyage round the world in 1768–71. President of the Royal Society for 41 years. He did much to encourage the introduction of useful food-producing plants, such as bread-fruit and mango, to many parts of the world.

Above The best barley is used for malting, in the manufacture of beer. Most of the crop however is used to feed livestock.

Above Ornamental gourds are sometimes dried and used to make instruments. This is a snake-charmer's flute from northern India.

The uses of plants

Economic botany deals with the plants which are used by man for some purpose, such as eating and providing materials for building, fuel, clothes and medicines. Although many plants were used originally by primitive and ancient people just as they found them growing wild, nowadays the majority of really useful plants are cultivated to give better crops or a plentiful supply of materials for manufacture.

Often the wild species of plants are not efficient enough to supply man's needs and it has been necessary not only to cultivate them in large numbers, but to raise new varieties. Crossing between species (to make hybrids) or the selection of more vigorous plants, give larger fruits than the wild species (compare wild strawberries with garden varieties). Thus new plants are raised which give better flavoured fruits and which are better able to resist disease and hard frosts. So we find that in practically all plants of any importance man has a choice of variety according to the conditions in his particular area.

Foods

Probably the most important food crops are those belonging to the grass family (Gramineae) which includes such crops as wheat, rice, maize, barley, oats, rye and millet. These are known as cereals, and contain a large quantity of starch and vitamins. They form the main food of people in many countries, for example rice in India and South-East Asia. Wheat is produced in many of the cooler parts of the world, while maize is grown mostly in the United States and Canada. The grass family provides the farmer with the greater part of the food for his cattle and other livestock, which is either eaten as it is grown or harvested as hay and straw and saved up for the winter.

Many members of the pea family (Leguminosae) are widely used by man for food, or as fodder for his cows (for example lucerne). They are also valuable as food because of their high protein content. It may be the seeds which are eaten, for example in peas and broad beans, or sometimes the whole pod (runner and french beans). Plants of this family, such as clover and lupins, are sometimes grown in fields and before they get too large are ploughed into the ground to provide compost to improve the conditions of the soil.

The crucifer family (Cruciferae) provides us with a great many of our green vegetables and most of these are garden varieties of wild cabbage, which is a very poor vegetable compared with the cabbages, brussels sprouts, cauliflowers and kales which have been raised from it. Mustard is used in the same way as clover as a green crop to improve the fertility or fruitfulness of the soil.

The so-called root crops are those with underground swollen roots or stems which are particularly useful as they can be stored for use at a later date when other vegetables are scarce. These include such things as potatoes, carrots, parsnips, turnips, beetroot and radishes. Potatoes belong to the solanum family (Solanaceae) together with tomatoes, and it is the dream of the people who raise new varieties to produce a hybrid between the two which will have edible fruits above ground and potatoes underground. Sugar beet is a root crop grown to provide sugar in colder countries where sugar cane will not grow.

Sweet potato is a common food in many tropical countries, eaten raw or cooked, and is the swollen root of a plant called *Batatas*. Yam is the very nutritious root of another tropical plant, the genus *Dioscorea*, which is usually a climber. Manihot is also cultivated for its large root and produces tapioca to be ground up as flour.

The lily family (Liliaceae) includes such plants as asparagus, the young shoots of which are a great delicacy, and the onion and its relatives. In onions, leeks, shallots and garlic it is the swollen leaf bases and stems which are eaten, and in chives and spring onions the young leaves which are used as salads.

Marrows, cucumbers and melons all belong to the same family, Cucurbitaceae. It is a large family consisting mostly of trailing or climbing plants which are rather fleshy and produce swollen watery fruits, many of which are highly coloured, as in the ornamental gourds.

The daisy family (Compositae) is not used very much for food, but does provide us with lettuce and chicory, which is eaten as a salad or combined with drinks to give a bitter flavour. Several of the root crops already mentioned belong to the Umbelliferae family, which also includes celery and parsley – in which the leaf stalks and leaves are used – caraway, and herbs such as fennel, rue and dill.

Above Fertile slopes of land in India and South-East Asia are terraced into elaborate rice paddy fields. Some of these fields are hundreds of years old. The rice seedlings are often grown in boxes and transplanted to the fields. The terraces produce high yields of rice in heavy soil.

Fruits

Fresh fruit is a very necessary part of our diet as it is a valuable source of vitamins. It is also preserved in the form of jams, jellies, marmalade and pickles, and many fruits are tinned. A number of fruits in the botanical sense are used as vegetables, for example marrow and cucumber; whereas melon, in the same family, is eaten as a fruit.

The citrus fruits are an important group giving us oranges, grapefruit and lemons. There are quite a few other fruits belonging to the same family (Rutaceae) which are used in other parts of the world, such as the lime and citron. The banana (*Musa*) is grown throughout tropical regions, and some varieties have very small fruits which are used for cooking (plantain bananas).

In temperate regions the most important fruits are those belonging to the Rosaceae family, which give us such things as apples, pears, plums,

Above Although the tea bush is a hardy plant it needs a warm and moist climate to be grown successfully on a commercial scale. To produce the normal black tea, the leaves are picked and allowed to ferment in the sun before roasting and drying. The green tea which is popular in China is obtained by very rapid drying of the leaves, without fermentation.

Above right The sunflower is not only a beautiful flower, with its colourful head which tends always to turn towards the sun, but a useful source of an oil, which is made from its seeds.

strawberries, raspberries and peaches. Most of these are hybrids raised from wild species which have small fruits. By constant hybridising and selection of the better varieties man has achieved a size of fruit which seems almost impossible when one looks at the original species.

The coconut belongs to the very distinctive family of palms, called the Palmae. It is known in Europe mainly for its edible nut, but it is cultivated in tropical areas for the fibre which surrounds the nuts. It also provides oil from the kernel, wood from the trunk, roof-covering from the leaves, and 'milk' from the liquid inside the nut. The date is another palm grown in dry areas for its fruit. Many other palms are useful for the fibres in their leaves, or for the oil in their fruit. Pineapple (*Ananas*) belongs to the family Bromeliaceae, and is now cultivated widely in the tropics for its fruit.

Mango is especially important in South-East Asia where it is grown for its very large and nutritious fruit. The papaw or papaya is another tropical fruit either eaten green as a vegetable or, if allowed to ripen, as a fruit.

The grape is a vine grown out of doors in areas with a Mediterranean climate either for the fruit or for making wine. Some varieties are grown to provide fruit for drying to make raisins and currants. Pomegranate is grown in similar conditions and is a large fruit with a refreshing clear flesh, but filled with a lot of seeds. Melons and water-melons are widely grown throughout the world, in the open in warm regions and under glass in colder areas, for their large fleshy fruits.

Oil crops

Most oil products are from plants grown in subtropical or tropical regions. We have mentioned the coconut, the oil of which is thick, fat-like and edible. Similar is palm oil from *Elaeis guineensis*, a West African plant which is used mainly in the manufacture of margarine and soap. Several oils from plants are liquid and useful for cooking and lubricating. Olive oil (from the olive tree fruits) and peanut (groundnut) oil both come into this group. So too does castor oil, used as a medicine.

Other oils dry on exposure to air and are useful for making paints and varnishes, for example linseed oil from a species of flax (*Linum*). Sunflower seed gives one of the oils which do not dry out completely and these are used in soap manufacture, in food or for cooking. Wax, used in polishes, is obtained from a Brazilian palm tree (*Copernicia*) where it occurs on the surfaces of the leaves as a hard layer.

Above There are several ways of growing grape vines: they may be trained on a trellis or on wires, or grown separately on stakes. The grapes are used mainly to produce wine, but they may be eaten raw, or dried and used as raisins in cooking.

Above left Bananas grow in large bunches on the tropical plant called *Musa sapientum*. Each plant bears only one bunch of bananas and when it has fruited the plant dies. When bananas are grown for export they are cut when they are green. The banana is a fruit which has been grown and used as a food since ancient times.

Beverages

Drinks can be made by extracting the flavour from part of a plant with hot water. Thus tea is made from the leaves of a small bush closely related to the garden camellia. It is grown in warm regions where there is plenty of rainfall. India and Ceylon are the main tea-growing areas in the world. The young tips of shoots are picked and put through a process which allows the tea flavour to develop.

Coffee is made from the seeds of *Coffea* species, a group of small trees and shrubs from Africa. They need a hot, wet climate and are now grown in a lot of tropical countries where conditions are right. The fruit of *Coffea* is red and fleshy when ripe, with two seeds inside (the coffee beans) and after a series of operations to remove the outside layer the clean seeds are obtained. Before they can be used to make coffee they are roasted and ground.

Cocoa and chocolate also come from a tree, the *Cacao* from South America, although it too is now widely grown in other parts of the world. The cocoa seeds or beans are produced in fruits which hold several beans on the trunks and branches of the trees. The fruits are removed and opened and the beans are processed to bring out the chocolate flavour, the final product being cocoa or chocolate.

There are many other drinks which are produced from plants and some of these are alcoholic and made by fermenting the extract from a plant with the aid of yeast: this converts sugars to alcohol. Beer is most commonly made from barley and hops, while most wines are made by fermenting grape juice. Wines can however be made from most fruits and quite a few vegetables as well, and many homemade wines are produced in this way. If stronger alcoholic drinks, such as whisky and brandy, are required, the fermented liquid must be distilled, a process in which the alcohol is separated from the liquid by the process of evaporation.

Wood

The trunks and branches of trees have supplied man with one of his most easily obtained sources of fuel for burning. If wood is burned slowly under a pile of turf and away from the air, it changes into charcoal – a black soft form of carbon used for various purposes such as an art material for sketching, as a smokeless fuel, and for making explosives. The softer woods (for example deal) are used today mainly for building, and the hard woods (for example oak and mahogany), which are generally more expensive as they are slower growing, are used for furniture making.

Above Among the many problems facing timber-producing countries is the transport of logs from the forest to the factory. One method, where the tree trunks can be rolled or carried to a river, is for a ship to tow vast numbers of logs held within a kind of net.

Compressed sawdust is made into various types of artificial boards and these are used in building and furniture making. If wood is crushed and treated with chemicals it becomes pulp and this is used to make paper. The cellulose in plants is used in the production of rayon, but most modern plastics are completely artificial.

All trees have a layer of cork on their bark, but the cork oak in Spain produces a thick sheet of it and is very valuable. The cork is removed from the trees about once every ten years and this does not damage them. It is used for a great range of purposes, since it is very light, a good insulator and does not get damaged by many liquids. Thus it is used as fishing floats, for stoppers in bottles, for gaskets in engines (it is not destroyed by oil or grease), for making linoleum and for insulation against cold.

Fibres

Various plants are grown to provide fibres either from their wood or from some other part of the plant, such as in cotton. Here, the seeds are covered with hairs which when dead form the cotton fibres. Different species and hybrids of cotton plants are grown, and they range from annuals to small trees and shrubs. An oil (cotton-seed oil) is also obtained from the seeds by crushing them. The remainder of the seed is fed to cattle as an oily cake.

Jute is a stem fibre made from annual plants which grow mainly in warm regions. The stems are cut, soaked in water and beaten to extract the fibres. Sisal is a plant cultivated to a great extent in East Africa for the fibre in its tough leaves. The leaves are cut and put into machines which expose the fibres; these are then washed, bundled and dried. Flax gives us linen, and hemp the material for strong ropes, and in both the fibres come from the stems.

There are other plants used on a smaller scale for fibres, but many synthetic, or man-made materials are now being produced and these will to some extent replace the natural fibres.

Medicines and drugs

The use of plants for healing is a very ancient practice and was probably known to prehistoric man. Although some medicines are now produced synthetically a great many plants are still used for this purpose. Many well-known drugs, such as morphine, cocaine and quinine, come from plants, although these too are now being replaced by artificial drugs. Some drugs made from plants can be dangerous if used wrongly and the plants themselves are poisonous if they are eaten when growing.

Another drug, curare, was used by the natives of South America as a poison on the tips of their blow-pipe darts, but it has the power of relaxing muscles and is used in the treatment of spastics and the diseases lockjaw and rabies, and also as an anaesthetic in surgery.

Some drugs can relieve tension and reduce blood pressure, and there are many other uses for plants in the field of medicine. This extends from trees right down to the lower forms of life, some of which have already been mentioned, such as penicillin.

Sugar

Sugar is obtained from various sources, the most important being sugar cane and sugar beet. The sugar used in the home is cane sugar (*Saccharum officinarum*), a member of the grass family. It can be four and a half metres high with thick jointed stems produced in a clump. The stems are harvested and squashed between rollers to extract the juice, which is very rich in sugar. This liquid is then evaporated and the sugar obtained. It is put through various processes, and charcoal is used to take away the natural brown colour and give the more popular white sugar. Sugar cane is grown in tropical countries, but temperate countries make their contribution to the world's supply of sugar by growing sugar beet. This is closely related to the garden beetroot and is a swollen root containing a useful amount of sugar which is extracted by shredding and soaking in hot water. It is then evaporated and purified to obtain solid sugar.

Rubber

One of the most interesting stories of plant life is the history of the rubber tree (*Hevea brasiliensis*). From the very early days of its discovery in South America, when the conquering Spanish saw children playing with rubber balls it was realised that rubber had waterproofing and other properties which made it valuable. The real boom for the rubber industry came when rubber tyres were made. Whole books have been written about it and the way in which world history has been changed by this indispensable substance.

Although originally from South America, rubber trees are now grown throughout the tropics, especially in South-East Asia. The rubber begins life as a white latex which is obtained by cutting grooves in the bark of the trees. First it goes through a chemical process which results in a sheet of crêpe rubber and in this form it can be transported. Further processing is necessary before it is made into such items as tyres. Nowadays synthetic materials are generally mixed with natural rubber.

A few other plants have been used to produce rubber, particularly in war-time when the transport of tropical rubber was difficult. A species of dandelion was used for this purpose

Above The white sticky liquid which is drawn from rubber trees is called latex. To obtain this latex a shallow curved cut is made in the bark and the liquid is gathered in vessels attached to the tree.

Below Much of the world's wood pulp is turned into the paper on which newspapers are printed. Modern newspaper presses like this rotary press which prints the *Calgary Herald* in Canada, combine highly reliable performance with quality printing and reproduction speed.

Above Land can be carefully restored after it has been used for such things as mining and quarrying. These drawings depict the same area of land before and after its restoration.

Above This little figure is taken from an Aztec manuscript and shows a warrior smoking tobacco in a wooden pipe.

in the Second World War, the white sticky latex producing a rather inferior grade of rubber. Another form of latex, from trees of the Sapotaceae family, is used for chewing gum.

Dyes

Here too synthetic materials are replacing those made from plants. Probably one of the most famous dyes is woad, the blue dye used by ancient Britons to colour their bodies blue. It is obtained from the plant *Isatis tinctoria* in the Cruciferae family and was cultivated on a large scale from the 13th to the 17th centuries. Henna, an orange dye obtained from the leaves of an Indian shrub, is employed in colour mixes for hair, but there are very few of these natural dyes still used.

The red colour in lipstick is obtained partly by using the dye called annatto, from the seeds of a South American tree which is now widely cultivated in the tropics.

Tannins, obtained from the bark of many different trees, are dyes used in the production of ink. The same substances are used in the tanning industry to give animal skins toughness, producing leather.

Tobacco

This is a strong-growing leafy plant which grows almost two metres high and is thought to be a hybrid between South American species of *Nicotiana*. It has been cultivated for a very long time, certainly before Columbus sailed to the West Indies in 1492, and its exact origins are unknown. Although by far the greatest quantity is now grown for smoking tobacco, the leaves have been and still are used for chewing, for snuff and to produce nicotine, an insecticide. The leaves are dried after harvesting either by allowing them to hang in sheds, or by artificial heat, and are then allowed to 'ferment' or 'age' in boxes. This process brings out the well-known tobacco smell, and the leaves can then be turned into cigars and cigarettes.

Finding new plants

Although so many of the plant products are now being replaced by artificially produced materials, as far as food is concerned man's reliance on plants will become even more marked as the world population grows. Over the past few decades, the intensive use of fertilisers and insecticides has greatly increased crop yields. However, this 'green revolution', as it became known, had drawbacks – for example, fertilisers are very costly, and insecticides may build up in the animals which eat the sprayed plants. Scientists are trying to overcome these problems partly by developing new plants, such as cereals which need no fertilisers.

Single-celled plants are grown on a commercial scale to produce high-protein food for farm animals. If this food can be made appetising enough, people may start to eat it too.

However, one thing is certain – above all man must conserve the vegetation here on earth for if by his own foolishness the green plants die, then he too will perish.

Above Many species of animals are in danger of becoming extinct because they are hunted by man and also by their natural enemies. National parks and nature reserves, especially in countries like Africa, have been created to protect and encourage wild life so that it is preserved. In these parks and reserves the balance of nature is maintained so that each species has an equal chance to grow and develop.

The world of animals

The magnificent Blue Whale is the greatest animal on earth, reaching a length of thirty metres, and weighing up to one hundred and eighty thousand kilograms. No other animal has ever reached this size. Even the dinosaurs would have looked small beside it. Although a mammal, the whale looks fish-like only because it lives in water and has a streamlined body. Also, the flat fish-like tail and the two flippers look like fins. Actually the flippers are closed-up hands for swimming with, and have finger bones inside. Apart from a whisker or two the Blue Whale is hairless. Hair would not help it to keep warm since it would always be wet. Like our clothes a mammal's hair must be dry to keep in the body heat. Instead of hair, there is a thick layer of fat – the blubber – which acts as a blanket.

Unlike the hunting Sperm Whale, which has teeth, the Blue Whale is toothless and harmless. From the upper jaws there hang two rows of bristle-like curtains, called whalebone or baleen. With this the whale catches its minute food. Every year when the long spring days bring light and sunshine to the Antarctic Ocean, the baleen whales travel south. The sea is then swarming with small shrimp-like creatures, called krill, drifting near the surface. The Blue Whale sifts this out of the water with its baleen. A mouthful of krill is caught, the seawater is then pushed out with the tongue, and the krill caught on the baleen bristles.

As winter approaches the pack-ice forms and the whales are forced northwards. Here, in the warmer waters, the females, called cows, produce their calves. A baby Blue Whale can be seven or eight metres at birth, and weigh up to ten thousand kilograms! For about six months it feeds on its mother's milk, then the whales return to the Antarctic to feed again on krill. Blue Whales travel hundreds of kilometres, eat huge meals and produce enormous babies.

The microscopic amoeba or ghost animalcule can spend all its life in a drop of pond water, where it lives the

Above The Blue Whale is the largest animal in the world and is shown in this picture alongside a man, drawn to the same scale. The Blue Whale has so much weight to bear that it would be impossible for it to live out of the water which supports it.

Above In the food chain of nature, small animals tend to be eaten by larger animals, who in turn are preyed upon by even larger animals. But all food, if it is traced back far enough, comes from plant life, since the smallest creatures live on microscopic plants. Some animals live entirely on plants.

simplest of lives. Even so, just like the whale, it moves, feeds and reproduces. Amoeba is a single-cell animal, a tiny speck of living matter covered by an elastic skin. It moves by pushing out parts of its tiny body, gliding along in a ghostly fashion. It seems to have some kind of sense because it will move away from something unpleasant, like a bright light or a poison in the water. If things get too bad, or the water dries up, it rolls into a tight ball and waits until all is well again.

To feed, the amoeba approaches a smaller animal or plant, and wraps its body around it, making a kind of stomach in itself, called a food vacuole. Inside this the food can be digested. Afterwards the stomach disappears, then is made again for the next meal. Meanwhile, another hollow collects any waste material and gets rid of it by bursting. To reproduce, the little animalcule simply acts like a mother and father in one, and divides into two. In this way its whole body goes into making two creatures and nothing is wasted. These activities, whether performed by a Blue Whale or an amoeba, are going on all the time in the animal kingdom – moving, eating, growing, reproducing and dying.

How animals live

Living things are divided into two kingdoms – plants and animals. In order to stay alive they require energy, and this comes from food. It is because plants and animals feed in different ways that we can tell them apart. Plants can actually make their own food, then use it to live and grow on. It comes from the gas carbon dioxide in the air, and water from the ground. As this is all around them plants do not need to move. They have the special chemical chlorophyll in their leaves and with this they change the carbon dioxide and water into food such as sugar and starch. Leaves are the great chemical factories of nature.

Animals have no chlorophyll and cannot make food, but must get it from plants. This is why they need to move about – to find food. They must also have a nervous system for smelling, seeing, hearing, tasting and touching. This helps them find their way about and know what is going on around them. Because plant food is a solid, animals need a mouth to take it in. Food is then broken up by the teeth or beak, and digested in the food canal by juices so that it can be carried away and stored up in fat or in the liver. Later it can be used as 'fuel' for growing and moving about. Any unused food or waste is passed out of the body.

Waste from animals may be useful as a fertiliser by making the soil in which plants grow richer and more fruitful. Also, when animals or plants die they are broken up by bacteria and what is left helps to improve the soil. In this way, by making food out of air and water, plants give life to animals. Then, animals and plants put back food into the soil when they die.

Since no animal lives for ever it must have young to carry on its kind:

this is called reproduction. The young of animals are either born or hatch from eggs. In this way we can recognise an animal – it moves and grows, it senses things, it feeds and digests with a mouth and food passage, it excretes or gets rid of waste food and poisons, and it reproduces. The remarkable thing is that all animals do these things, in spite of the great variety of shapes and sizes, and different ways of living.

Food chains

No animal can live entirely on its own. Sooner or later it must feed, and this means a plant or another animal. An amoeba feeds on tiny plants or animals. In turn it gets caught by a slightly larger water creature, such as a water-flea. These can sometimes be seen swarming in ponds, jerking about in the water. Next, a newt catches water-fleas for food. Then a water-beetle pounces and kills the newt with its powerful jaws. A little later a fish catches the beetle. Suddenly the fish too becomes a victim: from above a watchful heron darts forward with its sharp beak – and the fish is caught.

Joining up animals in this way, one catching the other, is called a food chain. This always begins with a plant because this is where all animal food comes from. Think of anything we eat and you will find it began with a plant. Food chains are working everywhere – in ponds and rivers, in the sea and on the land. Baleen whales feed on krill, and the krill feeds on tiny sea plants called diatoms.

In a woodland, caterpillars feed on leaves, and are then eaten by songbirds. Then a bird of prey such as a sparrowhawk catches the songbird. In this way a food chain can be built up like a pyramid with the leaves, which grow all over the woodland, at the bottom. Next come the caterpillars – not so many but yet in great numbers. Each moves about on a single branch and may eat two or three leaves. Then the songbirds catch the caterpillars, eating them in large numbers and feeding them to their babies. There may be about a hundred or so of these little birds in the wood. Finally, the sparrowhawk: probably there is only one pair in the whole area, hunting small birds and with a single family to feed.

Near the bottom of this pyramid are the important 'key' animals – the caterpillars. In the sea these would be the krill, and in the pond the water-fleas. At the top of the pyramid are the 'apex' animals – the sparrowhawk, the whale and the heron. Notice how all the key animals have large families and are eaten in great numbers. The larger apex animals have small families and few enemies apart from man.

Should a key animal become scarce then the food chain may be upset. When the rabbit, a valuable key animal, was nearly wiped out by myxomatosis, the buzzard which preys on rabbits stopped breeding for a while. Upsetting food chains can also be very harmful to apex animals. It is believed that some of the poisons we use on our crops and hedges can be picked up by caterpillars. They pass it on to the songbirds, and so to the sparrowhawk. This could kill the bird of prey, or make its eggs infertile, and cause the species to become rare.

Above The buzzard is a bird of prey which hunts the rabbit, an important key animal in the food chain.

Above The Peppered Moth originally had white wings speckled with dark spots, which helped it to camouflage itself against the pale lichen-covered bark of trees and thus avoid being seen and eaten by birds. During the time of the Industrial Revolution in Britain smoke from chimneys killed the lichens and turned the trees black. Over the years the Peppered Moth has gradually changed its colour to match the dark trees. This demonstrates evolution in action, and survival of the fittest, since it is vital for this insect to camouflage itself successfully.

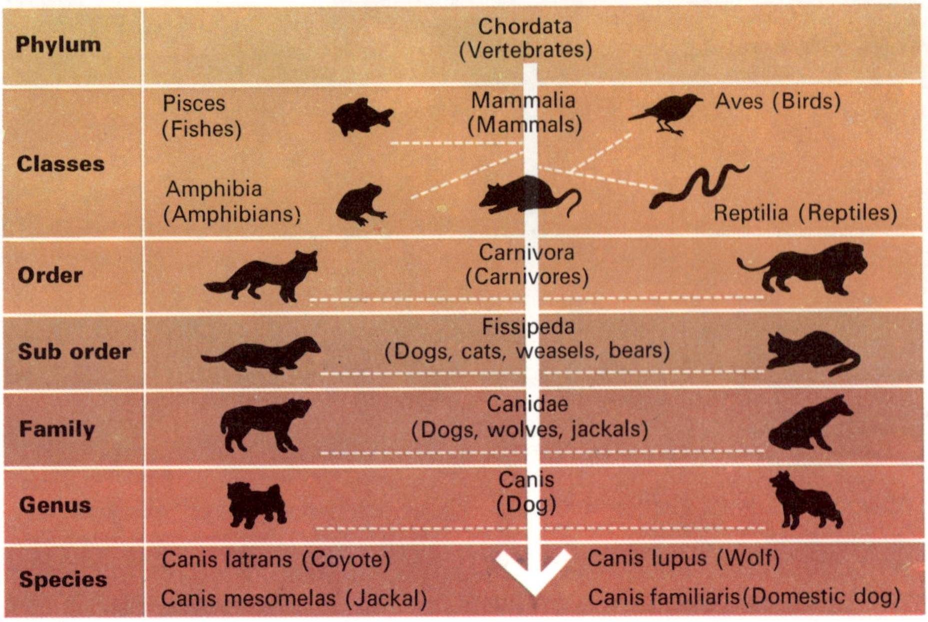

Above right This chart shows the relationship of the dog species to the phylum of Chordata or Vertebrates.

Classification of animals

To help study and recognise different kinds of animals zoologists have divided or classified them into groups, and given them scientific names. These names are made up from Latin or Greek, two 'dead' languages which are shared by every country. Each type of animal or plant, called a species, has a double name. For example the Common Frog is called *Rana temporaria*, meaning the frog of mild or temperate countries. It is known by this name all over the world. Common frogs breed only among themselves and not with other frogs, and this is the general rule with all species. The Edible Frog of Europe, called *Rana esculenta*, is not very different from the Common Frog, so these two and a number of other similar frogs are placed in a group called a genus. This would be the genus *Rana*.

The Common Toad (*Bufo bufo*), however, is built differently from a frog, so belongs to another genus, called *Bufo*. Another toad, the rare Natterjack (*Bufo calamita*), joins the Common Toad in this genus *Bufo*.

Next in grouping comes a family. The frogs belong to the family Ranidae and the toads belong to the Bufonidae. Frogs and toads have something in common – they hop. This puts them together in the next highest group, an order: it is called Salientia (from Latin, to leap).

Orders are then grouped into classes, in this case Amphibia (this is Greek for two lives). Both frogs and toads grow up in water as tadpoles, then change into adults when they come out. This also happens with newts and salamanders, but there is a difference – they have tails, and they crawl instead of hop. Their order is called Caudata (Latin for a tail).

Finally, the class Amphibia, like the Mammalia (mammals), Aves (birds), Reptilia (reptiles) and Pisces (fishes), have backbones. These make up one of the major groups of animals, called Vertebrata (Latin *vertebra*, a joint). Such a group is called a phylum. Another phylum is Mollusca (soft animals like slugs, snails and squids). A third is Arthropoda (meaning jointed legs – for example insects, scorpions and millepedes). When all the phyla are put together, the animal kingdom, or Animalia, is complete.

This method of classification is rather like the way in which an army is built up. Soldiers are put into platoons, platoons into companies, companies into battalions, then into regiments, brigades and so on to an army corps. With animal classification, however, the different species and other groups are based on how they are related. Each living species today may be compared to the buds on a tree. These lead back to the main trunk, via twigs, branches and boughs.

Classification is a kind of animal tree, but there is a lot missing. Only the 'buds' are living. All the rest is gone, or is buried in the rocks as fossils. Fossils are valuable, since they tell us what life was like long ago. People who study fossils, called palaeontologists (palaeontology meaning ancient life), have discovered many ancestors of modern animals, although they looked quite different from the ones we know today. Complete stories of animal groups have been worked out from fossils, particularly that of the horse.

The evolution theory

The idea that animals change slowly from one kind to another is called evolution and it has been going on for millions of years. This theory of evolution was explained in the last century by two great naturalists, Charles Darwin (1809-82) and Alfred Russel Wallace (1823-1913).

Until 1858 it was generally believed that life did not change. Lions always remained lions, buttercups never altered, humans were created as humans, and so on. Then, the idea that life did change – that it evolved – was proposed by Darwin and Wallace in London. Darwin called his theory 'the survival of the fittest'. So long as an animal was fitted to its surroundings, like a worm in the ground, a fish in water or a monkey up a tree, it would survive. However, in nature the surroundings are constantly changing. At one time the land in many parts of the world, for example the British Isles, did not exist, but was under the sea. This we know from sea-fossils found in the rocks. Then there were ice ages, when the woolly mammoth roamed along the Thames valley. This animal was fitted for a cold climate.

To live successfully in an ever-changing world life itself must change as well. We cannot really see evolution taking place around us because it happens too slowly. But an interesting discovery was made some years ago which shows how evolution can work – and this concerned a moth.

A common British moth, the Peppered Moth, which depends for its life on successful camouflage, gradually changed its colour to match the changes in the appearance of its surroundings.

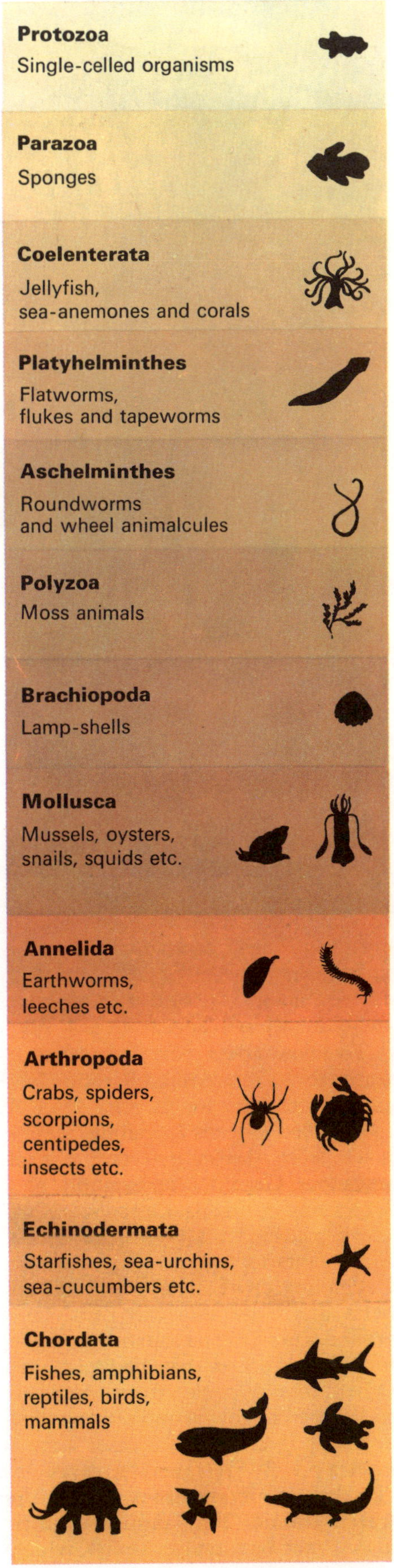

Left The animal kingdom is divided into a number of different groups, called phyla. This chart shows some of the most important of these groups and the types of animals that are included in them.

Charles Darwin (1809–82) English naturalist. World famous for his work on natural selection. In 1831–6 he went on an expedition in the waters around South America and in the Pacific as naturalist on HMS *Beagle.* His observations of animal and plant life in the Galapagos Islands in the Pacific led up to his theories on evolution. His great work on *The Origin of Species by Means of Natural Selection* was published in 1859.

Above The fossil of a bony fish some 50 million years old, which was an ancestor of the pompano fish, and once swam in the waters around Italy.

Below The colour and form of protozoans such as these can only be seen through the microscope.

The story in the rocks

Our planet was born out of the Milky Way some 4,700 million years ago. At first it was probably a swirling cloud of gases and stardust where life could not have existed. At an early stage it must have been tremendously hot, due to its own radioactivity. Not until it cooled enough to form a hard crust could life begin to appear.

To know about past life we must search for its remains in the rocks. Not all rocks contain fossils. One kind of rock, called igneous (meaning fire), is made from the molten lava out of volcanoes. Granite is an example, and it contains no fossils. Other rocks are slowly made from tiny particles of land and mountains worn away by weather. Depending on the size of these particles they form into clay, limestone or sandstone. In them can be found the fossils of creatures that died long ago. Other fossils come from lake-bed rocks, or from gravels and sand washed down by rivers. In rare cases almost perfect fossils are found in caves or, like the mammoths from Siberia, in frozen ground. Tiny animals such as insects may be found in amber, which is the hardened resin from prehistoric trees. Other fossils turn up in tar pits where they drowned long ago.

Usually only the hard pieces of an animal are preserved, such as bones, teeth and shells. Palaeontologists try to piece them together and tell us what the animals looked like, also how they lived. With the help of models and drawings we can learn something about the prehistoric animals which form part of the evolution story of life.

The first fossils

Scientists think that the earliest rocks formed about 3,800 million years ago, and the earliest life may have developed about 3,500 million years ago, 1,100 million years after the planet formed. Little is known about the life that may have existed then. It evolved in the seas and may have resembled the blue-green algae found today. The earliest creatures were tiny and fragile, with no hard parts to leave clear fossils. Also, the surface of the earth was going through tremendous upheavals.

However, a number of interesting

fossils have been found. One, named *Xenusion*, was a sea-creature, half worm and half centipede in shape and belongs to the Pre-Cambrian period.

Life must have existed for ages before we find the first clear fossils. These belong to the Cambrian period, named after Cambria, the Roman word for Wales, where these fossils were first studied. The Cambrian is the start of the first great age of life, the Ancient or Palaeozoic era, 570 million years ago. By then there were many kinds of animals living. They had three things in common. They were small, few being more than fifteen centimetres long, they lived in the seas and they had no internal skeleton. We call such animals invertebrates (animals without backbones). Many had a hard skin or shell-covering for protection.

By the end of the Cambrian most of the modern groups of invertebrates had come into being. Among the smallest were the Protozoa with bodies of only a single cell. Some called radiolarians were covered with spiky shells made of silica. Others, called foraminiferans, had shells of chalk. Descendants of these two groups are still in the sea today. Countless numbers of them in the past have filled the seas to make rocks. Some beaches today are full of their tiny shells.

Also drifting about the Cambrian seas were jellyfish. Imprints of their soft bodies have been found in rock. Curious markings resembling pencil marks are the remains of graptolites. These were colonies of tiny animals joined together on stalks which floated in the sea. Crawling on the sea-bed, and sometimes swimming, were great numbers of trilobites, the commonest of Cambrian animals. They had many legs to crawl with and a shell for covering. This was hinged so that a trilobite could curl up like a woodlouse does today. Also on the sea-bed, but usually stuck to rocks, were crinoids, creatures looking like starfishes joined to stalks. Spiny worms crawled everywhere, also a centipede-like creature resembling the ancient *Xenusion*. There were sea-cucumbers looking like those which exist now, and others more shrimp-like, also many sponges.

All this life was not so very different from that of today, except that there were no fishes or whales, which came much later. From fossils found in Cambrian rocks it seems that there was still no life on land at this time.

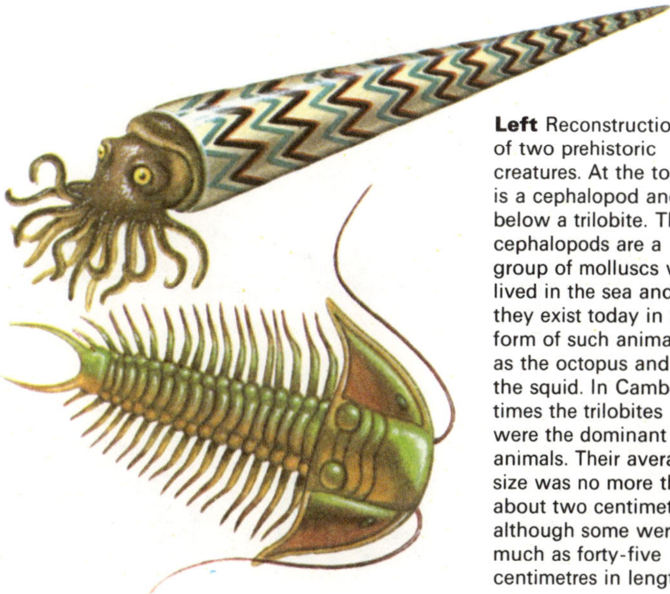

Left Reconstruction of two prehistoric creatures. At the top is a cephalopod and below a trilobite. The cephalopods are a group of molluscs which lived in the sea and they exist today in the form of such animals as the octopus and the squid. In Cambrian times the trilobites were the dominant animals. Their average size was no more than about two centimetres although some were as much as forty-five centimetres in length.

The age of shellfish

In the next period, about 500 million years ago, called the Ordovician after an old Welsh tribe, life was still in the sea. Trilobites were there, also graptolites, sea-urchins and corals. The crinoids or sea-lilies waved their arms about, catching food. Most numerous, however, were the molluscs, a group of shellfish consisting of single-shelled snails, double-shelled bivalves, and cephalopods. These last had tentacles, like a squid has today, but carried a shell. Those with long, pointed shells are called belemnites, a word meaning a dart. At one time people who found these fossil shells believed they were thunderbolts. Others had curled up shells, called ammonites after an ancient Egyptian god Ammon who had the head of a ram. Ammonite shells look like a ram's horns.

All these animals were invertebrates, but in Colorado, North America, were found some tiny pieces of fossil, probably of a fish with a bony skeleton. This was the first sign of a vertebrate, or animal with a backbone.

The early vertebrates

In the period called the Silurian, some 440 million years ago, and named after another Welsh tribe, trilobites, corals, starfishes and cephalopods continued

Alfred Russel Wallace (1823–1913) English naturalist. Travelled in the Amazon basin (1848–52) and in Malay Archipelago (1854–62). His travels furthered his interest in the problems of evolution. In 1858 he formulated his ideas on the survival of the fittest. He sent his notes to Darwin, who was surprised to find Wallace's ideas were almost identical to his own. A joint paper by Darwin and Wallace was read to the Linnean Society in 1858.

Right An impression of what a landscape might have looked like in the Devonian period. The land was partly covered with vegetation but it was only in late Devonian times that plants like ferns and horsetails developed.

Below The mudskipper is a fish adapted for life on land as well as in the sea.

to flourish. Very common were the brachiopods, called lamp-shells from the shape of the shell which was like an old-fashioned oil lamp. In the Silurian seas lived one of the largest invertebrates that ever existed, called an eurypterid. It was a kind of prehistoric sea-scorpion over two and a half metres long.

At this time the invertebrates dominated the sea. On land the first known plants were beginning to appear. But there were also newcomers – primitive vertebrates, small and jawless little fishes called ostracoderms. Apart from a bony backbone they had a hard outer coat as protection against enemies like the sea-scorpions. Of these two the ostracoderms were to survive, but the eurypterids died out.

The walking fishes

The Devonian period, named after the county of Devon in England, comes next, some 395 million years ago. It is often called the Age of Fishes. By now many kinds swarmed in the seas. There were also great coral reefs, many kinds of lamp-shells, sponges, sea-lilies, starfishes and a few eurypterids. Trilobites, however, were beginning to die out, so were the graptolites. The number of fishes had increased enormously and there were many kinds – big and small, slow and fast, some scaly and others bony.

Devonian fishes were of four kinds. Firstly, there were still a number of ostracoderms about. Then there were the ancestors of the shark. Because of their soft skeletons only teeth of fossil sharks are usually found. There were also armoured fishes with bony coverings called placoderms. Some grew into giants such as the nine-metre *Dinichthys*. The fourth group were true fishes with hard skeletons and jaws. These were of two kinds. Some called 'ray-fins' are quite common today. Their fins are shaped like a fan, with rows of bones spreading out from the base. Others, the 'fringe-fins', had fins placed on little bony stalks like miniature legs. These fringe-fins could also take in air to breathe with, since their nostrils led to a kind of lung or air-bladder inside the body. Similar fish, called lungfish, still exist today.

The ability to breathe was very useful to the fringe-fins because there were heavy drought periods in the Devonian, when whole lakes and rivers dried up. Fishes which could not breathe air would have died, but the fringe-fins could crawl away to another lake. Gradually they became more and

Below Eurypterids, prehistoric sea-scorpions, were like early forms of crabs. They were powerful swimmers in water.

more used to land, and their fins slowly turned into legs and arms with fingers and toes. They became amphibians, the first vertebrates to walk out on land. The word amphibian means 'a double life'. A few fossils have been found in Devonian rocks in Greenland, also footprints in other places.

As these early land vertebrates moved away from the water, the invertebrates were also experimenting on land. There were scorpions, insects and millepedes, but none of them could yet fly.

The 'halfway' animals

During the early part of the Carboniferous period (Coal Age), about 345 million years ago, there were clear and shallow seas in many places, containing much lime. The mud which formed turned into limestone rocks. These contain many fossils of coral, shellfish, cephalopods, lamp-shells and sea-lillies. Not many amphibians have been found in these rocks except a few bits and pieces, also footprints. In the second half of the Carboniferous, however, great changes took place. The sea-bed rose up to make low-lying land on which lagoons and swamps developed. In these surroundings the great forests grew up and died, slowly changing into coal. The black substance carbon, of which much of coal is made, gives the name to this period.

In the swamps lived many amphibians, some growing up to three metres long, called giant salamanders. Their food was probably the many kinds of snails, centipedes, scorpions and cockroaches which lived among the ferns. Larger salamanders probably preyed on the lungfishes and king-crabs living in the swamps. Some insects could fly, such as the giant dragonflies with wings seventy-five centimetres across.

Some time during the Carboniferous something important took place which made it possible for the vertebrates to leave the water entirely. An amphibian, such as a frog, must usually lay its eggs in water because life for it starts as a gilled tadpole. A change took place when some amphibians began laying eggs, which they covered with a shell, on land. From such a shell-egg there hatched out a new kind of vertebrate – a reptile. What happened then was that the babies, instead of growing up in the swamps, did so inside their eggs, in little 'private ponds'.

Above The period known as Carboniferous is usually split into two, called the Lower and the Upper. This picture represents a scene during Upper Carboniferous times. There were great swamps and the many trees formed the beginning of the coal forests of later periods. Seen in the picture is one of the giant dragonflies which existed then.

The great invasion

A reptile does not need to stay close to water to produce a family. Instead she takes her eggs with her, then lays them when and where she chooses on dry land. This could be the reason why the reptiles became so successful, and started the greatest invasion this world has ever known – the conquest of the land. Living out of water they went everywhere.

This invasion started in a small way during the Permian period, about 280 million years ago. It is named after a place in the Ural mountains of Russia. One interesting Permian fossil is *Seymouria*, a kind of half amphibian and reptile. But true reptiles were turning up everywhere. Some of the most curious were the sail-backs. They had high fin-like growths on their backs, and because they lived in desert surroundings these 'sails' could have acted as radiators to get rid of extra heat. Sail-backs were scaly, and this is

Right A number of the most important dinosaurs are grouped together in this picture, but they did not all live at the same time. **1** *Pteranodon* and **6** *Rhamphorhynchus* were flying reptiles. **2** *Stegosaurus* and **9** *Triceratops* were protected by armoured skins. **3** *Mastodonsaurus* resembled a gigantic frog. **4** *Iguanodon* probably ran upright on its back legs. **5** *Diplodocus* was a giant plant-eater. **7** *Tyrannosaurus* was one of the most terrible flesh-eating dinosaurs. **8** *Phororhacos* was a large flightless bird

Richard Owen (1804–92) English zoologist. Curator of Hunterian collections at Royal College of Surgeons. Produced series of catalogues. His knowledge of anatomy helped his researches into the life of prehistoric animals and fossil reconstruction. Was superintendent of the Natural History section of the British Museum and was responsible for the present museum buildings in South Kensington, London. Because he opposed Darwin's theories his scientific influence declined in later years.

common to reptiles, helping them to stand the dry atmosphere and to keep in the moisture in their bodies. Reptiles today can bask for long periods in hot sun, whereas amphibians with soft and naked skins would soon die of exposure.

These two things – laying shell-eggs on land, and being protected by scales – must have helped reptiles to travel far from water. By the end of the Permian the amphibians were losing their hold and reptiles were on their way to dominating all other animals. In the sea the trilobites and sea-scorpions were almost finished. Over the next three periods, land, sea and air were to be taken over by reptiles, ending up with the world's greatest land creatures, the dinosaurs. The Middle or Mesozoic era is about to begin with the Triassic.

Early reptiles

The Triassic period, some 225 million years ago, is so called because it shows three distinct layers of rock (*tri* means three). In those days life in the sea had not changed much. Ammonites, corals and sea-lilies were abundant, so were the molluscs. Lamp-shells were dying away, and the trilobites had disappeared. Bony fishes were increasing and there were even flying fish. Except for giant salamanders the amphibians were getting rare. For one thing there were not many swamps left owing to a much drier climate. A few lungfishes shared the remaining swamps with the salamanders.

Reptiles with scaly skins were much better suited to the dry, sandy country. On land there were various kinds, none very large. There were clumsy, four-footed ones, and others more graceful on two legs – these could hop and run about quite swiftly. No more than about a metre high these lively reptiles were actually the ancestors of the dinosaurs which were to appear as giants to dominate the animal world during the next two periods.

Other interesting reptiles were the dog-tooths. These were mammal-like reptiles with sharp dog-teeth, like *Cynognathus*, which caught and tore

up their animal prey. We do not know whether these early mammal-reptiles were warm-blooded or coated in hair, because this does not show in a fossil. Others like *Triassochelys* were the first turtles, which also had teeth for eating meat.

Crocodile ancestors appeared in the Triassic, but most remarkable of all were the sea-reptiles which must have looked just like fish. They are called ichthyosaurs, meaning fish-lizards. They had streamlined bodies, a fin on the back and a fish-like tail. Their feet were shaped like paddles. Like all reptiles they breathed air and kept coming to the surface of the sea (a fish breathes with gills and can stay below). The ichthyosaur's long beak was studded with sharp teeth for catching fish. Other sea-reptiles, called nothosaurs, had long necks. The fish and ammonites in the Jurassic seas had to avoid these reptiles, or be eaten.

The age of dinosaurs

About 150 million years ago in the Jurassic period, named after the Jura mountains on the borders of Switzerland, great reptiles flourished, especially the dinosaurs (this word means terrible lizards). From simple beginnings in the Triassic they evolved into monsters like the *Apatosaurus* or thunder lizard. It was over twenty-four metres long and must have weighed some thirty thousand kilograms. Its tiny head contained a brain no larger than a hen's egg. It was clumsy and slow-moving and probably quite harmless.

Because of its great weight *Apatosaurus* and similar dinosaurs may have spent most of their lives in swamps. There the water would have supported their weight and they could have eaten water plants.

However, it is possible that *Apatosaurus* may have lived on dry land. It would have been rather like a giant reptilian elephant. It would have moved around in herds and used its long neck to reach leaves at the tops of trees. It is is also thought that the young *Apatosaurs* lived with their parents and were protected by them if

Thomas H. Huxley (1825–95) English biologist. He studied medicine and was an assistant surgeon in the Royal Navy. His early researches into marine animal life led to his election as a member of the Royal Society. Naturalist to the Geological Survey and lecturer in natural history at the Royal School of Mines, 1854. He was one of the most important scientific men of his day, a great champion of Darwin's ideas and a brilliant public speaker.

a meat-eating dinosaur attacked.

Another giant, *Stegosaurus* or plated lizard, had a bulky body with a curious frill of bony plates down its back, a spiky tail and a tiny head. It too weighed about thirty thousand kilograms but it had only a very tiny brain. In the hips was a kind of second brain, very much larger. This was used only for controlling automatic movements, called reflexes, and not for thinking.

On land a sub-tropical countryside of palm-like trees, called cycads, grew everywhere. They were evergreen and produced cones. As yet there were no flowers. Insects such as dragonflies, grasshoppers, beetles and flies abounded among the cycads, but the giant salamanders had gone. In their place were the first frogs and toads. In the sea the ichthyosaurs flourished, joined by long-necked plesiosaurs, great sea-monsters which were sometimes over nine metres. Plesiosaurs used their fins like oars to twist and turn, even back-paddling, to catch the elusive fishes and squids. They shared the seas with sharks and rays, sea-cows and turtles.

Above In 1811 at Lyme Regis on the Dorset coast in Britain, eleven-year-old Mary Anning found the first known fossil of an ichthyosaur. She spent her time hunting for fossils and whenever she found one Mary put her little dog Tray on guard, and then she fetched workmen to dig out the fossil.

The ichthyosaurs must have looked very like fishes. We know this from some beautifully preserved fossils found in slate quarries in Germany. The slate was made from fine chalky silt laid down in a shallow Jurassic sea. Apart from the skeleton the outline of the body is also shown, a very unusual thing for fossils. It shows a fin on the back, a fish-like tail, and feet covered in as paddles.

The chalk period

The Cretaceous period is named from the Latin *creta*, meaning chalk. An enormous layer of chalk, more than a hundred metres thick, lies mainly in south-east England under the downs, and can be seen as tall cliffs at Dover and Eastbourne. At first, however, the shallow Cretaceous seas were slowly filled with mud brought down by rivers. These formed coloured rocks with names like Blue Gault and Greensand. In them are found many fossils of sponges, corals, molluscs, ammonites, sea-urchins and starfishes.

Later, when the land had been worn flat, most of the mud was formed in the sea itself. This came from tiny bits of broken shell of sea animals, also from minute plants. In this way the white chalk was made, very slowly, at the rate of about ten centimetres every ten thousand years.

Chalk often contains a stone called flint. This comes from the tiny spicules (needle-like bodies) of silica, a mineral which supported the bodies of soft sponges. When the sponges died the spicules fell out and washed into the gaps in the chalk. Sometimes a flint

Left The large animal skeleton is that of *Diplodocus*, a giant dinosaur up to 27 metres in length. Alongside it are a man and a boy drawn to the same scale. The fossil skeleton is a well-preserved example of an ichthyosaur. A reconstruction of the *Archaeopteryx* is also seen above. The fossil of this prehistoric animal was a key find, for it is a creature halfway between a reptile and a bird.

fossil may be found in a chalk cliff, a cast of the original animal. It died on the sea-bed, rotted away, and the space then filled up with flint spicules. One day, millions of years later, Stone Age man would be making his tools out of flint from the downs where he lived in prehistoric Britain.

In the chalk seas lived starfishes, sea-urchins, sponges and many shell-fish. Ammonites and belemnites were very common. The ichthyosaurs were becoming rare, but plesiosaurs had increased, becoming huge and powerful. They shared the sea with giant turtles, also a vicious reptile called a *Mosasaur*. It was shaped like a huge snake and had long, spiky teeth for catching its prey. Sharks and rays also dwelt in these shallow seas, so did an enormous herring-like fish, about four and a half metres long.

In the sky flew the pterodactyls or wing-fingers. These remarkable reptiles had greatly lengthened little fingers to support the wings with which they managed somehow to fly. One of them, *Pteranodon*, had a wing span of about six metres.

On the land were dinosaurs somewhat different from those of the Jurassic, but no less huge and domineering – it was still very much a reptile age. One of these was *Iguanodon* which moved about on powerful hind legs and used a long tail for balance. This was the first kind of dinosaur ever discovered. One morning in 1822 Mrs Mantell, the wife of a country doctor, found a fossil tooth just outside Horsham in Sussex, England. Further pieces turned up in a nearby quarry, and from this Dr Mantell built up an image of this dinosaur.

Iguanodon was a plant-eater, so too was *Trachodon*, sometimes called a duckbill. It had a curious flat beak crammed with some 2,400 teeth which it used for crushing and straining water plants. There were webs between its toes, and it could probably swim – at least paddle. Like many other dinosaurs it lived by swamps and lakes, so that fossil footprints have been found. In those days a large inland sea covered much of south-east England and Belgium.

Of all the giants one of the most terrifying must surely have been the *Tyrannosaurus* or tyrant lizard. It stood about six metres tall and measured some twelve metres from nose to tail. The teeth were fifteen centimetres long and it had great claws on its toes. Whereas *Iguanodon* and *Trachodon* could escape enemies by running away or leaping into the water there were other dinosaurs that were equipped for defence. The armoured kinds had thick coats of bony plates and scales, and were like living tanks. Others like *Triceratops* had horns on their heads, and a curved bony hood over the neck.

One of the most exciting discoveries about dinosaurs has been the finding of eggs. An American team searching in the Gobi Desert in Mongolia in 1922 found a nest of eggs laid by a small dinosaur, called *Protoceratops*. They were so perfectly preserved that

Above Footprints of dinosaurs have been found in sandstone which dates from the time of the Triassic period, particularly in valleys in America.

Above The earliest ancestor of the horse lived about 70 million years ago. It was a tiny creature no bigger than a fox terrier (top), called *Eohippus*. Later fossils of horses show a gradual increase in size. There was a later horse about the size of a very large dog, then another of donkey size, and so on until we come to the horse of today, which seems a giant compared with *Eohippus*.

when the eggs were carefully cut into very thin slices and placed under a microscope the outline of babies could be seen. They died some eighty million years ago!

By the time the chalk was being built most of the dinosaurs had passed away. The great reptile age was coming to an end. So were the evergreen cycads on which they fed. Instead there were flowering trees like elm, maple and oak, also pines. Perhaps this is why dinosaurs did disappear, because of a changing climate with not enough food to go round, since flowering trees lose their leaves during winter. The pterodactyls, pleisosaurs and ichthyosaurs were gone by the end of the Chalk age, sixty-five million years ago. The mammals were about to take over.

The dawn period

The Eocene, meaning dawn period, starts a third era called the Tertiary. With the dying out of reptiles the Age of Mammals began. With little competition from other animals they rapidly developed and spread everywhere, and in them we can recognise the ancestors of most of the present-day mammals. On land there were still a number of shrew-like mammals resembling the earlier Jurassic forms. Others, called creodonts, were primitive flesh-eaters. They had sharp claws and cutting teeth, and hunted the many plant-eaters. A number of these had hoofs for fast running and grinding teeth for eating grass and leaves. One of them was the little *Eohippus* which one day was to develop into the modern horse.

Another midget was the elephant's ancestor, *Moeritherium* – no bigger than a pig. It had no trunk but a pointed snout, and probably rooted about like a pig. In the trees lived tiny animals with hands and long tails. Called tarsioids, they were early primates which later evolved into monkeys, then apes, and finally man. In the air above the Eocene forests there were bats, and in the sea were whales. Birds were everywhere, and they shared the countryside with the mammals.

Birds and mammals have one important advantage over their reptile ancestors. They have warm bodies protected by fur or feathers, so they can stand up to cold weather. Also,

their babies are given special protection. Whereas most reptiles lay eggs, then leave them to be hatched by the heat of the sun, a bird builds a nest, sits on the eggs to hatch them, then feeds the fledglings. A baby mammal is even more protected. It grows inside its mother's body where it is warm and safe, then feeds on mother's milk when it is born.

Most of the Eocene mammals were small, but a few did grow to enormous size, like the *Uintatherium* and the *Arsinoitherium*, two giant hoofed mammals with horns sprouting from their heads. Like other giants they died out, whereas the little *Eohippus* and *Moeritherium* and the tarsioid evolved into the modern horse, elephant and man.

The plants among which these early mammals roamed were very much like those of today, such as magnolias, water-lilies and palms, swamp cypresses and pines. The sea, too, contained much which is seen today – cockles, cowries and oysters among shellfish, and crabs, starfish and sea-urchins in plenty. The ammonites had nearly gone. Bony fishes were dominant, and lived beside the sharks and whales.

Left All modern apes and eventually man himself have descended from the small tree-dwelling ape called *Proconsul* (far left). A later ape who walked upright was *Australopithecus* (centre) who may have used tools and weapons in his hunt for food. Peking man (right) belonged to a group of fossil men who lived about half a million years ago and is named from remains found near Peking in China.

The rise of mammals

In the next three periods – the Oligocene, Miocene and Pliocene – various kinds of mammals developed and died out, but all the time numbers were increasing so that today mammals are the dominant animals of the world. Apart from whales and elephants most of the giants became extinct, including a huge kind of giraffe over four and a half metres tall. It belonged to the Oligocene about 38 million years ago.

From our point of view the Miocene is perhaps the most interesting period. About twenty-five million years ago a small tree-dwelling ape lived in the Central African forest. A fossil of it was found in Kenya. This is called *Proconsul* and is another famous missing link between the ape and man.

The beginnings of man

From *Proconsul* there have descended all the modern apes, and also man. Another link in the fascinating story of man's evolution appears with the finding of many fossils of the man-apes who also lived in Africa. This was at a time of drought when the climate was much drier, and open grassy plains took the place of forests. A few apes existed in the remaining trees, but there was also a ground ape which walked upright. It is called *Australopithecus*, meaning the Southern Ape, and many remains have been found, especially in a deep ravine in Tanzania, called the Olduvai Gorge. Southern Apes go back nearly two million years. With their remains have been found primitive tools made out of bone and stone. These helped them to kill and skin animals, and so add meat to the berries, nuts and insects which their tree cousins fed on.

Another chapter in the story of man goes back about half a million years. In two places – on the island of Java, and close to the Chinese city of Peking – remains of some more advanced Stone Age hunters have been found. Called *Homo erectus*, they were quite skilled in making weapons and tools out of stone, bone and sticks. They also used fire for warmth and protection.

The ice age

We now shift to Europe where, in 1848, some workmen found a skull buried in one of the caves on the Rock of Gibraltar. It was so battered that its

Above *Uintatherium*, the largest of Eocene mammals, had curious bony projections on top of its skull. It had a heavy body with short powerful legs. It did not eat meat but lived entirely on plants.

Above Neanderthal man lived at the same time as the woolly mammoth, which he hunted for food. He lived in caves and wore rough clothing made from the skins of animals.

importance was not realised until 1856. A second, and more complete, skull was found on the banks of a small river in north Germany – the Neander. We now know a great deal about these early humans called Neanderthals (meaning men of the Neander valley) who lived during the ice age.

In fact, the ice spread down over Europe four times. In between each spread the ice melted and the weather warmed up. This is why, during a cold ice period, all life was pushed southwards. In Britain, for example, the ice sheet stopped just north of the Thames valley. The mammoth, woolly rhinoceros, reindeer and Arctic fox lived along its borders, and their remains have been found underneath London. When the ice melted everything moved north, and the southern animals took their place. In those warmer spells lions lived in the Thames woodlands and hippos swam in the river.

Neanderthal man lived south of the ice during the cold period, about 50,000 years ago. About one and a half metres tall, he had a heavy face with powerful jaws, thick eyebrows and sloping forehead. His brain was much smaller than ours, yet he could outwit the ice age animals, even catching the mammoth in traps. Sometimes he shared his home with the cave bear. Skins from the kill were used as clothing. He must have had a kind of religion because he buried his dead. The Neanderthals lived a wild and difficult life in the cold climate, and in time they died out.

Modern man

As the last ice invasion began to move north, another race of man moved up from Africa, slowly advancing into Europe to clash with the Neanderthals. This was our own ancestor, who bears our name *Homo sapiens*. Some scientists name him Cro-Magnon man after a place in France where his home used to be, about 30,000 years ago. In fact, he has been found in many European countries including Britain. Cro-Magnon had a much more human face than Neanderthal, with a noble forehead and pointed chin, and a better brain. He also grew taller and was far superior in his handiwork. He made beautiful weapons and tools out of stone and bone. He was also a fine artist, famous for his cave paintings and for carvings. A splendid art gallery containing hundreds of coloured drawings was found in a cave at Lascaux in France by two schoolboys. It shows pictures of deer, horses, bison, wild ox and many other animals, all of which Cro-Magnon must have hunted.

Gradually, after thousands of years roaming about as hunters, men began to settle down in one place. They built homes, tamed the wild animals and grew crops. Man was turning into a farmer. The oldest traces of such a farming village lie under the walls of the ancient city of Jericho, and are 8,000 years old. At long last man had reached the Neolithic or New Stone Age. It was the dawn of civilisation, leading into history.

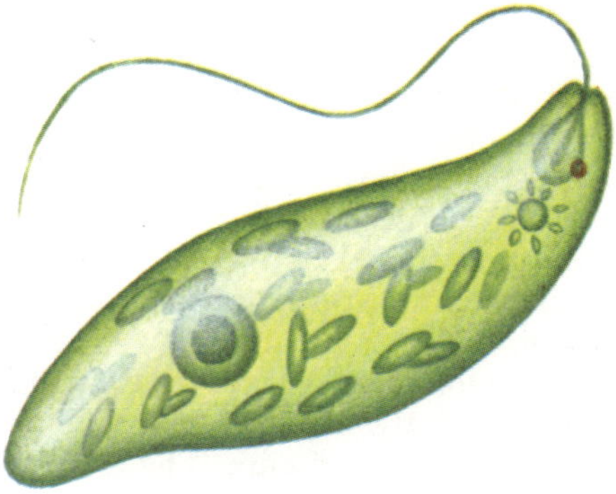

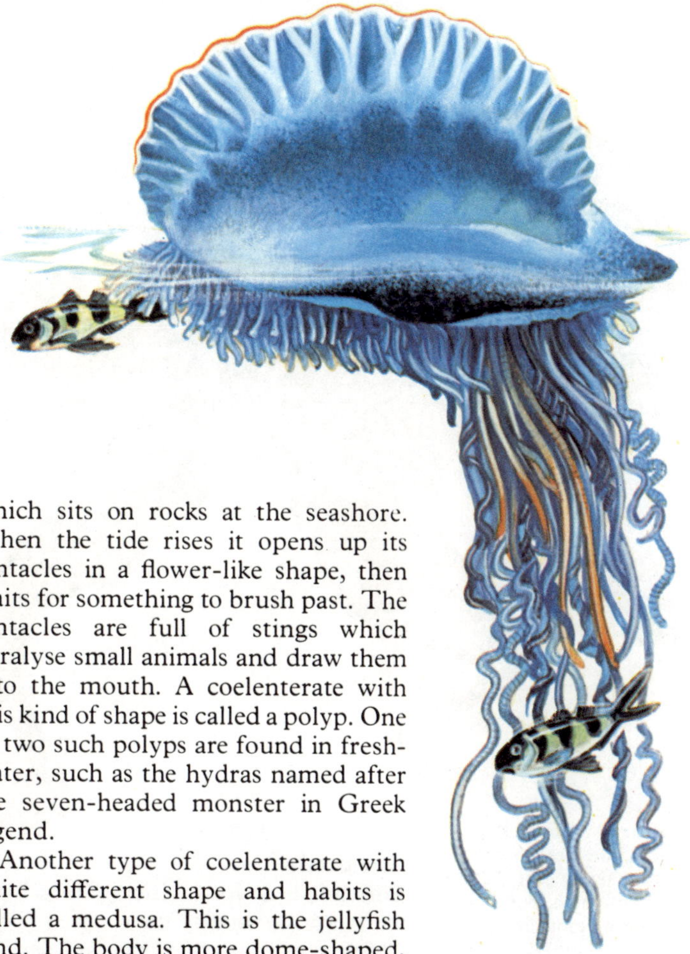

Animals of today

The Protozoa (meaning first animals) are the simplest animals and there are about 30,000 different kinds, all of which have something in common. Their tiny bodies are composed of a single unit or cell, and they are descendants of some of the earliest animals. Because they are so small most of them are hidden from our eyes, yet they swarm in vast numbers all around us – in the soil, in lakes and ponds, and in the sea. Some, like *Amoeba*, crawl about in ghostly fashion. Others like *Euglena* have a little whip-like cord, called a flagellum, which twirls in the water to pull it along. A third group have their cells covered with tiny threads, called cilia, which beat the water like oars and push the protozoan along. A common example of this group is *Paramecium*.

The fourth group is somewhat different. This includes motionless cells which live and feed inside other animals, including man, and behave as parasites. Some can be dangerous, and only through a microscope can they be seen. This is how malaria was discovered in the body of a mosquito. At one time people thought the disease came from the bad smell of the swamps (malaria is French for bad air). Another protozoan disease is sleeping sickness, carried by the tsetse fly.

Coelenterates

Most animals have an outer body wall with a food passage passing through it. Food enters at the mouth and waste passes out through the anus. The 9,000 species of coelenterates have just a body wall and a single opening ringed with tentacles. An example is the sea-anemone, a soft-bodied little animal which sits on rocks at the seashore. When the tide rises it opens up its tentacles in a flower-like shape, then waits for something to brush past. The tentacles are full of stings which paralyse small animals and draw them into the mouth. A coelenterate with this kind of shape is called a polyp. One or two such polyps are found in freshwater, such as the hydras named after the seven-headed monster in Greek legend.

Another type of coelenterate with quite different shape and habits is called a medusa. This is the jellyfish kind. The body is more dome-shaped, the mouth underneath, and the tentacles dangle. A jellyfish drifts with the sea currents, and can sometimes be a nuisance to bathers. One species, the Portuguese man-of-war, can cause a painful burn, and has an air-filled bladder acting like a sail.

A third type of coelenterate is called coral. This is really a whole mass of polyps which are joined up as a branching colony. To protect and cover up this living coral, lime is taken from the sea-water and built into a hard skeleton. This can form a reef which may be a hundred metres deep. Since coral builds very slowly some reefs must be millions of years old.

As the sea-bed slowly sinks the living coral grows to keep level with the surface of the sea. A reef which forms along a tropical coastline cuts off some of the sea to form a lagoon. In the clear and still water live a great variety of fishes and other sea-life, including beautiful worms, molluscs, anemones and sea-urchins. The reef may be visited by sea-birds and turtles who go there to lay their eggs.

Above The Portuguese man-of-war is a jellyfish which lives mostly in open seas. It has a large float and long tentacles from ten to thirty centimetres long. Its sting can be dangerous to man.

Above left *Euglena*, shown in this drawing greatly magnified. There are many species in this genus of tiny protozoans and one characteristic clearly seen in this picture is the whip-like flagellum with which it pulls itself along.

Above Although the Common Octopus does move by jet propulsion it also crawls along by using its tentacles.

Annelids

Annelids is a word which comes from the Latin *annulus*, meaning a ring. There are about 7,000 species of worms in this group and they have segmented bodies which show as rings on the outside. Earthworms are the best known because we find them in gardens and fields. There are many kinds of earthworm and they burrow in the earth by eating their way through the soil. What they cannot digest is passed out as worm casts on the surface of lawns. Garden worms feed mostly on leaves and other plant matter, sometimes pulling this into their burrows. They prefer damp and dark surroundings, coming out after rain or at night. British earthworms are about fifteen centimetres long, but in Australia giant worms may grow to about three and a half metres.

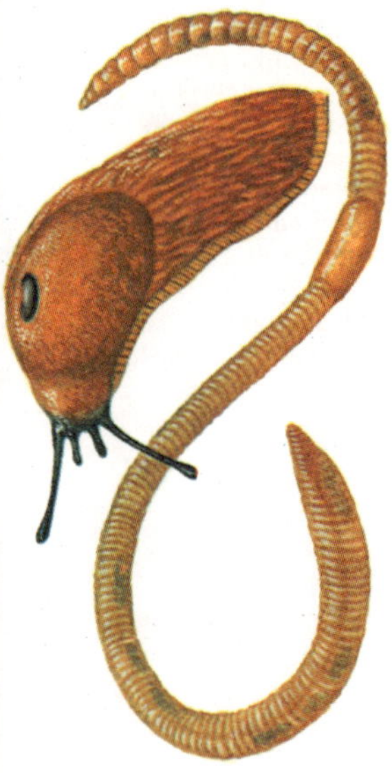

Above Some slugs are highly coloured, as seen in this drawing. Slugs and worms are not always popular with gardeners, though worms help to keep the soil sweet by turning it and letting in air.

Bristleworms are related to earthworms and live in the sea. They have small feet on each segment for crawling and burrowing. Most of them live in the sand, coming out of their burrows when the tide is in. Their long, plume-like tentacles wave through the water to catch minute animals and to breathe oxygen. Worm casts can be seen along the beach at low tide, and perhaps a fisherman will be digging worms up for bait. Shore birds such as waders also hunt for worms. Some marine worms are very beautifully coloured.

Other annelids, called leeches, cling to their victims with strong suckers, feeding on blood. They are parasites and sometimes attack humans, especially in jungle surroundings. At one time doctors used leeches for drawing off a patient's blood, called blood-letting, as a kind of cure. The doctors themselves were called leeches, and there is a British species called the medicinal leech.

Parasitic worms

Most annelid worms live freely in the soil or water, but some worm-like groups live inside other animals, even man. One of these is the group called Nematoda, or roundworms, containing some 10,000 species. They are pale in colour, without segments, and have pointed ends. They move about in a curious figure-of-eight fashion. Some of these nematodes, can be up to fifteen centimetres long, but many kinds are microscopic. All told there are vast numbers of these nematodes living in all sorts of animals, also plants, and a great number in the soil.

Each animal victim of a parasite is called a host. The human is host to another kind of worm, called a tapeworm. This belongs to the group of 6,000 species called Platyhelminthes or flatworms. In this case there are two hosts, the human and another animal which he may eat as meat, such as pork or beef. The pig or bull may pick up a tapeworm egg and swallow it. This hatches into a larva and bores into the flesh.

Another type of flatworm, called a fluke, has the shape of a small leaf. One example is the liver-fluke which attacks sheep.

Molluscs

These invertebrates (about 80,000 species) have soft bodies (*mollis*, Latin for soft) but may cover themselves with a shell. This can be single as in snails (called univalves), or double as in mussels (called bivalves). The snail type of mollusc crawls about on a broad foot, and rasps at its food, usually plants, with a tongue covered in horny teeth rather like a file. Some snails live in freshwater but they need to surface for air.

Many more univalves live in the sea, and can be found in rock pools. One of the commonest is the limpet which has a tent-shaped shell and clings tightly to rock. In this way it can live out of water when the tide is low, as there is enough moisture under the shell to prevent the limpet from dying. When the tide is in the limpet glides over the rock, feeding on the film of plant life, but always gets back to its old spot before the tide goes out.

Periwinkles, top-shells and dog-whelks can also be found in rock pools. There are many tropical snails with shells of beautiful patterns, such as cowries, cameo shells (*Cassis*) and mother-of-pearl shells (*Haliotis*). These are collected by people and some are rare and valuable.

Slugs live on land and in the sea, feeding on plants and debris. Garden slugs and snails are unpopular with gardeners because of the damage they do to plants. Some very handsome slugs live in coral reefs, brightly coloured and graceful in movement. One slug, called a sea-hare, gives off a cloud of dark poison for protection.

Bivalves live only in water, either fresh or salt. They usually stay in one place, or move about slowly by pushing out a narrow foot into the mud or sand. This foot swells at the tip, then it contracts and so pulls the shell along after it. The pond mussel moves in this way, but the common sea mussel on our shore stays in one place tied to its neighbours on the rocks or breakwaters. Out of water a mussel shuts tight, but once the tide comes in it opens its shell to uncover two openings, called siphons. Water passes in at one siphon and out through the other. In this manner a bivalve filters the water through its body and feeds on the microscopic water life.

The oyster is a bivalve which is eaten as a delicacy. One kind, the pearl oyster, may grow a pearl under its shell. This is due to an irritation, probably a tiny speck of sand, which the oyster covers with mother-of-pearl.

The third group of molluscs have tentacles instead of a foot, and can swim about. They are called cephalopods, meaning a head-foot. The tentacles surround the head and mouth, and have suckers for catching or holding food. One group, the squids, have ten tentacles and are called decapods. They can shoot through the sea backwards by squirting water out of their siphon – a kind of jet propulsion. The Pearly Nautilus is a cephalopod with a shell, and resembles the ancient ammonites.

There are some deepwater giant squids which grow to eighteen metres long, and are hunted by sperm whales. The octopus has only eight tentacles (an octopod) and is not so dangerous as people imagine. It hides between the rocks, darting out its tentacles to catch crabs. Cuttlefish are also cephalopods which contain a skeleton called cuttlebone. This can be found on the beach, and is sold in pet-shops for cage birds to sharpen their beaks on.

Molluscs are egg-layers, and their spawn can be found attached to plants or buried in the soil. Land molluscs usually remain hidden until dark, or after rain, before they show themselves. Some of them have a strong 'homing' instinct, and the slime trail of a garden snail can often be seen forming a wide circle and finishing up where it started. The snail will be hidden somewhere behind a stone or flower-pot.

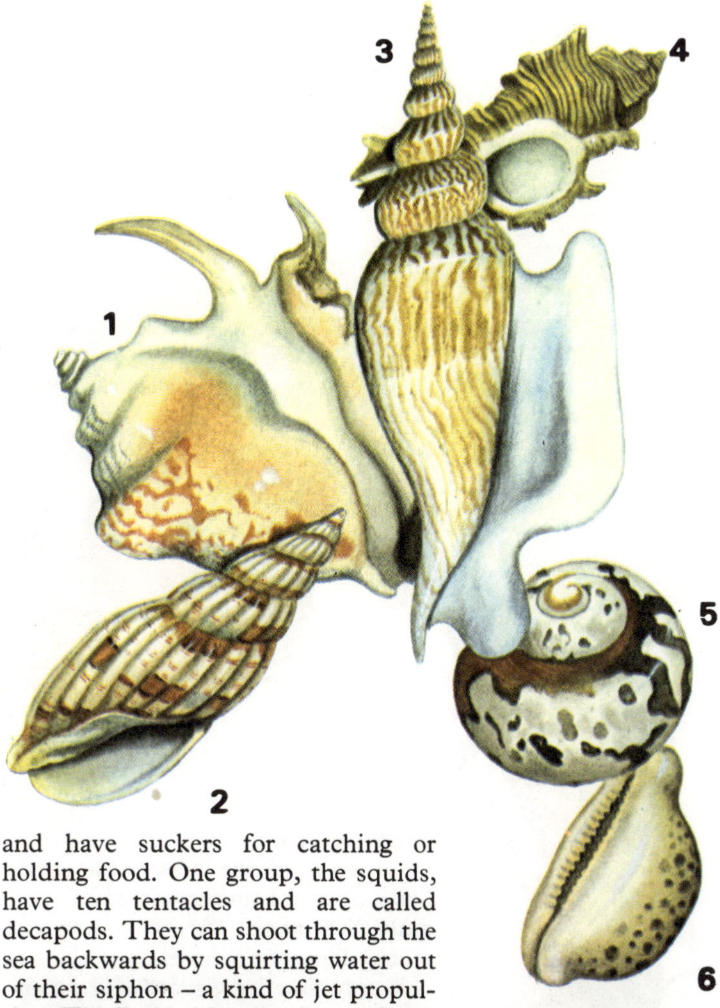

Above Shells of tropical animals have a vast range of form and colour. Some shell collections are very rare and valuable. The names of the shells in the drawing are **1** *Lambis violacia,* **2** *Lyria lyraeformis,* **3** *Strombus listri,* **4** *Murex,* **5** *Turbo sarmaticus,* and **6** *Cypraea tigris.*

Above Beetles form the largest order of insects with over 250,000 species. Shown above are (from top to bottom) the Hercules Beetle which comes from Central and South America and measures over twelve centimetres long, then the Museum Beetle and the Six Spot Tiger Beetle.

Arthropods

This is one of the most widespread divisions of the animal kingdom, certainly the largest. Arthropod means jointed legs but whereas vertebrates have only four legs, some of these invertebrates have many more. The main classes of arthropods are insects, arachnids (spiders, scorpions and mites), millepedes and centipedes, and crustaceans (crabs, lobsters and shrimps).

Insects

Insects are the biggest class of all animals, numbering nearly one million species. They are found everywhere except in the sea. Insects (from Latin *secare*, to cut) have six legs, bodies divided into three parts (head, thorax and abdomen) and go through several stages in their life history – egg, larva, pupa and adult. Whereas some insects are useful to man by providing him with honey, also helping to pollinate flowers, others can be harmful. Locusts attack crops and termites damage homes. Flies and mosquitoes spread disease. In turn the insects provide food for other animals. There are about thirty groups or orders of insects, and the following are the best known.

Butterflies and **moths** are attractive insects which do little harm, except in a few cases, such as the Cabbage White Butterfly. Also, some caterpillars of moths can damage trees. The word butterfly comes from butter-coloured fly, and was originally given to the species called Brimstone. Butterflies usually fly by day, and visit flowers for nectar. Some, like the Painted Lady, migrate to Britain each year from Africa. The most spectacular migration is that of the large Monarch Butterfly which travels hundreds of kilometres through North America. Large and colourful butterflies occur in tropical countries, some with wings fifteen centimetres across.

Moths, which are mostly night flyers, are more dully coloured, and camouflage well against their resting places during the daytime. There are giant moths, too, like the Atlas Moth of India. This is a member of the silk-moth family. Their caterpillars weave a cocoon of silk inside which they pupate, or undergo a stage in their development.

Beetles are insects with hard skins and wings which are protected by horny outer covers, called elytra. The true

Above Shown here are two moths and three butterflies. They are (left to right), **1** *Pholous labruscae* (Gaudy sphinx), **2** *Arctia caga* (Garden tiger), **3** *Papilo antimachus*, **4** *Leptocircus meges indistincta* (Green dragontail) and **5** *Hestia durvillei.* The last three are the butterflies and their characteristic antennae with clubbed ends can be seen. The antennae of moths are usually more elaborate and feathery and without knobs at the end

wings fold up underneath when the beetle is not flying. Beetles are found on and below ground, and in water. Some of their grubs, like those of the Maybug, damage plants. The so-called 'woodworm' is the larva of the furniture beetle, and the meal-worm is a grub of another beetle which eats stored food. Ladybirds and their grubs, however, are useful since they feed on greenfly. The tropical Goliath Beetle of Africa is the largest species, with a fifteen-centimetre body.

Bees, wasps and **ants** are called social insects because each group lives and works together in colonies. These fascinating insects have been studied in detail to find out how they live and organise themselves. Each individual insect has a job to do and this is done by instinct. In the beehive the queen bee lays eggs and little else, surrounded by workers. Some workers look after the queen and feed her, some act as nurses to the grubs and others go out and gather nectar and pollen. There are workers which cool the hive by standing in the doorway and beating their wings and others on guard outside it. The job of the drones is to mate with the young queens each year, after which they die. The rest of the hive keeps alive for another season.

Social wasps on the other hand do not store food, and the whole colony dies each winter, except for the young queens. They hibernate somewhere by themselves, then each makes her own queen nest, lays a few eggs and tends the grubs. From these, workers emerge, and as more appear they take over the jobs of adding to the nest and collecting food for more and more grubs.

There are also many solitary wasps and bees which rear their own small families. Bumble bees, which are solitary, usually live in this way.

Ants also live in colonies, making tunnels underground or in heaped-up nests. In Europe the large Wood Ant uses pine needles, piling them into a heap. In the garden there may be a nest of the small Black Ant beneath a concrete path. Ants are attracted by human food, especially sugar. Sometimes on a warm summer day, as if by a signal, thousands of winged females appear. They fly off, land and bite off their wings, then start a new colony.

Bugs have sharp, sucking mouths for piercing plants or animal prey and sucking out the juice. Some have their

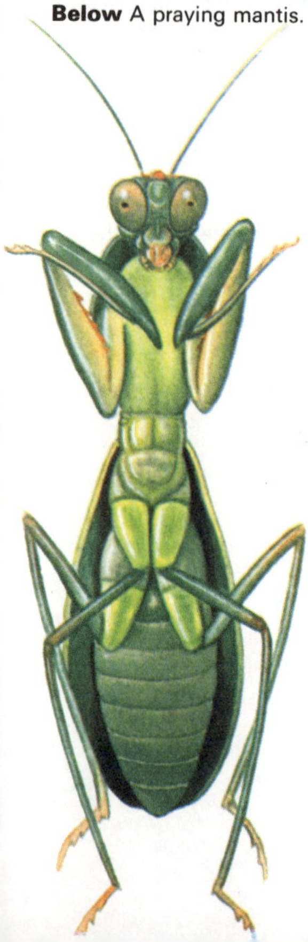

Above 1 Blue-winged grasshopper. **2** Short-horned grasshopper. **3** Great green bush cricket. **4** *Libellula quadrimaculata.* **5** Mole cricket. **6** Tree cricket. **Below** A praying mantis.

fore-wings half hard and half soft. The bedbug is attracted by warmth, and sometimes attacks humans. In the garden and fields are a number of small plant bugs, such as greenfly and blackfly, which can harm plants. In doing so they can spread disease. In ponds there are water bugs which catch small animals. Water boatmen are common examples and others called pond-skaters can be seen darting about on the surface of the water. Other well-known bugs called frog-hoppers live on plants and cover themselves with a white froth called cuckoo-spit.

Dragonflies live their young life as nymphs in water. A nymph hatches from an egg laid by the mother on water or in a water plant. It grows up by catching other water animals and feeding on them. This is done with its powerful jaws which are fitted on to a hinge, called a mask. This darts out to catch any passing prey. When it is fully grown the nymph climbs up a water plant out of the pond. It rests a while, then the dried skin splits along its back and an adult dragonfly crawls out. There is no pupa stage. Some dragonflies are large and powerful, called hawks, and they dart about in the air, even backwards, and are also able to hover. Prey is caught and eaten on the wing. Other more graceful and slender dragonflies, called damselflies, fold their wings back when resting, but the hawks keep them spread out.

Flies, unlike most insects, have only one pair of wings instead of two. The back pair are reduced to tiny knobs which are said to help them keep their balance when in the air. Some flies are among man's most dangerous enemies, since they spread disease and death. One of these is the House Fly. It has a pad-like mouth which is pressed on to its food. It sucks up filth on a rubbish dump where it lays its eggs, and then enters the house and settles on food. In this way diseases like typhoid, cholera and dysentery are passed on. One way to prevent this happening is to cover up food when flies are about.

Another dangerous fly is the African tsetse fly which spreads sleeping sickness. Far more serious is the mosquito which spreads malaria. It lives in many countries and breeds in stagnant water. One way to fight malaria is to spray the ditches and marshes with an insect poison to kill the mosquito larvae, or to drain water from the land. This was done along the east coast of England where malaria was common during the Middle Ages. In those days, it was called the ague or shivering disease because of the violent shivering attacks which happen during the fever. Not all mosquitoes carry malaria: the Common Mosquito, or Gnat, bites but is usually harmless.

There are vast numbers of smaller mosquitoes, usually called midges, which can be a nuisance during summertime, but form a valuable food for bats and birds.

Grasshoppers are harmless insects found in grass during summer where they can be heard 'singing'. Allied to them are crickets, which like warmth and were once common in people's homes when there were open fires. Few people object to grasshoppers, but cockroaches, which are related to them and are often called black beetles, are disliked. They live in the dark, and have an unpleasant smell, and spoil

Above 1 *Anax imperator.* **2** Desert locust hopper. **3** Desert locust. **4** *Rhyothemis graphiptera.* **5** Leaf insect. **6** Stick insect. **7** Termites (the larger one is a queen, the smaller a worker).

food. They are found especially in neglected kitchens, cellars and bakeries.

Stick insects and leaf insects have the shape and colour of the twigs and leaves among which they hide, and are splendid examples of camouflage. They eat plants, whereas the Praying Mantis waits for a victim, then catches it with its pincer-like fore-legs. It could easily be mistaken for a leaf.

Of all insects the locust is perhaps the most destructive. Resembling a large grasshopper, a locust and its off-spring will do no harm for years. Then mysteriously, a swarm begins to build up as the locusts increase and remain together. At first they move on the ground, as their wings have not yet developed. These are the hoppers. Then, with the last moult, the flying locusts emerge to make a swarm. This can be so thick that the sun is blotted out. An average swarm can weigh more than a million kilograms, and the locusts eat this amount of food each day. To fight the locust poisoned bait is put in the path of the hoppers. Aeroplanes attack the flying swarm with contact poison, but by then it is usually too late to stop them.

Fleas have no wings, but make up for this by jumping. They are parasitic, living on other warm-blooded animals and feeding on blood. Not only is man attacked by fleas but almost all other mammals and most birds have their individual fleas. A flea has hooked legs for hanging on to its host, and a body flattened sideways for creeping between hair or feathers. Usually a flea species will stick to one kind of host, but dogs and cats may pick up fleas from rabbits, hedgehogs and rats. The flea from the rat can be very dangerous, as it may carry the germ of bubonic plague.

Termites or **white ants** are sociable nest-builders, but in a different group from the true ants. They are the only insects which can feed on wood, and may do serious harm to buildings and furniture in the tropics. Some live inside wood, others underground, and a third kind build hard mud nests anything up to six metres tall. This is a common sight in places like Africa and Australia. Termites will gather and grow 'fungus gardens' inside their nests as a source of food.

Below Termites have a highly developed social life and the nests they build can be more than twice the height of a man.

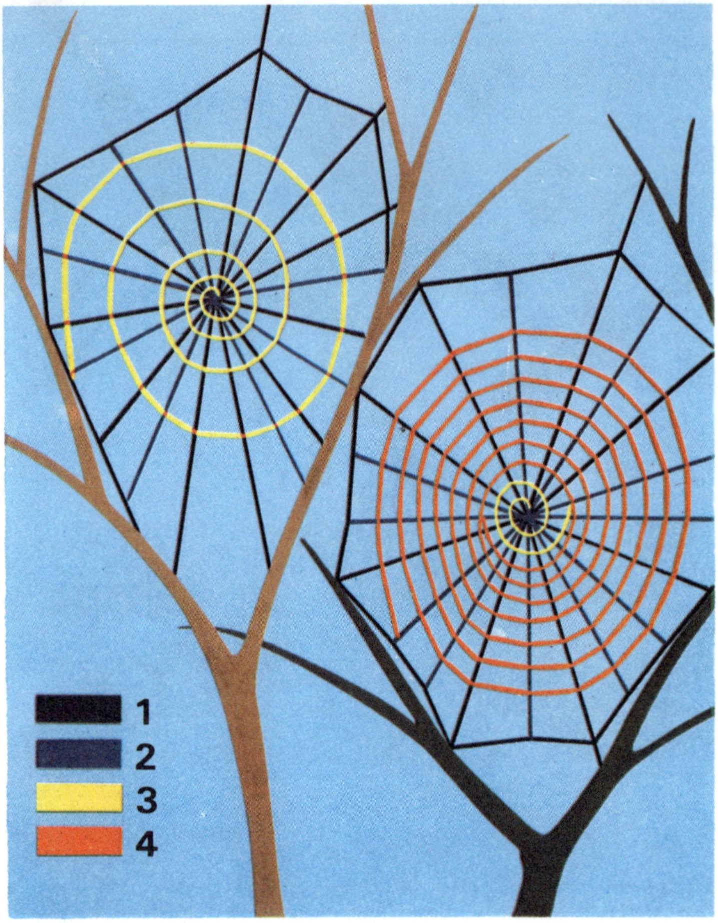

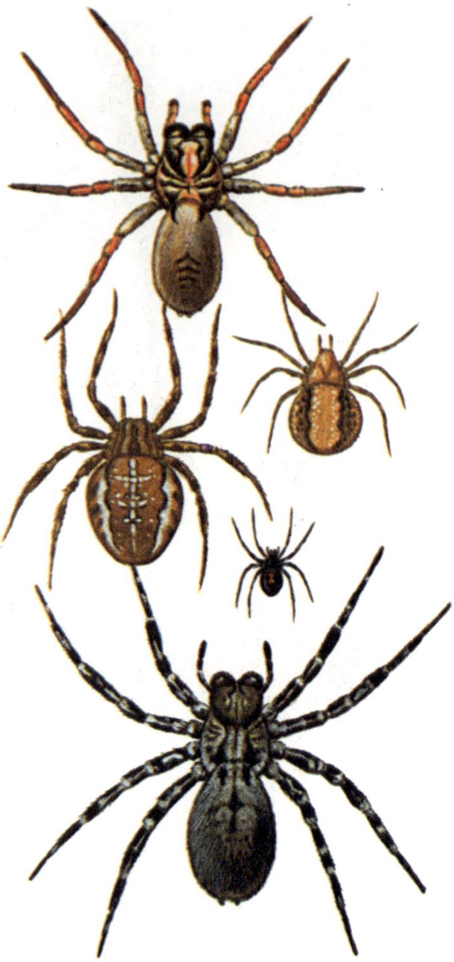

Above The stages by which an orb-spinning spider spins its web are shown. **1** Outer framework, which secures the web to its support. **2** The spider spins strong anchoring lines to the outer edge. **3** Next comes the temporary spiral pattern which supports and gives guidelines for the final web, in the same way that tacking is a temporary stitch in sewing. **4** The spider then spins its way back from the outside to the centre of the web, this time replacing the temporary 'tacking' with permanent threads. The spiders shown on the right are (from top to bottom) *Lycosa maderiana, Theridion melanurum* (House spider), *Araneus diadematus* (Garden spider), *Latrodectus mactans* (Black widow) and *Lycosa ingens.*

Arachnids

The arachnids are a class of arthropods which includes spiders, scorpions and mites. The adults have eight legs (six in insects), and a body in two parts, the head and thorax joined and the abdomen. The orb-spinning spiders, so called because the web they spin is circular and wheel-like, are well known, particularly the Garden Spider with a cross on its back. Its wonderfully built web is made by instinct, without any learning, and helps the spider to catch food. Spiders are graded according to their webs. The most primitive are the hunting spiders which merely pounce on their prey. Others build simple traps of a funnel shape, and can be found in grass along the hedgerows, or in cellars. Trap-door spiders build tunnels which are lined with silk and covered with a door on a hinge which fits so well that it cannot be noticed. When something comes close the trap-door spider darts out and catches its victim.

The large, hairy tropical spiders which look so dangerous are really timid and only bite if handled. Although called tarantulas, the real tarantula comes from the Mediterranean area. Its bite was once believed to cause madness. It was said that to get well it was necessary to dance madly and sweat out the poison. The dance was put to music, called the tarantella. The poison of the tarantula is not deadly, and a far more dangerous spider is the small American Black Widow Spider, which has been known to cause death.

Spiders are world-wide, but scorpions usually belong to warm and dry places such as deserts. They hide beneath the stones and plants, catching and killing their prey with their claws, not with their sting – this is used mainly for defence. Before mating there is usually an elaborate courtship among scorpions. The young are born alive and carried for a while on the mother's back.

Mites are small arachnids which live mostly in soil and leaf litter. They help to break up the leaves and dead plants. In one hectare of a beech wood there may be as many as 400 million mites. Others live in ponds and may be brightly coloured green or red. Many mites live as parasites on other animals. Some, called ticks, swell up with the blood of their hosts, fall off and lay eggs on the ground. The young tick climbs a plant, waves its legs about and waits to be picked up by a passing animal. In this way dogs, cats, and even humans can pick up these parasites. Some mites can cause disease.

Millepedes and centipedes

These are arthropods with long, slender bodies and many legs. Millepedes have the greater number of legs since there are two pairs to each segment. Their bodies are rounded and they can curl up like a watch spring. Millepedes are plant-eaters and can do harm in the garden. Centipedes, however, can be useful as hunters, catching other creatures in their powerful jaws. Centipedes have more flattened bodies, one pair of legs to a segment, and can usually move faster. Large tropical centipedes can give a painful bite.

Crustaceans

Sometimes called shellfish, these invertebrates have hard skins and many legs, some of which act as breathing organs. They live mostly in the sea and number about 25,000 species. The more familiar kinds are the ones caught for food, such as crabs, lobsters and shrimps. There are vast numbers of smaller crustaceans hiding in rock pools, also drifting as part of the floating world of plankton (a word meaning 'wandering') – small drifting organisms in seas and rivers. The plankton in the Antarctic includes the shrimp-like krill eaten by the giant whales.

One of the largest crustaceans is the giant Spider Crab with legs up to one metre long. It lives in warm seas in the Pacific. Crabs and lobsters – the kind we eat – are sometimes caught in the trawl net, but more usually in traps baited with food. Like shrimps and prawns they only turn red when boiled. The many microscopic crustaceans are a main food supply for sea fish, also for pond creatures. The little freshwater *Daphnia*, or Water-flea, is one of the 'key' animals in ponds.

The crayfish, which resembles a small freshwater kind of lobster, lives in rivers. It hides under stones and if disturbed darts along backwards by flapping its tail. Like the lobster, it lays eggs called berries, and when these hatch the mother carries the young.

Echinoderms

This is a group of about 4,000 sea creatures consisting of starfishes, sea-urchins and sea-cucumbers. The term echinoderm comes from two words meaning spiny and skin. Starfishes usually have five arms, and creep about slowly on rocks. Their underside is covered with hundreds of little suckers, called tube-feet. With these a starfish can grip the shell of a mussel and slowly force it open to get at the contents. Starfishes can sometimes be a nuisance if they get into an oyster bed.

Sea-urchins get their name from the old English word urchin, for a hedgehog. Their globe-like shells are covered with spines. They also cling to rocks and move about slowly. Some can burrow into the sand. Sea-cucumbers also have spiny skins and live on the sea-bed. The body is shaped like a cucumber, and collected by divers as food, called bêche-de-mer.

Above To represent the crustaceans in general and crabs in particular the picture shows a Common Shore Crab, which is typical of a section of the animal kingdom that contains over 4,000 living species. Below it is a starfish, and finally a sea-urchin, the shells of which are often collected as ornaments.

Above Puffer fish have sacs in their bodies which can be filled with either air or water to inflate their bodies.

Vertebrates

The animals we know best – for man is one of them – are called vertebrates, or animals with a backbone (*vertebra*, Latin for a twisting joint). There are five classes: mammals, birds, reptiles, amphibians and fishes. Some zoologists give this group another name, the Chordata, so as to include a few very primitive sea-creatures like sea-squirts and lampreys which also have a kind of simple backbone, called a notochord. In the true vertebrates this is found in the embryos only (when the animal is in its earliest stage of development) and is slowly replaced by a bony, jointed vertebral column down the back.

Fishes

Fishes are gill-breathing, aquatic (living in water) vertebrates built for swimming. Their bodies are usually streamlined and have fins, two in front (pectoral) and two behind (pelvic). The tail fin is vertical. There are about 20,000 species. In the bony fishes the gills are covered with a shield called the operculum.

Most fishes lay eggs but a few have live young, as those who keep tropical fishes will know. Such a 'live-bearer' is the little Guppy or *Lebistes*. Some fishes have very large families and may lay up to several million eggs. Usually there is no parental care and the baby fish must fend for themselves, but some fish rear small families and give them protection. The Stickleback, for example, selects a spot in a pond in which to build a nest, then invites a female to lay her eggs. The young which hatch are guarded from enemies. The red throat of the male acts as a warning to other males. Also some tropical fish fight fiercely to guard their nests, especially the famous Siamese Fighting Fish. It builds a nest of floating bubbles and will drive off any rival.

Members of the large **carp** family include the largest bony fish, the Nile Carp, which can weigh ninety kilograms and measure nearly two metres. Then there are the roach, tench and little minnows well known to anglers. The pet goldfish is an ornamental fish bred from the wild Chinese Carp which is a dull olive-green in colour. Carp are plant-eaters, whereas pike and perch, which belong to different families, are hunters. They hide in the reeds waiting for prey, then rush out to catch a smaller fish, a frog or sometimes a baby duckling.

1

Below Sea-horses can be found in waters of the Atlantic and the Mediterranean and off the coast of Australia. They are the only fishes with prehensile tails capable of grasping on to an object.

Hunters of a different kind are the **salmon** family. The Brook Trout of rivers and lakes is caught with special rods using a long line to which is tied a hook with an artificial fly. The fly is dropped on to the water to attract the trout. These fish normally rise to the surface to catch passing insects which have fallen in. Salmon are caught in a similar manner.

The Atlantic Salmon grows up in the sea. When mature it enters the cleaner rivers and can be seen leaping waterfalls and weirs to reach the spawning beds. Here the hen fish scoops out a hollow in the gravel, called a redd, and lays her eggs late in the year. The cock salmon then fertilises the eggs and the hen covers them. The fry (as the newly spawned fish are called) hatch in spring and the babies, called parr, remain in the area for about two years. Then they change into silvery-looking smolts (another

Above Fishes display an extraordinary range of colours, which in general are used for camouflage or as a recognition pattern. This is also true of special markings and shapes, for fishes can disguise themselves to look like logs or even leaves. The fishes in this drawing are **1** Zebra striped surgeon fish, **2** Queen trigger fish, **3** Blue gularis, **4** Squirrel fish, **5** Butterfly fish, **6** Clown fish, **7** Black banded wrasse.

name for young river salmon) and make their way to sea, where they grow up. One day they will return to the river to spawn.

The **eel** also migrates but does so the other way round. A tiny eel larva called a *leptocephalus* (meaning slender head) hatches from an egg laid in the Sargasso Sea. This larva is then carried by the Atlantic currents a journey of nearly five thousand kilometres towards Europe, taking about two years. Finally it reaches the shores of Europe as an elver (a young eel). Elvers enter the rivers in millions, and some grow into eels which, in their turn, eventually make their way to sea.

The **herring**, a valuable food fish, also travels a long way in search of its plankton food. Fishermen wait for herrings with drift nets which hang in the water on floating corks. The herrings swim into the nets and get caught in the mesh by their gills. Flatfish, such as plaice, sole and halibut, live near the bottom of the sea. These are caught in a trawl net which is dragged along the sea-bed. The cod is caught on rod and line and is another useful food, but some fish are caught in this way merely for sport. These include the mackerel and larger fish related to it such as the tunny, sailfish and swordfish. These can weigh hundreds of kilograms, and the fisherman has to be strapped into his seat to keep him from being pulled overboard.

A common sight at sea in tropical waters is the **flying fish.** It darts along the surface then becomes airborne on its 'wings', which are the large pectoral fins. Sometimes these fish land on the deck of a ship. It is among tropical coral reefs that some of the most brightly coloured fishes are found. Many are dotted or striped and are difficult to see against the corals and seaweeds on which they feed. Some can escape enemies by darting between tentacles of anemones without getting hurt. Others live on the bottom, half buried in the sand. One of the most remarkable cases of camouflage is the little sea-horse which carries its eggs in a pouch. With its tail used as an anchor to hold on to something, it could easily be mistaken for a piece of seaweed.

Above From top to bottom are shown the Manta Ray, which has pectoral fins up to six metres across; the Blue Shark; the strange Coelacanth, which is a living fossil related to ancient Devonian fishes; and finally two deep-sea fishes.

Deep in the ocean depths where it is always dark live strange fishes which can light up to see their way and to find one another. Some of them, called **angler fishes**, are fitted with a kind of rod and tassel on top of the head. When this is jerked it attracts other fish which, if they swim too close, are caught by the angler fish. Its wide open mouth and elastic stomach make it possible for the angler fish to swallow fish as big as itself.

Some of the most ancient of bony fishes are called **lungfish**. They date back to the Devonian period when fishes were turning into amphibians. As well as a pair of gills the lungfish has an air bladder so that it can live out of water. This happens when the swamps in which it lives dry out. The lungfish buries itself in the mud and forms a hard coccoon with a chimney through which it can breathe air. Later, when the rains fill the swamp it swims out and behaves like a fish once more. Lungfishes today are found in South America, Africa and Australia.

Another main group of fishes consists of **sharks** and **rays**. They have soft skeletons and their gills are uncovered. Little is known about their ancestors because no skeletons have survived – only teeth. Judging by the size of some fossil teeth, up to fifteen centimetres long, there may have been giant sharks at one time, up to eighteen metres in length. Today's largest shark is the Whale Shark, up to twelve metres long, and it is quite harmless. The teeth are small and it lives near the surface in warm seas, feeding on plankton. With each mouthful of sea-water this food is caught as it passes over the gills. In this way the Whale Shark eats as it breathes. Second in size is the Basking Shark. This comes much farther north than the Whale Shark and is sometimes seen on the coasts of Ireland and Scotland, where it used to be caught for its oil.

One of the more dangerous sharks is the Great Blue Shark, but it would seem that most sharks do not attack man unless provoked, according to what skin-divers tell us. The real danger is when sharks smell blood. With their sharp cutting teeth, which grow in rows inside the mouth, sharks tear at their prey. Many sharks, and rays also, have flatter, crushing teeth with which they crush shellfish and crabs. Skates and rays are related to sharks, having much flatter bodies for living on the sea bed. The large 'wings' of the rays are really enlarged pectoral fins.

Amphibians

The name amphibian comes from two Greek words meaning both and life. Amphibians usually start life in an egg which hatches in water into a larva called a tadpole. This has gills to breathe with and swims with its tail in a fish-like fashion. Later it grows legs and a pair of lungs, then leaves the water. There are about 3,000 species of modern amphibians, composed of frogs and toads, newts and salamanders, and caecilians.

Frogs and **toads** are without tails as adults and move in hops, also using their webbed hind legs for swimming. Most frogs and toads meet together in ponds and marshes during spring in the northern hemisphere, and in the rainy season in the tropics. Here they pair off and the females lay spawn. Frogs lay their spawn in clumps, whereas toads lay theirs in long strings. In each case the tadpoles which hatch must fend for themselves, and great numbers get caught and eaten. In rare cases the eggs are protected, as they are by the little Midwife Toad in Europe. The father carries the egg strings around his hind legs and takes them to water just as the tadpoles are hatching.

Some tree-living species which can cling to leaves and the bark of trees with their sucker-like feet lay eggs on the leaves, always over water. In this way the tadpoles can slip out of the eggs as they hatch and fall into the water. One rather primitive toad found in Africa, called *Xenopus*, or the Clawed Toad, never leaves the water. Frogs and toads catch food with their sticky tongues, whereas tadpoles usually feed on water plants at first.

The world's biggest frog is the thirty-centimetre long Goliath Frog in Africa. South America has the biggest toad, the Giant Water Toad, whose body is fifteen centimetres across. The Common Frog, which is found all over Europe, is native to Britain. Two other European frogs, the Edible Frog and the Marsh Frog, can be very noisy. The Edible Frog in particular can croak very loudly by blowing up two bladders on the sides of its mouth. Of all frogs perhaps the American Bull Frog is the loudest. The Common Toad is a typical representative of the toad family, with a strong instinct for finding its own pond. On waking from hibernation these toads make their way to certain chosen ponds, and it is still a mystery how they find their way. The little Natterjack Toad is now a rarity and can be recognised by the yellow stripe down its back.

Above From top to bottom: European Fire Salamander, with very contrasted markings which are a warning to other animals; East African Tree Frog, a brilliantly coloured amphibian; Horned Toad, which is in fact a reptile and should more properly be called Horned Lizard.

Frogs and toads are the noisy members of their group, but **salamanders** are silent. They have long bodies on weak legs, but when they grow up they keep their tails to swim with. Salamanders are found only in the northern hemisphere and include the largest amphibian, the Giant Salamander of China and Japan, about one and a half metres long. Some salamanders lay eggs on land in damp places, while others enter water to breed. There may be a kind of courtship by the male before mating. The male salamander is more brightly coloured than the female and is adorned with a crest along its back. It dances before its mate in the

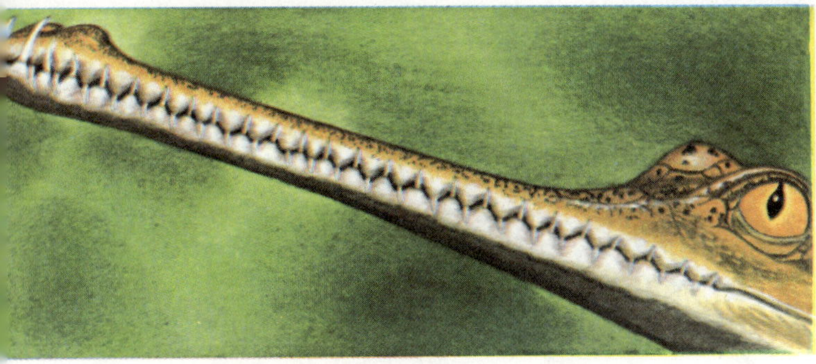

Above Crocodiles, alligators and gavials are living relatives of reptiles which existed in Mesozoic times over a hundred million years ago. They are amphibians and well suited to life in water. Their eyes, ears and nostrils are all placed on top of the head so that their senses are alert even when they are almost totally submerged. The pictures above show an Indian Gharial (top) and below it the Nile Crocodile with its shorter and broader snout.

water, after which she lays little clumps of eggs, or places them on water plants. The babies which hatch have gills at first, then develop lungs and climb out of the water.

Those salamanders called newts (from an old English word eft), such as the Smooth, Crested and Palmate Newts, can make attractive aquarium pets, and the courtship, egg-laying and growth of the tadpoles can be watched at close hand.

Caecilians are amphibians resembling large worms which live below ground in the tropics. Little is known about this curious group of animals.

Reptiles

Reptiles are air-breathing vertebrates which have limbs (except snakes and some lizards), are cold-blooded and have a horny covering of scales or horny plates. There are about 3,000 species. The four orders of modern reptiles are the crocodiles and alligators, tortoises and turtles, snakes and lizards and the Tuatara.

The last-named order means beak-headed, and the **Tuatara**, which is a Maori name, is the only survivor of it. Looking rather like a lizard with a beaked face it lives on some of the lonely islands off the coast of New Zealand. It is truly a precious living fossil, since this reptile order goes back to the time of the dinosaurs. The Tuatara seems to be slow in everything it does, even to its movements. It lives in underground burrows, often in company with a sea-bird, a species of petrel. The reptile sleeps there by night and the bird by day. The eggs have a long incubation period and it is sometimes as much as eighteen months before the young hatch out.

Crocodiles and **alligators** also belong to an ancient order dating back to dinosaurs. The true crocodiles, such as the Nile Crocodile, the Indian Mugger and the eastern Estuarine Crocodile, live mostly in the tropics along the sides of rivers and lakes. The Estuarine Crocodile can swim out to sea and has been known to reach a length of nine metres. Crocodiles can be recognised by their narrow snouts which have a notch near the front on both sides. Into these fit the two large lower teeth which can be seen when the jaws are closed. Closely related is the Indian Gharial, a large fish-hunting crocodile with a very slender snout. Alligators have broader snouts and belong mainly in America. Here the large lower teeth fit into sockets inside the upper jaw and cannot be seen when the mouth is shut. The Mississippi Alligator is found in rivers and swamps in the southern United States, especially in the Everglades of Florida. In South America are found the caymans, which is an Indian name. The word alligator comes from the Spanish *lagarta*, meaning a lizard. The Spanish settlers in America thought these reptiles were large kinds of lizards.

Such large reptiles are built for swimming, using their powerful tails as paddles. When submerged the ears and nostrils can be closed with flaps, so can the windpipe. This means that the mouth can remain open under water and when prey is caught it can be dragged under and drowned. Resembling a log, or drifting slowly just below the surface, a crocodile or alligator can surprise an animal coming down to drink, or on the surface of the water. Eggs are laid on shore, in a

rough pile of rotting vegetation. The mother may remain on guard to protect the eggs and newly born young from enemies. These reptiles are usually feared, and many are shot for their skins so that they are becoming rare in places. Yet they have a useful role to play in nature, acting as scavengers and eating up animals which are dead or sick.

Tortoises and **turtles** are unique among animals, having their whole bodies enclosed in a bony box. This is built from the rib cage which grows and joins up outside the limbs. The earliest tortoises show separate ribs but even these are already flattened as if about to join together. This peculiarity goes back even before the dinosaurs, so that chelonians (the name of the order to which tortoises and turtles belong) are the oldest group of reptiles. They even have the oldest individuals on earth today – the giant tortoises which can live to a hundred and fifty years or more. Chelonians are of three kinds – tortoises, turtles and terrapins. Tortoises are land reptiles with domed shells and stumpy legs. They move about clumsily and feed mostly on plants and fruit. The largest are the giant tortoises of the Galapagos Islands in the Pacific, and the Aldabra Islands in the Indian Ocean. They can weigh up to 550 kilograms and measure almost two metres in length. Tortoises sold in shops as pets come from the Mediterranean countries, and have been known to live up to a hundred years. Eggs are laid in the ground and left to hatch in the sun.

Turtles are sea-going chelonians, with flatter shells than tortoises and more paddle-like feet for swimming. At night the females come ashore on some lonely tropical beach where there is sand. They dig pits in which up to 150 eggs may be laid. These are covered up and the mother then returns to the sea. Later the babies hatch out, struggle to the surface, then make as fast as they can for the water. On the way many are caught by the waiting sea-birds. Because turtles are also caught for food and their eggs dug up, some are now becoming rare. One or two countries do protect turtles by fencing off some of the beaches where they lay their eggs, later collecting the young and taking them out to sea where they will be safe to grow up. The largest turtle, up to 400 kilograms and one and a half metres long, is the

Above Three species of tortoise are shown. Biggest is the Giant Tortoise, which is found in the Seychelles and Aldabras in the Indian Ocean and in the Galapagos Islands in the Pacific, where Darwin made some of his first discoveries about evolution. The tortoise on the right is a Radiated Tortoise and the smallest one is the common tortoise often kept as a pet. The other animal is the remarkable Tuatara.

Above Constrictors crush their prey to death. Among them are the largest snakes, the Malay Python and the South American Anaconda, or Water Boa. The snake in the picture is the Green Python. On the right is the Egyptian Cobra, which belongs to a different family.

Leathery Turtle. The Green Turtle is the species usually caught for making turtle soup, and the Hawksbill Turtle for its shell, called tortoiseshell.

Terrapin is an American Indian name for freshwater tortoises which swim in rivers and marshes, catching fish and water animals. They spend hours basking in the sun at the waterside, but dive in at any sign of danger.

Snakes and lizards have bodies with a covering of small scales, and the order has the largest number of species among reptiles, some 2,300 snakes and 2,500 lizards.

Snakes have long and slender bodies minus any visible limbs, and move about with a swimming motion by twisting their bodies into sideways curves, not up and down as is sometimes shown in drawings. They can also move their loose skin in a 'rowing' motion over the ribs, so that the scales catch on to rough surfaces and push the snake along. Some are good at swimming, climbing or burrowing, and others can even glide through the air. Serpents have always been feared by man, and often misunderstood, because some happen to be poisonous. These are in the minority, and even dangerous snakes nearly always avoid man. Poisoning is caused through a bite, not the tongue. The snake uses its tongue to catch particles of scent from the air, and to test its surroundings, even to track its prey. Poison is injected by special teeth, called fangs. These are either hollow or grooved and work like the needle of a doctor's hypodermic syringe. Poison in the glands is passed through these teeth and into the wound.

Venomous snakes include the mambas of Africa, the cobras of Africa and the Far East, the brightly coloured little kraits of India, the Taipan of Australia, and rattlesnakes in America. Vipers such as the Puff Adder and Fer-de-lance curl up before striking, then dart their heads forward. This is how the little British adder will bite, but only to kill its prey or to defend itself. It is shy and never attacks. Rattlesnakes also strike with high speed but will give a warning first by shaking their tails. The rattle is made out of a row of hollow dried skin segments which move against each other and sound like the noise of a tambourine. Rattlesnakes are also called pit-vipers. On each cheek is a hollow pit which is very sensitive to warmth. It is said that a rattlesnake can 'feel' the presence of a mouse in the dark. Cobras rear up to strike, and some spread out a hood behind the head to look more fierce. They are used by snake-charmers who are supposed to

Below A snake is able to swallow large eggs because of special jaw bones which permit its mouth to open wide.

charm the cobra with music. Actually a snake is deaf and is swaying its body only to keep an eye on the moving flute. Mambas have an evil reputation and their bite is certainly deadly, but again they do not normally attack unless provoked. Neither do the sea-serpents which live along the coasts of the Far East.

Snakes are not slimy creatures but have soft and often beautifully coloured bodies. Some of them, such as the Grass Snake, make popular pets. This is a harmless member of a very large family called Colubridae which is world-wide. Like most snakes the Grass Snake lays eggs with a soft shell covering. The babies cut their way free on hatching. Some families such as the vipers and boas have young, but there is no mothercare. Most snakes leave their eggs or young, but a python will sometimes curl up around its eggs to keep them warm.

Lizards resemble snakes in some cases, having long bodies and limbs that are either reduced in size or missing altogether. This is so with some of the skinks which live in desert surroundings and burrow a lot. The Slow-worm may be mistaken for a snake. One difference is that lizards can close their eyes. Also, unlike snakes, the jaw bones are fixed and can only move like ours do. Scaling on the head is also different. Lizards usually have long tails, and because some can shed them they need to be handled carefully. Most are quite harmless, like the Green Lizard and Wall Lizard most commonly seen in Mediterranean countries, basking on the rocks and among the ruins. The only lizards with a poisonous bite are the Gila Monster, marked a bright black and white, and the Arizona Lizard, which is black and yellow. They live in desert country, move sluggishly but have a very fast bite for catching prey. Monitor lizards of Africa, India and Australia grow up to almost two metres, are fast in movement, can climb and swim and hunt small animals. They will also raid crocodile nests. The world's largest lizard is a monitor – the Komodo Dragon, which reaches over three metres in length and lives on the small Indonesian islands of Komodo and Rintja. It is harmless.

Like some snakes, monitors are caught for their skins to make reptile leather. In America live the iguanas, brightly coloured lizards with frills along their backs, often caught as human food. They are plant-eaters. In warm countries can be seen the little geckos – climbing lizards with suckers on their toes. They often enter houses and are useful for catching insects.

Above On the left is a pair of coral snakes. On the right is a chameleon, one of the strangest lizards. It catches food with a long sticky tongue, can swivel its eyes in all directions independently of each other, hangs on to branches with its feet and curly tail, and can change the colour of its skin. Most chameleons are found in Madagascar, off the coast of Africa.

Above The Kiwi has a long and flexible bill with nostrils that open at its top. It feeds on earthworms and insect grubs.

Above The penguin's name probably came from the word pinion, or pin-wing, because it cannot fly. The name was first given to a large northern sea-bird called the Great Auk, seen here, which looked similar to a penguin but is now extinct. Below is the largest penguin, the Emperor.

Birds

Birds are descended from reptiles and share one thing in common with them – they both lay shell-eggs containing yolks, in which the embryos develop. Obvious differences in birds are the covering of feathers, the beak for a mouth, the absence of teeth, the warm blood, and the care given to the young. Birds will provide a nest, incubate the eggs, then feed their young or at least give them some protection. Their most spectacular achievement is flying. The fore-limbs are used as wings. There are about 8,600 species of birds in the world.

Running birds include the largest and heaviest birds, which are unable to fly. Their wings are very much reduced to stumps, but their powerful legs make them swift runners. The African Ostrich is the world's largest bird, two and a half metres tall and weighing about 130 kilograms. It can run up to fifty kilometres an hour. The black-coloured cock bird, which has white wing and tail feathers, mates with a number of greyish hens who lay their eggs all in one nest. The father incubates and guards the young. Few really wild birds exist today; most are protected in game parks, or kept on farms for their feathers. The ostrich which 'buries its head in the sand' does nothing of the sort. It is only hiding from danger by kneeling down and stretching its neck along the ground.

The Rhea of South America and the Emu of Australia have rather similar habits, leaving the cock to take charge of the chicks. New Zealand's little Kiwi is a night bird which forages in the undergrowth with its long beak. The nostrils are at the tip so that it can sniff out any hidden food. There are three species. Kiwis get their name from their whistling call. The most colourful of the running birds are the three species of Cassowary found in Australia and New Guinea. They have bright blue, red and yellow coloured heads and necks.

Penguins belong to the southern hemisphere, coming ashore to lay their eggs. There are fifteen species ranging in size from the Emperor Penguin to the Little Penguin of Australia and New Zealand. Only two penguins actually nest on Antarctica – the Emperor and the Adélie. The rest visit islands in the south Pacific and Atlantic. The Emperor actually breeds during the terrible Antarctic winter. There is no nest and the single egg is carried on top of the feet of either parent, who 'sit' on it to keep it warm. The penguins huddle together for warmth during the sudden icy blizzards. Penguins may look comical as they waddle about or toboggan on their bellies, but in water they are graceful and swift. They use their wings in a flying motion, and can move very quickly as they chase after fish.

Some water birds, such as **grebes** and **divers**, are expert fish hunters. The Great Crested Grebe, once rather rare, has become quite common near towns because of the building of reservoirs. Its small cousin the Dabchick, or Little Grebe, may even turn up in town parks. Divers, which used to be classified with grebes but now belong to a separate order, are much more shy and they belong to quiet waters of northern lands. The Red-throated Diver nests close to water – it is clumsy on land. Its feet are placed far back on the body – ideal for swimming but of little use for walking. In the far north, especially in Canada, lives the Great Northern Diver. Its weird cry – 'the call of the loon' – is heard only in lonely places far away from man.

Above 1 Great Crested Grebe. **2** Little Grebe. **3** Wandering Albatross. **4** Ostrich. **5** Common White Pelican, and **6** The Secretary Bird, which is one of the oddest birds of prey. It is stork-like in build and walks about on the ground. Its name came from the feathers on its head, which look rather like the quill pens once carried by clerks behind their ears.

Petrels or tube-noses spend most of their lives at sea, only coming ashore to breed. Their name comes from St Peter, who is said to have walked on water. The little Storm Petrel flies close to the waves, even paddling along the surface at times. At night it comes ashore to nest in dark burrows. It has a larger cousin called a Fulmar which looks somewhat like a gull. Petrels, however, can easily be recognised by their nostrils, which open at the end of tubes on top of the beak. The largest petrels are the albatrosses which spend their lives wandering over the southern oceans where there is always wind. Without this to help them they would have difficulty in flying, for their very large wings are built for gliding. Of the thirteen species the Wandering Albatross is the biggest, with a wingspan of over three metres. These birds, called Mollymawks by sailors, have always been treated with superstition. They are supposed to carry the souls of drowned seamen, roaming for ever over the oceans. The Greater Shearwater is another great traveller. It spends the summer in the Arctic, then travels south to breed, to the lonely island of Tristan da Cunha in the south Atlantic.

Pelicans may look clumsy with their large beaks and deep pouches, but they are graceful in flight and good swimmers. They fly in a V formation and work as a team to catch fish. A flock will splash the water with their wings to drive fish into the shallows. Then, as if by a word of command, all the heads dive under the water and the pouched beaks scoop up the food. Cormorants also catch fish, and in some parts of the world are still used by man in fishing. The birds are kept on a long line attached to a ring around the neck. In this way the cormorant is prevented by the ring from swallowing the fish it catches for its owner. The Northern Gannet, Britain's largest sea-bird, dives into the sea from a

Above Among the more beautiful and graceful birds is the flamingo. The most wide-spread variety is the Greater Flamingo which can be found in Asia, South America and Africa. In colour it ranges from whitish with pink tinges to the deep red of birds which breed in the West Indies.

Below Swans are typically white but for two exceptions: the Australian Black Swan (seen here) and the Black-necked Swan of South America.

height to catch fish. It breeds in colonies on land and islands around the northern Atlantic. Frigate birds roam the tropic seas and are called man-o'-war birds because they dive on other sea birds, forcing them to disgorge or give up their catch. The frigate bird then catches the falling food expertly without entering the sea.

Members of the **heron** family stand in water, waiting patiently for a fish or other animal to come close enough for them to stab at it with their long beaks. The Grey Heron will stand for hours like this waiting to collect food to take back to its noisy youngsters at the heronry. The famous White Stork which, according to legend, brings human babies into the world, usually nests by itself. It winters in Africa, then travels up to Europe to breed. People place cartwheels or platforms on the roofs of their houses or barns in the hope that the stork will nest there. In this way the spot may become a permanent yearly nest site.

The feathers of a beautiful but rather rare tropical cousin of the heron, the Large Egret or Great White Heron, were once used as decorations for women's hats. It was at one time so severely hunted that it nearly died out, but today it is protected. The smaller Cattle Egret is often seen with big game animals, catching the insects which are disturbed by the animals' movements. A species of a kind of short-necked heron, called a bittern, lives in the reed beds in marshland, where its famous booming mating call may be heard. The flamingo is a lakeside bird of Africa. A flock of these pink-coloured birds reflected in the water, or flying over it, makes a beautiful picture. A flamingo sweeps its curved beak sideways through the water to pick up microscopic life.

Swans are large, graceful water birds with long necks for probing underwater in search of food. The familiar Mute Swan, recognised by the S-shaped curve of its neck and the black knob or 'berry' on the beak, is a tame bird of parks and rivers. In Britain it has been treated for centuries as a royal mascot. Each year a ceremony called swan-upping takes place near London on the River Thames, during which swans and their cygnets are caught and marked according to whom they belong. Wild swans such as the Bewick and Whooper Swans usually visit the Arctic to breed. In North America the Trumpeter Swan is now a rare species. Australia has its own Black Swan, which gave its name to a river.

Ducks are small relatives of swans. The well-known Mallard is a friendly and common bird in parks. The drake has bright colours, whereas his mate is a dull brown – for a good reason. Like other birds which nest on the ground she must not give herself away while sitting, so she is well camouflaged. Some duck species travel to the Arctic to breed, as do the wild geese. One of these, the Grey-lag Goose, is the ancestor of the farmyard goose. Geese that winter in Europe settle on the coast in lonely places, coming on to the mudflats and fields to feed at dawn and dusk.

Birds of prey are the hunters among birds, catching their victims in sharp talons, then swallowing them whole or tearing them up with a curved and pointed beak. The most majestic of them is the Golden Eagle of northern mountain areas, spoken of as the king of birds, and chosen by many peoples as their emblem. The Romans, for example, decorated their standards with its image, the *aquila*, and carried it into battle. The Golden Eagle hunts grouse and mountain hare, and will also take the occasional lamb and deer calf.

A splendid and noble hunter is the Peregrine. It dives on its prey with tremendous speed, usually killing it with one blow and catching the lifeless body in mid-air. Like its beautiful cousin, the Gyrfalcon, it was once used in the ancient sport of falconry. A smaller falcon, the Kestrel, hovers in the air, then drops on its prey – probably a vole – on the ground. Smaller still is the little Merlin of the moorlands which hunts birds. The Sparrowhawk catches its prey by surprise. It dashes along hedgerows or through trees, knocking a small bird off its perch. The Osprey, or Fish-hawk, is found all over the world and it normally lives entirely on fish which it hunts by diving into lakes.

In Africa and other warm countries vultures can wheel and soar for hours, lifted by the warm air currents. The Griffon Vulture of Africa has a wing span of almost two and a half metres, but the largest vultures – in fact the largest of all flying birds – are the American condors, which have a span of about three metres. In spite of their size these birds are not hunters, but will wait until an animal dies, or take over the remains of another animal's kill. The vulture has excellent eyesight and soon spots a source of food. As one vulture drops to earth another a mile away sees it and comes over. This attracts a third bird and so on until quite a number are gathered at the kill. Although they are despised, vultures – like crocodiles – play a useful part as scavengers.

Owls take over when the day hunters are asleep. Their large eyes help them to see in the dark, but it is their hearing which is particularly acute. An owl can hear the faint movements of a mouse in the leaves and, because of its soft feathers, can fly and pounce on its

Above (top to bottom) **1** Mallard, which dips in the water with its tail stuck up in the air when searching for food. **2** Mandarin, which comes from east Asia and Japan and is often bred in captivity. **3** Barrow's Goldeneye from North America, Greenland and Iceland. **4** Hooded Merganser, which lives on North American inland waters. **5** Shoveller, which is common all over the northern hemisphere. **6** Shelduck, which is large and looks rather like a goose.

Above left Owls are nocturnal birds of prey, that is they hunt at night, and their silent flight enables them to pounce on a victim without giving warning of their approach. This is the Screech Owl which lives in North America.

victim silently. The Eagle Owl is one of the largest species and is capable of catching a small antelope. In the Arctic lives the beautiful Snowy Owl which, during bad winters, can be seen further south in northern Europe. Also pale in colour – a kind of creamy white – is the Barn Owl, which nests in barn lofts and churches. It has an eerie call. More familiar and homely is the hooting of the Tawny Owl, which often appears in town parks and suburban gardens. One of the few day-hunting owls in Europe is the Little Owl, which has a cry like a cat.

At one time man hunted animals for food, including birds. Now that he keeps farm animals and poultry he hunts them mostly for sport. With birds this is done with a gun, and certain **game birds** are bred for this purpose. One of the best known is the Ring-necked Pheasant, introduced into Europe from its native China many centuries ago. The bright-coloured cock with his ringed neck and long tail is easily seen in wooded country, whereas the dull-looking hen can be overlooked. Also from the Far East are the Golden and Silver Pheasants. The Lady Amherst Pheasant comes from Tibet and the Copper Pheasant from Japan. These are usually kept as ornamental birds, rather like the peacock.

The wild Common Peafowl belongs to India and Sri Lanka. Peafowl fly quite well and will roost in the branches like most game birds. The barnyard chicken does the same in the hen house at night. Its wild ancestor is the Red Jungle Fowl of India. The fighting cock once used in Europe for sport is the nearest resemblance to the wild bird. In Malaya lives the handsome Argus Pheasant. When courting, the cock spreads out its long wing feathers like a fan.

On the open moorland in Britain lives the Red Grouse, a bird found in no other country, unless taken there. Its cousin, the male Black Grouse, grows a curious forked tail often used as a hat decoration. These grouse meet at the courting grounds called leks, and the males perform mock battles. In North America the Prairie Chicken, another grouse, gives an impressive display. The cock birds blow up their bright-coloured throats as they dance and threaten one another. Also in America lives the Common Turkey, ancestor of the bird we see on the dinner table at Christmas. It was well known to early travellers in the wagon trains, and many a turkey was eaten around the camp fires. It has nothing to do with the country of Turkey, and the bird now bred on European farms was first brought over from Mexico by the Spaniards.

Gulls, auks and **waders** are found nearly everywhere in the world. Gulls which nest on cliff ledges include the Herring Gull, familiar at the seaside. It follows ships at sea, also the ploughman on a farm. The Black-headed Gull comes inland in wintertime and is now a common sight in towns on rivers and on reservoirs where it roosts. In spring it will go north to nest on the shores of the Baltic Sea or on the lochs of Scotland. The most sea-going of gulls is the Kittiwake, whose call sounds like its name. After breeding on the cliff tops it spends the rest of the year at sea. Terns are attractive relatives of the gulls, with forked tails, and they are also called sea-swallows. They nest in colonies on pebbly beaches, and some make long journeys. The Arctic Tern nests in the north, then for the rest of the year journeys to the Antarctic, a round trip of some 16,000 kilometres.

Auks are sea-birds which nest on cliffs, laying their eggs on bare rock. This happens with the black and white Guillemot. Its eggs are pear-shaped so that they spin in circles if knocked and do not fall off the cliff. The Puffin, with brightly coloured beak, is also called the sea-parrot, and it nests in rabbit burrows.

Waders are mostly dull-coloured birds with long legs and beaks, which haunt the seashore and marshy places, paddling in shallow water and probing the sand and mud for food with their beaks. A common species is the Redshank, which has a whistling call. The Curlew, with down-curved beak, has a musical cry which can be heard over the moorland where it nests during summer. An easy wader to recognise is the black and white Oystercatcher. It feeds on mussels and limpets rather than oysters.

Above The Dodo formerly inhabited the islands of Mauritius and Réunion, but is now extinct. It was a very large bird with a hooked beak and short stubby legs, related to the pigeon family. Clumsy and defenceless it was destroyed by sailors who visited the islands in the early part of the 17th century The Dutch who found the Dodo called it *walgvögel* or nauseous bird, because it was unpleasant to eat. They were extinct by the end of the 17th century.

Above A group of gulls, auks and waders.
1 Herring gull,
2 Little tern,
3 Guillemot, **4** Godwit (a wader), **5** Puffin, and **6** Little Auk.
Below The Common Peafowl, or peacock, is usually kept as an ornamental bird and when it displays it spreads out its long colourful feathers.

Pigeons are familiar birds and a number have been tamed. This happened with the wild Rock Pigeon which inhabits rocky coasts in Europe and Western Asia. It was bred into many varieties, such as the Fantail, Pouter, Tumbler and Racing Pigeons. Over the years numbers of birds escaped from their dovecots, and instead of returning to the sea cliffs they settled and nested on buildings. Today the so-called London Pigeon is found in most towns and villages all over the northern hemisphere, but only a few really wild pigeons can be seen. The Ring Dove or Wood Pigeon, which is native throughout Europe, can be a nuisance to farmers and gardeners by raiding crops. In summer the gentle, slender Turtle Dove arrives from Africa. Looking rather like it is a newcomer to European shores, called the Collared Dove, with a black half-ring behind its head. It is spreading rapidly from its original home in the Middle East.

Above A nest full of hungry young Golden Orioles. This bright coloured bird is about 20 to 30 centimetres long when it is fully grown and is the only one of its family to be found in Europe. Both male and female birds share the duties of incubation and rearing. The young orioles stay in the nest for two weeks after hatching before they take flight

Right The Kingfisher is well known for the brilliant colour of its plumage. It feeds mainly on fishes, which it catches expertly.

Parrots make popular pets, especially the talking kinds, like the African Grey Parrot. A number of smaller species, called lovebirds, keep together in pairs, even in cages. The brilliantly coloured parrots of South America, called macaws, are noisy, screaming birds. So are the white, crested cockatoos of Australia. But the little green budgerigar is aboriginal for 'good bird'. The Kea, a New Zealand parrot, was once unpopular as it used to attack sheep, tearing at their backs to eat the flesh.

Not all **cuckoos** lay their eggs in other birds' nests. Some build their own and rear their young. But the Common Cuckoo which exists all over the warmer parts of Europe and Asia is a parasite. A hen will look carefully for a number of nests belonging to other birds. She always sticks to one kind, whether it be a robin, a hedge sparrow or a meadow pipit, or some other species. Then she lays one of her own eggs in each nest in turn, and removes one of the original eggs. On hatching, the cuckoo chick tips out the other eggs, even the young, and gets all the food from the two hard-working foster parents. One day it flies away to Africa, and how it does so unaided and without any guidance from its parents is still a mystery.

Swifts and **humming birds** are birds of the air with extraordinary agility and speed in flight. The world's tiniest birds are the delightful humming birds of tropical America. They dart about with dazzling speed, hovering, moving up and down, sideways and even backwards. They sip nectar from flowers in mid-air, and make a humming noise with rapid vibrations of their wings. The smallest of these little gems is the Cuban Humming Bird, about five and a half centimetres long from the tip of its beak to the end of its tail. With a body about the size of a bumble bee it weighs no more than two grams.

The swifts are well named. The Common Swift, with its coal-black plumage, lives for most of the summer in Europe. It spends a lot of its time in the air and nests on tall buildings. In countries of the Far East such as Malaya and Myanmar there are colonies of small swiftlets which build nests out of their saliva on the walls of cliffs and inside caves. This is where the delicacy bird's nest soup comes from.

Some **kingfishers** live up to their name, and the brilliant little Common Kingfisher, the only species found in Europe, often catches a fish as long as itself and yet manages somehow to swallow it. It dives straight into the water from above. The nest is a hole dug into a bank alongside water. The majority of kingfishers come from central and eastern Asia and Africa, and many of these live in forests far from water. The famous Kookaburra or Laughing Jackass in Australia hunts small animals, including snakes. The hornbills of Africa are related to kingfishers and have very large beaks.

Woodpeckers are real tree-dwellers, where they dig for insects and grubs. The loud 'drumming' made by the beak is a male's warning to other males, and also an invitation to a female. A hole is bored in a tree for a nest. Common in Europe are the Lesser Spotted (no larger than a sparrow), the Great Spotted and the Green Woodpeckers. The largest European species is the Black Woodpecker, as big as a crow. Largest of all is the Ivory-billed Woodpecker of Mexico, fifty centimetres long.

Some gaudily coloured birds related to woodpeckers are the toucans of South America, which have enormous beaks and look top-heavy. In fact the beak is quite light, and a toucan can hold and play with a grape or an egg without damaging it.

Perching birds are the largest group of birds, in which the feet are built for gripping perches such as the branches of bushes and trees. Many are familiar to us as garden birds. The friendly House Sparrow is now almost worldwide as a town and village bird, and was probably well known to the cave man as it nested on rock ledges by his home. The Tree Sparrow prefers holes in trees. So does the Starling, another hole-nester, unless it can find a way into a building under the roof. The Starling has taken on a curious habit of flying into towns every night, to roost on the buildings. The Hill Mynah of India is a dark-coloured starling which is a wonderful mimic and is kept as a cage bird. The Chaffinch, Greenfinch and Bullfinch are common examples of finches. They have a brightly coloured relative in America, called the Cardinal. Waxbills are African finches also kept as cage birds.

Thrushes are somewhat larger in size and have wider tastes. As well as seeds they will eat snails, worms and fruit. There are some fine songbirds among them, such as the Song Thrush and Blackbird. Two northern thrushes, the Fieldfare and Redwing, visit Europe in winter. In summertime the Nightingale arrives and gives his nightly performance during May and June. He also sings in daytime. A great favourite all over Europe and a permanent resident in Britain is the confiding Robin. It appears almost as soon as the gardener gets to work, waiting for grubs to turn up. Although it appears friendly the Robin is a jealous owner of the garden and will drive off any rival. The red breast, like the red throat of the stickleback which

Above Noisy and brightly coloured, the Toucan is instantly recognised by its large beak. Perched alongside it is one of the equally colourful members of the parrot family, the Military Macaw.

Above There are over 300 known species of humming birds in all parts of the Americas. Brilliantly coloured, they have been given popular names like flamehead, golden belly, topaz and bluebeard.

Above At the top of the picture is the House Martin, which is common in Europe and returns to its nest during March or April. Alongside is the Magnificent Bird of Paradise, and below it the Raven, largest of the crows. Finally there is the Hoatzin from South America, a curious bird which is probably some primitive relic from the past.

also guards its nest, is a warning sign. Robins, thrushes and finches commonly nest in gardens. Some, like the Blue and Great Tits, will use wooden nest boxes put out for them – so will the Spotted Flycatcher. Most of these birds occur in woodlands which they share with the shyer perching birds such as warblers. These drab little birds from Africa have a pleasing song, and go about searching the trees for insects.

Wagtails will also catch insects and can usually be seen near water catching midges, or in fields where the horses and cows disturb the insects as they move through the grass. Larks have a way of singing in the air for long periods, especially the Common Skylark. It nests on the ground. Wrens are among the smallest birds. The most widespread is the Common Wren, which flits about in the undergrowth, searching for food. In the pine woods may be seen the even smaller Firecrest.

The 'rogues' of the bird world are the various members of the crow family. They steal eggs, hunt small animals and feed on carrion (the putrid flesh of dead animals). The Carrion Crow has developed a habit of visiting motorways in early morning to look for any creatures that have been run over. They also wait at laybys where motorists stop to eat. The handsome magpies and jays are egg-robbers and unpopular with gamekeepers. The Raven is the largest crow, a fine bird which is becoming rare in Britain. Ravens have been kept in the Tower of London for centuries, and it is said that if they ever leave, London will face disaster. One of the more sociable crows is the Jackdaw. It lives in colonies, nesting on cliffs and old ruins. There is a leader of the flock who takes charge, then a second-in-command, and so on down to the lowest jackdaw. This is called the pecking order, and can be seen any day among hens on a farm. Jackdaws are very intelligent and make delightful pets.

Some close relatives of the crows are the handsomest of all birds – the Birds of Paradise, found in New Guinea. The fine feathers of the cock birds are used in displays before the hens. The Papuans of New Guinea use the feathers as head-dresses for their ceremonies. Also of great beauty is the Lyre Bird which lives in the forests of the eastern half of Australia. It gets its name from the two curved tail feathers which are in the shape of an old musical instrument. The male uses a clearing in the bush in which to dance. The tail feathers are spread forward over its head, and while it dances it sings. It is an expert mimic of other birds, also of human noises. The hen builds a tall nest of debris and lays a single egg on top. Another Australian bird which displays is the Bower Bird. It constructs a kind of archway by twisting stems of grass together, then dances through and around this to attract a mate. It will collect bright objects like flowers and scatter these around the bower. After mating, the hen builds a separate nest for her eggs.

Below Here are three of Australia's pouched mammals. On the left is the Common Wombat, which is sometimes called a badger in Australia. Centre is the Red Kangaroo, and on the right the Koala or Native Bear.

Mammals

The word mammal comes from the Latin *mamma* for a breast. It is this breast-feeding of the young on mother's milk which is special to mammals, also the hair which grows on their bodies. There are about 3,200 species of mammals and today they dominate the world, with man as the most highly advanced of all animals. A few primitive mammals still exist as a link between ourselves and our reptile ancestors. These are the egg-laying Platypus and Echidna. The Platypus or Duck-mole was a puzzle to the early settlers in Australia who first saw it swimming in lakes and streams, and digging nest burrows in the bankside. It is covered with a thick coat of short hair, has webbed feet for swimming and claws for digging, and a curious duck-like bill for a mouth. The babies hatch from eggs, usually twins, and lick milk which oozes from the mother's milk glands. The Platypus feeds on water creatures such as crayfish, and worms on land. This odd looking mammal is a precious 'living fossil'. The Echidna or Spiny Anteater is covered in sharp spines, has powerful claws for digging into termite hills, and a long snout and tongue for catching ants. It also lays eggs, but its young are carried in the mother's pouch. Echidnas live in Australia, Tasmania and New Guinea.

Australia has many pouched mammals, or **marsupials**. These give birth to their young, which are so small and helpless that they grow up in their mother's pouch where they are warm, protected and well fed. The two largest marsupials are the Red and Grey Kangaroos, both about one and a half metres tall. The newly born baby is about two centimetres long, yet it can find its way to its mother's pouch without assistance. Most of Australia's mammals are marsupials and take the place of the true mammals that exist in the rest of the world. There is, for example, a pouched 'wolf' or Thylacine, now very rare – if not extinct. Then there are the Marsupial Mole and the Native Cat, one digging below ground and the other climbing trees to catch birds and small animals. The lovable 'Teddy bear' or Koala is a kind of marsupial bear in miniature. It lives in trees and feeds exclusively on gum leaves. The Cuscus takes the place of the squirrel, and the kangaroos are Australia's grass eaters. All these animals are marsupials: the true mammals introduced by man are cattle,

Below The Platypus or Duck-mole, one of two egg-laying mammals in Australia.

Above The entrances to the beavers' home are clearly shown in this drawing. They are underwater and safe from attack from unwanted visitors. Beavers are the great engineers of the animal kingdom and build their lodges and dams from sticks and branches with hands and teeth.

Above The little Pygmy Shrew is one of the smallest mammals and is found all over Europe and Asia.

sheep, rabbits, the camel and the dingo. Rabbits are unpopular with farmers because they eat the grass needed for the sheep and cattle. This is just one example of how man can upset nature's balance when he moves animals into strange countries.

A few small marsupials also live in America, one of which is the Virginian Opossum. Once, long ago, marsupials were world-wide. Then, as the more advanced true mammals multiplied and spread, those with pouches were slowly driven out. Some moved into what is now Australia at a time when it was still joined to Asia. When the continents moved apart and the sea broke through, this saved the few marsupials and egg-layers which we have today.

The great advantage which the true mammals have over the more primitive kinds is probably the way they care for their young. The unborn baby grows up inside its mother, joined by a special filter. Through this filter mother's blood and food can pass into the developing baby. This union is called a placenta. There are some placental babies so well developed that they can run about almost as soon as they are born. The deer fawn, the calf, the baby horse or foal, and the young hare or leveret are examples. Placental mammals range in size from the Pygmy Shrew to the giant Blue Whale.

Shrews are not mice but belong to the order of insect-eaters called **insectivores**. This includes the underground mole and the hedgehog. These mammals are restless hunters, often quarrelsome, and have long sensitive noses for searching among the leaves and earth for insects and worms. They have sharp little teeth. In tropical countries there are also tree-shrews which climb actively.

Rodents, which means gnawing animals, make up the largest order of mammals. They nibble at plants with their chisel-like front teeth, the incisors, and can open the hardest shell or bark. This constant nibbling is necessary, in order to keep the teeth sharp and the correct length. Rodent incisors never stop growing. Rats, mice, voles, squirrels and dormice are rodents which sometimes do a great deal of damage. Being shy and small, often nocturnal (that is active at night) and rapid breeders, they are not easy to keep down. The Black or Ship Rat was brought to Europe from Asia, it is said, by the returning Crusaders during the 13th century. Today it is much rarer and its place is being taken by the larger and bolder Brown or Sewer Rat, introduced much later during the 18th century. It lives in undisturbed basements, sewers, rubbish dumps, on farms and in warehouses, wherever it can steal food. Rats not only do damage but can spread disease and spoil our food, so must be kept in check.

Squirrels are rodents built for climbing, although some species live on the ground in tunnels. Chipmunks, marmots and hamsters usually do this. In Europe the Red Squirrel is not common enough to be a nuisance, but the Grey Squirrel, introduced from America, has increased so much that shooting and trapping has become necessary. Too many squirrels can damage trees, even killing young ones by nibbling the bark. The Common European Hamster is found in eastern Europe and parts of Asia. The Golden

Left The Flying Squirrel cannot really fly, but it uses the furry membranes between its limbs to glide when it jumps from branch to branch of a tree.

Above The curious looking Star-nosed Mole comes from America. It has twenty-two feelers around its nose, which is a very sensitive organ. It lives mostly in water, and is a good swimmer.

Hamster is a popular pet, descended from a single family found wild in Syria.

Mice include the House Mouse, the Field or Wood Mouse, the Yellow-necked Mouse and the little Harvest Mouse. The last species used to live in cornfields, building its nest around the stalks, but today harvesting machines have driven it out and it is more difficult to find. Voles can be confused with mice and rats, but have blunter faces, small ears and short tails. The Field Vole of Europe is perhaps the commonest species, living in rough pastureland. The larger Water Vole is seen by the waterside, feeding on water plants and diving in the water when disturbed. It is sometimes wrongly called a water rat, a name which should only be given to a swimming rat. An even larger American vole, called the Musk Rat, once ran wild in Europe, having escaped from the fur farms where it was bred for its fur – musquash. It has since been exterminated, at least in Britain, but the Coypu, a large rat-like rodent also bred for fur – called nutria – is still about. One of the most valuable fur animals is the Chinchilla. Today it is rare in its high mountain home in the Andes, but large numbers are bred on farms for their soft expensive fur.

Beavers are water rodents which dam streams with branches to deepen the water. In this way their home or lodge is surrounded by water and is safe from enemies. The entrance is below the surface. Beavers belong mainly to Canada, but a few still exist in parts of Europe and North Asia. The constant flooding of land caused by

Left Many rodents are attractive little animals and some are kept as pets. In this picture can be seen **1** field mouse, **2** yellow-necked mouse, **3** lemming, **4** water vole and **5** hamster.

Above The fox has a long body and short legs and runs close to the ground with its tail raised.

Right Domestic dogs probably come from mixed ancestors. Nobody is certain because dogs have been tamed since prehistoric times.

Above The Arctic Fox, which has a white coat in winter and a brown or slate-coloured one in summer.

Above The common Wild Rabbit which is still to be found all over Europe is not a fast runner over any distance. It relies for protection on being able to take refuge in its burrow when it is attacked.

beavers has produced some of the richest farmland in America. At one time beavers were widely trapped for their fur, and this is how the Hudson's Bay Trading Company made its name. It traded goods for beaver pelts brought in by the trappers and American Indians. Today the beaver is given protection. Porcupines are also American, as well as African. Like the hedgehog (an insect-eater) and the Echidna (an egg-layer) the hair, which is soft in the young, hardens into a stiff prickly coat for protection in the adult. The porcupine is a good climber and feeds on fruit and the bark of trees. If it is attacked it charges backwards with its quills erect and can cause injury. Since the quills come out very easily if touched, it is as well to keep a distance.

Rabbits and **hares** are no longer placed with rodents, but belong to a separate order, the Lagomorpha (meaning shaped like a hare). They have long ears and long hind legs, double incisor teeth, and all live underground. The rabbit lives in warrens and digs burrows. A doe will dig a separate nest-hole in which her naked babies are born. Hares, unlike rabbits, are solitary mammals. The young, called leverets, are born with eyes open and fully furred. They can run about almost at once. In Europe the Brown Hare lives in open lowland country, whereas the Mountain Hare belongs to the hills.

Carnivores are flesh-eaters and the main hunters among mammals. They include cats, dogs, bears, weasels and seals. A feature of such mammals is the enlarged canines or dog-teeth used for catching and tearing up their prey.

Cats are hunters with shortened faces, sharp claws and slender tails. They usually stalk their prey or lie in ambush, waiting to pounce. The smaller cats include the European wildcat which is still found in the Scottish Highlands. It is untameable and hunts rabbits, hares and ground birds. Tame domestic cats are descended from the African wildcat, and have been kept as pets since the days of Ancient Egypt. When man was beginning to farm the corn, the cat came in useful in keeping down the mice. Other small cats include the African Serval, Indian Caracal and Canadian Bobcat. The lynx is found in mountains of Europe and in North America.

Among the big cats the Lion of Africa lives in the open grassland of East Africa, its tawny coat blending with the dry bush country. Although lazy in habit, spending much of its time lying about in the shade, a lion when aroused can move at speed to run down its prey, such as a zebra or antelope – even a giraffe. Lions also live in a game park in north-west India. India is the home of the Tiger which ranges across the Far East to the Indonesian islands, and north through China as far as Siberia. Here it can survive the severe winters in the snow. A tiger's stripes help it to blend with the tall grass and bamboo thickets in which it hides. Also very widespread, from Africa to Siberia, is the Leopard. In places it is becoming rare because of

Above Three members of the cat family are shown here. At the back is a male lion, with its distinctive tawny or black mane. Lions are said to be the least ferocious of the big cats and kill only when they need to eat. Sitting proudly in front is a cheetah, which is often trained for hunting. Crouching is a tiger, which is known only in Asia and can grow almost three metres long: it is the largest of the cats.

the demand for its fur. The same applies to the Cheetah or Hunting Leopard, the fastest running animal. It can reach a speed of up to eighty kilometres an hour. America has two big cats – the Jaguar and the Puma. The Jaguar of tropical America looks somewhat like a well-built leopard with large spots. The Puma or Mountain Lion has a wide range but has been driven into the mountains and deserts because of its habit of raiding farms. It is one of the most harmless of cats, in spite of all the bad stories which are told about it.

Hyenas, although dog-like in build, are really more closely related to cats. They are scavengers and usually wait for the lion to make its kill, when they will feed on what is left of the carcass. Their powerful jaws can crack bone. The Striped Hyena lives in north Africa and the Spotted Hyena occurs south of the Sahara.

Dogs have long snouts, bushy tails, and usually hunt in packs. They follow their prey by scent and wear it down. The wolf has a wide range through Canada, parts of Europe, and in Asia as far south as India. Its reputation as a man-killer is much overrated. In America lives the wild dog of the prairies, called the Coyote. Another wild dog with large ears roams in packs in Africa. The jackals belong to Africa and India, and Australia has the Dingo. The Old World Red Fox is a wild dog which roams over most of Europe and northern Asia. Even though it has been hunted for many years it seems to be on the increase, and can occasionally be seen in the suburbs of large towns. The Arctic Fox, which turns white in winter, lives in the far north. An attractive little fox, the Fennec, has big ears and belongs to desert country in Africa. Domestic dogs may come from mixed wolf and jackal ancestors.

Right The Kodiak Bear is named after Kodiak Island in Alaska. It is the largest land bear – the equal in weight and size to the Polar Bear.

Below The tusks of the Walrus are really long teeth and can grow as long as seventy centimetres.

Below A mongoose will attack snakes, particularly vipers. Despite its ferocity a mongoose can make an attractive pet.

Bears are among the largest and strongest of carnivores, and the Brown Bear is the most widespread. It ranges from North America, through northern Asia down into India, and can still be found in parts of Europe. At one time, like the wolf and the beaver, it lived in Britain. A bear's food is varied, from deer to insects – also fish, fruit and roots. In the cold north bears hole up for the winter, and during her sleep a she-bear may give birth to her babies. Even in zoos bears hide away in their dens, and do not show their cubs until they are well grown. Polar bears roam over the ice and snow of the Arctic wastes and hunt seals and fish. They are hunted by the Eskimos for meat and clothing, but otherwise are given protection. The Polar Bear is the world's largest bear, reaching a length of over two and a half metres and a weight of up to 450 kilograms.

Seals are found in all oceans, from the Arctic to the Antarctic. Two northern seals which appear particularly along the coasts of the British Isles are the Atlantic or Grey Seal, and the Common or Harbour Seal. The larger Grey Seal prefers the rocky coasts of Wales, Scotland and Ireland, and comes ashore to a rookery (breeding place) where the pups are born in autumn. Many are drowned during the gales. The Common Seal is seen more on flatter, sandy coasts and in river mouths. Sea-lions, or eared seals, have short outer ears and hind flippers which bend forwards under the body. They are much more lively than seals and very popular in zoos and circuses, especially the Californian Sea-lion. It is taught to balance things on its nose and to play music. Eared seal rookeries are mostly on islands in the Pacific. Some species are hunted for their fur. In the Antarctic is found the world's greatest seal, the giant Elephant Seal. It can be six metres long and weigh 2,500 kilograms. In the Arctic lives a seal with tusks – the Walrus. It uses its tusks to pull shellfish off the rocks, and for hauling itself out on to land.

The weasel family contains the most bloodthirsty of hunters. Most of them have long and slender bodies on short legs, and are able to track their prey through tunnels. Many have strong scent glands. The tiny Common or European Weasel hunts rats and mice, and the larger Stoat chases rabbits and small birds. In northern countries the Stoat usually turns white in winter – then it is called an ermine – but always keeps a black tip to its tail. The Polecat is a larger weasel found only in France, parts of central Europe and in Wales. From it has been bred the Ferret, which is trained to catch rabbits. The Pine Marten, which lives in woods and forests in northern Europe, is an expert tree climber and can even catch squirrels. The Common Badger is a powerful digger. It makes a home underground, called a sett, which consists of many tunnels and entrances. Being nocturnal it can only be seen at dusk by sitting quietly near a hole it has used. Other weasels are the Mink of North America, and the Sable of Russia, both valuable for their fur. In Arctic regions lives the largest weasel, called the Wolverine. America has a weasel, the Striped Skunk, which has a

reputation for its awful smell. Actually the skunk rarely uses this and is sometimes kept as a pet.

Mongooses resemble weasels in their build, although they belong to a different family, and are supposed to be good at catching snakes, even dangerous cobras. This does happen, but they do hunt many other creatures as well. Mongooses make friendly little pets, so does the American Raccoon. It has a silvery coat with striped head and ringed tail. At one time its skin and tail were used as clothing and for hats worn by American trappers and Indian scouts. Pandas are related to raccoons and there are two kinds. The small Red Panda belongs to the Himalayas. The black and white Giant Panda, a favourite in zoos, comes from Tibet and South China. Panda means bamboo-eater, which is its main food in the wild.

Ungulates (a word from the Latin *unguis*, meaning a hoof) is the name given to those mammals which have the tips of their toes covered in horny pads. They are mostly harmless vegetarians, swift footed, and may be quite large. Their slender legs are raised on to the tips of the toes. Some ungulates are odd-toed and others are even-toed. The odd-toed ones include horses, which have a single toe on each foot. At one time the ancestors of the horse had separate toes. Horses today are mostly domesticated, and range in size from the Shire Horse on the farm to the small pony. The ponies running loose in places like Dartmoor and the New Forest in England have been put there by man. The wild ancestor is now a rarity, called the Mongolian Wild Horse. A few still exist on the northern steppes of Siberia. The most numerous wild horses are those we call zebras, of which Africa has four kinds. There are also a few wild asses in the desert lands of Arabia and Asia.

The Tapir is related to the horse and had the same early ancestor. It resembles a large pig with a short, trunk-like snout. It is a harmless and shy

Above left The Giant Panda was first discovered in the late 19th century in the Himalayas. The lovely otter (above) is a kind of water weasel and is a graceful swimmer.

Above Sea-lions belong to a family of eared seals, differing from true seals as they have visible external ears.

Above The Moose (left) is the largest of all deer. It lives in North America and is related to the European Elk. The smaller animal is the Springbok, an antelope from South Africa.

Above (top) Herds of reindeer numbering several thousands used to be common, but hunting by man has reduced their numbers.

jungle animal, often entering water. One species marked in black and white lives in south Asia, and another of a uniform brown colour belongs to South America.

In a third odd-toed group are the rhinoceroses. Africa has two species, both two-horned. The Black Rhino is still fairly common, but the White Rhino is much rarer and bigger. The Indian Rhinoceros has a single horn. Rarest of the five species are the small Javanese and Sumatran Rhinos of Indonesia. Attempts are being made to protect all these animals, but poaching still goes on. The horn when powdered down is supposed to be a powerful medicine and is much valued in the East. A rhino's horn is made of hair tightly matted together.

Even-toed ungulates are more numerous and make up the bulk of the hoofed mammals. They are mostly cloven-hoofed, that is with the hoof divided and having two toes to each foot. On the outside there may be two smaller toes, called dew-claws. The deer family are a northern group in which the male grows antlers. These are branched and drop off each year to grow afresh. The moose is the largest species. The only female deer to bear antlers is the reindeer. They are mostly tamed and used by the Laplanders for meat, clothing and milk. In America is the wild reindeer called the Caribou. Britain has two native deer, the Red Deer, the country's largest wild mammal, and the tiny Roe Deer. Roe deer occur mostly in woods, and red deer on the open mountains of Scotland and the moorlands of the west country. The pretty spotted Fallow Deer seen in parks also runs wild, but this is thought to have been introduced centuries ago by the Normans for hunting.

Antelopes are a large family of more tropical regions, especially Africa. Their horns are fixed and do not branch, although they may twist and curl: also most of the females grow them as well. They range from the large Kudu, up to nearly two metres at the shoulders, to tiny dik-diks and duikers, some of which are only forty-five centimetres high. Large herds of antelopes can still be seen roaming the open grassland of eastern Africa, such as the graceful Impala, the Springbok, Gnu, Wildebeest and many gazelles. One or two species such as the Arabian Oryx are now very rare. Prongbuck in North America are a curious mixture of deer and antelope: on the permanent horny base grow branched antlers which then drop off each year.

Cattle are large ungulates which chew the cud. After feeding, when food is stored in a huge compartment called a paunch, they rest for a while, then bring up lumps of food called cud. This is then properly chewed and swallowed a second time. The breeds of domestic cattle seen in western Europe and America are descended from the ancient wild Aurochs which was hunted by Stone Age man. The cattle most nearly resembling this giant are the famous white cattle kept on private estates in Britain. The mountains of India and Tibet are the home of the Yak. It is mostly tamed and used as a beast of burden. So is the Domestic Buffalo throughout tropical Asia. It pulls carts and ploughs and does most of the farm work in place of the horse. The African Buffalo is still wild and can be dangerous. The North American Bison (called buffalo in the United States) once teemed the prairies in millions, then was nearly wiped out by hunters. Fortunately the United States and Canadian governments stepped in just in time to save it, and it is now protected and fairly common in some of the game parks. Very much rarer is the European Bison or Wisent, but there are enough of them still about in private parks and zoos to be able to build up a fresh herd. Bison were widespread at one time, even in Britain, where fossil remains have been found. There are also many fine cave paintings of these animals.

Left There are two species of rhinoceros in Africa. The one in the picture, shown with one of its young, is the more common Black Rhinoceros. The other species is the White Rhinoceros. Both types tend to be grey in colour but the White Rhino is more docile and less solitary.

Camels, too, have been used for centuries to carry and pull things. They are able to live in dry desert surroundings or in mountains, and can go for long periods without a drink. Water is stored in the lining of the stomach. The hump is a store of fat. Camel's feet are cloven, but covered with a broad pad for walking on loose ground. The one-humped or Arabian Camel is the desert species of the Sahara, from which has been bred a fast racing camel or dromedary. This is used by desert nomads and is capable of covering long journeys. The Asiatic or Bactrian Camel has two humps and a more shaggy coat, especially in winter. It is more at home in mountains and rocky country, and is widely used for transport. In olden times, before cars and trains, it was the only means of covering the caravan routes from the East. Its name the 'ship of the desert' was truly deserved. South America has a smaller cousin of the camel, called a Llama. This is also a beast of burden in the Andes mountains. It has a wild ancestor from which it was bred, called the Guanaco. The other domestic species is the small Alpaca, bred for its wool. The Vicuna is another wild kind hunted for its skin and meat.

Above The Arabian Camel or dromedary (top) has long legs and is built for speed. The Bactrian Camel is a sturdier animal and is used more as a pack animal for carrying loads.

Right Instead of a hairy coat, armadillos have bony plates covered with horn. It was fossils of the Giant Armadillo and the Giant Ground Sloth which so fascinated Darwin when he visited South America in HMS *Beagle*. He realised that because of the changes that had taken place in these animals his theories about evolution were possible.

The African Giraffe is the world's tallest animal and can reach almost five and a half metres. In spite of its ungainly shape it can travel at speed, also it camouflages extremely well against trees. It was originally called the Cameleopard because of its camel-like shape and spotted coat like a leopard's. A small and shy cousin called the Okapi lives in the dense equatorial forest of the Congo in Africa. Its chestnut body and horizontal white stripes around the legs make it difficult to see among the trees.

Apart from cattle there are other farm animals domesticated from the wild. Living on hills are sheep descended from the Mouflon, which still occurs on the two islands of Corsica and Sardinia. Other wild sheep include the Rocky Mountain Bighorn and the Barbary Sheep of the Atlas Mountains. Farm goats are probably descended from the Bezoar Goat of south-west Asia. Other wild species are the Rocky Mountain Goat, the Ibex in Spain, the Chamois of the Alps and the Markhor of the Himalayas. In goats the billy, or male goat, usually wears a beard. Both goats and sheep are mountain animals. In the far north is a large and related species, called the Musk Ox.

Pigs on farms have almost certainly come from the Wild Boar which is still found in European forests, and spreads right across to India. Once it roamed the woodlands of Britain. Another wild pig is the Warthog of Africa, possibly one of the world's ugliest creatures. In South America are some pigs called peccaries. They have uncertain tempers and may attack humans. The large pig-like Hippopotamus (meaning river horse) is a waterside giant which will wallow in mud for hours on end. It is quite harmless unless annoyed. It can weigh over 4,000 kilograms. In deeper forest country lives the much smaller Pygmy Hippo. It has a more oily skin and can stay out of water for long periods.

Elephants have a peculiar but very useful 'nose' in the shape of a trunk, and enormous upper incisor teeth – the tusks. The African Elephant is the world's largest land animal, and can grow over three and half metres tall and weigh up to 5,000 kilograms, about the same as a London bus. It lives in open bush country in East Africa, mostly protected in the game parks. It has large ears, a rounded forehead, a hollow back and two lips to its trunk.

Below From left to right: zebra, African elephant, hippopotamus, a young giraffe and an African warthog. The zebra is really a striped horse. These stripes vary in the different species, all of which live in Africa. The African elephant is larger than its Indian cousin: many are now protected in game reserves. The hippopotamus has also needed to be protected from man, who hunted it for its tusks. The mother giraffe has only one baby at a time, which can walk almost as soon as it is born. The warthog, which gets its name from the wart-like bumps on its head, is one of the ugliest of all animals.

The smaller Asiatic Elephant of India and South-East Asia has small ears, a square forehead, a rounded back and one lip to its trunk. Also, the female – or cow – is often without tusks.

Training elephants is a slow business, and expensive. A grown animal can eat over 250 kilograms of food a day, and drink up to eighty litres of water. This is done with its trunk, a useful implement for smelling, eating and drinking, taking a shower, gathering food, smacking a baby elephant, and killing a man. There is no such thing as a 'clumsy elephant'. On its huge padded feet this giant can move like a shadow. The elephant's tusks have been its downfall. In the past thousands of animals were killed for their tusks, or for sport. Even today it is still poached for its ivory, although most of Africa's fine game animals are now being protected. A baby elephant suckles between its mother's fore-legs, using its mouth and not its trunk. It stops feeding in this way in its third year. At birth it is over a metre long and weighs some ninety kilograms. The baby elephant is born nearly two years after mating, and it will live for about fifty years. Stories of elephants over a hundred years old are probably untrue.

Edentates belong to the order Edentata, meaning without teeth, and consist of an odd collection of mammals found in South America and Africa. Actually some of them have teeth at the back of their jaws for chewing but none has teeth in the front. Armadillos are ground animals with a hard, shell-like skin which is hinged so that it can be rolled up when there is danger. Armadillos dig a lot and feed on termites. So do anteaters, tearing open ant-hills with strong claws and pushing into them with their long snouts. Only the tip of the snout can open, and through this flicks out a long tongue to catch a meal. In the trees live the plant-eating sloths which hang on to the branches upside down with their claws shaped like hooks. In the humid Amazon jungle a sloth is hard to see because tiny green plants sometimes grow on the hair, so that it camouflages well against the leaves. All these edentates are South American, but pangolins, also tree-dwellers, live in Africa. They are called 'scaly' anteaters because their bodies are covered with a hard scale-like skin.

Above Until about sixty years ago the Okapi was unknown, hidden in the dense forests of the Congo in Africa. It was not until about 1900 that a specimen was caught. The Okapi is a shy and solitary animal and its home in the remote Congo jungle makes it difficult to study in the wild.

Above The Killer Whale is a swift and vicious animal. It will attack sea-birds and seals and, when hunting in packs, will overcome larger whales than itself. The males grow some nine metres long.

Above Sea-cows belong to the order Sirenia, which gets its name from the legendary sea-maidens in Greek folk-lore. There are two living species, the Dugong and the Manatee, seen here. It is believed that the Dugong may have started the legend of the mermaid.

Bats were once thought to be flying mice, i.e. flitter mice. Actually they are a quite separate order. By means of their long finger-joints covered with skin, bats can use their hands for flying, and are as expert as birds. They can even fly in total darkness, though they cannot see. This is done by giving out a very high-pitched note which we cannot hear, called ultrasonic. If this hits an object it is reflected as an echo and heard by the bat. By means of this echo location or sonar a bat can even pick up its prey in the dark, and catch it in mid-air.

Insect-eating bats are the most numerous and inhabit various parts of the world. As well as eating insects some of the larger ones eat other small animals. The Pipistrelle is one of the commonest and is often seen flying round parks and squares, even in towns. The Long-eared Bat is easy to recognise because of its big ears. Two bats called Horseshoe Bats have curiously shaped noses. They usually hide away in caves. During winter many bats hibernate. Some tropical bats feed on the nectar of flowers, and others like the Vampire Bat of tropical America feed on blood. Horses and cattle are sometimes bitten and disease can break out. Humans have also been bitten at night and occasionally a form of rabies sickness has been passed on by these bats. Giant bats called Flying Foxes feed on fruit and do much damage. Bats give birth to young in the usual way, and sometimes the mother takes the baby with her on hunting trips, clinging to her body.

Whales, dolphins and **porpoises** are sea-going mammals built for life in water. There are two groups, the baleen whales and the toothed whales. Among the first is the world's largest mammal, the Blue Whale, which uses its baleen to feed on the krill. The various kinds of right whales, although not so large, have similar habits. These giants have been hunted by man for centuries to obtain blubber from their bodies. From this comes whale oil which is used in soap, margarine and cooking fats. Baleen can be made into brushes and brooms. Some people eat whale meat, and the skeletons are crushed into bonemeal which goes on to the land as fertiliser.

Toothed whales have only one giant, the eighteen-metre Sperm Whale or Cachelot. This hunts squids and fish, and was once feared by the whalers when they used only hand harpoons in the longboat and ran the risk of being capsized. This dangerous hunting is vividly described in the famous story of Moby Dick, a white sperm whale. Today whalers are safe in their steel boats, called catchers, and they use a deadly weapon, the harpoon gun. As a result whales have no chance of escape and are becoming rare. At the present rate of killing there is grave danger that the majestic Blue Whale will be wiped out for ever. Most whales are harmless, but the Killer Whale lives up to its name. A pack of them will tear a Blue Whale to pieces, and can cause havoc to shoals of fishes and herds of seals.

Small cousins of the Sperm Whale are the various porpoises and dolphins. Porpoises belong in the north, whereas dolphins tend to keep more to warmer seas. They often accompany ships by swimming just in front of the bows. Dolphins kept in large oceanariums show how intelligent these mammals really are. They play with their keepers in a gentle fashion, quickly learn all sorts of tricks and, like bats, have their own sonar. They can move about quite easily when blindfolded without hitting anything. One curious whale is the Narwhal of the Arctic. The bull has a long, single tusk in its upper jaw, probably used for fighting with. At one time the whalers would sell these tusks for a high price, pretending that they were horns of the legendary unicorns, and full of magic.

Although whales have the appearance of fishes they are true mammals, and this is perhaps more obvious in the unborn baby. It has tiny hands with fingers which close up by the time it is born. There are also some definite traces of an outer ear, which becomes just a small hole in the adult. Baleen whale embryos show traces of teeth, but these are absorbed to make way for the baleen. All this suggests that the whales had distant ancestors which once moved about on land.

Primates are the most highly evolved animals. From smallest to largest they have something in common. Their fore-limbs are fashioned into hands for holding and picking up things, and for gripping branches. Most primates live in trees. The four groups consist of lemurs, monkeys, apes and man.

Lemurs are the smallest and most primitive of primates, confined to tropical regions of the Old World, such as Africa, India and the Far East. They are tree-dwellers, mostly nocturnal, with large eyes for night vision, and they feed on fruit and small animals. Like other primates they have nails on their fingers and toes, except

Above There are many species of dolphin, and the one which is becoming so popular for its amusing antics in oceanariums is the Bottle-nosed Dolphin.

Left Bats are often considered unclean animals and they have at one time or other been classified as birds, rodents and even primates. Now they are in a separate order of their own and no one can deny their fascination, especially their ability to fly in the dark using a built-in 'radar'. The bats in this drawing are (top to bottom): the Long-eared Bat, the Horseshoe Bat, the Grey Bat and the Barbastelle.

Above The apes are the animals closest to man. There are today four kinds of apes in the world, two in Africa, the gorilla and the chimpanzee, and two in Asia, the gibbon and the orang-utan. The chimpanzee (left) is perhaps most like man in his body and in his brain. His intelligence is greater than any other primate and because of this the chimpanzee is often the subject of tests to prove how far an animal is capable of reasoning. Certainly chimpanzees are popular with people, performing man-like acts in zoos to win applause. In the picture above, seen alongside the chimp, is a baboon. This animal is not an ape but belongs to the Old World monkeys. A devoted parent, it lives in family groups.

for the second toe which ends in a claw and is called the 'toilet digit' because it is used for combing the fur. Madagascar is the main home of lemurs, and they include the Ruffled and the Ring-tailed Lemurs often seen in zoos. The little Tarsier with its huge eyes belongs to the Philippines and is a real 'living fossil' descended from one of the earliest primates of the Eocene Period. The charming little galagos or bush-babies of Africa actually cry like babies. They have long tails and are lively jumpers in the trees. Far more sedate and living up to its name is the Slow Loris of Malaysia. It is somewhat like the Potto of Africa. One of the more peculiar lemurs is the rare Aye-aye of Madagascar. It has a very long slender middle finger used for poking into holes to catch insects.

Monkeys are of two kinds. The Old World monkeys extend from Africa to Indonesia. Baboons are monkeys with dog-like faces which live in packs, mostly on the ground. In searching for food these powerful monkeys may hunt animals after the fashion of wolves, and can be dangerous if approached. Sometimes they damage crops. The even more powerful Mandrill with its vivid blue face and hind quarters also occurs in Africa. In India the Langur is treated as sacred, and is usually seen near temples in the hill country. The footprints found in the Himalayan snows and said to be the track of some strange giant called the Yeti, or Abominable Snowman, could be made by this monkey as it travels over the snow, or perhaps by a mountain bear. Langurs leap along so that all four feet come down together. In the snow this would appear as one footprint. Other African monkeys include the Colobus, Vervet and Diana monkeys, which have been widely hunted for their skins. The Rhesus Monkey has been used in large numbers for experiments. It has proved valuable in understanding about the different groups of blood in humans.

New World monkeys from Central and South America are somewhat different. They have much broader noses and can use their tails to hang on with. Some of them make attractive pets. The popular sailor's monkey of years ago is the Capuchin Monkey. It used to be seen sitting on top of a barrel organ in the street, dressed in a jacket and hat, holding out its hand for pennies. Other favourites are the little Squirrel Monkey and the Marmoset.

Above On the left is a fine specimen of a gorilla. It lives in Africa and is the biggest and strongest of all primates. It is a very difficult animal to train and when kept in captivity often becomes listless and sullen. The gorilla feeds on enormous quantities of fruit and roams the jungle looking for food. On the right is a small orang-utan, known locally as the 'old man of the woods', which is what its name means in the Malay language. Unlike the gorilla, it responds well to training and appears happy in captivity.

Both these pets become very attached to their owners. A really beautiful creature is the Golden Marmoset which is covered in golden-brown fur.

Apes are man's nearest living cousins. Like us they have no tail, and can stand upright, although normally they walk about on all fours. The largest ape is the Gorilla which may grow to one and a half metres and weigh over 250 kilograms. It is a shy animal which roams the Congo jungle in Africa in small family parties. There is also a mountain race. The Gorilla is a vegetarian, searching for fruit, bamboo shoots and leaves. At night it builds platforms in the trees in which the family sleep, the male gorilla usually staying below on guard. This ape has tremendous strength and can become dangerous if annoyed. At one time there were strange tales about these hairy 'ape-men' of the jungle. Actually the gorillas are delicate in captivity, and can quickly catch illnesses such as colds from humans. This is why their cages are covered with glass – also to keep in the warmth.

One of nature's animal clowns is surely the Chimpanzee, another ape living wild in tropical West Africa. Intelligent and friendly when reared as a baby it is the favourite in zoos and circuses where it performs many tricks. Wild chimps are like gorillas and roam through the forest in search of fruit and shoots. They will also raid birds' nests, and catch other animals to eat.

In Borneo and Sumatra lives the Red Ape, called the Orang-utan, a Malay name meaning 'man of the woods'. It has a thick reddish coat and spends much of its time in the trees. Leaves and fruit are its food and it has a fondness for the durian fruit, a large and sweet tasting fruit with an unpleasant smell. Because it is so gentle in captivity the orang-utan has become popular in zoos. Hunters kill the parents in order to capture the young. Also the forest home of this ape is gradually being cut down, and this makes its future very uncertain.

Gibbons are the smallest apes, and most agile. There are five species living in the forests of the Far East. They are expert tree climbers, and can swing about in a way that no humans can copy. This ape can also walk upright quite easily. When excited, gibbons make loud whooping cries, filling the jungle with their noise. Apes show much intelligence, but are slow to work things out, unless by accident.

Right Four stages in the development of man, showing a specimen of the skull, some typical tools, and from skull remains an impression of what the creatures may have looked like. Reading from top to bottom are shown: **1** *Australopithecus*, the oldest man-like primate, came from the Transvaal. He was small, lightly built and agile, and lived about a million years ago. **2** *Homo erectus*, or *Pithecanthropus* was so named as erect man. He is known from specimens found in Java dating from 500,000 years ago. **3** Neanderthal man lived in many parts of Europe during the Old Stone Age. He was a cave dweller and a very skilled hunter. **4** Cro-Magnon man replaced Neanderthal man and had a modern brain and features. The well-known cave paintings of animals date from his time.

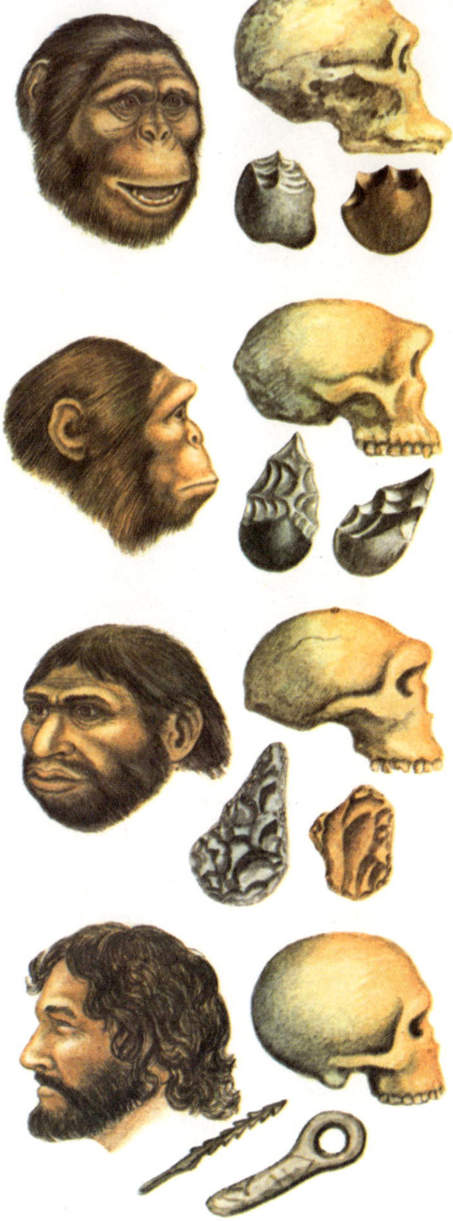

Right If the age of the earth is taken as about 5,000 million years and man has lived on earth for some 500,000 years, then on a twelve-hour clock which represents the span of the earth's life man's life has lasted about four seconds.

Humans have superior brains to all other animals, and this is what makes them the dominant animal on earth today. They can live in almost any climate and altitude, from the equator to polar regions, and from ground level to high mountains. With the skill of his hands and the thinking ability of his brain, man can work out many problems. This all began with his venture on to the ground as a walking ape-man. He first experimented with stone and bone to make his tools and weapons. Because he can make things the zoologist calls him 'a tool-making animal' and gives him the scientific name of *Homo sapiens* – 'man, the wise one'. Recently it was discovered that wild chimpanzees are just beginning to make use of objects. They will strip a big leaf down to the midrib, and poke it into a termite's nest. The ants bite on to this, then the chimp pulls it out and licks off the ants to eat. Another trick is to get at water which is out of reach in holes in trees. Leaves are pushed into the hole to soak up the water, then the leaf is sucked to get a drink.

Although we are the only living species of the family called Hominidae, some anthropologists (students of primates) have divided us into races, largely based on our colour. This is why we speak of whites, blacks and yellows. In some societies where races are mixed, as in the West Indies, there may be different shades of colour. We humans have little hair on our bodies compared with apes. Being warm-blooded it is necessary to wear clothing in the colder climates. Nobody is certain why we lost our hairy coats, unless it was because our ancestors had to run swiftly to catch their food, or to avoid enemies. Maybe this is why we developed naked skins to keep cool, especially as early man lived in Africa. Later when he spread north to colder parts he started wearing animal skins, then learned how to weave clothing from hair and wool, also to use fire and shelter in caves. Today with the aid of tools and machines which he has made with the skill of his hands and the intelligence of his thinking brain, man can live almost anywhere on earth. One day he will be spending his holidays on Antarctica, or even making pleasure trips to the moon.

The world of science and invention

Contents

243 The world of science and invention
Scientific method – Scientific models
Ancient science
Early machines

250 The microscopic world
The nature of matter – Solids, liquids and gases – Chemical substances – Atomic weights – Radioactivity – Electrons and ions – Discovery of protons – Neutrons and the Bohr atom

258 Time
Sidereal and solar time – Longitude and time – Clocks and watches – The atomic clock – Relative time

263 Motion
Motion on earth – From Aristotle to Galileo – Newton's laws of motion – Universal gravitation – Work and energy – Perpetual motion – Power – Kinetic theory – Steam power – The steam turbine – The internal combustion engine – The diesel engine – The jet engine – Rocket motors – Circular motion – Vibrations – Waves – Sound waves – Velocity of sound – Ultrasonics – Supersonics

284 Equilibrium
Adding up forces – Levers and machines – Stress and strain – Structure of metals – Organic compounds – Equilibrium in fluids – Equilibrium in the air

294 Controlling the electron
Electron currents – Potential differences and the volt – Electrical resistance – Electromagnetism – Electrical engineering – The electric telegraph – The telephone – The electric light – The electronic age – X-rays – Radio waves – The electromagnetic spectrum – Radar – Television – Solid state electronics – Infra-red rays – Visible light – Moving pictures – Lasers – Ultra-violet light – Gamma rays

307 Numbers and calculations
The computer – Automation

311 Controlling the nucleus
Natural radioactivity – Radioactive detection – Splitting the atom – Nuclear fission – Atomic energy – The atom bomb – The nuclear reactor – Radioisotopes – Fundamental particles

316 Inventions and discoveries

319 Medical science
Hippocrates of Cos – Early medical schools – Roman medicine – Galen's theories – Arabic medicine – The Middle Ages – The revival of learning – Medical books – New inventions – Great doctors – Thomas Sydenham – The 18th century – The nervous system – The key to life – Treatment of diseases – Techniques of surgery – Quarantine regulations – The 19th century – Antiseptics – First nursing services – The 20th century – Discovery of penicillin – Modern aids to health – Transplant surgery – Psychology – Sigmund Freud – Cybernetics

Above Many of the scientists whose names appear in these pages were men and women who dared to doubt what seemed to others to be an obvious and clear explanation of something. Only by patient research and by having the courage to discard old models and construct new ones can the scientist really progress.

The world of science and invention

For many thousands of years the earth was inhabited by creatures who lived and died without passing on their experiences to following generations. These early fish, reptiles, birds and mammals could only 'talk' to each other through the roars, calls and screams of the jungle. Yet, somehow, from these prehistoric beings a more intelligent animal evolved with a brain able to form the controlled sounds of speech.

At the same time, this human being began to use rocks and trees to fashion weapons to help him hunt for food. Stones and spears were probably the first tools used by humans as extensions of their own bodies – the spear could travel faster in flight than man could run – and this ability to invent tools and pass on knowledge gave man a growing control of his surroundings. His search for new ways to survive and improve his way of life continued through the ages and the story of this search is the story of man's world of science and invention.

As knowledge grew and the art of writing developed, parts of the story were recorded – some in one book, some in another. No man could remember all there was to know and writers found it useful to classify their knowledge under separate headings – much like a library arranges its books in sections so that the reader will know where to look for each subject. Science became separated into various branches such as physics (the study of natural forces), chemistry (the study of materials), and biology (the study of living things). These various branches of science progressed at quite different rates. Biology, for example, was for many thousands of years simply the accumulation of man's experiences in the rearing of animals and the sowing and reaping of crops, while human biology was left to the witch-doctor, until the practice of medicine became well established.

Yet time after time one branch of science received new and exciting ideas from another which enabled it to make further progress. As knowledge in each subject grew, the subjects themselves began to overlap, producing new branches of science such as

Right This drawing reconstructs an invention by Hero of Alexandria, the Greek mathematician who lived during the 1st century AD. It was a device for opening temple doors by heated air. A fire kindled on a hollow altar caused air to expand down a tube, driving water from one vessel to another. Extra weight in the second vessel caused it to drop and move round the pivots on which the doors were fixed.

Euclid
(4th century BC) Greek mathematician. Little is known about his life but he is thought to have founded the school of mathematics at Alexandria in Egypt, where he taught. His chief work is the *Elements*, still used as a geometry textbook and one of the best-known mathematical books. He has been called the most successful textbook writer of all time.

physical chemistry and bio-physics. Some men used this knowledge to build better machines and structures and later found it necessary to form special branches of what is called applied science. These engineers were the founders of civil, structural, mechanical and electrical engineering societies in many different countries.

Man's adventure into space is one example of the way in which scientists and engineers must today work in teams so that physicists, chemists, biologists, mathematicians, astronomers, doctors and engineers can all combine their own special knowledge of science to achieve a common aim.

Because the story of science and invention is so inter-related it is not told in the following pages under special headings like 'physics' or 'chemistry'. Instead it is traced through some of the ways in which man has successfully found and used the laws of science to satisfy his physical needs as well as his curiosity.

Throughout history, man has thought about the nature of matter – it is, after all, the 'stuff' from which he is made. Step by step he gained a deeper understanding of **The microscopic world** (the title of our next chapter) of simple particles and the behaviour of atoms.

To know when to sow and when to reap his crops he learned how to measure **Time**. The control of moving bodies has been one of man's greatest achievements, first on earth and now in outer space. This science of dynamics, or the study of **Motion**, began with the first hunters as they watched their spears travel through the air. To build houses, towns, roads and bridges, man had to keep things still and make sure that what he built would remain standing: therefore, he developed the science of **Equilibrium**, which means maintaining even balance.

Only when man's curiosity and physical needs had led him to the discovery of the electron and the principles of electricity and magnetism, did he find the answers to many of the problems of science. **The control of the electron**, now the responsibility of the electrical and electronic engineer, opened up new means of communication such as the telephone, radio and television. **The control of the nucleus** followed, and knowledge of the atomic nucleus has led to the development of atomic energy, an achievement which has offered man life-giving energy independent of the sun's rays.

Though this may be the last chapter of our present story, it will certainly not be the final chapter of man's world of science and invention.

Scientific method

Scientific progress has been achieved in many ways. Early man learned by experience and tried to repeat from memory the best way to hunt, to build or to keep himself out of harm's way. He was an inventor but had not yet become a scientist. Only when he began to search for natural laws and principles, and so produced theories, did he begin to use scientific method, that is: observation, deduction, hypothesis and experimentation. The ability to use that part of his brain – called imagination – to do this, was slow in developing. The first evidence of it can be seen in the cave paintings of primitive man.

Much later, the Egyptians carved imaginative scenes of their sun gods on rock faces, but it was the Greeks who were the first to develop a scientific imagination. Greek philosophers, such as Plato (427?-347? BC) and Aristotle (384-322 BC), created mental pictures of matter, while Archimedes (287?-212 BC) used mathematical pictures to explain physical principles.

The cave painters could not draw imaginative pictures of things they had never seen and many people today are in the same position, yet this is just what scientific invention is about. New ideas have often developed not only because an inventor had the ability to combine his knowledge with patient investigation, but because he could also use his imagination to make new and original scientific pictures and models.

Scientific models

Model building starts when we are very young with bricks and pieces of cardboard. A model plane can be built from two pieces of card or wood tied together with string. It is a very simple model but in imagination it can become the latest jet aircraft diving down through the clouds. With a construction kit and an elastic-powered engine, however, a real flying model is a possibility. Not perhaps as realistic a craft as one of the more advanced radio-controlled models, which are so perfect in detail that from a photograph it is difficult to tell the difference between the model and the real thing.

Scientists, too, like to build models and some of them appear in this book. These scientific models are used to explain how and why things behave as they do. For example, in the following pages we will trace the development of atomic energy from the time when early scientists built their first model of an atom. Like the model plane made of pieces of wood, the model atom was a very simple toy – something like a small billiard ball.

Above and **below**
These two photographs show how difficult it can be to identify the real thing from a model. Before reading to the end of this caption see if you can tell which is the real aeroplane. Both these photographs show the famous RAF bomber aircraft of the Second World War, the Lancaster. The real one is above and the model is below.

Right This model structure shows the DNA molecule. The letters DNA stand for deoxyribose nucleic acid and it is formed of two strands which spiral around one another. This molecule plays an important part in the passing on of hereditary characteristics from parents to children.

Eratosthenes (276?–194 BC) Greek mathematician, historian, astronomer, poet and geographer. Born at Cyrene in north Africa he went to Alexandria to take charge of the great library there. He was the first person to calculate the circumference of the earth. He did this by measuring the lengths and angles of shadows cast by the sun at two towns in Africa about 800 kilometres apart. His estimations were very near to the true figure.

But new facts about the behaviour of atoms could not be explained by this means and so a more complicated atom model was constructed. This was a miniature solar system with a sun, or nucleus, at its centre and planetary electrons rotating around it. This model worked extremely well, so well in fact that there was a danger of thinking that the atom was exactly like this. As we have seen, models can easily be mistaken for the real thing.

During the 1920s, as a result of further research, an even more complicated atom model was constructed which could not be represented in terms of particles at all. This model, too, is likely to be replaced as scientists discover further facts about the behaviour of the atom.

This is how science has progressed in many fields, and it is easy now to laugh at the earlier simple models and think how wrong they were. But like the crude model plane made from pieces of wood they did have something of the right shape and proved to be very useful in helping to develop many early inventions.

If you look at the number of important inventions and discoveries that have been made over the last 1,000 years you will find that most of them occurred in the last 300 years. Why is this? What prevented progress being made in the previous 700 years? One reason was the mistaken belief that once a scientific model had been built, it was a complete picture of the real thing. Anyone who doubted this ran the risk of being ridiculed by his fellow men and even in some cases of losing their lives by carrying on with their investigations.

Many of the scientists whose names appear in these pages were men and women who dared to doubt what seemed to others to be an obvious explanation of something. They helped to build the new models of the scientific age. It is no different today. Our models are not the real thing, and there are many new inventions and theories waiting to be developed. More names will be added to the growing list of scientists and inventors who have understood the need for simple models, but are prepared always to modify them when new facts demand a different explanation. Who knows? – perhaps in a few years' time one of these names may be yours.

Ancient science

From very earliest times man had to transport himself and his belongings over the face of the earth to find food. When loads became too heavy for him to carry they were tied on packs slung over an animal's back, or later tied to long poles trailing behind it. This system of transport is still used in

Left The wheel, one of man's most important inventions. No one knows how or when the idea of a wheel first occurred. Certainly it was a gradual process which must have developed from the rollers used in the ancient world to transport heavy objects. Seen in these drawings from left to right and from top to bottom are **1** The wheel of a cart from Ur in Mesopotamia, which is reconstructed from a relief dating from about 2500 BC. It is made from joined pieces of wood. **2** A chariot wheel from ancient Egypt. **3** 11th-century Anglo-Saxon cart wheel. **4** A chariot wheel from ancient Greece. **5** The wheel of a 1932 Alfa Romeo car. **6** A wheel from the scale model of a locomotive.

Siberia. When man began to build houses and live in communities he needed to transport heavier loads and found that tree trunks could be used as rollers. At what point in time the roller became a wheel is uncertain but early drawings suggest that tying the trunk or roller to a cart was an important stage in the development of the wheel and axle. The rollers had to be made wider at the ends so that they would turn freely and move the cart over rough ground. Smooth rotation of the wheel about a fixed axle was a much later development of the Bronze Age, and required the skill of the metal worker and some knowledge of geometry and engineering design.

Nowadays we describe these early periods of history in terms of the materials which were used at the time. The Stone, Bronze and Iron Ages were followed by the Classic Age of the Greeks about 600 BC.

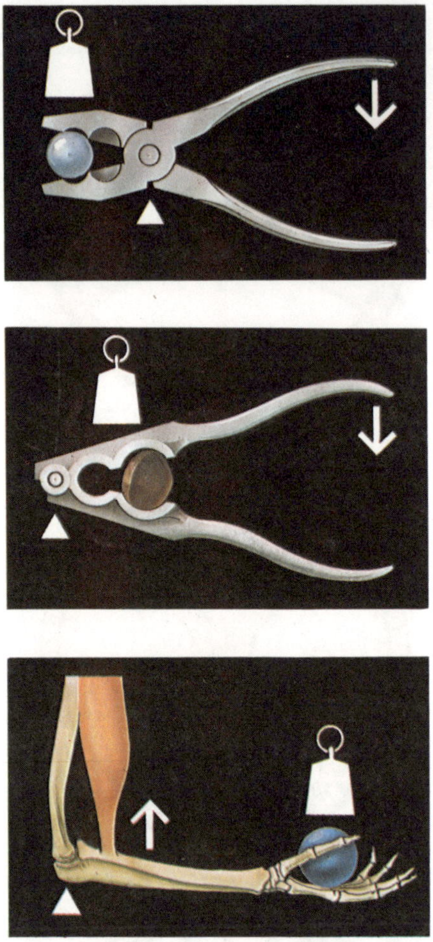

Right The three kinds of lever are demonstrated in these diagrams. At the top is a first order lever where the hinge is between the applied effort (the handles of the pliers) and the load. In the centre is a second order lever where the hinge is at one end, the applied effort at the other and the load in the centre. The final diagram shows a third order lever where the hinge is at one end and the effort is applied between the hinge and the load.

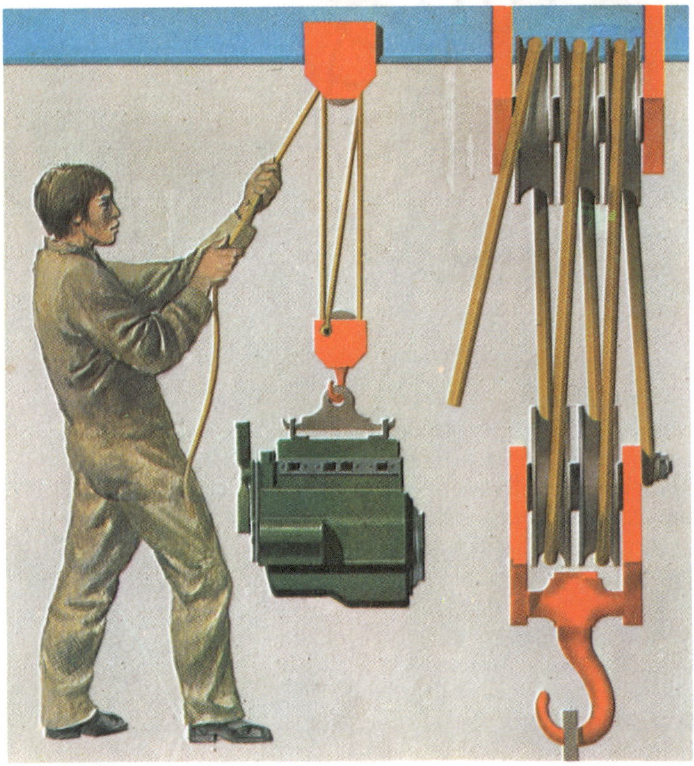

Below The pulley, which enables heavy weights to be lifted easily, developed from the wheel. The system of pulley wheels lessens the direct effort that is needed to lift the weight.

Early machines

Pulleys to hoist large stone blocks developed naturally from the wheel, while simple lever systems – the earliest machines used by man – were used to raise water from wells and shift large stone building blocks.

There are three kinds of lever. First order levers have the axle or hinge between the applied effort and the load. The single pulley and the balance arm are both examples of this kind of lever. Second order levers have the hinge at one end. Despite the fact that the oar of a rowing boat rotates in its rowlock, the real hinge of the lever is in the water. The load is the boat's weight acting at the rowlock and the effort is applied at the handle – a second order lever. Third order levers again have the hinge at one end, but the effort is applied between the hinge and the load. In this case the effort must always be greater than the load. Surprisingly, most human joints form third order levers.

Man's need to find food was again what inspired him to make traps – themselves early forms of machines – and invent the bow and arrow, one of the earliest methods of slowly storing energy. The quick release of this stored energy propelled the arrow farther than man could possibly throw it. (Was the twang of the string man's first introduction to a musical note, or did he discover his first instrument by blowing through a hollow bone to fan the flames of his fire?)

Without water, man could not live for very long, and the effort to obtain it, for himself, and for his animals and his crops, led to the invention of many methods of controlling this precious liquid. The early Egyptians, who had only the River Nile as a source of water, needed to store it in times of drought. They found that clay could be moulded into pots for this purpose – the beginning of chemical engineering. Pottery led to the potter's wheel, and artificial irrigation to water-lifting machines like the wheel and axle which could be driven round by an animal.

In South America, the Incas of Peru became expert engineers, transforming the sides of mountains into terraces on which they could grow their food. They too invented lifting machines and cut canals for irrigation.

Archimedes
(287?–212 BC) Greek mathematician and inventor. First to discover how to measure density, he proved the theory that a body placed in water will displace a volume of water equal to its own volume. Among his inventions are the endless screw and the Archimedes screw, which is a spiral pump for raising water.

In this way, through the ages, man's physical needs led him to invent new machines. When he first asked himself how and why these machines worked he began the story of science.

Early civilisations formed in areas where man could settle for long periods and obtain food from the earth around him. They were therefore situated in large river valleys such as those found in Mesopotamia, Egypt, parts of India and China. The races who settled in these areas were the first to record their inventions and pass on their knowledge by writing as well as by word of mouth. Scientific information began to accumulate and could be examined by later generations.

Warfare between the races destroyed many of these early civilisations and it is only through the ancient Greeks that much of this knowledge has been preserved. Later, the Greeks were able to apply scientific theory and principles to the inventions of the past because they were also mathematicians. The mill, windlass, pump and press were a few of the machines which resulted from this combination of theory and practice.

Archimedes laid the foundations of the theory of machines in his *Elements of Mechanics*, and also founded the theory of the two sciences, statics – why things remain stationary, and hydrostatics – why things float. Yet his writings were ignored by later civilisations and remained unpublished throughout the dark ages, until brought to light again in 1543.

Leonardo da Vinci (1452–1519) Italian painter, sculptor, architect, engineer and musician. Born in Vinci in Italy, he studied painting with Verrocchio and worked as an artist under the patronage of Lorenzo the Magnificent. He painted 'Last Supper' in 1498 and 'Mona Lisa' in 1503. He accomplished more than any other man in history in a wide range of arts and sciences. His understanding and knowledge of most of the sciences was far beyond that of his age. His original thoughts were contained in a series of notebooks and drawings, such as those reproduced above.

The microscopic world

A visitor from outer space, taking his first look at our world from high in the sky, might very easily think that the countryside was filled with a series of channels through which flowed a curious black liquid. From his position high above the earth he might not realise that he was looking down on a stream of cars moving bumper to bumper along a congested road on their way home from the seaside.

On taking a closer look he would perhaps be able to detect that the 'liquid' was in fact made up of separate moving objects. Some of these objects would be moving faster than others, and now and then an object would leave the main stream and travel along on its own, while occasionally two or more of the objects would collide! The space man would not find it easy to form any idea why or how all this was happening. Any conclusions he offered in a report to his own world could only be based on the facts he had observed.

The nature of matter

The early Greek philosophers were in much the same position as our space visitor when they attempted to think about the nature of matter. They were unable to observe matter close up and could only guess why and how it acted as it did. One of them, Democritus (5th century BC), believed that matter was made up of indivisible atoms (from the Greek word *atomos* which means something that cannot be divided). It was not a popular idea for it also suggested that the gods of the Ancient World were not in complete control of the movement of these atoms and this, to the Greeks of that time, was certainly unthinkable.

Little progress was made in the understanding of the nature of matter for nearly 2,000 years. Then, in the middle of the 16th century, a Dominican monk, Giordano Bruno (1548-1600), attempted to revive the atomic theory. He was, as it happened, burned at the stake for his 'outlandish' ideas and it was left to Pierre Gassendi (1592-1655), a French philosopher and mathematician, again to suggest that matter was made up of moving atoms. Gassendi was careful to explain that in his view atomic movement was under the complete control of God. This made his theories acceptable, but still almost impossible to prove one way or the other.

Today, with modern electron microscopes, we can examine the structure of matter much more closely and obtain some direct evidence of the existence of atoms, though even now we cannot actually see them as separate particles. We have still not moved as close to the atom as our imaginary space visitor to the line of cars on earth. But there is no need to see these atoms directly, for their existence has been confirmed in many ways, and they have enabled scientists to explain chemical and physical phenomena.

Solids, liquids and gases

One of the commonest substances on earth is water and we are well aware of its presence all around us in liquid form. Yet it is very easy to change the liquid state of water into a gas by boiling it in a kettle until it becomes steam, or to change it into a solid as ice in a refrigerator. Why do these three states of the same substance have such very different physical properties? The explanation appears to lie in the fact that particles of matter attract each other. This in itself is hard to believe, for in the ordinary way we do not sense that all the particles around us, making up the matter in our world, have any forces acting between them.

While magnets will attract each other if they are brought together in the right way – and really strong ones can be made to jump at each other along a table – it would be most surprising if the cups, plates, knives and forks on the dinner table jumped at each other in this way. The forces of attraction between particles of matter are there, however, but are much smaller than those between magnets. The forces are so small that their presence is not 'felt' until the particles are quite close together.

How does one particle 'know' that another particle is nearby? How do magnets 'know' when other magnets are attracting or repelling them? Scientists have been trying to answer these questions for many years and have not yet found a complete answer. It could be that some message is being sent from one particle to another. Is this message always being transmitted, like the flashing light on a beacon?

For want of a better scientific model, scientists invented message lines called 'fields of force', and imagined these fields to be radiating outwards in all directions from particles of matter. The particles have gravitational fields, but we will see later that they also have electrical fields and magnetic fields as well. All these fields have one thing in common – like light signals from a beacon, they grow weaker as the distance from them increases.

In solids, however, where the particles are very close together, the forces become quite strong so that the particles cannot easily escape one another's clutches. Some solids need saws, knives or even sledgehammers to separate them. Furthermore, in a number of solids the particles arrange themselves in orderly patterns to form crystals, and these crystal structures can become very strong indeed. One crystal pattern can be seen when ice forms on a window pane, and other patterns are revealed by taking photographs of the pictures formed in modern electron microscopes.

There is another way of making the particles move apart without using a saw or a hammer, though this method, too, requires a certain amount of energetic work. The energy can be

Above About 1590 a Dutch spectacle maker, Zacharias Jansen, placed two lenses, one concave and one convex, in alignment and was able to magnify a small object. This is usually considered to be the moment when the first microscope was invented. It was an important moment as, for the first time, man was able to observe the structure of matter in close-up. The ornate microscope seen here is known as the Adams' Universal.

Right The alchemist in the Middle Ages was concerned with the search for a 'medicine' called the 'philosopher's stone', of which there were two sorts: one was white for turning metals into silver and the other was red for turning them into gold.

John Dalton
(1766–1844) English chemist and physicist. Son of a Quaker weaver. In 1785 became head of a boarding school and began his life-long interest in physical studies and mathematics. Best known for his atomic theory (1803) and his efforts to formulate a table of atomic weights and a system to classify chemical compounds. Kept a diary for 57 years of his meteorological observations. Suffered from colour blindness, which he was the first to describe in detail.

supplied in the form of heat which, we say, 'melts the solid'.

When solids melt, the distances between the particles increase, while the forces between them grow weaker. Now the particles have more freedom, allowing the liquid to flow and be poured from one container to another. Some particles can escape from the surface of a liquid and shoot off into space like little spacecraft: very energetic particles can even escape from a solid, as anyone will sense in the presence of moth balls. The liquid then evaporates into the atmosphere.

Given even more heat the liquid reaches its boiling point and particles begin to form vapour bubbles deep down inside the body of the liquid. The liquid boils and turns into vapour. Vapour particles in the atmosphere are now much farther apart, and the forces between particles are so small that the particles dash about in space hardly noticing each other unless they happen to have a head-on collision.

Chemical substances

Men interested in chemistry in the Middle Ages were called alchemists and most of them were concerned with the fruitless search for a secret compound which could turn base metal into gold. But by the 17th century the first true chemists were discovering some of the real reactions that take place between chemical substances and what happened to them when they were combined.

In 1808, John Dalton (1766-1844), an English chemist, brought together the idea of the chemical combination of elements with the atomic theory of matter. Much of the evidence for his theories was based on earlier work by such scientists as Robert Boyle (1627-91) and Antoine Lavoisier (1743-94). In 1789, Lavoisier had listed thirty-three 'elements' and although only twenty-eight of these were later shown to be acceptable, they were recognised as the basic building blocks of matter.

Dalton's theories about chemical substances slowly took shape. Matter was formed of elements, such as iron, copper, carbon and oxygen (modern science now recognises ninety-two basic elements in their natural state and another eleven which have been made by man) and every element had

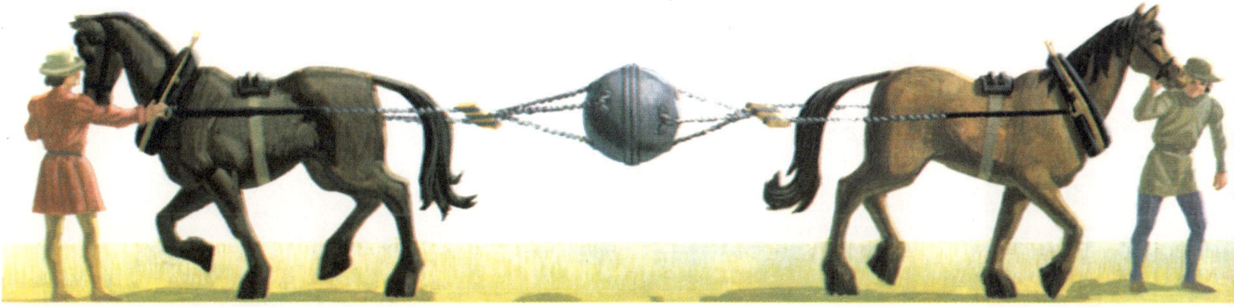

its own set of special physical and chemical properties.

The smallest particle of such an element that could exist on its own was an atom. At this time it was thought that the simplest possible particle of anything was a single atom, although compounds of several elements would contain more than one atom from each element, stuck together by some kind of attractive force.

And the atom itself? This still remained, in scientists' minds, as a mysterious, unsplittable, miniature billiard ball. Iron atoms were in some way different from copper atoms, but all iron atoms – no matter where they came from – would be identical to each other.

Dalton's atomic theory explained much, but was still incomplete. It could not predict how many atoms of each of the combining elements were contained within a single particle of a compound.

It was left to Amedeo Avogadro (1776-1856), an Italian chemist, to introduce the idea of molecules. These, he suggested in 1811, were composed of atoms, and some molecules contained more than one atom of the same element. A helium molecule, we now know, contains one atom. Hydrogen and oxygen molecules in their natural states each contain two atoms, since individual atoms of these elements do not exist under normal conditions. However, when the two elements combine to form water, the resulting compound molecule is made up of two atoms of hydrogen, and only one atom of oxygen.

From early times certain mystical symbols had been allocated to the known chemical substances. This practice was changed in the 19th century when scientists started using letters to represent the elements. These new symbols had a very special meaning. Each represented one atom of a particular element, and it was now possible to represent chemical reactions by equations.

This system remains in use today. A hydrogen molecule, containing two atoms, is represented by H_2. When more than one molecule is involved, this is indicated by a number in front of the symbol; thus $2H_2$ means two molecules. To represent the way in which water is formed by the combination of two molecules of hydrogen with one molecule of oxygen to form two molecules of water, the equation is written: $2H_2 + O_2 = 2H_2O$.

Atomic weights

From the middle of the 19th century, scientists were hard at work on experiments designed to reveal the composition, formulas and chemical properties of their new-found compounds. They tried, like stamp collectors, to arrange the elements in a kind of album. In the same way as stamp collectors might arrange their stamps according to value or nationality, so chemists grouped the known elements according to certain common chemical properties. For example, the elements potassium, sodium, calcium and magnesium, as a group, behaved in much the same way; while bromine, chlorine and iodine belonged to another group which again had many properties common to each other.

As a kind of 'value' chemists used the weights of the atoms of each element as another method of arrangement. Strictly speaking this 'atomic weight' was not a measure of actual weight, but a number representing how much heavier the atoms of one element were than those of another. Since hydrogen was the lightest known

Above Otto von Guericke (1602–86) was a German scientist who invented the first air pump in 1650. The drawing above depicts the famous Magdeburg experiment in which two hemispheres held together only by air pressure could not be pulled apart by teams of horses. Below is Von Guericke's air thermoscope which was a primitive device for measuring temperature.

The Russian chemist, Mendeleyev, in 1869, first saw the order in the then known elements. His periodic table, which arranged the elements in ascending atomic weight, has stood the test of time including the discovery of many new elements. It not only brought together all the groups of elements which had similar properties but also allowed Mendeleyev to accurately predict the properties of the new elements before they were discovered.

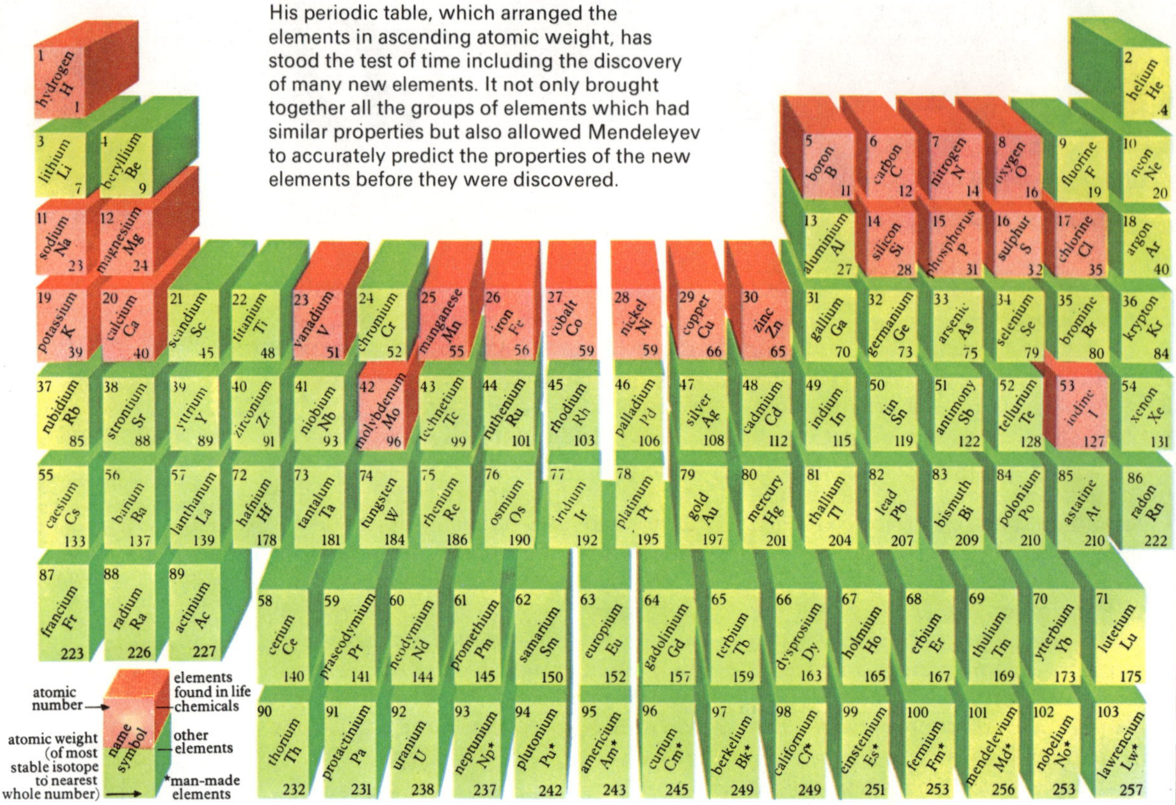

element this was used as a standard, and by careful experiments other elements were compared with it. Oxygen turned out to have an atomic weight of 16, while lead was found to be 207 times as heavy as hydrogen.

A very large number of these atomic weights appeared to be whole numbers. This led scientists to think that hydrogen might be the basic element from which all others could be built. But several of the elements refused to fit into this neat pattern, even when oxygen and then carbon were taken as the standard units, and the idea of a hydrogen atom building block had to be abandoned.

Nevertheless, using this atomic weight as a value, an English chemist, John Newlands (1837-98), arranged the elements in ascending order of atomic weight and discovered a curious, regular pattern. With one or two exceptions, every eighth element in his list was one of a group which had common properties. The exceptions to this pattern left his table incomplete, but the 'octave law' (law of eight) did encourage other scientists.

Quite independently of each other a German chemist, Lothar von Meyer (1830-93), and a Russian, Dmitri Mendeleyev (1834-1907), produced a better collection of the elements which not only took into account the octave law, but purposely introduced gaps into the list. It was suggested that the gaps represented elements as yet undiscovered, which would eventually complete the collection. This album, or Periodic Table as it came to be called, had later to be changed in the light of new knowledge, but it enabled a large number of the apparently unrelated facts of chemistry to be united.

Once the position of an element in the Periodic Table had been established by means of its atomic weight, its chemical properties could be predicted with reasonable certainty. This was a very great help not only to the research chemist, but also to the coming generations of students of chemistry who now had a framework on which to build their knowledge without having to memorise many unrelated facts.

Radioactivity

The 19th-century scientists had achieved a great deal and it was tempting for them to believe that the ultimate truth of the nature of matter was just around the corner. They had great confidence in the wonderful structure which the Periodic Table had given to chemistry. The truth was, however, that the unsplittable atom, which Dalton believed was the fundamental particle of matter, had hardly begun to reveal its secrets.

For the scientists of that time there were, of course, some questions still to be answered. For instance, what decided an atom's chemical properties? Some believed that shape was important and imagined that molecules contained atoms of different shapes. Oxygen was considered to be like a doughnut which could hold two ball-shaped atoms of hydrogen at its centre. Many models such as this were suggested, but none could explain all the facts.

Then, just before the end of the century, chemistry received a severe jolt. Professor Henri Becquerel (1852-1908), working in Paris, had as his assistant a young Polish girl named Marie Sklodowska. One day, in the laboratory, she used some old pieces of uranium to weigh down photographic plates. When the plates were developed, they revealed a curious pattern of lines. There was little doubt that the lumps of uranium were responsible. Becquerel experimented with his uranium rays and found them to be in some way rather similar to the X-rays discovered by Wilhelm Röntgen (1845-1923) only a year before.

Marie Sklodowska, fascinated by these 'radioactive' rays, decided to write a thesis on them, and so began one of the most remarkable investigations in the history of science. The young assistant, who is better known today as Marie Curie (1867-1934), devoted her whole life to the study of natural radioactivity and, together with her husband, Pierre, discovered two new elements which she called polonium after Poland and radium from the Latin *radius* meaning ray.

These new and very strange elements emitted three types of rays, named after letters of the Greek alphabet: alpha rays, which do not appear to be very energetic; beta rays, which move quite fast and were soon to be identified as electrons; and gamma rays, which appeared to be very similar to X-rays. What was really amazing was that her radioactive elements were turning themselves into new elements as a result of the radioactive emissions – doing of their own accord what the alchemists of old had tried to do for centuries.

The important discovery from the chemist's point of view was the fact that the alpha rays closely resembled atoms of the gas helium. How could an atom of one element suddenly be shot like a bullet out of the centre of another when atoms were supposed to be unsplittable? This single piece of evidence destroyed for ever the belief in an indestructible atom, and made scientists realise that their billiard ball model, though useful in explaining many phenomena, had not enough detail to enable them to understand the principles behind natural radioactivity.

Modern scientists will never claim that all is known to them, or that their models are in any way perfect. In the light of experience, they realise that scientific progress in any one branch of science is almost impossible without corresponding progress in another. One science feeds another with new ideas and all are inter-related. Chemistry, in the latter half of the 19th century, had to wait until the science of electricity was firmly established before it could progress further.

Left All rocks on earth are made of minerals, which are in turn composed of the various natural elements. Shown here are copper (left), one of the first metals to be used by man, sulphur (centre) and cinnabar (right), a mercury ore.

Right Diagram to illustrate the combination of positive and negative charges which make up different atoms. This is called the electron structure of atoms. The positive charge is at the centre of the atom and the negative charges, the electrons, are arranged in concentric circles about the nucleus. From left to right the atomic structures of hydrogen, helium, beryllium and chlorine are shown.

Ernest Rutherford (1871–1937) British physicist, born in New Zealand. He was a pioneer of modern atomic physics. His researches were mainly into radioactivity and his discoveries of the nuclear nature of the atom won him the 1908 Nobel prize in chemistry. During the First World War he worked on methods of anti-submarine warfare. In 1919 he succeeded Thomson as professor at the Cavendish Laboratory. President of the Royal Society (1925–30).

Electrons and ions

Michael Faraday (1791–1867) established laws governing the way in which electric currents break down certain solutions (known as electrolytes). It is now known that these electrolytes contain charged atoms or groups of atoms known as ions. If a potential difference (see page 296) is applied to the electrolyte, the positive and negative ions will move in opposite directions to each other resulting in an electric current.

However, it was not until 1874 that George Stoney (1826-1911), an Irish physicist, took a hint from the atomic theories of Dalton and suggested that electricity itself may also have an atomic structure. He proposed the name electron to describe this atom of electricity. Today, we accept the electron to be a negatively charged particle of matter, but Stoney originally thought of the electron simply as an electrical charge which could be either positive or negative. The electrons were concealed in some way within the atoms and only made their presence felt when the compounds were split into Faraday's ions.

Meanwhile other scientists in Germany had begun to investigate the conduction (or transmitting) of electricity in gases. As early as 1859, Heinrich Geissler (1814-79) demonstrated that when electricity was passed through a gas at low pressure in a glass tube, the walls of the tube began to glow with a strange fluorescence. Further work in this branch of physics by Faraday and William Crookes (1832-1919), an English chemist and physicist, finally led Professor J. J. Thomson (1856-1940) at Cambridge University to the conclusion that both positive and negative charges were produced when gases conducted electricity.

Thomson made a brave attempt to create a new model of the atom from the evidence now available. He suggested that the atom was a drop of matter which was positively charged, but contained an equal number of negatively charged electrons distributed evenly inside it, like currants in a bun.

Discovery of protons

Scientific investigations, like detective stories, introduce evidence from many sources before the mystery is 'solved'. Research work in chemistry and electricity could not, alone, supply all the facts needed to make the next scientific model of the atom. Some parts of the theories of light, heat, magnetism and electrostatics (the branch of science which deals with electricity at rest) were concerned in the process. Mathematics, too, contributed many ideas without which progress would not have been possible.

The great 'detective' who finally brought all the evidence together, and at the same time encouraged so many others to follow in his footsteps, was a

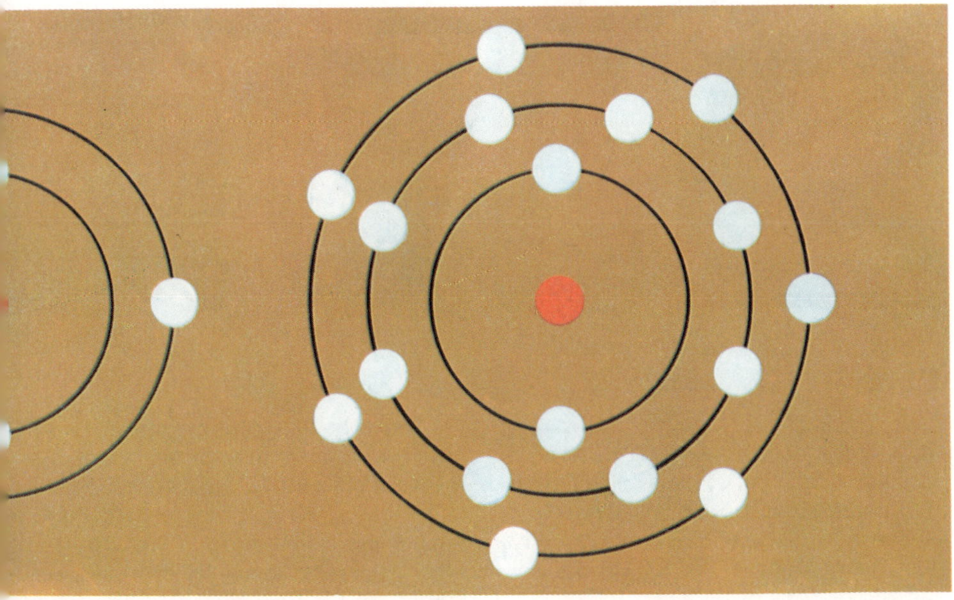

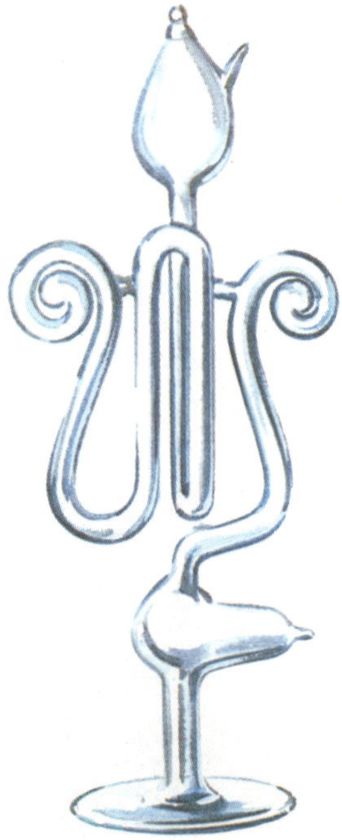

Above A Geissler tube. These tubes were devised by Heinrich Geissler and were made in a great variety of complex patterns. A rarefied gas was contained in a sealed tube and an electric spark then passed through it by means of platinum connections inserted at each end. As the spark darted from one end of the tube to the other, beautiful effects were created by waves and bands of light.

New Zealander, Ernest Rutherford (1871-1937). Following Thomson at Cambridge University, Rutherford, in a series of brilliant yet quite simple experiments, uncovered new evidence which suggested that the atom was, like a miniature solar system, mostly empty space.

The mass of the atom, he suggested, was concentrated in a central nucleus or 'sun', and the electrons rotated around this sun in miniature orbits. The nucleus contained a positive charge which attracted the negative electrons, normally preventing them flying off into space. Hydrogen, the lightest nucleus, had one unit of positive charge, equal exactly to the negative charge of the single electron rotating around it. Rutherford called the nucleus of the hydrogen atom a proton, and this became the new building block of the Periodic Table.

There was, however, a very serious difficulty in accepting this new model of the atom, since it did not agree with certain well established laws of electricity. It was a Danish physicist, Niels Bohr (1885-1962), who had the courage to suggest that it was not the new model that was at fault but the old laws. He insisted that these laws could not apply to the microscopic world of the atom.

The German physicist Max Planck (1858-1947) had already suggested that energy, like matter, existed in 'lumps', or quanta as he called these minutely small particles of energy. His Quantum Theory (the Latin word *quantum* means a definite amount) was used by Niels Bohr to justify his new atomic model.

Neutrons and the Bohr atom

Although there was now a great deal of experimental evidence to support the latest atomic model, there were still one or two elements which did not fit exactly into the picture. It was not until 1933 that this mystery was solved.

In that year, the physicist James Chadwick, one of Rutherford's research workers, discovered that the nucleus contained another particle of matter which, unlike the proton, possessed no electric charge but was very nearly the same mass. This new particle, the neutron, was the missing link which enabled the whole of the Periodic Table of the elements to be explained in terms of the so-called fundamental particles of matter.

From a chemical point of view, at least, the model appeared to be complete and scientists accepted this model of the atom as a 'good working likeness'. Like all other attempts, it proved in the end to be inadequate, and was replaced by an even more complex model. Although the Bohr atom is now considered not accurate enough, it is a helpful aid in the understanding of many chemical and physical changes, and can act as a useful model, providing it is not mistaken for the real thing.

Right Before clocks were invented, men had many different ways of telling the time. Shown here are (from left to right) a sundial used in ancient Greece and Rome from about 500 BC, called a hemicycle. Next is a candle clock, which burns down to show the passing of time. Then a shadow clock used in Egypt about the 10th century BC, and an Egyptian water clock. The green box-like object is a Chinese fire clock, and next to it are a pocket sundial with compass and a set of sand glasses.

Roger Bacon (1214?–92) English philosopher who became a member of the order of Franciscans in 1250. He was one of the most remarkable men of his time and although he remained interested in alchemy and the 'philosopher's stone' his discoveries in the field of science were much ahead of his time. His interests included optics, astronomy and medicine. He invented a magnifying glass and had a knowledge of gunpowder, suggested a revised calendar and a lighter-than-air machine.

Time

Every living thing is influenced by time, and since the days of early man we have accepted the passing of time as something natural and inevitable. Our early ancestors linked time directly with the position of the sun in the sky and the seasons of the year. The sun's angle of elevation (how high it stands above the horizon) was the natural way for man to estimate the time of day, and days were grouped into months according to the periodic appearance of the new moon. It is no accident that we continue to measure angles in terms of 'minutes' and 'seconds' and that our full circle contains 360 degrees. For early man learned by experience that there were on average twelve months in a year and roughly thirty days in a month, giving a total of 360 days in a year. Sub-dividing the full circle was probably the beginning of geometry.

The reappearance of leaves on the trees and the breeding seasons of animals gave man his first indication of an annual division of time. But these signs could not be relied on, for spring could arrive early or late. Then, in the more civilised communities, it became important to know the correct time of year to sow and reap the harvest. The temple priests found they could map out the position of certain bright stars which proved better timekeepers than the leaves of the trees.

As a result, many religious festivals were associated with some significant position of the moon or stars. Even the design of pyramids and temples was often controlled by the direction of the sun or moon's rays at these important times. Mythology, astrology, superstition and genuine scientific observation developed hand in hand, until man's fear of the unknown and the power of the priesthood took the upper hand and condemned him to an age of almost total scientific stagnation.

He emerged from these dark ages, as they are called, in the 15th century, when printing became more widespread and people began to read and educate themselves. Life became more civilised, trade flourished, and as men explored the world aids to navigation became increasingly important.

From the very early days, sailors had used the stars and the position of the sun and moon to decide the direction of their course across the sea, but they also needed to know the time before they could calculate their actual position. Three things – time, a position on the earth, and the angle of elevation of a star – are mathematically linked; knowing two of these, the third can always be calculated. It was only in the 16th century that the influence of the navigator became more important than that of the priest in the development of machines to measure time.

Sidereal and solar time

There is no absolute measure of time – that is, there is no natural law which demands that a year must start at any given moment. Night and day occur at different times in different places around the earth's surface. The Egyptians were the first to use the fact that the sun arrives back at a certain point in the sky with respect to the stars around it once every 'year', and the year we use today, called a sidereal year, is based on this measurement.

Unfortunately this span of time does not correspond exactly with the solar year, which is based on the movement of the sun with respect to the earth. It is the solar year which repeats itself in time with the seasons, but it does not

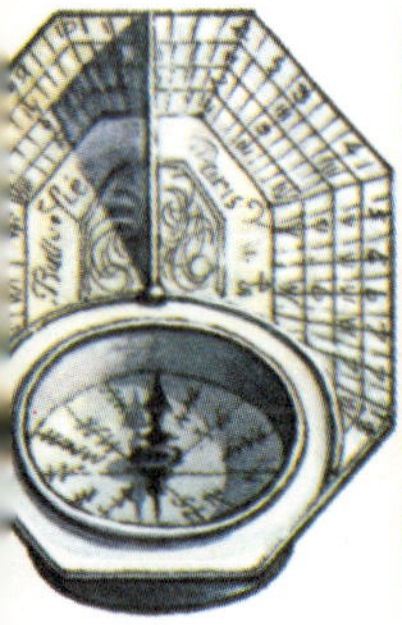

Left The principle of the water clock is illustrated in this diagram. Water is made to drip gradually from one container to another, causing a float to rise and thus turn the pointer on a dial. The water clock was known as a clepsydra and was used by the ancient Egyptians.

contain a complete number of days. If we adopted a sidereal year of exactly 365 days every year, it would mean that after about 700 years, winter would occur in June in the northern hemisphere.

Many methods were proposed to adjust the sidereal to the solar year and the one finally adopted by the Western world involved the addition of an extra day (now 29th February) every fourth or 'leap' year. It was Julius Caesar who decided that the year should start on 1st January, and it was he who named the seventh month July, after himself. But his proposals were not universally adopted.

In those days timekeeping was the concern of religion rather than science, and the church candle had not yet been replaced by a mechanical method of measuring intervals of time. The church was, however, also aware of the small error which occurred in the difference between sidereal and solar time. The extra day every leap year had proved slightly too large an adjustment to keep the seasons and religious festivals in step with the calendar, and the Catholic church ordained that leap years would not apply when the full century year was not divisible by 400. For example, the year 1700 was not a leap year in Catholic countries. There was much opposition to the change by Protestant and Greek churches, and in England it was 1752 before the calendar was reformed and the date of New Year changed from 25th March to 1st January.

Below A calendar clock. In the 17th century clocks began to be adapted to show the day of the month, the phase of the moon, and the course of the planets. Some clocks even had tidal dials.

Longitude and time

The position of a ship on the earth's surface is described in terms of its latitude and longitude. The equator provides a natural reference circle around

Above A copy by Larcum Kendall of John Harrison's fourth chronometer. Harrison won a prize of £20,000 with the original, which was used by Capt. Cook as a navigational aid on his second and third voyages of discovery. On the right is Harrison's first chronometer, a larger and more elaborate mechanism which he completed in 1735.

Christiaan Huygens (1629–93) Dutch physicist, born at The Hague. Studied at Leyden and Breda. In 1655 he discovered Saturn's ring and fourth satellite. He developed many of Galileo's ideas, chiefly the pendulum clock made in 1657. Visited England in 1660 and became member of the Royal Society. He also improved the air pump and worked in optics.

the earth which can be called zero latitude, and the latitudes north and south of this zero can be obtained by observations of the pole star and other heavenly bodies.

Longitude, that is measurements east or west around the earth, have no natural zero line and by international consent a line round the earth, through the poles and Greenwich Observatory in England, has been accepted as zero since 1884. Before this date there were thirteen different zeros from which the navigators fixed their longitude and took their time.

A ship having a bearing of 50 degrees north, 30 degrees west, indicates that it is in the Atlantic Ocean, about midway between Ireland and the North American coastline. To locate such a position by day or night requires a knowledge of time and since Greenwich is the zero of longitude it is also accepted as the standard reference of time.

Greenwich Mean Time is used as navigational time for both shipping and aircraft over a large part of the earth's surface. The earth revolves 360 degrees in twenty-four hours, that is 15 degrees every hour. Greenwich Mean Time is set so that the sun is at its highest point in the sky (its zenith) at noon. If a ship observes that from its position at sea the sun is at its zenith at 10 o'clock GMT, two hours before noon, this indicates that it is 15 × 2 = 30 degrees west of Greenwich, or longitude 30 degrees west.

Up to the beginning of the 16th century, sundials, candles, sandglasses and water-clocks were for most people the only available means of keeping time, and these devices could not be used on board ships at sea. Navigators still relied on complicated observations of astronomical events such as eclipses and star positions for their estimates of time. In fact, on long voyages they had to carry with them trained astronomers as part of the ship's crew.

Clocks and watches

The forerunner of the modern clock was a rather clumsy, weight-driven mechanism used mainly in observatories, churches and public buildings. The discovery by Galileo Galilei (1564-1642) of the laws governing the motion of a pendulum led the Dutch physicist, Christiaan Huygens (1629-93) to the construction of the first pendulum clock, containing a mechanism which could operate at sea. Still powered by weights, it proved unreliable, and it was not until Robert Hooke (1635-1703), English chemist and physicist, had established the laws governing the stretching of springs that a good marine clock became a possibility.

To encourage interest in the design of a reliable and accurate clock the British government, in 1713, offered three prizes to anyone who could invent a suitable means of measuring longitude. To win the first prize of £20,000 the rules stated that the method must be able to predict the longitude of a ship to within fifty kilometres after a voyage to the West Indies. Not an easy job, in view of the variations in clock time caused by different temperatures on the voyage.

A Yorkshire carpenter, John Harrison (1693-1776), dedicated his life to the task and after a number of attempts submitted a clock which, in 1761, proved its worth on a number of voyages. Harrison was very badly treated by the government of the day, who brought up various trivial objections to his invention but eventually agreed to pay half the reward. Only after a long legal action was Harrison given his just reward in 1773 after forty years of determined effort.

Above The clock in Salisbury Cathedral in England is said to be the oldest working clock in the country and possibly in the world. It was made in or before 1386 and it is possible that it was built by a craftsman from Burgundy brought to England by the then Bishop of Salisbury between 1375–88.

As clocks, and eventually watches, became more accurate, scientists were able to study the laws of motion in greater detail. The introduction of the canon and rifle into warfare was, no doubt, an added stimulus to the study of dynamics (the science of matter and motion) and the invention of even more reliable clocks. The Industrial Revolution caused life to move at a quicker pace. The engines of the new age moved faster, factory life worked to the clock and time eventually became the master of man.

In the 20th century discoveries in electronics and atomic physics have demanded clocks which can measure millionths, and even million millionths of a second. Only through the invention of electronic clocks could such measurements be obtained. Until very recently, however, the hair-spring watch, with its mechanical movement based on the principles first discovered by Galileo and Hooke, remained the ordinary man's timepiece.

Now, watches powered by a miniature battery and regulated by, for example, the vibrations of a quartz crystal, are common. Many of these show the time in numbers on the watch face, known as a digital display.

Right The first pocket watch is thought to be one made by Peter Henlein (1480–1542) in Nuremberg, Germany, known as the 'Nuremberg Egg' England was for a long time the centre of watch-making in Europe, particularly in the days of Thomas Tompion (1638–1713). Seen in the picture is the inside of a pocket watch of 1825. Below it, in contrast, is part of the works of a caesium atomic clock, the most accurate type of clock in the world.

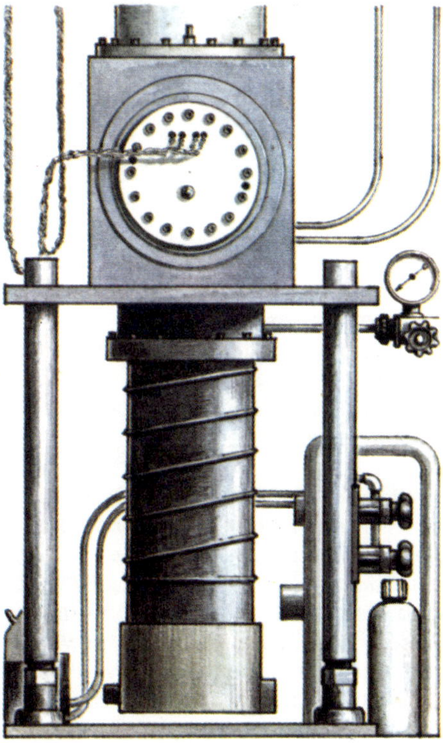

Albert Einstein (1879–1955) German-born mathematical physicist. Between 1905 and 1916 became world famous for his theories of relativity. Einstein merged the traditional concepts of space and time and did important research into the speed of light. Left Germany and became a citizen of the United States in 1940. Predicted the possibility of a 'super-bomb' based on atomic fission, but urged the control of atomic weapons after the war.

The atomic clock

Within the atom, when electrons jump from one place to another, they absorb energy, which is later released in the form of a wave. All kinds of waves have one thing in common: they cause a movement to be repeated at intervals. Sea waves, for example, make a small buoy bob up and down with a regular motion.

The waves that are emitted from atoms are so regular and occur so many times in a second that they can be used as a standard of time. Different atoms produce many different wave movements, and the most suitable of these has turned out to be the element caesium. In 1967 a certain wave emitted from the caesium atom was adopted as an international standard of the second. One second was defined as 9,192,631,770 vibrations of this particular wave.

Caesium clocks can be built anywhere in the world and will give exactly the same measurements and remain extremely accurate: a caesium clock will not gain or lose more than one second in 6,000 years. More accurate clocks are contemplated using hydrogen atoms, which will even improve on the accuracy of a caesium clock by as much as a hundred times.

With such clocks, which do not depend on the motion of the earth, sun or planets, irregularities in the rotations of these heavenly bodies have been discovered. It is now known, for example, that our solar year can alter by as much as three seconds. So the basis for our measurement of time has changed from an astronomical one depending on the solar system, to a sub-microscopic one depending on the atom.

Relative time

Science fiction, which nowadays seems to become fact with alarming regularity, delights in stories of time machines which can transport man forwards or backwards in time. There are good scientific reasons to believe that we will never be able to reverse time; but in 1905 and 1915 Albert Einstein (1879-1955), in his theories of relativity, showed that time can behave in a curious way.

It is not really possible to explain or understand Einstein's theories about time, matter and energy without going deeply into physics and mathematics. But these theories completely altered previous ideas which scientists had about the nature of the universe. Einstein showed that there is no such thing as an absolute measurement of time or space and that speed and position were *relative* things. He also proved that there is no real difference between matter and energy.

It was through a study of the relationship between time, space and speed that Einstein was led to his theory of relativity, one of the most important landmarks in the history of science.

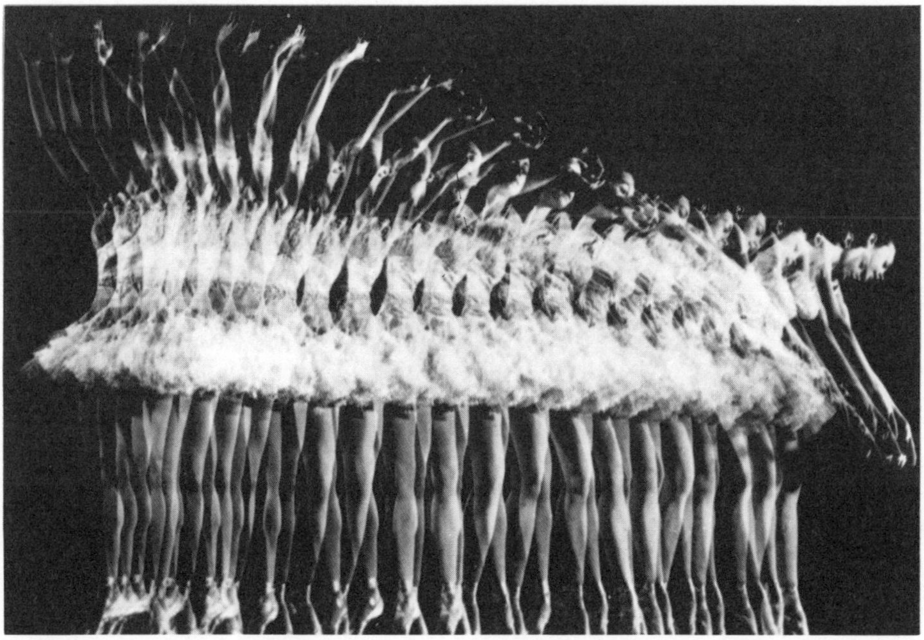

Left Stroboscopic photographs of a dancer taken by light flashing at twenty times per second reveal a flowing pattern of arms and legs as the dancer completes a movement. Such photographic techniques help the scientist to study dynamics, or motion.

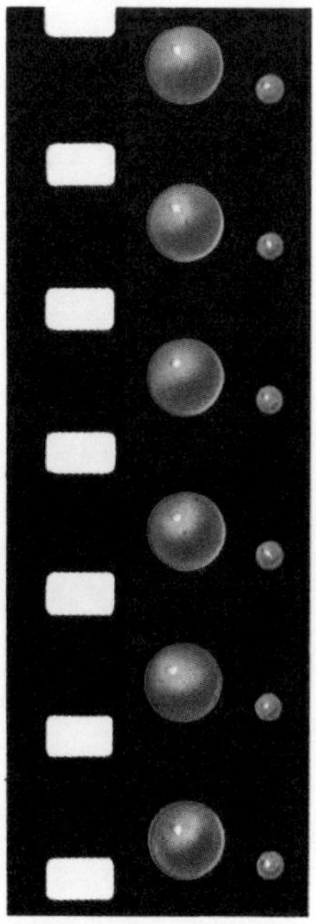

Above Galileo's belief that freely falling bodies of unequal weight would fall with the same acceleration can be proved by the camera with multi-exposure photographs which show that the bottom edges of the balls remain level as they fall.

Motion

Dynamics, the study of motion, is today assisted in many ways by modern electronic instruments and high-speed photography. One of these instruments, called a stroboscope, produces very sharp flashes of light at a steady rate so that a moving object is illuminated many times in a second. If a photograph of the object is taken with the camera shutter open for as long as a second, a large number of positions of the object are recorded one after another on the film.

For example, these photographs reveal many details of the motion of the human body which cannot be seen under normal viewing conditions. The movements of a dancer photographed under stroboscopic light flashing at twenty times per second produce a flowing pattern of arms, legs and body positions. When photographing things that happen very quickly, such as a golfer swinging his club, the number of flashes per second, or the 'frequency' has to be increased.

The term frequency is used in many branches of science: the frequency of rotation of a motor car wheel is the number of turns it makes a second: the frequency cf an alternating electric current is the number of cycles or changes which occur per second. Recently, it has been decided to measure all frequencies in a new unit called a hertz (hz for short) after the German physicist Heinrich Hertz (1857-94).

Stroboscopic photographs of moving objects, or bodies as the scientist calls them, show that there are many different kinds of motion. The simplest, but not the easiest to produce, is a constant speed. The body moves an equal distance in every interval between the flashes of light. Quite a different motion occurs when a body falls freely through the air. The increasing distances travelled between flashes indicates that the body is accelerating, that is, increasing its speed in each interval of time. If the body is thrown upwards, the distances between flashes decrease, indicating de-acceleration, or slowing down. Photographs of a ball thrown forward at an angle show that projectile motions of this kind combine acceleration, de-acceleration and constant speed. To understand how all these motions can occur at the same time requires some study of the types of motion involved.

Motion on earth

The study of motion on earth is made more difficult because of the many forces which act on a moving object. Motion through the air is not the same as motion in a vacuum, where there is no air. Stroboscopic photographs of a

Above When a sky diver jumps from an aircraft, after the initial acceleration, the speed at which he falls remains constant. This is known as terminal velocity and on reaching it several divers can join hands and fall together.

Below The teaching of Empedocles, the Greek philosopher (5th century BC) was based on certain 'elements' wherein four primary qualities (hot, cold, wet and dry) combined to form the primary substances – fire, water, air and earth.

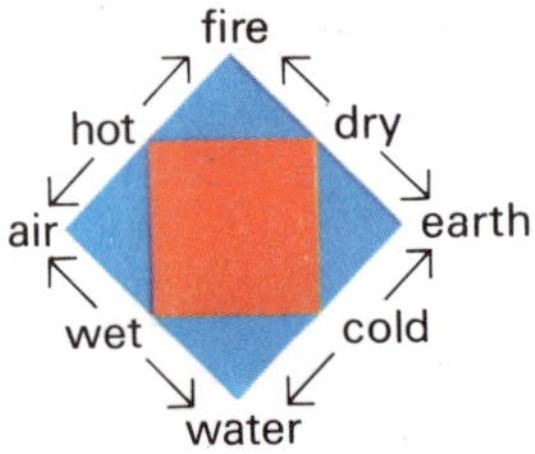

feather falling in air show a small acceleration of the feather at the start of the motion, followed by an almost constant speed. The same feather falling in a vacuum drops 'like a stone', since it now has only the gravitational pull of the earth acting on it.

The effect of the air is obvious in the case of the feather, but though less obvious with a heavier falling object, it is still there. It may be some consolation to you to know that if you fall out of an aeroplane, your speed does not continue to increase. You will, in fact, reach a point where your speed remains constant, called terminal velocity.

The word velocity is often used in the same way as speed, but it will be seen later that velocity does not quite mean the same thing. Sky divers are able to use the effect of the atmosphere in this way and can, on reaching their terminal velocity, link hands and all fall at this same constant velocity. They would all be travelling at well over 45 metres per second.

We can, with the help of modern equipment, examine the motion of bodies under the influence of various forces, and then, to make things easier to understand, set up experiments to see how each force, on its own, affects the motion. This scientific method of discovery was not so easy in earlier times and it is not surprising that scientists often came to the wrong conclusions. This was because they were forced to examine very complicated motions, involving a number of effects, all at the same time.

From Aristotle to Galileo

The Greek philosopher Aristotle considered rest to be the natural state of things on earth and that everything was made of some mixture of what he called 'the elements' – earth, water, air and fire. Each of these elements had a 'natural place' and when disturbed would always return to this natural resting place. A stone, being part of earth, would return to earth, but air and fire had resting places above the earth and would always rise above it.

These ideas led Aristotle to believe that heavier objects would fall faster than light ones. He would certainly have been surprised had he seen a modern stroboscopic photograph of a stone and a feather falling in a vacuum with the same acceleration. Aristotle's teachings, although wrong, were hardly doubted for many hundreds of years and no one took the trouble to perform experiments to test these theories, since it was thought that true understanding could only be obtained by reasoning things out. Asking *why* things happened, without first observing *how* they happened, was the method most used until the Middle Ages.

It was Galileo, considered by many to be the first modern scientist, who questioned this method of discovery. He concerned himself with observations and experiments which eventually led others to an understanding of why things move as they do. Galileo made the first scientific observations on freely falling bodies, distinguished between constant speeds and accelerations, and stated that 'within a finger or two' bodies of different weight released at the same time would fall equal distances in equal times.

There is some doubt whether he personally ever performed any experiments by dropping objects from the top of the leaning tower of Pisa, but he certainly encouraged others to challenge Aristotle's belief that heavy objects fall faster than light ones. One instance of this was in 1586, when a Dutch scientist, Simon Stevinus (1548-1620), reported an experiment with two lead balls, one ten times the weight of the other. He found that when released from the same height, the balls fell upon a hollow board and 'gave the same sound', indicating that they had fallen at the same speed.

Galileo, hampered by lack of accurate timing equipment, found he could not investigate the motion of freely falling bodies as he would have liked, so he ingeniously slowed down the motion by experimenting on bodies rolling down slopes. He would have been pleased to see a modern photograph of this type of motion which confirms one of his conclusions: the distances travelled depend on the squares of the times taken. This special kind of motion, under the influence of the earth's gravitation, is called a constant acceleration. This does assume, however, that the air has little effect, or that the body is moving in a vacuum.

Galileo Galilei (1564–1642) Italian astronomer, born at Pisa. In 1583 he stated his theories about the pendulum in the exact measurement of time. It is said that Galileo first began to think about the pendulum when watching a lamp swing in Pisa Cathedral. When he was professor of mathematics at the university of Pisa, he proved the theory that all falling bodies, large or small, descend with the same velocity. He perfected the refracting telescope and his astronomical investigations led him to support the theories of Copernicus.

Newton's laws of motion

Even today, many people are misled into believing that force is always necessary to make bodies move. Everyday experience indicates that when bodies are not being pushed or pulled they stay still. It therefore seems natural to assume that when bodies are stationary there are no forces acting on them. Yet it is just this misunderstanding that prevents many people from obtaining a clear grasp of the laws of motion. Galileo was the first to realise that when bodies have no forces acting on them they can, once set in motion, continue to move without being pushed or pulled in any way.

In the year in which Galileo died, one of the world's most brilliant scientists was born – Isaac Newton (1642-1727). Not only did Newton believe in an experimental method of approach, but he also had the ability to express his ideas mathematically, and this combination of theory and

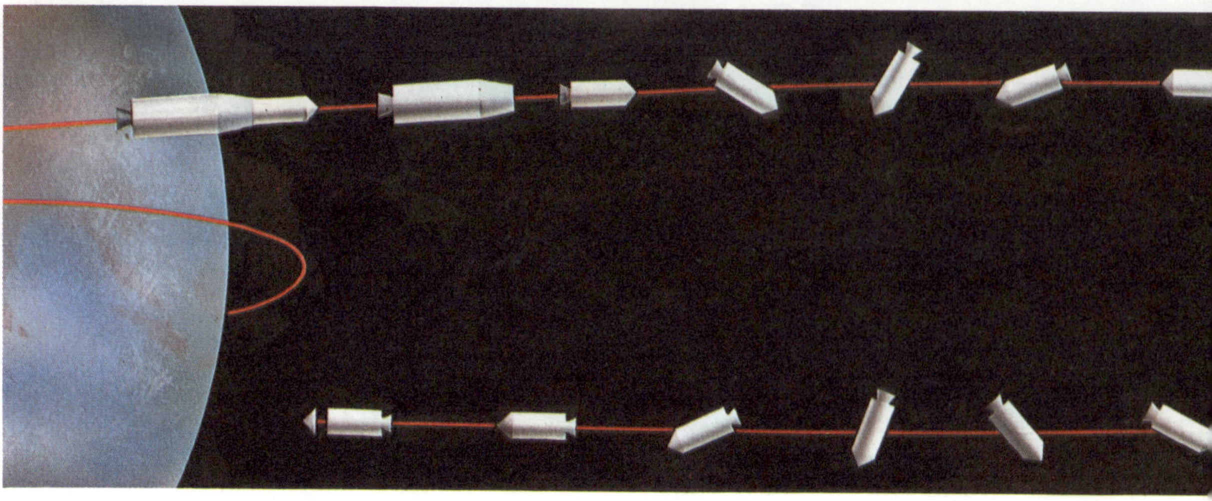

Isaac Newton
(1642–1727) English mathematician and scientist. Educated at Trinity College, Cambridge. It is said that the fall of an apple inspired him to think about the laws of gravity. He studied the nature of light and the construction of telescopes. Published his calculations on gravitation in his greatest work, called *Philosophiae Naturalis Principia Mathematica* (1687). Was president of the Royal Society from 1703 to 1727.

experiment made it possible for him to see further and deeper into the secrets of nature than man had ever done before.

He expressed Galileo's ideas in more precise laws and these formed part of his famous book *Principia* (1687), a scientific masterpiece, written entirely in Latin. His laws, expressed in modern language, are as follows:

1. A body will continue in its state of rest, or uniform motion (constant speed) in a straight line, unless acted upon by an external force.
2. The force applied to a body causes it to accelerate in the direction in which the force is applied and the acceleration is directly in proportion to the force applied.
3. To every action there is always an opposing reaction, and action and reaction are always equal and opposite.

It is perhaps only since man has accepted space travel as a reality that he has been able to appreciate the full meaning of these laws. Only in space are bodies free to move without being influenced by the resistance of the air and frictional forces, and it is under these conditions that Newton's laws can clearly be seen in operation.

Once a spacecraft has travelled far enough away from a planet's gravitational field to make the forces on it small, it continues to move through space at a constant speed with its rocket motors cut off, as the first law predicts. The thrust of the rocket motors, when they are switched on, will *change* the speed, that is either accelerate the spaceship or de-accelerate it, depending on which direction the thrust is applied. This is in agreement with the second law of motion. The third law is best illustrated by coming down to earth. On the earth's surface bodies can be moved by towing them with a rope. The rope transmits a force or pull on the body, but according to the third law, the body also exerts an equal and opposite pull on the rope, caused by frictional forces, air resistance and gravitational pull.

One other factor is involved which influences the force required to move a body, that is its mass, or the amount of matter that has to be moved. The larger the mass, the larger the force required. All units of force are based on a relationship between mass and acceleration and the unit now recommended for use in most branches of science and engineering is called a 'newton'. One newton is the force required to move a mass of one kilogram with an acceleration of one metre per second per second.

Universal gravitation

Of all Newton's contributions to science, perhaps his greatest was the law of universal gravitation – a law which enabled him to answer so many of the questions which had puzzled scientists for centuries. His answer to why things happen was based on observation and measurement rather than on the so-called logic favoured by the ancient Greeks. Why do all bodies

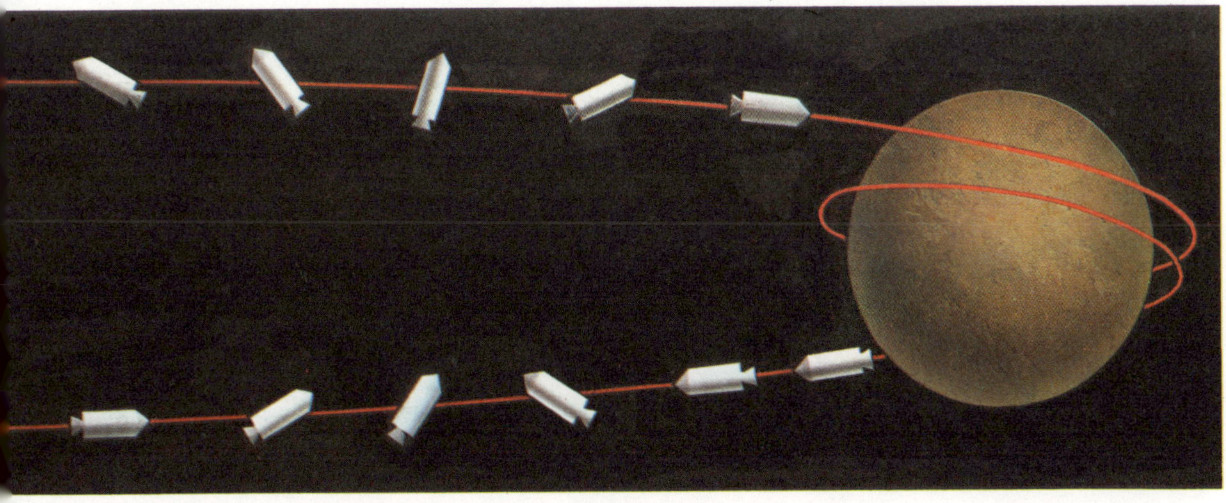

fall to the ground with the same acceleration regardless of their mass? Why do the planets revolve around the sun and not fly off into space and why do these planets have different speeds which are in some way related to their distances from the sun?

Newton suggested that the pull of the earth extended outwards in space like the pull of a magnet, but he did not claim that his theory explained why this gravitational pull existed in the first place. He extended this idea further to include every particle of matter in the universe and gave a precise account of the strength of this gravitational pull. Whereas this pull of gravity decreases as the distance from its source increases it never disappears altogether. The space traveller who claims to be outside the earth's field, or to have escaped from the earth's gravity, is no scientist for he implies that the pull stops somewhere in space.

The force of gravity depends on the size of a planet. Large planets, made of very heavy materials, have strong gravitational forces. As might be expected, the moon – which is smaller than the earth – has far less pull. The weight of an object (which is its gravitational pull) on the moon is much smaller than on earth.

By using the gravitational law, Newton was also able to show that astronomical observations by Tycho Brahe (1546-1601) and predictions by Brahe's assistant Johann Kepler (1571-1630) about the motion of the planets were correct. This happy marriage of theory and practice confirmed the law of gravitation, which, together with the laws of motion, became the foundation stones of the science of dynamics. Even though the laws are not completely true when applied to the world of atoms, or when bodies are moving at speeds approaching the speed of light, they are still of tremendous value to scientists and engineers and will continue to be used as basic principles in modern technology.

Work and energy

It is true that doing work makes people feel tired; yet feeling tired after standing for a long time in a train, or holding up a heavy weight, does not indicate that work has been done in a scientific sense. The opposing teams in a tug-of-war may fall exhausted to the ground after a 'drawn' match, neither side having moved from their starting positions, but they have done no scientific 'work'. Only when one side begins to pull the other over the line is mechanical work done, and this work is measured as the force applied multiplied by the distance moved: therefore, work = force × distance.

In some ways work, and its near relation, energy, is to physics what wealth and money is to economics. Wealth can exist in many forms. In the pocket it is usually found as coins or notes, but it can be spent in shops to buy goods, saved in a bank account, or invested in property or shares.

When a man lifts a heavy weight high into the air, he 'spends' an amount of work in the form of energy. But this work is really invested, for the weight

Above Newton's laws of motion can best be seen in operation by considering the way a spacecraft travels in space. When the craft has travelled far enough away from the earth's field of gravity it continues to move through space at a constant speed with its motors cut off, demonstrating Newton's first law: a body will continue in its state of rest, or constant speed, in a straight line, unless acted upon by an external force.

Above By 3000 BC the Egyptians were already skilled architects and builders. Stones weighing more than 15 tonnes were worked with copper tools. Temples like the one at Abu Simbel (about 1250 BC), re-erected recently on a different site, show how vast blocks of stone could be cut to make immense statues. They are remarkable because the stone blocks had to be pulled on sledges by gangs of men. Ramps were built and the blocks were pulled up these, again by gangs of men.

Above An idea for a perpetual motion machine. But energy cannot continuously be taken from a machine unless more is added; for energy is lost through friction.

he has lifted now has more energy than it had before. It is in the bank waiting to be released again. In scientific language, the weight is said to have increased its 'potential energy'. When the weight is allowed to drop towards the ground, the energy is withdrawn from the bank and converted into a new form. The weight gains what is called 'kinetic energy' – that is, energy of motion.

Just before hitting the ground the weight possesses the same amount of energy in this new form as was used by the man to lift it. Then the weight hits the ground and, one could say, fritters away its wealth in a number of new kinds of energy – heat and sound energy. The sound can clearly be heard, but the heat is not quite so evident in this case. Continually dropping the weight would, however, soon heat up the surroundings just as a large nail becomes quite hot as it is hammered into a block of wood.

All these transactions are based on the very important principle known as the law of conservation of energy. Energy can never be created or destroyed – it is simply transferred from one form to another.

Until the 20th century it was thought that man's only available source of energy was the sun. The sun's energy, transmitted as light and heat energy to the earth, was invested in prehistoric times inside the forests of the world and this energy only came to light again when it was dug up as fuel from the ground in the form of peat, coal or natural gas.

Man eventually learned to convert this energy into other forms and even temporarily to re-bank it as electrical energy inside accumulators and batteries for further use. He did not, until very recently, realise that there was another completely new source of energy available to him – atomic energy.

Today atomic energy plants are being built all over the world which are gradually replacing the conventional power stations run on coal or oil. These stations operate by converting matter directly into energy. Matter we now know is itself just another form of energy and this energy is not only the 'wealth' of the universe, it is also the 'stuff' from which the universe is made.

Perpetual motion

In the world of commerce, buying or selling usually involves paying a fee to an agent or stockbroker to cover the cost of the transaction. Nature, too, charges a commission on its energy transactions and, as a result, it is not possible to transfer energy completely from one useful form to another.

When petrol is burned in a motor car engine, chemical energy stored in the petrol is changed into the energy of motion and heat, but the useful energy of motion is far less than is theoretically available in the petrol. Furthermore, if the car moves along the road, nature continues to demand a fee by absorbing some of this energy as frictional energy in the moving parts of the machine, and also in work done against air resistance. Even here, however, the energy is not lost but converted into other unwanted forms.

Engineers have tried to reduce nature's fee by better lubrication of the bearings, streamlining the car's body and re-designing the engine, but even today a petrol engine is only about twenty per cent efficient. Nature gets an eighty per cent commission. Some inventors have given much time and effort to the creation of machines which they hoped would be one hundred per cent efficient. Such perpetual motion machines, once started, would continue to operate without any further assistance. None has ever worked and there are good reasons to believe that none ever will.

The search for more efficient engines inspired scientists to delve deeper into the theory of energy and they found that although one hundred per cent efficient engines were impossible, efficiency could be increased by raising the working temperature of the engine. This led to a search for materials which could stand up to very high temperatures and still maintain their physical properties, such as strength and resistance to wear. Metallurgy, the study of metals, was and still is the highly important branch of science responsible for the development of new alloys which can be used at high temperatures in spacecraft, atomic power stations and jet engines.

Power

Man himself is a very complex engine, converting the chemical energy contained in the food he eats into various other forms of energy. He does this quite efficiently, but is nevertheless not a very powerful machine. To build any of the ancient wonders of the world, such as the pyramids of Giza in Egypt, required enormous numbers of slaves, who toiled for many years to pull the huge slabs of rock up sand slopes piled against the sides of their buildings. Modern building machines could, no doubt, have finished the job in a fraction of the time, but in doing so would not have produced any more energy. The difference lies in the *power* of the machine used.

Power measures the amount of work a machine can produce in a given time. Modern machines are 'powerful' because they can give out large amounts of energy per second. This does not necessarily mean they are more efficient. In fact the very powerful motors of a launching rocket require enormous supplies of fuel to put quite a small satellite into orbit around the earth. They are, therefore, very inefficient.

Above Contrast the ease and speed with which we move earth and rock with the way the Egyptians did it. One man can drive this machine to help make a modern motorway, but hundreds of men were needed for such mighty constructions as the pyramids in Egypt.

Kinetic theory

It was a German mathematician and philosopher, Gottfried Leibniz (1646-1716), who in 1695 first suggested that heat and kinetic energy, or the energy of motion, had some connection. In 1780 Lavoisier and another French scientist, Pierre Laplace (1749-1827), came to the conclusion that heat given to a body was in some way absorbed by the particles of the body as kinetic energy.

A German scientist, Julius Mayer (1814-78), extended the idea to other forms of energy transfer and gave the world its first understanding of the law of conservation of energy about the middle of the 19th century. At about the same time, James Joule (1818-89), an English physicist, began a series of measurements which confirmed that different forms of energy were equivalent to each other. Appropriately his name is now used as the modern unit in which all energy measurements are made – the joule.

Above Thomas Savery, born in Devon, England, was one of the first to invent a practical steam engine. In 1698 he patented a water raising machine. It was used in mines and for raising water to supply houses and towns.

By combining the billiard ball model of the atom with the concepts of energy, scientists can obtain a much clearer picture of the behaviour of solids, liquids and gases. The particles present in a solid are continually vibrating at room temperature and when more energy is supplied, such as when an electric fire is switched on, or a frying pan put on a gas stove, the molecular vibrations increase as the temperature rises.

If the energy is removed, as in a refrigerator, the vibrations die down, and if this process is continued they almost come to a stop. At this very low temperature, the particles have almost no kinetic energy and this indicates the lowest possible temperature that can be achieved, called absolute zero. Physical apparatus has been built which can reach to within a millionth of a degree of absolute zero, but the last trace of kinetic energy has proved very difficult indeed to remove.

To convert solids into liquids and then gases, the particles of the solid must be moved further apart, and the energy absorbed during these changes of state is called latent heat.

If it were possible to watch the movements of gas particles in a transparent box, they would present a brilliant display of activity, more energetic than the busiest hive of bees and certainly less organised. Even at room temperature, air particles can attain speeds about a hundred times faster than an average man can run. Particles dash in all directions, some more energetic than others. They collide with each other, change direction continually and whenever they reach the walls of the box, bounce back into the centre of the gas to re-join the fun. Every impact against the wall of the box contributes towards the total pressure of the gas.

Heating the gas gives the particles more energy and, as might be expected, this results in even greater chaos as the particles get more excited and fling themselves at the walls and each other with ever increasing speed. The pressure of the gas rises until the box can stand the strain no longer and it finally explodes. Harnessing these pressures was the ambition of the early engineers who were attempting to control and organise the random motions of particles to make the first steam engines.

Steam power

No single person can be credited with the invention of the steam engine, though it is fairly certain that the cooking pot inspired many to investigate the possibility. As far back as 1680 Robert Boyle and his French assistant Denis Papin (1647-1712?) introduced the first steam pressure cooker at a meeting of the then recently formed

Left Newcomen's engine derived its power from atmospheric pressure on the upper side of a piston **1** which was drawn to the top of its stroke by a counterpoise weight **2**. As the piston moved, steam was admitted into the cylinder **3**, and when this was filled the valve **4** was closed. A jet of cold water then entered the cylinder **5** causing the steam to condense and form water, so creating a vacuum. Then atmospheric pressure on the outside of the piston was able to force it to the bottom of the cylinder. The condensed water was expelled on the next admission of steam, and escaped by a valve **6** and the whole cycle of events began again.

Royal Society of London. Papin dedicated his life to the development of a working steam engine, but like many other inventors died in poverty without realising his ambition. His plans may have been used by others, for not long after his death simple steam engines built to his designs were being used to drive pumps in the tin mines of Cornwall.

James Watt (1736-1819), perhaps the most famous of the steam engineers, started life as an instrument maker in Glasgow and became interested in steam power as a result of his attempts to mend a working model of an early steam engine built by Thomas Newcomen (1663-1729), the Englishman who invented the atmospheric steam engine. This machine was very inefficient and although Watt devised a number of improvements he was not able to perfect an engine which could use the full power of the expanding steam.

Like many other inventors who came after him, Watt's ideas had to wait development in other branches of engineering before they could be put into practice. Nevertheless, on his retirement in 1800, he was able to look back on a successful career as a creative engineer, which had included the founding of the profitable engineering firm of Boulton and Watt, developing steam engines that could power ships and factory machinery, and inventing the first automatic speed regulator or governor. He was also one of the leaders of the Industrial Revolution which, from the beginning of the 19th century, began to change the life and habits

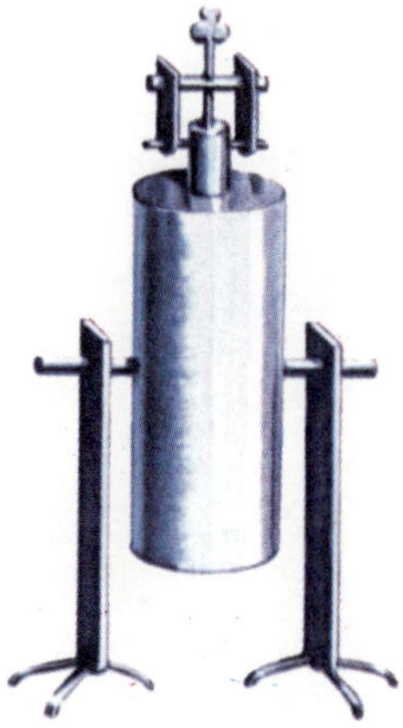

Above Denis Papin's 'steam digester' (1674) was the forerunner of the modern pressure cooker. Controlled by a safety valve it generated steam at high pressure.

Above Nicolas Cugnot, the French engineer, built a steam carriage which was first tried out in 1770. It still exists in a museum in Paris and is probably the oldest surviving mechanical road vehicle.

Right *Locomotion 1* built by George Stephenson in 1825 for the Stockton and Darlington Railway.

Below Goldsworthy Gurney's steam carriage was a stage coach without horses. In 1829 it travelled from London to Bath and back at an average speed of 24 k.p.h.

of men and women in many countries of the world.

In 1825 George Stephenson (1781-1848), following in Watt's footsteps, opened the first railway, which ran from Stockton to Darlington and, in 1830, after a great deal of opposition from those who feared this new steam age, opened the first passenger train service in the world.

The line, which ran from Liverpool to Manchester, was the scene of the famous Rainhill competition in 1829 to discover 'the most improved locomotive engine . . . the said engine effectively to consume its own smoke . . . be capable of drawing after it, day by day, on a level plane, a Train of Carriages of the gross weight of Twenty Tons'. The engine designed by George Stephenson and his son Robert (1803-59), the *Rocket*, now preserved in the London Science Museum, was the undoubted winner, reaching a speed of nearly fifty kilometres per hour during the journey.

Locomotives based on the Stephensons' designs were eventually to open lines in many parts of the continent of Europe. Although improved locomotives were built as the steam age developed, no new principles of motive power were introduced into public rail services until the arrival of the electrical motor.

The steam turbine

Even the best piston steam engine of the 20th century is unable to reach an efficiency of more than twenty per cent because of the low working temperature of the engine, caused by the cooling down of the cylinder walls between each injection of steam. In 1884 Charles Parsons (1854-1931) built his first turbine engine which used the pressure of steam to blow continuously against a system of blades built around a central shaft.

In fact the turbine works in much the same way as the water wheel or windmill, converting pressure into rotary motion, but it works at a constant high temperature and is therefore more efficient. Its advantages as a ship's engine were soon recognised and today it has found a new lease of life as the most effective method of converting the heat produced in atomic power stations into useful electrical energy.

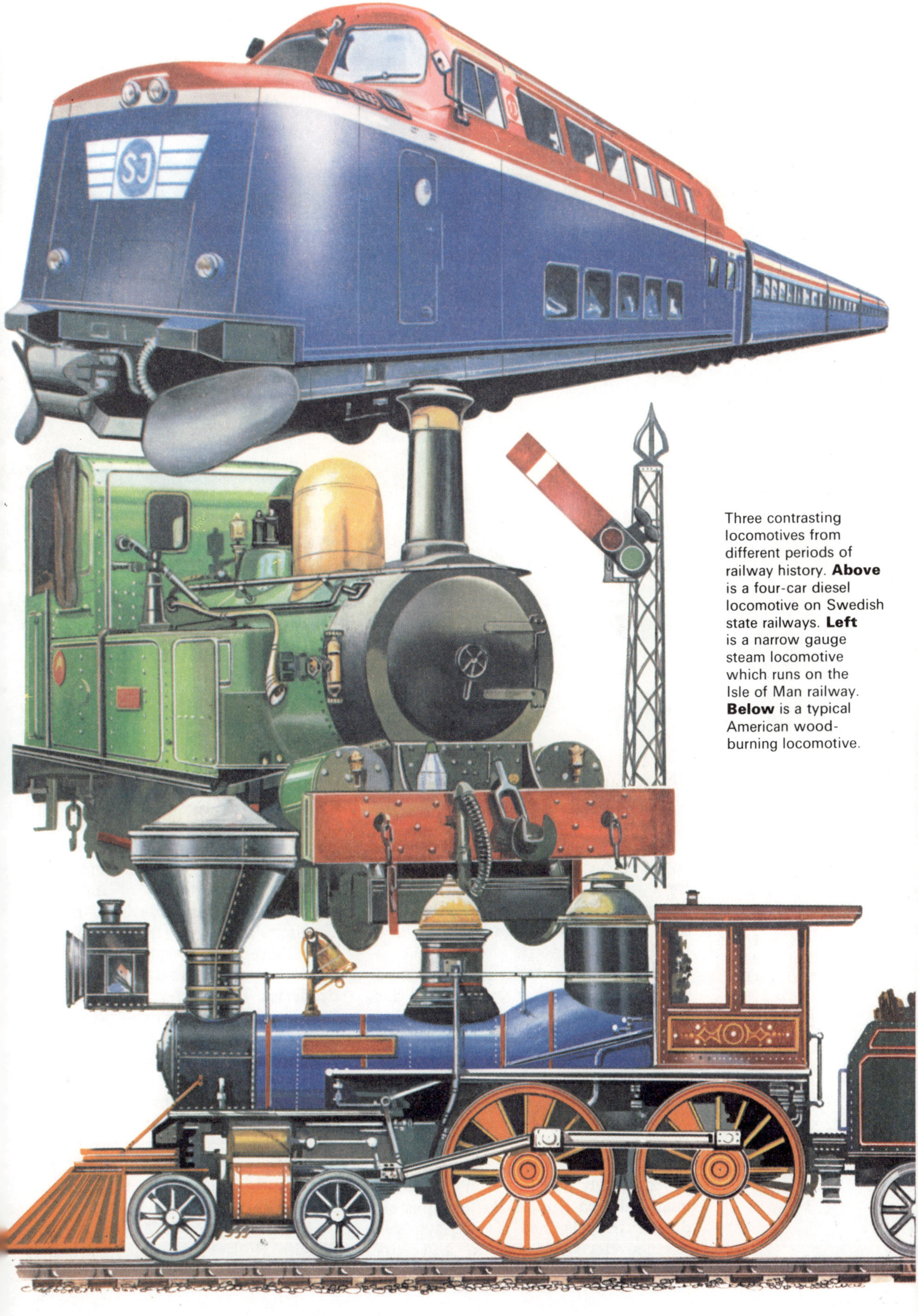

Three contrasting locomotives from different periods of railway history. **Above** is a four-car diesel locomotive on Swedish state railways. **Left** is a narrow gauge steam locomotive which runs on the Isle of Man railway. **Below** is a typical American wood-burning locomotive.

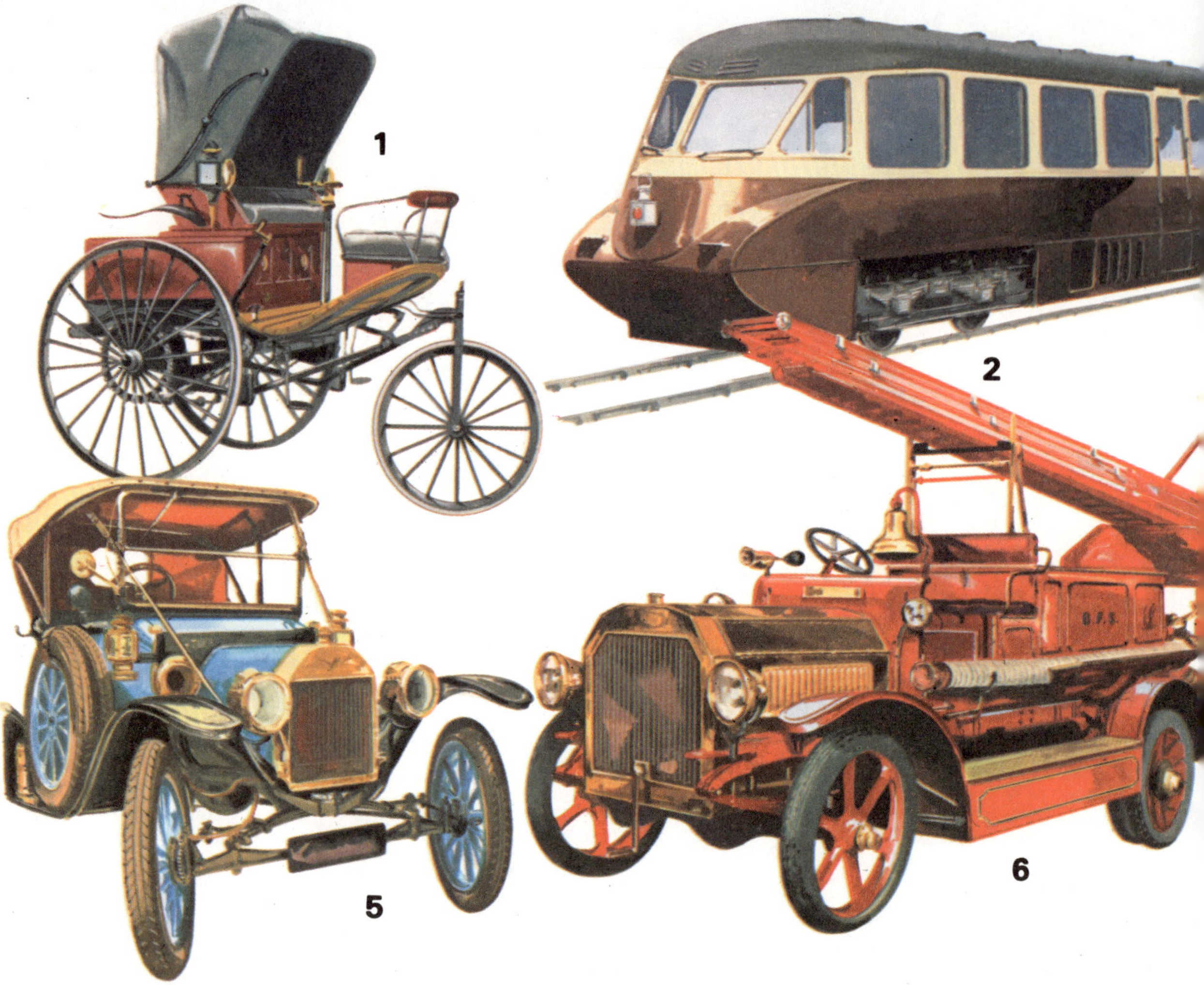

Above These vehicles represent a selection of models powered by the internal combustion engine or the diesel engine. **1** Benz three-wheeler car, 1888. **2** GWR diesel railcar, 1934. **3** Rolls-Royce Phantom II, 1932. **4** MGB Roadster, 1962. **5** Ford Model T, 1909. **6** Dennis fire engine, 1913. **7** Subaru estate, 1980. **8** Mini-Minor, 1966/70. **9** London diesel taxi, 1969/70.

The internal combustion engine

The demand for a simple, yet efficient, lightweight engine which could be operated by an unskilled driver and be switched on at will, without the need for a head of steam, led scientists to investigate other sources of energy such as inflammable gas, hot air, and finally petrol vapour.

The Otto four-stroke engine, named after its Bavarian inventor, Dr Nikolaus Otto (1832-91), adapted many earlier ideas into a machine which could be used with these new fuels, which led to the modern car.

In 1875 petrol gas was tried for the first time in the Otto engine by the Viennese engineer, Siegfried Markus (1831-99). His experiments were followed closely by those of an Englishman, Edward Butler. Butler's petrol-driven tricycle had a two-cylinder engine, electrical ignition and carburettor to feed in the air and petrol mixture in much the same way as it is done today.

In many countries inventors were busy improving and developing the internal combustion engine and laying the foundation stones of industries which today are household names. Gottlieb Daimler (1834-1900) and Karl Benz (1844-1929) in Germany, René Panhard (1841-1908) in France, Frederick Lanchester (1868-1946) in Britain, and Henry Ford (1863-1947) in the United States are some of the automobile engineers who pioneered the way.

By the beginning of the 20th century the motor car had become an accepted and reliable means of transport and by 1910, the petrol-driven bus and taxi had almost replaced the horse-drawn carriage and cab.

Henry Royce (1863-1933) and Charles Rolls (1877-1910), although late starters in this field of technology,

founded the firm of Rolls-Royce in 1906 and set new standards of near perfection in automobile engineering which were soon to be recognised all over the world. The reliability and the quality of Rolls-Royce engines made them especially suitable for use in aircraft and during the early part of the Second World War, when the freedom of the world hung in the balance, the pilots who won the Battle of Britain depended on Rolls-Royce Merlin engines to power their Spitfires.

The diesel engine

The petrol engine was a marked improvement on the steam engine and it achieved its greater efficiency of twenty-eight per cent by working at a higher temperature. In the same way, the diesel engine, with an increased efficiency of up to thirty-five per cent, obtained this figure by working at even higher temperatures.

An English inventor, Herbert Akroyd-Stuart, had been working for some time on the design of an engine which could use cheap, unrefined oil as fuel. He had also suggested that by compressing the cylinder gas sufficiently it could be made to ignite of its own accord as a result of the increase in temperature caused by the quick compression.

The German engineer, Rudolf Diesel (1858-1913), working along the same lines and backed by industrialists, perfected the idea and in 1897 completed his first engine. Diesel engines do not require a carburettor. Because of their high efficiency they are now used all over the world to drive heavy lorries and buses, ships and trains, electric power plants and submarines. The weight of the diesel engine has prevented it from being used in aircraft, where power is of greater importance than efficiency.

Right The jet engine and rocket aircraft seen in these drawings are **1** Gloster E28/39, 1941. **2** Gloster *Meteor* III, 1943. **3** Messerschmitt Me163B, 1941. **4** Messerschmitt Me262A, 1942. **5** De Havilland *Comet* 4, 1954. **6** Boeing *Super Fortress* carrying a Bell X-1 rocket research aircraft, 1947. **7** North American X-15. **8** Hansa jet 320 HFB, 1964. **9** Hawker Siddeley *Harrier* VTOL, 1968/9. **10** Boeing 747 (Jumbo jet), 1968/69.

The jet engine

When a toy balloon is blown up and then released, the air rushing out in one direction causes the balloon to fly off in the opposite direction, illustrating one of the basic principles of dynamics – action and reaction are equal and opposite. The rockets propelled into the sky during firework displays and the recoil of a rifle butt are other examples of the same principle.

As far back as 1930 Frank Whittle in England was attempting to use this principle in his early jet engines, performing highly dangerous experiments with little or no support from government or industry, but convinced that he could tame this source of energy. By 1939, when the Second World War began, the first jet engine was already built and Whittle's small engineering firm was soon a centre of highly secret work which resulted in Britain's first jet aircraft, the Gloster E 28/39. This was followed by the Gloster *Meteor*, a twin-engined jet aircraft, which appeared in time to join battle with Germany's first jet fighter, the Messerschmitt Me 262.

After the war, commercial aircraft using jet engines of various kinds were soon in production, and many variations of the basic jet engine principle, such as the turbo-jet, were introduced. In the turbo-jet engine, air is sucked in through the front of the engine, sent through a compressor and mixed with fuel in a combustion chamber.

Another version is the turbo-prop engine, in which the turbine is used to drive a propeller shaft as in an ordinary piston engine. Though this does not result in high speeds, it is more economical and finds its main use in long range aircraft.

The simplest engine of all is the ram-jet, which is little more than a specially shaped pipe. Air enters one end of the pipe and is compressed by the forward motion of the aircraft. The compressed air, sprayed with fuel, is ignited in the combustion chamber and escapes at high speed through the other end.

The pulse-jet is a rather similar device, but contains valves which feed the air into the combustion chamber in a series of pulses. The ram-jet and the pulse-jet cannot operate on their own, since the aircraft must already be in motion to produce the necessary compression of air. They are, however,

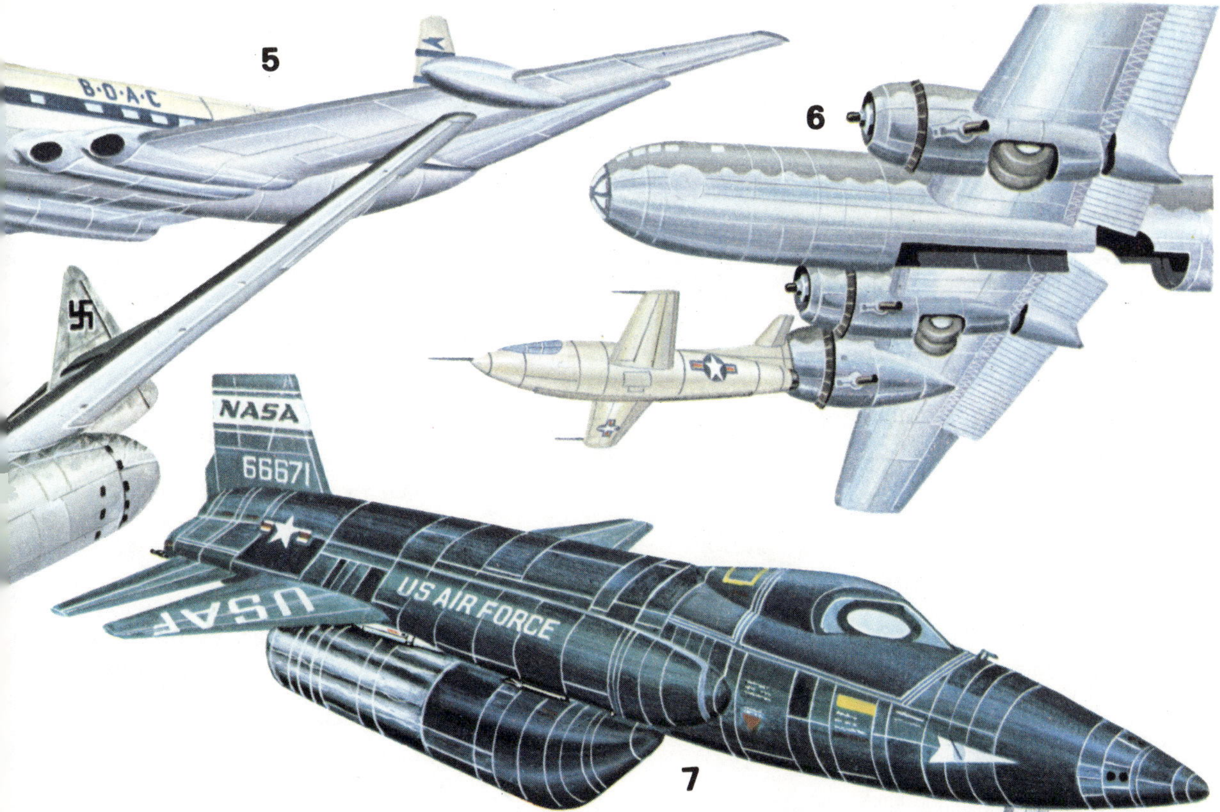

of great use as boosters to obtain high accelerations and climbing speeds with heavy loads.

Rocket motors

The rocket motor, used for interplanetary travel and spacecraft, must be capable of operating in a near vacuum. It has therefore to carry its own oxygen supply and fuel, which, brought together in the combustion chamber and ignited, produce gas particles moving at high velocity through the exhaust tubes.

No doubt new rocket motors are already contemplated by space research scientists to drive future transport craft into space. Atomic energy has yet to be successfully controlled for this purpose and other powerful new fuels are also under investigation. All have the same end in view, the conversion of stored energy into useful kinetic energy without paying too great a price for the transaction.

Further research into the basic laws of physics and chemistry must go hand in hand with the invention of new materials and manufacturing processes before the science fiction of today becomes the reality of tomorrow.

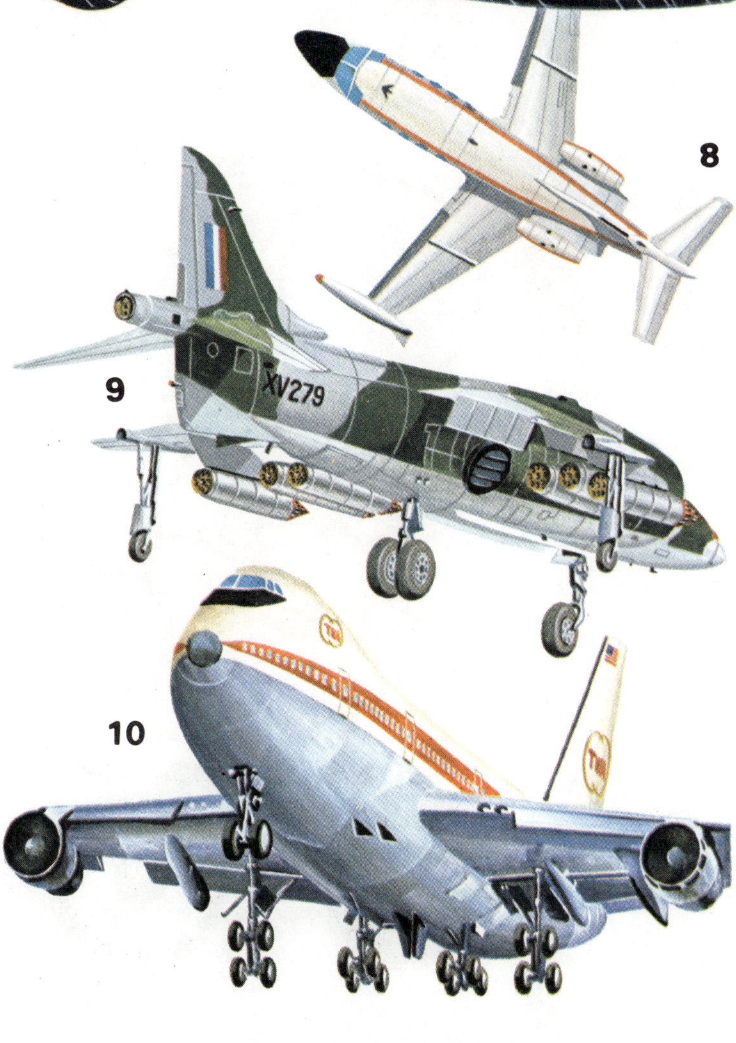

Right It is not until about 1790 that historians can identify an actual machine which resembles the bicycle of today. This consisted simply of two wheels joined by a frame on which the rider sat and propelled himself by pushing along with his feet. Illustrated here are some of the most important machines which, through the years, have developed from that primitive design. From top to bottom they are: a hobby horse, of about 1800; a velocipede, or boneshaker, about 1860; an ordinary, or penny farthing, about 1870; a Rover safety bicycle, about 1885; a Moulton bicycle, 1970; and the revolutionary racing bicycle used by Chris Boardman when he won the 4,000 metres individual pursuit gold medal at the Barcelona Olympics in 1992.

Above The first ball bearings were used on the safety bicycle about 1876. The balls and races, as the inner and outer rings are called, need to be very hard and accurately fitted to work efficiently.

Circular motion

So many things go round in circles that this kind of motion would appear to be a natural way for things to move. Planets revolve round their sun, electrons around their nucleus, and wheels rotate round their axles. But, once again, sensations can lead to wrong conclusions.

Riding in a car being driven round a corner, for example, produces a sensation of force on the passengers which appears to be pulling them outwards. In the same way, rotating the washing in a spin-drier forces the clothes to the outside of the rim.

It seems hard to believe that, in fact, under such circumstances, the forces are acting inwards towards the centre of the circle. Circular motion is not 'natural' because, as Newton discovered and stated in his first law, moving bodies left to themselves always move in straight lines. Only when a force is continually applied towards the centre of the circle will a body start to rotate.

It is the tension of the safety belt, the frictional forces of the seat and the pressure from the side of the car body, all acting inwards, which move the passengers round the corner, just as the pressure on the tub sides of a spin-drier, acting inwards, makes the washing rotate.

The planets have gravitational forces pulling them towards the sun, electrons are attracted to the nucleus by the protons' positive charge, and cars rely on frictional forces between wheels and the road to take them round corners. When roads are slippery and tyre treads worn down, the frictional forces acting inwards are not large enough and the car does what is natural. It refuses to go round in a circle and skids in a straight line.

In discussions on circular motion it is important to distinguish between 'speed' and 'velocity'. A small piece of Plasticine placed on the rim of a gramophone turntable will revolve at a constant speed. For long-playing records, making thirty-three revolutions per minute, this constant speed is slightly less than fifty-two centimetres per second. Yet, because velocity depends on both size and direction, the Plasticine is changing its velocity since it is continually changing its direction.

Left James Watt's famous 'sun and planet' engine, erected at Birmingham, England in 1788, is now housed in the Science Museum in London. It was so called because of the way the two driving cog wheels revolved around one another. Watt was compelled to dispense with the usual crank drive on his engine because the idea was protected by patents and so he evolved the 'sun and planet' drive.

James Watt (1736–1819) Scottish inventor. Settled in Glasgow in 1754 to become a mathematical instrument maker. Interested in the use of steam as a motive force, he did much to improve steam engines, describing the steam locomotive in one of his patents (1784). Between 1781 and 1785 he obtained patents for many engineering devices. The watt, a unit of power, is named after him. He was also the first to use the term horsepower.

Acceleration, which measures change in velocity, occurs in circular motion as a result of this change in direction. Theory shows that the Plasticine, revolving at a constant speed around a circle, must be given a certain acceleration towards the centre of the circle. Accelerations are, by Newton's second law, produced by forces, and the force which the Plasticine will require to make it revolve is provided by its sticking properties. If the speed of the turntable is doubled the Plasticine may not have a large enough sticking force for this speed and will therefore fly off the turntable in a straight line.

The same facts govern the motion of a planet around the sun or an artificial satellite around the earth, but here it is the gravitational force that matters. By feeding mathematical equations into their navigation computers, astronauts can predict and adjust a spacecraft's velocity of rotation and make it orbit at a given height above the earth or moon. Fortunately, the mass of the rotating body does not enter into the problem, which means that a heavy command module and a light moon craft can remain in the same orbit and still travel at the same speed. The manoeuvre of 'docking', that is, joining up two craft in space, would be very much more difficult if this were not so.

Vibrations

The problem of making wheels rotate from the up and down motion of a piston was solved by the early steam engineers, and the reverse process of making things move up and down, or to and fro, from a circular wheel can be done in much the same way. When, for example, a car engine is rotated by the electric starter motor, the pistons are driven up and down until the petrol ignites and causes the engine to 'fire'.

This up and down movement is one example of 'simple harmonic motion' and the word 'harmonic' suggests that there is some connection with harmony and music. If a length of rubber is stretched horizontally, pulled down in the middle and then released, it too moves up and down, or vibrates. The rubber will emit a faint musical sound as it does so. In just the same way, when violin strings are plucked they vibrate and produce musical notes, though these vibrations are not so easy to see.

Right This machine is a harmonograph and it draws patterns at random caused by the swinging of two pendulums. Examples of these patterns are shown below.

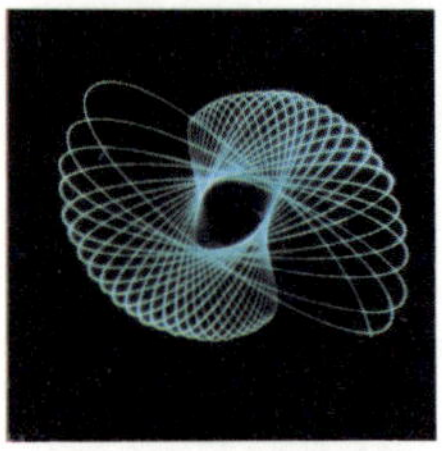

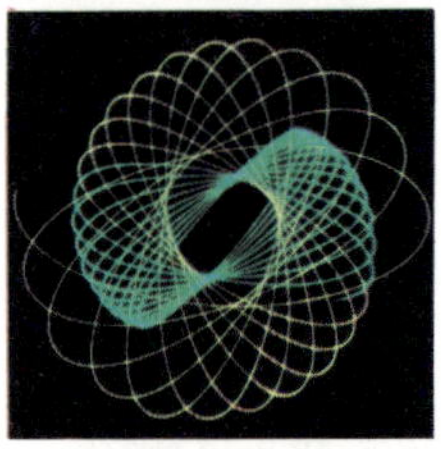

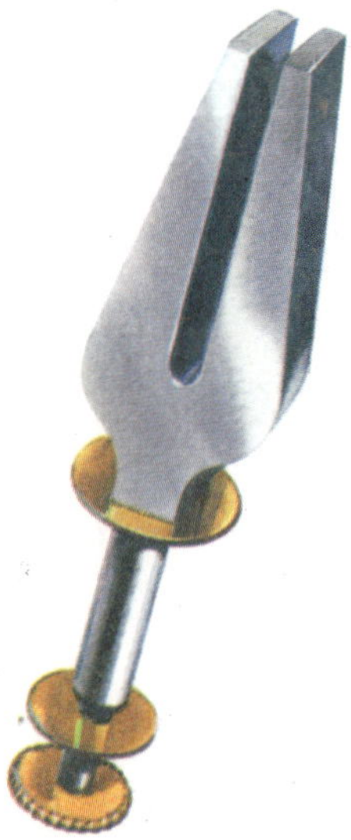

Above A tuning fork in music is a small two-pronged instrument made of steel which, when struck, gives off a note of accurate pitch. It was invented by John Shore, a trumpeter at the Chapel Royal in London, in 1711.

Simple harmonic motion can be studied in the following way. On a large sheet of paper draw a circle by tracing round a saucer. Then take a piece of string about fifty centimetres long and tie a loop on each end. Insert a finger in one loop and hold a pencil through the other. Place your finger on the outline of the circle and hold the pencil upright on the paper keeping the string taut. Rotate your finger continuously at constant speed around the outline of the circle and, still keeping the string taut, guide the pencil in a straight line like the motion of a piston. For every rotation of the finger around the circle there is one forward and backwards movement of the pencil which will draw a line on the paper equal to the diameter of the circle. One rotation is one vibration of the pencil and if it were possible to move your finger quickly enough to complete two rotations in one second, there would be two vibrations or cycles per second.

The pencil swings either side of the centre point of the line by a distance equal to the radius of the circle, and this swing is called the amplitude of the vibration. Even though the finger is moving at a constant speed there are changes in the speed of the pencil as it moves along the line, and these changes can be sensed in various positions. At either end of the line the pencil stops for an instant and then changes direction, gaining speed as it travels towards the centre. Past the centre point it begins to slow down or de-accelerate as it travels towards the opposite end of the line.

If this motion is imitated without the string and the pencil is moved across the sheet of paper at a constant speed, as well as up and down, a wavy line is produced which is closely connected with the simple harmonic motion of the pencil. The wave shows how the pencil moves with respect to time and the picture is not unlike those 'drawn' on a cathode ray oscilloscope by electrical methods.

Simple pictures such as this can be used to help scientists understand the behaviour of light, sound, alternating currents, mechanical vibrations and, at a more advanced stage, the latest model of the atom itself.

Waves

When the surface of a pool of water is disturbed by a stone, circular ripples or waves travel outwards across the pool in ever increasing circles. The disturbance is transmitted across the pond, but the water itself does not travel in this way. A small float some way from the source of the disturbance simply bobs up and down as the ripples reach it, indicating that the water particles are themselves only moving up and down. They are performing harmonic motions in a vertical direction but the disturbance travels horizontally over the pool's surface.

This kind of vibration is called a transverse wave motion. By continually disturbing the water at one end of a rectangular transparent tank, the waves can be watched as they travel along the surface. The wave shapes are very like the wavy pencil line. In the time that elapses between vibrations, the waves travel a certain distance along the tank, and this distance is called the wavelength.

Sound waves

When an electric bell is switched on inside a vacuum chamber and the air

pumped out, the sound slowly fades away. It is unable to pass across the empty space, indicating that a medium, such as air, or other material, must play some part in the transmission of sound. The air has elastic properties and behaves rather like a long spiral spring. When one end of such a spring is suddenly compressed, the adjoining layers are disturbed as the coils bounce back again and a compression wave travels along the spring at a constant speed.

In much the same way, the explosion of a firework causes the layer of air around it to be compressed. This layer bounces back, disturbing adjoining layers, which in turn affect layers further away from the source of the sound. The air particles vibrate backwards and forwards about their centre positions (like the pencil point drawing its line in simple harmonic motion) and since the line of the vibrations and the direction in which the sound travels are the same, the effect is called a longitudinal wave motion.

The vibrations of the air particles, on reaching the ear, make the ear drum vibrate and these movements are finally registered in the brain as a sound. It is some strange function of the brain which interprets the arrival of a single compression as a noise, yet if this noise is repeated many times in a second the brain 'hears' a note of music.

All musical instruments give out compression waves and the simplest of these, a tuning fork, is capable of producing a note of constant pitch. The number of vibrations made by the prong of the fork, that is, its frequency, decides the pitch of the note. If we say that middle C of the musical scale corresponds to a frequency of 256 cycles per second, then a smaller tuning fork, which gives out double the frequency – 512 cycles per second – corresponds to top C one octave higher up the scale.

Sound waves can also be represented by wavy lines. Such diagrams of sound waves are graphs showing the displacement of the air particles from their centre positions and must not be confused with the water wave diagrams which do actually represent the shape of the water surface.

If middle C is played first by a piano and then by a violin, the different sounds result in different wave shapes, though the number of wave crests is the same. Each instrument produces a

Above The whispering gallery at St Paul's Cathedral in London. A person whispering against the wall in one part of the gallery can be heard perfectly by someone sitting with his ear to the wall on the opposite side of the gallery. This happens because the dome is built to catch and carry the sound waves.

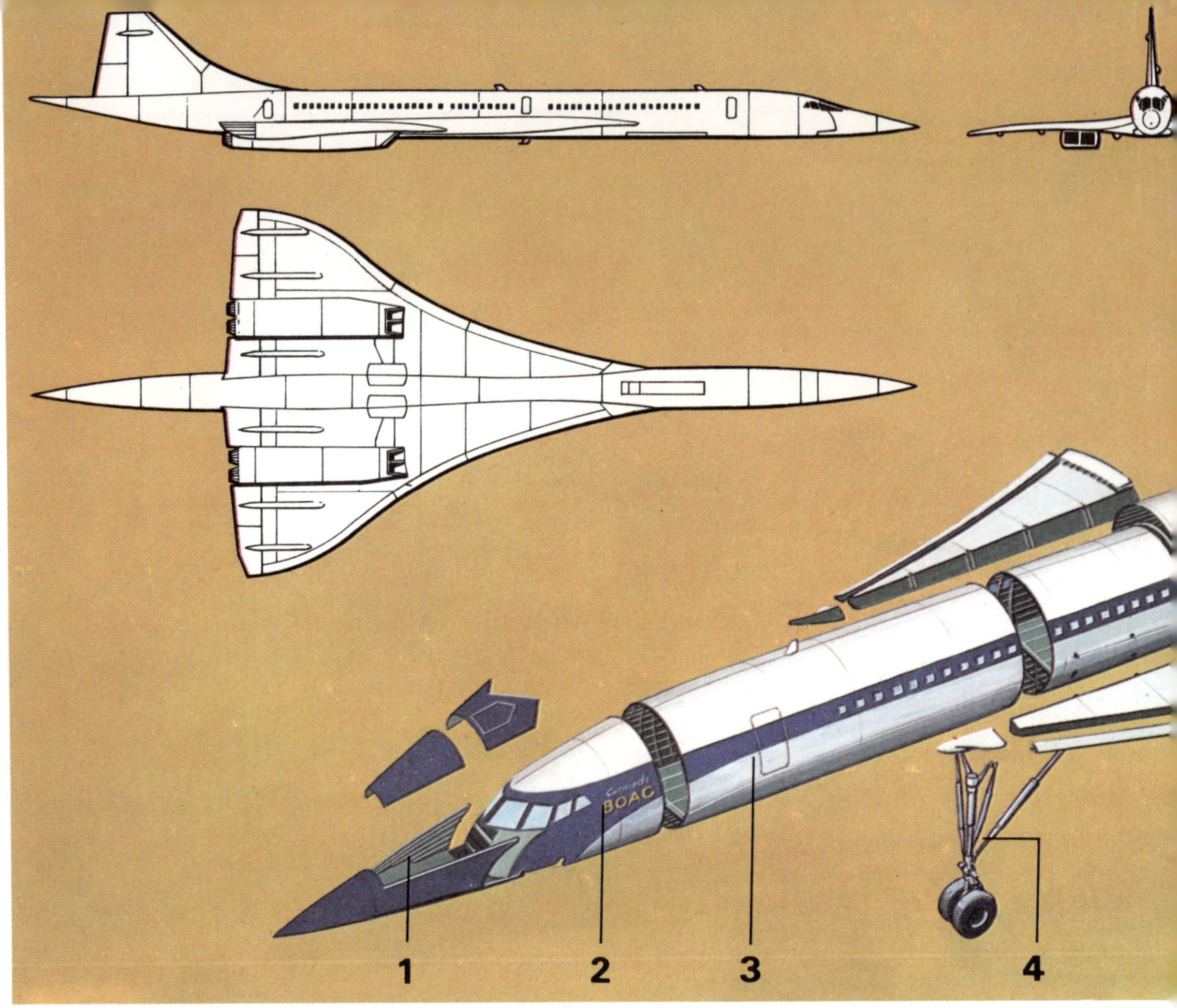

Above *Concorde* the Anglo-French supersonic aircraft, which can fly at speeds greater than the speed of sound. This drawing shows the design and some of the main parts of the aircraft.
1 droop nose. **2** fuselage nose. **3** flight deck.
4 landing gear nose.
5 passenger cabin.
6 forward wing. **7**. **8**, **10**, **11** and **18** centre wing.
9 landing gear main.
12 air intake. **13** Rolls-Royce (Bristol) turbojets. **14** engine bay.
15 outer wing.
16 elevons. **17** variable exhaust nozzle. **19** rear fuselage. **20** rudder.
21 fin.

different wave shape and it is this shape which determines the 'quality' of the sound.

Velocity of sound

Sound travels through the atmosphere at around 340 metres per second, which is slow in comparison with the speed of light. A flash of lightning, travelling at a speed of 300,000,000 metres per second can arrive many seconds before the clap of thunder caused by the same explosion.

Changes of atmospheric pressure have no effect on the velocity of sound but it is increased in warm air, and winds, which result in a movement of the medium carrying the sound, naturally affect its velocity relative to the listener.

A curious phenomenon occurs when sound is emitted from a moving source: for example, the whistle of a train suddenly drops its pitch as the train passes through a station. This 'Doppler' effect, named after Christian Doppler (1803-53), the Austrian physicist who discovered it, occurs with all forms of wave motion, and theory shows that the change in pitch is directly related to the speed of the source.

If the engine of an aircraft travelling directly towards an airport at half the speed of sound emits a note of frequency 256 cycles per second, corresponding to middle C, listeners on the ground will hear this note as top C, one octave higher. As the aircraft passes directly overhead the note will change to middle C, but as it recedes the note drops, this time by only two-thirds of an octave.

A somewhat similar change of pitch occurs when a moving listener approaches a stationary source of sound, but the changes do not occur in quite the same way. These changes of pitch can be measured quite accurately by

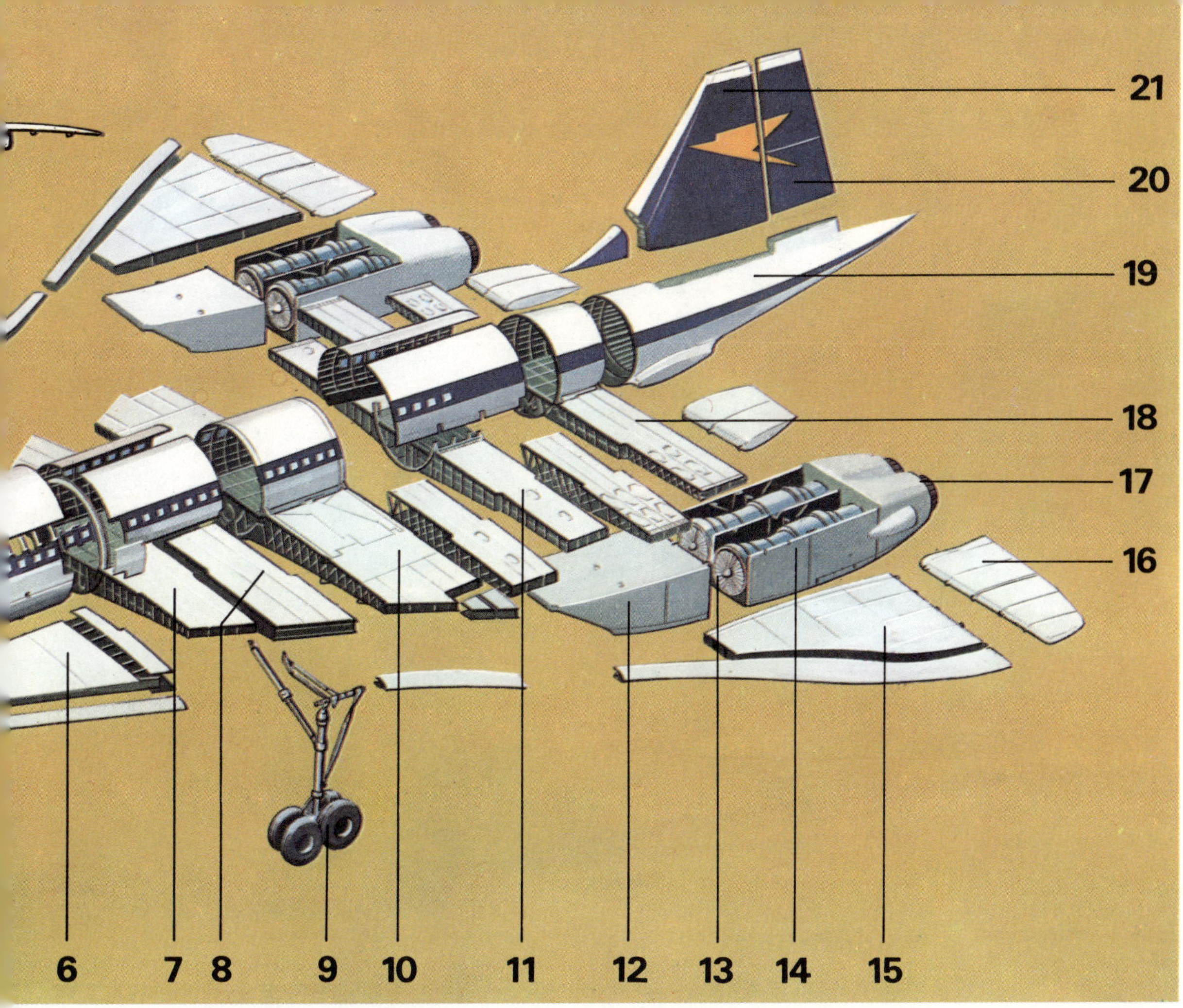

electronic equipment and enable a stationary observer to predict whether a source of sound is moving towards or away from him and at what speed it is travelling. Police radar checks depend on this effect as do the latest ultrasonic aids for the blind.

Ultrasonics

Ultrasonic sound, that is sound waves which have frequencies above 20,000 cycles per second, cannot be heard by human beings. In fact, as people grow older this upper frequency limit drops to below 13,000. Animals, particularly dogs, can hear ultrasonic whistles above 20,000 cycles per second and by emitting these sounds, bats are able to detect and avoid obstacles in their path while flying in the dark.

Industry uses ultrasonic sound waves to clean materials by making them vibrate at these high frequencies. They are also employed to cut materials and drill teeth. Perhaps their most surprising use is in hospitals where 'ultrasonic' ray machines are being used to take photographs of babies before they are born. In these circumstances X-rays could have harmful effects and are not usually used.

Supersonics

Supersonic aircraft such as the *Concorde*, designed to fly at speeds greater than the speed of sound, present a serious 'sound' problem. At speeds below the sound barrier, the atmospheric disturbances caused by the aircraft can travel faster than the aircraft and produce no more than a loud noise. But at the speed of sound a very large pressure wave builds up which on reaching the ground has an explosive effect. The resulting supersonic bang can break windows and remove roof tiles as a result of the rapid change in atmospheric pressure.

Above The Pont du Gard at Nîmes in France, a Roman aqueduct built about AD 14, still stands today as a monument to Roman engineering.

Below One theory to explain how the ancient Egyptians erected obelisks. The obelisk was hauled up a ramp and lowered into a hole filled with sand. The sand was gradually removed from below until the obelisk sank into an upright position. The ramp was then removed.

Equilibrium

In the ordinary sense of the word equilibrium means a state of even balance – a tightrope walker has to maintain his equilibrium, or keep his balance, when he walks on a rope high in the air. To the scientist, equilibrium has a more exact meaning. When an object on earth is still it is said to be in a state of equilibrium, that is, all the forces which might tend to move it one way or another cancel each other out.

How to stop matter from moving, that is, to keep it in a state of equilibrium, has been one of man's main problems since he gave up living in caves and started to build his own home. The simple dwellings of early man, built of wood, leaves and mud, were the first examples of structural engineering. Without knowing very much about the forces which were holding his building together, man found by experience how he could best keep a roof over his head.

As human beings began to live together in tribes or communities, they started to make larger buildings, such as meeting halls and temples. In time roof structures and foundations became more complicated, stone replaced wood as a building material, and simple machines were invented to lift these heavier loads.

It was the Egyptians who discovered some of the first principles of structural engineering and used this knowledge to construct many of the ancient wonders of the world, such as the pyramids. They also developed the basic principles of the movement of liquids, so that they could bring water to their fields in the very dry seasons. They were, therefore, the first hydraulic engineers (hydraulic means something that is worked by the power of water, or some other liquid, carried through pipes or channels) as well as being pioneers in the manufacture of glass, bricks and pottery.

Early Greek civilisations borrowed many of these Egyptian inventions and discoveries and at the same time developed new methods of constructing buildings, one of which, called 'cyclopean masonry', used huge blocks of stone which were held together by frictional forces without any form of mortar. To later civilisations it seemed impossible that these buildings could have been built without the assistance of the mythical Greek giant Cyclops.

Much of the engineering knowledge of the Egyptians and Greeks was passed on to the Romans, who were expert civil engineers, able to build roads, bridges and fortress towns over the whole of western Europe. By the time the Roman empire collapsed this engineering ability, first developed by the ancient Egyptians, had been passed on to the craftsmen of many countries who formed themselves into guilds. Through the ages, from generation to generation, they handed down their knowledge of stonework, plumbing, carpentry, metalwork and such crafts to their apprentices.

Today, the constructional engineer must not only understand the basic principles of equilibrium, or what it is that keeps matter at rest – which have become part of the science of mechanics – but must also have studied the physics and chemistry of new materials such as plastics, concrete and fibreglass which are now replacing metal, stone and wood in many modern buildings.

Adding up forces

Objects at rest on the earth's surface are motionless, or in a state of equilibrium, because all the natural forces on them balance out. A book placed on a table is being pulled towards the centre of the earth by the force of gravity, but the table offers an upward force called a reaction equal to the downward force, and these two forces cancel each other out. No resultant force acts on the book, which therefore remains at rest. In the same way a light bulb hanging from the ceiling remains where it is because its weight, acting downwards, is balanced by an equal tension force in the wire which acts upwards.

There are also cases of equilibrium in which the forces come, not just from above and below, but from all sides pushing and pulling at a stationary object. Such forces must be made to balance out if buildings are to remain at rest.

For example, the force which presses down upon the walls of a building due to the weight of a sloping roof can be thought of as two component forces. One acts vertically downwards and the other horizontally.

The vertical component force is balanced by an upward reaction due to the wall, which itself is supported by ground reactions in the foundations. However, unless some opposing force is provided in the design of the building, the horizontal component force will push the wall outwards. This has been known to happen in a badly designed building. A tie-bar fixed across the roof pulling inwards is one solution, but this can look unsightly in churches and large halls. The huge buttresses built outside such buildings provide an alternative method of balancing the horizontal component of the roof force and keeping the walls in position.

When three forces act on a body they may not be correctly balanced and if they are not the body is bound to move. The three forces must also act 'at a point'. They need not be connected to the body at one point, but the direction

Above Because of modern synthetic building materials, architects and engineers are able to design and construct buildings in ways that could not have been attempted before today. An example is the structure seen above – a geodesic dome made of fibreglass. This type of structure was pioneered by Richard Buckminster Fuller, the American architect.

lines along which they act must, if extended, all pass through the same point.

A large liner can be held stationary by three tugs if the directions of the ropes, when extended, all pass through one point and the force diagram is a complete triangle. But if just one of the tug ropes is tied to the liner in a different position, the liner will begin to rotate, though it will still not move forwards or backwards.

Levers and machines

When a door is made to rotate on its hinge by a force applied near the handle, the effort needed is small, but a much greater effort is needed if the door is pushed near the hinge. Two things control the rotation effect: the force of the effort and the distance between the hinge and the point where the door is pushed.

These rotation effects are called 'moments of force' and the 'principle of moments' was probably one of the first laws of mechanics to be discovered by man when he used a long tree trunk pivoted on a stone to lever a large boulder or perhaps a dead animal out of his path.

Machines enabled man to overcome his lack of strength and to take his time in operations requiring large amounts of power. He found gravitational and frictional forces were always fighting against him and overcame them by inventing wheels to decrease friction, and levers and pulleys to increase his 'mechanical advantage'. A system of pulleys may have a mechanical advantage of about 6, meaning that a load of about six kilograms can be raised by an effort equal to only one kilogram weight.

Every tool used by man is some form of machine, though not all machines are designed to have large mechanical advantages. Many accurate instruments, which are also machines, are designed to produce large movements of pointers or scales by a system of levers. One such instrument is used to magnify the changes in a length of steel rod while it is being tested for stress in a stress machine.

Stress and strain

The metal girders of a bridge are continually being stretched, strained,

compressed and twisted as heavy loads travel across by road or rail, and careful estimates have to be made of all these forces to ensure that the steel sections are strong enough before they are built into the structure.

It was Robert Hooke who first established the law of stress and strain in the 17th century. In simple terms, he discovered that the length by which a material stretches is proportional to the stretching force. There are however certain limits of stretch beyond which the law does not apply. The ordinary spring balance is an example of Hooke's law in action, but if too large a weight is placed on the balance it is likely that the spring can be overstretched.

One of the most important applications of this law is to be found in the machine used to test the strength of materials. Sample rods of steel are clamped into the jaws of a stretching machine and pulled slowly apart. Some machines can register automatically on a graph the force applied and the increase in length of the sample, and it is from the slope of this graph that an estimate of the strength of the material can be obtained.

But the graph can also indicate other important properties of the steel. As the stretching increases the line of the graph changes into a curve, finally stopping at the breaking point of the specimen. Just before the final break occurs, however, the metal rod begins to thin out rather like a roll of soft Plasticine when it is pulled at both ends. Most metals will return to their original length if they are not stretched too far, but after a certain increase in length, the metal reaches its 'elastic limit'. A further increase in length will result in a permanent stretch or 'set' when the forces are removed. This is why the metal girders of a bridge, if taken beyond their elastic limit, would produce a permanent sag in the centre of the span.

To explain why materials behave in this way, scientists have had to examine closely the atomic and molecular structure of matter, and in doing so have discovered new ways of giving them extra strength.

Structure of metals

Steel is made by feeding iron ore, mainly iron oxide, into a blast furnace together with limestone and coke and

On the **opposite page** (top) the iron bridge near Coalbrookdale, Shropshire, England. Built in 1779 it was the first bridge in the world to be built of iron. Tower Bridge, London (centre) is a bascule drawbridge built in 1894. Sydney Harbour Bridge in Australia (bottom) is a steel arch span bridge. On this page (above) is the Golden Gate Bridge in San Francisco, United States, a suspension bridge; and (below) the cantilever Forth Railway Bridge in Scotland.

Henry Bessemer (1813–98) English inventor. His first interest was in the improvement of the typesetting machine and the development of electro-typing. During Crimean War he designed a new rotating artillery shell. Finding traditional cast-iron cannon too weak, he developed his famous steel-making process, by which molten pig-iron, disturbed by a current of air, is turned directly into steel. The factory scene shows a Bessemer converter at work.

heating it to around 1,500 degrees C. The impurities contained in the ore, which melt and float above the molten metal, are allowed to run out through one hole while the iron is drained through another.

This crude iron is then purified in a Bessemer converter, or, more usually, in a basic oxygen converter (in which oxygen is blown over molten iron) or an electric furnace. The resulting steel is poured into moulds and left to cool down. During this cooling process, many thousands of 'seed' crystals appear in the mass of molten metal to which more atoms of iron attach themselves as the temperature drops.

One could imagine the growing crystals to be like small townships dotted about the countryside, each built to the same pattern, with a main square, or nucleus, and side streets all running parallel to each other. In time each town grows larger as more streets are built out into the countryside, until eventually the boundaries of one town get very close to those of another. Since no one made the main squares line up with each other in the first place, there are very few 'through roads' from one town to the next.

Thousands of crystal 'towns', or 'domains' as they are called by metallurgists (people who study the science of metals), grow in this way until their boundaries meet when the liquid has finally solidified. Polished specimens of steel reveal these domains when examined under the microscope and they can also be detected by sprinkling fine iron filings over the surface of the metal. The boundary walls appear to attract the iron filings like the sides of a magnet.

Many physical properties of metals such as strength, elasticity and brittleness are governed by the size of the domains, and scientists have learned how to control domain size by heat-treating the metal in various ways.

In the interior of a rod of steel a number of different kinds of force keep the metal in one piece. The electrical bonds hold together the crystal atoms within the domains, but the domains themselves are tied together by much smaller forces. These wall forces, partly frictional and partly electrical, are the weakest link in the chain and it is along these boundary walls that the metal is likely to crack first.

When a small stretching force is applied to a rod of steel the crystal shapes distort but the electrical bonds are not broken and the crystal springs back to its normal shape when the force is removed. This occurs up to the elastic limit of the material. Larger stretching forces can however make the domains begin to slide past each other and once this has happened, the metal rod can never return to its original length.

Malleable metals are those which can easily be pulled out into new shapes because of the weak forces at the boundaries of the domains. In fact, blocks of these metals are squeezed out in powerful rolling mills until they finish up as long thin sheets no more than a few millimetres thick. The sheet metal used in very large quantities to make car bodies is manufactured in this way.

Organic compounds

In 1848 the experiments of Louis Pasteur (1822-95), the French chemist, with certain crystals led to the discovery of a huge family of chemical compounds which we now know are also present in most living matter. These compounds came to be called organic to distinguish them from non-living substances like rock, iron ore and salt. As a result chemistry became divided roughly into the study of organic and inorganic compounds.

A great deal of early organic chemistry was developed in the second half of the 19th century by chemists such as Friedrich Kekule (1829-96) in Germany, and Jacobus van't Hoff (1852-1911) in the Netherlands. New chemical industries were developed to deal with the organic by-products of coal and oil, which resulted in a wide variety of new compounds based on the three main building atoms – carbon, hydrogen and oxygen.

As chemists found out more about the shape of organic molecules they were able to build up artificially new and very large molecules which were almost exact imitations of those created by nature in plants and animals.

Above The ICI works at Billingham in England, where raw materials for plastics, dyestuffs and paints are produced. This is one of the centres for research into the processing of new materials for industry.

Synthetic materials such as nylon and Terylene (synthetic means built up from simple parts) are now household names. These fibres start life as molecular chains which, when laid side by side, are persuaded to interlink themselves into strong threads by being squeezed through a small hole. Plastic materials, however, are made from molecules shaped like monstrous weeds whose arms spread out in all directions. When these molecules are formed in layers on top of each other their arms intertwine to such an extent that they become very difficult to separate. In fact, when heat is applied to some plastics the arms bond the material together until it becomes one solid molecule.

Perhaps the most recent addition to the family of synthetic materials is carbon fibre. British scientists have found a way of using long molecular chains of carbon as reinforcing rods lined up inside sheets of resin. Layers of this material are placed across each other so that the fibre lengths strengthen the material, like crossed wood fibres in a sheet of plywood. When these layers or laminations have been bonded together the finished plate can be twice as strong as steel, yet only one-quarter the weight. Since the material does not rust it has many possible uses as a building material. Its ability to be formed into complicated shapes by moulding will also make it possible to produce complete bodies of cars, or even aeroplanes, all in one piece. It has even been suggested that this strong, rustless, yet light material will make perfect artificial bones for human beings.

Above Stress patterns on metals are produced under the microscope which enable scientists to investigate physical properties such as strength, elasticity and brittleness.

Right 1 A coracle used by the people of ancient Britain, a circular boat with a framework covered by animal skins. **2** An Egyptian warship of the time of Ramses III, 1200 BC. **3** A Viking longship, or drakar, of the 10th century. **4** *La Reale*, a French galley of 1680. **5** Nelson's flagship the *Victory*, in which Britain's most famous admiral was killed, 1805. **6** The Atlantic liner *Mauretania*, 1906. **7** A modern French missile frigate. **8** The Russian ice-breaker *Lenin*, 1959. **9** The liner *Q E II*, 1969.

Inset The hydrofoil.

Equilibrium in fluids

Liquids and gases are described as 'fluids' since, in both cases, the weak inter-molecular forces allow each particle to have some freedom of movement. A fluid will flow easily through pipes and only come to rest when the pressures acting upon the fluid are balanced out.

The atmosphere itself is a fluid which exerts tremendous pressure. Fortunately, air pressure acts equally in all directions so that the effect on the human body is not noticed.

The famous Greek philosopher Archimedes first discovered the principle of flotation, which in modern language states that 'when a body is partly or wholly immersed in a fluid it loses weight, this apparent loss in weight, or upthrust, equalling the weight of fluid displaced'.

An object placed in water will float providing its weight is balanced by the weight of the water it displaces. It is for this reason that large ships, consisting of a tremendous weight of steel, can float on water, for their hulls are designed so that they contain a great deal of air and their shape ensures that they will displace an equal weight of water.

The submarine is controlled by similar forces. On the surface its weight is balanced by the upthrust due to the water displaced by its hull, which again contains a great deal of air. In order to submerge it must upset this equilibrium and does so by letting water into large tanks in its hull, which replaces the air and thus increases its weight. To surface, the process is reversed by blowing the water out again and letting in air.

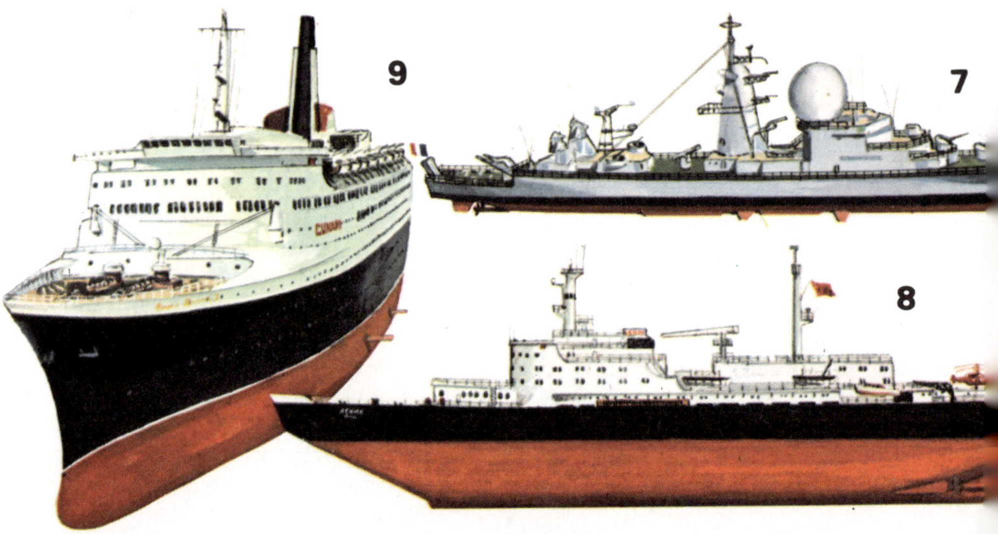

3

4

The hull of a boat must force its way through the water and this slows it down. The hydrofoil is a craft which travels with its hull above the water, and so it can reach much greater speeds. It has 'wings' or foils attached to its hull. These lift the craft in a similar way to an aircraft's wings (see page 292), although in this case there is a difference in water pressure above and below the foils. Hydrofoils are commonly powered by water jets. Many commuters now travel by hydrofoil.

Hydrofoil with fully-submerged foils

Hydrofoil with surface-piercing foils

6

5

Above In this selection of lighter-than-air craft are seen **1** Charles Green's Nassau hot-air balloon, 1836. **2** Henri Giffard's airship, 1852. **3** The Wright brothers' *Flyer*, 1903. **4** Fokker triplane DRI 1916/7. **5** Fokker tri-motor PAA, 1930s. **6** Graf Zeppelin 1930s. **7** Vickers Supermarine *Spitfire*, 1939/45. **8** Boeing B-17 *Flying Fortress*, 1943. **9** Convair XFY-1, 1954. **10** North American Bronco OV-10A, 1968.

Equilibrium in the air

A balloon 'floats' because its weight is balanced by the upthrust due to the very large volume of air displaced. Once filled with a lighter-than-air gas such as hydrogen or helium, a balloon's volume changes as it rises, because of changes in atmospheric pressure and temperature. If too much gas was allowed to enter the balloon on the ground, the chances are that it would burst at high altitudes.

Left to itself the balloon reaches a maximum height decided by its weight, the volume of gas it contains, atmospheric pressure and temperature. To descend, the balloonist has simply to allow gas to escape, reducing the volume of air displaced and therefore the upthrust. To ascend, it is the weight which must be reduced and this is normally done by pouring sand from bags on the side of the basket. In an emergency, however, instruments, or any movable object could be thrown overboard to maintain height.

The first successful airship was built in 1852 by a French engineer, Henri Giffard (1825-82). This cigar-shaped craft was powered by steam, but was difficult to control in flight. Eighty-five years later, on 6th May 1937, the giant zeppelin *Hindenburg* exploded at the end of a journey from Germany to America and the world lost faith in this form of air transport.

Today the balloon is employed to carry instruments into the upper atmosphere or used as a simple indicator of wind speed and direction. The development of new, strong, lightweight materials and the production of cheap non-inflammable gas may one day give to the lighter-than-air craft a second chance to prove its worth in other ways.

All aeroplanes in level flight are in equilibrium, even though they may be moving horizontally at great speed. In a vertical sense, the weight of the aircraft is balanced by an upward force produced by the air flowing past the

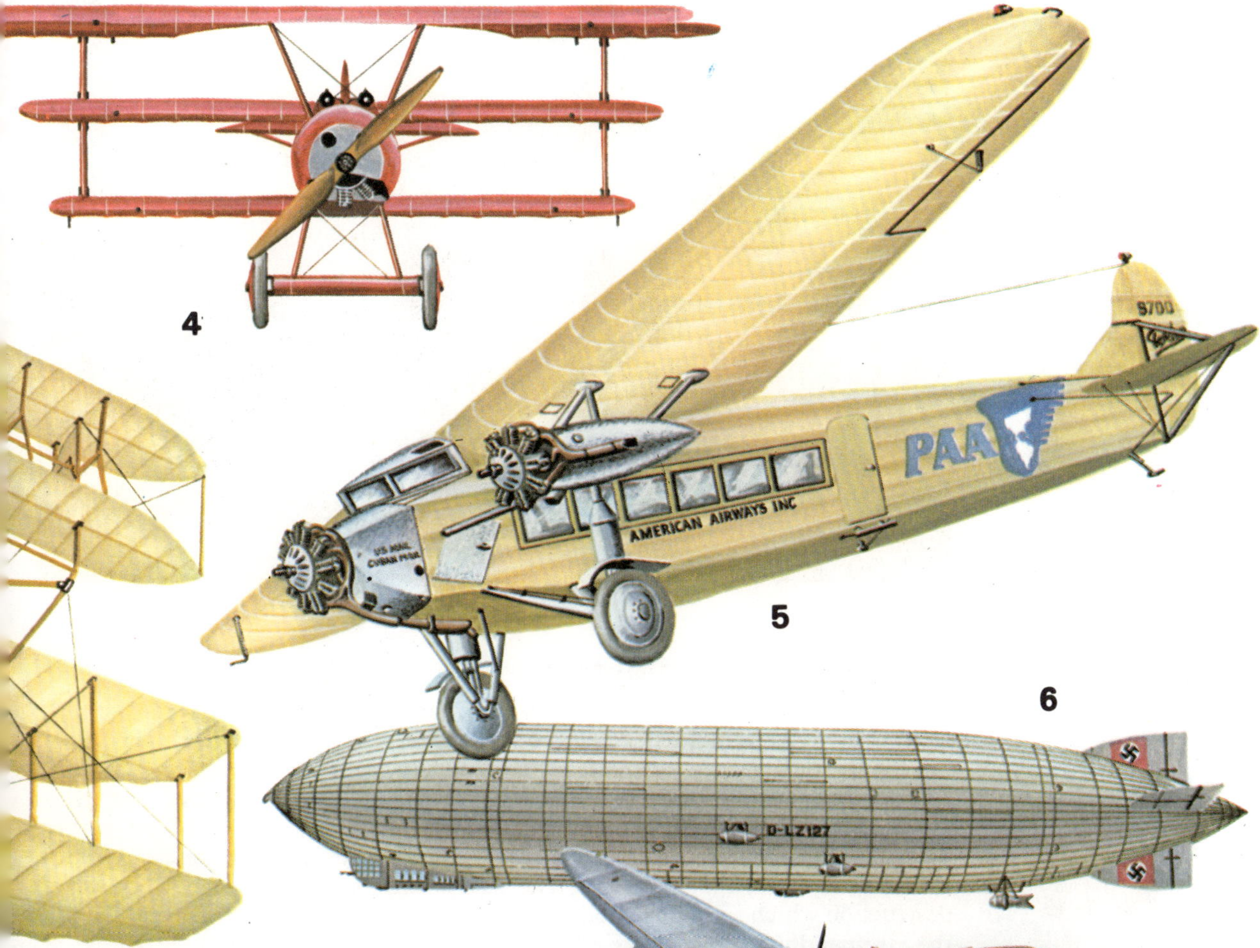

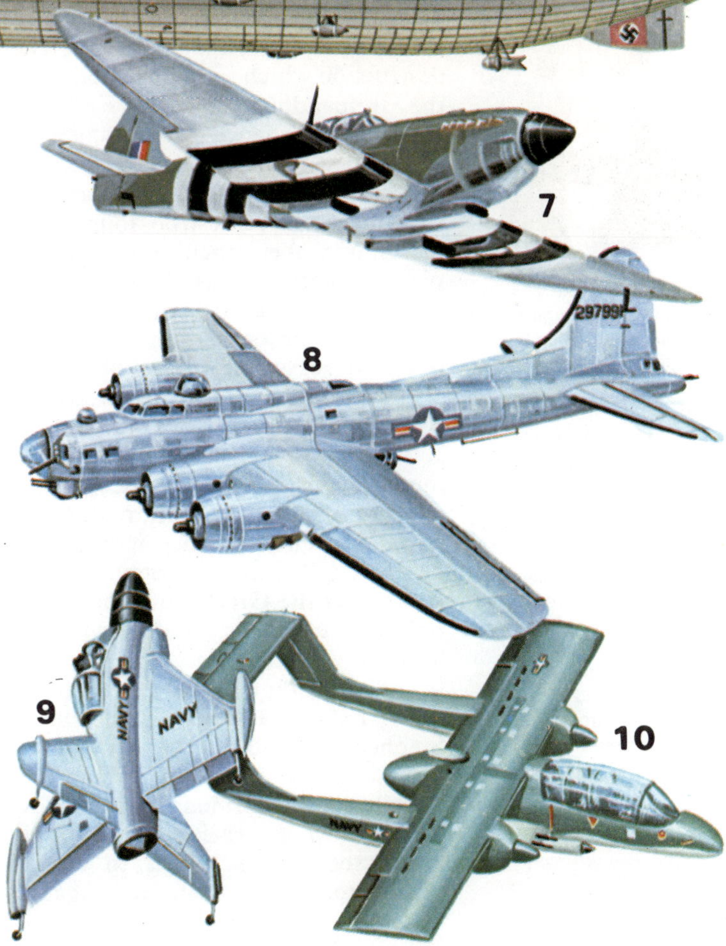

carefully shaped wings of the aircraft. The air flowing over the top of the wing is moving at a greater speed than that underneath. This results in a reduced pressure just above the wing, but a greater pressure below it. The pressure difference acting over the large wing area produces the required 'lift' to balance the downward weight of the aircraft.

In recent years a new method of producing equilibrium has been developed which also relies on balancing pressures. The hovercraft, as it floats only a few metres above ground or water, can move easily without losing frictional energy. A large fan draws air into a chamber below the hovercraft and maintains this air above atmospheric pressure. The craft floats on this cushion of air and can travel over quite irregular surfaces with ease. This craft is proving to be a most efficient way of travelling over water, and over rough or marshy ground, and allows exploration of difficult terrain.

Right Faraday's laboratory at the Royal Institution, where his discoveries were made. It was at the Institution that the scientist began the series of Christmas lectures for children that still take place every year. His long association with the Institution began in 1813 when he occupied two rooms in the building in Albemarle Street, London.

Controlling the electron

Man experienced the frightening effects caused by a sudden release of stored electrical energy long before he had any idea of its nature or importance. The brilliant flash of lightning during a thunderstorm was taken to be a signal from the gods, and the destruction which sometimes followed the tremendous flow of electrical charge was evidence of their anger

The first scientific discovery of the existence of electricity was made by the ancient Greeks, who found that pieces of amber when rubbed could pick up small objects. The same effect can be demonstrated by rubbing a plastic comb on clothing and using it to attract small pieces of paper. William Gilbert (1540-1603), a famous English doctor in the days of Elizabeth I, became fascinated by the effect and found many more substances, such as sealing wax and sulphur, that behaved like amber. Since it was Gilbert who called these substances 'electrics', after the Greek word for amber *elektron*, he may be credited with the 'discovery' of electricity.

It was nearly a century later, however, before another Englishman, Stephen Gray (1696-1736), discovered that some materials could hold the electric effects for long periods (insulators) while other substances allowed the electric effect to escape (conductors). A French investigator, Charles François Dufay (1698-1739), was the first to suggest that there might be two kinds of electricity – vitreous electricity (made on glass) and resinous electricity (observed on amber and other resinous substances). Vitreous and resinous have now been replaced by positive and negative but Dufay's theory that like kinds of electricity repel while unlike kinds attract is even today one of the most important rules of electrical theory.

A few years later in America, Benjamin Franklin (1706-90), a newspaper reporter and politician, found a new interest in science when almost forty years old. He began a series of experiments on electrostatics which led him to the conclusion that all matter contained 'electric fluid', and that rubbing matter did not, as others believed, make electricity but simply redistributed the electric fluid. If glass when rubbed with wool became positively charged, then the wool having lost this positive charge now held an equal negative charge.

Michael Faraday developed the idea further in his experiments on the conduction of electricity through liquids and became convinced that matter and electricity were closely related, but it was nearly a hundred years later before Franklin's electric fluid was identified as a flow of negatively charged electrons.

Michael Faraday (1791–1867) English physicist and chemist. Studied science as a young man in his spare time. In 1813 he became Humphry Davy's assistant at the Royal Institution. His greatest work was his *Experimental Researches on Electricity*, published over a period of more than forty years. His discoveries included electrical induction, the relation of electric and magnetic forces and atmospheric magnetism.

An Italian professor of anatomy, Luigi Galvani (1737-98), was the first to observe that electric currents could affect living tissues. One day, while dissecting a frog's leg he touched a muscle with two different metal rods, one of copper and the other of zinc, causing the leg to twitch. He wrongly considered this to be evidence of some source of electrical energy in the frog's leg. Galvani's name has become linked with many electrical ideas and devices such as the galvanic cell (an electric battery), the galvanometer (an instrument for measuring small electric currents) and galvanised iron (iron coated with zinc to stop electrical corrosion).

Another Italian, Alessandro Volta (1745-1827), later showed that it was the presence of two different metals which produced the electrical energy in the frog's leg. In 1800 he proceeded to build the first electric cell made from discs of zinc, moist paper and copper. It is quite easy to make Volta's 'pile' by building layers of milk bottle tops (aluminium), wet blotting paper and copper coins on top of each other. This home-made battery can generate sufficient electricity to power a small transistor radio.

Volta, whose name was given to the electrical unit called the volt, was the first to demonstrate the existence of electric currents, which we know today to be moving electrons. Those before him, such as Gilbert, had observed only the electrostatic effects of stationary charges.

Left Lightning is a sudden high-voltage discharge of electricity in the sky from the positively charged upper part of a cloud to the negatively charged lower part. Sheet lightning is simply the reflection on distant clouds of ordinary forked lightning which is hidden from view.

Humphry Davy (1778–1829) English scientist. Took up chemistry seriously in 1797. Experimented with gases. Lecturer to the Royal Institution 1801, where he was enthusiastically received. In 1803 began researches into agriculture. Discovered new metals strontium, sodium and potassium. In 1815 investigated fire-damp in mines and invented his safety lamp. President of the Royal Society, 1820.

Electron currents

Elements like silver and copper are good conductors of electricity because they contain 'lone wolf' electrons which are easily removed from their parent atoms and can move freely through the body of the metal. If a single electron is injected into a copper wire it can persuade a nearby electron to leave its atomic home and move one step along the line of atoms. This electron in turn affects the next atom and so on down the line, until one electron becomes homeless at the other end.

One could imagine a similar kind of disturbance occurring in a large bed containing ten men. If one man pushed his way in at one side he could persuade all the others to roll over one place until the man at the other side of the bed fell out.

In an electrical circuit connected to a battery, millions of electrons are being injected into the wire at the same time as a similar number are being expelled at the other end. On average the number of electrons passing any part of the wire in one second will be the same and this is the measure of the electron current.

As this is likely to be a very large number, a more useful unit of current to use is the ampere, named after the French physicist André Marie Ampère (1775-1836). When a current of one ampere is flowing through the wire, 6,240,000,000,000,000,000 electrons pass by any part of the wire

Above and **right** Electric tram and train which work from an overhead wire system and **below** an electric colour light signal which replaced the old semaphore signals.

every second. This is known as one coulomb of charge and is named after Charles Augustin Coulomb (1736-1806), who was the first to measure the repulsive force between like charges and discover how this force depended on the distance between them.

Potential difference and the volt

What causes a flow of charge through a conducting wire? A battery is needed to keep a small torch bulb alight by maintaining a flow of charge around the circuit. For many purposes this flow of charge can be thought of as the flow of a continuous stream of small spheres rolling down a slope. Spheres do not of their own accord roll along horizontal tables, but if one end of the table is raised then the spheres will roll from the highest to the lowest point. Similarly charges do not flow along wires without reason and a battery voltage or some other source of electrical energy is needed to 'lift', in an electrical sense, one end of the circuit above the other. This 'lift' is called a potential difference and is measured in volts. A potential difference between two points in a continuous electric circuit makes positive charges flow from the highest to the lowest point.

Electrical resistance

Elements like sulphur and compounds such as glass, plastic and rubber do not at ordinary temperatures contain any free, 'lone wolf' electrons and are therefore non-conductors, or insulators of electricity. Although charge may be held on the surface of these materials, it cannot flow from place to place as in a conductor. Certain elements such as carbon can produce electrons, but need more energy to lift them to freedom. Such materials are said to possess a high electrical resistance.

Georg Simon Ohm (1787-1854) was a German school teacher who took up the study of electrical resistance in order to become better qualified. His first achievement was to construct a galvanometer to measure the current-conducting properties of many materials. He eventually produced an 'order of merit' for the metals. Silver turned out to be the best conductor, followed in order by copper, gold, zinc, brass, iron, platinum, tin and lead.

In 1827 Ohm established his famous 'law', which defines the relationship between potential difference, the resistance of a circuit and the flow of current through it. It was twenty years later before Ohm's work was recognised, by which time scientists all over the world had agreed to name the unit of electrical resistance the ohm.

Electromagnetism

When a natural magnet, called lodestone (a magnetic ore), is suspended it always settles with the same end pointing north. Such magnets had been known for centuries, but the connection between magnetism and electricity was not discovered until 1820 when Hans Christian Oersted (1777-1851), a lecturer at the University of Copenhagen, showed that a compass was disturbed by being placed near a wire carrying electric current. There seemed to be a most unusual type of attractive force acting on the magnetic needle.

It was Ampère who unravelled the mystery and laid down rules for measuring the force between magnets and electric currents. But he was in the same difficulty as Newton and his gravitational forces when it came to explaining the origin of the magnetic forces. Even today the way in which one magnet makes its presence felt to another magnet can only be imagined. One way of doing this is to invent message lines running between them. These magnetic field lines can be traced by iron filings and reveal the direction of the forces which exist in the space between magnets and the way in which electric currents create magnetic effects. The same method has been used to map out the electrostatic forces between electric charges. We now know that a combination of magnetic and electric field lines drawn in space can help us to understand how light and radio waves travel through space.

Electrical engineering

Up to the beginning of the 19th century electrical experiments were often performed rather like conjuring tricks to amuse audiences by their novelty. The scientific discoveries of the pioneers found few practical applications, yet the next century was to see Ampère's currents used to produce artificial light and Oersted's electromagnets become the means of communicating over long distances by telegraph and telephone as well as providing a new source of power in the electric motor. Pure scientific research continued but a new breed of applied scientists – the electrical engineers – began to find everyday uses for electricity and prepare the way for the electronic and atomic engineers of the 20th century.

The electric telegraph

Samuel Morse (1791-1872) was in 1832 a portrait painter and member of the American National Academy of Design. Yet a chance encounter with an electrical conjuring trick sparked off an idea which was to make Morse famous throughout the world for a new method of communication. The conjuring trick demonstrated the way in which an electromagnet, a current-carrying coil of wire wound

Left Cooke and Wheatstone's five-needle telegraph used to convey messages on the Great Western Railway in 1842.

Charles Wheatstone (1802–75) English physicist. Notable principally for his experiments in sound. In 1837 took out a patent for an electric telegraph. In 1838 lectured to the Royal Society on principle of the stereoscope. Invented a sound magnifier for which he first used the term microphone.

Right Morse's first apparatus built upon the old frame of an artist's easel, which was capable only of receiving messages over short distances sent by the transmitting key seen below it.

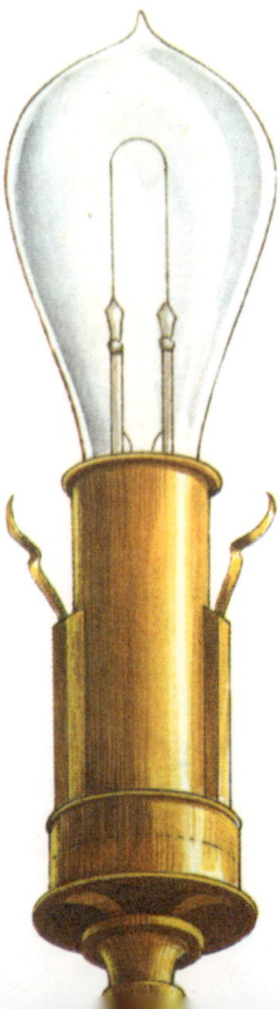

Below Joseph Swan's incandescent electric lamp, which he produced at about the same time as Edison did in the United States. These two men were joint pioneers in the invention of the electric light.

round a soft iron core, could pick up iron nails. Morse saw the possibility of making the electromagnet move a piece of iron attached to a pencil. Pressing a switch in the connecting wire up to fifteen metres from the electromagnet produced a pencil line on a continuously moving piece of paper.

Morse spent two years developing his first apparatus, built on an old painter's easel, but realised that the weak currents then available would be unable to transmit signals over long distances. He sought the advice of a famous American physicist, Joseph Henry (1797-1878), who encouraged him to continue despite the fact that many other inventors were at work on the same idea. Morse realised that a magnetic relay, a switch operated by an electromagnet, could be used at the end of one line to pass on signals to a second circuit containing another battery, and that this system would enable him to transmit over long distances using a number of 'staging posts' along the line.

His most famous achievement however was the creation of Morse code. By counting letters on the page of a newspaper he found that E was used more than any other letter in the English language and so represented E by a dot on his telegraph machine. T came next, represented by a dash, and so the code was built up through the alphabet. Morse code, first transmitted in 1838 along sixteen kilometres of cable, was later adopted by wireless operators and has been used ever since for the purpose of worldwide communications.

The telephone

The introduction of the telegraph not only gave instant communication over long distances but inspired many inventors to find a means of transmitting sound over these same electric wires. Almost forgotten now is the electric violin invented by Phillip Reis (1834-74), a German teacher of science. Reis converted violin notes by a mechanical method into electrical signals and then passed the signals along wires to a receiving violin where they were converted back into sounds. Around 1860 he first used the word telephone to describe his invention, which in those days was dismissed as another amusing scientific toy.

Alexander Graham Bell (1847-1922) was at that time studying science at Edinburgh University and on his return to his home in Boston, Massachusetts, he became a teacher of deaf-mutes. He invented many electrical deaf aids to assist his pupils and at the same time became fascinated by the problems of transmitting and recording speech. In 1876, with his assistant, Thomas A. Watson, he built a telephone system based on the scientific principles of magnetic induction first discovered by Michael Faraday in 1831. Oersted had shown that electric currents produced magnetic effects. Faraday carried the idea one step further and found out how to produce electrical effects from changing magnetic fields. It was Bell, however, who first combined these ideas in the loudspeaker and microphone to produce a successful telephone system.

The electric light

Thomas Alva Edison (1847-1931) had, by the age of thirty, already become recognised in America as a highly successful inventor. After producing many new devices to increase the

Left A contrast in telephone design between an early Siemens instrument with separate earpiece, and a modern fully transistorised phone which simply relays a conversation by means of microphone and loudspeaker.

Thomas Edison (1847–1931) American inventor. Began as a railroad newsboy. Published the first newspaper printed on a train. Was taught telegraphy and then invented an automatic repeater which sent messages from one wire to the next. Took out patents for many instruments and among them was the phonograph. His first machine was turned by hand and the cylinders were covered with tin foil. Later he invented a motor driven machine, an example of which is seen below.

efficiency of the Western Union Company's telegraph and telephone services he went on to invent one of the first speech recording instruments. His phonograph used a revolving cylinder covered with tin foil on which mechanical vibrations of a needle attached to a membrane left a permanent impression of the sounds falling on the membrane microphone. Edison then rotated the cylinder by hand, using the needle and membrane as a loudspeaker, to reproduce sound.

But his most famous invention was still to come. Like the British scientist Joseph Swan (1828-1914), Edison was determined to produce a successful electric light bulb. One which could be manufactured easily and cheaply and which would continue to glow for a long period without burning out. The secret lay in the material to be used for the filament of the lamp and many materials were tried and rejected, some too expensive, others too weak. Then, on 21st October 1879, a filament made from a length of carbonised sewing thread, mounted in an evacuated glass bulb, produced a steady glow for over forty hours. Three years later, on 4th September 1882, New York marvelled as Edison switched on the first successful electric light system in the world.

Today, countless numbers of incandescent lamps containing tungsten wire, instead of a carbon filament, and filled with nitrogen or argon gas, rather than a vacuum, are used to light the homes, streets and cities of the world. Yet millions of these lamps still bear the stamp of those two famous names, Edison and Swan.

The electronic age

Up to the end of the 19th century 'electric fluid' was put to work in many ways, yet the real composition of this curious fluid remained in doubt. We can only 'see' what is happening inside a solid or liquid carrying an electric current by using ammeters, to measure the current, or voltmeters to observe the potential

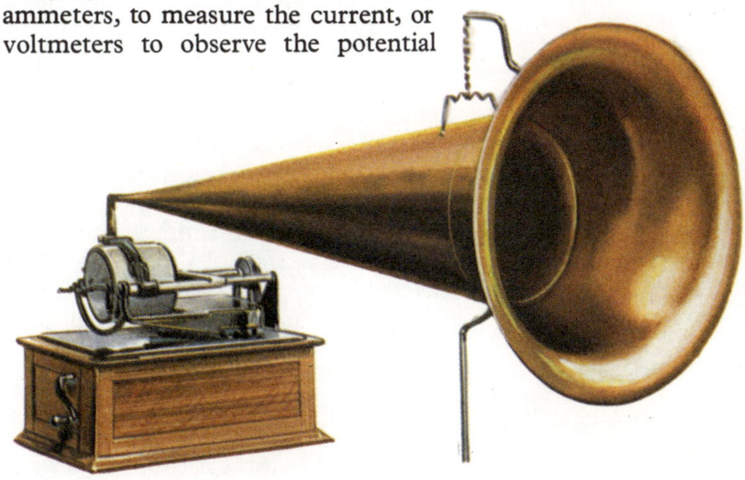

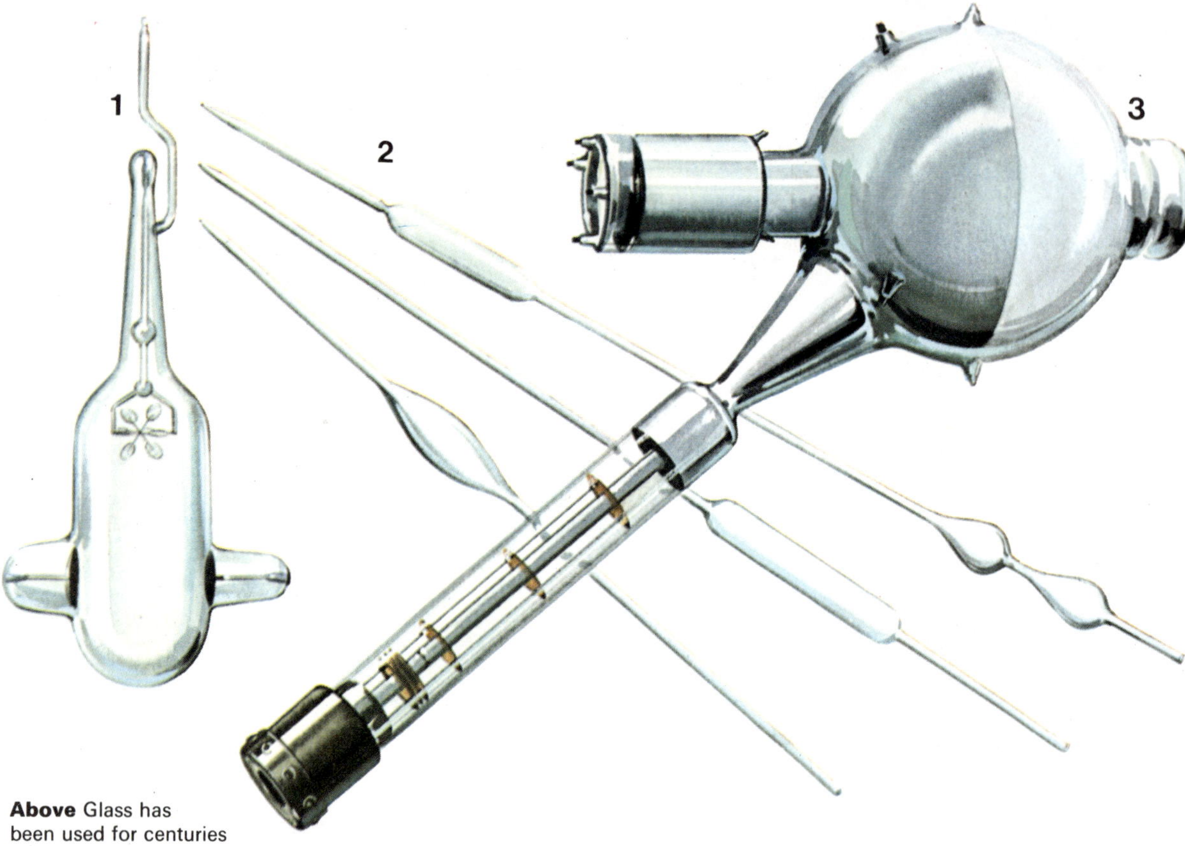

Above Glass has been used for centuries for both useful and decorative purposes. Glass-blowing was known to the ancient Egyptians and much fine glass survives from the Greek and Roman eras. Glass today is much used in the manufacture of scientific apparatus and these pictures show **1** A high vacuum electric discharge tube which dates from 1898. **2** Three pipettes, which are tubes used for transferring fluids. **3** The iconoscope used to be used in the television camera to convert the optical image into electric signals.

difference. In gases, however, even a small current can produce quite spectacular displays of flashing lights and colours, providing the conditions are right. These conditions were investigated by many scientists during the 19th century. Amongst them, William Crookes found that when a potential difference of a few thousand volts was applied across two electrodes sealed into a glass tube, he could watch a multi-coloured electrical performance as the air pressure was gradually reduced.

As vacuum pumps became more efficient, lower pressures were reached at which the flashing lights disappeared, to be replaced by a rather ghostly glow from the walls of the tube. Metal plates placed in the tube near the positive electrode (anode) created shadows in the glow. These cathode rays, streaming from the negative electrode (cathode), were deflected by magnetic and electric fields. The electron, the fundamental particle of negatively charged matter, was for the first time making a personal appearance in these experiments.

In 1897 Professor J. J. Thomson established that the cathode rays were streams of negatively charged particles travelling at high speed through the vacuum until they dashed themselves against the walls of the tube. These electron streams are responsible for the television pictures of today, but a great deal of research had to be done before they could be made to produce such organised patterns of light.

By the beginning of the 20th century, the electron proved to be responsible for many other phenomena which had been first discovered by 19th-century scientists.

X-rays

Wilhelm Röntgen was the first to notice the curious rays which escaped from a cathode ray tube when electrons travelling at high speed hit an aluminium anode at one end of the tube. This new radiation, called X-rays, could pass through thin sheets of various materials and cause a weak glow on a fluorescent material (barium platino-cyanide) placed far beyond the reach of the electrons.

The first X-ray picture, taken by Röntgen in 1898, showed clearly the bone structure of his wife's hand which had been exposed for fifteen minutes to the rays while placed on top of a photographic plate.

The discovery of X-rays was just one more piece of evidence to support a theory first proposed by a brilliant Scottish mathematician, James Clerk Maxwell (1831-79), in 1864. He suggested that moving charges could emit into space electromagnetic waves and showed that these waves would have properties very similar to light. As early as 1803, Thomas Young (1773-1829), a British scientist, had demonstrated that light passing through two slits, from a single source, could produce an interference pattern of dark and light bands on a screen. Only if light was some form of wave motion could these effects be explained. Clerk Maxwell predicted that his electromagnetic waves would behave in the same way and went on to suggest that these waves could be used to pass information over very long distances. He nevertheless left it to more practical minds to realise these ideas and invent the apparatus which eventually made his prediction come true.

Radio waves

Joseph Henry, in America, had suspected that there was some connection between light and electricity while experimenting with changing electric currents. He had, like Faraday, observed how to produce electrical effects from changing magnetic fields and contributed a great deal to the invention of the induction coil and transformer. Henry noticed that the sparks produced by the high voltage discharges of an induction coil could influence other electrical instruments placed some distance from the coil.

In 1887, Heinrich Hertz, in Germany, demonstrated for the first time the possibility of transmitting signals without wires by picking up the waves emitted from an induction coil on a distant ring of wire. Small sparks jumped across a gap in this ring whenever the coil was switched on. But it was a young Italian, Guglielmo Marconi (1874-1937), who won the race to send wireless messages through space. In May 1897, he transmitted morse signals from Lavernock Point, near Cardiff in Wales, to a small island in the Bristol Channel about five kilometres away. When, on 12th December 1901 in Newfoundland, Marconi received the morse signal for S, transmitted from an aerial in Cornwall, England, the world realised the tremendous possibilities of this new means of communication.

The suspected connection between radio waves, light rays and X-rays proved to be their common source, the moving electron. We now know that there are many other members of this family or 'spectrum' of electromagnetic waves, all of which owe their existence to moving electrons. Each has its own personality, due entirely to the frequency of the oscillation, but all travel through space with the speed of light at 300,000 kilometres per second.

The electromagnetic spectrum

Many of the inventions of the 20th century have arisen as a result of man's desire to produce, receive and use electromagnetic waves. Although theoretically all the waves are emitted by very hot bodies, such as the sun, special devices are needed to produce them efficiently on earth.

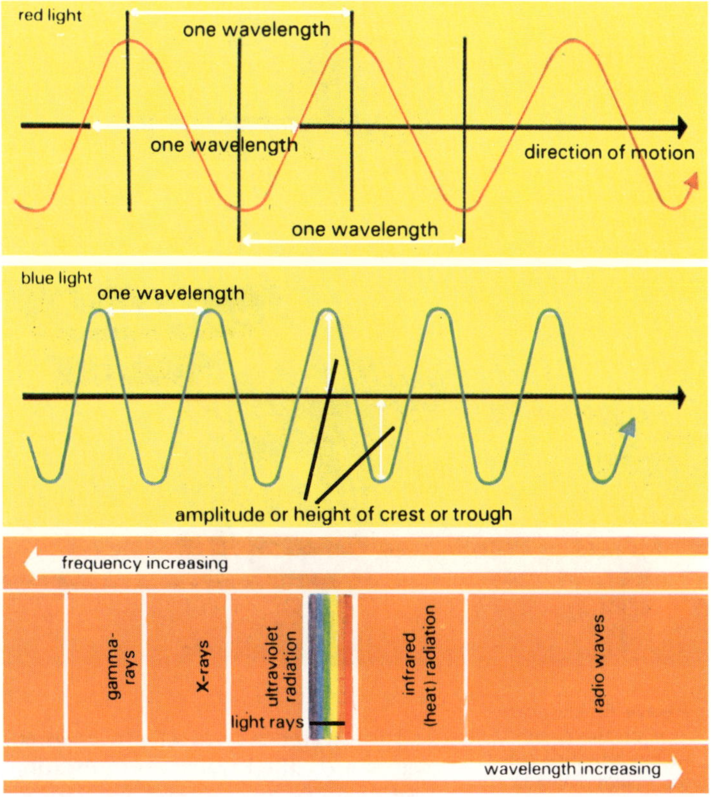

Above The wavelengths of red and blue light and the electromagnetic spectrum (bottom). The wavelength of red light is almost twice that of blue light. The frequency (the number of complete wave cycles in one second) is almost half that of blue light. Radio waves have much longer wavelengths than light waves which in turn have greater wavelengths than X-rays and gamma rays. The visible part of the spectrum is very narrow compared with other parts.

Above An electronic 'eye' on this paper-cutting machine stops the guillotine blade working until the man has moved back to a safe position.

John Logie Baird (1888–1946) Scottish television pioneer. In 1922 began his researches into television. In 1925 he transmitted the image of a face from one room to another. The system he developed was adopted by the BBC in 1929, but was superseded in 1937 by an electronic system invented by Zworykin in the United States. Baird worked on and produced images in three dimensions, in colour.

Like water waves, electromagnetic waves are called transverse vibrations and their frequency and velocity are connected with their wavelength (the distance from one crest of a wave to the next).

'Long' radio waves have a long wavelength of a few kilometres and therefore a low frequency. These were the first wireless waves produced by induction coils, but the invention of the thermionic valve by John Fleming (1849-1945) in 1904 opened up new methods of producing and receiving these electrical oscillations. Fleming's diode valve was an adaption of J. J. Thomson's cathode ray tube, but included a heated filament which could 'boil' off electrons from the cathode. This one way street of electrons, flowing only from cathode to anode, proved to have many applications, not the least of which was its ability to change alternating currents such as those produced by the mains supply into direct currents like those given out by a battery.

When an American, Lee de Forest (1873-1961) added a third electrode, called a grid, to the diode valve he produced the first triode amplifier which enabled Marconi and others to magnify weak incoming signals. These signals, picked up by the aerial as small changing electric currents, were passed to the grid of the triode, producing much larger current changes between cathode and anode.

The triode valve was soon being employed in a number of ways. It formed the electron gun of the cathode ray oscillograph, forerunner of the present day television tube, and in an oscillator circuit could maintain continuous oscillations. This device became the heart of numerous radio stations throughout the world. The heart beats, or frequencies, of these stations were eventually fixed by international agreement so that stations would not interfere with each other.

As more stations were installed, more frequencies had to be found using medium and short electromagnetic waves. Indeed short waves, unable to bend round the earth, proved to have their own special property of bouncing back from electrically charged layers high above the earth's surface. By a series of reflections between earth and sky these waves could travel right round the globe and became very useful for long distance communications.

Between 1920 and 1924 public broadcasting stations were installed in many countries to carry entertainment programmes and news items, but the home radio receiver was still a crude affair of earphones and untidy

wire. Only when mass production had made the triode valve into a cheap amplifier did the wireless set begin to resemble the modern radio receiver.

Radar

In the early thirties, the British Post Office became concerned over the annoying interference to their transmissions caused by reflected signals from aircraft and decided to set up a small research unit to investigate the problem. It was soon realised that the interference could be put to good use as a detector, and by 1935 a team of investigators led by Robert Watson-Watt was hard at work developing the first radiolocation stations along the east coast of England. These stations were designed to detect the approach of enemy aircraft by transmitting short, high powered packets of electromagnetic waves. When these waves were reflected by the target they returned to a receiver where they were displayed as pulses on a cathode ray tube. The direction, elevation and distance of a target could be estimated from these reflected signals.

By 1940 radar stations, as they were later called, using very short waves, maintained a secret and continuous watch on the seas and skies around the coast of Britain and enabled a very few Royal Air Force pilots to intercept and destroy hundreds of enemy aircraft. Radar, in those crucial days, changed the history of the world.

Television

There was another lonely inventor who in the early twenties had the germ of an idea, but little money to spend on his equipment. John Logie Baird (1888-1946) could be found any day in the little attic room of his house at Hastings in England, surrounded by wire, tin cans, old timber and string, patiently rotating a cardboard disc in front of a light beam. He watched carefully the patterns of light produced by this strange assortment of rubbish until one day, in 1924, he saw the beam trace out the faint outline of a Maltese cross. It was on that day that Baird, one-time sock manufacturer, jam trader and travelling salesman, invented television.

He moved later to London in search of funds to develop his ideas, but like many other inventors found little help or encouragement until in 1926 he demonstrated his invention to the Royal Institution of Great Britain. At last he gained some support, but other inventors were hard on his heels, particularly Vladimir Zworykin in America, who had perfected an electronic method of transmitting and receiving pictures which

Above A television camera filming in a studio. The scene is focused on to a photo-conductive surface inside the camera where electrons are built up into a pattern. In the receiver a picture is built up on the screen line by line, varying in intensity according to impulses from the transmitter. Because of the speed at which this happens the eye sees it as a complete picture.

Above left On a radar screen the picture of an object, such as the outline of the shape of land, can be built up by reflected echoes from radio waves sent out by a scanner.

Above The camera used by this 19th-century photographer is a daguerreotype whole-plate mounted on a tripod by Fox Talbot. His assistant is developing pictures in a mobile darkroom.

Louis Daguerre (1789–1851) French photographic pioneer, painter and physicist. He was a scene-painter in Paris until, in 1826, he began to work on his daguerreotype process in association with Nicéphore Nièpce. Daguerre tried to find a substance which would be influenced chemically by light to make a reproduction of natural objects. He perfected the process in 1839.

proved in the end to be more reliable than Baird's mechanical device. It was this system which was eventually adopted by broadcasting stations and has since been improved by teams of research engineers.

Colour television transmissions are now given in many countries. CEEFAX, a new information service developed by the BBC, was first announced on 23rd October 1972; a television receiver can display screen-size pages of information at the touch of a button.

Solid state electronics

In 1948 W. J. Bardeen and John Brattain, at the Bell Telephone Laboratories in America, demonstrated a new device which was able to control the flow of electrons within the crystal structure of certain solids. These solid state devices can do the same jobs as vacuum valves, yet are only a fraction of the size and weight. One device, the transistor, performs – like the triode valve – as an amplifier or oscillator, while the semi-conductor diode has proved to be as good a one way street as Fleming's vacuum valve. In this age of technology, engineers have been quick to see the advantages gained by small sized components. After only a few years of development work, transistor radios – portable, robust and worked by small dry batteries – were produced by the million.

Soon, a bewildering number of solid state devices appeared such as the photo-transistor which can convert light signals into electric currents, the thyristor, a new form of control switch, and the thermistor, sensitive to changes in temperature. All these devices have proved to be invaluable in the development of automation and space technology.

This miniaturisation of gadgets is continuing. Thousands of integrated circuits, containing transistors and other components, can now be contained on a tiny slice of silicon, called a microchip. A microchip only 5 millimetres square could contain the main circuits of a large computer of the nineteen-fifties. And tape recorders, virtually the same size as a tape cassette, are now available.

Infra-red rays

Infra-red rays, or heat radiations, are also electromagnetic waves, but have much shorter wave lengths than radio waves. They are the main carrier waves of the sun's energy, and though known to man from earliest times as a source of heat, they have only recently been employed by him in other ways. These rays can expose certain kinds of photographic plates, so that cameras can now take pictures in the dark of warm objects. Photographs of the human body taken in infra-red 'light' show up those parts which are hot and can reveal physical disorders by this means.

Infra-red photographs taken high above the earth from orbiting artificial satellites show many details of geographical interest which are not visible in ordinary light.

Visible light

Much of the early knowledge of the behaviour of electromagnetic waves came from the study of visible light. Early investigators such as Galileo, who produced the first efficient terrestrial telescope, and Newton, who discovered the light spectrum, believed that light rays were rather like very small bullets travelling in straight lines. Geometrical optics treats light in this way, using lines to represent the paths of narrow beams of light. The laws of reflection and refraction, which lead to an understanding of how rays are affected by mirrors and lenses, can all be illustrated by ray diagrams.

When, in 1837, a Frenchman, Louis Daguerre (1789-1851) developed a photograph from the inverted image produced by a pin-hole camera, he had no reason to believe that he was experimenting with electromagnetic waves. Nor did he realise that the reactions of the silver, iodine and mercury vapour he used to develop his first photographic plate were the result of electron movements within atoms. Indeed the early pioneers of photography were mainly amateur investigators with little scientific and certainly no electrical knowledge. A retired French Army officer, Nicéphore Nièpce (1765-1833), developed one of the first box cameras containing a convex lens; Daguerre himself was a decorator, and W. H. Fox Talbot (1800-77), the first to perfect a method of taking positive prints from negatives formed on glass, was an English gentleman of leisure.

In 1887, an American, George Eastman (1854-1932), was able to fix a layer of sensitive emulsion on to celluloid, making the first roll film and paving the way for the invention of moving pictures.

Left A number of silicon chips compared with a postage stamp to show how tiny they are.

Moving pictures

No one person can be credited with this invention. In England, around 1889, William Friese-Greene (1855-1921) produced moving pictures of a London street scene which could be projected on to a screen, while in America, Edison concentrated on his kinetoscope. This very early coin-operated machine presented a series of small photographs to the viewer as he rotated a handle, giving the impression of a moving picture.

In France the brothers Lumière, Louis (1864-1948) and Auguste (1862-1954), were also working on their *Cinématographe* using celluloid film to project moving pictures on to a screen and in 1895 opened the world's first cinema in Paris.

Many attempts to produce talking films were made over the next twenty years, but it was Lee de Forest's triode valve and the invention of the photo-electric cell that finally solved

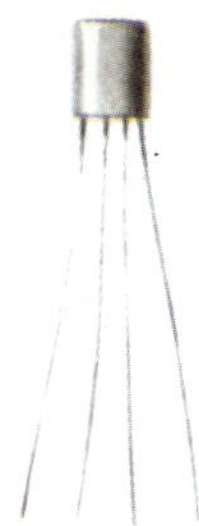

Above Contrast the size of the older type of radio valve (top) with the transistor which does the same job in a portable set.

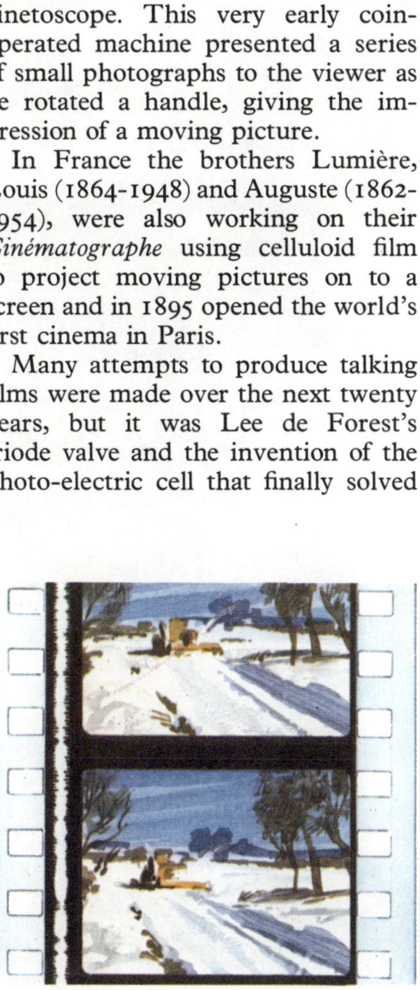

Left A section of 35 mm film showing the variable sound track on the left.

the problem. In the Warner Brothers' film *The Jazz Singer*, shown in 1927, Al Johnson's voice was recorded photographically on the film by using a microphone which converted the sound waves into variations in the intensity of a light beam to expose the sound track. During projection the light and dark areas of the track were sensed by a photo-electric cell and the small variations of current then amplified and fed into loudspeakers to reproduce the voice. Film with an adjacent soundtrack is still used.

In the late forties an alternative, video tape, emerged. This plastic tape can record both sound and pictures by small changes in the fields on its magnetic coating. Unlike film, it does not need to be processed and can be played back immediately. The quality used to be poor but has now improved sufficiently to compete with film for many purposes. Videotapes are packaged in cassettes, for use in cameras and recorders.

Below This picture shows the dramatic moment when a laser beam cuts a hole through metal. Laser is short for Light Amplification by Stimulated Emission of Radiation, and it was discovered by Theo Maiman in the United States in 1960.

Lasers

Ordinary beams of light contain a range of frequencies – the visible part of the spectrum. Laser light, on the other hand, contains only one frequency and so is known as coherent light. Since its discovery in 1960, an enormous range of applications have been found for it.

A laser is powerful enough to cut through metal, and yet can be directed so delicately that it can be used in eye surgery. It is also used in communications and for military purposes. Three-dimensional 'photographs' called holograms can be made using lasers. Perhaps the most important potential application is still being investigated. It is hoped that lasers will allow the production of energy by nuclear fusion. This is the process which produces the sun's energy, and if developed could solve the earth's energy problem.

Ultra-violet light

These waves, of frequency higher than the blue light near the end of the visible spectrum, are also emitted by electron motions within atoms. Mercury vapour in fluorescent tubes emits ultra-violet light as well as violet, blue-green, yellow and orange waves. Quartz tubes allow the ultra-violet light to escape in the 'sun-ray' lamp, but the strip lighting used in schools, offices and shops is mercury vapour light which has had the dangerous ultra-violet radiations absorbed by a glass tube.

Gamma rays

The X-rays, emitted by gas discharge tubes, are of even higher frequencies than ultra-violet light and by stepping up the voltage across these tubes it is possible to produce even higher and more penetrating waves which are called gamma rays.

However, as Marie Curie found during her experiments with radioactive materials, one source of gamma rays was to be detected right inside the core, or nucleus, of radioactive atoms. To understand this source of energy scientists began to discover more about the atom itself and its mysterious core. This was the beginning of the story of atomic energy.

Left The adding machine constructed by Blaise Pascal in 1642 was the first to use counter gears. These had ten teeth and were numbered from 0 to 9. There were six gears ranging from one for units to one for hundreds of thousands.

Above Napier's numerating rods, known also as Napier's bones, were the forerunners of a modern slide rule. They could be used for simple multiplication and division.

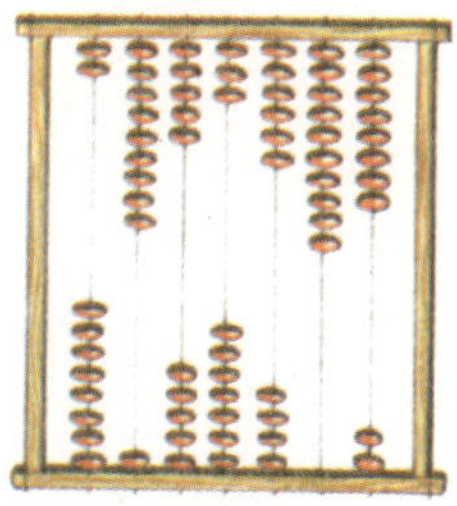

Above The abacus was probably the first computing machine. Known in the ancient world, it is still in use today, notably in China and Russia.

Numbers and calculations

Thousands of years ago, Egyptian traders, who had to account for large quantities of cargo, devised a system of making some grooves in the sand into which they placed small stones to represent numbers of things. Here, no doubt, was the origin of our own method of addition in columns. The Egyptians moved stones from groove to groove as we 'carry' tens from column to column.

The first counting machine arrived when the stones were replaced by beads threaded on to wire. This machine, called an abacus (from *abaq* the Arabian word for dust), is still in use today.

As painting and writing developed, symbols were used to represent numbers of things and in many countries the symbol for 'one' became a drawing of an upright finger. At first many drawings were needed to represent large numbers, until somewhere in India a new system developed using only ten symbols. Among these was the symbol for zero. This Hindu-Arabic system is the one we use today though the drawings have been simplified so that they appear as 0 1 2 3 4 5 6 7 8 9.

Counting machines developed slowly as man's need for more complicated measuring instruments grew. The development of the clock, the tape measure and the balance are all part of the story of how man came to measure time, length and weight by means of machines.

In 1614 John Napier (1550-1617) produced his logarithmic tables which simplified the multiplication and division of numbers by using a method of addition and subtraction. Representing these logarithms as numbers along moving scales led later to the invention of the slide rule.

The great French scientist, Blaise Pascal (1623-62), realised that the toothed wheel could be made to represent ten fingers drawn round a circle and that addition and subtraction could be performed by revolving such wheels when they were suitably meshed together. The device which records the number of kilometres travelled by a car and the mechanical cash register use the same method of operation today. Yet the most important idea was that developed by Leibniz, who introduced a system of counting which used only

Above One of the uses of a computer is to design objects as diverse as shoes and bridges. All the relevant information is first fed into the computer. The design may then be displayed on a screen, and amended if necessary using a light pen, as shown here.

two symbols 0 and 1. This binary system was little used at the time because it seemed more complicated than the decimal method.

Charles Babbage (1792-1871) designed a calculating machine based on the decimal system, but found that his machine could not be made to handle the ten symbols with sufficient speed.

It was over one hundred years later, in 1946, that the first electronic computer began to work. This machine used the binary system because the 0 and 1 symbols could easily be represented by 'on' and 'off' states.

Today, calculations can be done on a pocket calculator. This is a kind of small computer that can do instant calculations with numbers. When you press the keys of the calculator, the numbers are changed into on-off electric signals. Each number has a different signal. Then the 'brain' of the calculator adds the signals together to produce another signal, which is then changed back into a number that gives the answer. The brain of the calculator is a microchip (see page 304). It contains thousands of electric circuits that handle the signals. Because it is very small and the signals travel around the circuits very quickly, the calculator does additions very fast indeed. More difficult calculations are done by making additions one after the other, and the calculator carries them out so fast that it appears to get an instant answer.

The computer

The hub of a computer is its central processing unit (CPU). This performs calculations and controls all its functions. The information and instructions which have been fed into it are stored in its main memory, and it may also have additional memory on discs or tapes. People instruct and communicate with the computer through terminals. These may be keyboards (which are similar to electric typewriters), VDU's (visual display units, similar to a television screen) and high-speed printers.

Special languages are used to communicate with a computer. The computer has already been programmed to understand these languages and translate them into the binary code in which it works.

A computer can only do what it is programmed to do, but a skilful programmar can tell it how to make decisions, and so allow it to act independently to a limited extent. In many other ways, too, the computer has little in common with calculating machines. It can store vast amounts of information and rearrange and update it. This is useful, for example, for airline bookings and police files. It can do the numerous repetitive calculations necessary for weather forecasting in a short enough time to make the predictions useful. And the complex calculations needed for a Space Shuttle flight, or indeed any space flight, are only possible with a computer. It may be instructed to design a component, and can even control the machines which then build it.

Computers are available in a large variety of sizes and capabilities, from large business computers to small or microcomputers. Children tend to be familiar with microcomputers for many homes and most schools now have one. These can be used to teach subjects to a wide age range, as well as training their users in techniques of computing. They can provide entertainment as well – space invaders swept to popularity over a decade ago and has been succeeded by a vast number of computer games.

Automation

Automatic is a word borrowed from the Greek which describes any pro-

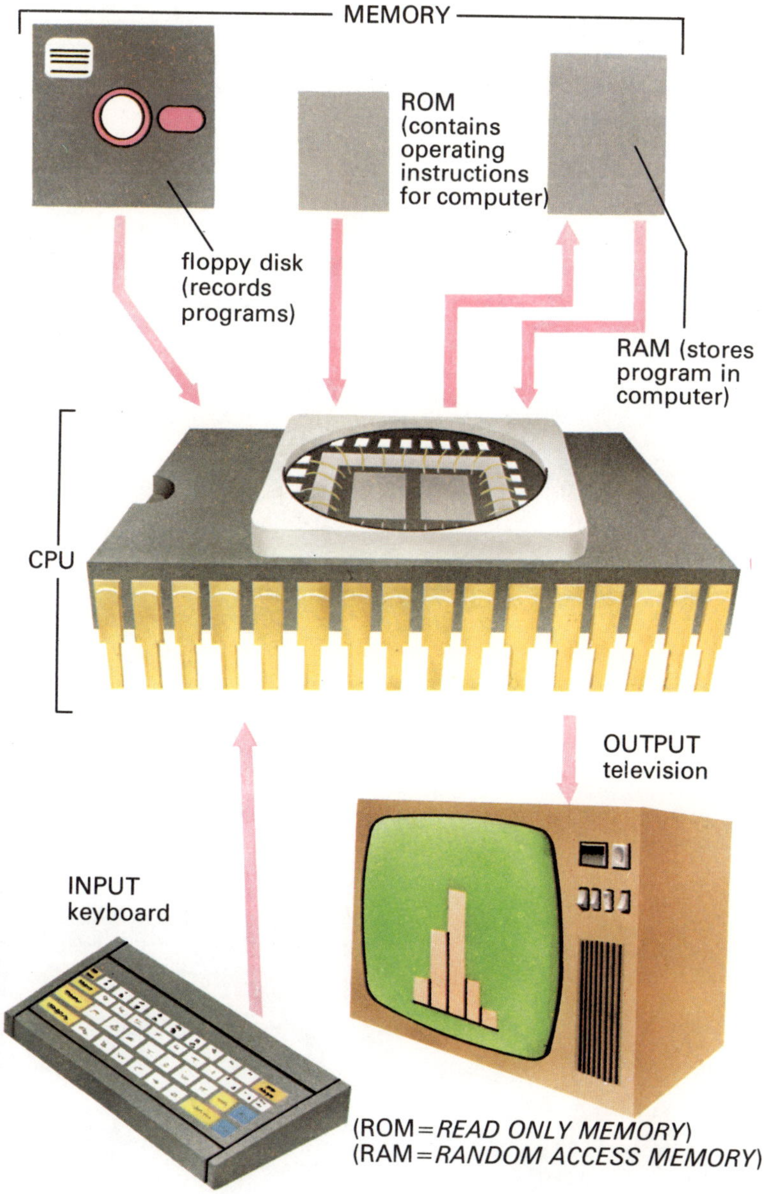

cess which can carry on without human help. Automatic rifles reload themselves and automatic machines serve the customer without help from the shopkeeper. The gradual development of automatic processes in many fields has been closely linked with the inventions and discoveries of science. It started when man first put to work the natural sources of energy around him such as the winds and flowing rivers and streams. Converting this energy into the motion of ships and wheels relieved man of many tiresome and exhausting jobs.

He had still to keep a watch on his machines however and alter their method of working from time to time. The sailor needed to control the rudder and set the sails when the wind changed while the miller in his windmill would have made little profit by just watching the wheels go round.

As machines developed, more efficient methods of control soon followed and led to the mechanisation of many processes formerly done by hand. During the 18th century the spinning of fibres and the weaving of cloth were transformed from occu-

Above The four main units of a computer are the input unit, the memory, the central processing unit (CPU) and the output unit.

Above left Drotz's draughtsman, a mechanical toy which could write its own name, and a mechanical music box which played a tune when its lid was raised.

Above A typical automatic assembly plant in a car factory.

pations carried out in hundreds of small cottages into a textile industry carried on in factories using many automatic machines.

At first the patterns woven into the cloth were controlled by operators who had to adjust the machines day and night to follow the designs. Later, pins set into rotating drums were used to produce a sequence of operations, and in 1890 a punched card method of control was introduced. This was the forerunner of the punched tape used in today's computers. Early mechanical musical instruments used many of these ingenious automatic systems. The musical box contained a rotating drum and mechanical organs churned out their music to the orders of punched slits on long rolls of paper.

Yet these control systems did not include one important device which is at the heart of any modern automation machine. Perhaps one of the earliest examples of this device was the speed regulator introduced by James Watt to control the speed of his engines. By coupling the driving shaft to this regulator he introduced what is now called 'feed-back', that is, messages sent back from the output of the machine to the input operating controls.

Today automation has come to mean the complete control of a whole factory system by sensing devices which feed back information to the machine control unit, checking all the processes for possible errors and making the necessary adjustments to the machines. The first automatic assembly plant was built at Detroit in America by the Ford Motor Company in 1955, and it produced a motor car engine every two and a half minutes.

Since then chemical plants, oil refineries and even complete cargo ships have been automated so that they can run with the minimum number of human hands, but at maximum efficiency.

In the future, many of today's boring and repetitive jobs will be done by automatic machines, but this does introduce a new problem for society. We must find new occupations for all the factory workers so that they can earn money to buy the products of the automatic machines which have relieved them of work.

Unless the science of living in a community keeps pace with the science of technology, civilisation as we know it may collapse completely and we will have to return to living in caves. Then we will have to start all over again.

Henry Ford (1863–1947) American automobile engineer and manufacturer. He built his first motor car in 1893 and in 1903 he founded the Ford Motor Company. He studied and created assembly line mass production techniques and produced 15 million of his Model T between 1909 and 1928.

Right This craft carries an automatic light to aid navigation and can be guided by computer to any point on the oceans.

Above A scientist handling radioactive isotopes through a special screen and using mechanical 'hands' which protect him from contamination.

Controlling the nucleus

The patient work of scientists like the Curies, Rutherford, Thomson and Chadwick revealed that the core, or nucleus, of the atom was composed of two particles, the proton and the neutron. In the 1930s these two particles appeared to be the main building blocks of the atom world.

Rutherford's estimate of the diameter of the nucleus of the atom made the size of the atom itself, including the electrons which orbit around it, ten thousand times larger than the nucleus. If the atomic nucleus is represented by a glass marble then the atom, to the same scale, would occupy a space bigger than the world's largest sports' stadium, and in this empty space the electrons would appear about the size of a pin head.

What scientists could not understand was how a nucleus, containing many positive charges, could possibly remain in one piece. By all the known laws these positive charges should repel each other with enormous force at such close quarters. Some other binding force must be at work and there seemed good reason to believe that the neutrons helped to keep the atom core together.

Natural radioactivity

When natural radioactive substances such as uranium and radium break up into other elements, they reveal much information about the composition of the nucleus by emitting, or giving out, some of the inhabitants of this nuclear world.

There seems no reason why a particular atom should decide to erupt suddenly in this way, yet by examining the breaking up of many atoms over a period of time, a kind of timetable can be established for each element.

This shows that a given sample of radioactive material will always break up at exactly the same rate. For example, 200 grammes of uranium will in 4,500 million years be reduced to 100 grammes of active material. In theory, after another 4,500 million years 50 grammes of the element will remain and after a further 4,500 million years only 25 grammes will be left that are active.

This period of 4,500 million years is, for uranium, its half-life – that is, the time it will take for it to change half of its mass by radioactive disintegration, or break-up. Half-life times vary from a few millionths of a second to many millions of years and, as yet, there is no complete theory as to why this should be.

Radioactive detection

Many ingenious devices have been invented to detect and measure radioactive events. One of the simplest, a fluorescent screen made of zinc sulphide, emits a small flash of light every time it is bombarded by an atomic particle.

Another detector, the geiger counter, is a small tube containing a gas at low pressure. A single atomic particle entering the tube produces

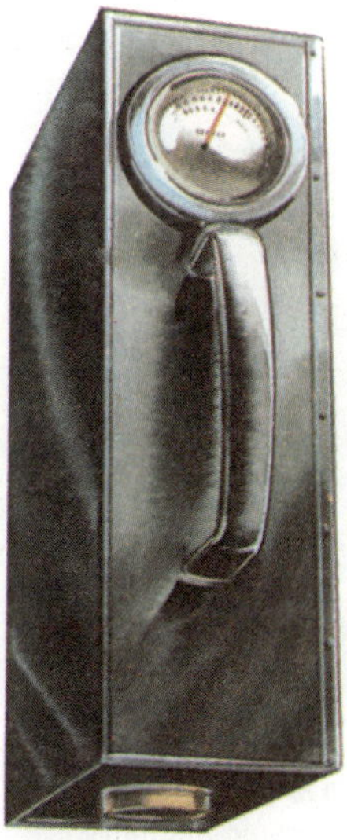

Above The geiger counter is used to detect and measure electrified particles from radioactive sources. It is an essential instrument in nuclear engineering and atomic research.

Right Calder Hall, Cumberland, opened in 1956, was the world's first atomic power station, and is a fine example of the harnessing of atomic energy for the production of electricity. Its essential part is the nuclear reactor in which the chain reaction of some fissionable material, usually uranium, is 'moderated' and controlled by heavy water. A gas, usually carbon dioxide, is passed through the reactor where it becomes intensely hot. The hot gas heats the water and converts it into steam which then drives the turbines for the electricity generators. The spent gas becomes cool and is fed back into the reactor to be used again.

Above People working in atomic research centres where there is any danger of radiation from radioactive materials take special precautions such as this technician who passes through a shower which cleans his clothing.

an electrical pulse which, after amplification, can be used to trigger a counting device called a scaler, or be heard as a click from a loudspeaker. The number of counts in a given time, that is the counting rate, drops to half its initial value after the half-life period has elapsed. Radioactive measurement of this kind, using geiger counters, enable 'decay curves' to be drawn for each active element, from which very long or short life times can be calculated.

Another detection device called a cloud chamber enables a particle to trace its own path by forming a line of bubbles as it passes through a wet vapour. From photographs of these tracks scientists can determine the charge, mass, speed and energy of the particles as they are emitted from a nucleus which is breaking up, and so learn more about its internal structure.

Splitting the atom

Because experiments on natural radioactive elements did not provide enough clues to solve the riddle of the nucleus, Rutherford suggested that it might be possible to destroy a stable nucleus by bombarding it with very fast-moving particles. In 1919 he was able to watch for the first time atoms being transformed by artificial means.

Unfortunately, the secrets of the nucleus are well guarded by the surrounding army of electrons, which can repel other negatively charged particles. The nucleus, too, being positively charged, can fend off positively charged particles unless they are moving at great speed. Other means of making atomic bullets are therefore needed to penetrate these electrical defences.

One such machine, the linear accelerator, is rather like a huge cathode ray tube using millions of volts to accelerate charged particles towards a target plate at one end of the tube. An even more powerful machine is the cyclotron, developed by an American physicist Ernest O. Lawrence (1901-58).

A whole family of new, more powerful atom-splitting machines, such as betatrons and synchrotrons are now at work in atomic research laboratories all over the world. One of the biggest of these built near Geneva in Switzerland hurls protons around a circular track as big as a race course.

Nuclear fission

Among all the possible atomic bullets used to split atoms, one particle, the neutron, can succeed where many others fail because it does not carry any electrical charge. The atom's defences have no effect on the neutron, which can penetrate easily into the nucleus and disturb the balance of the forces within it. In Rome the Italian physicist, Enrico Fermi (1901-54), began to bombard the uranium atom with neutrons, and in Germany the experiments were repeated by Otto Hahn and Fritz Strassman.

The atoms were split into two almost equal parts and this was the first time that atoms had been cracked open rather than just 'chipped' a little. Scientists then began a search for other targets capable in the same way of nuclear fission (which means the splitting of the nucleus of an atom into two parts).

Although by 1939 many of Germany's famous scientists had already left the country, they were still interested in the work being done by those who had remained behind, such as Hahn and Strassman. Lisa Meitner, a former colleague of Otto Hahn, and her nephew Robert Frisch were in close contact with Niels Bohr in Sweden and Albert Einstein, who had made a new home in the United States. Hahn continued to experiment with neutron bullets in Germany, passing on his results in papers to his friends abroad.

In 1939 Frederick Joliot-Curie, working in France, found that uranium was quite easily split by neutrons into the elements barium and krypton and in addition three new neutrons were released. It was this reaction that led scientists to believe they were on the brink of discovering a completely new source of energy.

Atomic energy

Careful measurements showed that the mass of an atom of uranium was greater than the 'bits' produced when this atom was split apart.

It would be very difficult to explain how the bits of a cracked nut could weigh less than the same nut in one piece. On the other hand, if every small piece was collected together and then glued back in place, the reconstructed nut would weigh more due to the extra amount of glue.

Meitner and Frisch came to the same conclusion about the atom. It must contain a kind of glue (called binding energy) which stuck the barium, krypton and neutron bits together, but was no longer needed when the atom was split apart and so transformed itself into various other forms of energy. This conversion of matter into energy had already been predicted by Einstein as part of his theory of relativity.

It was not only the release of energy that made nuclear physicists so interested in the splitting of the atom. The production of three neutrons in the process was also a very important result. If even two of these three neutrons could be persuaded to split another two atoms of uranium, then six neutrons would be produced. Four of these neutrons could then produce twelve more, and so every split would produce more energy as a chain reaction, as well as more neutrons, so that one single 'starter' neutron should be able to release from a block of uranium an enormous amount of energy in a very short time.

John Cockcroft (1897–1967) English nuclear physicist. Did research under Rutherford at the Cavendish Laboratory. In 1932 he and Ernest Walton succeeded in splitting the nucleus of the atom for the first time, and they shared a Nobel prize in in 1951. First director of Britain's Atomic Energy Establishment at Harwell in 1946. Awarded Order of Merit in 1957 and appointed first master of Churchill College, Cambridge, 1959.

Right During 1946 the United States carried out a number of atom bomb tests at Bikini atoll in the Pacific both from the air and from under water. The test fleet of warships beneath the explosion looked like toys.

Alfred Nobel (1833–96) Swedish chemist and inventor. In 1867 discovered how to make the explosive dynamite. He also invented blasting jelly and in 1889 several kinds of smokeless gunpowder. From the manufacture of explosives he amassed a fortune of over £2,000,000 which he left to endow the annual Nobel prizes in physics, chemistry, physiology or medicine, literature and peace.

The atom bomb

By the time the Second World War began in 1939, most of the leading nuclear scientists of the world were well aware that an atomic bomb was a possibility, but that to manufacture such a device would require a great deal more research and the assistance of many branches of engineering.

In the United States, Einstein, Fermi and their colleagues advised President Roosevelt to start production of an atom bomb immediately. On 2nd December 1942 an American research team headed by Enrico Fermi demonstrated the first controlled release of atomic energy at the University of Chicago.

Meanwhile at Oak Ridge, Tennessee, engineers began the construction of a huge factory to obtain relatively large amounts of the element Uranium 235, and six years after Einstein had first spoken with President Roosevelt the first atom bomb was ready for test.

On 16th July 1945 at a secret testing ground near Alamagordo in New Mexico, the bomb was exploded and produced a 'huge multi-coloured surging cloud'. It was estimated that the temperature at the centre of the explosion reached about 10 million degrees C. and that it was equivalent to a 20 kiloton bomb, that is, about the same as exploding 20,000 tonnes of ordinary chemical explosive.

Only three weeks after the first test in Mexico a bomb was dropped on Hiroshima in Japan; and three days later a second bomb was dropped on Nagasaki. The results were horrifying but brought the Second World War to an immediate end.

The nuclear reactor

Even before the atom bombs were dropped, scientists were constructing the first experimental nuclear reactors designed to produce atomic energy for peaceful purposes.

The first atomic power station in the world was opened in 1956 at Calder Hall, Cumberland, in England, and has operated successfully ever since. Breeder reactors such as that built at Dounreay in Scotland in 1959, which produce plutonium as well as useful electrical energy may, however, one day prove to be even more efficient.

There is an entirely different method of producing atomic energy called nuclear fusion, but this type of reaction has yet to be controlled on earth, although scientists are working towards this end. It is fairly certain that most of the sun's energy is obtained in a similar way.

Above The first nuclear powered merchant ship was the NS *Savannah*, seen here, which was launched in 1959 in the United States.

Radioisotopes

By bombarding elements with neutrons, nuclear reactors are now providing man with many new and useful radioactive elements. Radiations from elements like radium have been used for many years in the treatment of certain diseases but because of their very long half-life they must be removed from a patient's body by a second operation when their radiations have destroyed the diseased cells: otherwise they will continue to bombard healthy cells with damaging results.

New substances called artificial isotopes, with half-lives ranging from a few minutes to one or two months, can be left to do their work until their activity has dropped to a safe level, since they are transformed into harmless inactive elements which the body removes of its own accord.

Many common elements like carbon can now be obtained in a radioactive form and these have a number of useful applications. Fertilisers which contain radioactive substances, or radioisotopes, can give a good indication of the type of plant food which produces the best growth.

Mechanical engineers can use these same radioisotopes, embedded in the gearings of an engine, to discover how best to lubricate the moving system. Since radioisotopes can also expose photographic plates, they are a very good substitute for X-rays in many engineering applications. Flaws can be detected in the joints of a welded pipe in much the same way as an X-ray picture can disclose a broken bone.

Treated with caution, these new elements can be very useful to man, but over-exposure to any form of radioactivity or X-rays can be very dangerous. It is for this reason that all workers who have to handle any of these materials are regularly checked by doctors to ensure that they are not being affected by too much radiation.

Fundamental particles

Much of the original research into the nucleus was aimed at discovering the nature of the forces within it which held the protons and neutrons together. It became increasingly clear that protons and neutrons were not so simple as might first appear and that actual particles in some way passed between them. The size of these particles and some of their properties could even be predicted and they were eventually called mesons. Rather similar particles were known to exist in the cosmic radiations which are continually arriving on earth from outer space.

When, in 1948, the nuclear meson was first made on earth, physicists were inclined to believe that another scientific problem was nearly solved. It now appears that there are very many fundamental particles which make up the matter of the universe and a number of these have already made their appearance in the latest atom splitting machines. These new inhabitants fall into four main classes called hyperons, nucleons (which include the protons and neutrons), mesons and leptons (the electron is one of these).

It is the aim of modern physicists to understand how these very small masses are created and in what way they fit into the jigsaw puzzle of the nuclear world.

Above A coastal marine light to warn shipping. Instead of the old type of light which needed regular attention this one is powered by radioisotopes and will operate for years on its own.

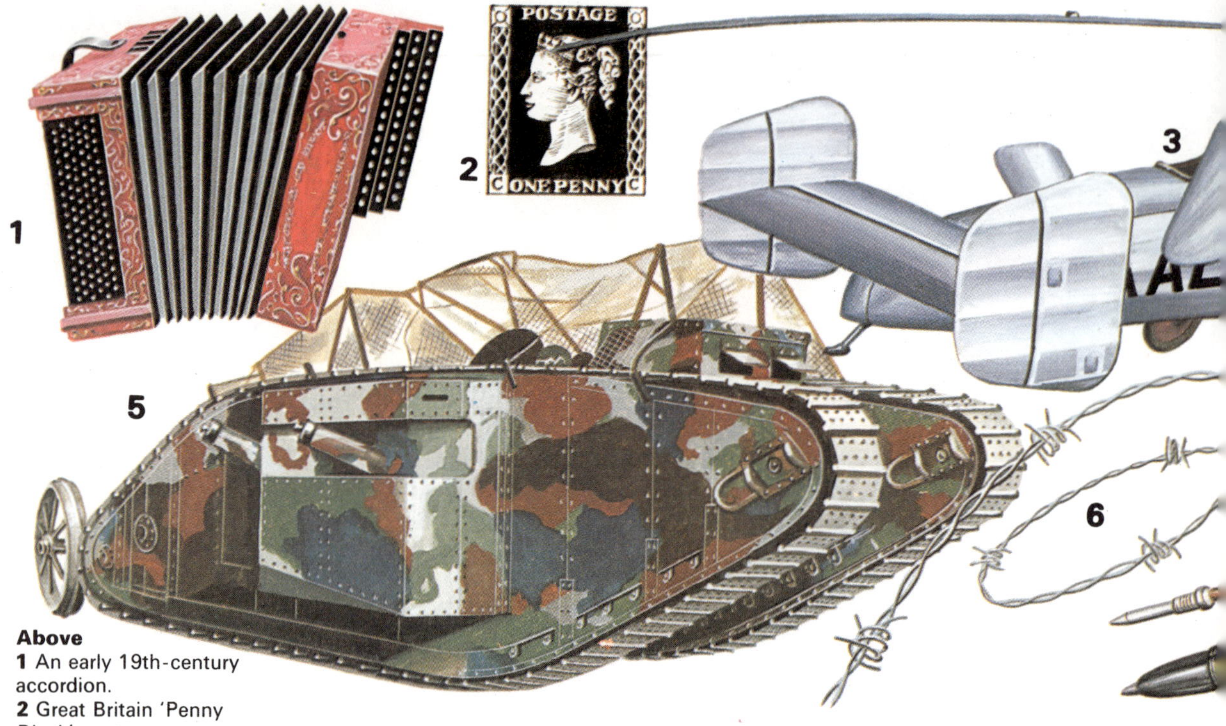

1
2
3
5
6

Above
1 An early 19th-century accordion.
2 Great Britain 'Penny Black' postage stamp.
3 Juan de la Cierva's autogiro.
4 The first hovercraft, SRN1.
5 The first military tank, 1916.
6 Barbed wire.
7 Georg Biro's ball-point pen.

Inventions and discoveries

This list includes some of the most famous landmarks in the history of scientific discovery. It gives the names of the people, and the countries from which they come, who are generally accepted as the originators of an invention or discovery, but it should be remembered that in many cases the first successful development of an idea came only after a long period of experiment in which many people may have taken part. Also, the same thing has often been 'invented' by two or more people at about the same time, working independently. For these and other reasons authorities often differ on both names and dates.

Accordion Buschmann (Germany) 1822
Adding Machine The first simple calculating machine. Blaise Pascal (France) 1640–50
Aeroplane The first sustained flight in a powered heavier-than-air machine. Orville and Wilbur Wright (United States) 1903
Airship non-rigid Henry Giffard (France) 1852
Airship rigid Ferdinand von Zeppelin (Germany) 1900
Algebra Probably used in Alexandria in the 3rd century AD but usually attributed to Al-khowârizmî (Arabia) 825
Anaesthetics James Simpson (Britain) 1847
Anemometer The rotating cup anemometer for measuring the force of winds. Dr Robinson (Ireland) 1846
Antiseptics Joseph Lister (Britain) 1867
Astrolabe Said to have been used by the Greek astronomer Hipparchus in the 2nd century BC. Also used by the Arabs in the 9th century AD
Autogiro Forerunner of the helicopter. Juan de la Cierva (Spain) 1922
Bakelite Leo H. Baekeland (Belgium/United States) 1909
Balance spring For use in watches. Robert Hooke (Britain) 1658
Balloon hot-air Montgolfier brothers (France) 1783
Ball-point pen The original invention is attributed to John Loud (United States) 1888. The first practical ball-point pen Georg Biro (Hungary) 1938
Barbed wire Joseph F. Glidden (United States) 1875
Barometer Evangelista Torricelli (Italy) 1643
Bathysphere W. Beebe (United States) 1934
Bicycle Kirkpatrick Macmillan (Britain) 1838
Bunsen burner Robert Bunsen (Germany) 1850
Carpet sweeper Melville R. Bissell (United States) 1876
Cash register James Ritty (United States) 1879
Cellophane J. E. Brandenburger (Switzerland) 1912
Celluloid Alexander Parkes (Britain) 1855. So named and developed by J. W. and I. Hyatt (United States) 1873
Chronometer John Harrison (Britain) 1735
Cinematography The first film of a 'real life' event – a train arriving at a station. Louis Lumière (France) 1895
Clock Earliest known mechanical clocks date from about 1330. Galileo and Christian Huygens applied pendulums to clocks in the 17th century.
Computer Charles Babbage (Britain) 1834, designed a calculating machine, a forerunner of the computer.
Concertina Charles Wheatstone (Britain) 1825.

Contact lens J. F. Herschel proposed use in 1827. Not manufactured until some sixty years later. First plastic lens 1938. Corneal contact lens 1950
Cotton gin A machine for separating seeds from cotton fibre. Eli Whitney (United States) 1793
Diesel engine Rudolf Diesel (Germany) 1897
Dynamite Alfred Nobel (Sweden) 1867
Dynamo Electromagnetic induction, basis of the dynamo. Michael Faraday (Britain) 1831. Early forms of dynamo by Picinotti (Italy) 1860 and William Siemens (Britain/Germany) 1867
Electric battery Alessandro Volta (Italy) 1800
Electric blanket Simmons Co. (United States) 1946
Electric flat iron H. W. Seeley (United States) 1882
Electric lamp carbon filament Thomas Edison (United States) 1879 and independently Joseph Swan (Britain) 1880
Electric motor Michael Faraday (Britain) expounded principle in 1821 also Joseph Henry (United States) 1829
Electromagnetic machine William Sturgeon (Britain) 1825
Electron microscope Vladimir Zworykin (United States) 1939
Flying shuttle Used on weaving machines. John Kay (Britain) 1733
Gas lighting Although there were earlier attempts this is generally attributed to William Murdock (Britain) 1792
Gunpowder It is reputed to have been used by the Chinese from about 200 BC but the earliest reference to its use in the western world is by Roger Bacon (Britain) 1240
Gyro-compass The first successful one. Elmer A. Sperry (United States) 1908
Gyroscope Jean Foucault (France) 1852
Hovercraft C. S. Cockerell (Britain) 1955.
Hydrofoil Enrico Forlanini (Italy) 1909.
Hypodermic syringe Alexander Wood (Britain) 1853
Internal combustion engine
gas-driven Etienne Lenoir (France) 1860.
petrol-driven Gottlieb Daimler (Germany) 1883
Jet engine Frank Whittle (Britain) First patent 1930. First engine 1937. The first successful jet aircraft was the Heinkel He 178 with engine designed by H. von Ohain (Germany) 1939
Kaleidoscope David Brewster (Britain) 1817
Knitting machine Rev Willian Lee (Britain) 1599
Laser Theodore Maiman (United States) 1960
Lift Elisha Otis (United States) 1852
Lightning conductor Benjamin Franklin (United States) 1752
Linoleum cork Frederick Watson (Britain) 1860
Loom power Edmund Cartwright (Britain) 1785
Macadam roads John McAdam (Britain) 1815
Machine-gun Richard Gatling (United States) 1862
Margarine H. Mège-Mouries (France) 1863
Matches First modern friction sulphur matches. John Walker (Britain) 1827. **Safety matches**. J. E. Lundström (Sweden) 1852
Micrometer William Gascoigne (Britain) 1638
Microscope compound Zacharias Jansen (Netherlands) 1590
Miners' safety lamp Humphrey Davy (Britain) 1815
Monorail Louis Brennan (ireland) 1909
Morse code Samuel F. B. Morse (United States) 1838

Above
1 A Sholes and Glidden typewriter which bore the name Remington.
2 Samuel Colt's revolver, 1871.
3 A decorative oriental umbrella.

Mouth-organ Buschmann (Germany) 1821
Motor-car Karl Benz (Germany) 1885
Motor-cycle Edward Butler (Britain) 1884
Neon light tubular Georges Claude (France) 1911
Nylon W. H. Carothers (United States) 1938
Paper-making machine Francois Robert (France) 1798
Parachute The first descent from by André Garnerin (France) 1797
Parking meter C. C. Magee (United States) 1935
Penicillin Alexander Fleming (Britain) 1928
Phonograph Later to become the gramophone or record-player. Thomas Edison (United States) 1877
Photography Joseph N. Nièpce (France) made a photograph on a metal plate in 1826. He and Louis Daguerre developed photographic process in 1829. Daguerre produced first daguerrotype in 1839
Piano Bartolommeo Cristofori (Italy) 1709
Pneumatic tyre Robert Thompson (Britain) 1845
Polythene P. H. Fawcett (Britain) 1933
Postage stamps Rowland Hill (Britain) 1840
Pressure cooker Denis Papin (France) 1679
Printing Movable type was probably used by the Chinese in the 7th century but the first practical use of it was by Johannes Gutenberg (Germany) 1454
Radar Robert Watson-Watt (Britain) 1935
Radio-telescope Karl Jansky (United States) 1931. First dish-type Grote Reber (United States) 1937
Radium Pierre and Marie Curie (France) 1898
Revolver Colt's first patent 1836 (U.S.)
Razor electric Jacob Schick (United States) 1931
Razor safety King C. Gillette (United States) 1895
Safety-pin Walter Hunt (United States) 1849
Screw propeller J. Ressel (Italy) 1826
Seed drill Jethro Tull (Britain) 1701
Sewing machine Elias Howe (United States) 1845. First practical machine by Isaac Singer (United States) 1851
Sextant navigational John Hadley (Britain) 1731
Slide-rule circular William Oughtred (Britain) 1622
Spectacles Mentioned by Roger Bacon in 1268 and by Marco Polo in 1270. Also attributed to Alexander de Spina (Italy) 1285
Spectroscope Gustave Kirchoff and Robert Bunsen (Germany) 1861
Spinning frame Some authorities claim this for Thomas Highs (Britain) but is generally credited to Richard Arkwright (Britain) 1769
Spinning jenny Again this is claimed by Thomas Highs in 1764 but James Hargreaves (Britain) introduced his improved jenny in 1767
Spinning mule Samuel Crompton (Britain) 1774
Stainless steel Henry Brearley (Britain) 1914
Steam-engine atmospheric First practical model by Thomas Newcomen (Britain) 1705
Steam-engine condenser James Watt (Britain) 1765
Steam locomotive Richard Trevithick (Britain) 1803
Steam road carriage Nicolas Cugnot (France) 1769 (not successful). Richard Trevithick (Britain) 1801
Steam-ship John Fitch (United States) 1787 and William Symington (Britain) 1788
Steam turbine Charles Parsons (Britain) 1884
Steel converter Henry Bessemer (Britain) 1856
Stethoscope René Laënnec (France) 1816
Tank military Ernest Swinton (Britain) 1916
Telegraph electric railway Wheatstone and Cooke (Britain) 1837
Telephone Alexander Graham Bell (Britain/United States) 1876. Also magnetic telephone by Phillip Reis (Germany) 1860
Telescope refracting Hans Lippershey (Netherlands) 1608
Telescope reflecting Isaac Newton (Britain) 1669
Television John Logie Baird (Britain) first demonstrated television in 1926
Thermometer Attributed to Galileo (Italy) 1595
Transformer electric Joseph Henry (United States) 1829 and independently Michael Faraday (Britain) 1830
Transistor Bardeen, Brattain and Shockley (United States) 1948
Tuning fork John Shore (Britain) 1711
Typewriter First commercially successful machine. Sholes and Glidden (United States) 1874
Umbrella Samuel Fox (British) 1852
Vaccination Edward Jenner (Britain) 1796
Vacuum flask James Dewar (Britain) 1892
Washing machine First self-controlled model. Alva J. Fisher (United States) 1907
Watch (The Nuremberg Egg) Peter Henlein (Germany) 1504
Wireless telegraphy Guglielmo Marconi (Italy) 1895
X-ray tube Wilhelm Röntgen (Germany) 1895
Zip fastener W. L. Judson (United States) 1891

Medical science

Nobody knows when medicine began. As long as there have been men there have been wounds to heal and illnesses to cure, and men have tried as best they could to heal and cure them. In this way the history of medicine ought to begin with the history of man. Perhaps it ought to begin even before that, before there were men, because from watching animals today it can be seen that they too make some attempt to cure their hurts. But because we can only guess how animals behaved before man evolved, and because we know so little about medicine amongst primitive men, the proper place to start a history of medicine is in Greece.

Primitive medicine was very much connected with magic and religion. The first people to regard medicine as a science were the Greeks. The poet Homer, writing in the 8th or 9th century BC, tells of two doctors, Machaon and Podalirius, who were the sons of Asclepius, himself an eminent physician. It appears that even in Homer's time doctors were divided into surgeons (who treat injury or disease by manual operation) and physicians (who use medicine and treatment in order to heal), for Machaon seems to have been a surgeon and Podalirius a physician – but we know nothing of their methods. Asclepius was regarded as the god of healing by later writers. His descendants were called the Asclepiads and were believed to have inherited special powers of healing.

Hippocrates of Cos

The first truly scientific doctor, some of whose writings have come down to us, was an Asclepiad: he was Hippocrates of Cos, who was born about 460 BC and is said to have lived for over one hundred years. It is the theory and practice of Hippocrates that still underlies modern medicine. In his writings (some of which may in fact be by other doctors of his circle) is found the still-accepted theory that every disease is subject to natural law just like everything else, and should therefore be carefully observed; and that since all bodies have a natural tendency to recovery the proper duty of medicine is to seek the best ways in which to help it. Doctors today still sometimes take the 'Hippocratic Oath' when they qualify, which binds them always to treat their patients with all the skill they possess, never to betray their patients' secrets, and to live and work honestly and well.

Although the idea was probably that of a later writer of his school, it is Hippocrates who was credited also with the 'Theory of Humours' which

Above In ancient Greece there were a number of temples to Asclepius, the most famous of which was at Epidaurus. At these temples miracles of healing were said to be performed by Asclepius, who became a god to be worshipped by the Greeks.

Asclepius
In classical mythology he was the god of medicine. The son of Apollo, he was supposed to be able to restore the dead to life. His use of this power is said to have angered Zeus, who killed him with a thunderbolt. The Latin form of his name, by which he is perhaps better known, is Aesculapius.

Above The medicine man in a primitive community has great power. He guides the tribe through all its natural disasters. He heals the sick, wards off disease and offers the appropriate rituals to please the gods, so that crops are good and the hunt succeeds.

Above The practice of acupuncture is common in the east, particularly in China and is now sometimes used in the West. Needles are inserted and rotated at various points determined by the illness.

was to dominate medicine in western Europe from his age until the 18th century. The theory stated that the body contains four substances or 'humours' – blood, phlegm, yellow bile (or choler) and black bile (or melancholy). These were associated with the four elements – earth, air, fire and water, of which Aristotle thought all creation was made in different proportions, a doctrine which he derived from the Greek orator-surgeon-magician Empedocles (5th century BC).

The perfectly sane and healthy man was believed to have an exact balance of the humours in his body. This was, admittedly, rare, and most people were characterised by having more of one humour than the rest, which caused them to have the 'complexion' or temperament associated with that particular humour.

Thus there grew up the notion of the 'sanguine man' (sanguine meaning confident and hopeful), the 'phlegmatic man' (meaning cold and not easily excited), the 'choleric man' (meaning angry and excitable), and the 'melancholy man' (meaning depressed and sad). These are 'types' which we still recognise and even refer to today, although the theory behind them is no longer accepted.

Developing from these types of temperament, it followed in the original doctrine that when the humours were ill balanced in a man then his sanity and physical health were greatly affected, and it was the duty of his doctors to bring about a more perfect balance of the humours within him. This was, undoubtedly, the most important and longest-held theory ever produced by ancient medicine.

Early medical schools

The conquests of Alexander the Great in the 4th century BC meant that Greek medical knowledge spread throughout the then-known world, and the first great medical school was started in Egypt, in Alexander's own city of Alexandria. Probably because they practised embalming (which means to preserve the bodies of the dead by use of balms or chemicals), and to do this successfully the 'innards' had to be removed, there was no feeling among Egyptian doctors that it was wrong to dissect, or cut up, dead bodies in order to find out more about anatomy.

The first man to dissect a human body in front of his students was Herophilus (died 290?BC), and he distinguished between arteries and veins (although he was not wholly clear about *why* they are different), and had some idea of the nervous system, recognising the brain as the central organ.

Erasistratus (304?–245?BC) attempted to explain respiration, or breathing, and because he believed that most diseases come from an excess of blood (which he called a plethora), he began the idea of 'bleeding' a patient as a standard treatment for most diseases, a habit which continued to be practised, far more intensively than Erasistratus would have approved, well into the 19th century.

It was the followers of Erasistratus who began what was called the empiric school. They relied not on knowledge of anatomy, but on *experience* based on observation. The three most important things in the empiric school (the so-called tripod) were observation, history (that is recording what had been observed) and judgement by analogy (or comparison) with other similar cases.

Left The reason why the ancient Egyptians took such trouble to preserve the bodies of the dead is because they believed that after death the body had to make a long journey to the next world and only if it arrived in good condition could the spirit re-inhabit it for a new life.

Galen
(AD 130–201) Greek physician. Born at Pergamum in Asia Minor, he studied medicine there and at Smyrna, Corinth and Alexandria. He produced some 500 works on medical and philosophical subjects but most of these have been lost. He gathered so much medical knowledge together that for centuries after all other writers on the subject referred to him as the authority.

This theory too was long-lived, into the 18th century at least, and it was the chief basis on which Roman medicine was founded. This was not surprising for, although the Roman writer Pliny the Elder (AD 23–79) had said rather scornfully that the Romans had got on healthily for 600 years without doctors, they had been in the habit of importing physicians from Greece, at least since sometime in the 3rd century BC.

Roman medicine

The earliest medical work in Latin which we still possess is the *De Medicina* or *Concerning Medicine*, written about AD 30 by Aulus Cornelius Celsus (1st century AD). This is something of a brief history of medicine from the time of Hippocrates, but it also shows how remarkably efficient and up-to-date Roman medical ideas had become, particularly on surgery and the subject of a balanced diet of food.

The Romans, great organisers of the ancient world, were outstanding in the way they arranged their medical services. The army had an efficient system of medical officers and army hospitals. Large towns, by the end of the 1st century AD, had public hospitals and 'National Health' doctors who looked after poor people and were paid by the town.

Possibly because of the way in which Roman doctors seem to have worked as part of a large medical system, few names of famous medical men have come down to us, and of these few only one is of real interest today. He was Claudius Galenus or Galen (AD 130–201), and he was not a native of Rome but of Pergamum in Asia Minor, although he studied medicine at Corinth and Alexandria as well as in the school of his home town. He eventually became physician to the Emperor Marcus Aurelius (AD 121–180) and his writings were to influence medicine for some fifteen centuries.

Above Drawn in the style of a Persian miniature this scene shows the great Arabic physician, Avicenna, surrounded by his disciples. He is often called the Persian Aristotle because of his philosophies. Avicenna's medical thinking took over from Galen and dominated the world for six centuries

Galen's theories

His main theory was that every part of man's body is there for a special and particular purpose, and that it is possible to understand that purpose fully by constant study, and that an understanding of the body will bring an understanding of God's plan in creating it, and so a better understanding of the purpose of all nature.

Galen had learned anatomy on a human skeleton, but for physiology (which means the science of the processes of life in animals and plants) he had to rely on the bodies of cattle, monkeys and pigs. He tried to explain respiration (breathing) and also how the blood came into being and what its function was, and it was here that he made a major, though understandable, mistake, which was accepted as the truth until well into the 17th century. He thought that food when eaten turned into a thick whitish fluid which was carried to the liver where the best part of it was turned into blood, the humours, and the 'natural' or 'vegetable spirits' whose function was to control all the normal bodily processes of growth and nutrition. Vegetable spirits were converted into 'vital spirits' in the heart, and these, Galen believed, kept the body alive. The vital spirits reached the brain and were purified there to become 'animal' (or soul) spirits which, by flowing along the nerves which were thought by Galen to be hollow, allowed the whole body to obey the brain in movement and emotion.

Galen's theories, which were not necessarily his own invention, but were probably derived from all such earlier medical thought as he considered worthy of note, were never seriously questioned by doctors until well into the 17th century. This happened because for a century after his death Galen was still the accepted authority whom no one dared to question. After that, by AD 400, the Christian Church began to oppose both ancient and new medical thought; the first because of its pagan, or non-Christian origins, the second in case it should cause men to question their faith or to treat any form of God's creation – even dead bodies – disrespectfully, by dissecting them to find out more about how they worked. Therefore, for about 800 years medical knowledge slowly declined, although the monastic libraries preserved many ancient medical writings.

Arabic medicine

By the 9th century advances in medical knowledge were once more being made, but they came not from the west, but from the Moslem nations in the east. By the 8th century the Moslems had conquered much of the near east, and had absorbed the surviving system of Greek medicine. Greek manuscripts were translated into Arabic, and Arabic-speaking doctors developed Greek medical ideas along new lines. Arabic translations of the writings of Hippocrates and Galen, with commentaries, were still being printed in Latin translation in

16th-century Europe. Rhazes of Basra (860–932) was still accounted an authority in 16th-century England, and the Persian Avicenna (980–1037) wrote a medical encyclopedia at the beginning of the 11th century which, at the beginning of the 17th century, was still the chief medical text-book in both east and west.

Much of the medical work written in Arabic was that of Jewish doctors living in places conquered by Islam. Of these, perhaps the most famous was Isaac Israili of Kairwan who was born in Egypt about AD 850, and whose study of fevers remained the best text-book on the subject throughout the Middle Ages. In Moslem-dominated Spain there were other outstanding medical men, among them the Arabian, Averroës of Cordova (1126–98) and the Jew, Rabbi Moses ben Maimon, or Maimonides (1135–1204), also born in Cordova, now remembered as a philosopher but more famous then as personal physician to Saladin.

The discoveries of physicians of the Arabian school were made known to the western world by means of Latin translations, for Latin was used by scholars all over Europe, and the names of some of these translators have come down to us. One of them was Constantine (died 1087), who was called 'the African'. He may have been a Jew or a Moslem, certainly he was a convert to Christianity, and he came to the medical school at Salerno bringing with him a number of medical books in Arabic which he translated there into Latin.

At this time Salerno was probably the most famous medical school in Europe, and was especially remarkable in having both Jews and Gentiles together on its staff and among its students. Even more surprisingly there were women among the lecturers and professors. The first woman doctor of history was called Trotula, and was a professor at Salerno in the 11th century.

The Middle Ages

By the 13th century a number of new universities and new medical schools were being founded in Europe. Bologna opened a medical school at its university in about 1160, and there the practice of dissection first became a regular part of the students' work. Montpellier in France had another famous medical school, and the first British physicians to gain an international reputation were associated with this university. These included Gilbert, known as 'the Englishman', who was writing in about 1290, and Bernard Gordon, a Scottish professor at Montpellier in the early 14th century.

The period from the 13th to the 16th centuries was not one of great new discoveries, but of small ones which were nevertheless important. Anatomy became much more accurate, surgery more widely practised and a little safer. The habit of making and keeping 'case-histories' of patients was started by doctors at this time,

Above This picture shows an apothecary dispensing medicine in the Middle Ages, and it is copied from a medieval painting. The apothecary was recognised as a person who carried out the art of mixing drugs for medicinal purposes as long ago as the 12th century. In England the Society of Apothecaries has the right to license medical practitioners.

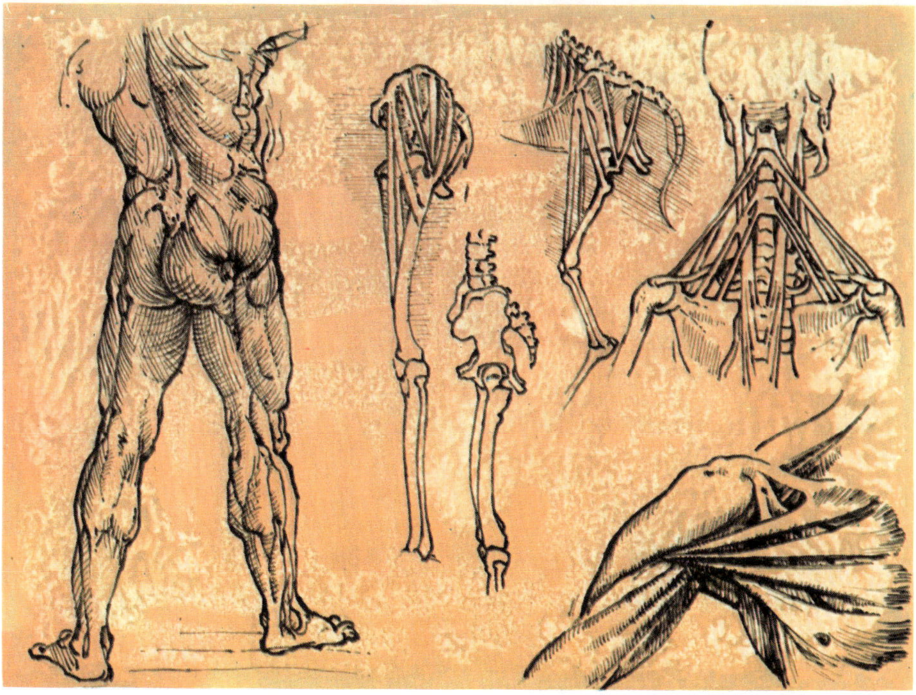

Right Among the many drawings of Leonardo da Vinci there are those which portray human anatomy in great detail. Leonardo is said to have dissected over thirty corpses to make drawings for a massive work on anatomy that he planned. Certainly his art benefited from intimate knowledge of the structure of the human body.

Above During the time of the great plague epidemics in Europe, surgeons would walk the streets clad in protective masks and wearing thick gloves in an effort to ward off infection.

some of which were of great interest to medical men of later generations. It was, too, the period of the great plague epidemics called the Black Death, which killed about a quarter of the whole population of Europe, and which all the medical knowledge of the time was powerless to prevent.

The revival of learning

The next stage in the history of medicine is that of the Renaissance, or the Revival of Learning, and the 'learning' was that of Greece and Rome. It was brought about when Constantinople fell to the forces of Islam in 1453 and numbers of Greek scholars fled west, carrying as many of their books and manuscripts with them as they could.

They brought them first to Italy, where scholars eagerly sought the knowledge they contained and the new areas of scholarship they opened to them. Gradually this enthusiasm for the 'new learning' spread westward until all Europe was infected by it. The spread of learning was encouraged even more by the invention of printing halfway through the 15th century, which meant that books became cheaper than ever before and could be circulated in far greater numbers, so that scholars had much better opportunities for study.

In medicine the Revival of Learning first brought about the publication of the Greek medical texts of antiquity. Although these were of interest they did little more than clarify and expand what was already known. In the collection and preparation of these texts one of the greatest names was that of Thomas Linacre (1460?–1524). He was physician to Henry VIII and to many other eminent men of his time, and he is remembered as the founder of the Royal College of Physicians in London, to which he left his library and his house.

During this period the interest in anatomy and physiology which had marked the ancient world was renewed, and for this interest the improved conditions in most medical schools gave greater scope. One result was the first really reliable book of anatomy, written by the Belgian anatomist Andreas Vesalius (1514–64) at Padua in 1543 and beautifully illustrated. This book was reprinted again and again. It was used in almost every country of Europe, and most of the medieval books on anatomy were forgotten.

Medical books

The study of botany became more systematic and, as a result, the existing list of drugs and their uses, called a pharmacopoeia, was considerably enlarged. The rapid spread of printed books meant that famous doctors such as the Frenchman Ambroise Paré (1517–90) could become internationally known by their publications. Improved techniques in the making of metal instruments led to an improvement in surgery, though this was still very hazardous. Perhaps the most important development of the period was the beginnings of a theory about infection and the spread of disease made by Girolamo Fracastoro (1483–1553) of Verona.

But the Revival of Learning had also brought about a deep split between doctors who still followed the Arabian school of medicine and those who thought that the ancient Greek tradition was the better one. Now, in the first quarter of the 16th century, a third course was presented by the Swiss physician, alchemist and philosopher Paracelsus (1493–1541).

He began a series of lectures at Basle by publicly burning the books of Avicenna, and he declared that his shoe-buckles knew more than Galen. He said that medicine should not deal in a set of man-made rules but in knowledge of all creation. He considered the human body to be the 'microcosm' (meaning a little universe or world) which mirrored the 'macrocosm' (the great universe itself), and that all diseases were spiritual not physical in origin and must be treated by something which would attack the spiritual root of the disease – not its mere physical symptoms. The drugs he used in this were most often derived from mineral or chemical sources, so that his followers were often called 'Chemical Physicians'.

The disciples of Paracelsus were hated and condemned by other doctors of the time, but his theories continued to be held until, in the 17th century, they were expanded and adapted and eventually became part of accepted medical thought.

New inventions

Between about 1590 and 1640 the science of medicine was dominated by what has been called the 'empiric' method, which, as in the time of Erasistratus, meant obtained from experiment and experience. Experimental physics had progressed enormously with such men as Galileo, and new medical techniques were often the indirect result. The thermometer first became possible because of the experiments of physicists. The importance of the pulse rate was realised and accurate methods of timing the pulse were invented. Doctors became interested in the effects different foods had upon health and now found means to assess them. From the somewhat vague theories of Paracelsus, the Flemish chemist Jean van Helmont (1577–1644) managed to construct a fairly successful system of practical medicine. Above all, in 1628, the English physician William Harvey (1578–1657) published his discovery of the circulation of the blood.

Until now, Galen's theories, which included a belief that there was a double system in the blood stream, had never been seriously questioned. Now Harvey discovered that there is only one system which circulates throughout the body. This discovery did not only disprove the old theory, but it also made some people begin to question the old ideas about the humours and the spirits, though it was many years before they were finally abandoned.

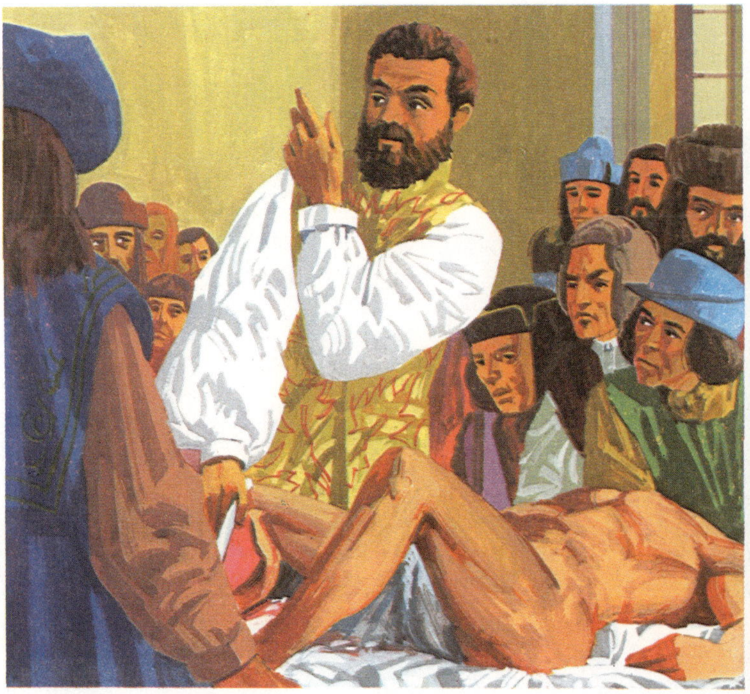

Above Andreas Vesalius dissecting a corpse during a lecture given at the University of Padua in Italy where he was professor of surgery from 1537 to 1544.

William Harvey (1578–1657) English physician. Discovered the circulation of the blood. Took degrees in medicine at Padua and Cambridge in 1602. Settled in London and became a physician. Published his treatise on the circulatory system in 1628, and publicly demonstrated his theory at Nuremberg in 1636. Physician to James I and Charles I, and was with Charles at the battle of Edgehill during the Civil War.

Above The Great Fire of London lasted four days and nights in September, 1666. It broke out near London Bridge and destroyed all but one sixth of the city. Nearly the whole of medieval London was wiped out. One good effect it had was to help defeat the Great Plague of 1665 as it swept away a large area of overcrowded, narrow and insanitary streets. Although some 100,000 people were made homeless it is believed that only about a dozen people were burned

The earliest form of the microscope had been invented by the beginning of the 17th century, and by 1661 Marcello Malpighi (1628–94) of Bologna had used it to show that the arterial blood reaches the veins by tiny tubes called capillaries, a fact not understood by Harvey. Anton van Leeuwenhoek (1632–1723), a Dutch scientist, first demonstrated red blood corpuscles with his microscope and also made other remarkable discoveries, including seeing bacteria, though he had little idea of their function.

All these new discoveries meant that 17th-century doctors split themselves into schools or factions, depending on which discoveries they accepted and regarded as the most important. There were five main schools, which varied between those who rejected new discoveries and stuck to the ideas of the ancients, and those who tried to explain life and the body in mechanical terms so that disease too became a mechanical fault.

Great doctors

Although this was an age of many and conflicting theories, it was also an age of great doctors. We have already referred to William Harvey's great discovery of the circulation of the blood and the effect it had on old theories. But new discoveries were being made about other parts of the body too, by such doctors as Malpighi, John Mayow (1640–79) and Gian Borelli (1608–79).

A number of major discoveries about the nervous system were made by Charles Lepois (1563–1633), sometimes called by the Latin form of his name Carolus Piso. The ancient writers had all described hysteria as arising from the stomach, and they thought it was confined to women. Lepois showed that men as well as women could suffer from hysteria, and said that it comes not from the stomach but from the head, and therefore involves the whole of the central nervous system.

The first complete treatise on the nervous system was published in 1664 by the English physician Thomas Willis (1621–73), and in it he supported many of Lepois's observations. He also showed that the nerves are not channels, as had previously been believed, but are quite solid. Clearly he no longer thought that actual fluid ran through the nerves, but rather that they were the invisible means by which the senses convey impressions – and this is very much closer to the actual case.

The work of various scientists and mathematicians brought new knowledge of the eye and of the mechanics of sight. In 1683 Joseph Duverney (1648–1730), the French professor of anatomy, published his book on the ear and hearing which was to remain a classic for many generations. There were also many discoveries concerning the reproduction of animals, those of R. de Graaf (1641–73) being perhaps the most famous.

Thomas Sydenham

All these men made great discoveries about the physiology, or working, of the body, but the man who was perhaps the greatest doctor of the age in the sense in which most of us think of that word, that is as someone who cures us when we are ill, was Thomas Sydenham (1624–89), an English physician. It was Sydenham who put forward the theory still accepted today that a disease is the result of the body trying to get rid of something harmful to it; that the symptoms are, so to speak, evidence of the fight going on between the body and whatever is attacking it.

The function of the doctor is therefore to help the body in its struggle rather than to attempt to cure the symptoms – which may in themselves be evidence of the success of the body in its fight rather than of the disease itself. Sydenham believed that the cause of disease is 'putrid matter' floating about in the air, but he never reached the idea that there are as many different kinds of 'putrid matter' as there are diseases, and he had no idea that infection is caused by living organisms rather than those that are not alive.

But modern medicine was, in some ways, not far off. In 1657 Christopher Wren (1632–1723) suggested that medicines might act more rapidly if they were injected directly into the veins, and this was at once tried, anticipating the inoculation methods of today. And in 1665 a doctor called Richard Lower showed that patients in a very weak state could sometimes be helped by a transfusion of blood. At first animals' blood was tried, but later in the 17th century young people became the first blood donors, and the practice became accepted in Europe in general.

Thomas Sydenham (1624–89) English physician. Left Oxford, where he was studying, to fight as a captain in Cromwell's army during the Civil War. Severely wounded at battle of Worcester. From about 1663 he practised in London. He was one of the greatest independent medical thinkers of his time. He introduced new treatments for smallpox and fevers.

The 18th century

The schools into which 17th-century medicine was divided were few compared with the number which arose in the 18th century. At the beginning of the century a number of doctors began what was later to be called the school of organicism. Briefly, this school believed that the most important thing in medicine is to study the 'mechanism of phenomena', or the

Above The arms of the English Royal College of Surgeons, founded in 1800.

Albrecht Haller (1708–77) Swiss botanist, anatomist and physiologist. In 1728 began the collection of plants which was to form the basis of his work on the flora of Switzerland. Started a medical practice in Berne, 1729. He was given the chair of medicine, anatomy, botany and surgery in the new university at Göttingen in 1736. As well as his large bibliographies of botany, anatomy and medicine he also wrote philosophical romances.

way in which the human body works in health and in disease, and by means of observation and reason to enlist the help of nature in restoring the patient to health.

Another school of the 17th century developed into the humoral school of the 18th century. They held to Galen's original (though wrong) theory that the symptoms which a disease produces *are* the disease, and not merely the signs of it. As their name suggests, they also held to the theory of humours, so they divided all illnesses into those affecting the humours and those affecting the 'solid' parts of the body. Some went even further and said that *all* diseases come from an upset in the humours.

The nervous system

The great advances in knowledge of the nervous system made in the 17th century were continued into the 18th, but now that the work had progressed from an exploration of what the nervous system is, to the theory of how it works, this progress included a good deal of guess-work. As we have seen, Thomas Willis, by showing that nerves are not tubes or canals, had exploded the old theory of a 'nervous fluid' which conveyed sensation. The fact that electricity had been discovered at about this time meant that a new explanation was to hand. Sensation was now believed to be conveyed along the solid nerves by a 'nervous force' which travelled just like electricity along a wire, and in the same way could not be 'seen' by the senses.

However, a most important contribution was made to medical thought by the Swiss anatomist, Albrecht von Haller (1708–77) when he showed that only the nerves in man are *sensitive*, that is only the nerves transmit messages to the brain; but that only the muscular tissues are *irritable*, which means they automatically contract (or shorten) when they come into contact with any object. This made, for the first time, the distinction between movement or action controlled by the brain – or willed – and reflex or involuntary action, as for example the instant contraction, or moving away, from a hot iron or pin-prick. And this distinction destroyed the old idea of all men's actions being governed by 'animal' or soul spirits. Von Haller made little of this discovery, and it was left to his successors to develop it; and 'irritability' in particular was used as the basis of many strange theories which were fashionable for a short time.

The British physician John Brown (1735–88) is remembered for his 'Brunonian Theory', which was to be of immense importance for over a quarter of a century. Brown believed that all life needs an outside force or stimulus without which it cannot continue, and which operates upon what he called the 'excitability' of the living organism. As long as the stimulus acts upon the excitability to the correct degree, healthy life results; but if the stimulus becomes either too strong or too weak then disease follows, and this can only be cured by correcting the degree of stimulation.

The key to life

The 18th-century medical movement which became a school called organicism believed that 'vital movement' is the most important thing in the functioning of all life. Thus, in man, this school tried to understand health, disease, and even life itself in terms of the working of the separate bodily organs, and they thought of one human life as the sum total of the individual lives of each of his organs.

From these basic beliefs the vitalist school developed, believing that while movement is the key to life, there are two kinds of movement, the one due to the 'thinking soul' (voluntary action) and the other to the 'principle of life'. It was this principle, according to the vitalists, which was responsible for all other bodily activity such as sensitivity, digestion and so on.

The most famous doctor of the vitalist school was undoubtedly the Scot, John Hunter (1728–93). For him, the 'vital principle' was to life as magnetic force is to the magnet. Hunter put an end to the old quarrel between the humoralists and their opponents the 'solidists' by saying that the proper functioning of the vital force in any body depends on the harmonious way in which solids and liquids are combined. Disease, for Hunter, was not a natural change of the humours or solids, as Galen had

Left The Chelsea Royal Hospital in London was founded by Charles II in 1682. The main buildings were erected by three different architects, Christopher Wren, Robert Adam and John Soane. The soldierly Chelsea pensioners who live there are a familiar sight with their scarlet frock coats which they wear in summer.

John Hunter (1728–93) Scottish surgeon and anatomist. Studied surgery at Chelsea Hospital and St Bartholomew's, London. In 1763, after service in the Army, he started practising surgery. Fellow of the Royal Society 1767 and in 1776 appointed surgeon-extraordinary to King George III. Built an anatomical museum in London 1784 and when he died his collection was bought by the nation in 1795 and presented to the Royal College of Surgeons.

said, but a morbid or unnatural action which caused such changes. Hunter himself never received the credit due to him for his medical theories, possibly because of his outstanding fame as a surgeon, and it was the Frenchman Marie Bichat (1771–1802) who was thought of as the leader of the vitalist school in his own time.

Treatment of diseases

In the last years of the 18th century came the only one of these movements still active today, and the only one which cannot be traced directly to earlier theories. This was the homoeopathic method, begun by the German physician Samuel Hahnemann (1755-1843). Hahnemann disregarded the idea which had dominated almost all medical practice from ancient times, namely that treatment *opposes* particular symptoms, as for example that a runny nose should be treated with some drug which will dry it up. He developed the revolutionary idea called in Latin *similia similibus curentur* (let likes be treated by likes) – that is, that drugs should be given which would act upon a healthy person to produce symptoms similar to those the patient was suffering from.

Hahnemann had, in fact, hit on the theory on which modern immunology is based (immunology is the practice of giving a person protection against a disease by injecting germs of that disease). His system included some odd-sounding notions but his methods produced some very remarkable results. In 1854, during a cholera epidemic this fact was borne out when the death rate of the London Homoeopathic Hospital, which used his methods of treatment, was 16·4 as against 51·8 of the other metropolitan hospitals. Alone of 18th-century theories homoeopathy is still practised all over Europe and in America.

Techniques of surgery

These were the chief 18th-century theories. In actual discoveries much of the work done in the first half of the century consisted of a much closer examination of some 17th-century

Right This drawing of a sculpture of Edward Jenner shows the occasion when he first inoculated a boy with cowpox virus in 1796. The boy was afterwards found to be immune from small-pox and the practice of vaccination began to be accepted all over Europe. A society named after the inventor was formed to promote it. Jenner was born at Berkeley in Gloucestershire, England, and after studying under John Hunter in London he returned to his home town to practise medicine and there he remained until his death in 1823.

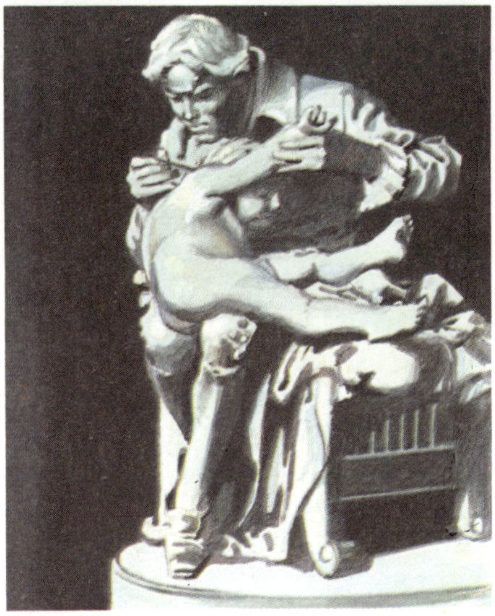

discoveries. Thus the heart, the organs of respiration as well as the nervous system were further studied, and the reproductive system was at last explained in detail. In the second half of the century the chemist Lavoisier finally dispelled the idea of any unseen 'vital spirits' or mysterious 'vital force'. Much work was done on the brain, also on the gastric (stomach) juices and the actual process of digestion.

Surgery was still often fatal, and there were as yet no anaesthetics, but surgical techniques were improving with the growth of other medical knowledge. Comparatively early in the century an English chemist Stephen Hales (1677-1761) discovered that the pressure of the blood can be measured and that it changes with different conditions. Later, the Breton doctor René Laënnec (1781-1826) invented the stethoscope, and by the beginning of the 19th century a medical examination by a competent doctor must have differed in only a few respects from a similar experience today. The disease of scurvy, which had been responsible for the deaths of many sailors, was conquered in 1753 when James Lind (1716-94), a Scottish naval physician, showed that it could easily be prevented if seamen were given a constant supply of fresh fruit or lemon juice.

Public health became important again for the first time since the decline of the Roman Empire. In the first quarter of the 18th century 154 hospitals were built in the British Isles. People began to realise the importance of hygiene to public health, and in the second half of the century many large towns had installed some system of sanitation and a public water supply.

Right Louis Pasteur, the great French chemist, gave his name to the process of pasteurisation. This is the treatment of milk to reduce the number of tiny organisms it contains. The milk is heated for a period and then cooled rapidly, which results in harmful bacteria being killed. The picture shows a modern plant where milk is pasteurised.

Quarantine regulations

Quarantine regulations were then put into force at sea-ports in Britain to avoid the spread of epidemic diseases, especially plague. From the beginning of the century inoculation against smallpox had been practised in Europe by using blood taken directly from someone suffering a mild attack of the disease – as had been the custom from early times in the east. By 1780, thanks to the efforts of the famous traveller Mary Wortley Montagu (1689-1762), this was generally done in Britain. It was superseded in 1796 by vaccination, introduced by Edward Jenner (1749-1823), who discovered that to inoculate with the mild cowpox virus was far safer and just as effective against smallpox as the older method. It was with this major discovery and the beginning of what was later to be called preventive medicine that the century ended.

The 19th century

The 19th century continued the work on public health which the 18th century had begun, and in this it was very much helped by new discoveries of a purely scientific nature which were made in its early years. The actual structures of the kinds of

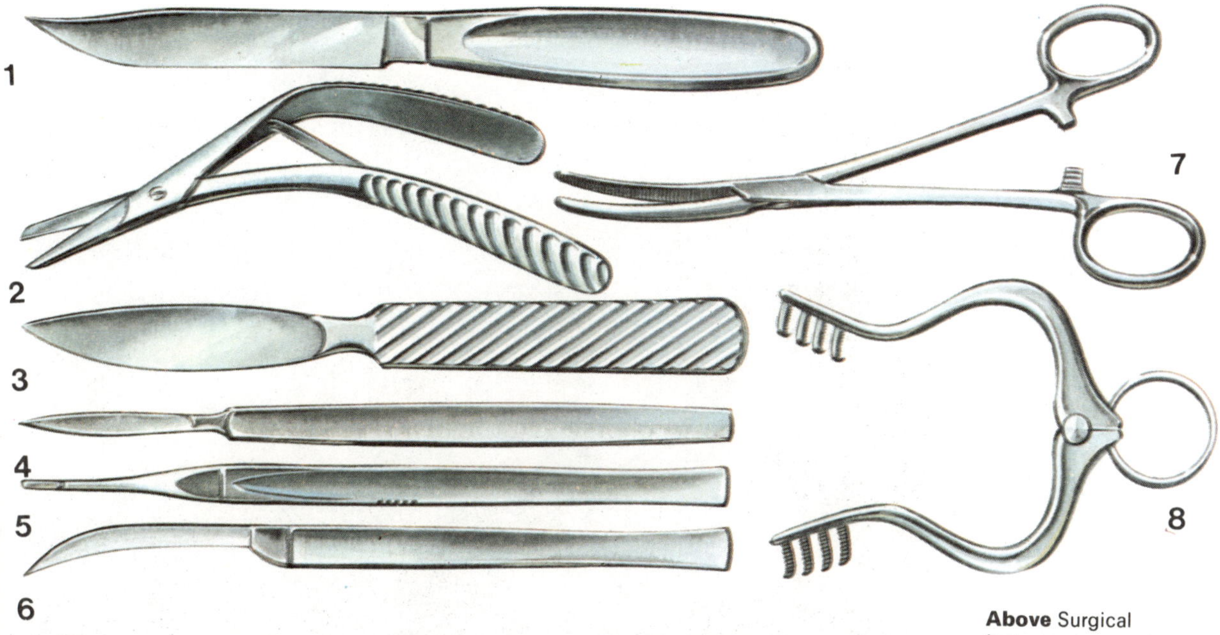

Above Surgical instruments seen in this drawing are **1** amputation knife. **2** stainless steel scissors for ligatures. **3** ankle joint knife. **4** and **5** are nickle-plated knives, with serrations on the handle of the second which serves as a guide, showing the cutting edge when the blade is hidden. **6** bistoury, a narrow knife for making incisions. **7** artery forceps. **8** self-retaining retractor. These all date from modern times, but even in the ancient world surgeons employed instruments, some of which are recognisable as crude forerunners of modern implements.

individual cell which make up all the tissues of the human body were first seen and then listed. The German pathologist Rudolph Virchow (1821-1902) said that 'the body is a cell state in which every cell is a citizen', and from this grew the idea of disease as a civil war among the citizens.

Another and very important discovery was that many diseases come from germs which invade the body and multiply in it. Most important here were the discoveries of Louis Pasteur, who discovered that many diseases, not only in man but in other living things, are the result of microbes, which are minute living organisms.

Pasteur discovered that to inject a living creature with a very weakened preparation or 'culture' of some of these disease-producing microbes would prevent that creature from ever developing the disease itself, and thus he discovered the new science of immunology. Vaccination was, of course, a part of immunology, but until Pasteur's discovery it had never been understood or regarded as useful except in the case of smallpox. Pasteur's work was added to by Robert Koch (1843-1910), a German bacteriologist (someone who studies bacteria or microbes), who managed to isolate and identify the microbes responsible for tuberculosis, cholera and sleeping-sickness.

Surgery in the 19th century advanced dramatically with the two discoveries of anaesthesia and antisepsis. An anaesthetic is a substance which makes the patient unable to feel pain. The first anaesthetic used was ether gas, but in 1847 James Young Simpson (1811-70) began the use of chloroform, which almost at once changed the nature of surgical techniques. Until this time a surgeon's most important skill was his speed. Now, with the patient asleep and insensible, neatness and care were possible, and more complicated operations were performed. By 1884 it was found that some operations could be done with the aid of a 'local' anaesthetic, usually cocaine, injected into one part of the patient's body.

Antiseptics

Antisepsis was the discovery of the English surgeon Joseph Lister (1827-1912). Before this, thousands of patients who were operated on, sometimes in quite minor ways, died a few days after the operation from an infection of the wound which resulted in blood poisoning. Lister had followed the work of Pasteur, and realised that such an infection was the result of microbes or germs carried in the air or on the hands or instruments of the surgeon. To cleanse the air of these he sprayed his operating theatre with carbolic acid and used this on the wound itself and on his hands. Later, he discovered other 'anti-septics' and found that heat is the best way of

Right A scene inside the hospital at Scutari during the Crimean War. Within the first six months of Florence Nightingale's arrival, with her team of nurses, the death rate in hospitals was reduced from 42 to 2 per cent.

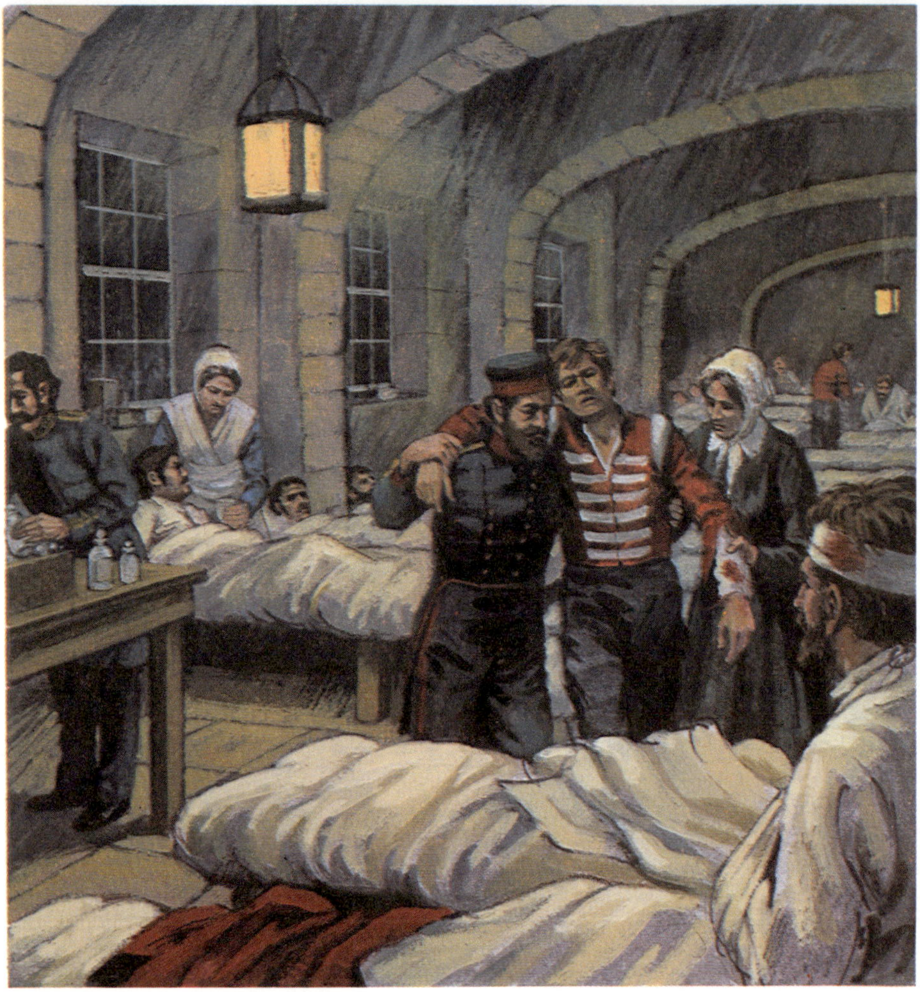

Florence Nightingale (1820–1910) British hospital reformer. Took an interest in hospital work when she was still young. Trained as a nurse at Kaiserwerth and Paris. When Crimean War broke out in 1854, she offered to organise a nursing department at Scutari. With a staff of 37 nurses she had some 10,000 men under her care. The bad sanitary conditions in Army hospitals caused her to devote her time to the improvement of nursing and general hospital conditions.

sterilising instruments and dressings. The results of Lister's discovery were dramatic, and surgery became safer than had ever been dreamed possible.

Working along the same lines as Lister, although independently, the Hungarian Ignaz Semmelweiss (1818-65) made the same discovery about the transmission of germs and was responsible for reducing the death rate among young mothers in Europe. These three men – Pasteur, Lister and Semmelweiss – probably saved more lives than had the discoveries of all the other scientists who lived before them.

The 19th century also saw the apparent conquest of some tropical diseases, and for a time areas of the tropics were safer to live in. Unfortunately, many of these diseases are difficult to eradicate. For example, malaria has been supposedly wiped out a number of times, only to reappear again.

First nursing services

Another great life-saving development took place in the 19th century with the revolution in nursing. In early times we have little evidence about the profession of nursing, but from the Dark Ages until the Reformation it was a task undertaken by monks and nuns, and all hospitals were religious institutions. This continued in countries where there was no religious upheaval, but in England, Germany and other countries where the monasteries and convents were destroyed the profession of nursing reached a very low ebb and there was no difference in status, nor often in skill, between a nurse and a general servant.

The first signs of change came from Germany where in 1836 Theodor Fliedner (1800-64) started an order of 'deaconesses', properly trained in nursing and hospital management. In

England, a few nursing orders of Anglican nuns were founded between 1840 and 1850, but the real revolution came with the work of the celebrated Englishwoman, Florence Nightingale (1820-1910). She had studied with the deaconesses at Kaiserwerth in Germany, and when the Crimean War began in 1854 she organised a nursing service to deal with sick and wounded soldiers, whose plight till then had been horrible. She returned famous from the Crimea and started a school for nurses and a nurses' home at St Thomas's Hospital in London, and with great rapidity other hospitals followed suit. Before the end of the century nursing was thought of as one of the noblest professions a woman could enter, instead of one of the most degrading.

The 20th century

The 20th century has already seen some astounding developments in medicine, and in some ways more progress seems to have been made in the past decades than in any previous century. Whether this is the case, only the future can tell.

The greatest discovery at the beginning of the century came when Marie Curie and her husband Pierre discovered the radioactive element radium. This was really a chemical rather than a medical discovery, but from it has developed the whole complicated science of radiotherapy which is of such importance in the treatment of cancer.

Another discovery which has had an immense effect on medicine, especially on diagnosis (that is identifying a disease through its symptoms), was that of Wilhelm Röntgen, who found and developed X-rays and began the science of radiography.

The science of chemotherapy was begun by the German bacteriologist Paul Ehrlich (1854-1915). This is treatment by means of chemical remedies which destroy the harmful bacteria in the body without damaging the living tissue which they are attacking. Ehrlich's success was moderate, but the discovery of new drugs in 1933 and 1953 produced a small revolution in methods of treatment.

This in itself might have been considered the most important dis-

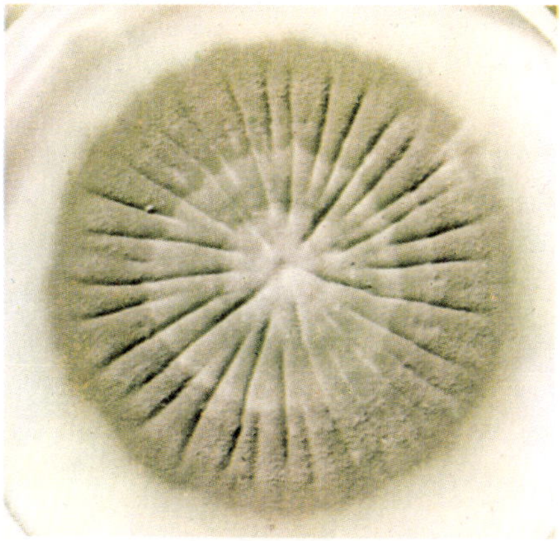

Left A close-up photograph of the mould, *penicillium notatum* (penicillin). It prevents the growth of many bacteria harmful to man.

covery of the century, had it not been for the discovery of effective antibiotic drugs (an antibiotic is a substance produced from moulds and bacteria which can kill or prevent the growth of other harmful substances), which happened at almost the same time. Pasteur, in 1887, had noticed that the growth of the bacteria which caused anthrax (a deadly disease which affects sheep and cattle but can be caught by man) was prevented by that of certain other bacteria. It was not until 1928 that the Scottish bacteriologist Alexander Fleming (1881-1955) found, quite by accident, that *Penicillium notatum*, one of the family of moulds which includes those of blue cheese and jam, was particularly deadly to many forms of harmful bacteria. This discovery of penicillin was taken further by Howard Florey and his work, together with that of other scientists, brought penicillin into general use during the Second World War. Now a huge range of antibiotics is available, and more are being developed all the time.

Huge strides have been made in understanding how the cells of the body work and what substances they produce. Some of these, called hormones, carry messages around the body and regulate its functions. Cortisone and insulin are examples of hormones. Many of these are now manufactured and used to treat illnesses.

Interferons are substances which seem to be produced when the body is attacked by viruses. Some can now be made and scientists think they may prove useful in countering a range of diseases. They are among countless new drugs which are being developed.

Alexander Fleming (1881–1955) Scottish bacteriologist. He qualified as a surgeon in London. He was the first to use anti-typhoid vaccines on human beings. In 1928 discovered penicillin, but had to wait eleven years before it was perfected. In 1945 he shared the Nobel Prize for medicine with Howard Florey and Ernest Chain, who developed the way to produce penicillin.

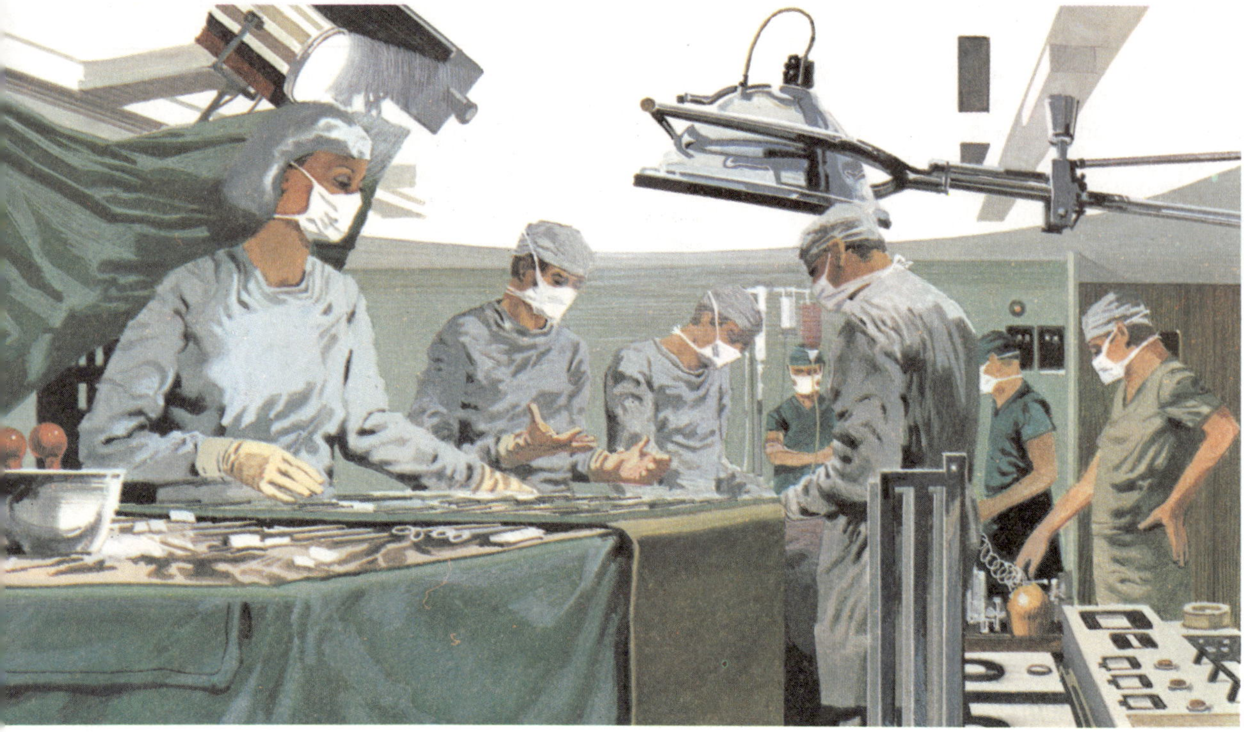

Above The scene inside a modern hospital during an operation. There are many challenges still before the surgeon, notably an effective remedy for cancer.

The body can produce a host of antibodies to counteract disease, each one specific to a certain disease. Preparations of antibodies (known as monoclonals, because each contains only one sort of antibody), can now be used to diagnose certain diseases and help cure them.

Modern aids to health

Immunisation, once used only against smallpox, is now available against a large number of diseases, from measles to plague. Anaesthesia has been made safer and more comfortable by the development of what are called barbiturate drugs, and there is a vast new range of pain-killers and mild sedative drugs which calm the nerves and prevent worry.

Nowadays blood transfusions are a matter of course, and hospitals carry 'banks' of blood grouped according to the main blood groups so that a patient can always be given blood of a group which will match his own.

In the past few years machines have been invented to which a patient's blood circulation can be connected, and which will pump the blood round the body so that the heart can be temporarily stopped for operation or observation. Kidney machines are available for some patients whose own kidneys have ceased to filter the impurities from their blood, and who would die within a few days without the help of the machine. 'Iron lungs' are used to make breathing possible for people whose chest muscles have been paralysed by disease or accident.

Surgeons are now able to graft skin from one part of a patient's body to cover another part where the skin has been destroyed by burns or other damage. This, the most important aspect of plastic surgery, was further developed during the Second World War to repair the damage done to airmen whose planes caught fire.

Other kinds of grafting that are now done successfully include corneal grafts in which the cornea (the transparent film which covers the front of the eye) is taken from the eye of a dead 'donor' and transplanted into the eye of a patient whose own cornea has had to be removed; and kidney grafts where a living donor freely gives one of his kidneys to save the life of a patient whose own kidneys have failed to work.

Transplant surgery

It is with this aspect of 'transplant surgery' that medicine is concerned deeply about today. Surgeons have discovered that kidneys can be grafted successfully where donor and recipient are closely related but, if they are not, the patient's body rejects the new organ. In 1967 Christian Barnard, a South African surgeon, performed the first heart transplant. Similarly, a transplanted heart may be rejected by the patient's body. Drugs are available to reduce the patient's reaction to the foreign organ, but these may leave the patient susceptible to disease. Progress has also been made in matching organs, so that patients now receive organs which are closer to their own. However, technical problems remain, and this surgery also raises moral problems.

Many challenges remain, including the discovery of a safe and wholly effective remedy for cancer, although constant progress is being made in overcoming this disease. In some ways scientists in the 20th century may have made too much progress too rapidly, for recent happenings suggest that some of the new drugs are more powerful and even more dangerous than their discoverers realised. But never before have so many lives been saved, and never has life been so free from disease as it is in the West today.

Psychology

Psychology, the science which studies the mind, is usually thought of as the newest of the medical sciences, but its beginnings are as much in the past as those of medicine.

It was Aristotle who divided the senses into five categories – sight, hearing, touch, taste and smell – and said that by means of our senses we feel pleasure and pain. He divided ideas into three kinds and stated that of all living beings only men *think*, and he speculated on the connection between mind and body, and mind and reason – and Aristotle died in 322 BC.

Hippocrates and Galen both held the view that men can be divided according to temperament, and St Augustine (AD 353-430) pointed out that man can obtain knowledge only through the senses.

After this the science developed little until the Dutch physician Johann Weyer (1516-88) attacked the standard book of his time on witchcraft, stating that all the illnesses which it attributed to witchcraft came from natural causes. The French philosopher René Descartes (1596-1650) was concerned with the way the mind works, as were many philosophers in the 18th century, who were helped by new knowledge of the anatomy of the brain and nervous system which was acquired at this time. The German philosopher Immanuel Kant (1724-1804) divided the mental faculties into knowing, feeling and willing, which are still part of psychological thought.

In the 19th century psychology became a science in its own right rather than an offshoot of philosophy or medicine, and 'psychological laboratories' were founded in Europe and America. In America the emphasis was on the study of human behaviour, which has been the chief concern of what is called experimental psychology since the beginning of the present century. In psychological medicine the old idea that mental disturbance was the result of some outside force acting on the mind was denied.

Sigmund Freud

The real founder of modern psychology was the Austrian Sigmund Freud (1856-1939). Freud first used

Left Many of the Surrealist paintings of the 20th century, such as this copy of one by Salvador Dali, portray the curious distorted world of dreams which Freud thought so important in his psychological studies.

Sigmund Freud (1856–1939) Austrian doctor and founder of psycho-analysis. Studied medicine in Vienna, then specialised in neurology (the study of the nerves). His great work, *The Interpretation of Dreams* was published in 1900. Freud did not use hypnosis in psycho-analysis but employed the method of free association. In 1910 he founded with Jung the International Psycho-analytical Association. In 1938 he left occupied Austria and settled in London.

Above and **right** Two intelligence tests to end with:
Above: Divide the picture by drawing only straight lines so that there are three hearts, three diamonds and three clubs in each section.
Right: Turn the large triangle upside down by moving three of the small triangles and placing them in different positions.

the method of 'free association', that is of getting the patient to report whatever comes into his mind without leaving anything out. He also analysed his own dreams over a long period and from them developed his ideas about man's unconscious mental struggles.

Psychology applied to the education of children had really begun in the work of Jean Jacques Rousseau (1712-78), a French philosopher who thought that education should bring out a child's individual qualities rather than fill it with unrelated and not very useful facts. The German educationist Friedrich Froebel (1782-1852) had applied these ideas to actual teaching practice, and his methods are still in use today.

By the first quarter of the 19th century psychology had divided into two main branches, one concerned with experiment, the other with the method of introspection which concentrates on inner thoughts and feelings. As the century progressed new movements and schools grew up, as in the case of medicine itself.

Child psychology had begun in the last years of the 19th century, and there was much interest in the possibility of testing intelligence and mental capacity. Test-methods derived from school work and ordinary life were developed and the idea grew up that a child could be graded by comparison with sufficient others of its own age group. Ever since then intelligence tests, aptitude tests and personality tests have been standard practice in many fields where a choice of candidate has to be made.

Cybernetics

It is possible to compare the nervous system in man with computers and calculating machines, and this has inspired the newest development in experimental psychology which is known as cybernetics. This is the name for a science which studies how systems organise themselves and learn. One aim of cybernetics is partly to replace man by machines by producing computers which would be capable of making decisions when presented with all the facts of a situation.

Social psychology has been developed by association with the work of anthropologists (those who study the science of man's natural history). This has shown that the origin of much social behaviour is due not to inborn drives common to all men, as Freud believed, but to their environment and way of life.

Psychology, which began with the philosopher Aristotle and was for many centuries afterwards primarily linked with medicine, is now far more broadly based. In the modern world it is linked, not only with medicine and philosophy, but also with anthropology, sociology (the science of human society), statistics (the study of numerical facts) and even with linguistics (the study of languages). It began as the study of man and has become the study both of man and of mankind.

The world of ideas and beliefs

Contents

339 The world of literature and drama
Indian literature – Chinese literature – Semitic literature – The poets of ancient Greece – Greek drama – Greek comedy – Prose histories – The fall of Athens – Roman literature – The Augustan age – Goths, Huns and Vandals – Scandinavian literature – Celtic literature – Beowulf – Songs of the troubadours – The romance – The Norman-French court – Castilian poetry and prose – Dante Alighieri – Chaucer and Malory – François Villon – The Renaissance – English 'New Learning' – Elizabethan drama – William Shakespeare – Ben Jonson – 17th-century France – 17th-century England – The new classical age – The novel – American literature – English romantics – French romantics – The French novel – 19th-century English novelists – 19th-century American literature – Victorian writers – Russian literature – Scandinavian literature – Modern drama – The modern novel – The novel in England – The novel in America – Modern poetry – The matter of literature

374 The theatre and popular entertainment
The Greeks and Romans – The church and the theatre – Italy advances the theatre – England's golden age – Spain's golden age – Molière's France – English theatre reborn – The German theatre – 18th-century France – Early 19th-century theatre – Late 19th-century theatre – Far eastern theatre – 20th-century theatre – The cinema – Radio and television – The circus – Puppets and marionettes – Mime and pantomime – The music hall

387 The world of religion and philosophy
The first hunters – *Homo sapiens* – The cave painters – The first farmers
Pre-literate societies
Power and taboo – The gods and spirits – Witch-doctors.

391 The ancient religions
The gods of Sumeria – The gods of Egypt – The gods of Greece – The gods of Rome – The gods of Europe – The gods of Mexico and Peru

401 The living religions
Hinduism – Buddhism – Jainism – Confucianism and Taoism – Shinto – Zoroastrianism – Judaism – Christianity – Islam – Sikhism

421 Philosophy
The science of reasoning
Greek philosophy
Evidence of our senses – The rule of law – Socrates – Plato – Aristotle – The Epicureans
Medieval and modern philosophy
René Descartes – The rationalists – The empiricists – Immanuel Kant – Political philosophy – Friedrich Hegel – Marx and Nietzsche – Existentialism – 20th-century philosophy

Above The world of ideas and beliefs comes together in this drawing, which shows masked actors inside a Greek theatre with the figure of the poet Homer in the foreground. The literary forms created by the Greeks have been used in western literature throughout its long history. Even today the true ancestors of modern literature are the writers of ancient Greece. Drama itself began in Greece as a form of religious ceremony in which man tried to persuade the gods to grant his wishes by acting and mime.

The world of literature and drama

Literature is what happens when human speech is used for something more than the ordinary needs of daily living. In a strict sense, literature is something that has been recorded, or written down, but the earliest 'literature' was made up in men's heads, given birth in their voices and retained in their minds. This is called an oral tradition of literature – spoken, not written.

Literature may be created for the amusement of either the creator or his audience or of them both, but it may also be created for the most serious of all human reasons, to please or persuade God or the gods, and to give men an understanding of themselves and their race. From the earliest times at which men believed in gods, and that is probably from the time of the earliest men, they have always tried to please them and to obtain from them an abundance of whatever they considered necessary for good living. Hence, the literature of prayer and praise is probably the oldest of all. And since men have always considered fighting as one of their greatest diversions, at times when they have not been wholly occupied in finding food for themselves, the literature of war is almost certainly the second oldest.

When men began to divide their society into priests, warriors and 'the rest', the priests became responsible for remembering the proper literature to be used towards the gods, for making new hymns and prayers when these were needed, and for the handing down of all this 'religious literature' to their acolytes, or students. The chief warriors remembered the battle-songs, and the poems telling of past glories and past heroes, and the young warriors learned them in their turn.

The earliest literature, whether it was religious, warlike or historical, was composed in 'poetry', not in 'prose'. Men talked in prose, as men do still, but for their literature they used poetry, and there seem to have been two reasons for this. The first is practical: poetry was easier to remember than prose. The second reason could be called aesthetic, or concerned

Above The *Arabian Night's Entertainment* is a collection of old stories written in Arabic which were first translated into English in 1707. Some have become very popular, notably the story of Ali Baba and the forty thieves, a scene from which is illustrated here.

Above The scribe in ancient Egypt was greatly honoured. In an illiterate country he was an educated man who could read and write. This limestone figure of a squatting scribe comes from the early Vth Dynasty and is in the Cairo Museum in Egypt.

with taste and proper conduct. Men clearly felt that words for ordinary day-to-day matters should not be used in exactly the same way for matters of high religious or tribal importance. So, for these, a 'heightened', or more ornate and important-sounding, language was used – the language of poetry.

The earliest poetry probably bore little relation to anything we think of as poetry now. And even today, the question 'What is poetry?' would certainly produce very different answers from a Frenchman, a Chinaman, a Bantu or an Eskimo. Distinct families of poetic tradition have grown up among the many races of the world. This has been partly because of the differences in the way their various languages work, and partly because their individual cultures, or ways of life, are different. But in the way in which family trees can show that one family may possess ancestors who came from different countries, so poetry – and literature as a whole – can be grouped into individual racial families. Modern English literature can be shown to have had Italians, Romans and Greeks among its ancestors.

The literatures of certain people, for example the African tribes, or the aborigines of Australia, or the Eskimos, were until recently almost entirely oral, and though each is of considerable interest in its own right, none has spread outside its own area. The same is true of the much greater literatures of India and China, and to a lesser extent of the literature of the Semitic peoples. Although all three developed early, and all continue to maintain a flourishing literary tradition, none has any descendants in the family trees of the literature of western Europe.

Indian literature

There are three main periods of Indian literature: ancient, medieval and modern. The ancient period extends from about 1000 to 200 BC and the surviving works from it are almost entirely religious. Scholars assume that there were other works of a more popular kind which have been lost. They are believed to have existed because of the amount of popular literature that has come down to us from the medieval period (200 BC–AD 1100), and which seems to have continued an already existing tradition. In this period popular work was composed and written in a large number of different dialects, while the more serious and still largely religious poetry and prose was in the literary language used by learned people known as classical Sanskrit.

In the modern period, which began either in the 12th or 13th century and continues today, the use of regional dialects and Sanskrit declined, and Urdu and Hindi became the two national languages used for literature. Most of the literature was in the form of poetry and poetic drama. There has been little prose written in either of these tongues.

Chinese literature

For most of its history Chinese literature, like that of India, has had a serious side written in a classical form of the Chinese language, and a popular side which uses ordinary language and was not written down until quite recent times.

In the earliest period (1700–600 BC) there are hymns, songs, charms and spells, but in the second period (600–200 BC), which was strongly influenced by the great philosopher Confucius, the first Chinese prose literature began. This was largely in the form of accounts of major historical events, but there are also essays on various subjects. Between the years 200 BC and AD 200 Chinese literature divided into the intellectual and popular streams which were never to join again. The intellectual writers produced very elaborate prose and much lyric poetry, whereas the people had ballads, songs and folktales. The fourth and fifth periods brought only small changes, but in the sixth (AD 900–1900) new styles of poetry grew up. Drama also developed, but the plays were all ones with happy endings and there were no tragedies. In the last and seventh period, from 1900 to the present day, the intellectual or classical form of the language has fallen into disuse, and for all kinds of literature ordinary language is used.

Today prose stories are being written but less poetry, and instead of Chinese literature (by far the oldest in the world) influencing the literature of western Europe, there is now evidence to show that western literature is influencing that of modern China.

Semitic literature

There are a number of Semitic peoples who belong to the Near or Middle East, each speaking its own language, and each having its own literature. They are called Semitic because traditionally they are the descendants of Shem, one of Noah's sons. Much of this literature has been lost or destroyed, but some early Arabic, Hebrew and Babylonian writings do exist.

Our knowledge of classical Arabic literature starts in pre-Islamic times, that is before the prophet Mohammed founded the religion of Islam in the early part of the 7th century AD. All that remains is a small part of the oral poetry, which was first collected and written down in the 8th century. The great literary and religious work of Islam – the Koran – written by the prophet Mohammed, dates from the 7th century. From that time Arabic literature continued to flourish until the 16th century, after which it declined and lost a great deal of its power, although it never ceased entirely.

The great monument of ancient Hebrew literature is the Jewish Bible, known to Christians as the Old Testament. The earliest parts of this are believed to date from about 800 BC. Apart from this there is an enormous bulk of classical Hebrew literature, most of it religious in character, and

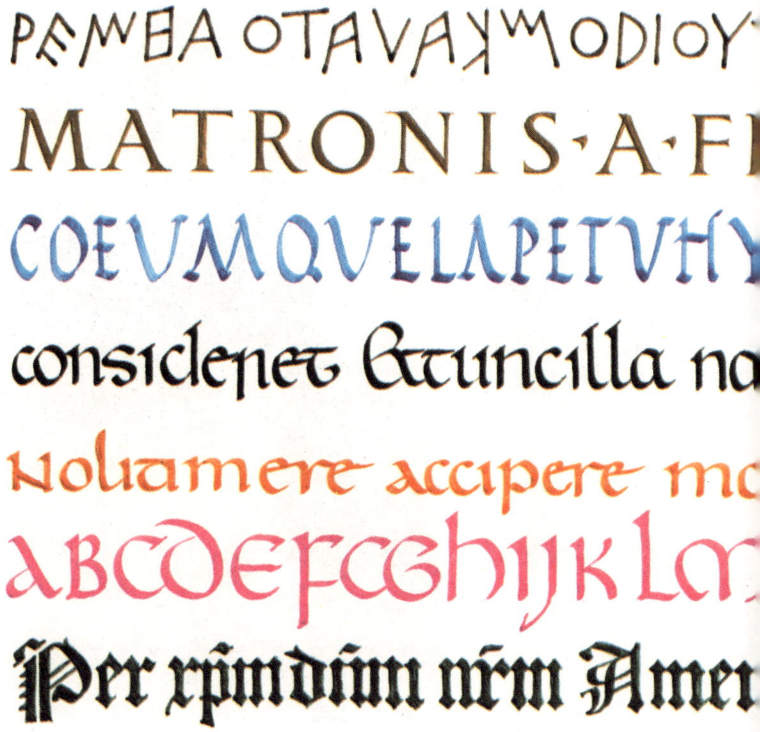

Above The history and development of scripts is shown very briefly in these examples of letter forms. From top to bottom they are Greek lapidary writing, 5th century BC; Roman lapidary writing, 1st century AD; Rustic capitals, 5th century; Anglo-Saxon half-uncials, 8th century; two examples of the celebrated Carolingian miniscule, 8th century, showing lower case and capital letters; and lastly Textura printed type from the 15th century.

Above The hero Gilgamesh holding a lion with which he fights during his epic adventures.

Above right Odysseus tied to the mast of his ship while it sails past the island of the Sirens. From a Greek vase painting.

Above The fables attributed to Aesop (6th century BC) were probably by several authors. Illustrated is the story about the race between the tortoise and the hare.

the tradition of such writing has continued up to the present day. In modern Hebrew there is a varied literature and Israel has a definite place in world literature.

What is probably the oldest literary work to be preserved, even though not all of it remains, is the *Epic of Gilgamesh* which dates from about 2000 BC. The earliest written form in which it exists today consists of twelve large clay tablets dating from the 7th century BC, on which much of the poem was inscribed.

The word epic raises the question of form in literature. In the beginning literature consisted of poetry. It had, generally, two subjects: religion and patriotism. Gradually, out of these two subjects, together with others such as magic, prophecy and the struggles of heroic figures – often against supernatural powers – grew a clearly defined poetry, later to be called epic.

Gilgamesh is not only the oldest surviving literary work, but it is also a good example of epic poetry. Its hero, Gilgamesh, sets out on a quest for everlasting life. He has many adventures, in which he descends to the underworld, finds and loses again a magic herb that restores youth, and fights with lions. He confronts many people and though finally his quest fails, he is seen at the end as the mighty and just ruler of his people. This epic poem, probably composed nearly 4,000 years ago, shows how little at heart the ideas and interests of men have changed.

The poets of ancient Greece

Despite its enormous interest in its own right, *Gilgamesh* apparently had little literary influence beyond its own nation. To discover the 'ancestors' of our modern western European literature we must turn to ancient Greece.

With the possible exception of the novel, scholars consider that no new literary form has been invented since the time of ancient Greece. The forms created by the Greeks, adapted to suit the needs of other European languages, but otherwise perfectly recognisable, have been repeated throughout the long history of western European literature.

The earliest Greek poetry which remains to us is epic. The *Iliad* and the *Odyssey*, both written by Homer (who lived about 900 BC), were composed to be recited or chanted, and were not written down until a much later date. These epics deal with the Trojan war, but while the *Iliad* tells of the actual fight for Troy, the *Odyssey* describes the wanderings and adventures of Odysseus, a Greek hero, on his journey home after Troy was won.

After the epic the next kind of poetry to develop in ancient Greece united the two original subjects of religion and patriotism: it was known as didactic poetry, that is poetry designed to give instruction. Hesiod's *Works and Days* is believed to date from about 735 BC and is made up of rules which a good farmer ought to follow if he is to be successful. As an illustration of one of its points Hesiod tells the earliest fable in Greek literature, that of 'The Hawk and the Nightingale'. Another poem thought to be by Hesiod is the *Theogony* which describes the beginning of the world and the birth of the gods, and finishes with an account of some of the most famous of the ancient heroes.

Lyric poetry, which expresses the poet's real or imagined emotions upon a particular subject, probably began on the island of Lesbos, off the coast of Asia Minor. Here Alcaeus (about 600 BC) and his contemporary Sappho, the only great woman poet of Greece, were probably the most famous writers. Other kinds of lyric poetry such as the elegy (a poem of lament), and the ode in celebration of a festival or a victory, were perfected by Simonides of Ceos (556–468 BC) and by Pindar (522?–440? BC), often called the greatest lyric poet of Greece.

Satire, or the exposure and correction of vice and folly by making it ridiculous, was first used with great effect by another poet – Archilochus of Paros (about 670 BC), but it did not become a really popular literary form until the great age of Greek drama.

Greek drama

For the beginning of Greek drama we must go back to the ancient idea that one way of persuading the gods to grant fertility and fruitfulness to man and his animals and crops was to mimic or act out whatever one wanted. By the time of the ancient Greeks such 'fertility rites' had become associated with the worship of Dionysus, god of wine and of all forms of natural fruitfulness. Processions were held in his honour, with choral singing and chanting, and in due course the part taken by the leader of the chorus became more and more dramatic. At length this turned into a dialogue between the chorus-leader and the rest of the singers, and this was the beginning of drama.

Dramatic performances consisting of one actor and a chorus continued until the time of the great tragic poet Aeschylus (525–456 BC). He is regarded as the founder of tragedy because he introduced a second actor, so that for the first time the dialogue became more important than the chorus's commentary upon the action. It was in the time of Aeschylus that the first permanent theatre was built in Greece, and it is believed to have been on his advice that the masks which the actors usually wore were improved, and the costumes made more gorgeous than ever before. Aeschylus is said to have written seventy tragedies but only seven remain to us. Of these the most famous are possibly the *Agamemnon*, the *Choephori* and the *Eumenides*, which together make up the trilogy, or linked group of three plays, called the *Oresteia* or the 'Story of Orestes'.

The themes of Greek tragedy are almost always taken from old legends in which religion comes into conflict

Above A scene from the *Iliad* during the battle between Achilles and Hector before the walls of Troy. Homer's epic poems the *Iliad* and the *Odyssey* deal with the ten years' siege of Troy by the Greeks and the return of the hero Odysseus (or Ulysses) from the war; in which he has marvellous adventures which prolong his journey home for another ten years. The poet Homer is a shadowy figure in Greek history. It is believed he lived during the 9th century BC and that he was blind.

Above Terracotta figure of a Greek comic actor from the British Museum, London, dating from the 2nd century BC.

Herodotus (485?–425 BC) Greek historian. Commonly called the father of history, a name given to him by Cicero. Born at Halicarnassus in Asia Minor he spent his early life travelling the Middle East and Africa. Then he settled (it is not known where) to write his great history of the Greeks and Persians, with the immortal stories of Marathon, Thermopylae and Salamis, which was virtually a history of the world as it was then known.

with morality, or patriotism, or family duty, and it is the essence of this conflict that it cannot be reconciled. In the *Oresteia*, Agamemnon on his victorious return from Troy is murdered by his wife Clytemnestra and her lover Aegisthus. Electra, Agamemnon's daughter, saves her brother Orestes from a like fate, and he later avenges his father by slaying both Aegisthus and his mother. But although he has done his duty as a son by avenging his father he has unavoidably angered the gods by murdering his mother, and he is pursued by the Furies and driven mad. Eventually he takes refuge with the goddess Athena who orders his trial at which he is eventually acquitted of guilt.

Aeschylus was the founder of tragedy but it reached its greatest glory in the work of Sophocles (496?–405? BC). In his work the subjects and the style are more human than in Aeschylus, and there is a sense that man is more in command of his own actions rather than doomed by fate to an heroic and tragic end. Of the seven plays which survive, the most moving are possibly the three grouped as the 'Theban plays' which deal with the story of Oedipus and his daughter Antigone.

The third great tragic author, Euripides (480–406? BC), is less interested than his predecessors in the moral problems of his characters and very much more in their emotions. He introduced some elements of romance into his tragedies, of which the most famous is perhaps the *Bacchae*.

Greek comedy

The form of comedy is thought to nave grown directly out of the very ancient 'fertility dances', and so it is probably in fact older than tragedy, but in the history of Greek literature the earliest comedy we have is that of Aristophanes (448?–388? BC). Comedy was then a part of the Dionysian festival and usually provided 'comic relief' by poking fun at some everyday political or social scandal, or at some old heroic tale. Aristophanes's comedy is really funny today, despite the fact that most of the personal or political scandals it shows up are scarcely relevant any longer. But his power of showing what men are really like, coupled with his sense of the absurd – which lets him present a chorus of frogs, or a pig grunting in verse – have carried him triumphantly from the 3rd century BC to the 20th century AD.

Aristophanean comedy is now known as 'old comedy', and this was followed by a period of 'middle comedy' (390–320 BC) in which the main emphasis was still on satire, but the targets were largely literary and social ones. This was a poorer age, which perhaps accounts for the near disappearance of the chorus, and the diminishing numbers of recorded productions. The only names of note are those of Antiphanes of Athens and Alexis of Thurii.

'New comedy' (320–250 BC) was of the type we would now call 'comedy of manners' and the plot, usually a story of love and intrigue, was of primary interest. Because of this the characters became more important in themselves and there was scope for witty dialogue. In this type of comedy Menander (343?–291 BC) is the most outstanding author, and it is his kind of comedy that is the ancestor of the bulk of comedy in Europe and the United States today.

Above The wars between the Greeks and Persians, which Herodotus recorded in his celebrated history, included the famous sea battle at Salamis. This was fought in 480 BC between a Persian fleet which is said to have numbered over 800 ships and a much smaller Greek force. Despite the odds against them the Greeks won a great victory and destroyed or captured a large part of the Persian fleet. Time and again in their battles with the Persians, both on land and sea, the Greeks proved their superiority as fighters.

Prose histories

Greek literature proves no exception to the rule that poetry develops before literary prose, and the first writer of prose whose work has survived is the historian Herodotus (485?–425 BC). He is considered as the first historian in the modern sense of the word. Ancient tribal histories in verse did not attempt to distinguish fact from legend. Herodotus, whose intention is to give a clear account of the wars between Greece and Persia, does use legend, but he attempts to distinguish it from fact wherever this is possible.

His successor, Thucydides (460?–400? BC), was the historian of the Peloponnesian war between Athens and Sparta, and apart from the speeches he wrote and put into the mouths of his chief characters, he remains a master of historical writing.

One of the greatest of Greek prose writers is the philosopher Plato (427?–347? BC). His work took the form of dialogues, a form of teaching which led the pupil to make his own deductions and discoveries. As a method it was already old but it had never been used in so masterly a way.

Although Aristotle (384–332 BC) is not perhaps as great a writer as Plato, it is two of Aristotle's works in particular which have had the greater influence on later writers. These are the *Rhetoric*, which deals with the use of language to argue and persuade, and the *Poetics*, which is the first text-book of literary criticism and the one on which we still depend for our basic definitions of tragedy and comedy.

The fall of Athens

This great period of drama, history and philosophy in Athens happened while the Peloponnesian war dragged on, and in 404 BC Athens at last fell to Sparta. During the troubled times which followed, literary work became steadily more difficult. Eventually all that remained was a trickle of pastoral poetry which dealt with the lives and loves of shepherds and shepherdesses in a kind of dream countryside remote from worldly strife. This, though apparently trivial in itself, was to have a great effect on the poets of later ages, but at the time it signified the end of the Greek literature of the ancient world.

Above The imperial city of Rome was the capital not only of a country but of the whole world during the greatest days of its glory. Edward Gibbon, the historian, declared in his *Decline and Fall of the Roman Empire,* 'if a man were called to fix the period in the history of the world during which the condition of the human race was most happy and prosperous he would name that which elapsed from the death of Domitian to the accession of Commodus (AD 96–180)'.

Roman literature

Although Greek power declined it was not the end of Greek influence. Before the final conquest of Greece by Rome in 146 BC, the Roman army captured the Greek city of Tarentum in 272 BC. A certain Livius Andronicus (284?–204 BC) was captured and became a slave and tutor in a Roman household. There he translated the *Odyssey* and later several Greek tragedies into Latin verse. His importance is that he started a fashion in Rome which eventually caused Roman writers to base their literature on that of Greece. After him, Gnaeus Naevius (264?–194 BC), who was already known as an epic poet, wrote several plays loosely following Greek models, and in doing so encouraged the development of Roman drama which was then only just beginning.

The first Roman playwright of real importance was Titus Maccius Plautus (250?–184 BC). His plays, like those of Aristophanes, are really funny, and his excellent dramatic craftsmanship has been imitated by many authors in later ages including Molière in France and Shakespeare in England.

Despite the work of Plautus, Roman drama never became a major part of Latin literature. Although Terence (190?–159 BC) was another writer of excellent comedy, and Ennius (239?–169 BC) became famous for his tragedies, the dramatic tradition in Rome was never strong.

Because Latin literature came under the influence of Greece before it had time to develop its own native characteristics, its development does not follow the usual ancient sequence of poetry, drama and prose: drama came first and prose second. The earliest outstanding prose work is the *Origines* of Cato the Censor (234–149 BC). Cato disliked the fashion for Greek culture and wanted the Romans to return to their own traditions and ways, and the *Origines* is a history of Rome showing its ancient splendour and promising further glory in the future.

Cato's work was highly praised by Rome's greatest political speaker Marcus Tullius Cicero (106–43 BC). Cicero's speeches and his *Letters* are probably at the height of Latin prose. Despite Cicero's greatness, however, it is easier to enjoy the clear, fast-moving style of Julius Caesar (102–44 BC), whose account of his own career as commander-in-chief, and eventually head, of the Roman state still captures the imagination.

The earliest Roman poet of general interest is Lucretius (99?–55 BC) whose *De Rerum Natura* (On the Nature of Things) had immense influence over the poets who came after him. The *De Rerum Natura* is a long philosophical poem which has aroused fresh interest in recent years because it propounds an atomic theory which modern science has shown to be at times remarkably near the scientific truth.

In lyric poetry Gaius Valerius Catullus (84?–54? BC) returned to the simple expression of sorrow and passion which the early Greek lyric poets had achieved. He also introduced a poetry of personal satire which was to be developed with great success by the next generation of poets.

The Augustan age

Catullus came at the end of the period during which Rome had been governed as a republic. The new age of the Emperor Augustus (63 BC–AD 14) was marked by a burst of patriotism and national sentiment which caused people to look back towards the great happenings of the past.

It was, in fact, the age which produced the national Roman epic, the *Aeneid* by Virgil (70–19 BC). As we have seen, the epic is usually one of the earliest literary works of a developing tribe or nation. The *Aeneid* however was written for a reading public, not composed to be recited to an illiterate audience. Virgil knew that great nations – and his example was Greece – celebrate their early triumphs in epic poetry. His *Aeneid* was the first conscious literary attempt to do this for a nation which had already been great, and was conscious of its greatness for many years. As well as his great epic, Virgil wrote the *Eclogues* – pastoral poems, and the *Georgics* – didactic poems which offer instruction in country and agricultural tasks.

Another very great poet of this time was Horace (65–8 BC), whose work includes lyric poetry, satires and verse letters. He also wrote a work on the art of poetry called the *Ars Poetica*, which proved second only to Aristotle's *Poetics* in its usefulness to later generations.

After Virgil and Horace it was clear that the greatest period of Latin poetry was over, and the next fashion looked backwards to Greek models once more. Nevertheless, the work of Ovid (43 BC–AD 17), particularly the *Ars Amatoria* and the *Metamorphoses*, a collection of legends dealing with transformations, ending up with the story that Julius Caesar after his death was changed into a star, was an enormous influence on later writers throughout the Middle Ages and the Renaissance.

History during the reign of the Emperor Augustus was represented by Livy (59 BC–AD 17) who writes of the glories and history of Rome from its foundation to his own day. The history of Rome under the later emperors was written by Tacitus (AD 55?–120), whose histories are more critical and, to a modern reader, more interesting than the work of Livy. In his *Life of Agricola*, Tacitus became the first biographer.

The period of the emperors who followed Augustus was one of great interest and political struggle, and the literature reflects this. Much of it is satire, directed at the vices and social evils of the age, and it includes the work of Persius, Petronius and Martial, all of whom lived in the 1st century AD. Above all, there are the satires of Juvenal (55?–140?) which deal graphically with all the stupidity, crime and greed of the worst period of Roman society.

The outstanding dramatist of this last age of Latin literature was Seneca (5? BC–AD 65), the first author to write 'armchair' dramas, intended to be read and not acted. His tragedies are all on Greek subjects, are of great moral seriousness, and although they may

Virgil (Publius Vergilius Maro) (70–19 BC) Latin poet, born near Mantua. Studied rhetoric and philosophy. Became a court poet at Rome about 41 BC. He left Rome, being wealthy, to settle in the country. He wrote his epic the *Aeneid*, which tells the story of Aeneas the Trojan, legendary founder of the Roman nation, at the request of the emperor. It was finished just before his death. He is regarded as the greatest Latin poet.

Above An initial letter from the *Book of Kells*, an early Irish illuminated manuscript of the four gospels which probably dates from about the 8th century. Generally reckoned the finest example of Irish illuminated art, it is preserved in Trinity College, Dublin. This shows the monogram page containing the three opening words of St Matthew.

seem remarkably dull today, they made a great impression on English playwrights of the time of Shakespeare and were constantly imitated.

With this last group of authors Roman literature virtually ended. The Roman civilisation was gradually broken up by civil wars, ineffectual emperors and barbarian invasion, and though literature did not suddenly stop, it was represented by isolated works which usually had little connection with the political events of the time.

Goths, Huns and Vandals

The gradual collapse of the Roman Empire lasted for nearly three hundred years before its final dissolution in AD 476, and it was in the middle of this long period of unrest that the emperor Constantine (274?–337) declared Christianity to be the official religion of the empire. In this way Rome's barbarian 'allies', such as the Franks and the British, and their enemies, the invading Huns and Vandals, came into contact with the new religion. The Goths were already Christian before they started to move westwards to Rome. The barbarian tribes were quick to accept Christianity. The Franks were Christian by the end of the 5th century and England by the 7th century. The various Germanic tribes (except the Saxons) were converted by the 8th century. Only the Scandinavian peoples, who were not concerned with the Roman empire, remained pagan till the end of the 10th century.

But the acceptance of Christianity did not at once lead to an upsurge of literature. In fact, the opposite happened. The old oral literature of the German tribes, which had never been written down, was now condemned as 'pagan' and ultimately lost. The Church, on the other hand, did not encourage secular, or non-religious, writing, and in its fear of heresy wiped out much work done in the ancient world when it destroyed the libraries of Carthage, Rome, Alexandria and Milan.

There is, therefore, a gap in the main stream of western European literature, which is somewhat thinly filled by the Gothic Bible of Bishop Ulfilas (311?-381?), other fragments of the New Testament in Gothic, two or three Latin legal and religious works, and the textbooks of Cassiodorus (490?-583?). It is hardly to be wondered at that the bishop and historian Gregory of Tours (538-593?) wrote of his own time, 'Woe to our time, for the study of books has perished from among us'.

Scandinavian literature

The oral literary tradition continued among those peoples who were not immediately affected by the fall of Rome's empire and the rise of her church, and some of this work was eventually written down and has been preserved. The Scandinavian peoples of Norway, Sweden and Iceland had a common literary inheritance. Some of this has been preserved in the

Icelandic poetry which seems to have been written down in the 10th and 11th centuries, though it was composed much earlier. The greatest example of this is the poetic *Edda,* which is a collection of poems dealing mostly with the ancient subjects of religion and the glory of the tribe.

The other kind of pre-Christian Scandinavian poetry was called skaldic, from the word skald, meaning a bard or poet. These poems are usually descriptive and they often include complex riddles and puzzles.

The earliest written work in Scandinavia was prose history, but by the end of the 12th century came the sagas – prose works with poems and songs in them – which tell of the kings, saints and heroes of Norway and Iceland. We do not know the names of many of the authors of the sagas, but we do know that the *Heimskringla,* a history of the early kings of Norway, and possibly the prose *Edda,* are by Snorri Sturlason (1179-1241). But the greatest of these works is the *Njala* saga, written in the 13th century. After this the art declined and never revived.

Celtic literature

Ireland was Christian from the 5th century and preserved, with other Celtic countries, a strong oral tradition. From this period dates the *Tain Bo Cualnge* (The Raiding of the Cattle of Cooley), an epic tale first written down in the 7th century. This epic, which deals with the hero Cuchulinn, is a great and tragic story.

Apart from this work, which although epic has a clear relationship to the sagas, and another which deals with the adventures of Finn and Ossian, the earliest Irish literature is religious and dates from the time of St Patrick (385?-461?). Three works are believed to be by St Patrick himself, but for the rest the authors are mostly unknown.

It was in the period between the 6th and 9th centuries that the greatest Irish literature was produced, and it covered almost every subject from the most serious to the most trivial. Ireland was known at this time as the 'land of saints and scholars', and was famous throughout Europe for its books and its learning.

Above A scene from *Beowulf*, the epic Anglo-Saxon poem of the 6th century, which shows the hero Beowulf about to be confronted by Grendel – half monster and half man, in the castle of Hrothgar, king of Denmark. Beowulf eventually slays the monster which had terrorised the castle and its inhabitants.

Beowulf

Irish literature, like that of the Scandinavian countries, had developed outside the influence of Rome, though it is recognised that Latin ways of writing poetry had some effect on Irish fashions after the 6th century. It is therefore rather surprising that we find almost no evidence of Roman culture on the earliest English literature, although Britain had been a Roman province. The answer lies in the two words Britain and England. Rome conquered the Britons, and although they probably had some literary tradition, nothing of this has survived. The name England comes from the Angles, a Germanic tribe, who, with Saxons and possibly some Jutes of the same stock, overran the Roman province of Brittania in the

Above El Cid (1040?–99) was a Spanish military hero born in Castile. His real name was Rodrigo or Ruy Diaz. Banished from Castile in 1081 he fought with the Moors against the Christians. After he had captured Valencia in 1088 he became the great champion of Christendom with a fabulous reputation for personal valour and skill as a soldier. His exploits were recorded in the 12th-century Spanish epic *Poema de mio Cid* and he has become a national folk hero.

5th and 6th centuries. Thus, the earliest English literature is entirely Germanic in culture. In fact, the great Anglo-Saxon epic *Beowulf*, which was probably composed in the 7th century though it was not written down until considerably later, deals with adventures which took place in Denmark in the 5th and 6th centuries. It is a splendid adventure story but seems to be the work of a man who lived in a simpler and more primitive society even than that which produced the story of Gilgamesh.

Apart from *Beowulf* quite a lot of Anglo-Saxon poetry, as well as prose, has come down to us. The poetry is primitive in its choice of subject, that is restricted to religion, war and tribal glorification. There are no love poems, no nature poems – nothing which from our knowledge of Greek poetry we have learned to call lyric. Anglo-Saxon prose is, on the whole, more interesting because of what we learn from it about the way of life than it is for its own sake.

Songs of the troubadours

For early lyric poetry we have to turn away from Anglo-Saxon England to southern France. From there came the songs of the troubadours, which may have originated in Provence. The troubadours, probably inspired by the great Latin hymns of the 7th, 8th and 9th centuries, composed both words and music of their love songs, in which the beloved is addressed in terms more suited to a goddess than to a mortal woman. From these songs came the idea of 'courtly love' in which the lover worships, serves and adores his beloved, whose every wish becomes his law. This tradition spread and influenced European love poetry for several centuries. In the 12th century the culture of Provence began to decline, and the poets of northern France took over Provençal traditions and continued them in their own dialect.

The *trouvères*, or professional poets of northern France, invented new forms of poetry, the most important being the *chansons de geste*. These were narrative poems dealing with great episodes of French history and the most famous is the *Chanson de Roland*. This poem, which exists in a manuscript dating from about 1170, is a kind of epic composed to be recited or chanted aloud by a *jongleur* or professional story-teller.

The romance

Another kind of narrative poetry began at about the same time, but this was intended to be read by the literate and cultured society of the court, and not to be recited aloud to an audience who could not read. It was the romance, and probably the most famous of the romances were those dealing with the stories of King Arthur and his knights. The original legends about Arthur were probably Celtic in origin, but they came into France from the work of Robert(?) Wace (1115?-83?), who translated, adapted and added to the *Historia Regum Britanniae* (History of the Kings of Britain) by the Welsh historian Geoffrey of Monmouth (1100?-54). The greatest French version of the Arthurian stories was that of Chrétien de Troyes, the earliest French poet whose name has come down to us. He was writing between 1165 and 1190, and four out of the five romances which remain of his work deal with King Arthur.

There were many other romances written at this time, but the most famous of them all is the *Roman de la Rose*, begun about 1230 by Guillaume de Lorris, and finished nearly fifty years later by Jean de Meung. This poem, which is in the form of a dream with a hidden meaning, was probably the best-known work of literature of the whole medieval period.

The romance proper was a serious and courtly kind of literature, but there were also other lighter forms. There were the *fabliaux*, funny and often highly improper narrative poems, and beast fables, especially the *Roman de Renart*, the story of Renart (Reynard), the clever fox, and his enemy Ysengrin, the stupid wolf. Altogether, northern France was the pioneer of literature in western Europe from the 12th to the 14th century.

The Norman-French court

In England the Norman conquest of 1066 put an end to Anglo-Saxon both as literature and, eventually, as a language. A Norman-French court meant that all serious literature was written in French or in Latin, and only a small quantity of poetry of a simpler kind was written in English. Even in such 'English' poems as Layamon's 12th-century retelling of part of the Arthurian legend, the *Brut*, and in the lyric poetry of the 13th century, the influence of France is very clearly seen. Many words adapted from French came into the English language, and a more obvious influence is the use of rhyme, a new development in English poetry.

Most prose written in England at this time was in Latin, though the *Anglo-Saxon Chronicle* was continued and religious books were written in contemporary speech, later to be called Middle English. Other, more famous Middle English works were written in the 14th century, and among those in which the debt to Anglo-Saxon literature is most clearly seen are the anonymous *Sir Gawain and the Green Knight* and William Langland's *Piers Plowman*.

Castilian poetry and prose

The influence of France did not extend only to England but to Spain also. There, the literary language was Castilian, and an epic tradition already existed, though only the 12th century *Poema de mio Cid* remains to us, among fragments of other poems. The 13th-century *Roncevalles* shows clearly that it is a version of the *Chanson de Roland*, and from this time on Spanish literature modelled itself on that of France. Castile had also possessed a tradition of pastoral poetry, while Galicia had come under the

Above The songs of the troubadours inspired the idea of 'courtly love'.

Above 16th-century statue of King Arthur. It shows the Romano-British chieftain, who probably lived in the 6th century, as a medieval knight in the tradition of Malory's great book *Morte d'Arthur*.

Right Florence, on the banks of the Arno in Italy, is one of the most beautiful cities in the world. It became a rich centre of commerce and banking in medieval times and during the Renaissance was the home of writers, artists, statesmen and musicians intent on reviving the ideals of Greek culture.

Dante Alighieri (1265–1321) Born in Florence, Italy. Poet. His life was dominated by his love of a young girl, Beatrice. For a time he fought as a soldier and later was involved with politics. The *Divina Commedia*, the most famous of his works, tells of visions of Hell and Heaven. It is an impassioned and imaginative summary of human history. Dante was the first classical poet of the modern world and the greatest figure in Italian literature.

lyric influence of the troubadours. It was not until the 13th century that these two traditions came together.

The earliest Spanish prose was also Castilian and consists of history, prose versions of some of the old (and now lost) epic poems, and collections of moral tales. The Arthurian story came into Spanish prose in the late 13th century, and was followed by other romances. From the 14th century there is a tradition of popular ballads, less serious and more dramatic than the stately literature of the court.

Dante Alighieri

It was under French influence that the earliest Italian literature began, with Provencal poetry written in Italy at the beginning of the 13th century. Then, in Sicily, at the court of Frederick II (1194-1250), Italian poets began writing in a language based on Sicilian but borrowing freely from Latin, French and Provençal. Provençal poetry was their model, but they invented several new forms of their own including the sonnet. Their influence gradually spread through Italy, and eventually reached Bologna where it encountered a young man, Dante Alighieri (1265-1321), who was destined to become the greatest of all Italian poets.

Dante's *Vita Nuova*, an account in verse and prose of his love for a mysterious lady, Beatrice, helped to create an Italian literary language. His greatest work was *Divina Commedia* (Divine Comedy) which he wrote as an unhappy and disillusioned man, his ideals shattered and Beatrice dead. The poem is a dream vision of a lover's journey through Hell and Purgatory in search of his lost beloved, whom he eventually finds safe in Paradise. Dante is the traveller, his guide through the underworld is the ghost of the poet Virgil, and the poem ends with his rediscovery of Beatrice. But more than this the poem has another meaning, for it is also an allegory of the soul's search for God.

Yet it was not Dante, but Francesco Petrarch (1304-74) who had the greater influence on the writers who came directly after him. Petrarch's allegorical poems and, more especially, his collection of lyrics, the *Canzoniere* (inspired by his beloved Laura), were to influence other poets of Europe for the next three hundred years. Italian prose was made equally famous by Giovanni Boccaccio (1313-75). He wrote verse also, but his prose romances and his collection of short stories, the *Decameron*, became a source of inspiration as strong and widespread as the poetry of his great contemporary Petrarch.

Chaucer and Malory

The poetry of France and Italy, the prose of Boccaccio, and the work of many Latin authors both classical and medieval were part of the background of Geoffrey Chaucer (1345?-1400), the first great English poet. He began a translation of the *Roman de la Rose*,

Left This drawing of Chaucer on his way to Canterbury with the pilgrims is taken from the Ellesmere manuscript of the *Canterbury Tales*. The host of the Tabard Inn in London, where the pilgrims assembled for the journey, offered a free supper to the teller of the best story on the road, and Chaucer includes twenty-four of the stories in his book.

wrote a number of other poems which show a clear debt to French poetry, including a romance about the Trojan war, *Troilus and Cressida*, and above all he wrote the *Canterbury Tales*. This is a collection of stories of widely different kinds, each told by a pilgrim on his way to Canterbury to the shrine of St Thomas Becket. The pilgrims themselves, whose journey links the tales, are a splendid and motley collection of people, all vividly alive, who show us what kind of men and women lived and worked in the 14th century.

After Chaucer there was no great English poetry for almost a hundred and fifty years, but English prose reached a new greatness with the *Morte d'Arthur* of Sir Thomas Malory (died 1471). This is a re-telling of the stories of King Arthur, gathered from a number of different sources. It appeared in 1485, fourteen years after the death of the author, and was one of the first books to be printed by William Caxton (1422?-91?) at his new press at Westminster.

The popular tradition of ballad-making continued in this period, and stories of great deeds, short romances and popular legends continued to be turned into ballads which were sung and remembered.

The Miracle plays also belong to this time. They were part of the celebrations of the Feast of Corpus Christi, and had grown out of the story told by the Christian year of Advent, Christmas, Lent, Easter, the Ascension and Pentecost. These plays were first intended to teach the people but there was plenty for them to enjoy.

After the Miracle Plays came the Moralities. These were usually less dramatic, most of the characters represented virtues or vices, and the aim was to show how the various qualities could aid or hinder a man in his quest for salvation. On the whole, with the notable exception of *Everyman*, they were dull.

François Villon

In France it was the age of Villon, one of the greatest of French poets. François Villon (born 1431) is remembered chiefly for two literary testaments or mock wills in verse, one called the *Petit Testament* and the other the *Grand Testament*. The subjects included are wide and are presented with great realism, as well as a strange blending of satire, humour and compassion. Like Chaucer, he stands alone and unrivalled.

The Renaissance

In England and France the 15th century was not a great literary age. This was true of Italy also, but there the new age of the Renaissance, or 'Rebirth of Learning', had already begun. The old capital of the Roman world, Constantinople, fell to the Turks in 1453, and from this time onwards many Greek scholars travelled to the west, bringing their learning and some of their books with them. They came first to Italy and there began a new interest in classical learning in all its

Above The printing trade mark used by William Caxton (1422?–1491). Caxton was apprenticed in 1438 to a London mercer. Went to Bruges in Belgium, became governor of the merchant adventurers' guild in 1463. Studied printing in Cologne. He printed *The Recuyell of the Historyes of Troye*, the first book printed in English, in 1474. He set up his press in England in 1476 at the Sign of the Red Pale. He produced ninety-nine works and he edited nearly every one.

Above The famous episode from Miguel de Cervantes's *Don Quixote* when the hero is about to tilt at windmills, imagining them to be giants. Don Quixote has read so many tales of deeds by knights of old that he rides out in rusty armour with his faithful servant Sancho Panza to do battle with the world. All kinds of everyday things are seen by him as fearsome and exciting but his adventures always end in a good beating and disillusion. The book was written as a satirical romance on tales of chivalry.

forms. At first it appeared that this would kill the creative spirit of Italian literature. Latin began to be used once more as the only language for serious writing, and study and research were considered of far more importance than poetry and romance. But towards the end of the century literature began to recover, and it was wonderfully enriched by the addition of classical learning.

From this period date the romance-epics *Orlando Innamorato* by Matteo Boiardo (1434-94), *Orlando Furioso* by Ludovico Ariosto (1474-1533) and *Gerusalemme Liberata* by Torquato Tasso (1544-95). In prose, the age produced Niccolo Machiavelli (1469-1527), whose *Il Principe* (The Prince), a work dealing with methods of government, was later of enormous influence politically in both France and England.

Scholars from the German states came in vast numbers to Italy to acquire the New Learning for their country, but for them it remained an interest in scholarship to be used mostly for theological purposes: it never flowered into literature.

In Spain, however, the effect of the Renaissance was just the opposite. Lope de Vega (1562-1635) and Pedro Calderon (1600-81) are still thought of as two of the greatest of Spanish dramatists, while Miguel de Cervantes (1547-1616) wrote his novel *Don Quixote*, the adventures of a foolish and charming knight which were to achieve world-wide fame.

In France the first truly Renaissance writer was François Rabelais (1494?-1553). His fantastic stories *Gargantua* and *Pantagruel* were too great to be imitated by later writers, and it was the *Essais* of Michel de Montaigne (1533-92) which were to prove the models to his own countrymen and to writers of other nationalities.

It was the poets of Renaissance France, and not the prose writers, who were more convinced that a study of Greek and Latin writers would benefit their work. A group of young poets known as the Pléiade after the constellation of stars called the Pleiades was led by Joachim du Bellay (1522-60). The most famous of this group was Pierre de Ronsard (1524-85), and with his fellows he concentrated on new forms of poetry and particularly upon the sonnet, which had come to France from Italy.

English 'New Learning'

The Renaissance came later to England, partly because the country is cut off from the Continent, partly because it was too deeply involved in the civil Wars of the Roses (1455-85), and it was not until the Tudors were securely established that the 'New Learning' began to be felt. Perhaps the greatest man of the early English Renaissance was Sir Thomas More (1478-1535), who was a statesman, a scholar and a saint. It was for the sake of his friendship that the greatest Dutch scholar of the age, Desiderius Erasmus (1466-1536), went to England and did much of his work there.

Ideas on education changed and broadened, and many of the most famous English schools were founded at about this time, among them St Paul's, built by John Colet (1467?-1519) – another friend of Sir Thomas More's. Just as a chance to learn was extended to more children than it had ever been before, so other scholars began to make English translations of the Bible, so that it would be available to all who could read. Their work, and most particularly that of William Tyndale (died 1536), was the foundation of the Authorised Version of 1611 which was to influence the prose of almost every notable English writer until this century.

Francis Bacon (1561-1626) imported the essay form of Montaigne into England as well as writing a history of the New Learning as it appeared to English eyes in his *Advancement of Learning*. It was at this time too that George Chapman (1559?-1634) produced the first English translation of Homer.

In poetry, Sir Thomas Wyatt (1503-42) and the Earl of Surrey (1517?-47) first attempted English sonnets, and they were followed by Sir Philip Sidney (1554-86), whose *Astrophel and Stella* is worthy to be compared with Petrarch's sonnet sequence to Laura.

As in France, it was a poet – Edmund Spenser (1552-99) – who thought most deeply about the uses of language at this time, but Spenser did not look as far back as Greece and Rome for his inspiration. He read Chaucer for old forms of words, or coined new ones to suit himself. His greatest work, the *Faerie Queene*, is a romance epic which looks back to Ariosto's *Orlando Furioso*, but blends materials from the Arthurian stories with patriotism and the high moral tone of the English Reformation.

It was the Reformation brought about by Henry VIII's rejection of the power of the pope in England, and the beginning of the Church of England, that made the Renaissance in England

a greater force in morals and education than it was anywhere else on the Continent. In England, the New Learning came at a time when an old way of life was changing, and the ideas it brought with it did not apply only to literature but affected the lives of quite ordinary people.

Elizabethan drama

People's lives were affected, too, by the sudden popularity of the theatre. This may have come from the personal delight which Queen Elizabeth took in plays, or there may have been other causes, but certainly this was the great age of drama in England.

The first really great English playwright was Christopher Marlowe (1564-93), who took the 'blank verse' introduced into the country by Wyatt and Surrey and made it sound as natural – or as glorious – as human speech can be. His life was mysterious and melodramatic. He may have been a spy, he probably did not believe in God and hence was an atheist, he was certainly stabbed to death in what seems to have been a tavern brawl, and, influenced by the ideas of Machiavelli,

Christopher Marlowe (1564–93) English dramatist, greatest of Shakespeare's predecessors. His life was violent, and he is said to have died after being stabbed in a tavern brawl. His verse is rich, powerful and imaginative.

Niccolo Machiavelli (1469–1527) Italian statesman (far left). Employed on diplomatic missions, but left politics because of alleged conspiracy. He turned to writing and his books on the art of war and statesmanship had great influence. His theme was that in order to maintain the position of authority in government all means are justified.

Thomas More (1478–1535) English statesman (above left). Was treasurer of the Exchequer and Chancellor of the Duchy of Lancaster, 1525. Speaker of the House of Commons. After Wolsey's fall was appointed Lord Chancellor against his will. He sympathised with those who wished to reform the church, but did not wish to break with Rome. He refused to acknowledge Henry VIII as head of the church, and was beheaded in 1535.

Above At the court of Queen Elizabeth I private performances of Shakespeare's plays were staged.

William Shakespeare (1564–1616) dramatist and poet. Little is known about his early life except that he was born in Stratford-upon-Avon and was married in 1582 to Anne Hathaway. He went to London about 1585 and eventually became an actor with a company of players led by Richard Burbage, and began to write his plays and poems. The range of his work is enormous and seems to express every emotion known to man. Thirty-seven plays are attributed to him although there is some doubt that he wrote all of them.

he was fascinated by the theme of power. In *Tamburlaine* he deals with the power of an emperor, in *Dr Faustus* with the power of the mind, in *The Jew of Malta* with the power of money, and in *Edward II* with the loss and gain of royal power. Yet Marlowe's plays lack shape and force when they are compared with those of William Shakespeare.

William Shakespeare

Shakespeare (1564-1616) is probably the world's greatest playwright, yet we know little more about his life than we do of Marlowe's. He was born in Stratford-upon-Avon, and after beginning his writing career with two poems imitating Ovid, and a sequence of sonnets which are among the most beautiful in English poetry, he came to London. Here, he became an actor, shareholder and writer with one of the leading theatrical companies. His early work was varied and included a comedy and a tragedy, several chronicle histories, one romantic comedy, *Two Gentlemen of Verona*, and one romantic tragedy, *Romeo and Juliet*.

In 1592 the London theatres were closed because of the Plague and did not reopen for two years. The companies went on tour but we do not know whether Shakespeare went with them. But when the theatres reopened, he was writing a new kind of romantic comedy for them, in which characters are more important than story. To this group belong *The Merchant of Venice, As You Like It* and *Twelfth Night*. His history plays were chronicles no longer, but history proper, selecting material to show the English people how England had become what she was.

By 1600 he had become interested in tragedy, and to this period belong perhaps the most famous of all his plays – *Hamlet, Macbeth, Othello* and *King Lear*. After this he turned to a new sort of romance comedy, more serious and more tender than before – sometimes seeming close to tragedy in form – and among these are *Cymbeline, The Winter's Tale* and *The Tempest*.

After this, Shakespeare apparently felt that he had no further urge to write and he returned to his home at Stratford-upon-Avon, where he lived for several years in the quiet obscurity which he seems to have preserved even in London. He was apparently quite uninterested in the preservation of his own work, and a complete collection of his plays and poems was not published until the First Folio edition of 1623, seven years after his death.

Ben Jonson

Shakespeare's only rival in his own age, Ben Jonson (1572-1637), had very different ideas on this matter. He himself prepared his work for the publisher, and although his fame rests on his plays he did not consider himself a man of the theatre. Jonson, unlike Shakespeare, was a classical scholar who looked back to the plays of Greece and Rome in his work. His tragedies *Sejanus* and *Catiline* were failures. Today they read more like translations and never come alive theatrically. But the comedies are the essence of life.

Jonson took the medieval theory of 'humours' – simple, strong traits of personality which determine a man's whole character – and his comedies show the results of these 'one-track' characters in conflict. He introduced the theory in *Everyman in his Humour*, whose success was such that it was followed by a sequel, *Everyman out of his Humour*. The satire in these plays is against folly and is not very strong, but Jonson, who hated above all things hypocrisy (that is the pretence of being other than one is), affectation and greed, moved on to sharper satire in *The Poetaster* and *Volpone*. Then, returning to his own theory that it is the duty of comedy 'to sport with human follies, not with crimes' he turned to lighter matters in *The Alchemist*. Jonson at his best is brilliant and wildly funny, but it is not until *Bartholomew Fair*, his last and greatest play, that he shows some of the feeling for human beings that makes the least of Shakespeare's characters come alive.

Although the playwrights of this age were many, none came up to the standards of Shakespeare and Jonson, although in their own time the works in collaboration of Francis Beaumont (1584?-1616) and John Fletcher (1579-1625) achieved at least as much fame.

After Shakespeare tragedy gradually became even more horrific, and dealt primarily with cruelty and corruption rather than with the greatness of human sorrow. Even so, there were some great plays written, such as *The Changeling* by Thomas Middleton (1570?-1627) and *The White Devil* and *The Duchess of Malfi* of John Webster (1580?-1625?).

Events of history in England had in the meantime brought first the Civil War and then the Commonwealth. In 1642 the Puritans closed the theatres, and they did not reopen until the Restoration of 1660. The Reformation, the Civil War and the Commonwealth had a profound effect on England and on the course of English literature.

Left Bartholomew Fair, the setting for Ben Jonson's most successful play, was held in Smithfield, London, from 1120 to 1855. At one time it was the chief fair in the country for the sale of cloth and although this remained one of its chief functions it later became an occasion for revelry and disorder.

Ben Jonson (1572–1637) English dramatist. Friend of Shakespeare. He worked as a bricklayer, served as a soldier, and was imprisoned before he became an actor and writer. His first play *Every Man in his Humour* was performed in 1598, with Shakespeare in the cast. His most famous plays were produced between 1606 and 1614. He also produced a number of masques. In 1625 fell out of favour at court, and was unable to repeat his earlier success.

17th-century France

In France, while there had been no sweeping changes, there had been much political and religious thinking, and in the 17th century there began a rebellion against both church and state in the works of several writers. Greater, however, than any of these was René Descartes (1596-1650), one of the earliest philosophers to attempt to base all his ideas on reason and logic alone. On the side of church and state, and opposed to the rebels, was Blaise Pascal (1623-62), who attempted to show that religion was necessary in the lives of men.

Descartes and Pascal were principally philosophers, but the age also produced men more concerned with the society of their time. Foremost among these was La Rochefoucauld (1613-80) whose *Maxims* criticise the pomp and fussiness of the society in which he lived. A possibly truer, though less obviously critical picture

Above Molière was a first-rate actor of comedy and his acting has been compared with Garrick's for forceful expression and use of gesture. He was also a great theatre manager and spent the whole of his life from the age of twenty-one involved in acting, producing and writing plays, some of which are the great masterpieces of comedy.

John Milton (1608–74) English poet. A brilliant scholar, his early poems won fame, particularly in Italy, where he went in 1638–9. Returned to England at the time of the Civil War and apart from political material on the side of Cromwell wrote little for twenty years. Became blind in 1652. Towards the end of his life he wrote his greatest works.

of that society is to be found in the *Caractères* of Jean de La Bruyère (1645-96). He began by translating the *Characters* of the Greek philosopher Theophrastus and then turned to writing 'pictures' of the men of his own time.

The only major poet of the age was Jean de La Fontaine (1621-95) whose *Fables*, inspired by those of Aesop, tell worldly-wise and moral tales of birds and animals in a clear-cut and elegant style which both children and adults can enjoy. His poems may seem trivial on the surface, but in fact he was dealing with universal characteristics of mankind and not merely with the temporary code of manners imposed by the society of his day.

Although there were few great poets, this was the greatest age of drama in France. The Renaissance had revived the ideas of Greek and Latin drama, and tragedy particularly was written according to the strictest of classical traditions. This is shown best by the famous quarrel which arose among the critics over the second play of Pierre Corneille (1606-84), *Le Cid*. Corneille's first tragedy *Médée* followed the classical pattern, but *Le Cid*, the story of the famous 11th-century Castilian hero, has a happy ending and many of the critics were outraged. Corneille never again violated classical rules.

In the work of Jean Racine (1639-99) love and glory are still opposed, but the struggle between them is more real and far more harrowing. Like Corneille, Racine used classical stories from Greek legend and Roman history for his plays.

French comedy was influenced by classical models, but also by the tradition of the *commedia dell'arte* brought to France by Italian actors. This was an art of mime, clowning and dialogue invented by the actors as they went along, and one of its last descendants is the Punch and Judy show. This tradition added lightness and a certain amount of slapstick humour to the more serious classical ideas of comedy.

The first great dramatist to write this kind of comedy was Jean-Baptiste Poquelin (1622-73), better known – for he, like Shakespeare, was also an actor – by his stage name of Molière. Molière made his name with *L'Ecole des femmes*, but he established himself as the greatest of French comic playwrights with such plays as *Tartuffe* and *Le Misanthrope*. Like Ben Jonson he was a satirist, attacking hypocrisy and pretence.

Like Jonson, too, Molière could not be imitated, and after him comedy became lighter and more trivial. Pierre Marivaux (1688-1763) wrote delicate, almost fairy-tale romances, while Pierre Beaumarchais (1732-99) returned to the slapstick and rapid intrigue of the *commedia dell'arte* in his *Le Barbier de Séville* and *Le Mariage de Figaro*.

It was only in England and France that the force of the Renaissance did not decline almost at once. In Italy in the 17th century and early 18th century there was little outstanding literature until the dramatic revival associated with the tragedies of Vittorio Alfieri (1749-1803) and the comedies of Carlo Goldoni (1707-93). Spanish literature was also in decline, and that of Germany, Russia and Scandinavia was still wholly involved with national topics of little interest outside the country of their origin.

17th-century England

The 17th century in England was certainly not one of decline. There were new ideas about the writing of poetry in the work of John Donne (1572-1631), George Herbert (1593-1633) and Andrew Marvell (1621-78). These poets were later called metaphysical poets because each of them used ideas

Above Samuel Pepys (1633–1703) the great English diarist was also an Admiralty official. His famous diary was written in cipher and covers the period 1 January 1659 to 31 May 1669. It gives a vivid picture of the court, official and social life of his times. The diary was deciphered by John Smith in 1819–22.

Left This drawing is based on a steel engraving from the original edition of John Bunyan's *Pilgrim's Progress*.

and methods from philosophy and other branches of learning in their poetry. Above all, the century produced John Milton (1608-74), one of the greatest English poets.

Milton was an ardent Puritan and Latin secretary to Oliver Cromwell. His prose work, which is mostly in support of the Puritan cause, shows the 'grand style' of English at its height. But he is best remembered for his epic *Paradise Lost* in which he sets out 'to justify the ways of God to man', and to write for England an epic worthy to be set beside Virgil's *Aeneid*.

The 'grand style' of prose – ornate and based on Latin – is again found in the *Religio Medici* and *Urn Burial* of Sir Thomas Browne (1605-82), but it is possible that today it is easier to appreciate the 'plain' style of John Bunyan's *Pilgrim's Progress*. Bunyan (1628-88) was another Puritan writer whose book is an allegory of the simple man's search for salvation, and his style shows his debt to the Authorised Version of the Bible of 1611.

Literary criticism had its real beginnings in the 17th century with the *Essay of Dramatic Poesy* of John Dryden (1631-1701). He was himself a poet and playwright, producing the best satirical poem of his age in *Absalom and Achitophel,* and inventing two new dramatic forms – the short-lived English heroic play, and the comedy of manners which was to dominate the theatre for fifty years. This type of comedy dealt wholly with the brilliant but artificial society of the court of Charles II, and as the work of William Wycherley (1640?-1716) and William Congreve (1670-1729) shows, it was a society where morals counted for little against wit, polish and gusto.

The new classical age

The 18th century brought to England a revival of the classical spirit in all the arts, and the chief aim of writers of the time was a blend of 'correctness', elegance and clarity. The way to this had been opened by Dryden, who had given much thought to the kind of language best suited for writing poetry, and who had begun to use the ten-syllabled lines rhymed in pairs which are called heroic couplets. Dryden began this new way of writing, but it was

Richard Lovelace (1618–57) One of the Cavalier poets, who were so called because of their loyalty to Charles I. Other important Royalist poets were Thomas Carew (1595–1639) and John Suckling (1609–42). All three wrote elegant and witty verse.

Right Alexander Pope made translations of Homer's *Iliad* and *Odyssey* from which he earned enough money to build this villa in Twickenham (1718). Pope had a great affection for the house and often said that he wished he could be free of the need to write so that he could retire and quietly cultivate his garden there.

Voltaire (1694–1778). Greatest of the French writers and philosophers who challenged the existing order and so prepared the way for the French Revolution. Was forced to leave France several times because of outspoken writings. He finally settled near the French border where many statesmen and writers visited him. There he condemned abuses of the law and the cruelty of the time. At the end of his life he returned to Paris.

the work of Alexander Pope (1688-1744) which showed the perfection which this style could reach.

Pope believed that 'the proper study of mankind is man', and that man should be seen in the context of his society as a 'social animal'. He was a satirist whose polished and biting wit has never been surpassed except perhaps by his model, the great Roman satirist Juvenal, though when he wished to he could describe nature with the same clarity and sureness of touch. His mock epic *The Rape of the Lock* is about the sly cutting off of a curl of hair from a young society lady by an admirer. The whole incident is blown up in a mock-serious way which is very comic and serves to show up 'society' manners.

After Pope poets turned to nature and to imitating the lyric and elegaic writers of Greece and Rome. Of these *The Seasons* by James Thomson (1700-48) enjoyed the greatest contemporary fame, but today the shorter poems of William Cowper (1731-1800) and Thomas Gray (1716-71) find more readers. Cowper was a very serious poet, yet his *Diverting History of John Gilpin* remains one of the most successful of English humorous poems, while Gray's *Elegy in a Country Churchyard* is one of the best-known poems in the language.

Later in the century George Crabbe (1754-1832), the doctor-vicar of a remote Suffolk town, returned to the heroic couplet for his exact and horrifying descriptions of the miserable reality of country poverty, by means of which he hoped to attract public concern. If a modern reader wishes to learn about 18th-century English rural life, he must read not only of the 'civilised' country of Pope's *Windsor Forest*, or of the comparatively well-off villagers of Cowper's *The Task*, but also of the misery of Crabbe's poor parishioners and patients.

The work of the Scottish poet Robert Burns (1759-96) is remarkable in that he was both a brilliant satirist and a lyric poet whose songs have achieved world-wide fame. Even the fact that he wrote his best work in the dialect of southern Scotland has proved no drawback to his admirers.

In the work of William Blake (1757-1827) it is the apparent extreme simplicity of style coupled with the extraordinary difficulty of the mystical and visionary experiences he was trying to convey that have made his work so hard to understand. Blake was a philosopher and an artist, and his philosophy is expressed in strange, haunting pictures and poems, and few people have ever felt that they wholly understood him.

The novel

The 18th century also saw the rise and development of one new and major literary form, the novel. There had been earlier works which were true novels, like *Don Quixote*, and there had been works which were close to the novel in form, such as *Gulliver's Travels* by Jonathan Swift (1667-1745). Swift intended this as a social and political satire, but it is also an excellent tale of fantasy–adventure in its own right and is more often read in this way today than as Swift intended it to be.

Daniel Defoe (1660-1731) was the first true English novelist, and his

Above Dr Johnson met his biographer James Boswell in 1763. The scene here shows Boswell and Johnson during their memorable journey to the Hebrides, about which Boswell wrote a journal that became the first part of his masterpiece the *Life of Johnson* (1891).

Above left The scene from *Gulliver's Travels* where Gulliver is captured by the Lilliputians.

Robinson Crusoe and *Moll Flanders* have never lost their popularity, but he too had a didactic, or teaching, purpose in writing them.

In France, too, the earliest novels, with the exception of those of Alain René Le Sage (1668-1747), were the work of philosophers who found them an excellent way of getting their ideas to the public. The two outstanding names are those of Jean-Jacques Rousseau (1712-78) and Voltaire (1694-1778), and it would be difficult to find two such opposed minds in any age. In his most famous novel, *Candide*, Voltaire satirises the work of a German philosopher by applying theory to a real-life situation with comic effect. He was one of the greatest writers of his time and was successful also in drama, history, poetry and short stories.

Denis Diderot (1713-84) was another philosopher who worked in story-form, while Antoine-François Prévost (1697-1763) achieved fame by his own novel *Manon Lescaut* and by his translation of the work of Samuel Richardson.

Richardson (1689-1761) was the true founder of the English novel, though *Pamela* and *Clarissa* are too deeply concerned with a narrow moral code to be satisfying today. His influence in France, however, was considerable. Although Richardson was admired in France, his closest English contemporary, Henry Fielding (1707-54), disliked his work exceedingly. He wrote a parody of *Pamela* entitled *Shamela*, and later another book, *Joseph Andrews*, which is directly aimed at Richardson. In *Tom Jones*, however, he wrote a novel that has remained popular until the present time, and which presents a living picture of 18th-century life.

Tobias Smollett (1721-71) in *Roderick Random* began a lasting fashion for tales of seafaring and adventure, while Laurence Sterne (1713-68) in *Tristram Shandy* was the first to attempt to explore his hero's mind as well as to record his deeds, and the result is a very funny and clever book.

Dr Samuel Johnson (1709-84), most famous for his great dictionary of the English language, can best be compared with Voltaire, for his novel *Rasselas* served to express his philosophical ideas. Like Voltaire he was a satirist, a pamphleteer, a poet and a great talker.

Oliver Goldsmith (1728-74) wrote one great novel, *The Vicar of Wakefield*, and is also remembered for his brilliantly funny comedy, *She Stoops to Conquer*.

With Goldsmith the first age of the novel ended, and a new fashion for tales of horror and mystery began. These were called Gothic novels, because of their frequent setting in the

Edward Gibbon (1737–94) English historian. Educated at Oxford, and served in Hampshire Militia from 1759–63. Decided to write *The Decline and Fall of the Roman Empire* in 1764, one of the greatest histories in English. It deals with a period covering thirteen centuries, its style dignified and eloquent. It is notable for accuracy.

Above Fenimore Cooper's *Last of the Mohicans* is an exciting tale about the American west.

Charles Lamb (1775–1834) English essayist and critic. Became a clerk with the East India Co., 1792. From 1796 until the end of her life he cared for his sister Mary, who suffered periodic attacks of insanity. His best-known works are the *Essays of Elia.*

medieval period, and their most famous author was Horace Walpole (1717-97), whose *Castle of Otranto* was enormously popular. In this fashion, too, was *Frankenstein* by Mary Shelley (1797-1851), which can now be regarded as the first science-fiction story to be written.

American literature

In the middle of the 18th century American literature had its beginning. One of the first writers to be known outside his own continent was Washington Irving (1783-1859), whose *Rip Van Winkle* and *The Legend of Sleepy Hollow* showed Europe that America already had her own legends and way of life. Fenimore Cooper (1789-1851) in *The Pathfinder* and *The Last of the Mohicans* described the existence of the settlers and began the romance of the Red Indian which has lasted so long. But it is not until the mid-19th century that American literature can really be considered in a manner comparable to that of western Europe.

German literature

It is in the second half of the 18th century that Germany for the first time began to produce literature which aroused interest in Europe and America. The two greatest writers of Germany, Johann Wolfgang von Goethe (1749-1832) and Johann Friedrich von Schiller (1759-1805), did their early work in this period, and it had considerable effect on other writers outside their own country. Goethe returned to a Greek story by Euripides for his *Iphigenie auf Tauris*, and his first *Wilhelm Meister* and the first part of *Faust* are written in a simple and classical way. Both Goethe and Schiller believed that if a man could develop all his powers equally he would find himself in perfect harmony with himself and his life. Schiller in his play *Wilhelm Tell* and Goethe in his epic *Hermann und Dorothea* both attempt to give examples of their beliefs.

From this part-classical, part-romantic literature came the real German romantic movement. This held that art was something above normal life and almost religious in feeling. To this period belong some outstanding lyric poetry, the fairy tales of the brothers Grimm, and Goethe's last and possibly greatest works, the second *Wilhelm Meister* and the second part of *Faust*.

The only outstanding poet outside the movement was Heinrich Heine (1797-1856), who excelled in both satire and lyric. He was neither classicist nor romantic in the way he wrote and stands alone in his age as a great and original talent.

English romantics

The English romantic movement borrowed from all sources, and its beliefs were in the power of the creative imagination, the necessity for genius to overthrow rules, and in Nature as a source of inspiration. It began with the publication of the *Lyrical Ballads* in 1798 by William Wordsworth (1770-1850) and Samuel Taylor Coleridge (1772-1834). The aims of these two poets were simplicity of form and the use of ordinary everyday speech for their poetry. The results were as far away as possible from the classical ideas of the 18th century.

It was not they, however, but George Gordon, Lord Byron (1788-1824), who enjoyed European fame as a romantic poet, and his romances and *Childe Harold* were praised by Goethe and even translated into Russian. Nevertheless, Byron's best work lies in his satire, especially in the witty *Don Juan*, and he is more properly a follower of Pope and Dryden than a true romantic.

The other two romantic poets of the age were Percy Bysshe Shelley (1792-1822) and John Keats (1795-1821). Shelley's lyric poetry has an unequalled delicacy but, despite his belief that poets are the prophets of their age, he produced no large works of any lasting quality. Keats was not really interested in literary fashions. For him the essential doctrine both for poetry and life was 'What the imagination seizes as beauty must be truth', in other words 'Beauty is truth, truth beauty', and his work is an attempt to show this. His odes are among the greatest in English poetry.

French romantics

Romanticism in French literature came after the Revolution, when society was very different from what it had been in the past. Alfred de Vigny (1797-1863) found most of his theories in the Bible, and his idea of greatness is the uncomplaining acceptance of suffering.

A greater writer was Victor Hugo (1802-85) who wrote poetry, drama and prose. He attempted a new form of the epic in *La Légende des siècles*, but this is something of a magnificent failure. He is, perhaps, at his best in his lyric poetry, where his style makes old situations and emotions suddenly come alive.

Possibly the greatest of all the French romantic poets was Alfred de Musset (1810-57). But his judgements were not always sure, and sometimes his poetry in its excessive emotion topples from passion to self-parody.

The last of the French romantics, Charles Baudelaire (1821-67), stood outside the movement. Like Keats he was searching for beauty and truth, but his work could not be more different. His collected poems *Les Fleurs du Mal* (The Flowers of Evil) produced a public storm and legal proceedings. The reading public was shocked by some of Baudelaire's subjects and by his treatment of them. Yet it was his work that was to inspire the greatest poets of the next generation.

The next school of poets to arise in France was the Parnassian, and the originator of this movement was Théophile Gautier (1811-72), who was both poet and novelist. In his novel *Mademoiselle de Maupin* he first expressed the theory of 'art for art's sake', an idea which developed naturally out of romantic theories and was

Left Byron in Greek dress, from the painting by Thomas Phillips in the National Gallery, London. As with so many poets Byron was a man of action at heart. A great lover of freedom he joined the Greek people in their struggle for independence from Turkey. He caught a fever during the campaign and died a national hero to the Greeks.

Left A scene from *Tom Thumb*, one of the fairy tales by the brothers Grimm. These two brothers were learned professors of the German language and literature but they are remembered today for their folk and fairy tales.

Johann Wolfgang von Goethe (1749–1832). German poet and dramatist. He first studied law at Leipzig, where he wrote his first two plays. Moved to Strasbourg, then in 1775 he settled in a ministerial appointment at the Weimar court. He was a universal genius and is said to have been the last man to have mastered all branches of knowledge. But his chief fame lies with his poems and plays.

Above In a lively encounter D'Artagnan and the musketeers cross swords with Cardinal Richelieu's men in an episode from *The Three Musketeers.*

Honoré de Balzac (1799–1850) French novelist. Studied law but did not wish to practise. Had novels published in 1821 but his real career as a writer did not begin until after a period in publishing during which he became bankrupt. After this his output of novels was immense.

to have considerable influence on later writers. The Parnassian ideal was detachment and pure description, and an escape from the lyric of personal passion.

The Parnassians were followed by the Symbolists, a movement begun, although unconsciously, by Paul Verlaine (1844-96). Verlaine attempted to get away from all literary devices and write delicate impressionistic poems, capturing changing moods and feelings. Arthur Rimbaud (1854-91) wrote a sonnet which 'sees' each of the vowels in terms of a different colour. He thought of the poet as an inspired figure who must suffer every emotion to the full, even to madness, before he is fit to write. His genius, like that of Coleridge, was short-lived and his poetic career ended at the age of nineteen.

Symbolism reached its peak in the work of Stéphane Mallarmé (1842-98). He wrote in a curious and difficult style, almost a new language, where sentences take on strange shapes in a kind of word-music.

The French novel

The pre-Revolution French novel had been largely an imitation of the English Gothic novel, but by about 1830 romantic ideas began to affect this literary form. Romanticism is first seen in the work of Marie Henri Beyle, known as Stendhal (1783-1842), who wrote *Le Rouge et le Noir* and *La Chartreuse de Parme,* in which motives and feelings are carefully explored.

The most prolific writer of the age was Honoré de Balzac (1799-1850) whose enormous output of about eighty novels form what he called the *Comédie Humaine,* in which he attempted to classify all the different kinds of men and women of his time. The more emotional and sentimental side of romanticism is found in the books of George Sand (1804-76), whose real name was Aurore Dupin.

Historical fiction became popular in France, especially in the work of Alfred de Vigny, Victor Hugo and Alexandre Dumas *père* (1803-70). Dumas wrote three books about the adventures of the three musketeers (Athos, Porthos and Aramis) and these and the *Count of Monte Cristo* were among the first books to appear in serial form in the magazines of the time.

Prosper Mérimée (1803-70) wrote a number of stories of romantic adventure, but he was the last of the romantic novelists. A fashion for realism, or truth to life in situation and character, was beginning. This is best seen in the work of Gustave Flaubert (1821-80). In *Madame Bovary* he shows how silly the romantic outlook on real life can be, while *Salammbô* was the first unglamorised historical novel.

This realistic style of writing lasted for about thirty years. Then with Emile Zola (1840-1902) realism passed into naturalism, which was an attempt to produce an absolutely true picture of life, with the unpleasant and disgusting treated in the same way as the beautiful and attractive. As usually seems to happen with this kind of attempt the author found more in life to disgust than to delight him, and his work is brilliant but depressing.

Naturalism in the short stories of Guy de Maupassant (1850-93) is rather different. Because he is not writing full-length novels he is forced to select the most important things and to let these speak for the rest. Alphonse Daudet (1840-97), also a writer of short stories, varies his style from romanticism, through realism to

Above Some of the best-known characters from the works of Charles Dickens are grouped together in this drawing.

Above left Scott's first novel *Waverley* tells the story of a young army officer, Edward Waverley, who joins Bonnie Prince Charlie's army during the Jacobite rising in 1745 in Scotland.

naturalism according to his subject, while Anatole France (1844-1924) seemed to return to the ironic, logical style of Voltaire.

19th-century English novelists

The 19th century is the great age of the novel in England. Jane Austen (1775-1817), the daughter of a Hampshire rector, lived a quiet and secluded life, yet produced an unequalled portrait of the upper middle-class society of her day. She writes with a beautiful gentle irony, and her six novels, *Pride and Prejudice, Sense and Sensibility, Mansfield Park, Emma, Northanger Abbey* and *Persuasion,* are witty and minutely observed records of the lives and loves of characters who remain perfectly real to us today.

Sir Walter Scott (1771-1832), Scotland's greatest novelist, returned to the traditions of romance and history. It was Scott's tales of the tragic and stirring past of his own people in such books as *Rob Roy, The Fair Maid of Perth* and *The Heart of Midlothian* that helped to make Scotland fashionable as a place to be visited.

Probably the greatest English novelist of the time was Charles Dickens (1812-70), whose best work reveals some of the dreadful social conditions of his age, the miseries of child-workers and of the poor: by bringing these things to public notice he did much to remedy them. Such books as *Oliver Twist* and *David Copperfield* are among these, while *The Pickwick Papers* is pure comedy, and *The Old Curiosity Shop* is a somewhat sentimental story.

William Makepeace Thackeray (1811-63) uses satire to show the social silliness of the age. His *Vanity Fair,* the title of which is taken from Bunyan's *Pilgrim's Progress,* is one of the wittiest novels of the time.

The three Brontë sisters, Charlotte (1816-55), Emily (1818-48) and Anne (1820-49), were, like Jane Austen, daughters of a country rector, but they were brought up at Haworth in the bleak moorlands of Yorkshire. Charlotte and Anne became governesses, then the only career open to middle-class girls, and their books describe their experiences in this capacity. Charlotte Brontë's *Jane Eyre* is the love story of a poor governess who ends by marrying her employer, but it also describes the terrible conditions at the boarding school to which the little Brontë sisters were sent. Emily Brontë remained at Haworth and her only novel *Wuthering Heights* is a strange and grim tale set in the bleak moors she loved so well.

Mary Ann Evans (1819-80), who wrote under the name of George

Thomas Carlyle (1795–1881) English historian. Although he was a talented mathematician, he soon turned to writing. He moved to London in 1834 where he wrote his famous book on the French Revolution (1837). His was probably the greatest influence on mid-19th-century literature.

Above One hot summer afternoon Alice chased the White Rabbit down a rabbit hole and began her strange *Adventures in Wonderland.* This story by Lewis Carroll is one of the most famous children's books ever written but it appeals to people of all ages. Carroll's real name was Charles Dodgson (1832–98) and he was a lecturer in mathematics at Oxford. The real Alice was Alice Liddell, who with her sisters went on river expeditions with Mr Dodgson, during which he told them the story, piece by piece. Alice's adventures also appeared in *Through the Looking Glass*, and the illustrations for both books by Sir John Tenniel have created a curious and familiar world to millions of children and grown-ups.

Eliot, deals with social conditions of farmers and tradesmen in the Midlands; while Anthony Trollope (1815-82) gives a picture of life in an imaginary English cathedral town and the country around it.

Thomas Hardy (1840-1928) returns to English country settings, but although many of his villagers are amusingly drawn he is aware of the hardships and sorrows of country life, and his books, such as *Tess of the D'Urbervilles,* are largely tragic.

After 1870 schooling became compulsory for all English children. As a result more people than ever before were reading books, and a demand grew for 'lighter' reading and more 'good stories'. This was met by such writers as the Scot, Robert Louis Stevenson (1850-94), whose *Treasure Island* and *Kidnapped* are among the best adventure stories of all time, and by Rudyard Kipling (1865-1936), who wrote some of the best children's books in *Puck of Pook's Hill* and *The Jungle Books*.

19th-century American literature

In the 19th century the scope of American literature began to grow. Edgar Allan Poe (1809-49) was a poet, novelist and short-story writer who excelled in tales of horror and mystery, and whose *The Murders in the Rue Morgue* was really the first detective story.

America also inherited the ideas of the romantic movement and these were expressed chiefly by Ralph Waldo Emerson (1803-82) and Henry David Thoreau (1817-62). Nathaniel Hawthorne (1804-64) also thought of his work as 'romantic', but he is much concerned with ideas of guilt and how men's consciences work, probably because of the strict traditions of the American puritan background.

In Herman Melville (1819-91), too, there is this strong sense of the power of evil, and his greatest novel *Moby Dick* shows men tormented by a sense of guilt set against their pursuit of the great, white whale, Moby Dick.

The American romantic poets looked to England for their inspiration, and to the ideas of Wordsworth in particular. Henry Wadsworth Longfellow (1807-82) and John Greenleaf Whittier (1807-92), the Quaker poet, are at

their best in simple accounts of country scenes and people, though in *Paul Revere's Ride* Longfellow showed that he could write excellent narrative poetry, while his *Hiawatha* continued the romance of the Red Indian.

In America, as in France, romanticism was followed by realism, and the link between the two styles is to be found in the work of Walt Whitman (1819-92). His experiments with new rhythms and new forms of poetry paved the way for modern writers of the 20th century. American realism was to be less grim and sordid than the French idea of it, and this is seen best in the work of Samuel Langhorne Clemens (1835-1910), better known as Mark Twain. He mixed truth to life with a wryly humorous view of it, and his *Tom Sawyer* and *Huckleberry Finn* are still a delight to both children and their elders.

Although realism was to remain the most popular American way of writing until the present century, the best writer of the second half of the 19th century was closer to Zola and the naturalistic school. This was Stephen Crane (1871-1900), whose *The Red Badge of Courage* dealt with the American Civil War in a vivid and down-to-earth way.

Good stories of romance and adventure are found in *The Call of the Wild* and *White Fang* by Jack London (1876-1916), while the *Uncle Remus* stories of Joel Chandler Harris (1848-1908) have now appealed to at least four generations of children.

The outstanding American novelist of his time, however, was Henry James

Left Moby Dick in the book by Herman Melville is a great white whale which Captain Ahab vows to destroy. He chases it half-way round the world before the final encounter which ends in an epic fight lasting three days.

Mark Twain (1835–1910) American writer. He worked as a Mississippi pilot and he adopted his name from the call of a man sounding the river, 'mark twain', meaning mark two fathoms. His real name was Samuel Langhorne Clemens. He travelled extensively in Europe and America and was famous as a humorist. His most famous books *Tom Sawyer* and *Huckleberry Finn* are drawn from his boyhood experiences in Missouri.

(1843-1916), whose work is international rather than American. His early work is in the tradition of realism, but he was later to become interested less in actions and events and more in the way people's minds work, and in their private feelings and responses to life. For this reason his later books such as *The Wings of a Dove* and *The Golden Bowl* were failures when they first appeared, and it was not until after his death that James became really famous.

Victorian writers

After the romantic period ended in 19th-century England there was no great literary 'fashion'. At the beginning of the Victorian age there were two outstanding English poets, Alfred, Lord Tennyson (1809-92) and Robert Browning (1812-89). Tennyson wrote lyric poems and verse dramas not intended to be acted, and in his *Idylls of the King* he returned to the stories of King Arthur. A weakness in his work lay in his feeling that only old, beautiful and romantic themes were suitable for poetry, so that the truth to life which makes poetry 'come alive' is, for the most part, missing.

Browning, too, preferred to set his poetry in past ages, but because he was chiefly interested in the kinds of moral and religious problems which have applied to all ages, his work is more alive and has remained so. Matthew Arnold (1822-88) also was interested in wider moral questions, and his poetry shows a return to the simple and disciplined style of classic times.

In the latter half of the 19th century a new movement grew up in revolt against the Industrial Revolution and all the ugliness and lack of grace to which the beginning of the 'machine age' had led. This was an association of poets, painters and craftsmen, whose ideals were those of medieval times, and for this reason they called themselves the Pre-Raphaelite Brotherhood.

This was led by Dante Gabriel Rossetti (1828-82), who was, like many of his colleagues, both painter

Left Rudyard Kipling's *Kim* is an exciting adventure story of an orphaned Irish boy who spends his childhood as a vagabond in 19th-century India and works for the British secret service.

Right The retreat from Moscow of Napoleon's army is one of the great dramatic moments in Tolstoy's *War and Peace,* regarded by many people as the greatest novel ever written. The book is on a vast scale and contains a great variety of characters whose lives are described with an extraordinary vividness and sympathy.

Gerard M. Hopkins (1844–89) English poet. One of the outstanding names in the poetry of the 19th century. He was a Jesuit priest whose work was not published until 1918. Even then it astounded its first readers because it was 'too modern'. Hopkins created a new language of poetry, with new rhythms and metres and it is only today that he has become recognised as a major poet and a great influence on modern poetry.

and poet. The Brotherhood included William Morris (1834-96), poet and craftsman, and Rossetti's sister Christina (1830-94), and its work shows the first conscious revolt against mass-production and the industrial uglification of what Blake had called 'England's green and pleasant land'.

Russian literature

It was during the 19th century that Russian literature began to be known outside her own boundaries. Until this time there had been little communication between Russia and the other nations of Europe. Because of the mystery which had wrapped that vast country, when Russian literature was first read abroad in translated form it immediately and justly became both famous and fashionable.

The work of the first great Russian poet, Alexander Pushkin (1799-1837), which includes the heroic poem *Ruslan and Ludmilla,* the romance *Eugene Onegin* and the historical drama *Boris Godunov,* did not in fact achieve the international fame it deserved. Poetry can seldom, if ever, be translated successfully into another language without losing most of its character in the process. It was, therefore, Russian novelists and dramatists who became most famous abroad.

The Russian novel began because of the popularity among Russian readers of the translated works of Richardson and Fielding, and the first really national Russian novelist was Nikolai Gogol (1809-52). Because he began the truly Russian novel he had great influence over the writers who followed him, particularly over Feodor Dostoevsky (1821-81). Dostoevsky led a poor and rather miserable life. At one time he was a political prisoner in Siberia and the scenes in his novels recall these grim events. His best-known works are *Crime and Punishment, The Idiot* and *The Brothers Karamazov.*

Another poet, who is better known to the west for his novel *A Hero of our Times* is Mikhail Lermontov (1814-41). Unlike Dostoevsky, he was more interested in the ways in which his characters' minds worked than in the actions in which they were involved. Lermontov's work also influenced later Russian writers, particularly Ivan Turgenev (1818-83) and Leo Tolstoy (1828-1910).

Turgenev was primarily interested in the society of his time, but Tolstoy preferred much grander topics. His famous *War and Peace* follows individual characters and the fate of warring nations during the Napoleonic Wars, when Napoleon set out to conquer Russia but was defeated by the cold of the Russian winter and the vastness of the country, not by human armies. Tolstoy's *Anna Karenina* is one of the greatest love stories of all time.

Short stories became the fashion in Russia, and the two most notable writers in this form were Anton Chekhov (1860-1904) and Maxim Gorky (1868-1936). Today, Gorky is

George Bernard Shaw (1856–1950). Irish dramatist and writer. Began his career as a music and drama critic. His plays tend to have little action but are full of witty and stimulating thought. He was a life-long socialist and reformer.

perhaps best remembered for his play *The Lower Depths,* and Chekhov also is thought of as the foremost dramatist of his age. His best-known plays, *The Seagull, Uncle Vanya* and *The Cherry Orchard,* are still constantly produced in translation in most countries of western Europe.

In 1917 came the Russian revolution and a new state emerged – the Union of the Soviet Socialist Republics. Since then we know comparatively few works from Russian literature. One of the books which achieved international fame is Mikhail Sholokhov's *And Quiet Flows the Don.*

Scandinavian literature

In the 19th century Scandinavia, which had been outside the main stream of European literature for many centuries, produced three writers who achieved world-wide fame. One was the Dane, Hans Christian Andersen (1805-75), whose fairy tales and stories include such small masterpieces as *The Ugly Duckling* and *The Snow Queen.* The other two were dramatists: the Swede, August Strindberg (1849-1912) and the Norwegian, Henrik Ibsen (1828-1906).

Of these, Ibsen is enormously important, not only in his own right but because of the influence he had upon the English theatre. Ever since the decline of Restoration drama there had been no great playwright in England, except for the witty and graceful writer Richard Brinsley Sheridan (1751-1816). Now, the production of Ibsen's plays in England, such as *The Doll's House, Hedda Gabler* and *The Master Builder,* gave new force and direction to English drama. These plays are really neither tragedies nor comedies, but are intended to make audiences think out many of the questions which confront most men and women.

Left Two writers who had an immense influence not only in their own countries but on the whole of western literature were Anton Chekhov (1860–1904), seen left, and Henrik Ibsen (1828–1906), seen right. Chekhov was a great novelist and playwright with a fine sense of comedy who was able at the same time to express the unhappiness in the world which often underlies its beauty. Ibsen was principally an influence in the theatre, and his plays of realism which deal with the actual problems which men and women experience in their lives, have more force than his poetic dramas, *Peer Gynt* and *Brandt*.

Modern drama

Ibsen's ideas on how drama can work were accepted and carried still further by other dramatists in England, notably by the Irishman, George Bernard Shaw (1856-1950). He made his plays into arguments for and against all sorts of topics that interested him, and his plays are still splendid theatrical entertainment.

This was an age of Irish playwrights, for Shaw's contemporary, Oscar Wilde (1854-1900), went back to the witty and light-hearted work of Sheridan

Above Joseph Conrad (1857–1924) was a Polish-born sea-captain in the British Mercantile Marine. He left the sea in 1894 and settled in England to become a writer. Nearly all his books are to do with the sea, mostly in the area of Malaya, which he often visited. After writing several short stories his first book *Almayer's Folly* was immediately accepted and he spent the rest of his life producing novels, many autobiographical, with a command of the English language that is remarkable.

for his inspiration and his comedies, particularly *The Importance of Being Earnest*, have lost less than Shaw's by the passing of time. Another Irishman, John Millington Synge (1871-1909), turned to Irish peasants and Irish legend for his subjects, while *Juno and the Paycock* by Sean O'Casey (1884-1964) remains the perfect story of Dublin life.

Drama in England now is difficult to judge. The verse plays of T. S. Eliot (1888-1964) are still produced, but he does not seem to have inspired a new fashion for the use of poetry in the theatre.

In neither Italy nor Germany was the first half of the 20th century remarkable for its drama. Each produced one major playwright: Luigi Pirandello (1867-1936) in Italy, whose *Six Characters in Search of an Author* explored new methods of dramatic writing; and Bertolt Brecht (1898-1956) in Germany, whose *Threepenny Opera* has been successful in America and England.

France has kept a tradition of good drama without a break from the first half of the 19th century. Romantic comedy was written by Alfred de Musset, while *La Dame aux camélias* by Alexandre Dumas *fils* (1824-95) shows that romantic tragedy can still appeal to an audience of today. So, too, does the work of Edmond Rostand (1868-1918) who wrote the comic fantasy about the longest nose in history, *Cyrano de Bergerac*.

The films of Jean Cocteau (1891-1963), such as *Orphée*, have brought him international fame as a dramatist and script-writer. Jean Anouilh, too, is almost as well known in England as in France, particularly for *The Lark* and *Becket*. Jean-Paul Sartre uses drama as a way of exploring his ideas about politics, religion and philosophy: as a result his plays often seem to lack action.

The most recent fashion in the French theatre is for 'drama of the absurd', where the plays are strange fantasies without plots and often without normal conversation. The playwrights associated with this school are Eugene Ionesco, Samuel Beckett and Jean Genet.

There was no real American drama before the 20th century, and even then it began in a very small way with amateur groups producing plays mostly for their own amusement. A member of one such group was Eugene O'Neill (1888-1953) and, from writing his first play for the amateur company to which he belonged, he went on to become America's greatest dramatist with such plays as *Mourning becomes Electra* and *The Iceman Cometh*. No other playwright was as successful until Tennessee Williams produced *The Glass Menagerie* and *A Streetcar Named Desire*. Arthur Miller was made famous by his modern tragedy *Death of a Salesman,* and he has written one extremely powerful historical play in *The Crucible.*

The modern novel

In France perhaps the most outstanding novelist of the first half of the 20th century was André Gide (1869-1951). Gide was most interested in how men's consciences work when they encounter difficult moral problems, so that he is a very serious writer. In his book which recalls his own life as a child and a young man *Si le grain ne meurt* he shows that life was always a serious thing for him.

Another author of the time, Marcel Proust (1871-1922), also wrote of his childhood in *Du côté de chez Swann,* but he is trying to recapture what being a child actually *felt* like. In his great work *A la recherche du temps perdu,* of which *Du côté de chez Swann* is the first part, he is chiefly interested in time and the effects of time on memory.

The greatest woman writer of the age was Colette (1873-1954), many of whose novels also recall her own childhood in Burgundy, and her girlhood in Paris, with simplicity, humour and great skill.

Among writers of this century Francois Mauriac, like Gide, preferred to write of the problems which beset men's consciences. Unlike Gide, he approached them from a strictly Catholic point of view. The books of André Malraux combine exciting action with the difficulties men have in being true both to themselves and to their fellow men. Albert Camus, like Malraux, was primarily interested in what makes men take decisive and heroic decisions. This is clearly seen in *La Peste.* The novels of Jean-Paul Sartre are a depressing, almost despairing picture of the uselessness of most lives, but brilliantly written.

In Germany, the greatest writer of this century is undoubtedly Thomas Mann (1875-1955), both in the full-length novel and short story. Franz Kafka (1883-1924), who was in fact a Jewish author from Czechoslovakia, also wrote in German and his two novels *The Trial* and *The Castle* are among the most outstanding of the century.

Left The history of journalism and the popular newspaper in modern times is very much bound up with the names of two men in particular: Alfred Harmsworth, Lord Northcliffe (left) and William Randolph Hearst (right). The name Harmsworth belonged to five brothers all of whom became newspaper magnates or politicians. The most celebrated was Alfred, who pioneered mass-circulation journalism. He published *Answers* in 1888, took over the *Evening News* in 1894, and the *Daily Mail* in 1896. Founded the *Daily Mirror* in 1903 and became proprietor of *The Times* in 1908. Hearst was an American newspaper owner who acquired the San Francisco *Examiner* from his father in 1867. It was he who revolutionised journalism by the use of banner headlines, pictures and sensational features – all of which earned his papers the nickname of 'the yellow press'. Took over the New York *Journal* in 1895.

The novel in England

England began the 20th century with 'novel-series' by John Galsworthy (1867-1933) and Arnold Bennett (1867-1931). Galsworthy's account of a wealthy family in his *Forsyte Saga* is still very popular today. Bennett deals with the poorer and more ordinary people of the industrial midlands of England.

The political struggle which at last gave women the right to vote in political elections was one of the things which inspired D. H. Lawrence (1885-1930) to consider the different ways in which men and women react to each other, and to consider the problems they encounter. Women, too, are at the centre of most of the novels of Virginia Woolf (1882-1941), though she is more interested in the way in which their minds work.

One of the greatest writers of this century was the Irishman James Joyce (1882-1941), who also explored the minds of his characters. To do this he invented a new style of writing – fascinating but often very difficult. His two most outstanding books are *Ulysses* and *Finnegan's Wake.*

Novels inspired by political and social ideas are associated particularly with the names of Hilaire Belloc (1870-1953), G. K. Chesterton (1874-1936), E. M. Forster (1879-1970) and George Orwell (1903-50). Evelyn Waugh (1903-66) and Graham Greene (1904-91) are thought of as 'Catholic' novelists, though Waugh can also be classed with Aldous Huxley (1894-1963) and Compton Mackenzie (1883-1972) as one of the best satirical writers of his generation.

The fashion for detective stories began in the 20th century, and some of the very best are still the earliest to be written. Wilkie Collins (1824-89)

Right Sherlock Holmes and Dr Watson are shown in a familiar scene of detection, where the great man is about to deliver his thoughts to his eagerly awaiting and admiring companion. Sir Arthur Conan Doyle began life as a doctor, but lack of success turned his hand to authorship. After his debut with a story in *Chamber's Journal* he introduced the great detective from Baker Street in a series which ran in the *Strand Magazine*. Holmes's utterance, 'Elementary, my dear Watson!' has become a household phrase.

Somerset Maugham (1874–1965) British writer and master of the short story. He qualified as a surgeon at St Thomas's Hospital in London and drew material from this for his novel *Of Human Bondage*. In both the First and Second World Wars he was a British agent. He travelled all over the South Seas and the Far East. Among his most famous works are *The Moon and Sixpence* and *Cakes and Ale*. His collected short stories were first published in 1951.

introduced the first great police detective, Sergeant Cuff, while the outstanding amateur at the job is certainly the immortal Sherlock Holmes, created by Sir Arthur Conan Doyle (1859-1930).

Science-fiction was partly the invention of H. G. Wells (1866-1946), and although this kind of book is often more sensational than literary, excellent stories have been written by C. S. Lewis and John Wyndham.

C. S. Lewis (1898-1963) will be remembered by children for his *Narnia* stories, for the 20th century has also been the age of novels for children. Arthur Ransome (1884-1967) deserves a mention for his enormously popular stories of the *Swallows and Amazons*, while for a younger age group *The Wind in the Willows* by Kenneth Grahame (1859-1922) and the *Winnie the Pooh* books by A. A. Milne (1882-1956) are outstanding.

The novel in America

The entry of the United States into the First World War (1914-18) meant that for the first time ordinary Americans experienced ways of life outside their own country and, probably as a result of this, post-war American writers began to question the value of many things which had become accepted as part of the American way of life. The most outstanding among these was Sinclair Lewis (1885-1951) whose *Main Street* and *Babbitt* attempted to show what was wrong in small-town and city life.

Ernest Hemingway (1898-1961) spent much of his life outside America and his interests covered a wide field. He wrote about men of action, and in such novels as *For Whom the Bell Tolls* he used his own experiences for background to his exciting stories. F. Scott Fitzgerald (1896-1940) wrote of people who were happy in their youth, wit and wealth, and his experience, too, included many years spent outside America.

John Steinbeck (1902-68) was concerned with the fate of the poor, particularly in California, but he was also fascinated by odd, out-of-the-way characters and his books such as *Cannery Row* and *Sweet Thursday* are as rich in humour as in sadness about the state of poor men. William Faulkner (1897-1962) was a native of Mississippi and is primarily interested in the problems of the 'deep south'. A very different author, James Thurber (1894-1961), was also a brilliant illustrator of his own fantasy stories. He achieved world-wide fame as a cartoonist and journalist, and his fairy tale *The 13 Clocks* is one of the best children's fantasies of the century.

One of the most interesting of modern American novelists was the Russian-born Vladimir Nabokov (1899-1977). He saw the vulgarity and silliness of middle-class Americans with fresh eyes, and brought this out with humour and style in such books as *Lolita* and *Pnin*.

Modern poetry

In the history of the poetry of this century the First World War inspired English poets as it did no others. Some, such as Rupert Brooke (1887-1915) and Julian Grenfell (1888-1915),

Left The Water Rat and Mole sculling up river after Ratty has spoken of the joys of boating in the immortal words from Kenneth Grahame's classic *The Wind in the Willows:* 'there is nothing – absolutely nothing – half so much worth doing as simply messing about in boats'.

saw the war as heroic and glorious. Others, like Wilfred Owen (1893-1918), found it a terrible experience, and their poetry is against war.

William Butler Yeats (1865-1939), an Irishman, was more involved in the struggle for the independence of his own country than with the war in Europe. But his best work is not influenced by politics or wars but is an expression of his own vision in a rich yet simple and musical style. Walter de la Mare (1873-1956) was another poet who wrote of his own fantasy world. A more complicated philosophy of life was expressed by T. S. Eliot in 'free verse' without rhyme or regular metre.

In France the greatest poet in the early years of the century was Paul Valéry (1871-1945). Paul Claudel (1868-1955) was an ardent Catholic and at his best in religious verse. André Breton (1896-1966) and Paul Eluard (1895-1952) were also outstanding lyric poets.

There has been little major poetry in Italy since the work of Gabriele d'Annunzio (1863-1938), and his work is now thought of as rather stiff and unreal.

In Germany Stefan George (1868-1933) and Hugo von Hofmannsthal (1874-1929) put new life into lyric poetry in the early years of the century, and this revival culminated in the work of Rainer Maria Rilke (1875-1926), who was probably one of the greatest European poets of the years between the two world wars. But the Second World War interrupted the literary life of Germany, as it did in Italy, and nothing of world-wide fame has been written there since.

America's greatest woman poet, Emily Dickinson (1830-86) died before the 20th century, but her work was not known until after her death, as apparently she never wished to have it published or to be known as a poet. A more 'modern' outlook on poetry and on life is to be found in the work of Carl Sandburg (1878-1967) and Nicholas Vachel Lindsay (1879-1931). Both these two loved life and adventure and write with enormous gusto and enthusiasm. Robert Frost (1874-1963) was a more retiring character who was a farmer as well as a poet, and he writes well of country life.

The first American 'school' of poetry in this century was started by Ezra Pound (1885-1972). This was the Imagist school which was inspired by the tiny, exact and perfect descriptive poetry of China and Japan.

The matter of literature

This review of the beginning and development of literature has shown many things. Literary forms have been invented, have flourished and then declined. Literary fashions have risen, to be supported for a while and then forgotten. The most significant thing of all is that literature arose out of the four main topics of battle, religion, love and death, and these four are still the subjects of almost all the literature of today. Men's ways of writing change: the subjects they most want to write about do not.

Ernest Hemingway (1898–1961) American author. He was a journalist, chiefly a war correspondent. His novels and short stories are mostly about physical courage and reflect the hard adventurous life he led. His style and gift for naturalistic dialogue and the understatement began a new way of writing. Won the Pulitzer Prize in 1953 and the Nobel Prize in 1954.

Above Greek theatres were built in the open air, usually on a hillside. This reconstruction shows what such a theatre in Athens probably looked like. The centre, or orchestra, is the space immediately in front of the tiered seats in which the audience sat. This was originally circular but in later theatres became a semi-circle. In the centre of this stands the altar to the god Dionysus.

The theatre and popular entertainment

Actors are sometimes called Thespians in honour of a Greek who lived over two thousand years ago. His name was Thespis, and he is said to have travelled round Greece with a company of strolling players and a wagon that could be converted into a stage.

Thespis was the first to use an actor in plays, which had been performed by a chorus and its leader until he arrived on the scene. He wrote and directed plays, and acted in them as well. He was the first 'man of the theatre'.

Although the very beginnings of the theatre date back to the dawn of human history, when primitive man first danced and then added words and music to his dances, it was in ancient Greece that the theatre proper, with playwright, actor and audience, was born.

In the fascinating world of actors and actresses, scenic designers, audiences and theatre buildings, there were some periods during which the actor was in command of the theatre – in others, the playwright. Just occasionally a miracle happened and playwright, actor and audience – and there can be no good theatre without a good audience – were all at their best together. This happened in the England of Elizabeth I and James I. From time to time during its history the theatre has almost disappeared – but never completely. It survived the dark ages – just! It will survive the space age.

The Greeks and Romans

Greek theatres were in the open air and were built into hillsides. Audiences sat on steeply-tiered seats in a semicircle overlooking a circular space called the orchestra. This was originally a dancing space with a central altar and was used by the chorus. Behind the orchestra was a permanent building. At first, perhaps, this was just a hut for the actors to change in, then it became a temple-like structure with a central double door. The restored theatre at Epidaurus, built around 340 BC, shows best what Greek theatres looked like, and it is still being used for performances of ancient Greek masterpieces.

Theatres held up to 16,000 people and everyone could hear perfectly. The theatre was regarded as a celebration for the whole community, so the whole community went to it. At first all seats were free, and later, when a charge was made, the poor were given the small amount of entrance money required.

Actors wore splendid robes, high boots and masks. There were many different types of masks, which enabled the actors to play several parts in the same play. Because his face was covered, the actor's voice was all-important, especially as his heavy robes limited movement. Comic actors had lighter costumes as they had to be somewhat acrobatic. There were no actresses, and the actors themselves were greatly respected.

Roman theatres were built on flat ground. They did away with the orchestra, and the action was concentrated on a raised stage and a theatre building with three doors. Many Roman theatres survive. But the Romans had little of the Greeks' flair for the drama. Their actors were not respected as people. Plays became broader and coarser, but could not compete with the Roman love of cruel sports and sheer bloodbaths in great arenas. The new religion, Christianity, frowned on the Roman theatre, and when the barbarians conquered Rome they despised what was left of a once great art. In the 6th century AD the theatre seemed to be dead.

The church and the theatre

The theatre was kept alive during the dark ages only by wandering groups of minstrels, dancers, acrobats and story-tellers. Its very survival depended on humble entertainers and even they were under attack from the church.

Yet it was the church that brought the theatre back to full life. All over Europe from about AD 1000 onwards, plays with stories from the Bible were being performed by the priests and choirboys. Most people could neither read nor write and plays helped get the Christian message across. Soon ordinary people as well, though not women, started acting in the plays. The churches were the theatres, and scenes ranged from Bethlehem to the Mount of Olives.

Then, from the 13th century onwards, the plays went out of doors and into the market places – and the language was changed from Latin to the language of the people. Sometimes, the different scenes of the plays, known as 'Mysteries', were mounted on carts, some of them two-storeyed, and taken round the towns. A scene would be repeated a number of times in different sections of the town.

By now the trade guilds were taking over the plays from the churches. The fishmongers' guild staged the story of Jonah and the Whale – Noah's Ark was staged by the shipwrights. And excitingly staged they were, with carpenters producing splendid fires and floods, with trap doors, with realistic torture scenes, with angels coming down from Heaven, and with the mouth of Hell belching forth clouds of smoke! Audiences thrilled to everything from the Creation to the Last Judgement.

Throughout Europe an exciting thing was happening. A true theatre audience of every sort of person was being formed. The time was ripe for great playwrights and permanent theatre buildings to appear.

Italy advances the theatre

Italy produced no great playwrights in the 16th and 17th centuries, but it has rightly been called 'the cradle of the modern theatre'. Though new types of theatres are now being built,

Above The Roman theatre had an elaborate stage: it was long and deep and scenery had been introduced by about 100 BC. The first permanent theatre in Rome was built by Pompey (106–48 BC).

Below A scene from one of the early travelling mystery plays in which the themes were usually religious. By the middle of the 14th century writers of plays had appeared and various towns began to stage their own productions, such as the great series of miracle plays from York, Chester, Wakefield and Coventry in England.

Above It is not known exactly when the unwritten comedies of the *commedia dell' arte all'improvviso* (meaning professional improvised comedy) were first performed. Certainly by the end of the 16th century they were acted all over Europe. Leading figures from the *commedia dell'arte* were popular as toy theatre characters such as Arlecchino, or Harlequin (top), and as porcelain ornaments, such as Pulcinella (bottom), the pierrot who became Mr Punch in England.

most of today's playhouses and opera houses are direct descendants of the Italian theatres of some three hundred years ago.

After trying to imitate ancient Greek and Roman theatres, Italian designers created the auditorium, curved like a horseshoe, where the audience sits, and the 'picture-frame' stage, so called because that is what it looks like when viewed from the audience. A proscenium arch formed the picture frame. It was originally built to disguise the marvellous scenic effects that Italian designers created. Clever machinery enabled 'gods' and 'goddesses' to descend from 'clouds' and other marvels.

Meanwhile, perspective – the method used by artists to give an impression of distance and space – was used to allow designers to show whole streets on the stage. Scenery was painted, and flat 'wings' were introduced, which were made of painted canvas stretched on wooden frames. These were stationary at the sides of the stage at first; then movable ones appeared, which could be slid on and off the stage to reveal other marvels behind them.

The newly invented art of opera gained most from these new ideas. Operatic productions in the 17th century were more spectacular than they have ever been since.

The other Italian contribution to the theatre of the period was the *commedia dell'arte*. There has never been a more truly theatrical entertainment than these plays, which were improvised (made up as they went along) by troupes of actors, each of whom always played the same type of part. One standard character, Arlecchino, we shall meet again as Harlequin; another, Pulcinella, hump-backed and stupid, later turned up in Britain as Mr Punch. Wearing masks, the actors in *commedia dell'arte* plays were expected to dance, sing, play the fool, perform acrobatics and act – and they did!

England's golden age

While the Italians were revolutionising theatre buildings and scenery, in England the golden age of theatre had dawned. From around 1576, when the first English theatre was built near Finsbury Fields in London by James Burbage (died 1597), until 1642, when the Puritans had every theatre closed, the theatre flourished more gloriously than ever before or since in any country.

The crowning glory of this age was William Shakespeare, the actor from Stratford-upon-Avon who became the supreme genius of the English race. But even a Shakespeare could not have flourished so successfully if conditions had not been right for him.

The first thing in his favour was a great audience. For generations, the Mystery plays had made people theatre-minded. The Elizabethans were tough and adventurous. Some of their sports, like cock-fighting and bear-baiting, were brutal. Yet all classes of people, even the toughest, seem to have loved music and poetry. Poetic dramas by Shakespeare, Marlowe and others stirred the people to their very depths, even though some of them cannot have understood everything they heard. Disappointed playwrights sometimes railed against the 'stinkards' who cracked nuts and ate oranges during performances, but there is plenty of evidence that Elizabethan audiences were marvellous. A friend of Shakespeare's wrote 'Oh how the audience were ravish'd, with what wonder they went hence!' It has been calculated that one Londoner in eight went to the theatre every week. A city of 160,000 people produced 21,000 theatregoers weekly. Until the cinema became universally popular there was nothing comparable to this in the history of popular entertainment.

The actual construction of Elizabethan playhouses is, alas, still something of a mystery. There were four theatres in London when a Dutch traveller named de Witt drew a picture of the Swan Theatre about the year 1596. It is the only really useful picture of an Elizabethan playhouse we possess. As for the immortal Globe Theatre, where so many of Shakespeare's plays were performed, scholars still argue fiercely about its structure.

Public theatres were roughly circular and enclosed a yard where people stood. Galleries surrounded them and they were open to the sky. The stage, which was a platform, projected into the standing area and, though ferocious

arguments still rage on the subject, there was almost certainly a curtained alcove behind the stage which was used for certain scenes in plays. A balcony above was used for other scenes. At the back was an actors' dressing room and a store room. The theatre held up to three thousand people, and a few privileged spectators sat on each side of the stage.

Little scenery was used and most costumes were 'modern' – in other words, Tudor or early Stuart, with sometimes just a suggestion of period: a cloak or a helmet, perhaps, to suggest Roman times. With so little scenery, the action was fast, as it is in all Shakespeare's plays, which have many scenes in them.

In the winter private theatres in indoor halls were used, the most famous being the Blackfriars Theatre. Probably more scenery was used in them than in the open-air theatres.

The actors were professionals under the protection of great lords. Shakespeare's company of actors was known as the Lord Chamberlain's Men, later – under James I – the King's Men. There were no actresses, and skilful boys took the women's parts. Every member of a company was

Above The Globe Theatre on the south bank of the Thames in London was established in about 1589. It opened with a performance of Henry V and here the Lord Chamberlain's Men became the first acting company in England with Burbage as its leading actor and Shakespeare as its playwright. In this drawing the wall of a typical Elizabethan theatre has been cut away to show inside.

Above Masques began as pastoral comedies in Italy in the 15th century. In their highest form they became court entertainments in Elizabethan and Stuart times, and claimed such writers as Ben Jonson and John Milton, and the designer Inigo Jones. Costumes and scenery were rich, colourful and ornate, and the acting was accompanied by music and dancing. Some of the most elaborate performances were staged in the Banqueting Hall at Whitehall Palace in London which was specially rebuilt to accommodate the performances.

expected to be able to dance and sing, though the 'low' comedy roles – like the gravediggers in *Hamlet* – were usually played by company clowns. A famous clown at the Globe was Will Kemp.

Shakespeare was undoubtedly inspired by having a great actor, Richard Burbage (1567?–1619), son of the builder of London's first playhouse, in his company. Burbage was the first Hamlet and the first Henry V. Another great actor was Edward Alleyn (1566-1626), who played the leads in Marlowe's plays at the Rose and Fortune theatres.

There were also private performances called masques at court and in great noblemen's houses. These were mixtures of singing and dancing and were performed by courtiers and their friends. Women were allowed to take part as the performances took place in private. They were often staged by professionals who had studied the latest scenic developments in Italy, and the masques were often spectacular.

In 1642 the Puritans closed all public theatres, and by that time the courtiers were too involved in the civil war to have much time for masques. The theatre went 'underground' – the few actors who risked trying to perform were imprisoned if they were caught. It was a black period for the theatre and it lasted eighteen years.

Spain's golden age

Other countries besides England enjoyed a theatrical golden age in the 16th and 17th centuries. Spain not only had a great playwright in Lope de Vega: it also had open-air theatres very like England's. The actors were professional and were greatly influenced by visiting troupes of *commedia dell'arte* players from Italy. One important difference in the audience was that men and women were kept apart, the women being forced to sit alone in a gallery at the back called the *cazuela,* or 'stew-pan', which sounds very hot and uncomfortable! However, women were allowed to act on the stage.

Molière's France

Like the Spanish, the French allowed women to act in plays from the start. Theatres in Paris were never unroofed, like those in England and Spain. At first, they were long rooms with a platform stage jutting out into the room. Spectators stood near the stage or sat behind on benches and in boxes. Candles lit both the stage and the auditorium.

The French theatre flourished, particularly in the time of the great comic actor and playwright, Molière. Spectacular entertainments were put on using Italian scenic methods. The court patronised the theatre, and after Molière's death his company was one of those incorporated by Louis XIV in 1680 to become France's most famous theatre, the Comédie-Française.

English theatre reborn

By the 1650s the theatre was alive and popular nearly everywhere in Europe except Britain. One small country, Holland, with its wonderful tradition of painting and drawing, provided posterity with many fine theatre illustrations, and also details of a famous theatre, the Schouwburg Theatre in Amsterdam, which was built in 1637. This was the first theatre of which we have reliable 'ground-plans' in front of and behind the stage.

Meanwhile, England remained without theatres. But when Charles II was restored to his throne in 1660, the theatre also was restored. Charles and his friends naturally wanted to continue watching the type of theatre they had enjoyed in exile in Europe. They were used to painted scenery, clever machinery and a stage with a curtain.

The old theatres being destroyed or unusable, new ones were built indoors, still with a platform stage but with a proscenium arch as well. There were doors for the actors on each side of the proscenium arch and boxes on each side of the stage.

Actresses appeared for the first time. Even before 1660 a few women had appeared on a stage despite the ban on theatres. Shakespeare's godson, Sir William D'Avenant (1606-68), had managed to produce some entertainments with music – the first English operas – in which women had sung. But from the 1660s onwards professional actresses took their place in the English theatre, one of the first being Charles II's favourite, Nell Gwynne.

Only two theatres functioned in London at first, one being the famous Theatre Royal, Drury Lane, built in 1663 and the first of four Theatre Royals on the spot. Shakespeare's plays were 'modernised' to suit public taste: *Macbeth* had singing witches and *King Lear* was given a happy ending! There was at least one great actor, Thomas Betterton (1635?-1710). Costumes were still in modern dress and theatregoing was now confined to the narrow court circle. Consequently, the brilliant, witty but often dissolute plays of Wycherley, Congreve and the other Restoration dramatists only reached and appealed to a handful of the population.

Gradually, the middle classes began to come back to the theatre, where the plays got more respectable but worse! The 18th century saw great acting in Britain – for by now many provincial cities had theatres – but few good plays. David Garrick (1717-79) dominated the century as an actor equally good in tragedy and comedy. In 1765, he introduced stage lighting concealed from the audience, having actually

Above A view from the stage of London's famous theatre, the Theatre Royal, Drury Lane, during its reconstruction in the 18th century.

For the Benefit of Mrs. CIBBER.

Theatre Royal in *Drury-Lane*,

This preſent *Monday*, being the 17th of *MARCH*,

Will be preſented a TRAGEDY, call'd

VENICE PRESERV'D.

Pierre by Mr. GARRICK,

(*Being the Firſt Time of his performing in that Character theſe Fifteen Years.*)

Priuli by Mr. HAVARD,

Renault by Mr. BURTON,

Jaffier by Mr. HOLLAND,

Bedamor by Mr. BLAKES,

Duke by Mr. BRANSBY,

Belvidera by Mrs. CIBBER.

End of the Play, the laſt NEW *Pantomime Dance* ... KEEPERS,

By Signor *Grimaldi*, Sign... ora

Giorgi, Mrs. ...

To which wi...

HIGH LIFE

The PRINCIPAL

Mr. PA

Mr. K

Mr. OB

Mr. YA

Mr. PAC

Mrs. CLI

No BUILDING *on the*

+ LADIES are deſired to ſend their Servants by Three o'Clock.

Tickets deliver'd for The ORPHAN of CHINA *will be taken.*

To-morrow, *The Funeral* and *The Way to keep Him*,

For the Benefit of Mrs. PRITCHARD.

Left An old theatre bill from the Theatre Royal, Drury Lane, in London. It advertises a performance of *Venice Preserv'd* with the great English actor, dramatist and theatre manager, David Garrick, in the leading part. Garrick was the most versatile actor of his day and could play tragedy and comedy equally well.

Right Caricature of Edmund Kean entitled 'The Theatrical Atlas'. Dressed as Richard III he carries the Drury Lane theatre on his shoulders. The sketch is a comment on the sad state of the English stage at the time. Kean 'carried' the theatre both as actor and manager and he worked himself to an early death, worn out at the age of 43.

Above Master William Betty as Young Norval in *Douglas*, after the painting by John Opie, 1805. London went mad over his Hamlet but his success did not last. As one critic said 'the popularity of that baby-faced boy was a disgrace to our theatrical profession'.

managed to banish spectators from the stage three years earlier.

After Garrick came the great tragedienne, Sarah Siddons (1755-1831). Both of them electrified the ever-growing audiences of their day and both were famous figures of their time. Yet actors were still regarded as little better than rogues and vagabonds, though they, not the playwrights, kept the theatre alive.

The German theatre

The German theatre got off to a late start. It was held back by continual wars in central Europe, by religious differences, by the popularity of touring Italian and French companies and by the fact that Germany was divided into many states. There was no capital city, theatrical or otherwise. The first theatre building was a converted church in 16th-century Nuremberg. Among the plays presented were those by Hans Sachs (1494-1576). Three hundred years later, Wagner made Sachs, the cobbler-poet, the hero of his opera, *The Mastersingers of Nuremberg*.

In the 18th century, serious-minded playwrights tried to raise the standard of the German theatre, but their plays were dull. Then Shakespeare, well-translated, reached Germany and the German theatre never looked back. Standards of acting, and the conditions under which actors worked, greatly improved. The world-famous poet, writer and thinker, Goethe, was a good amateur actor. He ran the Court Theatre at Weimar from 1784 to 1825, much of the time with the great playwright, Schiller.

Goethe's company was well-trained, but the acting was considered rather stiff and lifeless, rather as English acting had been just before Garrick's time. The best acting to be seen in Germany was in Berlin, where an actor-playwright named August Iffland (1759-1814) turned the national theatre there into one of the finest in Europe. In the early 19th century, Germany, like so many other European countries, went through a period of great actors and poor plays.

18th-century France

After Molière's death, the French theatre lost some of its former glory. More and more ordinary people (as opposed to courtiers) started going to the theatre, but there were few good new playwrights. The mighty genius Voltaire was also a good amateur actor, and he built several playhouses. He managed to clear the stage of spectators by 1759, even earlier than Garrick had done in London. Strangely enough, the treatment of actors was worse in France than in England. They were cast out by the church, and when they died could not be buried in consecrated ground. Even the great Molière had suffered in this way. Yet, by 1730, an English actress, Anne Oldfield, was buried in Westminster Abbey!

By the 1770s revolution was in the air in France, but when it broke out in 1789, the theatres survived the storm. They even remained open during the worst days of the Reign of Terror. But the new rulers of France were less tolerant than the old. Molière's plays were banned, Voltaire's were altered. The actors of the Comédie-Française were finally denounced by a member of the audience for performing a play which had a line in it praising tolerance. Only the end of the Reign of Terror saved them from losing their heads.

Early 19th-century theatre

The early 19th-century theatre in Europe was a strange but exciting mixture of great acting, bad plays and

Above At the time that Master Betty was all the rage in London, theatres everywhere were staging plays of little merit but great spectacle. Acting became less important than the number of horses that could be crowded on to a stage, or how spectacular and 'real' the effect of an earthquake could be.

sheer silliness. In Britain the bright side included the sensational career of Edmund Kean (1789?-1833), a genius who many regard as the greatest of all British tragic actors. There was also the rather odd career of the twelve-year-old boy wonder, Master William Betty, whose Hamlet so overwhelmed London in 1804 that the House of Commons adjourned early to go and watch him.

'Plays' starring horses and dogs, and sea-dramas with the stage flooded, were the rage in Britain and America. Shakespeare survived, which was fortunate for actors like Kean, but little else of note. Theatres such as Covent Garden and Drury Lane, the latter newly rebuilt after being burnt down in 1809, were so vast that it affected standards of acting. Melodramas simple stories with plenty of action and violence – were wildly popular: a typical one was *Maria Marten or the Murder in the Red Barn*. So were stage 'earthquakes' and 'fires'. Gas lighting was introduced in the early 1800s and it improved vision and, unlike candles, could be controlled for effects.

Audiences by now were very rough. The middle classes had deserted the theatre, except for the real enthusiasts, including great critics of acting like William Hazlitt (1778-1830). Many theatre audiences were little better than mobs.

The American theatre was established by now, though it relied at this time on visiting stars from Europe, especially Britain.

French audiences relished romantic dramas and strong acting. The most exciting stage artist of the day was the actress, Rachel, who died in 1858 aged only thirty-eight. Generally speaking, the Parisian theatre was in a healthier state than London's. Vienna was now the leading city of the German-speaking theatre world.

The most popular art-form at this time in Italy and many other European countries was Italian opera. The drama in Italy had never been able to compete with opera, which enjoyed the sort of universal popularity that plays had enjoyed in Elizabethan England. It was another case of great works, great performers and great audiences being present at the same enchanted time.

Right Kabuki plays are now more popular in Japan than the classical Noh drama because they are full of action and movement.

Sarah Bernhardt (1844–1923) French actress. She made her début in 1862 in the Comédie Française. She appeared all over Europe and America. Founded the Théâtre Sarah Bernhardt in 1899. Had a leg amputated in 1915 but continued to act. Probably the most versatile actress in theatrical history.

Late 19th-century theatre

From around 1850 until the coming of motion pictures in the early 20th century the theatre enjoyed a wonderful period of prosperity. It was not simply that great dramatists like Ibsen, Chekhov and Shaw appeared after years without any really good playwrights at all: the theatre regained its popularity with all classes and it deserved to.

It was another age of great acting. Sir Henry Irving (1838-1905) became Britain's first theatrical knight in 1895. The great Italian actor, Tommaso Salvini (1830-1915), performed the most volcanic Othello in history. The tempestuous French actress, Sarah Bernhardt (1844-1923), and the more restrained Italian actress, Eleonora Duse (1859-1924), thrilled hundreds of thousands of people all over Europe and America. More theatres than ever before were built. In Britain at the end of the century there were three hundred or so companies on tour most weeks of the year. And also in Britain, Shakespeare's plays started to be performed as he wrote them, without the 'happy endings' and other absurdities that had been tacked on after his death.

There was a passion everywhere for realistic scenery, in particular that it should be historically accurate if the play was a 'costume' one. Spectacle was popular everywhere. It was the age of actor-managers who ran companies and played leading parts. The profession of producer, now generally called director, had not yet arisen. The star actor arranged his own moves.

Yet gradually the play as a whole, and not just the star, was considered. The German Saxe-Meiningen company, which toured Europe in the 1870s, influenced every capital it visited from London to Moscow. Its crowd scenes were brilliant. Teamwork had come to the theatre. Acting styles gradually became less broad. Ordinary plays about ordinary people needed quieter, more 'true-to-life' methods of acting. And there were far more rehearsals than there had been in the earlier days. Electric lighting was introduced in the 1880s and audiences started sitting in the dark.

In the United States as in Europe the theatres were booming. There were now great American actors like Edwin Forrest (1806-72). There were also heroes of the Wild West like Wild Bill Hickok who performed as themselves in 'Western' plays.

Most countries supported one or more of their theatres with grants of money. Sometimes, kings or princes provided the money; in other capitals, like Paris, the state provided it. Britain and the United States had no national theatres of this sort, but in the 19th century the price of staging plays – even the more expensive ones – was not so impossibly high as it later became. However, it meant that the life of a British or American actor was often far more precarious than that of his colleagues on the Continent, where it was taken for granted that a theatre was as much a part of a town's life as a museum or library.

Far eastern theatre

The most remarkable form of eastern theatre is the Noh drama of Japan, which has not changed at all since the early 17th century. Noh plays are performed on a square, slightly raised stage, the audience being on two sides. A balcony houses a small chorus, another stage at the back contains four musicians and two stage hands. There are two actors, one of them masked, and the stories are legendary. The actors glide about and chant their lines in a set, traditional manner. A Noh performance of five plays and three comic interludes takes seven hours!

A more popular off-shoot of Noh is the Kabuki Theatre, which had an effect on the west when visitors discovered that it used a revolving stage. The first such stage in Europe was built in 1896.

The Chinese theatre mixes song, dance, acrobatics and speech, the most famous being the Peking Opera. The stories come from history and legend. Indian theatre, too, is traditional, but apart from its music and dance is little known in the west. In Japan there is now a great interest in western drama.

20th-century theatre

There have been many changes in the theatre in the last seventy years. It has had to adapt itself to the rivalry of films, radio and television. Today, it is no good trying to outdo the cinema with realistic scenery. Many designers now aim at symbolic scenery, which suggests rather than copies life.

Theatres are now rarely built in the old Italian opera house style. Some have stages which jut out as they used to in Elizabethan times. Others are 'theatres-in-the-round', with the audiences sitting right round the stage. The best modern theatres combine perfect visibility with not too great a distance between actors and audiences. But arguments still rage. The perfect theatres of the future will be able to vary their stages along with the methods of staging for each type of play. For instance, many of Ibsen's plays demand realistic scenery and staging, but his *Peer Gynt* does not.

A theatre director shapes and interprets a play in the way a conductor shapes and interprets a symphony – to the greater glory of the playwright or composer. At least, that is the aim of the good director, although it is possible for a director to distort plays much more disastrously than actors ever can. One of the first and most influential directors of modern times was the Russian, Constantin Stanislavsky (1865-1938), who produced many of Chekov's plays and inspired actors to 'live' their parts on the stage. He tried to produce the 'complete illusion of reality' in actors and productions. Not everyone accepts his methods: perhaps his greatest achievement was to make actors *think* more about their work.

Above A typical toy theatre stage and proscenium of the sort which became popular in England as 'juvenile drama' in the 19th century.

Below Mississippi paddle boats were floating theatres in the early 19th century. These showboats staged melodramas, vaudeville and musical plays for over 100 years.

Charles Chaplin (1889–1977) Film actor and director born in London. Came from theatrical family and went to Hollywood in the United States in the early days of motion pictures. In the first year alone he made thirty-five films and it was then he adopted the moustache, bowler-hat, cane and turned-out feet that made him a familiar and well-loved figure throughout the world in silent comedy films. His sound pictures were not as successful.

In the early part of the century theatre audiences were greatly increased by the spread of repertory theatres, some performing a different play every week. Television killed many of them, although some have survived, including the most famous of all British theatres, the Old Vic. Some theatres, such as the National, are repertory in the more usual sense of the word, having a repertoire of plays which are acted on different nights of the week, with new productions being brought in from time to time.

There is still a vast audience for theatre in the world and today's new playwrights and actors help to keep the flag of theatre flying as it used literally to fly over Shakespeare's Globe when a performance was taking place. From ancient Greece to today the theatre has flourished, faded, sometimes almost died, only to rise again in triumph.

The cinema

Until television began to sweep across the world in the 1950s, films were the most popular form of entertainment in history. During the 1930s and 1940s, vast sections of the world's population went to the cinema not only once but twice a week. These were the golden years of Hollywood, the American – and the world's – film capital. Millions went to the movies whether their idols appeared or not. Of course, it was better if one or more of the legendary stars were in a film, but the audiences always flocked in.

Today, although millions of people still go to the cinema, films have to be better or bigger, or both, before the 'house full' notices go up.

As with most inventions, no one person invented the moving film. Thanks to the work of Thomas Edison in America, the Lumière brothers in France, and William Friese-Greene and Robert Paul in Britain, the first silent films were shown in the 1890s, usually as part of a music-hall show. An early film of railway trains entering a station alarmed its audiences who thought the trains were coming straight at them.

By 1901 a Frenchman, Georges Méliès, was making story films. America's first story film was *The Great Train Robbery* in 1903. Two of the first filmstars were Mary Pickford and the immortal comic, Charlie Chaplin. While Europe was fighting in the early years of the First World War, American film-making shot ahead. Hollywood, near Los Angeles in California, was established as a film centre. Great comedians like Buster Keaton appeared. So did the first great director, D. W. Griffith, who made *The Birth of a Nation* in 1915. The director is the key man in film-making, as his name implies. He decides what scenes shall be seen, how they are shaped and how the actors interpret their roles.

During the 1920s, Germany, Russia and France were also centres of fine film-making. The Russian director Eisenstein (1898-1948) made a masterpiece called *The Battleship Potemkin.* The first sound film, *The Jazz Singer,* created a sensation in 1927. Soon, the era of silent films was over and the 'talkies' had come to stay. Europe continued to make films, but this was Hollywood's era, though many of its greatest stars and directors were European. During the 1930s, Walt Disney's cartoon characters, Mickey Mouse and Donald Duck, became world famous.

Three countries who became major film producers after the Second World War were Italy, Sweden and Japan.

Above The modern circus, with all the thrills of performing animals, acrobats and clowns began in the 18th century.

Noel Coward (1899–1973) English actor, dramatist and composer. The complete man of the theatre. Appeared on the stage as a child and then acted in many of his own plays and films. Wrote the music and lyrics of the famous operetta *Bitter Sweet* (1929).

The competition from television made film-makers experiment with improved sound, bigger screens and new spectacles like Cinerama. Colour films improved in quality from their early days in the 1930s. The perennial old stars were joined by new ones, but films remained chiefly a director's medium.

Now films are truly international. Hollywood, though still important, has been joined by London, Rome, Paris and Stockholm as world film capitals. Location work, when films are made out-of-doors, takes place anywhere on earth. As long as good films are made, the Big Screen will never lose its hold over millions.

Radio and television

Radio and television reach the largest audiences in the history of entertainment. Popular broadcasting began in the 1920s, and the world's first television service was started by the British Broadcasting Corporation in 1936.

Radio helped other sections of the world of entertainment: television at first did the opposite. Theatres and cinemas closed because people were sitting at home watching their TV sets. But today television creates interest in many forms of live entertainment and, what is important to the actor, it gives show people work. The big development in the 1960s was the beginning of transmissions in colour.

The influence of television can hardly be exaggerated. A great part of the world's population watched the American astronaut's trip to the moon and back in 1969, and many European countries have become so involved in watching serials and sports that streets have been deserted while they are being transmitted! Television has become the most powerful form of entertainment in history.

The circus

It is a far cry from the modern circus with its animals, clowns and acrobats to the circuses of ancient Rome. There, in great arenas, fights between gladiators took place, and later, as popular taste became more brutal, massacres were organised, as happened when the Christians were thrown to the lions. A less horrible form of circus in the ancient world took place in great rectangular arenas where thrilling chariot races were run. One such arena was the Circus Maximus in Rome, which held 200,000 people.

Modern circuses began in the 18th century. Astley's circus in London

Above Puppets date back to the beginning of theatrical history and have appeared in different forms all over the world. The puppets seen here are a Javanese Wayang shadow puppet (left), an Italian stringed marionette (right) and, in the foreground, the familiar figure of Mr Punch as a hand glove puppet.

had acrobats, clowns and riders, plus fireworks and scenes from history. France, Russia and the United States were among the countries that welcomed the travelling circus, which became so popular that every continent was visited. The 19th-century American showmen, Barnum and Bailey, called their circus 'The Greatest Show on Earth', while Buffalo Bill's Wild West Show, complete with real Indians and cowboys, caused a sensation in Europe in the 1880s. Circuses today are as popular as ever, and the thrill of the Big Top remains strong.

Puppets and marionettes

These date back to the very beginning of theatrical history, so the millions of children who watch puppet shows on television and Punch and Judy shows at the seaside are enjoying a very ancient entertainment. Italy and Japan are two nations with a particularly long history of puppets, and Russia has a famous puppet theatre in Moscow. Puppets are controlled from below the stage by the operators' hands or by rods: marionettes are controlled from above the stage by wires or strings.

Mime and pantomime

Mime in modern times has come to mean 'acting without speech' and has been practised most often in France. The French actor Gaspard Deburau (1796-1846) developed mime into a fine art. In the ancient world actors called mimes concentrated on comic acting and gestures, but were allowed to speak. Certain types of play, usually meant to be read rather than spoken, were also called mimes.

Pantomime to most nations means the same as mime, but the British form of pantomime is very different. It is often based on a popular story or legend like *Cinderella* or *Aladdin,* but usually includes popular modern songs and jokes, acrobatic turns, and a man playing the part of the Dame – a comic old woman. Until recently the 'principal boy' was always a girl: but now he is often played by a man!

Earlier British pantomimes used to be a variation on the harlequinade, which was a mixture of music and mime about Harlequin and Columbine, who themselves came from the Italian *commedia dell'arte*.

The music hall

In many countries, especially Britain, the United States and France, music halls were popular. In the United States they were called vaudeville or variety. The most famous surviving music hall is the London Palladium.

Music halls started in 18th-century taverns. By the early 19th century, every London tavern had its music room where comic and serious songs were sung and comedians entertained the customers. Soon, variety theatres sprang up throughout Britain. In America, vaudeville dates from the 1880s.

Great music hall personalities 'topped the bill' whenever they appeared and were loved by millions. But vaudeville was killed in America by radio and films, and the music hall in Britain by television. Today, many social clubs in Britain now have entertainers, much as their predecessors had in taverns.

Above This cave painting from Lascaux in France dates from between 15,000 and 10,000 BC. It is thought to represent a man in a bird's head mask being attacked by a wounded bison. In the centre is a wand with the figure of a bird on top that was probably the man's spirit helper. A spear seems to have pierced the bison's flank and wounded it. Cave paintings such as this were usually related with rituals to bring success in hunting.

The world of religion and philosophy

For half a million years or more man and his closest ancestors have lived on earth. During most of that time man has been without writing, which was first used probably about 3500 BC. Before then there is no clear record of what he thought or believed. We can never look into the mind of prehistoric man or know the names of his gods or the purpose of his rituals. Our only source of knowledge about him is archaeological evidence – that is, things dug out of the ground: his bones, and the tools and weapons that he used. These things give fascinating glimpses of prehistoric man and his way of life, and we can even make guesses about his religion.

The first hunters

We know little of prehistory before the time of Neanderthal man, so called because his remains were first dug up in the valley of a river called the Neander in Germany. He lived about 50,000 years ago, eating the flesh of the animals he hunted and killed, and wild fruit which he picked. His main concern was to stay alive, but although he lived in a very primitive way he did take the trouble to bury his dead. More than this, he sometimes trussed up the body or placed it under a stone slab, as though he were afraid it might escape to trouble him. Sometimes he buried tools with the body, as if he expected the dead to make use of them. These practices suggest that Neanderthal man believed in life after death.

The early hunters were faced with the problem of finding sufficient food. Success in the hunt was essential to their survival. It is possible that they practised rituals to help bring them success. In a number of Alpine caves the skulls of bears have been found which date from this period. Sometimes the skulls were found on a low ledge or wall or arranged on the

Above A ceremonial African dance mask from Dahomey.

Below Prehistoric man made little statuettes of female figures which were probably emblems of fertility. They are the oldest known figures of humans. This one is called Venus of Willendorf, found near Vienna in Austria in 1908.

ground in circles. This suggests that the caves were more than just storage depots or burial chambers and may have been the places where Neanderthal man carried out rituals to ensure a good hunt.

Homo sapiens

About 30,000 years ago another race of man, called *Homo sapiens* – our own species – moved into Europe from Africa. Life for *Homo sapiens* probably differed little from that of his ancestors. Burials have been found as before, although rather more elaborate. Sometimes the bodies are placed face downwards or in a crouching position, again as if to prevent them from returning to trouble the living. More often there seems to be a concern for the future well-being of the dead. They are generously provided with ornaments, weapons and even food. It must have been felt that the dead had need of these things for the living to have spared food from their own meagre supplies. Some of the bodies are coloured with a red pigment, as though to give them the appearance of being alive.

Further evidence of rituals has been found in a cave in the Pyrenees in France. A clay figure of a crouching bear was discovered, riddled with holes as if it had been stabbed many times with an arrow or spear. We can imagine the hunters gathered round the figure, which may have been draped with a bear skin and given a bear's head. After the leader had stabbed and 'killed' the clay bear, the hunters would go out to their task. By imitating the killing of the bear, the hunters believed they had a better chance of killing one in reality. If this picture is true, it is an early example of magic based on the idea of imitation.

The cave painters

The most exciting evidence which early man has left us is that of his paintings. The best are found in southern France and northern Spain. They are mostly of animals – bison, horses, deer, mammoths and many others. They are drawn with a vividness which delights us even today. Most of them are in caves, not the caves which were used as dwelling places, but remote and sometimes almost inaccessible chambers like those of Lascaux and Niaux in France. It therefore seems unlikely that the paintings were for decoration, and we have to imagine some other purpose. Perhaps by means of these drawings the painter-hunter hoped to gain control over the beasts. If this is so, it would be a further example of magic based on imitation. Having a reproduction of the animal within his power would give the hunter the feeling he had some kind of power over the animal itself.

There is also the possibility that these caves were places where some early god was worshipped, some lord of the animals who would deliver them into the hunter's hands. The most striking of these paintings are not of animals but of humans, often dressed in skins. One of these, the 'Dancing Sorcerer' from the cave of the *Trois Frères* in the French Pyrenees, shows a figure apparently wearing a deer's head with antlers, an owl's face, a wolf's ears and a horse's tail. Only the dancing legs are human. Is this strange figure the leader of some magical ceremony to gain power over the animals? Or is he perhaps the Great Sorcerer, the lord of the animals and the god of the hunters?

The first farmers

One of the great revolutions in man's existence was when he learned to farm: to sow seed so that he could later reap the harvest, and to keep animals for his own use. Neolithic (New Stone Age) man, as the first farmers are called, made his appearance about 8,000 years ago. His main interest was no longer in successful hunting, but in the sun, the rain, the wind and the soil – all the natural forces upon which the growing of crops depended. From the civilisations which sprang up after 3500 BC we know that man associated these forces with the gods of the sky and the heavens. It seems probable that Neolithic man also had the same beliefs.

The great sanctuary at Stonehenge in England, constructed at the very end of the Neolithic Age during the period 1900-1400 BC, was built with its axis pointing towards the summer sunrise. Almost certainly it was used for some kind of ritual linked with a belief in the gods of the sky.

Pre-literate societies

Scattered around the world are many societies where people still follow a simple way of life, probably not so very different from that of Neolithic man. Such groups as the Australian aborigines, the African bushmen and certain tribes in the Pacific regions remain largely untouched by civilisation as we know it. Because they do not know the art of writing they are called pre-literate. But since their way of life has survived to our own times, their religion can be known much more fully than that of prehistoric man. We have been able actually to observe some of their rituals and ask them about their beliefs.

Power and taboo

The pre-literate Melanesians of the Pacific Ocean use the word *mana* to describe anything which is powerful and unusual. *Mana* is shown in the supreme skill of a hunter or fisherman,

Left These carved and painted grave posts are from Melville Island, off the north coast of Australia. They are part of the mourning rituals and are erected near the grave. Sometimes they are regarded as gifts for the dead.

the success of a warrior in battle, the wisdom of a great chief. All these qualities are due not to the ability of a person but to the *mana* he possesses. Melanesian religion consists of obtaining *mana*, or power, and in using it for one's own purpose.

Other pre-literate societies have had different names for the same idea. The Iroquois Indians of North America called it *orenda* and the Sioux Indians used the term *wakan*. This was a mysterious power which filled the universe and showed itself in any unusual happening. When the Sioux first saw a gun they called it *wakan* iron, or iron filled with power.

Linked with the idea of power is *tabu*, or taboo. The Polynesians, also from the Pacific region, use this word to indicate those things and people which must not be touched because they are filled with power, and therefore dangerous. To say that something is taboo is like putting up a notice saying 'Danger! High voltage!'. Polynesian chiefs were not allowed to touch ordinary objects, nor to walk on the ground. They had to be carried everywhere because whatever they touched became dangerous to other people. It is said that a Polynesian would die of hunger rather than use the tools of a chief to light a fire. Most pre-literate societies have the same idea of things which are forbidden, either because they are dangerous, or because they lead to loss of power. If a hunter was unsuccessful, it was thought that he might have lost his

Above In many of the countries along the Atlantic coast of Africa images are made in metal, ivory and stone, as well as in wood. This jaunty figure is modern and cast in iron. It is the statue of a god from Dahomey.

Right A wooden dance mask from Alaska which is made up of two human faces and two hands, and parts of the various animals hunted by the Eskimos, such as webbed feet and furry tails.

Below right Painting on a sago leaf from New Guinea which shows two cockatoos. According to primitive myths in the Pacific islands the first woman was made of a sago leaf and given as wife to man.

Below The totem poles of the North American Indians include carved and painted figures of totem animals.

power because of some offence which he or his family had committed.

Any object which carries power is called a fetish. The Creek Indians of North America had a 'war bundle', or fetish, which they carried into battle with them to ensure they would not be defeated. Some Eskimos still cover the fur parkas (jackets) of their sons with fetishes: a hawk's wing to give them speed, a fox's tail for cunning, or the skin of a sea-bird for success in fishing.

The gods and spirits

Power is sometimes thought to belong to the gods. The Sioux use almost the same name for power (*wakan*) and for the supreme god (*wakanda*). Because the gods are filled with tremendous power and are able to give it to favoured people it is important to be on good terms with them. The supreme god may sometimes be a remote and distant figure, but below him there are more approachable gods who can be influenced with gifts and sacrifices. These gods provide success in the hunting of animals or in the cultivation of crops. The Fox Indians of North America cultivated tobacco not for smoking but for offering to the gods or spirits of nature.

Power is also believed to exist among spirits who make their homes within trees, rocks or other objects. The belief that these objects then contain a powerful spirit is called animism, and it is widespread in pre-literate societies.

Animals, too, may become the home of spirits, and for hunting people these animal spirits are very important. In the case of the Australian aborigines, each clan within a tribe is closely associated with a particular animal, and hence the spirit which is supposed to exist within it. This is known as totemism and involves rituals performed by the members of each clan on behalf of their totem animal.

Witch-doctors

In most pre-literate societies there are a few privileged people who are believed either to be possessed by a spirit, or to have some control over *mana*. They are popularly known as witch-doctors. Some of the most famous witch-doctors in any pre-literate society were those who operated among the heathen tribes of Siberia, and they were called shamans. These shamans were both respected and feared because the power they were supposed to control could be used for good or evil. They claimed to be able to cure sickness or disease by transferring some of their power to the patient, but they could also take away whatever power a person already had so that, in this case, the patient would weaken, fall ill and perhaps die.

Shamans, or witch-doctors, often appear to have fits or go into trances, as their power or spirit moves them. Dreams or visions about the future are also supposed to be part of their supernatural gifts. As a further mark of their authority they usually live apart from the rest of the tribe and are subject to certain taboos.

Above Sumerian cylinder seals were used as marks of personal ownership. The picture shows a seal of about 2800 BC with an impression taken from it.

The ancient religions

With the invention of writing man entered civilisation and history. One of the early centres of civilisation was in Mesopotamia, along the valleys of the rivers Tigris and Euphrates, which flow into the Persian Gulf. Here a people called the Sumerians held power some time before 3000 BC. From the excavations of their temples, and from writings found in them, we know a good deal about their religion. About 2350 BC they were defeated by a Semitic people, who were men of the Arabian desert, and some centuries later Babylon was established as their capital. Further north another Semitic group gained power in Assyria. Both the Babylonians and the Assyrians adopted the beliefs of the early Sumerians.

The gods of Sumeria

The Sumerian people lived in city-states, each city worshipping one of the gods. An, the god of the sky, was worshipped in the city of Erech, while Enlil, god of the wind, was the chief god of Nippur. The cult of the moon-god Nanna was centred upon Ur, while at Larsa the sun-god Utu was the chief deity.

As well as the worship of the gods, the Sumerians had a number of myths, or stories, about them. One of these, the myth of creation, tells of the goddess Nammu, who is the primeval ocean. She gave birth to the sky and earth who, in the form of a god and a goddess, produced the air-god Enlil, responsible in turn for the rest of creation.

The gods of Babylon and Assyria

The Semitic people who conquered the country took over the Sumerian gods and arranged them into a pantheon, or family. Chief in this pantheon were Anu, the god of heaven; Enlil – renamed Bel – the god whose wind moves over the face of the earth; and Enki or Ea, lord of the ocean. The most important goddess was Ishtar, the mother goddess or queen of heaven, who was the giver of love, fertility and motherhood. Linked with her was Tammuz, the god of vegetation, who died each winter and returned to life each spring, thus symbolising the new life of the vegetation and crops.

The chief god of Babylon was Marduk, and his power was linked

Below This figure of a worshipper is about 5,500 years old and comes from Mesopotamia.

Right The ziggurat at Ur and a modern reconstruction

Above The great lord Marduk was the highest of the gods in Babylon. At his feet is the sacred dragon of Babylon.

with the political and military rise of the city. Gradually he took over the duties of the other gods until he became supreme – the creator of men and the protector of Babylon. The national god of Assyria was Assur whose power also grew with his country's strength.

Early creation myths

The Babylonian story of creation, called *Enuma elish*, describes how the gods were born from the union between Apsu, the sweet water ocean, and Tiamat, the salt water ocean. The gods quarrelled and Tiamat unloosed a horde of monstrous beings upon them. But Marduk defeated the hordes of Tiamat, became ruler of the gods and created man for their service. In the Assyrian version of the story this part is played by the god Assur.

Another story called the *Epic of Gilgamesh* describes the search for a plant which will give immortality. Part of this story is the account of a flood sent by the gods to destroy all life on earth. One man only escaped by building a boat, on which he and the animals he took with him were kept safe from the deluge.

These stories of creation and the flood were later used by Hebrew writers in the Old Testament of the Bible.

Temples and worship

According to the creation story man was created by the gods in order to serve them in worship: man was their slave. The gods, in their turn, protected man and gave him long life as a reward for his services. Only the gods were immortal. When man died he went to the kingdom of the dead, a place without joy or hope.

The actual conditions of life in Mesopotamia had a lot to do with the religious attitude. Man's control over his natural surroundings was still very insecure. Storms, floods and drought could ruin crops for years and bring hunger and starvation. There were also constant wars, invasions and other upheavals to cause worry and concern. The people accepted the fact that their lives were completely at the mercy of the gods.

The gods were supposed to live in ziggurats, great temple buildings in the form of towers, and here they were worshipped. This took the form of

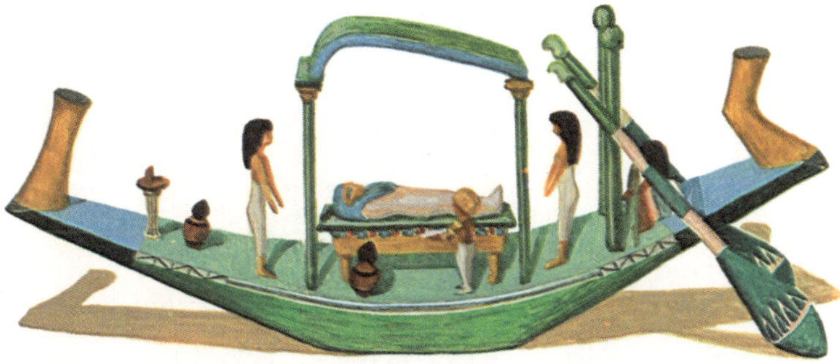

hymns chanted by the priests in honour of the god. Other priests were responsible for foretelling the future by studying such things as the entrails of slaughtered animals and the flight of birds.

Worship was dominated by the king, who represented the gods upon earth. The most important of the seasonal festivals was the celebration of the New Year. In the Babylonian version of this festival the creation story was recited and the victory of Marduk over Tiamat was reproduced in dramatic form. The climax of the festival was a marriage in which the king played the part of the god. In this way it was believed that new life for the coming year was created.

The gods of Egypt

About the same time as the rise of Sumeria, perhaps about 3200 BC, the Upper and Lower Kingdoms of Egypt were united under the rule of a single king, or pharaoh.

There were two types of gods in Egypt: the universal gods usually represented in human form, and the local gods often represented in animal form. The idea of universal gods may have come from outside Egypt, whereas local gods may be those which developed within Egypt.

Chief among the gods was Horus, represented as a man with a falcon's head, probably formed by a combination of a universal god with a local god. He was god of the sky and the sun, and also god of the kingship. Another god associated with the sun was Re, who was pictured as riding in a boat across the sky. Osiris was ruler of the kingdom of the dead. Among local gods was Khnum (represented as a ram) who created man; Thoth, the ibis-headed god, who was scribe to the gods; and Sobek, the crocodile, who stood for the power of the River Nile to rise and fertilise the land.

The gods have their origin in the basic natural forces which governed life in Egypt – the sun, and the River Nile whose annual flooding watered the land. But, as in Mesopotamia, the power of the gods became linked with the fortunes of the cities in which they were worshipped. Re was combined with the creator Atum, and under the name Atum-Re was worshipped in

Above The wooden model of an Egyptian funerary barque, XIIth Dynasty. On either side of the canopy which covers the mummy stand the gods Isis and Nephthys.

Above The ankh, an ancient Egyptian symbol of eternal life carried by the gods. It appears frequently on wall paintings and is thought to have originated in the shape of a sandal-string. It became later a symbol of the sign of the cross in the early Coptic church. The Copts were descended from the ancient Egyptians.

Above left A wall painting from the tomb of Ramses I in the Valley of the Kings in Egypt, showing the god Horus.

Above A bronze statuette of the goddess Isis, 4th century BC. Isis, a popular goddess throughout Egypt, was the divine mother of Horus and wife of Osiris. The god Horus is seen sitting upon her knee.

Right Re, the sun-god of Heliopolis, is shown with a solar disc on his head and a papyrus sceptre on his knees.

Heliopolis as the supreme creator-god. The priests of Memphis put forward their god Ptah as the god of creation. At a later period, when Thebes was the national capital, the Theban priests identified their god Amon with Re and in the form Amon-Re he was worshipped as supreme.

The worship of Aton

It was against the power of Thebes that the famous pharaoh Amenhotep IV (14th century BC) carried out his reforms. He replaced the power of Amon-Re by that of a new god called Aton, represented by the disc of the sun with rays stretching down from it. The king changed his name to Akhenaton, and built a new capital city to be the centre of the cult. Worship of Amon was forbidden and only the worship of the new supreme god was allowed. But this new cult did not survive the death of the king who supported it and the old worship of Amon was restored.

The divine king

There was no great divide between the gods and men in Egypt. Life was settled and ordered. Political upheavals were rare, and the annual flooding of the Nile provided a regular means of irrigation. Perhaps for this reason gods and men were pictured together as part of a settled order. Symbolising this order was the king, who was the human ruler and was also identified with the sun-god Horus. Just as the gods protected the cosmic order by ensuring that the seasons followed their normal course and the Nile flooded regularly, so the king protected the social order by conquering the enemies of Egypt and maintaining justice in the land. As the mediator between gods and men the king was responsible for worship and it was the priests who acted as his representatives.

Life after death

The Egyptians believed that their settled and ordered life on earth could continue after death, provided that certain rituals were closely observed. These were intended to help the dead person make the journey from this life to the next.

The pyramids, built mostly during the period 2700-2300 BC, were royal tombs in which the body of the king was preserved. In order to keep the corpse life-like, it was mummified by spreading oil on it and wrapping it with bandages. Preservation of the body was not enough: a lengthy ritual had to be observed to ensure the continued life of the king.

In the pyramids themselves are inscribed the Pyramid Texts, collections of stories which were recited as part of the ritual. These stories are centred around the god Osiris, who was killed by his brother Seth. Osiris was later brought back to life, after his wife Isis had given birth to the god Horus. Horus was appointed to have authority over the living, while Osiris went to rule over the land of the dead. In the Pyramid Texts recited during the ritual the living king is identified with Horus, while the dead king becomes Osiris. Thus as Osiris once rose from the dead, so the pharaoh – his body and many of his belongings preserved and placed in the tomb – would receive new life after death.

Book of the Dead

At first it was only the king whose life after death was a matter for concern. Then gradually the belief in another life was applied not only to the king but to all the people. Then it came to be believed that ritual alone was not enough to ensure new life. The dead had to undergo a judgement before they could be admitted to life after death. This judgement is described in the *Book of the Dead,* a collection of texts which was often buried in the grave. At the time of judgement the soul of the person was weighed in the balance. If the verdict was favourable the soul was welcomed to the kingdom of Osiris; if not, he was delivered to a monster who was the eater of the dead.

The gods of Greece

From about 2000 BC onwards waves of invaders moved down into the land that was to become Greece. They were an Indo-European people, using a language similar to that of the invaders of other parts of Europe, India and Persia. The religion of the conquered people was probably connected with the earth and fertility, while the religion of the invaders looked up to the sky. Out of the conflict between these two cultures Greek religion was fashioned.

The Olympian gods

The gods of the invading people, such as Zeus, the king of the gods, combined with those of the conquered people,

Above A scene from the war between the gods and the giants from Greek mythology which is depicted on an amphora (a two-handled jar) found at Melos and dating from the 4th century BC.

Below A Greek red-figured vase showing Apollo, the god of music, and Artemis, the goddess of the hunt.

Above The typical hero of Greek myth was Heracles, known also by his Roman name of Hercules. The twelve labours of Heracles were deeds of incredible strength and bravery. They included wrestling with the Nemean lion, clearing the Augean stables and the destruction of the Hydra, a monstrous water-snake with many heads.

Above Janus was a Roman god and appears in no other mythology. He was the god of doorways and had two faces so that he could see both ways.

such as Demeter, the goddess of motherhood and fertility, to form the pantheon, or family, of the gods. Zeus is the head of the family and with his brother Poseidon, lord of the waters, and Pluto, lord of the underworld, rules over heaven and earth from the gods' home on Mount Olympus. Hera is the wife of Zeus, and among their offspring are Athena, the goddess of wisdom, and Hermes, the messenger of the gods.

The Olympian gods formed the basis of the official Greek religion. Sacrifices were offered to them in order to ensure the welfare of the state. The gods were all–powerful, and the worst sin for mortals was *hubris*, the arrogance of putting oneself on a level with the gods. Since the gods held the future in their hands they were able to reveal to men what it held for them. For man to know the future he consulted the oracles. The most famous of these was at Delphi, where the god Apollo was supposed to speak. In the centre of the temple at Delphi there was a vent in the earth from which the fumes of minor volcanic activity sometimes emerged. Any words uttered by a priestess seated amid the fumes were thought to be inspired and the words of the god himself.

Philosophers and poets

The gods did not escape criticism. Greek philosophers challenged the behaviour of the gods and the stupidity of thinking that the supreme being was modelled on man. 'If horses could draw,' said Xenophanes, 'they would draw the shape of gods like horses.' The philosophers discarded the old picture of the gods and tried to discover some universal principle which was behind all things.

The poets also were not satisfied with the old religious ideas, and in their plays they pictured the gods administering justice not blindly but according to the moral law. Plato thought of a creator who was identified with the good and the true and the beautiful. He believed that man's soul needed to grow towards the supreme good which his creator had set before him.

The mystery religions

In ancient Greece neither the official religion nor the ideas of Greek philosophers and writers satisfied the religious needs of the ordinary people. These were met by mystery religions. The most famous of these were the Eleusinian mysteries and Orphism. Both involved secret rites, and those taking part in these rites were promised that

Left The Vestal Virgins performed the duty of keeping alight the sacred fire in the temple of Vesta. They were well-born girls who entered the service of the goddess when six to ten years old and served from five to thirty years.

they would share the immortality of the gods.

The Eleusian mysteries were celebrated in honour of the goddess Demeter and her daughter, Persephone. The rites included a procession to the sea, ritual bathing and a return to Eleusis near Athens for further secret rituals. Those taking part believed that they would receive the protection of Persephone beyond the grave.

The Orphic mysteries arose out of the exciting and at times savage rituals of the worship of Dionysus, in which wine was drunk to bring about states of intoxication, and the flesh and blood of a kid or a bull was consumed. The Orphic rituals were much milder: those who followed Orphism believed that the soul passed from one body to another at death. They thought that by leading a good life and by taking part in the Orphic rites, they might purify their souls and so escape the perpetual cycle of birth, death and rebirth.

The gods of Rome

According to tradition, the first settlement on the hills around Rome took place in the 8th century. Some time in the 6th century BC Rome was properly established as a city and from then on her power grew until the Roman Empire covered the whole of the Mediterranean world.

Early Roman worship

The earliest Romans formed small communities of peasant farmers. Among their gods three were supreme. Jupiter, who is the equivalent of the Greek Zeus, was the god of lightning and rain. Mars was the god who gave protection against enemies, and so became the god of war. Quirinus was the god who presided over peace and good government. Among the many other gods were Juno, protector of women, and Vesta, the goddess of the hearth-fire.

The Romans used the word *numen* to express the sense of power which belonged to certain objects and certain beings. The gods had much *numen*, and the object of the religious rituals was to ensure that they continued to be supplied with it. The gods had little personality and, unlike the Greek gods, there were few myths about them. The most important thing was the correct performance of the ritual, which had to be right in every word and detail.

The ritual was in the hands of the priests. Each god had his own *flamen*, or priest, who was responsible for his

Above An early Etruscan bronze figure of Minerva, the Roman goddess who is the equivalent of the Greek Athena.

Right The head of Mithras which was found when the remains of a Roman temple were discovered in London in 1954. Mithras was a Persian god who was adopted by the Romans, particularly by the army, in 68 BC. His cult rivalled Christianity in the 3rd century AD.

Above An Etruscan sculpture showing Romulus and Remus being suckled by a she-wolf. Romulus was the legendary founder of Rome and its first king. The story is that Romulus and Remus were twin sons of Mars who were abandoned and set afloat on the River Tiber. The twins were found and brought up by a shepherd and his wife. After the founding of Rome, Romulus is said to have murdered Remus. Romulus was later worshipped by the Romans as a god under the name Quirinus.

worship. *Pontifices*, or overseers, were appointed to ensure that the cult was properly performed. The Vestal virgins were responsible for tending the fire in the temple of Vesta at the Forum in Rome.

The Etruscans

The Etruscans were a race of people who lived in Etruria (present-day Tuscany), a large region to the north of Rome. They spread south to Rome in the early days of the city's history and introduced images into Rome for use in the cults. They also began the practice of inspecting the entrails of sacrificed animals in order to determine the future. From Greece came many new gods including Hercules (the Greek Heracles), the protector of traders. These new gods were more positive and colourful than the shadowy Roman deities.

From the time of the emperor Augustus (63 BC–AD 14), the emperors themselves were thought of as gods. In Rome itself it was only after death that they were raised to join the gods, but in the outlying provinces of the Roman Empire the living emperors were worshipped as divine.

The Oriental cults

For the majority of the people the more personal side of Roman religion was provided by the mystery cults, which were imported from lands further east. Of these, three were important: the cult of Attis and Cybele which came from Asia Minor; the cult of Isis which came from Egypt and was based on the story of Osiris rising from the dead; and the cult of Mithras which came from Persia. This last was especially popular among the soldiers of the Roman army. All these cults offered their followers the hope of a glorious future life.

The gods of Europe

Two of the principal races of central and western Europe in the pre-Christian era were the Celts and Teutons. The first settled in western Europe from the 6th century onwards, to be followed some centuries later by the Teutons.

The Celts

The Celts worshipped nature deities – gods of the sky and of the earth. Much of their religion was concerned with fertility, and two festivals were held annually. At the winter festival sacrifices were offered to renew the fertility of the earth. The gods included the Dagda, the great father; Belenus, the god of sun and fire; and Cernunnos, a horned god who was closely connected with the processes of fertility. The spring festival was held on May Day, and still survives in Maypole dances. It was held in honour of the renewal of the sun's strength, when fires were lit and the people danced round them. Possibly animals or even humans were sacrificed in the fire, in order to help the sun-god recover his power during the summer months.

These sacrifices were in the charge of the Druids, or priests, who probably held some of their ceremonies in sacred groves of oak trees. According to the Romans human sacrifice was widely practised by the

Left The Celtic white horse cut in the hillside at Uffington, Berkshire. The turf is removed to reveal the chalk beneath. There are several of these chalk figures in Britain, which are linked with early religious beliefs.

Below A god and goddess from north Germany made from two forked branches, 1st century AD.

Druids, who usually chose criminals or prisoners for their offerings.

The Teutons

The religion of the Teutons is known from a number of writings, in particular from two Icelandic works called the prose *Edda* and the poetic *Edda*. From these we learn that Teutonic religion was concerned mainly with gods of the sky. Tyr (the Greek Zeus) was god of the shining sky, but gave up his place as chief god to Wotan (or Odin), the warrior god who protected heroes and fighting men. Two other gods were Thor, the god of thunder and rain, and Frigga, the wife of Wotan. These gods lived in a place called Asgard, which was pictured as being at the top of a tree called Yggdrasil, which represented the world. At the roots of this tree dwelt Hel, the goddess of death. The names of some of these gods survive in the English names of days of the week: for example, Thursday is named after Thor. After death those who were warriors went to Valhalla, and others to the underworld ruled by Hel.

The gods of Mexico and Peru

When the Spanish came to the New World of the Americas in the early 16th century they found flourishing civilisations both in Mexico and Peru. The religions of these countries show

Left The silver Gundestrup bowl, found in Denmark, is decorated with figures of Celtic gods such as Cernunnos, seen in close-up below.

Above The Aztec religion seems to have been of peculiar cruelty. Human blood was thought to be the food of the gods and many sacrifices were made to appease the national god at the temple of this deity, Huitzilopochtli. At the top is seen a sacrificial knife made of flint, used to carve out the heart of victim, as shown in the brutal drawing copied from an Aztec temple. The smaller object is a ceremonial whistle which the victim played as he walked to his death. On the right is an Aztec skull overlaid with mosaic.

some interesting similarities with the ancient religions of the Mediterranean area.

The Aztecs

The empire of the Aztecs was founded in Mexico in AD 1325. Although their social life was well organised, their religion seems to have been of peculiar cruelty. They were a farming people and believed that the success of their crops depended on the power of the gods. The gods, like men, needed nourishment in order to maintain their strength and power. This nourishment was provided for them by human sacrifices.

The Aztecs made war on their neighbours in order to capture great numbers of prisoners. These prisoners were then killed by the priests according to a set ritual and their hearts were offered to the gods. When the temple of the national god, Huitzilopochtli was consecrated, thousands of prisoners were sacrificed.

The fate of the individual after death depended upon his manner of death. Those who were sacrificed to the gods entered the paradise of the sun-god. Those killed fighting or by drowning entered the realm of the god of wind and rain. All others entered the land of the dead.

The Aztec empire was brought to an end by the Spanish leader, Hernando Cortés, who conquered Mexico in 1520.

The Incas

Farther south, in the region of Peru, the Incas ruled over a vast empire from about AD 1000 onwards. This empire ended when the Spaniards under Francisco Pizarro conquered the Incas in 1532. The ruling family claimed to be descended from the sun-god, and the power of the emperor who represented the god was almost unlimited.

The chief temple for the worship of the sun-god was at Cuzco. It was a great building, beautifully adorned with gold. Its inner sanctuary contained an image of the sun-god himself, and in the main hall of the temple the mummified bodies of former rulers were seated on thrones.

In the 14th century one of the ancient gods, Huiracocha, was elevated above the sun-god, and the chief temple was re-dedicated to him. Below the supreme gods were a host of minor deities, all possessed of *huaca*, or power. Like the Melanesian *mana* this power attached itself to unusual objects, to natural phenomena like hills and rivers, and to the gods themselves.

Above Grouped together in this picture are various Hindu gods. From the left to right they are an early figure of a bearded god which comes from Mohenjo-Daro, an early civilisation in the Indus Valley, and is about 4,500 years old. Next are seen two Nagas, a fabulous race of snakes who sometimes take human form. Then a statuette of Vishnu mounted upon Garuda, an eagle, which is carved from wood and comes from Bali. Finally, there is a head of Siva from Java and below it two seals from the Indus Valley.

The living religions

As well as the early civilisations in Mesopotamia and Egypt, a third great community sprang up on the banks of the River Indus in what is now Pakistan. From about 2500 to 1700 BC cities flourished in this part of northern India. The people used writing, although it has not yet been deciphered. This civilisation came to an end at about the same time as invaders from the north (similar in language and culture to the Indo-Europeans who overran Greece and Europe) swept down into India.

Hinduism

The ideas and beliefs of the invaders and the original inhabitants were merged into a new kind of religion which was to develop into Hinduism.

We know little of the religion of the Indus Valley civilisation which existed before the Indo-European invasion. From the appearance of female statuettes that have been dug up in the area it is thought that a mother-goddess cult was practised. A god pictured as a seated figure wearing a horned headdress and surrounded by animals was also worshipped. It is likely that he is a forerunner of the later Hindu god Siva, lord of the animals. The great differences between Hinduism and the religions of countries farther west is likely to be due to the influence of these early inhabitants of the Indus Valley.

The gods and sacrifice

The invaders were a robust and cheerful people whose religion matched their character. Chief among their gods was Dyaus Pitar, the sky father, whose name is the equivalent of the Greek Zeus and the Roman Jupiter. Dyaus Pitar was later overshadowed by Indra, the god of the storm, who is pictured as rowdy and boastful – a fit leader for the Indo-European, or Aryan, tribes as they fought their way into India. The messenger of the gods was Agni, the god of fire. Sacrifices to the gods were laid on the fire, and it is believed that Agni carried the sacrifices to the gods. During the offering of the sacrifices, hymns were sung or chanted and these hymns were collected together in the first scripture of Hinduism, called the *Rig Veda*.

Rebirth and *karma*

Eventually the actual details of the sacrifice became more important than the gods. It was thought that the gods and the natural processes of the world were dependent on the correct performance of the ritual. Perhaps as a reaction against the formality of the rituals a completely different kind of writing appeared about 700 BC. These new sacred books, called the *Upanishads*, contained many new ideas. The most important teaching to be found in them is that of transmigration, or rebirth. This states that when a person

Above The temples at Mamallapuram in southern India, built in the 7th century A.D. This is one of a series of remarkable temples, mostly carved from outcrops of rock with hollowed-out interiors, which are of great importance in the long history of Indian art.

Above right This is one of the many stone figures which decorate the great Indian temple at Tanjore. It depicts the god Siva.

dies his soul passes into another life. He may then be reborn as a human, or as an animal, or in the world of the gods. Thus each person has not simply one life but a series of lives through which he passes.

Linked with the idea of transmigration is *karma*, which has to do with the quality of a person's actions while on earth: a good action will bring reward; a bad action will bring punishment. Everything that happens to a person is the result of his past actions, and his reward or punishment may come in the present life as good or bad fortune, or it may come in a future life as a good or bad rebirth.

One of the things determined by *karma* is a person's place within what is called the caste system. Before the time of the *Upanishads* four major divisions of caste existed. These were the result of the distinction between the invaders and the conquered people. The invaders were divided into priests, warriors and traders, and the conquered people formed the caste of slaves. A priest, or Brahman, was thought to have reached his high status by means of the good actions that he had performed in previous lives. On the other hand, a slave was born into the lowest caste as a result of his bad actions in previous lives.

This succession of rebirths seemed to Indians to be a burden from which they must escape. The thought of an endless series of rebirths was to them a horrifying one, and Indian religion might be described as the search for an escape from the round of rebirth.

Ways to salvation

The *Upanishads* describe a new religious class, not the priests who conducted sacrifices, but wandering hermits who left their homes and lived in solitary meditation searching for escape from rebirth.

One way of escape is given in the *Upanishads* themselves. Behind the world we see, there is a reality which is the only true principle of life, and part of it is in every person. If the soul can identify itself with this true reality and be absorbed by it, then that soul is released from the round of rebirth. The name Vedanta is used for this

teaching and it has been revived a number of times at later periods of Indian history and is popular today among some Indian philosophers.

Another way of release is described in the Yoga system. This is a set of physical and mental exercises, the object of which is to free the mind from the world around it until one passes into a state of trance. The experience of being completely detached from the world and isolated in trance is interpreted to mean that the soul has withdrawn from the body and from the round of rebirth.

Vishnu and Siva

In the *Bhagavad Gita*, written probably about the 2nd century BC, the ultimate reality is the personal god Vishnu, who is described as being the creator of the world. Vishnu is believed to reveal himself to the world in a number of guises or incarnations, called *avatars*, which include both historical and mythical figures. The *Bhagavad Gita* includes the story of one such mythical *avatar*, Krishna. Another popular god who is also described as supreme creator is Siva. Sometimes Siva is pictured as fierce and terrible, but the worship of this god has given rise to some of the most beautiful devotional poetry in the world.

Temples and worship

Most Hindus today are followers of one of the personal gods, Vishnu or Siva. A third god who is sometimes worshipped is the wife of Siva, known as Kali. The centres of worship are the temples in which there are statues of the deity or objects representing him or her. Daily rituals are carried out in the temple by the priests – waking, dressing, feeding and entertaining it. The ordinary worshippers are not present at these rituals, but come at other times to the temple to offer their gifts to the god and to make their requests.

In addition to the temple worship there is worship in the home which is still practised by many Hindus. Somewhere in the home is a small shrine where an image of the god is placed. At certain times of the day the head of the family will make offerings and say prayers before the image.

Caste

A unique feature of Hinduism is the caste system. There are thousands of caste groups differing from each other for reasons such as rules of descent, rules of marriage, ritual, occupation, ideas and beliefs. Although some Hindus still closely follow the traditions and ways of life of their group, the rules of each caste group have become less strict, most changes having taken place during the 20th century. One reason for this is the spread of modern education and ideas, and a greater movement of people through the country and to other countries due to among other things, an increase in economic and physical mobility. Some old practices have therefore lapsed into disuse and some new ones have been adopted.

Many paths and one goal

Hinduism, which today has over 250 million followers, has no set doctrine or creeds. It is simply the religion of the people of India, and there are no truths which one must believe in order

Above Detail of a wheel from the Surya temple at Konarak in India, built in the 13th century. This temple is dedicated to the sun-god Surya and is in the form of a gigantic chariot drawn by the seven horses of the sun. There are twelve of these wheels round the temple's base.

Above This massive elephant's head is a detail from the descent of the Ganges relief at Mamallapuram.

Above The north gate of the Great Stupa (a Buddhist sanctuary) at Sanchi in central India. This building dates from the time of Asoka, the Buddhist emperor who lived in the 3rd century BC. It is covered with reliefs carved in stone which depict incidents in the life of the Buddha.

Above right This fierce warrior is Shukongo-shin, an image in painted terracotta of a guardian god of Buddhism. Clad in full armour he wields a thunderbolt. The figure dates from about the 8th century AD.

to be a Hindu. The variety of teachings within the religion of Hinduism is expressed by the Hindu conviction that all beliefs and practices are ways of reaching the supreme goal. Even the popular worship of idols in the temples is well suited to people at a certain stage of development. All religious paths lead up the mountain to the same summit.

Buddhism

In the 6th century BC many Indians left their homes to exist as hermits or homeless wanderers. Their object in leading this way of life was a religious one, to discover the way of release from the cycle of rebirth in which all men were imprisoned. One such wanderer was Gautama, the founder of Buddhism.

Gautama the Buddha

The legends of Gautama's life date from long after the period when he lived, but there is little doubt that they refer to an historical figure, born probably about 560 BC. The legends say that he was the son of the chief of a small tribe living near the River Ganges on the borders of what is now Nepal. His personal name was Siddhartha but he was usually known by his clan name of Gautama. Brought up by his father in great luxury, Gautama was trained as the future ruler of his tribe. At the age of twenty-nine he saw four signs which caused him to rethink the meaning of life. The first three of these were an old man, a diseased man and a corpse. These sights brought home to Gautama the truth that life was not the luxury to which he had been accustomed but was marked by old age, disease and death. The fourth sign, a wandering hermit, made him realise that a way of escape from this life might possibly be found.

Leaving his home and family he spent six years living very simply in the forest and practising self-torture. He abandoned this life and tried instead the way of meditation, and at the age of thirty-five achieved the enlightenment for which he had been searching. He earned the title of Buddha, or 'enlightened one'.

He was tempted at that moment to cut short his life but decided that he would remain in the world as a teacher, trying to help others to see the truths that he had discovered. He gathered round him a group of followers and for forty-five years travelled around the north-east part of India. Those who wished to share his way of life were admitted to the Buddhist order. He died at the age of eighty.

The middle way

The enlightenment which the Buddha found was a middle way to release between the extremes of luxury and self-torture. It was a way based on meditation and a simple life of self-control. His teaching is contained in the Four Noble Truths.

The first of these truths teaches that all life is marked by suffering, by continual change and by 'no-soul'. No one can escape suffering; and continual change, or impermanence, is a characteristic of all things and all people. 'No-soul' means that man has no permanent inner soul or spirit. At death and rebirth the Buddha believed that all that passed from one life to the next was the *karma*, or the accumulation of a person's good or bad deeds. The second truth taught that suffering is caused because men and women desire things for themselves. From this followed the third truth, that to escape suffering one should learn to control desire for all things. Desire was like a fuel that kept the process of rebirth in motion. The ending of rebirth was called *nirvana* – the end of the road which brought to a close the long series of lives through which a man's *karma* had led him. The fourth truth taught the path which led to this goal: this was called the Noble Eightfold Path and set various standards of personal behaviour in life.

The community of monks

The Buddha laid down a code of discipline for the members of the inner community who shared the wandering life of their master. They were called *bhikkhus*, or beggars, because they used to beg daily for their food. Shortly after the death of the Buddha they began to gather in monasteries where they were subject to a strict code of rules. They ate only before midday, were not allowed to handle money and did not marry. They wore saffron robes as a symbol of joining the community. Their way of life was designed to encourage meditation and detachment from the desires of the world.

Left The Amida Buddha (seated), bronze, 13th century; and a Bodhisattva sculpted in wood, 14th century.

New teachings

The early form of Buddhism was a severe religion in which there was no worship, no prayer and no supreme god. It was primarily a religion for the *bhikkhus* and for those who had time to spend in meditation. In later centuries Buddhism developed new teachings which filled the religious needs of ordinary people. The Buddha, instead of being a human teacher, became a superhuman figure who could be worshipped. At a later period still the number of Buddhas multiplied and there were thought to be countless thousands of them. Behind them all lay one supreme reality. In addition to Buddhas another class of beings was worshipped: these were the *bodhisattvas*, or saviours, who helped people to

Gautama (The Buddha) (6th century BC) Founder of Buddhism. The son of a rich man he gave up his life of luxury because he was overcome by the poverty and unhappiness of his people. He led the life of an ascetic and when he died, at the age of eighty, he had influenced religion all over the Far East.

reach the final goal. These new teachings were called the *Mahayana* and the earlier teaching was called *Theravada*.

Below This graceful Jain pillar is part of a temple at Chandra-giri in India and was built in the 10th century.

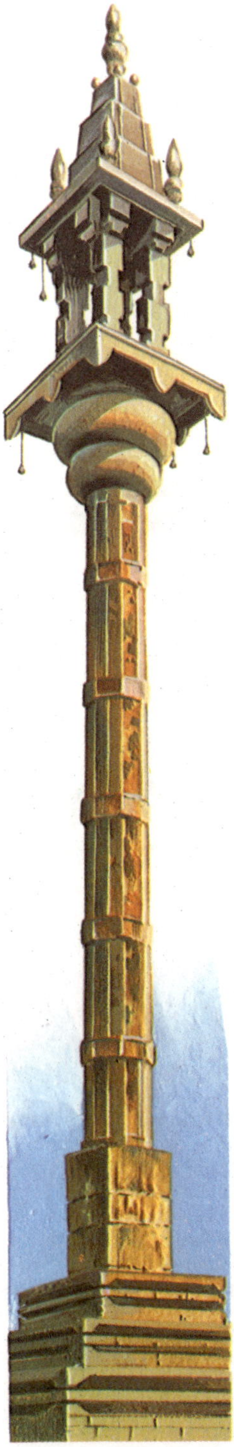

Spread and decay

For many centuries Buddhism flourished in India. Under the great emperor Asoka (264?-223?BC), who was a patron of Buddhism, it spread through India across Central Asia as far as China and Japan. In each new country the community took root and formed the nucleus of the religion, while the beliefs of the ordinary people were adapted to Buddhism. In Ceylon the people continued to pray to the old gods but they did so in Buddhist temples. In Burma the worship of spirits continued. In China Buddhism existed alongside the Confucian and Taoist systems, while in Japan it shared the allegiance of the people with Shinto.

From about the 5th century AD onwards, for reasons we do not know, Buddhism began to decay in India. The monasteries were destroyed, the Buddhist lay-people were absorbed back into Hindusim, and finally Buddhism disappeared altogether from the country of its origin.

Zen Buddhism

The one creative development that took place in Buddhism outside India was Zen. This system grew from about the 6th century AD onwards, first in China and later in Japan. Instead of enlightenment being an experience for which a long training was necessary, Zen taught that it was possible to reach it in an instant. All that was necessary was to stop thinking about things and instead to know and feel them directly. In order to bring about this experience Zen developed techniques including the use of beating and shouting to break the usual habits of thought. *Koans*, or riddles, were used to confuse and excite the mind until suddenly everything was seen in a new way and brought sudden enlightenment.

Lamaism

A form of Buddhism which included the use of spells and ritual charms found its way into Tibet and mingled with the ancient Tibetan religion to become Lamaism, so called from the

name *lama* given to the monks of high rank. These monks were also the rulers of the country. During the 15th century AD it was claimed that the lamas were the incarnations of the Buddhist gods. The Dalai or Great Lama was said to be an incarnation of the god of mercy, Avalokitesvara. When a Dalai Lama died his successor was chosen from among children born near the time of death, in one of whom the god was supposed to be reincarnated. Since the Chinese occupation of Tibet the Dalai Lama has gone into exile and the rule of the Lamas has now been abolished.

Modern Buddhists

Outside China and Japan, which were never more than partly Buddhist, there are about 150 million Buddhists today. Asian countries like Ceylon and Burma are sending Buddhist missions to western nations in order to spread the knowledge of the religion. Today Buddhist organisations exist in many countries in the world, such as Britain, France, Germany and the United States.

Left Many of the monasteries built in Tibet by the Lamas were sited on almost inaccessible hilltops. This drawing shows the north face of a monastery at Portala in Tibet.

Asoka
(264–223 BC) King of the Maurya dynasty and emperor of a large part of India. He is an important figure in the history of the east since he was a convert to Buddhism and he organised it as a state religion. He devoted his life to spreading the faith among his people.

Jainism

About the time that the Buddha was teaching his way to release, another teacher was putting forward a different way of escape from the round of rebirths. He was Vardhamana Mahavira, born probably in 540 BC, who founded the religion of Jainism.

Mahavira

Like the Buddha, Mahavira is said to have been the son of a chief. Brought up in great luxury, he left home at the age of thirty, and for twelve years lived in great hardship. At the end of this period he believed that he had reached full enlightenment and became a Jina – one who has conquered. His followers called themselves Jainas, or disciples of Jina. After his death at the age of seventy-two these followers formed themselves into a community of monks with a code of discipline. Jainism spread through southern India and for some centuries was influential in many Indian states. Like Buddhism it began to decline in the 5th century AD. Unlike Buddhism it did not spread beyond India.

Jain teaching

Jain teaching is based on two great realities, soul and matter. Souls are said to be imprisoned with matter. They are prevented from escaping by *karma*, which in Jain teaching is thought of as a kind of matter which weighs down the soul and prevents it from rising to release. To obtain release one must free the soul from all *karma*. This means undergoing hardship and discomfort to burn up all old *karma*, and being careful to avoid harming any living creatures, for this builds up new *karma*. The way of life for the monks is based on these two ideas. They carry brushes to sweep the ground before them to ensure that they do not step on any creature and harm it.

While the Jains have no supreme god, they do worship the Tirthankaras, great beings like Mahavira himself who have discovered the way to release. These beings are worshipped in the Jain temples. They cannot help their followers: release can be achieved only by a man's own effort. About 2 million Jains still live in India.

Right Two Shinto priests. Shinto, which means 'the way of the gods', is based on the belief that the gods were ancestors of the Japanese people. In the centre is a carving of Lao-Tzu and his green ox on which he is said to have ridden away, never to be seen again. At the bottom is seen the Shinto goddess Nakatsu-hime.

Confucius
(551–479 BC) Latin name for the Chinese philosopher Kung-fu-tzu. His early career was in politics and teaching and he was very popular with the people. After his death a collection of his sayings, called *Confucian Analects*, was published. He was a teacher of moral behaviour rather than religion but was revered after his death.

Confucianism and Taoism

The ancient Chinese religion was based on the worship of ancestors in the home, and on the great state festivals in which the gods of the earth and sky were worshipped. During the 6th century BC the two great movements of Confucianism and Taoism arose.

Confucius and conduct

Kung-fu-tzu, whom the Europeans call Confucius, was born probably about 551 BC. As a young man he made a close study of ancient Chinese traditions and then turned to teaching. He gathered a group of students who became his disciples. After a time some of these students were appointed to public office. Finally Confucius himself was made a magistrate, but he ended his life as a wandering teacher.

His teaching was concerned not with religion or philosophy but with conduct and behaviour. The ideal man of Confucian teaching was a man of virtue – even the expression on his face had to be correct. This is not empty ritual, for behind the formal behaviour there must be a heart which feels for others. Confucius was more concerned with what a man has to give to society than with his individual religious needs. Benevolence and kindness in elders and rulers; respect, obedience and loyalty in subjects: these were the great virtues.

The followers of Confucius, by their training in practical government, soon gained a great deal of power and became the chief administrators of the empire. They took into the Confucian system the domestic worship of ancestors and the strong sense of respect for parents. It was not until the 20th century that the Confucian system was overthrown.

Tao and harmony

While Confucius concentrated on conduct and behaviour within Chinese religion, there was another school of teachers called Taoists who were more concerned with philosophic thought. Taoist belief is explained in a book called the *Tao-Te-Ching*, said to have been written by a certain Lao-Tzu. Little is known about him, but he is believed to have lived just before Confucius, and there is the familiar legend of how he resigned from an official position to live a simple life.

The basic belief of Taoism is in the changeless reality of Nature, called *tao*. The ideal man learns to live in harmony with this reality. He becomes passive and receptive, so that *tao* is able to influence all his thoughts and actions. The supreme virtue is *wu-wei* (meaning literally 'do nothing') which means taking no action, not interfering, not opposing things, but living in harmony with Nature and all men. The Taoist submits to the power of *tao* and so grows in simplicity, generosity and contentment.

Shinto

For centuries the Japanese people remained separate from the rest of the world. Until 1945 they were never invaded or conquered. In the 6th century AD Buddhism spread from China to Japan, and Confucian thought also reached the country. These two movements filled much of the need of the Japanese for religious teaching, but the basis of their religion was Shinto.

Above The Altar of Heaven in Peking was first built in 1420 and later reconstructed in 1889. It was here that the emperor of China offered sacrifices to the god of heaven. The sacred building is approached by eight flights of steps which rise above the triple terrace that is a symbol of heaven.

The state worship

Shinto ('The way of the gods') is based on the belief that the gods were ancestors of the Japanese people. The sun-goddess Amaterasu was believed to have sent down her grandson to rule the islands, and the family of the emperor was descended from this first ruler, and thus from the sun-goddess herself. The other noble families of Japan were descended from other gods. These gods were worshipped at the great national shrines, the most important of which is at Ise and is sacred to the sun-goddess. At the twice-yearly Great Purification the emperor, as the descendant of the sun-goddess, pronounced absolution over the people.

Linked with this worship of the gods was a strong love of nature and the scenery of Japan. This was accompanied by a firm patriotism which saw Japan as the island especially beloved by the gods.

In the 18th century a great revival of national feeling led to Shinto becoming the state religion. The local shrines were purged of their Buddhist priests, and government-paid Shinto priests performed the daily cult at these shrines in honour of the national gods. After the end of the Second World War in 1945 the state Shinto was abolished and the shrines returned to their original purpose of serving the needs of individual worshippers.

Rituals in the home

In addition to the national rituals, Shinto also includes domestic rituals in which the Shinto gods who are also the ancestors of the nation are worshipped in the home. In one corner of the house is a shelf on which are placed memorial tablets with the names of the gods inscribed on them. There is a daily ceremony at which food is offered and a prayer is said. On special occasions candles may be lit while the family gathers to make its thanks and to pay its respects to the gods.

Zoroastrianism

Some time before 1000 BC an Indo-European people settled in Persia. They were of the same racial stock as the invaders of India and their gods

Above In the mythology of ancient Persia, the god Ahura Mazda eclipsed all others. This enamelled brick bas-relief shows the winged disc of the god surmounting two winged sphinxes.

Moses
(14th century BC) Hebrew prophet, law giver and leader who, according to the Bible, received the Ten Commandments, the basis of the Hebrew law, directly from God.

and their culture also were similar. But Persian religion developed in a completely different way to Hinduism. Indeed the boundary between India and Persia is also the boundary between two great types of religion. On the one side are the Asian religions like Hinduism and Buddhism, which are philosophical and mystic. On the other side are the western religions like Judaism, Christianity and Islam which are monotheistic (that is they believe in one supreme creator God) and prophetic. Zoroastrianism belongs to the western group.

Zarathustra

Zarathustra was born in about 630 BC. He was the founder of Zoroastrianism, which was called after the Greek form of his name, Zoroaster. He experienced visions or revelations which he believed were from the supreme god whom he called Ahura Mazda or Wise Lord. Some of Zoroaster's sayings have been preserved in the hymns of the Avesta, the sacred book of the religion. Zarathustra was a monotheist, believing in one god, the creator of all things.

The good and evil spirits

Below the supreme god, taught Zarathustra, there were two spirits representing the opposing forces of good and evil. The good spirit was responsible for all that was good and right and beautiful: he was the source of life. The evil spirit was responsible for all that was evil and ugly. In the early teaching both these spirits came from Ahura Mazda. Later they became separate gods. The good spirit combined with Ahura Mazda to become Ormazd, the good god, and the evil spirit became Ahriman the devil.

The world was a battleground between these two principles and man was given free will to decide on whose side he stood. Those who made a true confession of faith and did good deeds put themselves on the side of Ahura Mazda. By a false confession and a bad life they sided with the evil spirit.

This religion became the national faith of Persia, and some of its ideas passed into Judaism. Under the form of Mithraism it became powerful in the Roman Empire. Its only living adherents are the Parsees, an influential Indian community who live mostly around Bombay.

Judaism

According to the Hebrew tradition in the Old Testament of the Bible a small group of Semitic people led by Abraham migrated from Sumeria in about the 19th century BC. The descendants of this group finally entered Egypt. This may have been part of a much larger movement of people caused by the influx of invaders from the north. Many of the Semitic people were on the move at this time. For a while Egypt was ruled by the Hyksos, a Semitic group who held power from about 1750 to 1580 BC. The Israelites, descendants of Abraham, were settled in Egypt at this time and when the Hyksos were expelled the Israelites were at first undisturbed. In the 14th century BC their fortunes changed and they were compelled to provide forced labour. This was the setting for the escape from Egypt led by Moses.

The Exodus

Moses was born an Israelite but was brought up as an Egyptian. His great spiritual experience came when he

Above The Old Testament is full of dramatic scenes which tell of the power of God, such as the escape of the Israelites from Egypt into Sinai

was living as a shepherd in the desert. He saw a bush burning and when he approached a voice spoke to him. Moses believed the voice to be that of God. Moses was told to lead the Israelites out of Egypt to freedom. He returned to Egypt from the desert and confronted the pharaoh, who refused to release the people from their forced labour.

Moses then led the people into the desert. The Egyptian troops pursued them but were overwhelmed by catastrophe. The sea, or lake, which the troops were crossing, flooded suddenly, due possibly to an earth tremor or some other natural event. The Israelites believed that God had protected them by destroying their pursuers. Immediately after this dramatic escape Moses led the people to Mount Sinai where they entered into an agreement, or covenant, with God. On his side God promised protection to the people, and on their side the people agreed to keep the commandments which expressed God's will.

After many years wandering in the desert the Israelites finally entered Canaan. Probably they were only one of a number of Hebrew tribes to do so. Slowly the Hebrews made themselves masters of the land and all the tribes accepted the leadership of the Israelites, the group which had come from Egypt. The God of the Israelites became the God of the whole country. When King David (11th-10th century BC) conquered Jerusalem, the last of the Canaanite strongholds, he resolved to build a temple to house the Ark of the Covenant, the old symbol of the agreement between God and his people. The temple was actually built by David's son, Solomon.

The exile and return

Although God's power prevailed in Israel, there were many people who still failed to keep the covenant and the commandments. It was against such unfaithfulness that the later prophets such as Amos and Isaiah thundered.

During the 7th century BC Babylon rose to power and in 586 BC Nebuchadnezzar captured Jerusalem. The temple was destroyed and many of the leaders of Jerusalem were deported to Babylon. This was a supreme

David
(11th–10th century BC) The second king of Israel. He made great conquests after he became king and greatly enlarged the territory of Israel, giving unity to the scattered tribes. An accomplished musician he was called 'the sweet psalmist of Israel'. The encounter with Goliath is probably a legend.

Above In the Old Testament story of Belshazzar's feast a moving hand appeared before the king and wrote upon a wall. Daniel read the words 'mene, mene, tekel, upharsin' and he interpreted them to mean that the king had lost favour with God and that his kingdom was to be divided. That night Belshazzar was slain and Darius the Median became king.

crisis for the Israelites. It seemed as if God had deserted them. They were given new hope by the unknown prophet who wrote the later chapters of the book of Isaiah. He proclaimed that God was not only the protector of Israel but was also the supreme Creator who made all things and governed all nations. He had brought judgement upon Israel for her unfaithfulness but he had not deserted her. The people of Israel would be restored to Jerusalem.

This prophecy was fulfilled when the Persian king, Cyrus the Great, conquered Babylon in 538 BC. The new ruler allowed the exiles to return to Jerusalem to rebuild their city and temple. From this time on the people are known not as Israelites but as Jews, and their religion as Judaism.

New beliefs

During the next few centuries a number of beliefs found their way into Judaism, probably from Persia. Before the exile, the Israelites had no strong belief in a life after death. They believed that the dead went to Sheol, a grey, shadowy place where God was not known. After the exile some of the Jews began to believe in a life after death which would follow the resurrection of the dead. They also began to think of a judgement at which the dead would receive either reward or punishment. Other new beliefs were the existence of angels and a personal devil, or Satan.

The most important part of Jewish religion at this time was obedience to the law. It was the task of the scribes to work out what the law was, and what one was permitted or not permitted to do. A body of traditional law based on the scriptures came into being and provided a detailed guide for everyday living.

A number of parties sprang up. The Pharisees accepted many of the new beliefs, such as resurrection, while the party of the Sadducees rejected them. When the Romans made Judea a province of their empire in 63 BC the party of the Zealots appeared, determined to win back national freedom. Another group, the Essenes, withdrew to live a monastic life apart from the rest of the community. It was near such a monastery that the celebrated Dead Sea Scrolls were found. These included Old Testament manuscripts and writings on the monastic beliefs and discipline.

During this period the belief in a Messiah became steadily stronger. The Messiah was one who would come to save his people and establish the rule of God on earth. The Jews rejected the claim of Jesus's followers that he was the Messiah. Steadily their resistance to Roman rule increased until the Romans were forced to act. An army was despatched against Jerusalem and after a terrible siege the city was taken and the temple destroyed in AD 70. Sixty years later another rebellion by the Jews was savagely suppressed and the Jews were banned from entering Jerusalem. On one day in the year only they were allowed to return to part of the old foundation wall of the temple to mourn for the loss of their land.

Jewish festivals

Although dispersed from their homeland the Jews did not cease to exist. Their religion became centred upon the Talmud, a collection of the laws and traditions which was assembled in Babylon. As they travelled and settled in the lands surrounding the Mediterranean, they continued to observe the regulations preserved in the Talmud.

The Talmud laid down the three great festivals which are still observed by Jews today. Passover was originally an agricultural festival in which the people gave thanks for the new life of the spring season, but it became linked with thanksgiving for the Exodus, or escape from Egypt under Moses. Fifty days later the feast of Pentecost is held. This was originally a thanksgiving for the first harvesting of the crops, and it also commemorates the giving of the commandments at Mount Sinai. In the autumn the festival of Tabernacles gives thanks for the autumn harvest and also for God's protection to his people during their wanderings in the wilderness and throughout their history.

Besides these great festivals which look back to events in Jewish history there is also the New Year festival which is the celebration of the creation of the world. On this day Jews are called to repent of their sins and to turn to God.

By means of these festivals and of following the way of life laid down in the Talmud the Jews have been able to retain their sense of identity as the chosen people of God. They believe that God will continue to guide them until finally all nations come to believe in him and to worship him.

Zionism

There are about 10 million Jews in the world today. Many of them belong to the Reform movement which rejects the idea of a Messiah and does not believe that the Jews are a separate nation with a right to their own homeland. In contrast to this viewpoint the Zionist movement which believes strongly in the Jews having their own state has grown in the last century. In 1947 the United Nations agreed to the formation of a new state of Israel, and since then many Jews from all over the world have returned to the land which their ancestors entered three thousand years ago.

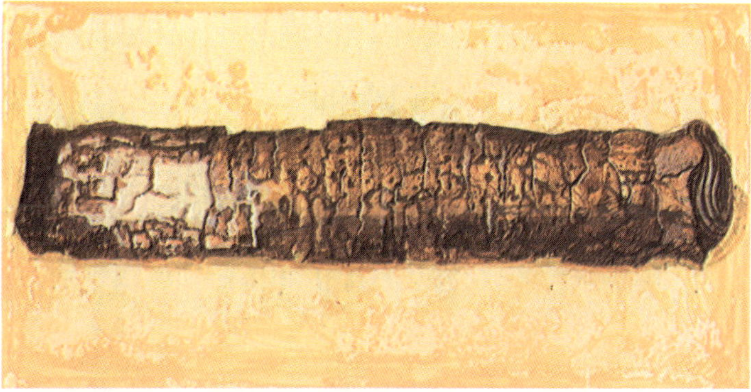

Above The first Dead Sea Scrolls were found in 1947. These ancient scrolls were either intact or in fragments and contained in jars The picture above shows an Aramaic scroll of Genesis as it was found.

Cyrus the Great (6th century BC) Founder of the Persian Empire. Began his conquests in about 550 BC and by 548 BC was king of Persia. He increased the extent of his lands until he was master of a vast area stretching from the Mediterranean to India.

Right Stained glass windows are said to have originated in the east. At first one central figure, such as the image of God, was portrayed, but later biblical scenes were introduced.

St Francis of Assisi (1181?–1226). Founder of the Franciscan order. Son of a wealthy merchant at Assisi, he spent his youth in gay and riotous living. A serious illness began his conversion and he devoted himself to the care of the poor and sick. The Franciscan brotherhood was founded on the principles of chastity, poverty and obedience.

Christianity

During the period of the Roman occupation of Judea many Jewish families lived quietly and devoutly, attending the synagogue and bringing up their children to know the Jewish law and the writings of the prophets. In such a family Jesus, the founder of Christianity, was born, probably about the year 4 BC.

Jesus the Messiah

Little is known of Jesus's childhood and youth. Probably he was brought up in a large family with many brothers or cousins. The story of his visit to the temple in Jerusalem when he was aged twelve shows his interest in religious matters, even at such a young age. When he was about thirty he went to the banks of the River Jordan to receive baptism, a symbol of repentence, from John the Baptist. As he came out of the water he had a profoundly moving experience of the Spirit of God coming down upon him. He received a conviction that he was called by God to a special task. After retiring to the desert for some weeks he returned to his home province of Galilee and began to announce that the coming of God's kingdom was near. As a sign of this he healed many sick people and exorcised those who were possessed by demons. He gathered round him a group of disciples, of whom twelve were especially close to him. He taught great crowds about the nature of God's kingdom and about the conduct and spirit required from those who wished to enter it.

At first the crowds seem to have listened gladly to Jesus, but later they began to fall away. There was much opposition to his teaching from the Jewish leaders, who mistrusted the authority with which he interpreted the Jewish law without respecting Jewish tradition. His close followers became convinced that he was the Messiah, and Peter, leader of the twelve, acknowledged him to be so. Neither the common people nor the Jewish leaders accepted this claim. When Jesus went to Jerusalem he gave a final challenge to the leaders by clearing the money changers out of the temple, demonstrating again that he believed his own inner conviction and authority to be superior to the Jewish tradition. The Jewish leaders resolved that he must be executed and had him arrested. The Roman governor Pontius Pilate was persuaded to agree to the execution and Jesus was crucified, the usual Roman method of punishing criminals.

The early church

The disciples at first were fearful and despairing after the death of their master. Then they came to believe that he was still alive, that he had risen from death and was appearing to them.

The climax of these appearances was at the Jewish feast of Pentecost. The disciples had an experience of power filling them. They described it as like a violent blast of wind and tongues of flame. They interpreted it as the Spirit of God filling them. From that moment onwards they took courage and began to proclaim that Jesus was the Messiah, or Christ. Like their master they suffered a good deal of persecution. When one of their number, Stephen, was stoned to death by the Jews, many of the little community of Jesus's followers left Jerusalem and were scattered over Samaria and Judea.

This was the beginning of a division within the Christian movement. On the one side there were those who believed that the new movement ought to remain obedient to the Jewish law. The other side, led by a convert from Judaism named Paul, believed that the new movement ought to be open to all, whether they observed the Jewish regulations or not. Paul was responsible for establishing Christian congregations in Asia Minor and Greece, and finally his view triumphed. The Christian movement began its history as a world-wide community embracing many nations and races.

As the church spread it developed a distinctive worship and organisation. From the beginning in Jerusalem there had been meetings on the model of the synagogue services at which there was prayer, preaching and the singing of psalms. There was also a ceremonial meal based on the Last Supper eaten by Jesus with his disciples before his death. This was linked to the belief that by his death Jesus had enabled God to achieve an act of rescue similar to the deliverance of the Israelites from the Egyptians. But this Christian deliverance was not from human enemies but from spiritual ones. By the death of Jesus the Christian was saved from sin and from the power of evil beings. The way of entering the Christian community was by baptism, which was interpreted as being a sharing of the death of Jesus so that one could rise to life as he had done.

The organisation of the church slowly became more rigid, and by the beginning of the 2nd century AD each congregation was led by a bishop, assisted by elders and deacons.

Above The Church of the Nativity in Bethlehem was built in the 4th century on the site of the stable in which Jesus was born. Below the High Altar is the Grotto of the Birth.

Above left This medallion of the Holy Lamb comes from St Mark's Cathedral in Venice and is a typical example of the beauty of Byzantine art.

The Gospels

The early beliefs of the Christian church were set out in the Gospels which tried to describe the meaning of Jesus's life, and the letters of church leaders, especially Paul. These writings put forward the idea that Jesus was more than a human figure: he was also divine and possessed the nature of God. As the church spread, various heresies, or different views about Jesus, arose. In order to make clear its teaching the church framed the creeds or statements of belief, and also made a list of the writings which

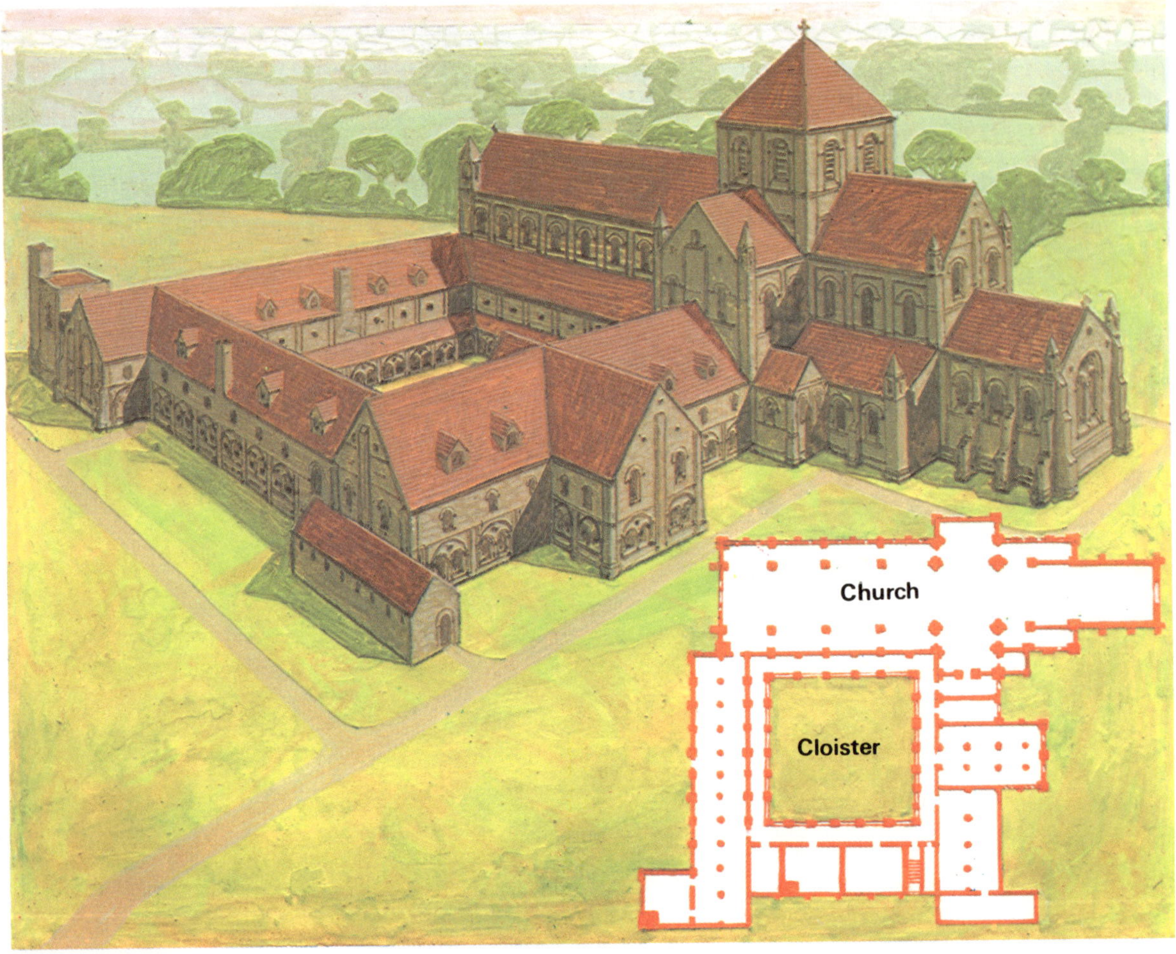

Above Monasteries are self-contained communities in which the monks live, work and worship.

Constantine I called the Great (274?–337) Roman emperor. Converted to Christianity in 312, he made it the state religion in 324. He chose Byzantium as the capital of his empire, renaming it Constantinople.

were to form the New Testament. During the 4th and 5th centuries AD the teachings on the Trinity and Incarnation were finally expressed. The teaching on the Trinity said that within God there were three persons, Father, Son and Holy Spirit. This did not mean three gods but three ways in which God showed himself to the world. The Incarnation claimed that Jesus was both divine and human, two natures in one person. By these teachings the church believed that it was safeguarding the truth that Jesus was the saviour of all men.

Spread of the church

For the first three centuries of its life the church suffered persecution. Under the Roman emperor Constantine (274?–337), who took office in 323, Christianity became more powerful, and in 383 it was declared the state religion. The power of the bishop of Rome was also growing. Leo I, who was bishop, or pope, from 440 to 461, declared that the church in Rome should be the leader of all the churches, because of its link with the Apostle Peter who was the leader of the twelve disciples of Jesus. The Eastern or Greek part of the church did not accept this claim and in 1054 the church split into two parts.

As the Roman Empire collapsed the church spread to other parts of Europe and the barbarians who overran the Empire became converted to Christianity.

Monasticism

In the 3rd century AD a number of Christians felt that they could practise their religion more fully in solitude. In Egypt especially there were a number of desert hermits. They began to live together in communities, and in the 6th century Benedict (480?–547?) worked out a rule of life for the monks which included manual labour,

Left John Wesley, (1703–91), the English evangelist and founder of Methodism, rode through every part of England preaching the gospel of the Christian religion. It is said he travelled some 8,000 kilometres every year on horseback and preached some 40,000 sermons in his life. His brother Charles (1707–88) helped him in his work and is best known as the writer of over 6,500 hymns.

reading and worship. The libraries of these monasteries preserved much of the ancient learning when the barbarians conquered Rome. From the 10th to the 13th centuries there were a number of reforms in the monasteries. New orders such as the Dominicans and the Franciscans were founded. The most famous of the Dominicans was Thomas Aquinas (1226–74), who showed that Christian belief could be supported by reason. Another Dominican, Meister Eckhart (1260?–1327), developed a mystic cult in which he believed that God and the individual soul were united.

The Reformation

In spite of the heights of thought and feeling reached by the great monks, the common people were not satisfied with the state of the church. The authority of the pope was used to establish taxation and the selling of pardons. These and other customs were unpopular and were also thought to be unscriptural. A widespread demand grew for changes within the church. The German Martin Luther (1483–1546) became the leader of the group making these demands, and he attacked the practices of the pope and the church. As he studied the New Testament he came to believe that true Christianity was not a matter of belonging to the church but of inward repentance and trust in Jesus Christ. Many people followed the lead given by Luther, and finally Lutheran churches were formed which rejected the pope's authority. Other Protestant churches were also founded. In Switzerland John Calvin (1509–64) formulated his ideas on the sovereignty of God which led to the founding of the Calvinist churches. Rejection of the pope's authority also led to the Church of England and the Presbyterian Church of Scotland.

Modern movements

In response to the Reformation the Roman Catholic Church which remained obedient to the pope undertook its own reforms. As a result new orders arose within the church, the most famous of which was the Jesuit movement. The Jesuits continued the missionary expansion of the church and carried Christianity to India, China, Japan and America.

At the end of the 18th century a revival of religious feeling in England led to the Evangelical movement and the founding of the Methodist Church. As a result of this awakening the Protestant churches began to organise missions. The beginning of the 19th century saw a number of missionary societies founded. Members of these societies carried Christianity to Asia, Africa and South America.

Today about 700 million people belong to the Christian church. The most important of recent movements within the church is the endeavour to unite the various separate churches which have resulted from the splits of 1054 and the Reformation. The Church of South India was formed in 1947 from the Protestant churches in southern India. In 1948 the first assembly of the World Council of Churches was held. This body continues to encourage churches to unite.

Martin Luther (1483–1546) German religious reformer. Entered a monastery at Erfurt when he was a young man. He attacked the selling of indulgences under papal authority and, in 1517, posted up 95 points for discussion on the door of Wittenberg church. This was the academic practice but Luther's points questioned the authority of the church. This moment marked the beginning of the Reformation.

Above The Dome of the Rock in Jerusalem built in 691, is the first monumental building erected by Moslems that has survived almost intact. At one time it was intended as the centre of pilgrimage to replace the Ka'abah.

Above right The interior of the mosque at Cordoba in Spain, begun in 785 and enlarged at various times during the following 300 years.

Islam

The word Islam means submission, and the followers of the religion of Islam are known as Moslems, or those who submit to the power of God. The religion of Arabia in the 6th century AD was a simple belief in a family of gods. Islam was founded as a reaction against this Arabian paganism. It is 600 years younger than Christianity, but includes many of the ideas of both Christianity and Judaism. The founder of Islam was the Arabian, Mohammed.

The prophet of God

Born in AD 570 in Mecca, Mohammed was orphaned at an early age and was brought up by his relatives. He earned his living as a caravan leader and at the age of twenty-five married a widow, Khadijah, some fifteen years older than himself. It was a strong and successful marriage. When he was about forty Mohammed entered a time of spiritual stress during which he saw in a vision the messenger of God, who told him that he was to be God's prophet. At first he doubted the reality of this call but at last came to believe that it was true. He began to preach in the name of God, whom he called Allah, calling men to repentance and warning them of the day of judgement to come. His following in Mecca was very small and finally he left for the near-by city of Medina. Here he quickly became the leader of the city and set about establishing the customs of the new religion. The first mosque was built and Friday became the day of community prayer. When war broke out between Medina and Mecca, Mohammed led the Medinan army, marched on Mecca and captured it. He made Mecca the centre of the new religion and its shrine, the Ka'abah, became the most holy spot in the Moslem world. In 632, two years after taking Mecca, Mohammed died.

The Koran

The sacred book of Islam is the Koran. This is a collection of the sayings of Mohammed, which Moslems believe to be the words of God himself given through the prophet. They believe that the Koran must always be right and true, being a copy of the scroll which exists in heaven with God. It is therefore the final revelation, which takes the place of the revelations given to the Jews and Christians. Mohammed and his followers believed that they were worshipping the same God as both Jews and Christians but that Christians especially were guilty of associating another being, Jesus Christ, on terms of equality with God.

The five pillars

The religious duty of the Moslem is summed up in the 'Five Pillars'. First, the creed. This states that 'There is no god but God, and Mohammed is the prophet of God'. According to Moslem thought, God is the one and only supreme Creator. He is compassionate and merciful, and will forgive all those who submit to his holy will. Mohammed is God's prophet or mouthpiece. He is not a divine being but an ordinary human. His only claim to uniqueness is that he is the last and the greatest of the prophets.

Secondly, prayer. The Moslem is required to pray according to a set ritual five times a day. During this prayer, which may be said either in private or in the mosque, he faces towards Mecca and praises God. Friday is the day of public prayer on which the worshippers meet together at the mosque.

Thirdly, almsgiving. This meant giving a proportion of one's income, originally one-fortieth, to the poor.

Fourthly, fasting. This takes place for a whole month, the month of Ramadan. During this month no one is allowed to eat or to drink during the hours of daylight. Only a few people – the sick, the aged, children and mothers – are excused this fast.

Left The Ka'abah in Mecca is the holiest sanctuary of Arabia. It was adopted by Mohammed as the symbolic spot towards which each Moslem should turn in prayer.

Fifthly, pilgrimage. Once in a lifetime, if possible, every Moslem is expected to make the pilgrimage to Mecca. There he will visit the Ka'abah and take part in the ceremony of circling the building.

The spread of Islam

When Mohammed died the leadership of the Moslem community passed to the caliphs, under whom the new religion quickly expanded into a vast empire. Mohammed had united the tribes of the Arabian desert into a political and military force, which quickly conquered vast tracts of territory. First Syria fell to the Moslem armies, to be followed by Palestine, Egypt, and Persia. Later the Moslem domination included Spain, Central Asia and India. Islam spread both as a religion and also as an empire.

Moslem sects

The orthodox Moslems are known as Sunni: they are the defenders of the traditions which go back to Mohammed. Their idea of religion is based on obedience to the law which expresses those traditions. Another movement within Islam was based on feeling and emotion rather than on law. It became known as Sufism after the Sufis (or wool-wearers), who were mystics. They believed that religion was above all a matter of learning to know God and to love him. The first Sufis wandered from place to place, reciting the names of God and living a simple life.

Another sect is the Shiah, who believe that the leader of the Moslem community should belong to the family

Above A feature of Moslem mosques is the minaret, a tower, often richly decorated in mosaic, from which the *muezzin* calls the faithful to prayer.

Below The Sikhs are a proud, warrior-like people, the true Sikhs wear what are called the five ks: *kes*, uncut hair; *kacch*, short drawers; *kara*, a bangle; *kanga*, a comb; and *kirpan*, a dagger.

of Mohammed. They consider that the only true caliph was Ali, who was Mohammed's son-in-law. When he was murdered the leadership passed into other hands, but the Shiites believed that the true succession should have passed to Ali's descendants. Now that the line of Ali's descendants has died out, they look for the coming of a *mahdi* or leader who will come from heaven and eventually lead them to success.

Islam today

There are between 500 and 800 million Moslems in the world today, and converts are still being made especially in Africa. Many of the countries of the Middle East and North Africa are Moslem. In 1947 the latest of the Moslem states, Pakistan, was created by the division of India into two parts.

Sikhism

When the Moslems first invaded India they strongly criticised some of the Hindu beliefs. In the 15th century AD a new religion began which drew upon both Moslem and Hindu teaching. This is Sikhism, one of the youngest of the world's religions.

The teaching of Nanak

The founder of the Sikh religion was a man called Nanak, born in 1469. Like many religious leaders he was subject to visions: in one such vision he was commanded to practise meditation, worship and the repetition of the true name of God. After this vision he emerged from the forest and pronounced that 'There is no Moslem and no Hindu'. He travelled to Mecca, the great Moslem centre in Arabia, and also to the Hindu places of pilgrimage. The only place where his preaching was successful was in his home neighbourhood of the Punjab in northern India. There groups of *sikhs*, or disciples, began to form. Nanak's teaching was based on the concept of a supreme Creator, such as is found in Moslem teaching. He taught the Hindu ideas on *karma* and rebirth: escape from rebirth came from thinking upon God and repeating his name.

The warrior faith

A succession of *gurus*, or leaders, built the Sikhs into a strong community separate from both Hindus and Moslems, but not strong enough to be a separate nation. The tenth *guru*, Govind Singh or Govind the Lion (1675–1708), aroused the Sikhs for a major struggle. He began an order within the religion, to which disciples were admitted by being baptised with sweetened water. Those who had taken this baptism were called Singhs or Lions, and had to conform to a number of customs, including the wearing of long hair on the head and chin. They pledged themselves to worship God, gave up alcohol and tobacco and were encouraged to eat meat. Good living and diet and a confident faith gave them strength and in time they dominated the Punjab. Their central temple is at Amritsar where a copy of the *Granth* or collection of Sikh hymns is enshrined in the Golden Temple.

The home territory of the Sikhs is now divided between India and Pakistan. Many Sikhs have emigrated to other parts of the world.

Philosophy

What is philosophy? The word itself comes from the Greek and means love of wisdom. In this sense philosophy is the study of the principles which underlie all knowledge. Throughout the ages, philosophers have asked a great many different questions. The oldest philosophical question is 'What is there?' or 'What exists?' Philosophers have answered this question in their own particular way, which is different from that of the scientist. All the different groups of philosophers have tried to convince us of their claims by long and often complicated arguments, which form the backbone of their philosophies.

The philosophers who attempt to answer the question 'What is there?' do not try to mention every single thing there is in the universe, or to say how many single things there are. On the contrary, they usually try to divide all the many things there are into one or two large groups. For example, instead of saying there are shoes and ships and stones the philosopher says there are material objects.

One who says there is nothing but material objects in the universe is a materialist. He is also called a monist (from the Greek word for one), for he says that all the things that exist are of one kind.

Many philosophers have not been materialists. They have said that thoughts and sensations (like pain) exist, and occur in minds or souls – which are not material objects. Philosophers who say there are both material objects and minds, which are quite distinct kinds of thing (and this is perhaps the view of most people and might be called the commonsense view), are called dualists.

Idealists, on the other hand, say that there are *only* minds in the universe. Many philosophers have claimed that the universe contains one very perfect mind, that of God. One set of philosophers, known as sceptics, have said that the commonsense view *may* be right but we have no way of *knowing* it is.

The question 'How do you know?' raises another important question: 'What is knowledge and when can we be *sure* that we know something?' Many philosophers have felt that there must be limits on what human beings can ever know. For instance, some claim that we may believe that there is a God, but we can never *know* that there is. Apart from 'How do you know?' we very often need to ask the philosopher 'What exactly do you mean?' It is not easy to say exactly what we mean by words like God, mind and space.

One branch of philosophy is particularly concerned with the meaning of 'value' words like good and bad, and is called ethics. Other branches of philosophy which deal in part with value words are political philosophy and aesthetics. The first deals, among other topics, with words like justice and freedom which crop up frequently in the discussion of politics. Aesthetics is the philosophy of art, and deals with words like beauty and good as applied to art.

Above *The School of Athens* by Raphael, on which this drawing is based, is in the Vatican and shows the triumph of philosophy, with Plato and Aristotle at the centre of a group of scholars.

Above Auguste Rodin's celebrated statue *The Thinker* (1904) has come to symbolise man's preoccupation with philosophic thought.

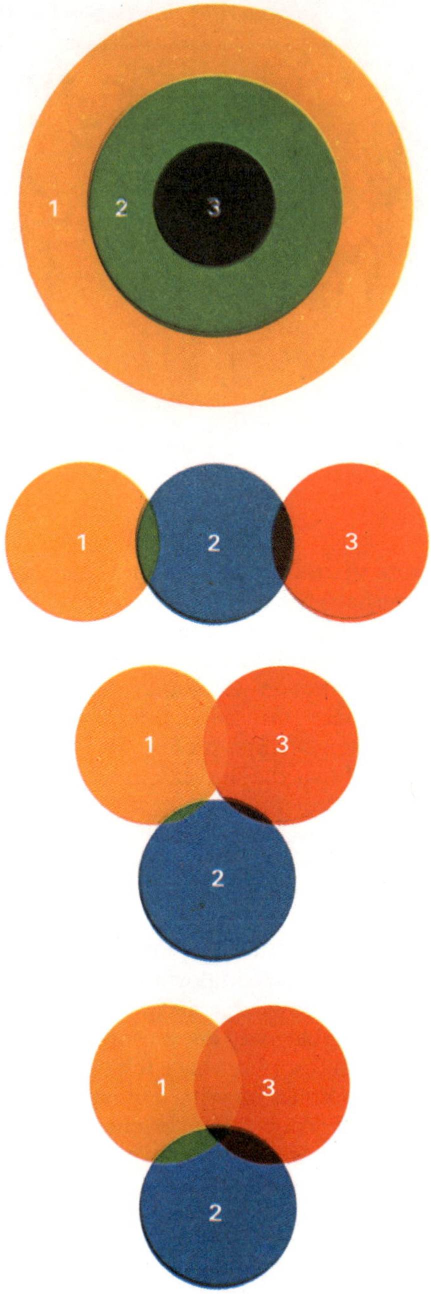

Right This diagram illustrates the process of formal logic. The top drawing shows that if all the area marked 3 is contained in the area 2, and all of 2 is contained in the area 1, then all of 3 must be in 1. This is a symbolic way of expressing what is called a syllogism: Socrates (3) is a man (2), and all men (2) are mortal (1), therefore Socrates (3) is mortal (1). The other three groups of drawings illustrate the fact that if some 2 is 1, and some 2 is 3, some 3 may be 1 (centre diagram) or may not be (top diagram). The bottom diagram shows that it is possible for some of the 1 that is 2 to be some of the 1 that is 3.

Democritus
(5th century BC) Greek philosopher. Travelled in the east, studying the works of other philosophers. The most learned thinker of his age, he was the most notable exponent of the atomic theory of the universe, which assumes an infinite number of atoms, from the combinations of which nature is formed. This theory has been revived by modern chemists and physicists.

The science of reasoning

Finally, there is logic, which may be called the study of reasoning. This can be dealt with quite separately from the rest of philosophy, but a knowledge of logic is necessary if we are to understand and be able to criticise philosophical arguments. Many philosophers claim that they know God exists because they have proved His existence. That is, they have started with a set of statements known to be true, and said that a certain conclusion must be true if these statements (known as premises) are true. The set of premises plus the conclusion form the proof. Logic is partly a study of different kinds of proof.

At this stage you might think that the answer to the question 'What exists?' should be left to the scientists. Surely they know what the world contains? But it is doubtful whether any but the earliest claims put forward by philosophers can be shown to be false by scientific experiment. To discuss 'What exists?' as philosophers we must stand 'outside' science. The findings of scientists are among the facts that philosophers consider.

In the history of philosophy several questions, like 'What are all things made of?' have split off from philosophy to be tackled by experiment in science. But the central questions in philosophy still remain obstinately outside the scientist's sphere.

Greek philosophy

The story of philosophy begins in Greece. The ancient Greeks provided the world with some of its greatest philosophers. The most famous are Plato (427?–347? BC) and Aristotle (384–322 BC), and Plato's teacher Socrates (469?–399 BC). Before Socrates came the first philosophers, the pre-Socratics (that is those who came before Socrates).

The earliest pre-Socratic philosophers were curious about the nature of the world as a whole. They believed that there was one kind of 'stuff' out of which the whole world was made. Thales (6th century BC) said that all things were made of water. No doubt he had his own reasons for saying this but we know little about them. One thing is certain – he had no microscopes to help him in reaching his conclusions.

Other thinkers put forward other claims about the basic stuff of the world. Anaximenes (6th century BC) said it was air. Heraclitus (6th century BC) did not feel so strongly that there was one basic stuff out of which all things are made. He was struck by the way the world was constantly changing. He said 'You can never step into the same river twice', meaning that although the river may look the same there is always a new body of water flowing through it. But he also felt that things changed in accordance with a definite law. Fire, according to Heraclitus, is the most important substance in the world, since it is the main cause of change.

Pythagoras (570?–500? BC) did not think that the clue to understanding the universe lay in finding one basic stuff of which all things are made. He claimed that measurement or number was the real key to understanding, and he made many striking discoveries about the numerical properties of things. Pythagoras also claimed that he knew the best way to live. He taught that in each human being there is a soul; when a man dies his soul goes into another body, perhaps that of an animal. Because of these beliefs (similar to those of the Hindus on reincarnation), Pythagoras claimed that we should spend our lives caring for that part of us which never dies – the soul. Pythagoras had many followers and influenced later thinkers.

Evidence of our senses

The views of the earliest pre-Socratics on the nature of the universe raised one of the most discussed philosophical questions: what is the best way of finding out about the world? In particular, how much notice should we take of 'the evidence of our senses' – the things we see, touch, hear and feel? We may *think* that the world is made up of one basic stuff, but can we be *sure* that it is, if we have not checked our belief against what we can see and feel?

Parmenides (5th century BC) and many later philosophers thought that we could work out the true nature of the world just by thinking about it. But we must think about it in one particular way. We must start with a premise or premises (that is propositions agreed after reasoning) – which we know to be true – and only allow ourselves to believe things which must be true, if the premises are true. In this way we can arrive at certainty about the world by thought alone. Parmenides believed that he had himself reached the truth and he thought he had proved that change and movement were impossible. He was so convinced that the conclusion of his proof was true, that he could not see how to believe the opposite, even if he was tempted to do so by what he saw.

Left Perhaps the most famous theorem in geometry is that attributed to the Greek philosopher Pythagoras: that the square on the hypotenuse (the side opposite to the right-angle) of a right-angled triangle is equal to the sum of the squares on the other two sides.

Parmenides's follower, Zeno (5th century BC), who became famous for his paradoxes (sayings which contradict most people's opinions), also argued that, in his opinion, motion was impossible.

After Parmenides's disturbing claims, some philosophers called atomists, led by Democritus (5th century BC), tried to 'save appearances'. We see change and movement, they said, so there must *be* change and movement. The atomists concluded that the world was made up not of one unmoving spherical mass – as Parmenides had suggested – but of millions of tiny atoms, which could change position among themselves and thus make up new things in time.

The pre-Socratic philosophers were mainly interested in the universe as a whole, and in man only in so far as he was part of that whole. There was much disagreement among them, and it was not easy for them to settle their disputes without the aid of scientific instruments.

The rule of law

Soon a new interest began to absorb Greek thinkers. The Greeks came into contact with people of many different lands, with very different ways of living from their own. This caused them to ask whether any law or rule of conduct was better than any other. Why should we do what the law tells us to do? This was the beginning of political and ethical philosophy.

A group of men called sophists (wise men) tried to tackle these new

Zeno of Elea
(5th century BC) Greek philosopher. Native of Elea, a Greek colony in Italy. Disciple of Parmenides. Best known for his paradoxes, particularly that of Achilles and the tortoise. These puzzles were the beginning of what is known as the dialectic or question and answer method of philosophic inquiry.

Above In his search for the truth, the great philosopher Socrates made many enemies. Eventually he was found guilty on a charge of corrupting the minds of the young and was condemned to die. This he did by drinking poison. When the appointed hour arrived Socrates gathered around him a circle of friends to help him pass his last hours. As he calmly discussed philosophic questions with them he took the poison and ended his life. The statuette is one of the earliest portraits of Socrates and was found at Alexandria in the 4th century BC.

questions. Protagoras (485?–411 BC), the most famous sophist, argued that if everyone obeyed some laws the life of each man, even the strongest, would be improved. So each man should be law-abiding. Protagoras also thought that some laws were better than others. A state could have bad laws but in general some law was better than no law.

The sophists took an important part in the education of the Greeks. There were no high schools or universities in their time. The philosophers took the place of school teachers; they accepted fees for their teaching and became rich. One of the things they taught was the art of making speeches in public. Often they stressed the importance of making one's audience think one was right, rather than actually being right.

Socrates

In this respect the Athenian philosopher Socrates was very different from the sophists. He took no fees and lived in poverty. He was not interested in sounding as if he had knowledge, but actually in finding knowledge. Socrates shared with the sophists their interest in the conduct of human life, rather than the workings of nature as a whole. He studied the pre-Socratic philosophies but soon turned to his own questions and found his own way of answering them.

One of Socrates's main questions was, 'How would a really good man live his life?' It seemed to him quite clear that one could find out what sort of life would be lived by a really good man. More important, we can only be truly good, Socrates thought, if we know clearly and definitely what *is* good. He believed that no one does wrong willingly. We all do what we *think* is right. But in order constantly to *do* right, we must know what really is right. So Socrates began to try to find out what makes an action right or good.

He went about his search in his own special way, which won him enemies as well as admirers. He did not begin by telling people what he thought goodness was, but tried to find out what *they* thought. He questioned poets, politicians and all kinds of men. 'What makes an action right?' he asked. 'What do we mean by "rightness" or "goodness"?' By such questions Socrates tried to make clear people's ideas about right and wrong. He tried to find out the exact meanings of certain important words which, without pausing to think what they mean, we all use freely in daily life. But Socrates made enemies in the course of his search, and was brought to trial by them and condemned to death for false teachings. Yet he died calmly, convinced that no harm could come to a man who had done his duty.

Plato

One of Socrates's pupils and admirers devoted his life to developing his master's teaching. This was Plato, who had once planned to become a politician, but changed his mind when he saw that a man like Socrates could be condemned to death in the courts. Instead he devoted himself to philosophy and founded the Academy at Athens.

Many of Plato's books, unlike the works of the earlier philosophers, have survived till today. These take the form of imaginary conversations, or dialogues, between various people. Socrates is often one of the characters and Plato gives us examples of the historical Socrates's method. The earliest dialogues are searches for the meanings of terms like 'courage' or 'justice', which often reach no definite conclusion. But gradually Plato developed his own philosophy, still in connection with the same problems.

What is special about Plato's thinking is that he felt sure that goodness was some one thing which existed by itself, quite apart from the many particular good things. He argued that goodness itself was something unchanging and permanent. A good man might perhaps change and become bad. Everything around us is constantly changing. But how can goodness itself change? The nature of goodness is always the same.

One aim of the philosopher, according to Plato, is to discover the nature of goodness. Without goodness we could be neither good men nor good rulers. This is very like Socrates's view that in order to be good we must be clear about what goodness is; but Socrates did not talk about goodness as something eternal and unchanging, as Plato does.

Perhaps noting the difficulties Socrates had in discovering the nature of goodness, Plato felt that a long training was necessary before one was ready to discover its true nature. He describes the education that he thinks a philosopher should have in his most famous book *The Republic*.

It should begin with training in music, literature and gymnastics – to take care of both mind and body. The next stage was a thorough study of mathematics. The reason for this is that in mathematics, although we draw particular triangles from which to work out our conclusions, in fact our conclusions are not about these particular figures. What we draw and see are only imperfect examples. What we learn about is the nature of triangularity itself. This is the last stage of the way, before philosophers can turn to the study of non-mathematical forms: this will not be before they are fifty years of age. Thus Plato saw philosophy as a long and hard task, needing a training which few men would be clever enough to complete.

In *The Republic* Plato also describes what he thinks would be a perfect city-state. In this, the rulers are philosophers who have reached the goal of their education – knowledge of goodness itself. Only with this knowledge, thought Plato, could a man know how to rule. How otherwise could he be sure what was good for the city-state? Plato did not think well of the Athenian democracy in which those who made important decisions were not experts. He believed that just as only a doctor, an expert in curing the sick, should be allowed to prescribe medicines for them, so only an expert should be allowed to govern.

Above The most famous university in the ancient world was at Athens, where Plato founded his Academy in 388 BC.

Plato
(427?–347? BC) Greek philosopher. Was a disciple of Socrates and attended his trial. Plato's *Dialogues* often have Socrates as the central figure but usually as a spokesman for Plato's own doctrines. Plato believed mind was more important than matter, and that the idea of 'the good' was the whole meaning of life. Among his best-known writings is *The Republic*, a plan for an ideal state.

Right A copy of an illumination from a 15th-century manuscript of Dante's *Divine Comedy* which is in the British Museum, London. It shows St Thomas Aquinas hovering above the figures of St Dominic and St Francis as he tells the story of St Francis to Dante and Beatrice.

Aristotle
(384–322 BC) Greek philosopher and scientist. For 17 years was with Plato at his Academy. After Plato's death he became tutor to Alexander the Great. In 335 he founded his Peripatetic School at the Lyceum in Athens. It was so called because Aristotle's habit was to walk up and down while delivering his lectures. He was accomplished in the study of science as well as philosophy.

Aristotle

Aristotle entered Plato's Academy at seventeen, and stayed for twenty years. His father was a doctor; this may help to explain the amazing scope of Aristotle's own interests. He worked and wrote on zoology and astronomy, as well as on logic, ethics, aesthetics, politics, the nature of change (in the *Physics*) and what he called 'first philosophy'. His writings on first philosophy were placed by his editors after the *Physics*, and in this way became known as the *Metaphysics* – which means after physics in Greek. When we talk of metaphysical theories nowadays we usually refer to theories about existence which are not based on scientific experiment.

Aristotle wrote one of the greatest books on logic. He regarded logic as the study of forms of reasoning which are the same for every subject. Aristotle made a careful study of a pattern of reasoning he called the syllogism, which is made up of a pair of premises and a conclusion. By this study Aristotle became the first really important logician.

In the period after Aristotle's death, philosophers concentrated again on the problem: how should life be lived? Their teachings were popular and well-known, more so than the teachings of most philosophers. The sciences began to be developed by other men, separately from philosophy.

The Epicureans

Epicurus (341?–270 BC) believed that men's souls did not survive their deaths, and so there was no need to spend one's life preparing the soul for life after death, as others had suggested. Epicurus noticed that all living beings seek pleasure and avoid pain. He concluded that pleasure is good for man. But he actually advised men to seek, in particular, calmness of mind. Thus the Epicureans recommended a quiet and simple life as the best one.

The Stoics said that men should not aim at pleasure or riches; they should try to make themselves as independent of other things as possible. Self-control was one main Stoic aim. The meaning of the adjective stoical reflects the Stoics' view of how to live. Theirs was a long-lived philosophy – the Roman Emperor Marcus Aurelius (AD 121–180) was a Stoic.

Modern philosophy

In medieval times philosophy took up a new role. The Greeks had lived before Christ and well before Christianity became an established religion. The most famous philosophers of the medieval period were Christians. Their belief in the existence of God was firm and unshakeable. Yet they wished to make clear the exact nature of their belief, and to see if it could be proved by a valid argument. Thus they were philosophers as well as Christians; but with them reasoning would not be allowed to overcome faith.

St Anselm (1033–1109) was archbishop of Canterbury. In his book, the *Proslogion*, he was the first to put forward a famous argument for the existence of God, known as the ontological argument. This argument runs roughly as follows: God is the greatest possible

Above It was in Amsterdam that Descartes settled in 1628, to be free to pursue his philosophy. Amsterdam was then the financial capital of the world. Because there was religious and intellectual freedom, the city also became a centre of the arts, science and philosophy.

being – it is part of the very idea of God that He is such a being. Now, the greatest possible being must exist. So God, the greatest possible being, must exist. Some later philosophers accepted the argument, but others rejected it.

St Thomas Aquinas (1226–74) put forward his own 'five ways' of proving the existence of God in his long book *Summa Theologica*. These all argue that there must be a God, starting from various facts about the nature of the world around us. Since they were put forward, these arguments have been much discussed and disputed.

René Descartes

Modern philosophy is often held to have begun in France with René Descartes (1596–1650). Descartes certainly saw himself as breaking away from all the earlier philosophical 'schools', and starting out on his own in a completely new way. In his *Discourse on Method* Descartes set out his method of reaching truth in all matters. In the *Meditations* Descartes tells us about the results he came to using this method. He began by asking which of his present beliefs could not possibly be false. Surely his belief that he was now sitting at his desk must be a true belief? But, he remembered, he had often dreamed that he was sitting up at his desk, when in fact he was really asleep in bed. So he *might* be wrong – he might be dreaming now.

Descartes concluded that the one belief he could not doubt was that he was thinking. He could be sure that he *thought* he saw a desk, even if he couldn't be sure that there *was* a desk in front of him. So Descartes found the first premise of his philosophy: I think. Further, if he could not doubt that he thought certain things, he certainly could not doubt that he existed. He is therefore quite certain of his own existence – at least insofar as he is a thinking being. 'I think, therefore I exist: *cogito, ergo sum*.'

Descartes was convinced that his mind and his body were two quite different things. He argued that whereas it was *possible* to doubt that his body really existed, he could not doubt that his thinking mind existed. So mind and body were distinct things. This view is known as mind-body dualism. One of the problems Descartes left with later philosophers was this: how is the mind of a man connected to his body? This became known as the mind-body problem.

The rationalists

Descartes, and those who followed him in the use of the 'mathematical' method in philosophy, have been called rationalists (from the Latin *ratio* meaning reason). Rationalist philosophers think that we can find out what the world contains by careful reasoning from obviously true premises; these premises can be known to be true without our needing to observe or experiment on the world around us. They sometimes call these premises innate truths – meaning that we are born (Latin *nati*) already knowing their truth.

Baruch Spinoza (1632-77), a Dutch lens-grinder, and the Prussian, Gottfried Leibniz (1646-1716), are two

René Descartes (1596–1650) French philosopher and mathematician. Dissatisfied with his teachers and what he could learn from books he sought a new form of rationalism by looking for truth within himself and in nature. He began by doubting all traditional beliefs and opinions. While serving as a soldier he began to study geometry and later devoted himself to pure mathematics.

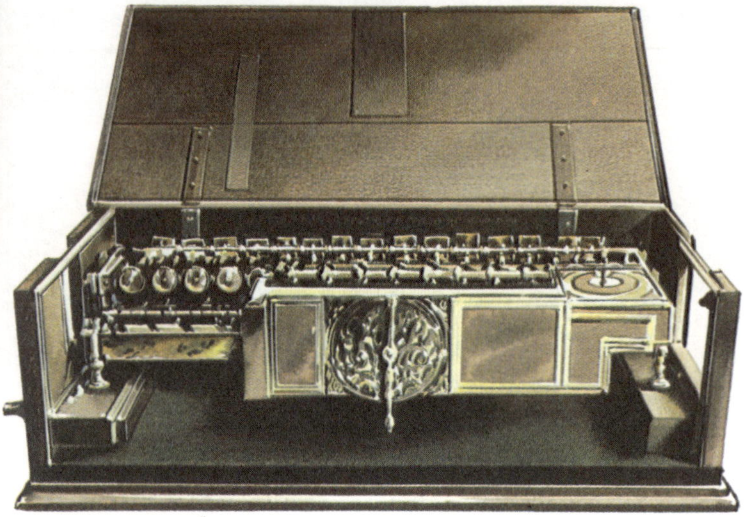

Above Leibniz's calculating machine, an improvement on Pascal's, was capable of adding, subtracting, multiplying, dividing and extracting roots.

Gottfried Leibniz (1646–1716) German philospher and mathematician. He is ranked with Newton as one of the two great intellects of the 17th century. There is some dispute whether he or Newton first discovered the infinitesimal calculus. His best-known work is *Monadology* and he left a vast correspondence with learned men of his day which expresses his views.

famous rationalists. In his main work, the *Ethics*, Spinoza tried to develop and improve upon René Descartes's philosophy.

Spinoza saw man as merely a part of nature; further, all events are connected and influence one another. An adult man's character is the result of the way other things and people acted upon him when he was a child. So, Spinoza concludes, we should not behave as if people could ever have acted otherwise than they did. We should not show anger or resentment, but only calm understanding, in the face of another person's stupid or wicked actions.

The view that all of a man's future actions are fixed in advance, or predetermined, is known as determinism. Philosophers today still discuss the view that we cannot hold a man responsible for his actions if they are all determined.

Leibniz, a brilliant mathematician as well as a philosopher, wrote out his main ideas in his *Monadology*; this title means 'theory of monads'. Monads are simple, mind-like substances of which, according to Leibniz, the world is made up. Leibniz tried to prove that the world must be made up of innumerable monads and that all that really exists are these monads. If his conclusions do not appear to be true according to our observations of the world, he would answer, like Parmenides, that our observations of the world do not inform us about what the world really contains.

The empiricists

Faced with conflicting views of what there is, we may begin to wonder how we are to decide between them. One way of telling if a statement is true or false is to look and see. If I say, 'There's a cat on the mat', and you see nothing on the mat, you will conclude that what I said was false. In this way we frequently use the evidence of our senses to tell if a particular claim about the world is true. A group of philosophers who claim that our *only* way of telling what there is, is by using the evidence of our senses, are the empiricists (from the Greek word for experience). A claim which cannot be tested by our senses can be ignored, they say: it can give us no knowledge of the world about us.

The first modern empiricists were John Locke (1632-1704), George Berkeley (1685-1753) and David Hume (1711-76).

In his *Essay Concerning Human Understanding* Locke attacked the rationalist view that there are some beliefs which are innate, or inborn, in the human mind. Locke claimed that, on the contrary, the minds of children at birth are like blank sheets of paper. The rationalist thinkers, Locke argued, had no right to expect us to believe certain premises because according to them they were innate. There are no innate beliefs.

Locke's own picture of the world was taken over from the scientists of his day, Boyle and Newton. Objects in space close to our bodies cause sensations (called by Locke 'ideas') to occur in our minds. When we have these sensations we say that we perceive (see, hear, feel, touch or smell) the objects themselves. Locke's theory suggests the question: 'How do we know that objects in space are in any way like the sensations they produce in our minds?'

Berkeley tried to answer this question in his *Principles of Human Knowledge*. He said that we cannot even know that objects outside our minds cause sensations. All we are ever conscious of are the sensations themselves, so our knowledge is limited to knowledge of our own sensations. For how can we have any grounds for our beliefs, if they are about anything but our sensations?

David Hume, who gave his ideas of the limits of knowledge in his *Treatise* and *Enquiry*, doubted the existence of all things apart from his own sensations and thoughts. He said that he had no idea what the human mind could be apart from a 'bundle' of experiences. His own experiences were all he knew about for certain.

Immanuel Kant

Immanuel Kant (1724-1804), the great German philosopher, felt challenged by Hume's scepticism, and began to think carefully for himself about the nature of human knowledge. He wanted to know what kinds of things we could know, and what kinds of things, if any, we could never know. His book, *The Critique of Pure Reason*, is perhaps the greatest masterpiece of philosophy. As Kant himself was aware, it is difficult to understand. But it is worth the trouble of trying to do so.

Kant is not sceptical, in Hume's way, about the existence of material objects in space. He argues that we must believe that there are enduring things around us in space, or how could we connect together our different sensations, and how remember them? Kant claimed that we needed to think of our experiences in terms of objects, if we were to have any grasp of our experiences at all.

Kant also wrote important books on ethics (the *Critique of Practical Reason*) and aesthetics (the *Critique of Judgement*). In answer to Socrates's question, 'How ought one to live?' he wrote that we act well only when we act as we would wish all men to act in our situation.

Two other philosophers who gave a famous answer to Socrates's question are Jeremy Bentham (1748-1832) and John Stuart Mill (1806-73). They developed the theory known as utilitarianism. According to this theory, one should act in such a way that one produces the greatest possible pleasure or happiness by one's action. The moral rule laid down here is sometimes called 'the Greatest Happiness Principle'. There have been many objections to this principle. One was this: if I have promised to pay you a sum of money tomorrow, then I *ought* to pay you that money, even if, by giving it to a beggar instead, I could produce more happiness than by giving it to you.

Above Immanuel Kant lived all his life in Königsberg in east Prussia, never moving more than 50 kilometres beyond the town. He used to take his meals in cafés where, so great was his fame, students followed him to wait for the opportunity to have an impromptu discussion with him.

Political philosophy

Political philosophy has not been neglected by modern philosophers. Thomas Hobbes (1588-1679) took up the sophists' question, 'Why should we obey the laws of our country?' in his great book *Leviathan*. He argued that men could only live happy lives if they lived in a society with one firmly established ruling body or sovereign which made laws for everyone. If men lived without a sovereign and without laws, their lives would be 'nasty, brutish and short'. In such a state of nature, as he calls it, each man would be at war with every other man. So, for their own good, all men should agree to abide by the laws of one sovereign. Having once handed over the right of law-making to the sovereign, men are duty bound to obey him and all his laws. These laws impose many further duties on the citizens, such as the duty not to kill other citizens.

John Locke, the empiricist, also wrote on political philosophy. His most famous work in this field is the *Two Treatises on Government*. He emphasised that the role of laws is to hedge us in from 'bogs and precipices'. Laws do not *only* provide us with duties, but also with rights. If other men have the duty not to kill me, then I have the right to live. Locke believed that everyone living in a society has a

John Stuart Mill (1806–73) English philosopher and reformer. He was a brilliant student and by the time he was 14 he could speak Greek and Latin and had a vast knowledge of logic, political economy, mathematics and history. Engaged in literary work from an early age. Published his *System of Logic*, 1843 and *On Liberty*, which contained his political views, 1859.

Above In this picture gallery of philosophers are seen **1** John Locke (1632–1704) English philosopher who, as well as writing on the nature of human understanding, was a political adviser to the 1st earl of Shaftesbury. **2** Jean-Jacques Rousseau (1712–78), French political philosopher, educationist and essayist, whose work was a great influence on Revolutionary France. **3** Friedrich Hegel (1770–1831), German philosopher who was interested chiefly in political philosophy. **4** F. H. Bradley (1846–1924), English philosopher, whose thinking on metaphysical ideas influenced Bertrand Russell. **5** Arthur Schopenhauer (1788–1860), German philosopher who was particularly concerned with freedom of will as the key to an understanding of all things.

duty to obey the laws of that society, provided that these laws actually protect the interests of society. He claimed that merely by continuing to live in a certain country one had given tacit (silent) consent to the laws of the government in power.

Jean-Jacques Rousseau (1712-78) also made use of the notion of consent or agreement in discussing whether or why we have a duty to obey the laws of our country. In *The Social Contract* he describes what for him would be an ideal type of society. This is one in which all the citizens together agree upon each law that is made. Rousseau felt very strongly that only such a process of agreement between citizens can create a citizen's duty to obey the laws.

Friedrich Hegel

In the years following the publication of Kant's great works, philosophy flourished in Germany. The most outstanding and influential philosopher was Friedrich Hegel (1770-1831). Hegel's thought covered all the branches of philosophy. He saw philosophy as a study demanding great learning and skill. He himself tried to present a view of the nature of the whole universe, not only as it is now, but as it has been and as it will be.

Hegel has been called an idealist since he claimed that the most important factor in the world was consciousness and knowledge. Sometimes he writes as if individual men's minds are part of one great spirit (the Absolute) which guides the course of the world. But human progress in knowledge was of great importance, and philosophy was the most important study of all. For philosophy had to consider the whole range of human knowledge – history, politics, art, science, religion – and discover how the different parts are connected. The business of the philosopher is to see the world as a whole, and to know how parts are related to one another. When human knowledge of the world is complete the world will have reached its state of perfection.

Hegel had many followers, including F. H. Bradley (1846-1924) in England. There were also anti-Hegelians, but, like Hegel, they often chose to describe the world as a whole, to give a 'total vision' of the world. Arthur Schopenhauer (1788-1860) disagreed with several of Hegel's basic ideas. His best-known work is *The World as Will and Idea*. Each of us knows what it is to exercise our will – to act with purpose, to decide we want something and to go out and get it. We ourselves have our own wills and we also have 'ideas' (sensations). We do not produce our ideas and what does, Schopenhauer says, is an unseen will which underlies the universe. Schopenhauer, unlike Hegel, did not believe in any

6 Karl Marx (1818–83) German philosopher, politician and founder of Communism. He settled in London in 1849 and there published his great work *Das Kapital*. **7** Friedrich Nietzsche (1844–1900), German philosopher who revolted against the accepted values of his time and published his views in a number of books. **8** Sören Kierkegaard, (1813–55) Danish philosopher. He attacked organised Christianity and influenced Sartre and hence all modern existentialism. **9** Jean-Paul Sartre (1905–1980) French philosopher, dramatist and novelist. Was very active in Left-wing politics and was a famous spokesman of existentialism. **10** Friedrich Engels (1820–95) German socialist who worked with Marx and with whom he wrote the *Communist Manifesto*. Edited *Das Kapital* after Marx's death. **11** Emanuel Swedenborg (1688–1772), Swedish thinker who wrote on mystical subjects, convinced that he had access to the spiritual world.

progress towards a state of final perfection. The will, he said, cannot ever find satisfaction or be calm.

Marx and Nietzsche

A philosopher who opposed Hegel in a different way was Karl Marx (1818-1883). Marx gave up Hegel's notion of a spirit which directed natural processes. As far as Marx was concerned there was only the material world plus human minds. He called his philosophy materialism, because he rejected the Hegelian world-spirit. He saw the process of human history as a gradual progression towards the ideal state of communism, in which there would be no exploitation of one person by another. Marx disagreed with Hegel's view that it is the philosopher's job merely to understand how the world works. Understanding should lead to criticism, and criticism to revolution. And Marx's doctrines have in fact had a revolutionary effect on recent history.

Friedrich Nietzsche (1844-1900) also attacked Hegel and denied the existence of some invisible guiding will behind the scenes. He says, rather, that there is a perfectly visible will to power everywhere in the world. All men desire power. Our desire for knowledge of the world comes from our wish for power over the world. The real goal of men is to become supermen.

Existentialism

A Dane, Sören Kierkegaard (1813-55), another philosopher who was hostile to Hegel's views, was also the first of one of the best-known modern groups of philosophers, the existentialists. He, in fact, first used the word existentialism.

Kierkegaard wrote many books, some of them with dramatic titles like *Fear and Trembling*. One title, *Either – Or*, expresses the core of Kierkegaard's philosophy, the notion of human choice between alternative courses of action. For Kierkegaard one of the most striking features of human existence is that each individual man can choose what he wants to do and, particularly in the sphere of religion, what he wants to believe. He objected to Hegel's view of the individual as merely a part of the universe, whose goal should be to understand the whole.

The most famous existentialist, Jean-Paul Sartre, also stressed the fact that we can all choose what to do, and what to become. Someone who is a waiter today does not have to be a waiter. He could decide to give up his job. Even if he does not give up his job, he does not have to carry it out in a particular manner. Men are not like machines, which have to do one particular job in one particular way. Each man is completely free to do what he wants, Sartre said, and must realise this if he is to know the truth

Bertrand Russell
(1872–1970) English philosopher and mathematician. One of the greatest logicians of all time. Twice imprisoned for his vigorous pacifist views. Despite his position as a great English philosopher of the 20th century, it is as a figure of protest, particularly against war and the use of nuclear weapons, that he is best known.

Albert Schweitzer
(1875–1965) German musician, philosopher and doctor. Studied theology at Strasbourg university. Also gained international reputation as an organist and authority on J. S. Bach. He abandoned these pursuits to become a missionary doctor. Set up a hospital at Lambaréné, in French Equatorial Africa in 1913, and he dedicated the rest of his life to his work there.

about himself. Sartre expressed all these views in a long philosophical work, *Being and Nothingness,* and also in novels and plays.

20th-century philosophy

Many 20th-century philosophers have tended to discuss limited problems in a detailed, careful manner. Studies in logic have developed rapidly. The work of Gottlob Frege (1848-1925) and Bertrand Russell (1872-1970) is among the best known in this field. Many logicians have also become interested in the nature of mathematics. With A. N. Whitehead (1861-1947) Russell wrote *Principia Mathematica,* an outstanding work in this field.

A home-grown American school of philosophy is pragmatism. The original pragmatists were C. S. Peirce (1839-1914), William James (1842-1910) and John Dewey (1859-1952). The pragmatic theory of truth says that a statement is true if it is useful for us to believe it.

One school of philosophy which became popular in Britain and America originated in Vienna, among the members of a group known as the Vienna Circle. These men were all mathematicians or scientists, and their doctrine is known as logical positivism or logical empiricism. According to their theories, only statements which can be verified (shown to be true) by our looking about us, by the evidence of our senses, can be said to tell us anything, or to be meaningful. This principle was used by members of the Circle in order to show that many of the doctrines of past philosophers had been meaningless. In Britain, A. J. Ayer's book *Language, Truth and Logic* brought logical positivism to people's attention. These philosophers and, later, many philosophers in Britain, were influenced by the work of an outstanding Austrian philosopher, Ludwig Wittgenstein (1889-1951). His early theories were to do with the need for a 'perfect' language which would picture facts in a clear way. He did not believe any actual human language was perfect. Later in his life Wittgenstein claimed that many philosophic problems arise because we are misled, or worried in one way or another, by our language. For instance, we might find ourselves talking about time – 'How much time has passed since I last saw you?' – and suddenly wonder, but what *is* time? Similarly we might feel puzzled or worried about the nature of reality – 'Is it real, or am I dreaming?' These worries lead to some of the oldest and most famous questions of philosophy. Wittgenstein suggests that they should be answered by carefully considering the actual use we make of words.

Many Anglo-American philosophers have said recently that the job of philosophy is to analyse concepts, which is roughly the same as to study and explain word meanings. They would agree with Wittgenstein that philosophy 'changes nothing'. The philosopher's business is *description* merely.

We know that not all philosophers have held this view of their subject. Some, perhaps, would have found this view helpful and useful. But it seems a long way from the theories of Leibniz, the doubts of Descartes, the scepticism of Hume, ard the answers of Kant.

The world of art and music

Contents

435 The world of art and architecture
The terms of the artist – The artist as craftsman – The first artists – Early civilisations
Primitive art
The Greeks – The Etruscans – The Romans – The early Christians
Indian art
The barbarians – The growth of the church – Romanesque art – Gothic art – The *Dance of Death*
Oriental art
Northern painters – Printing – The Renaissance – Leonardo da Vinci – Michelangelo
Pre-Columbian art
Mannerism – Germany – The Low Countries – France – Spain
Islamic art
The age of the Baroque – Baroque in Italy – Baroque and Rococo in France – Rubens and Van Dyck – The Dutch painters – The 17th century in Spain – English art – 18th-century Europe – North America – Neo-classic art – The Romantics – Vision and landscape – William Morris – 19th-century architecture – The Pre-Raphaelites – The Barbizon painters – Rural and urban life – The sculpture of light – Whistler – The Impressionists – Art Nouveau – Post-Impressionism – The Bauhaus – Photography – The 20th century – Architecture – Sculpture – The graphic revolution

493 The world of music and the dance
How music is made – Western music – The Greek modes – Plainsong – Polyphony – The Middle Ages – The Renaissance – Music of the Reformation – The birth of opera – The Baroque Age – Bach and Handel – Sonata and symphony – Haydn's symphonies – Mozart – Beethoven – The Romantic movement – Growth of the orchestra – The Viennese school – Richard Wagner – Italian Grand Opera – Strauss, Bruckner and Mahler – Nationalism – New sounds – Atonality – Music today

518 Music and the dance
Religion and magic – Forms of dance – Dancing in the ancient world – Folk dancing – Spanish dancing – Court dances – The waltz – The birth of classical ballet – The first ballet stars – The romantic ballet – Isadora Duncan – The Diaghilev Ballet – Ballet today

Above Joseph Turner, the great English painter, visited Venice in 1832 and the first of his Venetian paintings was shown at the Royal Academy in 1833. Turner found the Italian city to be his ideal painting ground and among the pictures he produced during the next twelve years was *Venice, from the Canale Della Giudecca* (1840), seen here. Turner himself described Venice as 'a city of rose and white, rising out of an emerald sea against a sky of sapphire blue'.

The world of art and architecture

The word art in its broadest sense has to do with the making or doing of almost anything which depends on a degree of personal skill and talent. In this way, basket weaving, judo, riding a bicycle, swimming or making model aircraft might each be thought of as an art. But for most of us the word art has to do with the way in which people try to communicate their thoughts or feelings by means of drawing, painting, sculpture, music or writing. To limit the meaning still further, Art – with a capital A – means the visual arts and does not include music and literature.

In order to paint a picture, or carve an image out of stone, or design a beautiful building, the artist needs to be able to see what he is doing. This may seem obvious, but it is important; for the visual arts are those most directly linked to our physical senses – more particularly, the sense of sight. This does not mean that the artist is limited by what he can actually see. Nothing could be further from the truth. For each human being has his own view of the world about him, and what the artist 'sees' and tries to express is personal to him. His work is influenced not only by his experience, temperament, knowledge and understanding, but by his particular emotions at a given time.

Vision is a very personal thing. Very often we 'see' only what we want to see. Sometimes we deliberately ignore sights which either displease us or simply fail to excite our interest – just as we all sometimes ignore facts which do not support our own private beliefs and opinions. As far as our eyes are concerned, it is the job of the artist to communicate through paintings, sculpture or architecture something of his extra awareness of the reality of things.

Art is both vision and communication, the one being useless without the

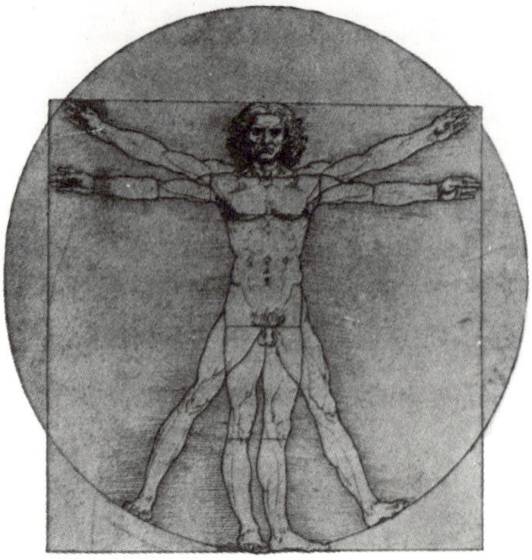

created it. And when we first meet the work of a new and unfamiliar artist, and perhaps find it rather puzzling, we should welcome the chance it gives of looking at the world afresh.

Above Milan Cathedral in Italy is one of the finest examples of Gothic architecture in the world. Its proportions are based on strict geometric principles. The building was begun in 1386 and continued in the 15th to 19th centuries.

Above right In this drawing Leonardo da Vinci illustrates a statement by the Roman architect and engineer Vitruvius (1st century AD) on the proportions of the human body, that the measurements of a man are such that the span of his outstretched arms is about equal to his height.

other. Communication means working to a generally accepted and recognisable set of rules – as, for example, a spoken language is made up of words with particular sounds and meanings which are understood by the people who use that language. And just as the language of words changes from one country to another, or from one century to the next, so the language of art is also constantly changing. It must do this, because unless something continually changes and grows, it will die. People who look at modern painting and say, 'Why can't they paint today the way they did three hundred years ago?' fail to understand this vital fact. A painting created today in the 'language' of three hundred years ago would not be a true work of art. We should try to see the art of every generation, including our own, through the eyes of the great painters, sculptors and architects who

The terms of the artist

When talking or writing about art we use certain words that help explain how a painting, a piece of sculpture or a building looks. Learning the meaning of these words is important. Being able to use them saves long, complicated explanations each time we try to describe a work of art.

One of the most important of these words is proportion. To understand it, imagine that a man you have not met before comes into the room where you are sitting. At once you know whether he is tall or short, fat or thin. How can you tell? Because, almost without thinking, you have considered the proportion of the man's height to his width, and compared his height and width to that of the door and furniture in the room. As we look at the world around us we are constantly comparing one shape with another in this way, and so forming our judgement of proportion.

Since the time of the ancient Egyptians artists have tried to create perfect proportion – that is, proportion completely satisfying to the human eye. If you take several pieces of paper and draw a line on each of them, and then ask some friends each to divide a line in a way that looks pleasing to them, you will find that most of them divide it in almost the same way – so that one part of the line is nearly twice as long as the other. The ancient Greeks worked out this proportion mathematically. The artists of the Renaissance also used it, calling it the Divine Proportion, and today we call it the Golden Section, or Golden Mean. This proportion, which the Greeks felt was in harmony with the universe itself, does not belong only to works of art. Plants, shells, crystals and many other forms in nature, including the human body, are based on the Golden Mean.

Another word that has to do with measurement is scale. This describes actual size. For instance, you may have seen a map with a scale of one inch to the mile, meaning that every inch on that map represents one real mile. Works of art are often measured by comparing them with the real size of the people or objects they represent: this real size is called life size. The scale of a statue, therefore, might be given as three-quarters life size.

Besides having proportion and scale, every work of art is made up of a number of different things. To begin with, each one has a complete, or outside, shape. If we look at a building or a piece of sculpture we would call this outside shape its mass. The terms of geometry, such as sphere, cube or cone, are often used to describe mass. Mass can have space inside it, or it can be solid – but either way, whatever is inside is called the volume.

In a painting or a drawing, such an enclosed space is called the area. This might be quite irregular, or it might be possible to describe it with other geometrical words like square, circle or triangle. An area is enclosed, not by mass, but by line, and this may be a fine stroke, a broad band, or simply an edge.

A work of art also has a structure (which is its basic framework, or skeleton), and it has surface. A completely flat surface is called a plane. Three-dimensional works, such as buildings and statues, have mass, volume and planes. Two-dimensional works, such as paintings, drawings or prints, have only a plane. However, although a plane has no depth, many paintings and drawings do seem to have depth. Any system of drawing which gives this appearance of depth is called perspective.

Above Towards the end of his life the great German draughtsman and engraver, Albrecht Dürer, was preoccupied with studies on the theory of drawing. The illustration is based on a woodcut by Dürer from an edition of his great work on geometry and perspective, published in 1525. It shows a painter studying the laws of foreshortening, using threads and a special frame.

Finally, every surface has texture – in other words, it may be hard or soft, rough or smooth, dull or shiny. The best way to learn about texture is, of course, to feel it. But even if this is not possible, the way light strikes a surface often tells us something about its texture, so that we can imagine what it feels like.

Proportion and scale, mass and volume, area, line, structure, texture – all these things put together give a painting or drawing, a building or a piece of sculpture what we know as its form.

The artist as craftsman

When an artist has decided what it is he wants to create, there is at once another vital decision to be made. What medium will he use – or, in other words, what means will be most suitable for communicating his message? This may not seem to be terribly important, but it is. Suppose, for instance, that the artist wishes to create the image of a horse, stressing above all its massive power. He is likely to be more successful if he carves it in stone than if he makes it of porcelain. Again, it may be the speed of the horse that interests him, and in this case a drawing may serve his purpose best. If, however, it is colour and texture he wants, he must make a painting. The artist may want more than one copy of his horse – if so, he will have to make prints of it.

Having made the first decision about a medium, there are other, finer points to be settled. There are many different

Above Some of the earliest signs of man's artistic expression are the abstract designs found on the stone blocks of prehistoric megaliths, or burial chambers.

kinds of pencils, charcoals and crayons for drawing, and a number of different methods of painting. If the artist wants to make prints there are several ways of doing this.

Today, there is an ever-growing variety of media in which an artist can work. The first half of this century has seen a huge increase in experiment with materials, and more and more will come to be used in the future.

Oil paint is probably the best-known medium today, as it has been for about six hundred years. It is so called because the granules of colour, or pigment, are bound together with linseed and other oils. This paint is usually applied to stretched canvas or to board, both of which are first treated to prevent their absorbing the paint. If these are well prepared and of good quality, a painting should last many years.

In water colour painting the pigment is bound by gums, such as gum arabic, and the colour block or paste is soluble in water. This is used mainly on heavyweight paper or board, and the transparency of the colour gives a luminous effect. Gouache paint is also water-soluble, but it is much more opaque than water colour and less difficult to apply, as a light colour may be painted over a dark one.

Other materials may be used to bind pigments, such as the white of egg used in tempera painting. This paint is used on a wet or dry plaster surface, and it also gives a glowing, transparent effect. When used on wet plaster it is known as fresco.

This century has brought many new methods. One of these is collage, which is painting by sticking down bits of various materials, such as paper, wood, cloth or metal. There are also new media for binding pigment colour, including polymer and acrylic resins. New methods of working, like the spraying of paint from aerosol cans, add to the number of choices now open to the artist. So, too, does the introduction of drawing instruments like ball-point and fibre-tip pens.

The invention of plastics has given the sculptor many new and exciting materials. These are now so numerous that they may be tough, brittle, soft, or even inflatable. And it is no longer necessary for sculpture to convey movement only through its form. Instead, sculpture really can move!

Technology contributes the materials, and art finds the uses for them. Structures like the Sydney Opera House in Australia are made possible only by advances in both fields.

Above The pictures on these two pages illustrate some of the different mediums used by artists. From left to right are shown an illuminated manuscript from a medieval book of hours; a woodcut by Albrecht Dürer; a painting in tempera on wood by Giovanni Bellini; an oil painting by Rubens; another oil painting, this time by Van Gogh and showing this artist's use of very thick paint on canvas; and lastly a modern collage by Kurt Schwitters.

Artists who use print-making are also experimenting beyond the traditional methods, which are: raised surface printing, such as linocut and woodcut; lowered surface printing, such as etching; and same-surface printing, such as silk-screen and lithography. The growth and development of photography has brought possibilities of new methods to add to these old ways.

The first artists

No one knows exactly when or how art began. The only thing we do know for certain is that no people in the entire history of the world has been without its own forms of art. It seems that the making of images is one of the most basic and important of human activities. The word images does not, of course, mean only fine portraits or impressive statues. It means anything made by man that has visual qualities as well as purely useful qualities. For example, a chair is just as useful whether it is covered with an old sack or a piece of beautiful tapestry. The tapestry is simply evidence of man's urge to beautify. At the same time, any object that is designed to work really well often gains very satisfying visual qualities at the same time.

The oldest surviving works of art belong to the Palaeolithic Age, or Old Stone Age, from about 50,000 to 20,000 years ago, when men sheltered in caves and lived by hunting. On their weapons of stone, ivory and horn, Palaeolithic men engraved images of the mammoths, boars, deer and bison they hunted. They also made engravings and paintings in underground caves (not those in which they lived) using the natural contours of the rock to emphasise the shapes they drew. They worked with sharpened flints, reed brushes, natural pigments of red and yellow ochre (called earth colours) and charred wood or bone. We do not know why they painted these animals, or made abstract patterns. It is clear, however, that these unknown, ancient artists were keenly observant and highly skilled.

Early civilisations

When the first civilisations came into being, the customs and beliefs of the people influenced their art strongly. In ancient Egypt, for example, it was important that the dead should have everything they might need in the spirit world – where, it was believed,

continued on page 442

Above Eskimo mask from south-east Alaska which probably dates from the 19th century. It is made from painted wood and feathers and would have been worn in dances and ceremonies.

Above right Bronze head of a queen mother from Benin, Nigeria (16th century).

Below Ornament of carved jade made by the Maoris in New Zealand in the 19th century.

Primitive art

Primitive art is timeless. It is still being practised in several parts of the world and yet has its beginnings with the cave paintings of the earliest hunters in about 30,000 BC. The only difference is that modern primitive art has become deadened by contact with our developed, commercial culture, while earlier primitive art is bold, imaginative and vital.

The art of the early hunters was centred on animals and on magic ways of capturing them. It survives today among the Bushmen of Africa, the Australian aborigines and the Eskimos, but its peak was over by 10,000 BC. As soon as the ice disappeared from the plains, and forests began to grow, man turned to an agricultural way of life. Fertility was all important and he carved figures which seemed to promise this – 'great mother' statuettes, or ancestor figures. Sometimes they are combined one on top of another on door-posts to make fertility even more certain, just as the nomads of Asia made ornaments in which horses, elks and even snakes were also mounted one on top of another.

Over the centuries man used art and ceremony to express his sense of kinship with nature or his fear of it. Gradually, he tried to impose order on nature and it was at this stage that the mature city cultures of the Middle East arose (5000 BC) to be followed by those of India, China and finally South America. These cultures were to reflect back on the primitive art surrounding them, sometimes to enrich it, more often to overwhelm it. The most interesting primitive art was produced in areas that received few influences from outside – that is, Africa and Oceania. Here the arts of woodcarving, bronze casting, pottery decorating and textile designing are richly expressive, direct, and full of confidence.

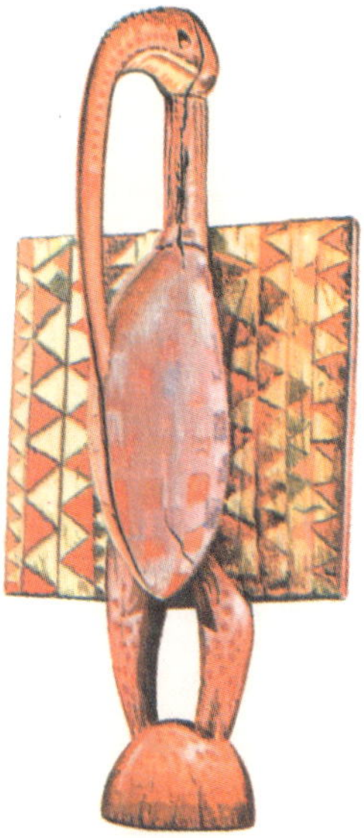

Above The figure of a standing bird made by the Senufo peoples of the Ivory Coast in West Africa. It is carved from wood and painted and probably played some part in the cult of ancestor worship.

Above left Tiger's head made from bronze and inlaid with silver. This beautiful piece of early Chinese metalwork dates from the Chou dynasty, which lasted from about 1027 to 221 BC.

Far left Hunter carrying an antelope, from Benin, Nigeria, cast in bronze (late 19th century).

Centre left Ancestor figure from the Babar Islands in Indonesia. It is carved in wood and dates from the 19th century.

Near left Shield from the Sepik River Valley, New Guinea. This grotesque face sticks out its tongue to ward off evil, a very ancient gesture.

Above The head of Nefertiti, one of the most famous works of Egyptian art. Queen Nefertiti was wife of the pharaoh Akhenaton and the sculpture dates from the XVIIIth Dynasty.

Above It was the custom for Egyptian artists to paint people in profile but with shoulders turned to the front so that both arms could be seen. A full-face eye was drawn into the side view of the face. This figure is taken from an XVIIIth Dynasty tomb painting in Thebes.

daily life would go on just as usual. The dead man's tomb was filled with his best possessions and decorated with paintings showing scenes of work and play from normal life. In these paintings it was the custom for people to be shown with head and legs in profile, but with shoulders turned to the front so that both arms were visible. In this way no limbs appeared to be missing from the image, and the dead man could take a complete body to the spirit world.

The later Egyptians built gigantic temples to their gods. The columns, some of which were as much as eighteen metres high, were decorated with figures and with stylised plant forms such as the lotus and the papyrus. Remains of a few of these temples still stand today, after some 3,500 years.

At about the same time that the civilisation of Egypt developed in the Nile valley, the Babylonian civilisation grew up in the valley between the Tigris and Euphrates rivers. Here, too, great temples were built. Unlike those in Egypt, the Babylonian temples, or ziggurats, were massive towers, several storeys high. The Tower of Babel described in the Bible was just such a building. Built of unbaked brick, these Babylonian ziggurats did not survive time as well as the stone temples of the Egyptians.

Much fine craft-work was produced in the early civilisations. The Egyptians made beautiful glassware, although the art of blowing glass was not invented until about the 1st century BC. Egyptians, Babylonians and Persians all created wonderful jewellery with precious metals and gems, and the Persians also wove silk fabrics of exquisite design.

The work left behind by the artists of long ago tells us a great deal about the kind of people they were. We know, for instance, that the Egyptians loved dignity and ceremony, that the Assyrians were fierce and warlike, and that the Minoans of Crete were gay, adventurous seafarers. It was this Cretan culture that finally spread to the mainland of Greece and influenced the beginnings of Greek art.

Among all these early peoples, however, artists were simply servants of the state, as were writers, poets, mathematicians and philosophers. We do not know the names of any of them. Only with the birth of the Greek civilisation did an interest in man's personal and individual ideas of the natural world arise.

The Greeks

The art forms that the Greeks took over from the Minoan civilisation can be seen in the geometric designs on decorated vases, and in the early simple wooden temples. Around the year 600 BC Greek civilisation settled down; temples and other buildings were made of stone, and cities like Athens were built. Gradually, there began the amazing changes which the Greeks made to the course of art.

Instead of copying the old way of representing the human body, the Greeks really began to look at it and to represent what they saw, rather than what they knew about it. In the course of time they also added drama and emotion to their art. This was the birth of the artist as an individual, making his own personal contribution to society. The works which have survived

for us to see are mainly buildings and statues, but in their own time the paintings of Greece were even more famous than the sculptures. Sadly, none of these now exists, though we know from decorated pottery something about the changes made in the drawing of the human body. A vase of about 500 BC, signed by Euthymides and called *The Warrior's Leavetaking*, shows figures that almost come to life, with the body standing naturally. For the first time in history, the artist had drawn the foot as seen from the front.

The people of Greece lived in small, simple houses, but built magnificent temples to their gods. The temples were all basically of the same design: a rectangular inner room surrounded by a colonnade, and over it a pitched roof with gable ends. Rites were performed outside at altars in front of the temple, and the temples themselves housed only the statues of the gods. The original versions of these statues have been destroyed, but we know from writings that, for example, the statue of Athena made by Phidias (5th century BC) for her temple in the Parthenon, stood some eleven metres high, was coloured and covered with precious metal and ivory.

Later Greek architects also planned cities and designed large public buildings, such as theatres and stadia (like the sports grounds of today), reflecting the growth and sophistication of their civilisation.

Greek art reached its peak at the time of Praxiteles, about 350 BC, when the purpose of making images was changing. A generation later, about 330 BC, a quality of likeness had been added to sculpture. A portrait head of Alexander the Great by Lysippus (360?-316? BC) shows a face with real character, quite unlike the formal, carefully expressionless faces that had gone before.

Alexander's founding of the Hellenistic Empire began the further changes in Greek art that eventually coarsened and debased it. Works of art lost their old connections with religion and magic, and strove only to look grand and impressive.

Above The most famous citadel in the ancient world was the Acropolis in Athens. Here, Phidias built Athena's temple, the Parthenon (top right).

Alexander the Great (356–323 BC) His conquests extended the Greek empire to the borders of India. More than a conqueror, he spread Greek culture and learning over the ancient world. This portrait head is taken from the surviving copy of a sculpture by Lysippus.

Above The ruins of the Colosseum, the greatest of all Roman amphitheatres, as they appear in Rome today. Begun in AD 72 by the emperor Vespasian it was dedicated by the emperor Titus in AD 80. During the inaugural games, which lasted for a hundred days, thousands of gladiators and wild animals were killed in the arena. The Colosseum is about 500 metres in circumference and it has been estimated that it could hold about 80,000 people. Inset is seen a cameo of the emperor Augustus (1st century AD).

The Etruscans

The Etruscans, who came originally from Asia Minor, were warriors who dominated the peoples of Italy from about the 8th to the 2nd century BC. Their society was probably lively, even violent, and their art was crude and vigorous. They lived well in luxurious, decorated houses, in towns which were planned along lines later to be followed by the Romans.

Etruscan sculptors used mainly clay and bronze, modelled rather than carved, as suited their quick, impetuous natures.

The Etruscan temple seems to have been based on the Greek, but with some notable differences. Its inner space was important, whereas the Greek temple was meant to be seen as a mass, from the outside.

In their later history, the Etruscans began to use the masonry arch. Their gates and aqueducts made on the arch principle were later to become an important influence on the Romans – who developed from the Italic peoples after they had eventually conquered the Etruscans.

The Romans

Strongly influenced by Greek and Etruscan art, the Romans absorbed both and changed them to suit their own needs, so making a recognisably Roman art.

By about AD 200 Rome was the capital of the greatest empire the world has ever known. Highly-skilled Roman civil engineers constructed roads, bridges, sewers and aqueducts that were not to be bettered for many centuries. Public buildings, such as circuses, theatres and baths, had to be large enough to accommodate huge crowds. As well as being vast in size, the Romans also liked their buildings to look splendid and impressive. While their architecture resembled the Greek style in its use of columns it also made use of the Etruscan masonry arch. The combination of these two features gave Roman architecture its distinctive appearance.

Roman painters were often commissioned to decorate the inside walls of the homes of rich citizens. They perfected a method of painting on highly polished plaster, producing paintings with a very brilliant surface. They also painted on wooden panels, using colours mixed with hot wax. This kind of painting, called encaustic, was used for the portraits in which they excelled.

Roman sculptors also specialised in portraits, which were extremely lifelike and had great vitality. Because of this, we know today exactly what the great generals and emperors such as Pompey, Nero and Vespasian looked like.

The Romans, like the Greeks, were fond of telling visual stories. In particular they liked to tell of their wars and victories. An outstanding example of this is Trajan's column, which was erected to commemorate the campaigns of the emperor Trajan (AD 53?-117) in Dacia (now Rumania). The reliefs covering the surface of the column are factual, realistic war reporting. In their matter-of-fact treatment they are very typical of the whole Roman attitude to art.

As their empire declined, the down-to-earth realism of the Romans gradually gave way to a feeling for mystical and spiritual qualities. This feeling was to be satisfied by Christian art.

The early Christians

Early Christian art had no real style of its own at first, and simply drew directly on late Roman art. Due to the breaking up of the Roman empire, Roman art itself was changing while the early Christian church was establishing itself.

Two events in history had a great effect on the development of both Christianity and art, as they brought together the cultures of east and west. The first was the edict of Milan in the year 313, by which the Roman emperor Constantine gave recognition to the Christian faith within the empire. The second was in 330, when the capital city of the Roman empire was moved from Rome to Byzantium.

Above St Mark's Cathedral in Venice is one of the largest Italian Byzantine churches and was consecrated in 1094. A great deal of detail in the Italian Gothic style was added in the 12th and 14th centuries.

The two major art forms in use by then in the Roman world were the Hellenic, derived from Greek art, and the Semitic, which was the decorative art of the eastern part of the empire. The first aimed to represent the appearance of real things, while the second was concerned with pictures about ideas, using symbols.

Early Christian art was an art concerned mainly with symbolism. The fish was particularly favoured as a symbol by the growing Christian community (because its spelling in Greek formed the initials of Jesus Christ, Son of God, Saviour).

The early Christian churches grew from the ordinary dwellings of the time, first becoming rectangular meeting houses, and then developing into basilicas – buildings which included a nave and side aisles as well as the central area. The most important basilica was Old St Peter's in Rome. A more elaborate kind of church was also built in the style known as Byzantine, on the principle of a great dome, or series of domes, resting on arches.

Mosaic was much favoured as a medium, worked in small cubes of glass or stone called *tesserae*. The play

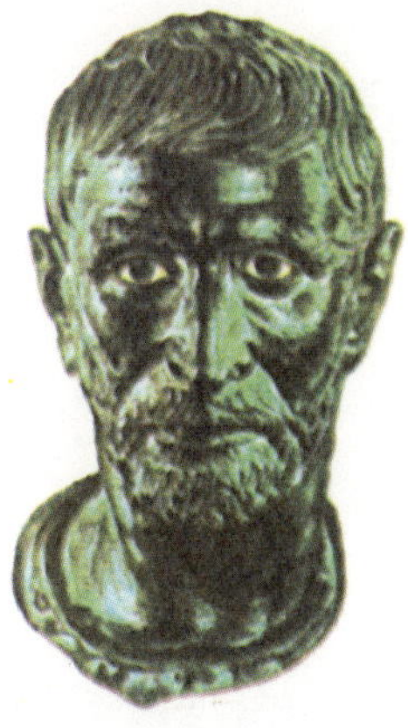

Above A bronze Roman head from the 2nd century BC, with eyes inlaid in enamel, which is Etruscan in character.

continued on page 448

Above This lively dancing girl is one of the remarkable bronze figures to survive from the Indus valley civilisation in Mohenjo-daro, which existed between about 2500 and 1000 BC.

Right Muktesvara temple, Bhuvanesvar, in India, built in the 9th and 10th centuries. Inset is a limestone head of a Buddha from Gandhara in north-west India dating from the 4th to 5th centuries AD.

Above Mogul sword hilt in the shape of a horse's head, 17th century. It is made of jade and inlaid with gold and precious stones and is typical of the style of the people who conquered India during the 16th century.

Indian art

About 5,000 years ago a civilisation in the north west of India left images of a sacred bull. The next peak of culture came after 500 BC, when Buddha inspired a new religion and his followers erected a number of commemorative mounds called stupas which were approached through ornamented gateways. Through war and trade they learned about the Greek ideal of the hero and were soon fashioning large figures of the Buddha, and painting scenes of his life on the walls of their cave temples, such as those at Ajanta. These were excavated into the rock of the hillsides and richly carved.

In the 5th century an older religion overwhelmed Buddhism. This was Hinduism, a religion of many gods which enabled the Indian princes to seem like gods too. The earliest Hindu temples copied the Buddhist versions, but soon a free-standing type evolved, taking the basic idea of the stupa but extending it into a much taller tower to represent a celestial mountain. These towers are carved with tier upon tier of gods and goddesses, dancing girls, musicians, gurus and all kinds of animals ranging from elephants and lions to cows and monkeys. Although they are really gigantic pieces of sculpture they are also feats of architecture.

Hindu sculpture is full of movement, and it is not by accident that Siva is often shown as God of the Dance in small bronzes as well as in stone sculpture, with more than two arms to show movement and to hold all the symbols of his power.

By the 16th century Hindu art declined, for the simple reason that India was conquered by the Mughals from Central Asia. Akbar the Great and his grandson Shah Jehan built superbly luxurious palaces and tombs based on Islamic models, and commissioned realistic portraits of themselves out hunting elephants.

Above The Taj Mahal at Agra in India. It was built (1630–48) by the Mogul emperor Shah Jehan as a mausoleum, or tomb, for his wife and himself. The most remarkable feature of the building is its brilliant white exterior and rich decoration in a style which some historians believe indicate that the building may have been designed by Italian artists.

Left In this drawing of the Mogul period (about 1605) a prince spears the flank of a lioness which is attacking his elephant.

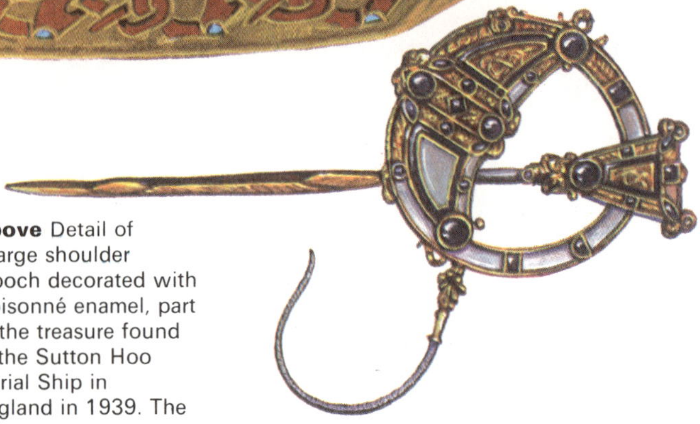

Above Detail of a large shoulder brooch decorated with cloisonné enamel, part of the treasure found in the Sutton Hoo Burial Ship in England in 1939. The ship was a monument to a 7th-century king from East Anglia, and the jewellery discovered in it is a rare example of the skills of Anglo-Saxon craftsmen. The other smaller brooch (above right) is a fine example of a Celtic ring brooch dating from the 8th century. It is known as the Tara brooch.

of light inside churches like Santa Sophia made these *tesserae* glow and sparkle as if lit from within.

Other artists made vivid pen and ink miniatures as illustrations for manuscripts, or worked in precious metals and jewels producing symbolic icons. The Christian church would not allow idols to be made, so sculptors worked mainly on low-relief carvings for church decoration.

The barbarians

For several hundred years after the fall of Rome there was a great difference between life in the eastern and western parts of the Roman empire. Countries in the western part were overrun by barbarian tribes from the north and north-east. These tribes were not always warriors, but simply semi-nomadic peoples looking for a more permanent place to live.

As a result of their nomadic existence these people did not make large heavy things like statues. They made only small objects, and were particularly skilled in metal work. Typical of the designs they used are the spiral, curving and interlacing patterns favoured by the Celts. Jewellery was made in the cloisonné technique, which means that fillets of metal, usually gold, were fixed to the body of the object and built up into patterns with spaces between. These spaces were then filled with enamel paste which was fired to harden it, or with semi-precious stones, like garnets.

Manuscript illumination, like that in the Book of Kells, an 8th-century copy of the Gospels in Latin which was made in an Irish monastery at Kells, resembled jewellery in its rich colour and pattern.

The growth of the church

A revival of interest in the arts took place at the court of the emperor Charlemagne (742-814), largely due to Charlemagne's enthusiasm for Roman craftsmanship. Manuscript illumination now began to progress beyond the achievements of the Celtic peoples, and the human form was once more used in art. This, together with a lingering interest in barbaric pattern, makes 9th-century manuscripts different from earlier ones.

An English abbot called Alcuin of York (735-804) helped Charlemagne to redesign the script then in use for writing. This resulted in a script known as Carolingian minuscule (from the Latin word for smallish), which has, in turn, developed into the handwriting we use today. A manuscript like the Utrecht Psalter, written in France about 832, is a charming example of the work of the time. It shows the renewed interest in story-telling, but uses human beings instead of symbols. The figures are drawn with honesty, and with the exaggeration of simple gestures which was typical of the Middle Ages.

We have only recently learned, through modern excavations and discoveries, the extent to which architecture had developed at this time. Roman

Left One of the most famous buildings in the world is the campanile, or bell-tower, which stands beside the 11/12th-century cathedral at Pisa in Italy. This 'leaning tower' of Pisa is built on shallow foundations and is gradually sinking into the ground on one side. It is about 54 metres high and now leans over 5 metres from perpendicular.

techniques of solid stone masonry had been revived, and the basilica adapted to the needs of monastic communities. From this time, too, dated the erection of towers as an important part of the general mass of buildings.

As the church slowly came to dominate the life of the people completely, more art forms emerged.

Romanesque art

The laws and customs of the later Roman empire, combined with those of the barbarian tribes, finally led to the beginnings of the feudal system in the 9th century. By the 11th and 12th centuries, life in western Europe was completely ruled by this system, and by the great, powerful monasteries. The style in which the churches were built is known on the continent of Europe as Romanesque. In Britain it is called Norman, after the invaders who introduced it.

The abbey church was the most important building in any community at this time, and it had to be large enough to house many pilgrims. Thick walls gave it a feeling of security, and massive pillars supported the rounded vaults of the roof, known as barrel or tunnel vaults. The Roman skill in vaulting huge buildings had been lost, so the pillars, or piers, had to be set very close together to take the tremendous weight of the stone vaults. In France, later Romanesque churches had carving around their porches and the capitals of their piers, showing rigid, solemn figures of great dignity.

Metalwork was still important. Altar vessels made of gold or bronze were elaborately decorated and enamelled. Murals (wall paintings) were often carried out on panels, and looked rather like enlarged pages from an illustrated Bible. Brilliantly-coloured miniatures with wide, decorative borders were still painted in the monasteries.

Little secular, or non-religious, art has survived from this period. This does not mean that none existed, for the feudal lords in the great castles did sometimes employ artists. However, in a Europe which suffered continual wars and unrest, castles were often destroyed while churches were spared. One example of secular art that has survived for us to see is the Bayeux Tapestry, which tells the story of the Norman conquest of England in 1066.

Gothic art

The Romanesque style lasted only for just over a hundred years. This was typical of western Europe. In the east, art styles lasted unchanged for thousands of years, but the west was always unsettled – looking for new answers to old questions, or even finding new questions! Even by the end of the 12th century, life in the west was changing, and art was changing with it. Trade had revived, and cities

Charlemagne (742–814) also known as Charles the Great. Roman emperor and Frankish king. He founded the Holy Roman Empire in the year 800 and was for the rest of his life the champion of the Christian faith and the most powerful figure in Europe.

Above The White Tower, or keep, is the oldest building in the Tower of London. It dates from about 1078, when it was built by the Normans. The cupolas on the towers replaced the original pointed spires in 1543.

Above The Gothic cathedral of Notre Dame in Chartres was built in the 13th century. It is notable chiefly for its tower and spire and for the splendour of its stained glass.

Above right The stained glass rose window in the north transept of Chartres Cathedral.

were growing up in place of the old monastic communities. The monastic schools were becoming the first universities, and the abbey churches were giving way to great city cathedrals.

The new style that evolved with this new way of life is today called Gothic. In a way it began with the discovery that the vaulting of a church with cross-arches could be carried much further than Romanesque architects had ever attempted. It was found that quite slim pillars, with the addition of 'ribs' to span the arches between them, could take the entire weight of the roof. There was, therefore, no need for massive stone walls – in fact, these could be almost completely done away with, and huge windows could take their place. As well as this, the arches could be made steeper by fitting two segments together, and so the typically pointed Gothic arch was born. Grotesque gargoyles and rainspouts ornamented the outside of Gothic churches.

It was at this time that the art of creating stained glass windows was perfected. The coloured glass was spun, rolled, and cut or broken into fragments. Some pieces were painted with a dark pigment to show detail in faces or clothes, then the pieces were joined together with strips of lead. The whole effect was like a glowing, translucent painting suspended in space. As most people at this time could not read, to them these windows were like a 'film' of the Bible stories.

It is only partly true to say that all this began with a discovery about methods of vaulting. The truth really lies somewhere in the search for new answers to old questions – each age finds the particular answers that suit it best. The vaulting does not explain, for instance, why Gothic ornament, furniture and even clothes were also tall, narrow and upward-pointing. If we look at the basic outline of the dress, head-dress and shoes of a fashionable lady of the time, what we see is remarkably like the shapes found in the Gothic cathedral.

Many beautiful examples of Gothic architecture are still to be seen today. Among them are the cathedrals of Chartres, Reims and Notre Dame (Paris) in France; those of Salisbury, Wells and Canterbury in England; those of Siena, Orvieto and Milan in Italy; and the *Hallenkirche,* or Hall churches, in Germany.

The mid-13th century was a period of prosperity and progress, and the cities of northern Italy were among the first to benefit from this. The ports flourished, and so did the financial and manufacturing centres such as Florence and Siena. A new interest in the classical art of Greece and Rome grew up, figures became less stiff and more secular art appeared. A sculptor called Nicola Pisano (1225?-84?), who lived and worked in the seaport of Pisa, carved reliefs with figures of almost classical realism.

Painters were slower to respond to the new spirit of the age. Gradually, however, two important and quite different schools of painting emerged. A school of painting does not mean a place for teaching painting, but the work of people with similar ideas, usually painting in the same geographical area and about the same period in history.

These two schools of painting are known as the Sienese and the Florentine. The best known of the Sienese painters is Duccio di Buoninsegna (1260?-1320?). In many ways Duccio was a Byzantine painter, for he clung to the use of pattern and fine detail, painted in brilliantly coloured tempera on a background of gold. At the same time, he succeeded in breathing new life into the traditional forms.

The Florentine school, and in particular Giotto di Bondone (1267-1337), broke right away from Byzantine and Gothic traditions. In his magnificent frescoes Giotto introduced a new use of light and shade. With this he created figures that seemed to have weight and to exist in space. Giotto's fellow citizens in Florence were very proud of him. They liked to talk about his wit and his skill, and they spread his fame far and wide. This was really quite a surprising thing. Until then, artists had been regarded in much the same way as skilled carpenters or stone-masons. Some were more efficient than others, but none was particularly remembered by name. In fact, many artists did not even bother to sign their work. Giotto's fame was an important pointer to even greater changes to come.

Left *The Raising of Lazarus*, a detail from the fresco painted by Giotto in 1305/9. This artist is a key figure in the history of art because of his understanding of the methods by which an illusion of depth can be created on a flat surface. For this reason Giotto's figures seem alive and full of movement.

The *Dance of Death*

In Europe the 14th century began well, but peace and prosperity did not last long. By 1345 almost every banking house in Florence had failed. In 1348 an even greater disaster struck – the Black Death, or bubonic plague. This horrible disease is estimated to have killed half the population of Europe during a period of two years. It spread rapidly as far north as England and broke out from time to time in different parts of the continent during the next 300 years. Meanwhile, the Hundred Years' War, which began about 1339 and lasted until 1453, was being fought out between England and France.

It is hardly surprising that the ideas of late Gothic artists were pessimistic and dramatic. One popular theme was the *Dance of Death*, which showed people of all ranks, each dancing with a dead partner of equal rank. Thus a king would dance with a dead king, a merchant with a dead merchant, and

continued on page 454

Above In this detail from an engraving by Hans Holbein, the grisly figure of Death plays on the drum, while at his feet the sands of time trickle slowly through an hour glass.

Above 'Famille Rose' bottle of the Yung-cheng period (1723–35). It is made of porcelain with coloured enamel decoration, probably for use in the Imperial Palace.

Right The Golden Pavilion in Kyoto, Japan. Originally erected in 1397 the building served partly as a villa and partly as a monastery.

Above The Chinese emperor Hui-tsung (1082–1135) was a gifted painter, poet and calligrapher. These characters are copied from an example of his writing from one of his poems.

Oriental art

Indian artistic ideas were carried by traders into South-East Asia where they inspired temples and sculptures based on Indian models, notably in Angkor Wat in Cambodia. In China, though, a sophisticated culture was already so well developed that foreign influences had limited impact.

From early times China was controlled by a strong centralised government with an emperor at the head, supported by a highly educated civil service. Although ancestor worship was important and the Chinese ruling class commissioned craftsmen to make superb bronze vessels and glazed terracotta figures for the graves of their dead, they did not consider that these were the highest art forms. What they really valued, and practised themselves, was calligraphy (handwriting) and the associated art of painting scenes on silk or paper scrolls, which were unrolled and contemplated at leisure. Later on, Buddhist monks were to make their contribution to this tradition which involved a sensitive response to nature as well as skill with pen and brush.

Buddhism was to gain enthusiastic support all over the Far East. The basic Chinese architectural form, the rectangular hall with heavy tiled roof, was built one on top of another to create a pagoda. Statues of the Buddha, his attendants and disciples were made from gilded and painted wood, terracotta, lacquer or bronze. By the 14th century, however, this sort of public display had given way to simplicity, as seen in the greyish white cups used in the tea ceremony, in the exquisite art of flower arrangement, and the dry rock and gravel gardens which were viewed like a picture. This emphasis on simplicity over several centuries (in spite of a violent history) enabled the Japanese to develop a fine sense of design and composition.

Above Drawing based on the colour print from wood-blocks, *The great wave off Kanazawa*, by Hokusai (1760–1849) the great Japanese artist and wood-engraver.

Near left This ceremonial axe is from the Late Shang period in China (12th to 11th centuries BC). It is made of bronze and was probably used for ritual execution.

Far left above A seated court lady holding a mirror, from the T'ang period (AD 618–906). These ceramic figures were provided for the dead as symbolic companions in the after-life.

Left Detail of a hanging scroll of the Ming period in the first half of the 16th century. It was painted by Ch'iu Ying and depicts an emperor fording a river.

Right The chapel at King's College in Cambridge is acknowledged as the finest example of the Perpendicular style in Britain, especially for the stone tracery and fan vaulting of its roof.

Fra Angelico (1387–1455) Italian painter. Entered the Dominican order of friars in 1407. He lived in the monastery of San Marco in Florence from 1436 to 1445 when he was summoned to Rome by the pope. He painted only religious subjects, chiefly frescoes and altar pieces, masterly in design and using beautiful colours. The devotional, angelic figures which appear in his paintings gave him his name.

so on. This theme appeared in manuscripts and in church mural paintings. Another favourite theme was the *pietà* – the Virgin mourning over the dead Christ.

Perhaps to get away from all the disaster and gloom, rich people began to hold lavish feasts, pageants and festivals. In the 15th century these grew more and more splendid. Manners became refined and costumes elegant, as can be seen in the jewel-like miniatures of the time.

The new elegance showed itself in architecture, too. Late Gothic buildings had elaborate vaultings, and fine lace-like stone tracery. This style is known as Perpendicular in England and as Flamboyant in France. Guildhalls, town halls and private houses were built in the Flamboyant style, but few completely new churches. The lovely fan-vaulting of the Perpendicular style can be seen in Henry VII's chapel in Westminster Abbey, London.

The medieval world was coming to an end. In Italy the Renaissance, or rebirth, had already begun, while artists in northern Europe were turning to a different kind of realism.

Northern painters

Up to the end of the 14th century, the artist in Flanders (which we now know as Holland and Belgium) was still treated as a craftsman. He had to belong to a guild in order to practise his trade. First, as a young boy, he would be apprenticed to a local master. Later, he would become a journeyman, travelling from city to city to learn from other masters. At the end of a certain number of years he would himself become a master painter, and would be commissioned through the guild to carry out work. Like artists in most western European countries, Flemish painters at this time worked in the decorative international Gothic style, painting miniatures and illuminations for manuscripts.

A great break with this tradition came quite suddenly in the work of the brothers Hubert (1370?-1426) and Jan van Eyck (1389?-1441). It has been said they invented oil painting, but this is doubtful. What they probably did, in fact, was to carry earlier experiments several stages further. Certainly they produced the first successful results with oil painting in Europe.

Painters in the 14th and 15th centuries (in fact, right up to the time of the 19th century) could not go into a shop and buy paints in tubes as we can now. Instead, they had to prepare their own pigments, mostly from coloured minerals and plants. After grinding these to a fine powder between two stones, the painter – or his apprentices – would add some kind of liquid to make a paste. Throughout the Middle Ages the liquid was usually egg. This egg tempera was quite effective but it dried very quickly. In the new kind of paint perfected by the Van Eycks, the liquid was a mixture of oils which made a much slower-drying paint.

Jan van Eyck was probably the first painter ever to make an exact visual copy from nature. His new method

Above A Book of Hours was a devotional book, commissioned by a private patron and often beautifully illustrated. This is a section from one of the pages from the *Très Riches Heures du Duc de Berry*, painted by the brothers Limbourg in about 1415.

Above left This painting by Jan van Eyck from one of the panels of the Ghent Altarpiece (completed 1432) in the cathedral of St Bavon, shows St Cecilia playing on the organ.

allowed him to work on fine detail until it was perfect – while the paint was still wet. He could blend light into shade softly and naturally, without any hard edges, and he could build up his colour with one transparent glaze after another. At the same time, Van Eyck's beautiful paintings, such as the Ghent altarpiece, are not like colour photographs. The detail may be true to nature, but the complex organisation and the unity of the picture as a whole are entirely his own. Van Eyck also broke with tradition in the subjects he painted. These were often secular, not religious, and included many portraits.

Other Flemish artists followed in the Van Eycks' footsteps. Rogier van der Weyden (1400-64) also used the new medium to show every crease, every hair and every stitch, but the rhythmic patterns his figures make are more true to Gothic tradition. On the other hand, the paintings of Hugo van der Goes (1440?-82), while also realistic, are tense and emotional.

In France artists were interested in what was happening in both Flanders and Italy. The leading French painter of the 15th century, Jean Fouquet (1420?-80?), visited Italy as a young man and was deeply impressed by what he saw there. And yet, though the figures in his paintings have the weight and the apparent existence in space seen in Renaissance paintings, his love of surface detail is truly northern.

Printing

Sometime between 1450 and 1460, in the town of Mainz in Germany, Johannes Gutenberg (1397-1468) developed the idea of printing from movable wooden blocks. The Dutchman, Laurens Janszoon (1370?-1440), known as Coster, also experimented with movable type, probably before Gutenberg, but little is known of him or his work.

The transfer of an image by impression is a very ancient art, and existed in the seals and stamps of the early Egyptian and Babylonian civilisations. Printing itself was probably 'invented' in China, where books printed from wooden blocks are known to have existed in the 9th century AD and may probably have done so as early as the 7th century. Movable type is first known in the 11th century and its invention is attributed to a man called Pi-Sheng. Probably because Chinese was not written alphabetically and

Above *The Rout of San Romano* by Paolo Uccello. This is painted on a panel and probably comes from a room in the Medici palace in Florence. The picture illustrates Uccello's preoccupation with perspective and his ability to make figures stand out from the flat surface.

Above The first trade mark of the Aldine press, a dolphin twined round an anchor, is seen here. Aldine editions were small volumes of Greek, Latin and Italian classics printed at Venice in the 16th century by Aldus Manutius.

was a language unsuitable for the use of movable letters, the idea died out in the east.

Books had certainly existed in western Europe before Gutenberg, but only in handwritten (manuscript) form. These manuscripts were copied by hand and no large numbers of the same book were ever available. The idea of providing several copies of one illustration by making a woodcut came later. The illustration may have had words with it, and if they were to print as well they had to be cut, in reverse, on the wood. All the surface of the wood that was not to print was cut away by gouges. By this method, many more copies of books could be made than was possible with manuscripts. Very early books of this kind are known as incunabula.

Gutenberg made it possible to cut individual letters in wood and fit them together to make words, holding these in place in a frame. The letters were then inked over, paper was laid on top and pressure was applied, so transferring the inked words to the paper. Possibly one reason why this idea developed when it did was that at this time paper began to be more plentiful, and therefore cheaper.

Within a very short time a peak in the art of book printing was reached at the Aldine Press, founded by Aldus Manutius (1450-1515) in Venice. In 1499, only forty years or so after movable type was effectively invented, Aldus was publishing books with beautiful letter forms and illustrations. With lovely balance of black and white on the page, these books were themselves works of art.

A book's main function is the communication of ideas, and the content of a book is every bit as important as its design. The most influential ideas at this time also came from Italy.

The Renaissance

While Gothic art was at its height in other parts of Europe, in Italy something quite different was happening. This was the rebirth of humanism – that is, an interest in the importance and value of life for all men. It is difficult for us to understand how little importance this earthly life had for the people of the Middle Ages. Their church had taught them to believe it was merely a preparation for the after-life to come. But now, in 15th-century Italy, the individual was once more becoming important as a reasoning human being.

A significant political change was taking place in Italy, too, which affected the everyday life of the people. The guilds were losing their power, which was passing into the hands of a new generation of princely rulers. One of the most famous of these was Cosimo de'Medici (1389-1464), who refused any rank except citizen, but was the virtual ruler of Florence. Such wealthy princes were great patrons of

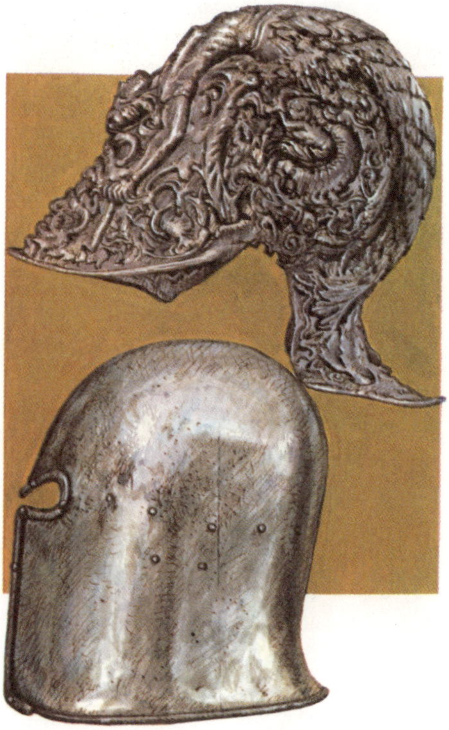

Left At the time of the Renaissance Milan was a centre for the making of armour. Milanese armourers held a privileged position in the city, which mass-produced and exported armour all over Europe. The two helmets shown here illustrate how the design of armour developed from the functional in the 15th century (below) to the decorative in the 16th century (above), when firearms had reduced much of armour's effective protection.

Left below This statue of a condottiere (a professional soldier, or mercenary) is by Donatello and was the first bronze equestrian statue on a large scale to be made since ancient times.

the arts. Under their rule trade flourished and times were prosperous. The wealthy merchants, the church and the nobility were able to commission a great flow of work from the artists of the day.

One of the first outstanding artists of the time was Filippo Brunelleschi (1377-1446). He is famous mainly as an architect, though he was a sculptor for much of his life. Also working in Florence at the same time were the sculptor Donatello (1386?-1466) and the painter Masaccio (1401-28?). These artists found their inspiration in the art of the Greeks and Romans. To them it seemed the most glorious art of all time, and they strove to revive it. But this did not mean just copying it. In Florence, each of them built on his inspiration: Brunelleschi beginning with the famous dome for the cathedral; Donatello with sculpture like the marble statue of St George for the church of San Michele; and Masaccio with paintings like *The Holy Trinity* in Santa Maria Novella.

These three artists, and those who followed them, were fascinated by the problems of movement and perspective. They wanted the figures in their paintings and sculptures to look as though they were standing firmly on the ground, correctly placed in relation to each other and within the space of the composition. They solved these problems by drawing up rules of perspective, and by using colour in increasing or decreasing intensity. Artists like Piero della Francesca (1420?-92), Andrea Mantegna (1431-1506) and Paolo Uccello (1397-1475) were among many working in a similar way at the time.

It is interesting to know that between 1409 and 1444 there were forty-one artist's shops (or *bottegas*) in Florence. A boy could enter such a shop at the age of ten or eleven years to become an apprentice. He would learn how to grind colours, to prepare panels of wood with linen and plaster, to use gold leaf and to transfer the master's drawings to the prepared ground. In time he would be allowed to do minor parts of the painting and, eventually, if he were good enough, he would become the master of his own *bottega*.

Side by side with this creative outburst in Florence, there existed a school grown from the Sienese tradition. The painter Fra Filippo Lippi (1406?-69) belonged to this, as did his most famous pupil, Sandro Botticelli (1444-1510). The Sienese school saw its finest flowering in Botticelli's mystical paintings and illustrations, with their mastery of rhythm and movement.

This was an age of great human endeavour and scientific invention, as well as an age of research and development in the arts. Ideas about

Lorenzo Ghiberti (1378–1455) Florentine sculptor and goldsmith. One of the greatest metal workers who ever lived. He was chosen to design the famous doors of the baptistery in Florence which Michelangelo called 'the gates of Paradise'. A detail from one of the doors, a self-portrait of Ghiberti, is seen here.

Above The Mona Lisa, called La Gioconda, painted by Leonardo da Vinci in 1503, is perhaps the most famous picture in the world. Although it is one of the most familiar images in the history of art, the mystery of the Mona Lisa's elusive expression, and the beauty and softness of the painting, shine through afresh each time the picture is seen. The original is in the Louvre, Paris.

Above right *The Holy Family* by Raphael, also from the Louvre, Paris.

flying machines and submarines, inventions like gunpowder and the movable-type printing press, and the great voyages of discovery, all made the 15th century a memorable one in history.

Leonardo da Vinci

By the early 16th century, Rome and Venice had become centres of the artistic world, as well as Florence. A number of powerful popes had brought famous artists to Rome to face them with challenging tasks, while Venice had stopped trading with Constantinople and turned its attention to the rest of Italy. It is interesting to wonder why, in this country and at this time, one of the most extraordinary geniuses in history should appear. The humanists of the Renaissance had their 'ideal man', who was a complete personality – artist, scientist and scholar. Now, it seemed that he had really come to life in the person of Leonardo da Vinci (1452-1519).

As a painter and sculptor, the perfection of Leonardo's work outshone all former artists; as a scientist, his ideas were centuries ahead of his time. He was also a skilled engineer, a botanist and zoologist, an accomplished musician and composer, and the author of the first standard book on anatomy. As if this were not enough, he was handsome, charming and exceptionally strong. It seems strange now to know that Leonardo was a worry to his parents and his schoolteachers: they complained that he started to do too many things, then gave them up.

One of the reasons we know so much about Leonardo is that he left behind many notebooks, full of his thoughts and drawings. The entries in these notebooks are written from right to left, and must be held in front of a mirror to be read. Leonardo may have done this because, at that time, it was unwise to write down really extraordinary ideas – ideas, for instance, like the entry which reads 'the sun does not move'.

Leonardo believed that sight was man's most precious possession, and that research would reveal the natural laws of the universe. He always insisted, however, that all his investigations were simply directed towards making him a better painter. He was one of the first Italian painters to work in oil paint, and he shared with the other great painters of his time an interest in calm, balanced compositions that still retained great vitality.

Another painter who was charming as well as talented was Raphael (1483-1520). Born in the region of Umbria, he studied there and then later for four years in Florence, where he came under the influence of Leonardo. In 1509, in Rome, he was engaged by Pope Julius II to decorate the pope's library with frescoes illustrating the paths of wisdom – theology, justice, poetry and philosophy. It is the last of these, a magnificent painting designed in a series of great arcs, that is known as *The School of Athens*.

Michelangelo

The third outstanding figure of the age is Michelangelo (1475-1564). Even as a child, Michelangelo wanted to be a sculptor. Unfortunately, his father, the chief magistrate of a small town near Florence, had other ideas. But Michelangelo would not be beaten out of his determination, and at last his father gave way and apprenticed him to the painter Domenico Ghirlandaio (1449-94) for three years.

Michelangelo's talent in modelling was soon noticed by Lorenzo de' Medici (1449-92), the ruler of Florence, who took the boy into his own household. But things were not to continue so happily for Michelangelo. Lorenzo died and his tyrannical successor, Piero (1471-1503), ordered Michelangelo to do stupid things like modelling a statue in snow. Florence changed, too, with the religious revival preached by Girolamo Savonarola (1452-98). People wept and shouted in the streets, and wealthy citizens gave up their positions to become monks. Eventually Piero fled, and Florence was declared a republic.

Michelangelo took no part in these upheavals, either then or later, when the city turned against Savonarola and burned him at the stake. Michelangelo's wonderful *Pietà* at St Peter's, Rome, had already established him as the greatest sculptor in the world, but he had not made his fortune. His family thought he must be very rich, and after he had starved himself to help them, they accused him of being mean. In 1501 Michelangelo returned to Florence from Rome to make the enormous statue *David*, which was to commemorate the city's deliverance from her enemies.

Above *Pietà*, carved in 1499 by Michelangelo and representing the Madonna tending the dead body of Christ, is the only work ever signed by the artist.

Although his greatest love was sculpture, Michelangelo won everlasting fame with his magnificent paintings on the ceiling of the Sistine Chapel in Rome. He had no wish to do the paintings, which were forced on him by Pope Julius II. Michelangelo quarrelled with all his assistants and finally undertook the enormous task alone. He worked in secret, on and off, for the next four years, lying on his back on high scaffolding. He had endless trouble with the fresco technique: one panel, *The Deluge*, became mouldy as soon as it was finished and had to be painted all over again. The effort made Michelangelo ill, and even his worst enemies were astounded at his almost superhuman achievement.

Michelangelo also worked as an architect, and in 1546 took over the great task of designing St Peter's in Rome. This was still not completed when he died in 1564.

In Venice, as in Florence, the early 16th century saw a move towards calmness and order in painting. This was started by Giovanni Bellini (1430?-1516), and brought to perfection by his pupils, Giorgione (1478?-1511) and

continued on page 462

Michelangelo (1475–1564) Italian artist. He claimed to be only a sculptor, but as a painter, poet and military engineer Michelangelo was the greatest figure of the Italian Renaissance. This portrait bust was made of him in the later years of his life by one of his followers.

Right The Pyramid and Temple of the Inscriptions at Palenque in Mexico. This temple belongs to the classic period of Maya culture, from the 4th to the 9th century AD. The Mayas belonged to an American Indian civilisation, remains of which have been found in Guatemala and British Honduras as well as in Mexico.

Above A stone figure called *The Adolescent* which may represent the god Quetzalcoatl as a young priest, carrying his son on his back. It comes from the Huastec culture (2nd to 4th centuries AD).

Pre-columbian art

As the Roman Empire declined, in far distant Mexico a city even bigger than Rome was built according to the instructions of a caste of priest-kings. This cult city, called Teotihuacan ('the place of the gods') was magnificently laid out in its mountain setting with terraced pyramids for religious worship, with painted temples and dwelling houses, all organised around a broad Avenue of the Dead. In this way order was imposed on nature by the priests, who somehow were to make the cruel god of death more important for their people than the life-enhancing gods of rain and maize. Even Quetzalcoatl himself, the god of spring, is depicted as a fierce plumed serpent on the pyramid dedicated to him.

This city was one of the earliest of many which were built by the pre-conquest inhabitants of Mexico and Peru. Their civilisations developed comparatively late, were apparently isolated from the rest of the world, and largely from each other. Nevertheless, they have characteristics in common, mainly because they preserved links with primitive culture.

Although they never learned how to construct a rounded arch, these people were superb builders, chipping their stones to fit each other exactly or to form bold geometric reliefs on the sides of their palaces. They were also masters of sculpture and left many free-standing monoliths.

When the Spanish conquistadors came to Central America in the 16th century they were amazed by all that they saw, especially the work in gold. Montezuma, the great Aztec chief, trustingly sent treasures back to Charles V, which Albrecht Dürer happened to see. He too marvelled at the 'subtle ingenuity of these men in a faraway land'. Sadly, the Spanish conquest was to put an end to such skills.

Above This gold pendant, worn on the breast, is only 11 cm. high. It comes from the Mixtec culture of the 15th century and represents the Lord of Death.

Left top Detail of a textile fringe covered with pictorial embroidery which comes from Peru and probably dates from the early centuries AD. The colours are from natural mineral dyes of great permanence.

Left centre Some 6,700 pieces of Pre-Columbian goldware are conserved in the Bogota Museum of Gold in Colombia. Among them are these gold ear-rings.

Left This colossal stone head, about 249 cm. high, of an Olmec chieftain is in the park of the museum at La Venta, Mexico.

Above Titian's *The Vendramin Family*. Titian was the most celebrated painter in Venice, a master of colouring, a portrait painter of genius and a revolutionary in his attitude to the conventions of his age.

Above The head of Cellini's great masterpiece, his bronze statue of Perseus slaying Medusa (1553). As well as being a sculptor and goldsmith Cellini was also an accomplished musician.

Titian (1490?-1576). The gentle nature of Giorgione shows in all his paintings, with their lovely soft light and subtle colour. Like Raphael he died young, and barely twenty of his paintings are known to exist today. The use of canvas for oil painting dates from the time of this Venetian school.

When Titian, who was taught by both Bellini and Giorgione, first came to Venice from his home in the Alps, he looked like a bronzed young mountaineer. This health and strength, and his carefree nature, are reflected in his vigorous paintings. When Bellini died, Titian was elected to succeed him as the official painter of Venice. He lived in a splendid palace there, where he entertained princes, scholars and all the distinguished visitors to the city.

Titian painted many portraits and gave all his sitters a touch of his own majesty. At the time, the freedom and simplicity with which these portraits were painted must have been astounding. They have none of the fine modelling of earlier portraits, and yet they are somehow much more alive and compelling. It is not surprising that when Titian died the whole of Venice went into mourning for him.

Mannerism

The word Mannerism was first used in the 16th century to describe the style of the artists who came after the great period of the Renaissance. It was used jeeringly, for many people believed that the artists of the late Renaissance had solved every problem that artists would ever have to face. Their successors used curious distortions just because there was nothing else left for them to do – or so it was thought. Recently people have begun to realise there is more to Mannerism than that.

To begin with, Mannerist artists did not live in the same kind of world as artists of the Renaissance. The Protestant Reformation, the French invasions of Italy and the sack of Rome in 1527 all helped to make life unsettled, and this feeling of tension and crisis was bound to show in art. Even the later works of Michelangelo and Raphael were affected by it.

Elongated figures – either stiff or unnaturally flowing and graceful – are typical of Mannerist painting and sculpture; so are violent contrasts of scale, odd proportions and abrupt changes of direction. It is as though the artist wanted to take his onlookers by surprise. All these things can be found in the paintings of Jacopo Pontormo (1494-1552), Francesco Parmigianino (1503-40) and the Florentine, Angelo Bronzino (1502-72). But it was the Venetian painter, Tintoretto (1518-94), who gave Mannerism its greatest fame. Using the same technique of 'taking by surprise' in his paintings, he seemed to be about to reveal the truth behind some tremendous mystery.

In sculpture, Mannerism was practised by Giovanni Bologna (1524-1608) and by Benvenuto Cellini (1500-71), who was famed as a goldsmith. Cellini was a true man of his times. His own book about his life shows him to have been proud, ruthless and boastful: a vivid personality, living in a vivid, restless age. He travelled from country to country, winning fame but picking many quarrels. One of the few examples of Cellini's work still in existence is a golden saltcellar he made for Francis I, king of France, at whose court he lived for some time.

Not every Italian artist in the 16th century worked in the Mannerist style. Two who did not are the painter Paolo Veronese (1525-88) and the architect Andrea Palladio (1518-80); to them, symmetry and balance were still important. Palladio's buildings, and also his ideas and drawings, were

Left The Villa Capra at Vicenza in Italy, called the Villa Rotonda, and built by Palladio in 1567. This classic Palladian villa has been the inspiration of many architects throughout the world. In its turn the style of the Palladian villa is derived from the buildings of ancient Rome.

to have a great effect on English and colonial American buildings in the 18th century.

Germany

The first of the German painters about whom we have any knowledge at all today is Matthias Grünewald (1480?-1528), who worked in Germany around the beginning of the 16th century. He either knew nothing about the great developments in Italy or took no notice of them. His work follows the German linear tradition, in which line was the commonest way of describing any shape. This strong line, along with raw, crude colour, can be seen in the *Isenheim Altarpiece*. The *Crucifixion* from this artist is harshly and cruelly pictured, and the artist has used the medieval custom of making the most important figures the largest.

By contrast, Albrecht Dürer (1471-1528), who lived about the same time, was deeply interested in Renaissance ideas. He lived in an age when, because of the ferment of the Reformation, there was a great demand for illustrations for religious books. Although he was also a fine painter, it was through his wood engravings for illustrations that Dürer really became famous. His prints spread throughout Europe and created a sensation. When he visited Venice in 1506 he found both admiration and jealousy among Italian artists. He was pleased, however, that Bellini – whose work he admired – praised him highly.

Dürer was the first northern artist to make a serious study of proportion

Above A section from Veronese's painting *The Family of Darius before Alexander*. Veronese gained his reputation as a painter of historical scenes.

Left Dürer's self-portrait, painted in 1500. In it he is seen posing as Christ. He is said to have been vain about his own appearance and often portrayed himself in paintings and drawings.

Above Detail from the painting by Hans Holbein the Younger of Erasmus, the Dutch scholar who recommended the painter to Thomas More in England. It was through this introduction that Holbein became court painter to Henry VIII, who was the subject of many of his most celebrated canvases.

Right Bruegel's *The Misanthrope* (1568). A misanthrope is a person who hates all mankind and the translation of the inscription beneath the picture reads: 'Because the world is so faithless I am going into mourning' The little figure in a glass ball represents the faithless world and he is engaged in stealing the misanthrope's purse.

and natural form, and to write books about these subjects. He was also the first to be treated with respect by the rich merchants of such places as Frankfurt, Antwerp and Nuremberg (his home town). In his own way he completely altered the northern attitude to artists.

Another German painter, born only a year after Dürer, was Lucas Cranach (1472-1553). This artist was fascinated by his native landscape, with its ancient forests of great fir trees, and his work aroused interest in this kind of Alpine scenery. After he became official painter to the Protestant court of Saxony, however, Cranach turned to paintings of fashionable, doll-faced young women. He is probably best known for his friendship with Martin Luther.

The Reformation brought about many changes for artists, mainly because Protestants would not have pictures and statues in their churches. As most artists had earned their living by supplying the churches, they had to look around for some other way to make money. Some found the answer in illustration, and others, like Hans Holbein (1497-1543), in portraiture.

Holbein was born only twenty-six years after Dürer, but in that short time the world had changed. Gone for ever was the awe and mystery surrounding the earth. It was no longer thought to be a great, flat plain encircled by sea, nor was it the centre of the universe. Geographers and astronomers had found out that it was merely a little globe, spinning round in space amongst countless others. For this reason the mystic, medieval feeling found in Dürer's work is completely missing from Holbein's paintings.

The years 1523 to 1527 were bad years for artists, as for everyone else in war-torn Europe. Holbein, living in Basle, revived the *Dance of Death* theme that had started during the plague of the Middle Ages. In a series of little woodcuts, he showed, that death must come to every man in the same way, whether he be pope, prince or peasant.

In 1526 Holbein left Switzerland for England with a letter from the great scholar Erasmus, in which he recommended Holbein to his friend Sir Thomas More. Holbein eventually became court painter to King Henry VIII. He designed jewellery, weapons and goblets, costumes for pageants and decorations for great halls, as well as leaving a vivid record of the men and women of the English court.

The Low Countries

Flanders, like Italy, was a centre for the weaving and trading of cloths. All through the 15th century trade between the two countries increased, and a growth in trade always means a growth in travel. Among the many Flemish people travelling to Italy, and bringing back Italian ideas, were artists, and they gradually absorbed these new ideas into their own tradition of painting.

A great painter in this tradition, who used some of the Italian ideas where it suited him, was Hieronymus Bosch (1460?-1516). We know that

Above The palace at Fontainebleau in France was rebuilt during Renaissance times in the 16th century during the reign of Francis I. It was a favourite residence of Napoleon and it has been the scene of many historic events.

Above left One of the finest examples of the black and white half-timbered style of building in England is Moreton Old Hall, Cheshire. It dates from about the middle of the 16th century and one of its most celebrated visitors was Queen Elizabeth I, who often stayed here.

Bosch lived in the little town of Hertogenbosch, but little else about him. Over the centuries painters in the Netherlands had developed their own ways of showing figures and objects as realistically as possible. Bosch made full use of these methods, but his purpose was different. His paintings are fantastic visions of Hell and Paradise, and his figures are creatures from a nightmare – part animal and part human. Bosch's realism, detail and enamel-like colours only help to make these visions more terrifying.

Peter Bruegel (1520?-69), another Flemish painter, again took Italian ideas and used them in a completely different way. The scenes in Bruegel's paintings are the everyday scenes of rural life. We see peasants going about their normal business – working, hunting, feasting or celebrating a country wedding. There is nothing mannered or elegant about these paintings; they swarm with hearty, boisterous life. But Bruegel himself was not a peasant, and he observed these rustic activities with a cool, townsman's eye. It was the custom at that time to regard the country 'yokel' as a sort of clown, and there is a trace of this mockery in Bruegel's work, too.

France

Mainly because France was made up of small, independent units, French art remained Gothic right up to the 16th century. Then King Francis I brought Italian artists to work in his court at Fontainebleau. Michelangelo, Leonardo da Vinci and Benvenuto Cellini all spent some time there. Under their influence a school of French painters grew up, which was known as the school of Fontainebleau. Patronage by royalty, rather than by the church, made it easy for these painters to work in the style of the Florentine Mannerists. This Mannerist style was brought into French sculpture, too. Cellini's influence can be seen in the work of Jean Goujon (1510?-68) – notably his nymphs on the Fountain of the Innocents in Paris.

The painter Jean Cousin the Elder (1490-1560) lived in the provinces and had little to do with Fontainebleau, but his paintings show signs of Mannerism as well. In his case, it is mixed with the typical northern element of mystery, gloom and foreboding.

Spain

Until the Moors were expelled from Spain in 1492, the country had no real unity. And yet, by the 16th century, Spain was a powerful nation, holding lands throughout Europe, as well as colonies in the Americas. The Renaissance style of architecture fitted well into this rich society. The vigorous Spanish version of this style is known as Plateresque (from the Spanish

continued on page 468

Above Detail from a painting by the Persian artist Mir Sayyid Ali called *Life in the Camp*, done in about 1540. This artist had a love of realistic detail and when he moved to India at the invitation of the emperor he started the Mogul school of painting.

Above right The magnificent Lion Court of the Alhambra Palace, Granada, Spain, built in the 14th century. This palace is one of the most remarkable examples of Islamic architecture.

Islamic art

Islamic art sprang from the desert when in the 7th and 8th centuries the Arab armies brought half the known civilised world under the banner of Mohammed – namely Palestine, Iraq, Syria, Mesopotamia, Egypt, part of Afghanistan, North Africa and even Spain. In the Arab camps a rectangular open space was set aside as a place of prayer and it is from this that the plan of their mosques developed – an open courtyard surrounded by shady arcades and a prayer hall against the wall facing Mecca.

The first mosques borrowed architectural features from the Romans, such as the dome and classical pillars, and used mosaics to decorate the mihrab, the focal point for worship. By the 9th century, though, when the Arabs gave up political control to the Turks of Persia, a confident Islamic style had emerged. This, as shown not only in religious buildings but in royal palaces and tombs, had a basic liking for clearcut monumental shapes outside and a feeling for space inside, in the high airy domes and careful organisation of halls, passages and courts to give wonderful vistas.

On to these buildings the Moslems imposed all sorts of intricate patterned decoration, in stone, marble, brick or tiles. Flat abstract patterns were very popular, including an interlacing star design and even Arabic lettering; these were not only used round walls and doorways but in pottery, furniture, metalwork and carpets.

The only place where human figures and animals appear at all frequently is in the superbly illustrated manuscripts made for the royal courts. The figures in early miniatures are used decoratively and set against flat backgrounds, but after the Mongol invasions, in the 13th century, painters got to know Chinese work and set their figures in natural surroundings.

Above At Samarra in Iraq is the largest mosque built by the Moslems, the Great Mosque of al-Mutawakkil, 848–52. The huge minaret had an external spiral staircase.

Far left The Cappella del Mihrab in the Umayyad Mosque, Cordoba, Spain, completed in 965 and one of the most beautiful Islamic religious buildings.

Left Ceramic mosque lamp from the Dome of the Rock, Jerusalem, about 1549. A brilliant translucent glaze is laid over a semi-porcelain body.

Below Isnik ceramic plate from Turkey, late 15th century.

Above The *Burial of Count Orgaz*, one of El Greco's most famous paintings, contains a self-portrait of the artist. He is seen, looking straight out of the picture, the seventh figure from the left in the background.

Above right One of the many Baroque fountains in Italy, the Fontana di Trevi in Rome.

El Greco (1541–1614) Greco-Spanish painter. Born in Crete, he settled in Toledo about 1577 where he worked as painter, architect and sculptor. This drawing is based on the self-portrait seen in the painting above.

platero, silversmith), because the fineness of the ornamental detail was very like the elaborate work of the silversmiths of the day.

When Philip II came to the throne in 1556 this warm, exuberant style was too rich for him. He was a cold, morose man, the austerity of whose nature is reflected in the style of the Escorial in Madrid, which is church, monastery and state building all in one. Philip's influence on the designers shows very strongly.

Spanish painters, who worked on the usual medieval frescoes and miniatures, had never developed any strong national style. It was left to a Greek, Domenikos Theotocopoulos (1541-1614), to bring fame to painting in Spain. El Greco, as he was called, studied in Venice under Titian and Tintoretto before going to Toledo and settling there about the year 1577.

The most powerful and determined enemies of Martin Luther's Reformation were the Spaniards, and El Greco's paintings were a perfect expression of their savage and mystical religion. The distorted forms of Mannerism were ideal for showing this kind of emotion; so were the strong, unnatural colours he used. Although El Greco's art was popular in Spain at the time, it had little or no effect, strange to say, on the work of other Spanish painters.

The age of the Baroque

Late in the 16th century, and early in the 17th, the gloom and uncertainty that had affected the Mannerist artists began to disappear. A more confident spirit grew up throughout western Europe. It was an age of violent contrast, and of a bewildering variety of ideas.

On the one hand the Catholic church was bringing back a medieval intensity of faith in its opposition to the Reformation, particularly in the dedicated activities of the recently-founded Jesuit order. On the other hand, the philosopher Descartes, although he remained a Roman Catholic, was challenging medieval faith with the arguments of reason. It was an age of invention, and of the discoveries of Isaac Newton and Galileo, but at the same time it was an age of renewed superstition and witch-hunting.

It is hardly surprising that the art of the time was just as varied, complicated and bewildering as the society in which it thrived. The word Baroque, which is used to describe it, may have come from the Portuguese *barocco*, meaning a pearl of irregular shape. It is a fitting description for an art so rich and lavish, but so full of contrast.

Baroque in Italy

One of the effects of the Counter-Reformation was a revival of interest in church building and decoration. The more the Protestants preached against outward show, the more eager were the Catholics for the kind of lavishness seen in the work of artists like Giovanni Bernini (1598-1680).

Above This massive and ornate table is typical of Baroque art in furniture. It is made in carved and gilt wood and comes from Paris where it was made in about 1680.

Above left *The Conversion of St Paul* (1601) by Caravaggio, which demonstrates the artist's use of strong contrasts of light and shade.

Bernini designed the major decorations for the inside of St Peter's, Rome, and built a huge, richly ornamented *baldachino* (a kind of canopy) over the high altar, under Michelangelo's great dome. He also designed the vast piazza in front of the church. His choice of an unexpected oval shape for this, rather than a circle or square, was typically Baroque. Bernini's greatest talent lay in his ability to blend sculpture and architecture into one complete whole, doing this by a skilful use of light, shade and colour.

Painters at this time were specially interested in creating as great a feeling of depth in their work as possible. And yet, at the same time, they wanted each painting to be a unified whole – just like Bernini's unified sculpture and architecture. They achieved this feeling of unity by using flowing movements and swirling draperies to link foreground to background.

The two leading Italian painters in this period were Annibale Carracci (1560-1609) and Caravaggio (1573-1610). Both worked in Rome, though Carracci came from Bologna, and Caravaggio from a small town near Milan, from which he took his name. Their work was very different, and soon each had a party of supporters in Rome. These opposing parties had endless arguments about which was the better artist of the two, but the painters themselves were good friends. This was all the more surprising as Caravaggio had a ferocious temper.

Carracci was not an experimenter. He modelled his work on that of great masters of the past, like Raphael, adding to them only the Baroque feeling for fluidity and unity. Caravaggio, on the other hand, cared nothing for tradition or ideals of beauty. His paintings are bold, and the common people in them look like common people. They are striking in their use of highlighted forms emerging from deep shadow, and for the play of light on all kinds of different surfaces – skin, hair, cloth, fur, glass and metal.

Baroque and Rococo in France

In the 17th century all traces of the Gothic style disappeared from French art, and a really French style began to emerge at last. The reasons for this were partly political, for Louis XIII and Louis XIV were both powerful kings who attached much importance to the arts, and used them to increase their own prestige.

In painting, the first important figures were Nicolas Poussin (1594-1665) and Claude Gellée (1600-82), who spent most of his life in Italy. These artists were the first to paint scenes in which the landscape itself was really more important than the figures it contained. Although the scenes the two artists painted are sometimes alike, Poussin's forms are solid and distinct, while Claude's are bathed in soft, golden light. When the French Royal Academy of Painting and Sculpture was founded in 1648, Poussin became its first president.

Above This portrait bust in marble of Louis XIV is by Bernini. The sculpture portrays the majesty of Louis, who ruled France with absolute power and was the most powerful figure of the Baroque period. The French court was maintained with the utmost splendour and the arts were greatly encouraged and supported.

Above A view of part of the chateau and gardens at Versailles as they appeared about 1668.

Below This elegant pavilion is a fine example of Rococo architecture. It is the Pagodenburg, Schloss Nymphenburg, Munich. It was designed by François de Cuvilliés about 1722. The gardens of Nymphenburg were laid out in imitation of those at Versailles.

The most famous building of the Baroque age in France is undoubtedly the Palace of Versailles, which was built for Louis XIV around 1660 to 1680. This is so enormous that it can only be seen as a whole from the air. Louis, the 'Sun King', employed an army of architects, designers and decorators to work on it. The firm of Gobelins, which produced not only the famous tapestries, but also furniture, metalwork and textiles, was bought for the Crown in 1662.

The gardens at Versailles were a vital part of the whole plan. These, with their formal avenues, clipped trees, terraces and ponds, extending over many miles, were designed by André Le Nôtre (1613-1700). No expense was spared; even the water at Versailles was expensive, for it had to be brought from some distance away to fill the pools and sparkle gaily in the fountains.

By the end of the century, France had taken over from Italy as the artistic centre of the world. And on the death of Louis XIV, the heavy dignity of the Baroque gave way to the carefree gaiety of the style known as Rococo.

The people of this age liked dainty rooms for conversation or card-playing. These were decorated with designs of shells and garlands of flowers, all painted in light colours and gilded. Everything was small and delicate, including the porcelain and marble statues by sculptors like Jean Antoine Houdon (1741-1828). Houdon even travelled to America, to model the statue of George Washington that is now in the Virginia State Capitol.

This taste for charm and delicacy was reflected in the paintings of Antoine Watteau (1684-1721). As a frail boy of nineteen, Watteau ran away from his unhappy home in Valenciennes and found employment in a workshop in Paris, where cheap religious pictures were mass-produced for selling in country shops. For his labours Watteau's pay was a small sum of money and one bowl of soup a day! Later he went to work for a painter of ornaments who was also a

Left Detail from a self-portrait by Rubens, who is seen with his first wife, Isabella Brant. This picture was painted about 1609.

Far left *Portrait of a young man with a hurdy gurdy,* by Watteau.

guardian of the Luxembourg Palace. In those days, the park attached to the palace was natural country, and it was here that Watteau learned to paint the lovely groups of trees that feature so strongly in his later works.

Above everything else, Watteau wanted to win the Prix de Rome, awarded by the Academy. He entered the competition and failed, but was noticed by the academicians and, to his amazement, was elected a member of the Academy himself. This was the turning-point in Watteau's career. He painted one of his finest works, *The Embarkation for Cythera*, as his diploma work for the Academy, and from then on was able to earn his living in comfort.

Rubens and Van Dyck

Although the Low Countries were not divided into Holland and Belgium until the Peace of Westphalia in 1648, there were always notable differences between the Dutch and the Flemish peoples. The Dutch were northern and Protestant, while the Flemish – Catholic and closer to the French in character – were less puritanical.

Peter Paul Rubens (1577-1640), a Fleming, went to Italy in 1600 and was deeply impressed by what he learned there. After travelling from Rome to Genoa he lived for eight years in Mantua as court painter to the Duke. By the time he returned to Antwerp in 1608 he was a rich man. He was so skilled in arranging large-scale compositions in the rich Baroque manner that he had no rival in his own country (Flemish painters always having worked on a small scale). All the same, Rubens had not lost his basic, northern belief that it was a painter's business to paint the world around him, truthfully and in detail. So although his paintings are sweeping and dramatic in the Italian manner, they also have beautiful, glowing flesh tones and contrasting textures.

Soon Rubens had more orders for paintings than he could possibly manage on his own. But he was a man of great charm and organising ability, and other gifted painters were only too happy to work under him and to learn from him. When an order for a new painting came in, Rubens would often just make a small, coloured sketch. His helpers would then transfer this to a large canvas and do the underpainting. Lastly, Rubens himself would do the final brushwork – and make the painting spring vividly to life.

Rubens travelled from court to court as an honoured guest, and was knighted by Charles I of England. On his travels he often undertook delicate political missions. He was also a scholar, and carried out long correspondences in Latin about archaeology and art. In spite of all this he found time to paint a large number of brilliant paintings.

Among Rubens's many famous pupils the greatest was Anthony van Dyck (1599-1641). He soon acquired his master's skill in the treatment of

Above This *Mirror in the Chinese Taste* was carved from wood about 1740, probably by an English craftsman.

Rembrandt van Rijn (1606–69) Dutch painter. He began to study under various masters when he was a boy, but his art was largely self-taught. One of the most hard-working and productive artists of all time, his genius was never acknowledged in his lifetime. Some of his greatest paintings were self-portraits, done in old age, one of which from the Louvre in Paris is seen here.

Right One of the many heroic portraits of Charles I painted by Van Dyck while he was artist to the English royal court.

textures, but he never had his gaiety and drama. Van Dyck suffered from poor health, and this is perhaps why his paintings so often have a languid, melancholy mood. Like Rubens he was a painter of court portraits, and he too had so many commissions that he could not do them alone. He had assistants who painted the costumes of the sitters arranged on dolls, and sometimes Van Dyck did not even paint the whole of the head himself. This probably accounts for the flattering, but lifeless, look of some of his portraits. At the same time, he was masterly in conveying the very spirit of royalty – the elegance, the authority, the natural dignity. No wonder his work was so popular! Van Dyck spent the last nine years of his life at the court of Charles I, and the way he painted the king and his court has influenced history's opinion of them to this day.

The Dutch painters

By the middle of the 17th century the Dutch were wealthy. During the Spanish rule of their country they had, like the Flemish, prospered. The East India Company had been formed and great commercial cities, like Amsterdam, were strong in civic pride. Protestantism meant that, for Dutch artists, any religious, pagan or even historical subjects would be frowned upon. So in order to make a living these Dutch painters looked to the daily life of their country and painted it with a realism that suited their northern taste.

The first notable Dutch painter was Frans Hals (1580?-1666), whose *Laughing Cavalier*, painted in 1624, is well known. There is a hint in his works of the sculpture portraits of Bernini, and he had a great ability to catch the character of sitters, especially the good-natured jolly ones.

It was Rembrandt (1606-69), however, who made Dutch painting outstanding in the history of western art. His story is that of a great man far ahead of his time.

Born in Leyden, the fifth son of a prosperous miller, Rembrandt quite early established himself as an etcher and a painter of wealthy merchants' portraits. But after the death of his beloved first wife in 1642, Rembrandt began to turn away from the easy, popular subjects. In fact he had already finished, in that year, the painting that was to ruin him as a successful portrait painter. This had been commissioned by a group of militia officers, who wanted a pleasing group portrait. But what Rembrandt gave them was a painting of a scene – the turning-out of the guard. The work had drama, movement and urgency,

Left *St John the Evangelist on Patmos*, painted by Velasquez in 1617–8.

but many of the faces are half lost in shadow and are unrecognisable. The officers were furious. They wanted to see themselves! This painting is now one of Rembrandt's most famous works, and is known as *The Night Watch*.

After this, Rembrandt became poorer and poorer, till he finally ended up bankrupt. But throughout the rest of his life, as his genius developed, he still refused to paint to please anyone but himself. The world has reason to be grateful for his stubbornness.

The mirroring of everyday Dutch life was left to the group of painters who specialised in domestic scenes. The best known of these painters – and there were many – is Jan Vermeer (1632-75). His portraits and interior scenes have a purity of colour and an honest simplicity that is refreshing.

The 17th century in Spain

Naples and Sicily were under Spanish rule for many years, and one of the results was that Spanish artists travelled to Naples and were influenced by artists working there. This happened in the case of José de Ribera (1588-1656). He was strongly affected by the painting of Caravaggio, who had settled in Naples, and he carried Caravaggio's ideas and techniques back to Spain.

This kind of naturalism was the main style in Spain when Diego Velasquez (1599-1660) was born in Seville. Velasquez's great opportunity came in 1623 when the young king of Spain, Philip IV, was persuaded to give Velasquez a sitting. Philip was so pleased with his painting that he at once appointed Velasquez to be court painter at Madrid.

From the beginning Philip and Velasquez were on friendly terms. In 1628 Rubens came to Madrid and for nine months he was constantly with the king and Velasquez. Perhaps on Rubens's advice, the king then allowed Velasquez to go to Italy, where he made a special study of the work of Tintoretto. On his return, Velasquez went on painting portraits of Philip, no doubt realising that it was not the subject but the treatment of it that made a masterpiece. Later, he also painted the king's family in brilliant works like *The Maids of Honour*, in which the artist himself appears before his easel.

Below The chief monument to the plain and rather gloomy form of architecture imposed on his designers by Philip II is the Escorial palace near Madrid, built late in the 16th century.

Until this time, painters had usually worked in a studio away from their sitters, having first made notes and sketches from which to work on the finished painting. Velasquez must have been one of the first painters to work directly and entirely from observation.

Among Velasquez's pupils, the most famous was Bartolomé Murillo (1618-82). This artist was notable for his soft, even pretty, treatment of religious subjects. When we look at his work it can be seen that the violent feelings of the Reformation and the Counter-Reformation were at last passing away, and Spain was becoming more serene.

Canaletto (Antonio Canale) (1697–1768) Venetian painter who is known chiefly for his detailed and colourful landscapes of Venice. He spent ten years in England (1746–56) during which he painted many well-known views in and around London.

Above Queen's House, Greenwich (1616–35) was designed by Inigo Jones. The main entrance is inside the building as it was originally built astride the old London to Dover road.

Above A miniature by Nicholas Hilliard of his wife Alice, painted in 1578 when the couple were living in France.

English art

Art flourished in England in the Middle Ages, thanks to the patronage of the church. Then came Protestantism with its teaching against visual imagery and, later, the destruction of the monasteries: patronage came to an end. The only kind of painting that survived the Reformation for any time at all was portraiture – particularly in miniature. The best known of the English miniaturists was Nicholas Hilliard (1537-1619), who worked for Elizabeth I and James I.

There was no real revival of art in England until the restoration of the monarchy in 1660. By that time the nobles had become much wealthier as a result of colonisation. They wanted to have large mansions again, and fill them with fine furnishings and portraits, but there were almost no artists left to meet their demands. Painters, especially, had to be brought from abroad. Only in the 18th century did a truly English school of painting grow up.

Inigo Jones (1573-1652), the first great English architect, and surveyor-general to James I and Charles I, visited Italy and was impressed by the ideas of Palladio. He used some of Palladio's systems of proportion in his work, but only as a basis for his own, very personal style. His buildings, such as the banqueting hall in Whitehall, London, show much of the 17th-century feeling for unity.

After the Great Fire of London in 1666, Christopher Wren (1632-1723) designed many new buildings to replace those that had been destroyed. They often had to be squeezed into small, awkward spaces between other buildings. Wren drew attention away from this by giving his churches towers that soared high above the neighbouring rooftops. These towers were circular or many-sided, and were surrounded by colonnades and topped by slender spires. With them, Wren completely changed the skyline of London.

Englishmen at this time liked their homes to be stately and classical; rich ornament and formal gardens did not appeal to them. Versailles they found absurd, but the scenery painted by Claude was exactly to their taste. They surrounded their Palladian villas with 'landscape gardens' based on this kind of painting. It is strange to think that the ideas of a French painter actually altered the appearance of large parts of the English countryside.

The fashionable English wanted paintings signed by Continental masters, not by their unknown countrymen. This was a very sad state of affairs for English artists. One of them, a young engraver called William Hogarth (1697-1764), tried to remedy it by producing paintings that would appeal to English puritanism. In several series of paintings, like the one called *The Rake's Progress*, he preached the rewards of virtue and the wages of sin. Although these paintings tell a story (and reach a horrible conclusion) they are as carefully composed as any painting in the classical tradition. They are also a keenly observed study of the English middle classes. Hogarth's picture-series earned him fame and quite a lot of money, not from the paintings themselves, but from the engraved reproductions he made of them which sold well.

The 18th century was known as the Age of Reason – the age of Addison and Steele, *The Spectator*, and the early English novelists. A generation

after Hogarth, it finally found a painter to please its own elegant tastes. This was Joshua Reynolds (1723-92), a man-about-town and a friend of Dr Johnson. Unlike Hogarth, Reynolds had visited Italy and studied the great masters there. In fact, he borrowed so much from each of them that he produced portraits startlingly different from each other in style. When Reynolds became the first president of the newly founded Royal Academy of Art, he gave long lectures about the rules of taste and the importance of choosing lofty and dignified subjects.

Reynold's greatest rival was Thomas Gainsborough (1727-88). Born in rural Suffolk, Gainsborough had never visited Italy, although he also painted portraits in the formal tradition. Gainsborough's feeling was really for landscape, which he treated with great charm. He confessed, 'I paint portraits for money, landscape for love'.

Throughout the 18th century these English painters, and English life in general, were admired by all those in Europe who longed for a similar 'Age of Reason'.

18th-century Europe

On the Continent, as in England, people had grown tired of the dainty Rococo style. The French philosopher Rousseau idealised primitive man and his emotions, and many artists felt the same way. One of them, Jean Baptiste Greuze (1725-1805), developed emotional expression through the subjects he chose to paint. These illustrated the domestic virtues, often in a rural setting.

It was in Spain, however, in the work of Francisco Goya (1746-1828), that the spirit of the late 18th century found its most powerful expression. Goya was a painter of portraits at the Spanish court. At first glance, his state portraits may look quite like the traditional paintings of Van Dyck or Reynolds. But as soon as we look a little harder at those elegant grandees, we begin to see that they are painted in a totally different spirit. In fact, Goya was mocking them. Under the surface grandeur, his merciless eye found greed, stupidity and conceit. No other court painter has ever left

Above Hogarth planned several series of paintings telling stories, usually about the rewards of virtue and the wages of sin. This picture is called *Chairing the Member* and is from his Election Series, 1754.

Lancelot Brown (1715–83) British landscape gardener, known as 'Capability Brown'. Was gardener at Stowe House in Buckingham and showed remarkable ability in planning gardens. It became fashionable among rich people to employ Brown and he became very wealthy. Two of his most famous gardens are at Kew and Blenheim.

Left One of the great architectural masterpieces of Christopher Wren is the Fountain Court at Hampton Court Palace.

Right Francisco Goya's painting *The Executions of 3rd May, 1808* was done in 1814 after the French armies of occupation had been expelled from Spain. The picture depicts the brutal execution of people who rebelled against the Napoleonic invasions.

us such a truthful record of his patrons.

But Goya is not famed only for his court portraits. He produced a great number of etchings – many of them fantasies, with witches or other uncanny creatures. He also produced paintings and etchings of war scenes, showing them in all their true horror and brutality. As well as being a social commentator, Goya was an experimenter with light and colour, and in this was a forerunner of the Impressionists of the 19th century. Goya himself said, 'There are no lines in nature, only lighted forms, and forms which are in shadow; planes which project, and planes which recede'.

Above The two-storey wooden house at Mount Vernon in Virginia in the United States where George Washington lived is now a national monument.

North America

The European colonists who settled in North America during the 17th century took their own ideas of art and culture along with them. The society set up by these colonists was one of equality, so there were no rich or royal patrons for artists. The growth of town life, however, brought opportunities for craftsmen, and later for artists. New England towns like Newport and Boston became centres for the production of fine furniture, and increasing wealth led to a demand for family portraits. The growth of trade also meant that items like paintings could be bought in Europe and shipped to America.

In architecture the English tradition was very obvious at first, but new styles were taken later from books of architecture.

The earliest painters in the colonies produced not only portraits, but inn signs, shop signs and funeral trappings. Some painters of note did emerge, like John Smibert (1688-1751), a Scot who had come to America with Bishop Berkeley on an unsuccessful expedition. He stayed and married an heiress, and from 1730 lived in Boston. His work, by European standards, was not great, but he was Boston's foremost painter of the day.

John Singleton Copley (1737-1815) and Gilbert Stuart (1755-1828) were the best known of the colonial painters working from the style of Smibert. London, as a centre of the arts, was always a great attraction. Copley returned there in 1776, and Benjamin West (1738-1820), a native American, had already settled in the city by 1763. West found wealth and fame, and eventually became president of the Royal Academy in 1792, on the death of Joshua Reynolds.

Neo-classic art

Neo-classic art was, as the name says, a new classic art – in other words, a revival of interest in Greece and Rome. This had happened before, during the time of the Renaissance, but now the outcome was very different. The first history of art appeared in 1764.

Called *History of Art among the Ancients,* it was written by J. J. Winckelmann (1717-68) and was probably one reason for the fresh interest in classical art.

More important, however, was the fact that between 1750 and the Revolution in 1789, growing unrest in France meant that the froth of Rococo art was no longer a real expression of the way in which people were thinking. The mood of the country had become serious, and the events of the time were thought to be just as important, and worthy of record, as were those of Greece and Rome.

The wave of new ideas which flowed around the time of the French Revolution introduced an important new range of subjects for artists. This was the era of Benjamin Franklin's experiments with atmospheric electricity, of the founding of iron works and the invention of the spinning frame. Adam Smith (1723-90) had published his *Wealth of Nations, The Times* newspaper was first published, and the philosophers Rousseau and Paine were writing about change and revolution.

The first important painter in the neo-classic style was Jacques Louis David (1748-1825), who used its clarity and order to express modern political events, like the *Death of Marat,* painted in 1793. David, in fact, became the official painter of the newly formed republic. But it was another French artist, Jean Auguste Ingres (1780-1867), who took this style to its highest peak in his use of line to create a real feeling for nature.

Above Typical of the Regency style of the English architect John Nash (1752–1835) is Park Crescent near Regent's Park in London.

His portrait drawings, made with a very hard pencil, are among the most outstanding works in the neo-classic style.

An interesting comparison can be made between these two masters of the neo-classic style and the imitators who followed them. One of these was Alexandre Cabanel (1823-89), whose *Birth of Venus* shows just how debased this style had become. Cabanel was famous and successful in his time, but now his paintings are thought to have little artistic merit.

Jacques Louis David (1748–1825) French painter. During the Revolution he joined Robespierre's party. Made court painter by Napoleon he died in exile in Brussels.

The Romantics

In France neo-classic was the 'official' painting style. Both the style and the subjects to be used were taught in government art schools. This way of teaching a style frustrated the more imaginative students, while helping to disguise the weakness of the less able ones. Artists began to revolt against it, and it was this revolt that led to the movement we call Romantic.

The Romantic movement did not happen only in art. It was a feeling that was sweeping Europe at the time. The growing use and acceptance of machines, and especially the growth of railways, had changed the social life of Europe. Essentially, the

Left The Arc de Triomphe in Paris, (1806–36) built by J. Chalgrin to celebrate the victories of Napoleon's armies, used the Roman triumphal arch as its model.

Above *Horses emerging from the sea* by Delacroix was specially commissioned in 1860. In some ways the painting, with its masterly rendering of the rhythm in the movement of the horses and their rider, is a souvenir of the artist's visit to Africa some thirty years before.

Romantic movement was one of protest against the rule of aristocratic society, and against the ideas that had grown out of new scientific laws. It seemed to many people that life was becoming too mechanical, with no scope left for imagination and feeling. In accord with the Romantic movement were the ideas of Darwin's evolutionary biology, and the new idea of socialism.

In painting, this movement was best represented by the painters Theodore Géricault (1791-1824) and Eugène Delacroix (1798-1863). Géricault's *The Raft of the Medusa,* painted about 1819, was controversial both in subject and treatment. It is a vivid account of a disastrous shipwreck, caused by official negligence, which drowned hundreds of French immigrants going to North Africa. Even the scale of this painting is dramatic – it measures about seven metres by five metres.

After Géricault's early death, Delacroix became the leading Romantic painter. The Romantics had no 'official' support, but they influenced French art till well into the 1870s. Delacroix preferred to paint exotic subjects, often Turkish or medieval. His illustrations for *Hamlet* and *Faust*, and for the poetry of Byron, are truly Romantic in feeling.

Right Detail from one of William Blake's drawings for an illustrated edition of Dante's *Divina Commedia*. This scene from Canto 19 shows the descent into Hell.

Vision and landscape

William Blake (1757-1827), an English painter and poet, may have been affected by the new Romantic approach to art, but in all other respects he was quite individual. Like Goya, he was an etcher and painter of fantastic visions. But whereas Goya's fantasies carry hidden messages about social conditions, Blake's are simply his personal visions. He was deeply religious, thought by some to be completely mad and by others to be merely a harmless crank. He was so indifferent to the demands of everyday life that only the kindness of a few friends who believed in his art saved him from starving.

Born in London, Blake began by copying the prints of Michelangelo, and by the age of fourteen was earning a living as an engraver. His inner visions were so important to him that he refused to draw from real life. This may mean there are technical faults in his work, but we should think of Blake as resembling the artists of the Middle Ages, who thought vision and faith much more important than accuracy. He certainly did not belong to any school of painters, and his work had no effect on other artists of the late 18th and early 19th centuries.

The Romantic movement had one very noticeable effect on art, and that was a new freedom of choice in subject matter. Until then, artists who painted 'views' had not been taken seriously. Figures were the important thing, landscape merely a background to them. Gradually, however, a feeling for landscape as a worthwhile subject in itself grew up. This was brought to its full flowering in England in the paintings of Turner and Constable.

Above Turner's *The Fighting Téméraire Tugged to her Last Berth to be broken up* (1838). With such pictures as this Turner introduced a new world of dazzling light and rich colour into English painting.

Joseph Turner (1775-1851) was a true Romantic painter. He worked by making a study direct from nature, and then letting his imagination take over. He used every possible trick to make his landscapes striking and dramatic: had he been less skilful the results might have been disastrous. But the tremendous daring and gusto of Turner's paintings convey the grandeur and drama of nature. His canvases are great areas of space alive with light and colour, in which forms lose all solidity in the golden, misty atmosphere. Turner led a solitary and private life and died leaving some 20,000 drawings and paintings to the nation – and a fortune of £140,000.

John Constable (1776-1837) painted in a very different way from Turner. He wanted nothing to do with what he called Turner's 'airy visions, painted with tinted steam', and tried to represent nature. Fashionable landscape painters who still modelled themselves on Claude had worked out a very simple recipe for making an effective picture: an impressive tree in the foreground, leading the eye to a distant view in the centre, brown and gold colours in the foreground, fading to pale blue tints in the background. There were tricks for painting clouds and water and the gnarled bark of trees. Constable despised all this. He made his own careful studies from nature and then composed them into an original, informal picture.

Constable loved the rural landscape of his native Suffolk. He recreated the warmth of its sunlight, the movement of its wind and rain, and the shadows of its passing clouds.

William Morris

Although he was only seventeen years old when the Great Exhibition was held in London in 1851, William Morris (1834-96) was appalled by the shoddiness and vulgarity of the things he saw there. It was this feeling that started his lifelong war against the machine age and its products. His belief was that 'the true root and basis of all Art lies in the handicrafts'.

Morris trained in architecture and painting and was a member of the Pre-Raphaelite Brotherhood, but this did not satisfy him. He wanted to revive the old traditions of honest workmanship in all the arts and crafts. Eventually, in 1885, he formed the Art Workers Guild, and in doing so marked the beginning of a new era in 'applied' art.

With the help of his Pre-Raphaelite friends, Morris introduced entirely different kinds of designs for interior decoration, fabrics and furniture. Although the group based their designs on medieval ideas, they brought a fresh eye to bear on them and never

Above Schloss Neuschwanstein in Bavaria, a celebrated castle built for Ludwig II between 1869–81. Its style of architecture has been described as Wagnerian Gothic.

Right One of the finest examples of architecture in iron is the Eiffel tower in Paris, built by Gustave Eiffel in 1889 for the Paris Exhibition. This view shows the base of the structure which supports the tower.

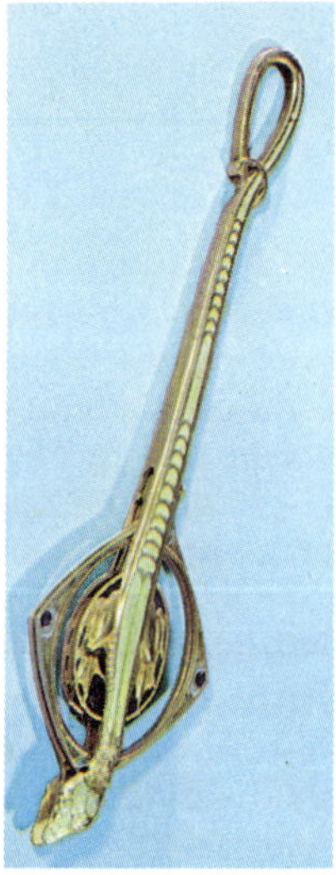

Above William Morris and his friends set up a business to produce furniture that was well-designed and functional. Seen here is one of Morris's 'Sussex' chairs.

Above right An example of Morris's rich textile designs is seen (left) in this detail from the pattern known as Wandle chintz, first made in 1884. The influence of Art Nouveau was felt not only in architecture but in all aspects of design, including jewellery. This lorgnette (right) from Paris is made in the form of a lizard.

relaxed their high standards of workmanship. They revived, among others, the old arts of tapestry, stained glass and calligraphy (the art of beautiful writing). Morris's own designs for textiles and wallpapers are in production again today.

What Morris was fighting was not only the machine age, but also the gap between art and artists and ordinary people and everyday life – a gap which had started to open in the Renaissance and had been widening ever since. By the 19th century it seemed it would never be closed, until Morris came along with his theory of an art 'by the people and for the people'. By starting to narrow this gap he had a very important effect on the art of the 20th century.

19th-century architecture

There were three main trends influencing architecture in the 19th century. First came reliance on the past. In the 19th century, looking back towards the past affected not only artists and architects but also poets, novelists and politicians of many countries. There was an upsurge of nationalism as each country looked back to its earlier days of glory. In England it is particularly difficult to distinguish between the survival of traditional forms and the revival of them.

When the old Houses of Parliament in London burned down in 1834, a competition for a new design was held. The winner was Charles Barry (1795-1860), an expert in the Renaissance style. Then it was decided that, as England's democracy rested on the achievements of the Middle Ages, the new building ought to be built in the Gothic style. So Barry had to consult an expert in that style, Augustus Pugin (1812-52). In the end, Barry designed the overall shape of the building and Pugin designed the decoration.

William Morris and his architect friend, Philip Webb (1831-1915), hated the products of the machine age and turned to medieval methods, materials and designs. An example of their work at its best can be seen in the Red House at Bexleyheath in Kent, which was Morris's own home.

France, Germany and the United States were also affected by the trend towards a revival of the past, and all shared a passing 'Italianate' movement, based on formal Renaissance models.

The second trend in the 19th century was unity of structure, materials and site. This led to the use of the new materials of the Industrial Age, in buildings such as the Crystal Palace in London and the daring tower in Paris designed by Gustave Eiffel (1832-1923). Also following this trend were architects working in the style known as Art Nouveau. The most famous among these is the Spaniard Antoni Gaudí (1852-1926), whose buildings are easily recognisable by their flowing, curving lines.

Lastly, there was the influence of classical proportion. This trend grew up very late in the 19th century, and its most important results can be seen in the work of the Bauhaus early in the present century. The Bauhaus was founded by Walter Gropius in 1919 and was an experimental centre for architects, engineers, painters and sculptors.

The Pre-Raphaelites

By the middle of the 19th century, Britain's character as the 'world's workshop' was established. For the first time the town and city population of a modern nation outnumbered its rural population. Victorian Britain was carried away with its industrial success, but never before had the gap between the technical arts and the visual arts been so wide. Objects on display at the Great Exhibition of 1851 included such things as four-poster beds modelled on cathedrals, 'Gothic' bookcases and cast-iron pianos.

Among the many people disturbed by all this, and by the loss of the old crafts, were some young English painters. A few years earlier, in 1848, they had banded together, calling themselves the Pre-Raphaelite Brotherhood. Their aim was to revive the best traditions in painting. The academies claimed to represent the tradition of the painter Raphael; if that was so, the Pre-Raphaelites argued, then art had obviously taken a wrong turning through Raphael. To reform art it would be necessary to go further back than Raphael, to the times when the artist was an honest and humble craftsman. The group included Dante Gabriel Rossetti (1828-82), Holman Hunt (1827-1910), Edward Burne-Jones (1833-98) and John Everett Millais (1829-96). They attracted the enthusiastic support of John Ruskin (1819-1900), the greatest critic of the day, who was also a supporter of William Morris's Arts and Crafts movement.

Unfortunately, the Pre-Raphaelites did not have the simple faith of earlier artists, and could not produce the honest and unsophisticated art they so admired. The road they had chosen to follow turned out to be a blind alley, and the movement did not last for long.

Above *The Death of Ophelia* by John Millais. The aims of the Pre-Raphaelites were expressed in terms that were often realistic and romantic at the same time. This famous painting shows the brilliant colour and minutely observed detail which appeared in many of their paintings.

The Barbizon painters

In France the annual exhibition held in the Salon d'Apollon in the Louvre by members of the French Academy tended to exclude artists who did not work in the traditional grand and noble style. It was partly for this reason that some painters began to move out of the city to paint in the

Above The French painter Millet was mainly concerned to portray peasant life and reproductions of many of his paintings made them world famous in the 19th century. This is *The Wood Sawyers*, painted in 1875.

Above right The English artist George Stubbs (1724–1806) is known chiefly for his exact and imaginative pictures of horses.

Above Daumier's caricatures of the French king, Louis Philippe, caused his imprisonment. He depicted the king with a pear-shaped head, the significance of this being that in French a 'pear' is a simple person who is easily deceived.

countryside. There were also other reasons of a more practical kind. France was in a state of unrest, the cost of city life was rising, and the fact that paint could now be bought ready-mixed in tubes made working out of doors more possible.

Among the painters who left Paris were Theodore Rousseau (1812-67) and Jean François Millet (1814-75). Along with Jean Corot (1796-1875), they worked around the small village of Barbizon in the forest of Fontainebleau, and it was by this name that their style became known. The important thing was that for the first time the painting was done out of doors, directly from nature. Until this time such landscapes would certainly have been observed and sketched outside, but the actual painting would have been put together in the artist's studio.

Rousseau painted landscapes like the 17th-century Dutch masters whom he admired. Millet's paintings were more controversial, for they dealt with subjects that the Salon found unacceptable. *The Winnower*, exhibited at the Salon in 1848, is typical of this. Its subject, which is peasants at work in a harvest field, led to accusations of socialism. But Millet's work marked the beginning of the great change in attitude that has made art from the 19th century onwards so different from everything that went before.

Until the 19th century, painters had made a fairly good living. They painted in the style of the day, and the work they left behind was typical of their age, since everybody else worked in more or less the same style. Now many styles began to be used at the same time. In fact, the word style came to mean the particular way one person worked, rather than the manner of a school of painters. This created new opportunities, but also new difficulties for the artist. It was no longer simply a matter of drawing and painting with accuracy, because a lot of artists could do this. Instead, it was essential to be individual. Many painters allowed only what would sell to influence their style, but it is the few who were true to themselves who are remembered.

An important event affecting art was the introduction of photography to the public in 1839. This undoubtedly had an effect on the painters of the Barbizon school, who said they wanted to interpret the 'mood' of the landscape, as well as merely recording it with accuracy.

Rural and urban life

Gustave Courbet (1819-77) was the son of a French farmer. His father sent him to Paris to study law, but once there he forgot all about the law and started to learn to paint. Courbet had a passion for realism, and a genuine sympathy for the working classes. To a young man of his serious nature, making pictures out of imaginary happenings from novels and poetry seemed a very stupid thing to do. He was annoyed when one patron asked him to paint a picture with angels in it. 'Angels!' exclaimed Courbet, 'but I have never seen angels. What I have not seen I cannot paint.'

Like Millet, Courbet did not care about the values of the academic schools. The academies were outraged when he showed a simple country funeral scene in *Burial at Ornans*. This kind of subject had only ever been painted before when it showed wealthy and powerful people.

While Courbet was recording rural life, another painter was recording the troubled times in Paris. He was Honoré Daumier (1808-79). Over a period of forty years Daumier made about four thousand satirical lithographs, mainly for the weekly humorous journals. In these he probed deeply into the life of the city, uncovering both the attractive and the unattractive things about it. He was also a painter of forceful simplicity, finding his subjects in the new poor of the industrial age.

The sculpture of light

Auguste Rodin (1840-1917), the sculptor, was born in Paris and in his own lifetime achieved a fame almost as great as Michelangelo's. He belonged to a poor family and early in life had to earn his living in a stone-mason's yard. There he soon became familiar with the sculptor's materials.

At the Salon of 1877 Rodin showed a statue called *The Age of Bronze* that was so life-like he was actually accused of having taken a cast from a living model! To prove his accusers wrong, he made his next statue, *St John the Baptist,* larger than life-size. In his work he went, as he said, 'to Nature, and when the artist follows Nature he gets everything'.

However, Rodin knew that blindly copying the 'lumps and bumps', as he called them, would not do. He made great use of light – the way it played along surfaces, the shadows it cast, and the glow of it on his materials. He also realised that when we look at any object we see the whole of it first, and the details later. Because of his opinions the critics lumped him together with the Impressionist painters, although he was in fact an admirer of classical sculpture.

Rodin's last work, exhibited in 1898, caused the critics to accuse him of not knowing his own craft. In this statue of the writer Balzac, Rodin had modelled the figure only in the roughest of outlines, with detail concentrated in the upturned face and tousled hair. Rodin showed in this great work how he despised outward 'finish' – that is, smoothness and polish which adds nothing to the meaning of the work.

Above In his painting *The Artist's Studio* (1855) Courbet shows himself absorbed in his work undisturbed by all the people who have crowded into his studio to watch.

Auguste Rodin (1840–1917) French sculptor. Was much influenced in early life by the work of Michelangelo and other Italian sculptors, but he became essentially an artist in tune with the Romantic ideals of his time. Like the Impressionist painters he was concerned to show the effects of light and shade in his work. He did many portrait busts, such as the one on the left of the French writer Victor Hugo.

Above Whistler's painting which he called *Harmony in Grey and Green* (1873) is a portrait of Miss Cicely Alexander.

Above right Manet's *The Balcony*, first exhibited in the Paris Salon of 1869.

Right Two other important members of the Impressionist group were Camille Pissarro (1830–1903) and Alfred Sisley (1839–99). Sisley's *Boat during a Flood* is seen here.

Right Seurat's *The Bathers* is one of his best-known pictures, in which he uses countless tiny dots of pure colour, arranged in such a way that combinations of them give the impression of other colours, rather in the way that printing in colour converts a picture into an arrangement of dots of primary colours.

Whistler

While the Pre-Raphaelites were following their own chosen path, a young American called James McNeill Whistler (1834-1903) was a student at the military college of West Point. Failing his exams, he took a job as a draughtsman and learned to engrave and etch. Then, in 1855, he went to Paris to study art.

Whistler was a very high-spirited young man, and thoroughly enjoyed the gay life led by the students in the Latin Quarter. At the same time he worked very hard and in less than four years produced his first notable work – *At the Piano*, painted in 1859. An admirer of Velasquez and of Japanese prints, Whistler (along with Manet, Degas, Monet and other French artists) was a frequent visitor to a Japanese shop in the Rue de Rivoli in Paris. There he was able to study the prints of Hokusai and Hiroshige. He invented a new kind of portrait painting, which blended Spanish realism with the Japanese feeling for flat pattern. Because he thought the composition and the arrangement of colours more important than the subject of a painting, he gave his paintings names such as *Harmony* and *Nocturne*.

Eventually, Whistler settled down to live in Chelsea and became friendly with his neighbour, Rossetti. He produced a wonderful series of etchings known as the 'Thames' set. Unfortunately his work did not appeal to popular taste, and he suffered a great deal of criticism. One of his worst enemies was John Ruskin, the defender of the Pre-Raphaelites. Ruskin's attacks were so savage that Whistler brought a libel action against him in 1878, but was awarded only one farthing in damages by a hostile judge and jury. He became bankrupt, and all his belongings were sold to pay his debts. However, he was a man of great spirit and determination, and in the end won his way to success.

Whistler was the first American painter to win international fame, and also the first artist to reveal to Londoners the hidden beauties of their own riverside.

Above Renoir's *The Luncheon of the Boating Party* (1881) includes a picture of the girl who was to become his wife, Alice Charigat (on the left holding a dog).

The Impressionists

It was Edouard Manet (1832-83) who formed the link between Courbet and the painters known as the Impressionists. Like Courbet, Manet was intended for a career in law, but took up painting instead. Manet saw very clearly how in real life one colour faded into another. Like Goya, he realised that 'there are no lines in Nature'. Another saying of his, which links him to the Impressionists, was, 'The principal person in a picture is the light'.

The Impressionist movement was born at an exhibition in Paris in 1863. Manet, along with Claude Monet (1840-1926) and Pierre Renoir (1841-1919), had been refused permission to show his paintings in the Salon exhibition. Because the artists protested so loudly, the emperor Napoleon III heard about it and insisted that they should be allowed to exhibit in another room. This became known as the *Salon des Refusés,* meaning the Hall of the Rejected. The name Impressionist was coined by a critic who jeered at a painting by Claude Monet in this exhibition called *Impression, Sunrise.* However, what started as a term of derision came to be used to describe the painters' aims.

It is difficult now to see why people were so outraged by the Impressionists. All through history, just as people have got used to one kind of art, artists have infuriated them by starting something quite different, and so it was with the Impressionists. In their case, they were working on the principle of simultaneous vision. This means that the human eye will focus only on one small part of any scene at any time, and detail within that part will be sharp. Over the rest of the scene, detail will be less clear. Use of this principle was not entirely new – Velasquez had moved towards it in his later paintings. What was quite new, however, was the palette of colour used by the Impressionists.

The scientist Michel Chevreul (1786-1889), while working for the Gobelins tapestry company, had written a book called *The Laws of Simultaneous Contrast of Colours.* This book made it clear that colour was not unchanging, but was affected by atmospheric light. If the light changed in the course of the day, every colour in nature would seem to change as a result. Chevreul pointed out, too, that shadow was not just black or grey, but depended on the colour of the object casting the shadow. He also wrote that the more colour is mixed, the more it loses its brilliancy, and that light destroys colour. Manet had been quite right to say 'the principal person in a picture is the light'.

Monet, Renoir and Edgar Degas (1834-1917) experimented with colour and light, too, but it was Georges Seurat (1859-91) who reduced it all

Below *The little dancer aged 14,* a sculpture by Degas.

Right A poster for Aristide Bruant's cabaret designed by Toulouse-Lautrec, who raised the art of the poster to a new level during the 19th century.

Above One of the most extraordinary churches ever designed is Gaudi's Sagrada Familia in Barcelona. It shows the strange effect of Art Nouveau on church architecture. The building was begun in 1884 and remains uncompleted.

Above An Art Nouveau motif for book illustration designed by Mucha in 1904.

almost to a scientific formula. He applied his paint in small, roundish dots, each with a very exact colour relationship to the other.

The very popular, newly imported prints from Japan also affected the Impressionists. Their influence is noticeable, too, in the paintings and posters of Henri Toulouse-Lautrec (1864-1901), who recorded the more colourful characters of Paris so vividly.

Art Nouveau

The decorative style known as Art Nouveau started around the early 1880s. Although it was never considered as a school of painting, its effects can be seen in the curved, elongated line used by painters like Paul Gauguin (1848-1903) and Edvard Munch (1863-1944), and in the drooping forms used by the Pre-Raphaelites. Whistler used Art Nouveau motifs both in his painting and in the typography of the books he designed, with their lovely title pages.

The style was widely used in illustration, achieving its most dramatic effects in the work of Aubrey Beardsley (1872-98) and Alphonse Mucha (1869-1939). Although Beardsley was only twenty-six years old when he died his work had already made a great impression both in England and on the Continent. His arrangements of short, curved lines and lines of little dots was quite different from the work of any other artist at the time; so, too, was his way of covering unlikely surfaces with flowers and small ornaments. But perhaps his greatest talent lay in his ability to give value to large areas of empty space.

In architecture the Art Nouveau style, at its most lavish, can be seen in the work of Antoní Gaudi. In buildings such as his *Casa Milá* in Barcelona, it seems the walls move and flow into one another.

Although the Art Nouveau style began in Britain, other developments soon overtook it there. On the Continent, however, it was much longer-lived – and in the United States, too, where Louis Tiffany (1848-1933) produced his famous glassware in this style. Meanwhile the English architect-designer C. F. Voysey (1857-1941) had taken something of William Morris's ideas, and something of Art Nouveau, and adapted them to form a very personal and original style, refreshing in its simplicity. Much the same might be said of Charles Rennie Mackintosh (1868-1928), who, working mainly in Scotland, produced buildings and interiors owing as much to the Scottish baronial style as to the Arts and Crafts movement and Art Nouveau. Although Mackintosh's influence on British architecture and furniture was slight, his work had a great effect in Europe, particularly in Austria. England herself turned her back on this influence and took up a fake classical trend.

Art Nouveau gradually became debased, as cheap typography and mass-produced ornament picked up its typical motifs and applied them with no knowledge of the purity and spaciousness of the original style. It was finally killed by the 'modernistic' zigzag line of the 1920s and 1930s – in itself a debased version of a Cubist motif. Until quite recently, Art Nouveau was thought to be decadent and superficial, quite inferior to later design. Only now do we recognise that, along with the Arts and Crafts movement, it was the basis of the great work done by the Bauhaus.

Post-Impressionism

Around the year 1880 western society began to change. The complete confidence built up in the last two decades of industrial invention and expansion started to crumble. In industry there were slumps, in science,

Above Vincent Van Gogh's *Cottages at Cordeville*, painted in the last year of his life, 1890.

Far left A detail from *Three Tahitians* (1899) by Gauguin.

Near left Detail from Beardsley's *Atlanta*, drawn for *The Yellow Book*, an illustrated magazine, in 1895.

completely new and less reassuring advances, and in society, revolution. All these separate, yet related, things led finally to the Great War of 1914-18. As always the pattern of events was reflected in the art of the time.

One of the most important painters was Paul Cézanne (1839-1906), who had been influenced by Impressionist ideas about colour, but never used their palette. What obsessed Cézanne was substance, solidity and weight. He said, 'I wish to make of Impressionism something enduring, like the art of the old masters'. The ideas behind his still-life paintings were closely connected with the scientific thought of the time. Basically, this was that space was curvilinear – in other words, the shortest distance between two points could be a curved, rather than a straight, line. Cézanne used colour, rather than light and shade, to give depth and weight to his works, often deliberating for a long time before making a single brush stroke. He is important both as an individual painter and as the main influence on the Cubists who followed him.

From Vincent van Gogh (1853-90), on the other hand, can be traced the growth of the Expressionist painters. Van Gogh's short, tragic life is well recorded in books and films. He began to paint when he was about thirty years old after several false starts, and his early work showed his great concern for the poor. Later, his painting became more personal, exciting and violent. He used colour at its full intensity and his effect on the later Expressionist painters is easily seen.

The third artist who was to influence those who followed was Paul Gauguin. We know him mainly from his paintings and prints of Tahitian life, for he gave up his business in Paris at the age of thirty in order to paint in Tahiti. This was the time when Europe was colonising Africa, and the feeling for native art was strong. It showed even in the work of

Henri Matisse (1869–1954) French painter. In 1905 he became leader of a group of young painters called *Les Fauves* (meaning the savages) which included Derain, Dufy and Rouault. They were so called because they ignored the forms of nature in their paintings and used violent colours. Matisse remained throughout his life a master of line and colour.

Above A typical work by the primitive painter Rousseau, called *L'Octroi*.

Right *Bust of a child*, a water-colour by Paul Klee, one of a related group of heads painted by him in the early 1930s.

Above This design for the jacket of a book published in Germany shows the influence of the Bauhaus teaching on graphic design.

the primitive painter Henri Rousseau (1844-1910), who spent most of his life as a customs official, hence his nickname *Le Douanier* (the customs officer). Gauguin's work was, therefore, of his time – which is not the same thing as saying he was financially successful.

The visual arts were not the only ones affected by the restless state of the world; it was also reflected in the music of composers like Debussy. This music found its visual counterpart in the paintings of Pierre Bonnard (1867-1947), with their soft, glowing light and colour.

The Bauhaus

With the death of William Morris in 1896, the new design movement came to an end in England. Later developments, leading to an acceptance of machine products, took place in Europe. Writers like Walt Whitman in America, and Zola in France, saw the marvellous possibilities of the machine age. Architects like Frank Lloyd Wright (1869-1959) understood and accepted the machine and its relation to architecture and design. The ideas of these men influenced the early German art schools, which were growing in size and number. Finally in 1919 all these threads of thought, from Morris and Art Nouveau onwards, were gathered together by one man, Walter Gropius, in one place, called the Bauhaus.

Gropius believed in the importance of building – in its widest possible meaning. So, the Bauhaus (or Building House) was a school and a workshop combined, where artists trained first in general subjects, and later in their chosen one. This might be architecture, or design for wood, glass, metal or ceramics; it might be photography, or design for theatre and film; or it might be graphic design – illustration, typography and advertising. For ten years the Bauhaus was the greatest centre of creative activity in Europe. Its effects reach into every corner of our lives, even today.

There were no famous designers of the day for Walter Gropius to bring to the Bauhaus as teachers, so he looked to painters – not the great and famous ones, but men like Paul Klee (1879-1940), Vassily Kandinsky (1866-1944) and Lyonel Feininger (1871-1956). With these and other teachers Gropius ran the course as a living, changing experience which did not rely on any set plans. The students came from many different countries, and so the ideas of the Bauhaus spread far and wide. It was a loss to the whole world when this wonderful school was closed by the Nazis in 1933.

In all kinds of design, and also in painting, the Bauhaus showed that mere ornament was useless. The shape of any object should only help it to serve its purpose better. This meant an enormous change of thought about the over-decorated machines, furniture and household equipment then in use.

The ideas of the Bauhaus never died. Staff and students who left Germany carried its teaching abroad. Some went to America, including

Left The Guggenheim Museum in New York, designed by Frank Lloyd Wright and built in 1943–59. Inside the building the museum exhibits are arranged round a continuous spiral ramp. This was the architect's last important work carried out in his lifetime.

Gropius, who took American citizenship and became an architect of international fame. Many of the products designed at the Bauhaus during the 1920s and 1930s are on sale again today – and perhaps appreciated by more people than ever before.

Photography

The word photography comes from the Greek, and means 'writing with light'. Men have known since the Renaissance that if a dark room has a tiny hole in one wall, light coming through the hole casts an upside-down image on the opposite wall. Around the middle of the 16th century a lens was substituted for the pin-hole, making a more brilliant image, and eventually in the 18th century the first camera was made. This was a box with a hole at one end, and at the other a ground glass screen on which an image could be seen from outside the box.

Modern photography, however, was not born till the 19th century, when someone had the idea of fixing the image permanently with chemicals. In fact, several people worked towards this without realising that they were not alone in their discoveries. The Frenchman Louis Daguerre (1789-1851) made his process public in 1839, and the word photography was first used in the same year, but by an Englishman, John Herschel (1792-1871). In 1844 Herschel's friend, Henry Fox Talbot (1800-77), published a book called *Pencil of Nature* with photographic illustrations. Gradually, throughout the 19th and 20th centuries, photography has been refined until, in its most basic form, it is available to everyone because it is cheap and easy to use.

The ways in which painting and photography have influenced each other are easy to see. Some early photographs, for instance, show strong traces of portrait painters whom the photographers admired. Equally, in the 1860s, Julia Margaret Cameron (1815-79) was making wonderful portrait photographs which must have influenced the painters of the day. But even at this time the place of photography as an art form was not settled. The mass reproduction possibilities of a photograph gave it other powers. A photographic portrait of Abraham Lincoln was made by Mathew Brady and distributed in large numbers for the presidential campaign, and Lincoln later declared, 'Make no mistake, gentlemen. Brady made me president'.

From the invention of photography came the new medium of film-making, which began very much in the theatrical tradition. Later, creative directors like the Russian, Sergi Eisenstein (1898-1948), showed the possibilities of film as a medium for the artist. Naturally, in both movie and still photography much of the work is purely technical, but as an influence on science, technology and the visual arts photography is of great and evergrowing importance.

Above One of Julia Margaret Cameron's portraits (top) of Marie Spartali, taken in 1868. Beneath it is a contemporary photograph of Henry Fox Talbot.

Above Picasso's *Woman Weeping* (1937). The strong, bright colours are in vivid contrast to the grief of the subject. Pablo Picasso (1881–1973) was considered a mature artist at the age of ten and held his first exhibition when he was sixteen. After his 'Blue' and 'Rose' periods in Paris (1905–7), his *Les Demoiselles d'Avignon*, painted in 1907, began Cubism.

Above right Braque's *Still Life with Fish* painted in 1909–11, is typical of Cubist paintings which treat familiar objects in a new way.

The 20th century

It is difficult to look clearly at 20th-century painting and see it as people will a hundred years from now. We are still too close to it. All that can be attempted is to list briefly some of the various movements and how they differ from one another.

Cubist is the name given to the paintings Pablo Picasso and Georges Braque (1882-1963) made between 1908 and 1914. These painters tried to show their subjects as though they could be seen from several points of view at the same time. All the different planes shown made them look as though they were composed of little cubes. The Cubist painters also rejected the Impressionist colours and worked mainly in browns and greys. Picasso's painting continued to change and develop after his Cubist phase. His mural *Guernica,* painted in 1937 on the theme of the Spanish Civil War, was partly Cubist but also partly Surrealist.

The first Abstract painter, in the 1890s, was Vassily Kandinsky, and he was soon joined by others, including Piet Mondrian (1872-1944) and Joan Miró. Their idea was to abstract (or take out) the essence of everyday things so that we could see them afresh. This tied in with much of the scientific work of the time. The geometric abstraction of Mondrian has had an influence on modern design and architecture.

After the 1914-18 war the movement named Dadaism grew up. Many people believed that respectable society was responsible for the horrors of the war, and they wanted to shock this society into looking at itself afresh. Dadaist artists, who included Marcel Duchamp (1887-1968) and Kurt Schwitters (1887-1948), introduced the idea of accident in painting, and also exhibited what they called 'Readymades'. When Duchamp presented a manufactured hat rack as a work of art, he was asking society to think again about even everyday things.

The growing science of psychology was largely responsible for the movement in art called Surrealism. The work of Freud at the beginning of this century was echoed in the paintings of Max Ernst, Giorio de Chirico and René Magritte (1898-1967), who presented us with bizarre images with a nightmare-like quality.

The Expressionist painters, beginning with Van Gogh, needed to express their personal reactions to the confusing world around them. The pioneer of this movement was Georges Rouault (1871-1958), and others who have followed in it are Chaim Soutine

Left Perhaps the best-known modern movement in art is Surrealism, a term that was invented in the 1920s. Its aim was to create something more than realism which went beyond into the wider realms of the mind's imagination. One of its most successful exponents is Salvador Dali, whose paintings often portray the strange, confused world of dreams. The picture shown is called *Metamorphosis of Narcissus.*

(1894-1943), Francis Bacon, Graham Sutherland and Oscar Kokoschka.

Two individual painters of fantastic works, quite different from those of the Surrealists, are Marc Chagall and Paul Klee. Chagall's fantasies are dream-like, while Klee's are intellectual and witty.

After the Second World War (1939-45) the Action Painters came into being. They explored the physical qualities of paint by spattering it on, or flinging it at canvas, so producing abstract, colourful images. Karel Appel, Sam Francis and Jackson Pollock (1912-56) worked in this way.

The important thing to notice about these modern movements in painting is that, unlike the old schools of painting, they are truly and immediately international. There is no question of new ideas slowly creeping from one country to another. They happen simultaneously in most countries of the world – we could almost say they explode into being! This is perhaps one of the most exciting things about the age we live in.

Architecture

The first signs of an international style in architecture can be seen in a building called Robie House, designed by the great American architect Frank Lloyd Wright in the year 1909.

Frank Lloyd Wright's continuous development of his own, very personal ideas spans a period of fifty years. He was not really appreciated in America until the 1930s, by which time he had already worked in Europe and Japan. But some of his finest work was on individual houses for the very wealthy, which was more possible in the United States than in Europe. At least two of these houses are world famous, and with good reason. They are *Falling Water,* built in 1936, and *Taliesin West,* begun in 1938.

Another very individual architect in the international style was the Frenchman Le Corbusier (1887-1965). He was particularly interested in building houses for large numbers of people, and in trying to perfect a 'machine for living'. Typical of his work is *Unité d'Habitation,* a housing unit for 1,600 people built in Marseilles, France, which puts forward one answer to the problems of communal living.

From the beginning of this century up to the present day, all developments in architecture have been so closely linked to technological advances that it is impossible to separate the two. Present trends suggest that interchangeable, prefabricated units will play a big part in the architecture of the future.

Above The Villa Savoye, Poissy, built by Le Corbusier (real name, Charles Edouard Jeanneret) in 1929, was designed in an entirely new style. Built in reinforced concrete, the walls of the structure are merely shells and allow the use of open planning. Instead of a staircase, access to the upper floors is by means of a gently sloping ramp.

Right The sculpture of Henry Moore has had a great influence in modern times. His work has always been concerned with the relationship of the internal and external shapes and forms of inanimate objects. This is his *Locking Piece* and is on show beside the River Thames in London.

Right Victor Pasmore is an English artist who believes in three-dimensional construction. This 'painting' is made of wood and plastic and called *Transparent Construction* (1962/3).

Above Typical of the elongated form of Giacometti's figures is this bronze *Man Pointing* (1947).

Sculpture

Most of the movements in 20th-century painting have their counterparts in sculpture. Jacob Epstein (1880-1959), who settled in England in 1906, certainly worked in the language of the Expressionists. His portrait busts show an intense, nervous energy in the way he handled the clay.

The Rumanian sculptor, Constantin Brancusi (1876-1957), on the other hand, carried Abstraction almost as far as it would go. His very simplified forms get the maximum effect from the materials he used – whether it is marble, metal or wood. The work of the Russian sculptor, Naum Gabo, is also abstract – but more than that, it is mathematical. He has made much use of new materials like transparent plastics and nylon. He is also among the sculptors who have introduced real, rather than suggested, movement into their works. Others who have done this are Jean Tinguely and Alexander Calder.

Among the sculptors whose subject was still the human figure were Henry Moore (1898-1986) and Alberto Giacometti (1901-66). Moore was famous for his many different versions of the reclining figure, and Giacometti for his elongated, wistful forms.

The graphic revolution

Today there is a tremendous growth in visual imagery of all kinds. It is easy to see how this has come about. Thanks to scientists and technologists, travel and communication have become faster and easier. Not only can we cross the Atlantic in a few hours, but we can sit in our own homes and watch events on the other side of the Atlantic as they happen. With the pace of life in 'civilised' communities increasing at such a rate, the printed word is at last in danger of losing the power it has held ever since the 15th century. People have got used to doing everything very quickly, and it is quicker to 'read' a picture than it is to read words. As well as this, we now have so many machines to help us at work and in the home that our leisure time is increasing. Formerly, only the rich and idle had time to spend on the arts. Now most people have, and the arts are benefiting.

All this has not happened suddenly. The growth of advertising has had a lot to do with the growth of visual imagery, and this has been going on since the last century. It was the custom for a long time to look down on advertising posters and commercial art generally, but today many of the early posters are collectors' items. It was the realisation that advertising is the crude and living art form of the people that led to the 'Pop Art' movement of the 1950s. Since then, it seems as though the gap between the 'art' of artists and the 'art' of ordinary people is closing at last. William Morris's dream is being realised, but not at all in the way he would have imagined.

And tomorrow? It is impossible to guess. We can only hope that the return of the artist to the community means a really exciting age to come.

Above *Dance to the Music of Time* painted by Nicolas Poussin (1594–1665), a French artist who worked for most of his life in Rome. Poussin was not in sympathy with the Baroque art of his time and, particularly in his later period, his subjects were taken from allegory and mythology, painted in the classical manner with great precision. An example is this scene in which four statuesque figures dance to music played on a lyre by Time.

The world of music and the dance

The urge to make music is very ancient. Simple rhythm and melody, two of the most important features of music, are as old as man himself. Rhythm is a steady beat, holding music together and giving it form. Melody can be found in the sing-song noises a mother may make when rocking her baby to sleep, or the half-sung cry of a hunter as he bolsters up his courage to run forward and face some savage animal. These kinds of acts are instinctive and are much more a part of our natural selves than words. We sing or cry out in such ways without thinking, almost as naturally as we breathe.

In its origins music is almost certainly older than painting, sculpture, poetry or any other means man has found for expressing his thoughts and feelings. But we know far less about the music of early civilisations than we do about their art, literature or religion. We have discovered a few examples of a kind of musical notation, or written music, used by the Egyptians. We also have examples of Egyptian wall paintings which depict people playing various instruments. But whereas we can actually see some of the architecture, sculpture and paintings of ancient Egypt, and their writing can be deciphered and read, the music they made cannot be conjured up out of thin air. We know what their instruments may have sounded like, but not how the peoples of the ancient world organised these sounds into music.

How music is made

Organised sound is a good definition of music. Sound is created by vibrations, or waves, in the air, and every note of music is produced by a set number of sound waves per second, called its frequency. When the frequency of a sound wave is increased the note we hear goes up, and when it is decreased the note goes down. In this way the note's pitch is raised or lowered.

There are three basic ways by which we can produce musical sounds: by striking an object, by plucking or scraping a stretched string, or by

Above Musicians from an Etruscan tomb painting (480–470 BC). The man in the centre plays a double pipe and on the right a man is playing a lyre.

Gregory the Great (540?–604) pope and saint. Born in Rome. After he became pope he sent Augustine to England in 596 to convert the country to Christianity. He was a great administrator and reorganised the ritual and services of the Catholic church. He gave his name to the newly-adopted Gregorian chant.

Right This copy of an old Japanese print shows a musician playing a samisen, a guitar-like instrument with three strings.

blowing into a tube. In each case – the object, or the string, or the air in the tube – vibrates and sets up sound waves. Instruments in general fall into one of these three categories; they are either percussion, stringed or wind instruments. A few instruments do not belong strictly to any one category. The piano, for example, combines the principles of a percussion and a stringed instrument. Also, during the 20th century, experiments have been made with electronic devices, which do depart from these basic principles.

No instrument would be very interesting if it could play only one note, however beautiful that note might be. Fortunately, there are many things determining the pitch of a note, which can be manipulated to give a wide range of notes on nearly every instrument. In the case of stringed instruments, for example, the pitch depends on the tautness, thickness and length of the string. In wind instruments, the length of the tube, as well as the way the player blows into his instrument, determines the pitch of a note.

The tone, or quality of sound, belonging to each instrument has also to be considered. In each case the tone of an instrument, and to a large extent the volume of sound it produces, is decided by its shape and size, and by the materials it is made from.

The musical instruments men have made for themselves down the ages have produced sounds of an amazing variety and range. However, we should remember that the most flexible and expressive instrument of all is the one we carry within us – the human voice. Here the sound waves are produced by air passing between the vocal chords. These are two bands of elastic-like tissue, contained in a space called the glottis, which in turn is found in that part of the throat called the larynx. Muscles attaching the vocal chords to the glottis can stretch them, bend them, bring them close together or hold them apart. No other instrument can match the range of pitch and tone which these physical actions produce.

Western music

Each civilisation has created its own kind of music. Today, the music of India, China or Africa has its own sound, and because of radio and the gramophone, this individual sound can become familiar to people all over the world. But the type of music that is now most popular and widespread belongs, in origin, to the people of Europe. We call it western music, in the same way that we speak of western civilisation. The fact that western music is so widespread is due to the influence of western civilisation itself. When European people explored and settled in other lands, they took with them western customs and culture – and part of this was music. It can be said of western music that it is richer and more varied than that of any other musical tradition, and therefore has more to offer.

Above The sitar is a stringed Indian instrument, played with a plectrum, which developed from the lute of the ancient world.

The Greek modes

The word music comes from the language of the ancient Greeks, who founded so much of western culture. Greek music was based on certain sequences of notes of varying pitch, called modes. These modes, such as the Dorian, Lydian and Aeolian, correspond roughly to our scales of today.

The Greeks believed that each mode was related to a certain state of mind. In the same way today different scales, or keys, are sometimes linked with particular states of mind. Some keys are thought to be 'happy' and others to be 'sad'. Such comparisons are a matter of personal feeling. For the Greeks, however, the character of each mode was definite, and music played in a particular mode was supposed to bring on a certain state of mind in the listener.

The philosopher Pythagoras went much further than this in his thinking. He believed that each of the planets produced its own harmonies, and that the discovery and true interpretation of this 'music of the spheres' would reveal all the secrets of the universe.

The Greek modes are important to an understanding of western music, for they were taken over by the early Christian church. St Ambrose (340?-397) and later Pope Gregory I (540?-604) adapted them for the chanting of prayers and scriptures, and these two kinds of chanting are now known as Ambrosian chant and Gregorian chant.

Plainsong

To chant means to recite to a melody, and for hundreds of years the only European music of which we have any definite record was religious chanting known as plainsong. It was exactly what its name suggests: a song, or melody, which everybody sang together, without any kind of accompaniment. It can still be heard in some monasteries and churches today, though to modern ears it may sound monotonous because it lacks both a recognisable rhythm and harmony.

Harmony is the playing or singing of two or more different notes at once. In ancient Greek music all the voices sang the same melody but, as would happen naturally when boys or women were singing with men, each group sang at a different pitch, probably an octave (eight notes) apart. Harmony first appeared in western music about the 9th century. Instead of everyone in the choir singing the melody on the same note, the lower and higher voices were divided so that the melody was doubled, sometimes an octave apart, and sometimes only four or five notes apart. This made singing easier for all concerned, because the basses did not have to struggle to reach high notes or the tenors to reach low ones. Basses sang the melody of the chant fairly low down in pitch, and the

Above Bronze Age trumpets called *lurs* have been found in various parts of Denmark, dating from the 14th century BC.

Right Notre Dame Cathedral in Paris. Begun in 1163 its western towers were completed about 1240. It is one of the finest examples of Gothic architecture in France. During the Middle Ages the church was the principal home of music and it was at Notre Dame that one of the most famous schools of choral singing flourished during the 12th and 13th centuries.

Above A figure from the Luttrell Psalter, an illuminated collection of psalms made for Sir Geoffrey Luttrell in England in 1340. It contains many illustrations of musicians and this one is playing an early form of bagpipe.

tenors followed them, note for note, at a constant interval higher up in pitch. This type of singing was called *organum*.

Polyphony

Organum singing was an important step forward, and it was soon followed by even more interesting developments. Instead of just one melody being sung at different pitches, two different melodies started to be sung together. The old style was single-voiced, that is, all voices singing a single melody. The new style was called polyphony, meaning many-voiced. And from the time when choirs started to combine different melodies, western music began rapidly to grow and develop.

One of the first places where the new polyphony flourished was Winchester cathedral in England during the 12th and 13th centuries. Even more famous was the Notre Dame School in Paris, so called because it was associated with the building of the great Gothic cathedral of Notre Dame. Belonging to this school of music were Leoninus (12th century) and Perotinus (12th/13th century), two of the earliest European composers we know by name.

Plainsong and *organum* had been fairly easy to memorise and required little practice or rehearsal. There were no separate or independent parts for the singers to learn. Once the chant had started, it continued in a leisurely manner, and musicians found it was sufficient to indicate the approximate course of the music by means of a few signs written over the words to be sung. These signs were called *neumes*.

Polyphonic music was more complex. If two or more separate melodic lines had to be sung together, it was necessary that each group of singers should know their parts thoroughly. A far more exact system of writing down the music was needed, so that it could be properly studied and learned.

This new system of notation took the form of a number of horizontal lines, called staves. One of these staves was made to represent a certain note, called the key note. All the notes written on or between the staves could thus be related accurately to the key note and to each other. The rhythmic beat of the music could also be indicated by placing vertical lines across the staves. This had the effect of dividing the music up into bars.

One of the pioneers of this kind of notation was a Benedictine monk called Guido, who lived in the monastery at Arezzo, in Italy. Guido d'Arezzo (990?-1050?) also invented a system for the easy memorisation of music, naming the notes by syllables. This enabled singers to recall the relative pitch of one note to another, and to sing a piece of music they had previously learned, once the key note had been established. This very useful idea was revised in the 19th century, when the English system of tonic sol-fa, with its familiar symbols – doh, ray, me, fah, soh, lah, te, doh – was introduced to bring it up to date with modern musical practice.

The Middle Ages

In the Middle Ages the church was the most powerful institution. It told people what to think and believe, it laid down many of the laws, it ran the schools and universities, and it had most of the money. All artists and craftsmen looked to the church for work, in building and decorating the great Gothic cathedrals, and in writing and performing the music that was required for the services.

However, the church did gradually lose a little of its control, especially over the arts. Miracle Plays, or Morality Plays as they were sometimes called, were organised by the clergy to teach congregations who could neither read nor write something of the lives of saints, and of the life of Christ himself, in a way they could enjoy and understand. These sacred plays were originally performed inside churches and cathedrals. But as time went on they began to be performed outside, where there was more room and more elaborate productions could be mounted. There they became public entertainments, often with musical items added. They became increasingly secular, or non-religious.

Much of the best secular music of the Middle Ages was played and sung by the troubadours. These were minstrels from southern France who earned their living by travelling from castle to castle, entertaining kings, princes and barons with their poems and songs. England had her own band of minstrels, called gleemen or bards. In Germany the minstrels were known as minnesingers, a word meaning love-singers. Walther von der Vogelweide was a famous minnesinger. Another was Tannhäuser, who went on one of the crusades to the Holy Land. The legend that grew up around him formed the basis for Wagner's opera of the same name.

The minstrels died out when the feudal system came to an end, and the power of the lords in their castles declined. Life became increasingly centred on towns and cities. It also became better organised and offered new opportunities for artists.

Musicians felt free to try out new harmonies and rhythms, and notation encouraged them to sit down and compose entirely new pieces of music, instead of simply carrying on the traditions of plainsong and *organum*. Guillaume de Machaut (1300?-77) was the most celebrated musician of this period and one of the first true composers. Most of his work was for the church but he wrote secular music as well. He and other musicians of the time called their music *ars nova*, the new art, to distinguish it from the *ars antiqua*, the old art, of the previous century.

Above In this painting by Fra Angelico, *Christ Glorified in the Court of Heaven*, a number of 15th-century instruments can be seen.

Left An illuminated music manuscript dating from the early Middle Ages. The music was drawn in by hand and the side panels and capital letter beautifully painted. To complete each page of such music would take many weeks.

Right The virginal is a small type of harpsichord in which the strings are plucked and not struck with a hammer, as in a modern piano. This instrument, made in Italy, is said to have belonged to Queen Elizabeth I of England.

Right The Italian sculptor Luca Della Robbia (1399–1482) created a musicians' gallery in Florence Cathedral and part of the decoration is this group of singers, or cantoria, carved in marble.

Giovanni Palestrina (1525?–94) Italian composer. For most of his life he was master of music at the Vatican, where he became the greatest 16th-century composer of unaccompanied choral music. His Masses are landmarks in the history of religious music.

The Renaissance

Throughout the Middle Ages the church had taught that man should be content to do things simply to the greater glory of God. The Renaissance, with its rebirth of interest in the philosophy, literature and art of ancient Greece and Rome, gave to men a renewed belief in their own importance in the scheme of life. People did not turn against the church but they did start to think more about their life on earth rather than being completely absorbed with the life to come. It was a fundamental change of attitude, in a time which produced the art of Leonardo da Vinci and Michelangelo, the scientific discoveries of Galileo, and the voyages of Columbus and other great explorers.

In music, composers like Guillaume de Machaut had already expressed something of the Renaissance spirit, when they thought of themselves as individual artists and not just as servants of the church. One of the first true Renaissance composers was an Englishman, John Dunstable (died 1453). His talents were so outstanding that he inspired a whole new school of musicians who were known as the Burgundians, because they lived and worked in the old French kingdom of Burgundy.

The Burgundian composers, of whom Guillaume Dufay (1400?-74) was the outstanding member, wrote a large number of *chansons*, the French word for songs. These were secular pieces and, because of their accompaniments, they were quite revolutionary in their time. During the Middle Ages the only instrument that mattered was the voice. Nearly all music was choral music. The Burgundians, in the accompaniments to their *chansons*, made imaginative use of such instruments as an early kind of flute, blown through its end like a recorder, and the viol, ancestor of our modern violin. From that time on, instrumental music gradually gained in importance and popularity.

Nevertheless, some of the finest choral and religious music was written during the Renaissance period. Josquin des Prés (1450?-1521) and Roland de Lassus (1530-94) were both born in the Low Countries, and belonged to another musical school called the Netherlands school. They wrote choral music of great distinction.

Even more beautiful was the music of Giovanni Pierluigi da Palestrina (1525?-94). Composers had become so absorbed in the techniques of polyphony, adding more and more melodic lines to their compositions, that very often it was difficult or impossible to hear the actual words they were setting to music. The church objected to such over-elaborate settings of religious texts, and insisted that the music should allow the words to be heard clearly. In meeting this requirement, Palestrina composed Masses, Lamentations and Magnificats of great purity and perfection.

Music of the Reformation

Palestrina wrote music for the Roman Catholic church. It was the only church in western Europe, until a monk named Martin Luther (1483-1546) led a revolt against the authority of the pope, and so started the religious movement known as the Reformation.

Luther established his own church. He did away with much of the ritual of the Catholic church, and encouraged his congregations to sing hymns and generally take a greater part in acts of worship. For his hymns he adapted a number of traditional German folk tunes. These hymns were called chorales, and they inspired Bach when he came to write his great choral works two centuries later.

In England the Reformation led to the establishment of the Church of England, but there was a long and bitter struggle between this new church and the old Catholic families. Consequently, composers of the time, like William Byrd (1543-1623) and Thomas Tallis (1505?-85), found themselves called upon to write music for both churches. Byrd was also the founder of the secular English madrigal. The madrigal was a musical setting of verses, usually to be sung by a small group of five or six people. Madrigals had already been written in other parts of Europe, but none could match the English madrigals for tunefulness and variety. In addition to Byrd himself, most attractive madrigals were composed by Thomas Morley (1557-1603), Thomas Weelkes (1575?-1623), Orlando Gibbons (1583-1625) and John Wilbye (1574-1638).

Even finer were the songs of John Dowland (1563-1626). These were mostly composed for solo voices, with an accompaniment written for the lute, an instrument something like a guitar. Dowland was so fond of the lute that he also wrote some pieces especially for it.

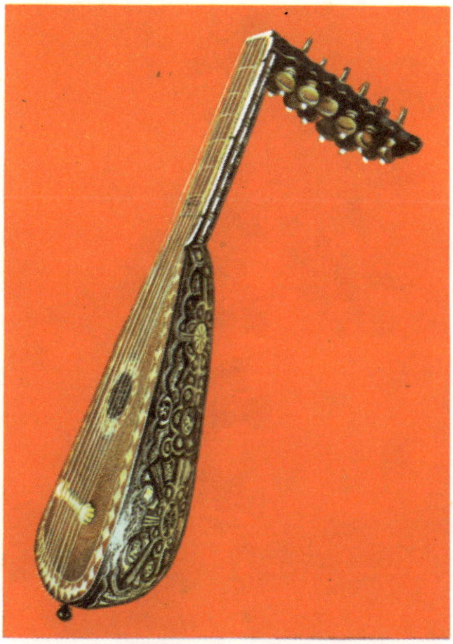

Left A soprano lute made at Milan in Italy in the 18th century. The lute is a very ancient instrument and was introduced into Europe from Arabic lands in the 13th century. In the 16th century it became the chief instrument both for playing in the home and for the professional musicians. The strings of the lute were usually plucked but there were also lutes played with a bow.

The birth of opera

During the 16th century, Count Giovanni Bardi (1534-1612), who lived in Florence, had the idea of setting some of the plays and legends of ancient Greece to music. The idea appealed to other Italian poets and musicians of the time, and they formed themselves into a group called the *camerata*. Vincenzo Galilei (1520-91), father of the astronomer and scientist, Galileo Galilei, was one of them.

This was how opera started. Opera is a combination of drama and music, requiring both a stage and an orchestra for its performance. Some of the first operas were written by Jacopo Peri (1561-1633). In them the dramatic action on stage was still much more important than the music. But with Claudio Monteverdi (1567-1643), music became the chief ingredient of opera.

Monteverdi lived and worked in Venice, which was particularly famous at that time for its instrumentalists. Monteverdi quickly took advantage of this and recruited the best of them for his orchestra. Before this time there had been no orchestras. Individual musicians supplied music

Claudio Monteverdi (1567–1643) Italian composer. Born at Cremona he was a violinist in the service of the Duke of Mantua. Became music master at St Mark's, Venice in 1613. His operas *Orfeo* and *Arianna* mark the beginning of modern opera.

Above Bach wrote many pieces for the organ, an instrument he loved, and for much of his life he was employed as a church organist and choir master.

Henry Purcell (1659–95) English composer. He was the son of a court musician and himself a chorister at the Chapel Royal. His most famous works are his operas and choral odes written to celebrate official occasions. He was recognised in his day as the greatest English musician and composer.

when and where it was required. An orchestra was a group of musicians who played together regularly. This way they could learn to play music which would have been too difficult and complex if they gathered together for just one occasion and then all separated again.

The great thing about Monteverdi's operas is their rich orchestral accompaniment. Such instrumental writing was entirely new. Monteverdi's opera *Orfeo,* based on the story of Orpheus in the underworld from Greek mythology, is still sometimes performed.

Jean-Baptiste Lully (1632-87) was Italian by birth, but French by adoption. His talents were recognised by Louis XIV. This king was known as *Le Roi Soleil* – The Sun King – because of the splendour of his reign. He attracted to his court many of the most gifted men of his day, and in this way Lully came to collaborate with the great French dramatist Molière. Out of this collaboration came the French operatic style, which included an overture (an orchestral introduction), ballet sequences and the use of a large chorus on stage.

Lully's influence quickly spread abroad, particularly to England, where Henry Purcell (1659-95) was the most gifted and original composer of his generation. Purcell wrote music in every style of his day: odes for festive occasions, instrumental pieces, songs and cantatas, and a large amount of church music. He also wrote music for the stage, including one very fine opera, *Dido and Aeneas,* based upon an event from the Trojan war. Purcell remained the greatest English-born composer for nearly 200 years.

The Baroque age

Monteverdi and Purcell composed with great skill and imagination for the orchestra, and the instruments they wrote for were being improved all the time. This was especially so with stringed instruments. During the 17th century the viols of the Renaissance and Tudor periods were gradually replaced by violins and cellos, which were both more expressive in tone and far more flexible to play. This change was greatly helped by the wonderful craftsmanship of the violin makers of Cremona, a town in northern Italy. Nicolo Amati (1596-1684) and Antonio Stradivari (1644-1737) were the two most celebrated violin and cello makers of this time and place. Instruments made by these two master craftsmen are today worth large sums of money.

The qualities of violins, violas and cellos were much appreciated by the new generation of Italian musicians. The two outstanding composers here were Arcangelo Corelli (1653-1713) and Antonio Vivaldi (1678-1741). Both were brilliant violinists themselves, and the music they composed for strings is especially rich and exuberant. It is called Baroque music, because in general character it matches the art and architecture which is given the same name. Good examples of the Baroque style of sculpture and architecture are the magnificent fountains which Giovanni Bernini built in Rome.

While Stradivari and his fellow craftsmen were making the world's finest violins, yet another Italian was doing equally important work with keyboard instruments. He was Bartolommeo Cristofori (1655-1731). By the 17th century there was a wide variety of keyboard instruments, including the virginal, clavichord, harpsichord and spinet. They were called keyboard instruments because of a series of balanced levers called keys which, when depressed by the fingers of the hand, operated a mechanism which plucked a set of strings. They were like mechanical harps. Cristofori invented a mechanism whereby a hammer struck the string instead of plucking it, and then immediately bounced back into its original position, leaving the string to vibrate. He called his invention the *piano forte,* literally the 'soft loud', because of the greater range of tone it produced. In reality it was some years before his pianofortes sounded very different from harpsichords, but he had achieved a technical breakthrough in keyboard instruments.

Just as some composers had specialised in writing for strings, so the development of keyboard instruments inspired other composers of the age. In Italy there was Domenico Scarlatti (1685-1757); in France, François Couperin (1668-1733) and Jean Philippe Rameau (1683-1764); and in Germany, Johann Sebastian Bach (1685-1750).

Bach and Handel

One of Bach's greatest keyboard compositions was a set of forty-eight preludes and fugues called *Das Wohltemperierte Klavier*. This title means The Well-Tuned Keyboard, and with the music Bach wished to demonstrate a new system of tuning keyboard instruments which enabled them to be played equally well in all the twenty-four major and minor keys. These preludes and fugues also established the entire system of keys and scales which, by the middle of the 17th century, had replaced the old church modes.

Bach's forty-eight preludes and fugues are a major landmark in musical history. They were written for technical reasons, but they are also wonderful pieces of music, covering a wide range of expression. The fugue, in particular, was Bach's favourite musical form.

Bach also wrote a large number of other fugues for the organ, many of which are most powerful pieces of

Above The pianoforte as we know it today was invented by Cristofori in about 1709. The one seen here dates from 1720 and is in the form of a mechanised dulcimer with hammered strings. The action which Cristofori 'invented' was probably known in the 14th century but was never developed. Even Cristofori's pianos were not properly recognised or used until the 1770s when Mozart began to write for the instrument and to play it himself.

Left A violin made by Antonio Stradivari in Cremona in 1722. The violins of the period combined features of several earlier instruments such as the rebec, the fiddle and the *lira da braccio*. The viol, although it sounds a similar word, is not a true ancestor of the violin.

Above During the 18th century the gardens at Ranelagh and Vauxhall in London were the resorts of fashionable society. They became places of entertainment where concerts and firework displays were given in the evenings. This drawing based on a late 18th-century print shows Vauxhall Gardens which, although first laid out during 1661, did not become popular until 100 years later. On the right of the picture can be seen the statue of Handel, whose music was often played at the concerts.

music. He loved the organ, and was employed as a church organist and choirmaster for most of his life. In this capacity he was also called upon to write sacred cantatas – a word coming from the Italian *cantare,* to sing – and composed well over a hundred, suited for every event in the church calendar. His three choral masterpieces are the *St John* and *St Matthew Passions* and the Mass in B minor. The two Passions are settings of the story of Jesus Christ, according to the gospels of St John and St Matthew, and they are two of the greatest choral works in the world.

Bach was a serious-minded man, but he could write very attractive secular music. This included arrangements for the violin, cello or harpsichord of various dances popular in his day, such as the courante, pavane and saraband. Such collections of dances are called suites. He was also commissioned by the Margrave of Brandenburg to write a set of six orchestral suites, which we know today as the Brandenburg Concertos. They are superb examples of the Baroque orchestral style.

George Frideric Handel (1685-1759) was born in the same year as Bach, in one of the old provinces of north Germany. The two men, however, were very different. Bach stayed in Germany, where he married and settled down. Handel, however, travelled to Italy as a young man, then to England, where he made his home and adopted British nationality. His fortunes fluctuated wildly, as he fell in and out of favour with the English court and London society.

Handel gained a name for himself in the one major form that Bach had not attempted – opera. Although the form suited his style, and some of his operas are still performed, it is the oratorios that are now world famous.

Oratorio is a kind of sacred opera. It gained its name from the fact that the earliest of them had been performed in an oratory, or small chapel, of the church of St Philip Neri in Rome. This was in the late 16th century. By Handel's time oratorio had grown considerably in size and popularity. The finest of Handel's oratorios is *Messiah,* containing the Hallelujah Chorus, first sung in Dublin in 1742. The English king, George II, was so moved by the music that he rose from his seat and stood for the remainder of the piece. This was one of the most celebrated tributes ever paid to a piece of music.

Handel also composed purely orchestral music. He wrote a number of works called *concerti grossi*, similar in style to many of the pieces for string orchestra written by Corelli and Vivaldi; a group of organ concertos; and two famous pieces written for festive occasions, *The Water Music* and *Music for the Royal Fireworks*.

Sonata and symphony

Bach and Handel brought the Baroque period of music to a close. By the middle of the 18th century music was moving in entirely new directions.

This was the period known as the Age of Reason. It was inspired by the work of philosophers and writers like Descartes and Voltaire, who believed that reason, tolerance and social justice were important in the search for a happier world. Though the mass of the people remained poor and ignorant a more reasonable and humane attitude to life did emerge, and those with the money and the time set about making their lives as agreeable as possible. Among other things, this gave rise to a light and decorative style of architecture known as Rococo.

There was a corresponding style of music also known as Rococo, and Georg Philipp Telemann (1681-1767) was a composer in this style. He wrote a great amount of music for the church, but also composed large quantities of light and attractive music for the elaborate social occasions which were a mark of 18th-century life among the rich. One of his pieces was written in honour of a pet canary's birthday!

The other important feature of the Age of Reason was a love of form and proportion. This was acquired from a study of the buildings of ancient Greece, such as the Parthenon in Athens, which had been designed on strictly mathematical lines. Again, music soon found its equivalent form of expression.

Previously, composers had taken one or more melodies and woven them together. Now they developed a method of composition which allowed them to use different melodies separately, like musical building blocks, and so construct a single piece of music, modelled on much the same principles of balance and proportion as those applied to architecture. The result was sonata form, so called because it was mainly used in pieces of music called sonatas. Like so many words in music, sonata comes from an Italian word, *suonare*, meaning to sound. It is a good choice of word because the much clearer and stronger sound produced by the improved keyboard instruments of the 18th century was ideal for the greater tonal contrasts of sonatas and sonata form.

An early composer of sonatas was Carl Philipp Emanuel Bach (1714-88), the most gifted of J. S. Bach's sons. C. P. E. Bach, in particular, took sonata form and general keyboard technique a long way forward.

The orchestral equivalent of the sonata was the symphony. This originated from the earlier sinfonia – an orchestral interlude in larger choral works and operas. Its development took place largely in Germany, because at that time Germany was still divided into dozens of separate kingdoms and principalities, each of which considered it a matter of pride and prestige to maintain its own opera house and court orchestra. Consequently, there were greater opportunities there than anywhere else for new experiments in orchestral music.

George Frideric Handel (1685–1759) German-English composer. Studied law but became organist at Halle Cathedral in Germany when he was 17 years old. Played in an opera orchestra. Appointed to the court of the Elector of Hanover, who later became George I of England. Thereafter, Handel remained in London and became very popular. He is remembered today chiefly for his well-known oratorios, which are often performed. In addition to these he wrote over 40 operas.

Above Joseph Haydn was twenty-eight years old when he entered the service of the Esterházys. Part of his duties was to compose chamber and orchestral music to entertain the family and its guests. Among the music composed by Haydn during this period were some 30 concertos, 40 quartets and many operas.

One of the best and most enterprising German orchestras of the time was in the Rhineland town of Mannheim, and the so-called Mannheim school of musicians was closely connected with the early development of the symphony. The leading composer of the Mannheim school was Johann Stamitz (1717-57). Other composers of the period were Karl von Dittersdorf (1739-99), Johann Christian Bach (1735-82), another of J. S. Bach's sons, and the Englishman, William Boyce (1710-79). All of them wrote symphonies, though in many cases they did not sound so very different from the operatic overtures and other pieces of the period.

Haydn's symphonies

The man who went further than any other to reshape the orchestra, and to establish the symphony as the most important kind of orchestral composition, was Franz Joseph Haydn (1732-1809). For a large part of his working life, Haydn was *kapellmeister*, that is, director of music, to one of the great aristocratic families of the old Austro-Hungarian Empire, the Esterhazys. He got on very well with his employers, and while he had to spend much of his time carrying out his official duties – writing music for special occasions and regularly rehearsing the court orchestra and choir – he was also given every opportunity to experiment with the new musical forms and styles of the period.

Bach and Handel had treated all the instruments of the orchestra in much the same way, simply dividing them up according to whether they were treble or bass. On this rough-and-ready basis, they often wrote for the trumpet in much the same way as they wrote for the violins. They and their contemporaries did not really think of the orchestra in purely orchestral terms.

Haydn grouped the instruments of the orchestra into definite 'families': the strings, woodwind and brass. He thought very carefully about what each instrument was best suited to do, and in this way ensured that when the instruments were playing together they always produced the clearest and most effective orchestral sound. The modern symphony orchestra is two or three times as large and complex as the orchestra Haydn wrote for, but the basic orchestral framework which he established remains.

Haydn wrote over a hundred symphonies. The early ones still show him experimenting with both form and orchestration, but by the time he was famous and had accepted an invitation to visit England, his style of composition had come close to perfection. All his best-known symphonies have four movements, that is, four separate pieces which go to make up the whole work.

Because he was such a success with the British public, Haydn visited London twice, and for each occasion he wrote six new symphonies. They are known as the Salomon symphonies because a London impresario, J. P. Salomon, was the man who arranged the visits. They are numbers 93 to 104 and carry such famous nicknames as 'Surprise', 'Military' and 'Clock'.

Mozart

The symphonies, sonatas, and other instrumental works of Haydn are almost completely free from any kind of emotional expression. They are what we might term 'pure' music; pieces which concentrate purely on matters of musical form and style. They belong to the classical school, which lasted from about 1750 to 1800.

Wolfgang Amadeus Mozart (1756-91) is generally thought of as a classical composer, because his symphonies, concertos and sonatas obey the rules of sonata form and other musical forms of the classical period. What is not at all 'classical' about some of Mozart's music is the very personal note which it strikes. Some of his finest compositions sound as though he were pouring his heart out in his music.

Mozart was a child prodigy. He could play the harpsichord when he was four, and began to compose little pieces of music at the age of six. Because of his extraordinary gifts, he was taken on tour round the courts of Europe, playing before kings and queens. But when he was no longer a child, people lost interest in him. He had to earn his own living as a fairly humble musician. For a time he was employed by the archbishop of Salzburg, but after a quarrel he lost his job and was never regularly employed again. He did not earn enough money to keep himself, his wife and children decently clothed and fed, and when he died he was buried in a pauper's grave.

During the last ten difficult years of his life Mozart composed some of the greatest music ever written. Despite the tragic tone of some of this music, and the fact that his experiences must have influenced his art to some degree, it is clear that the spirit of Mozart's genius transcends the circumstance of his everyday life. The delightful opera *Così fan tutte*, a joyous and witty masterpiece, was written against a background of poverty, debt and anxiety.

Above The young Mozart made his début when barely six years old, first at Munich then at Vienna. He played before the royal courts all over Europe. His first composition was published in Paris when he was seven and in 1766 a concert was given in Amsterdam for which he composed all the music. He first appeared as conductor when he was twelve. His success as a child musician was not repeated in adult life and he suffered many hardships before his early death.

The element of drama in much of Mozart's orchestral and instrumental music came from his wide experience as an operatic composer. During the early part of the 18th century, opera had become a trivial entertainment, full of meaningless conventions. Christoph Willibald Gluck (1714-87) had done much to restore some real power and purpose to opera, and Mozart was able to build upon Gluck's valuable reforms. The operas he wrote with the Italian librettist Lorenzo da Ponte (1749-1834) are among the finest ever created. *The Marriage of Figaro* and *Don Giovanni* contain music which is not only beautiful in its own right, but also reflects every change of

Right Beethoven was taught music from the age of four and his teachers predicted that he would be a second Mozart. It is said that when Mozart first heard him play in 1787, he exclaimed 'He will make a noise in the world some day'. Early in his career he met Count Waldstein who became his life-long patron. He began to go deaf early in life but it was 1822 before his hearing had entirely gone. Beethoven died during a violent thunderstorm and his funeral was attended by some 20,000 people.

Above The serpent is an instrument of the old cornett family. It consists of a wooden tube about 2·5 metres long which is folded into its serpent-like shape to make it manageable. It was first used in about 1590 and went out of fashion well over a hundred years ago.

mood and twist of plot. The characters are presented as real people rather than theatrical puppets.

Beethoven

Ludwig van Beethoven (1770-1827) identified his music much more closely with moral and political ideas. Two of his most important works, the opera *Fidelio* and the *Choral* symphony, are specifically to do with freedom from political tyranny and the universal brotherhood of man. His views were shaped largely by the French revolution, which started in 1789, when he was still only nineteen years old. Beethoven's imagination was fired by the revolutionary ideals of *Liberté, Egalité, Fraternité* (Liberty, Equality, Brotherhood), and some years later he dedicated his *Eroica* symphony to Napoleon Bonaparte as the liberator of Europe from the old order of kings and princes. He changed the dedication when Napoleon was himself crowned emperor. Beethoven saw this as a betrayal of the revolution and angrily struck Napoleon's name from the title page of the original score.

As far as his own life was concerned, though, Beethoven was prepared to forget his ideals and allow himself to be supported by aristocrats. His argument was that he had genius and therefore deserved the favours of people with more money but less talent than himself. Beethoven had the strength of personality to do what Mozart had failed to do – maintain his position as a largely independent artist, writing music that he wanted to write rather than music someone ordered him to write, and getting it accepted. It is significant that during his lifetime some of the first copyright laws came into force, which helped an artist to receive fair payment for his work. Beethoven ended up sick, penniless and alone, but this was largely through bad management of his domestic affairs. He had already done more than anyone else to raise the artist to the level we know today.

The real crisis in Beethoven's life came when he realised, at the age of thirty, that he was going deaf. This is about the worst thing that could happen to a musician. Beethoven's determination to rise above such affliction, and the way this determination expressed itself in his music, is the central feature of his art.

While Mozart wrote with every appearance of ease, Beethoven often composed with the greatest difficulty. This is because he would start off with some immense vision of what he wanted to express, and then had to struggle towards it. He left behind him a number of sketch books, and from them we can see how he hammered away at his material, continually revising it until it was eventually to his satisfaction. There is seldom any of the sheer grace and charm we find in Mozart. Instead there is a wonderful sense of growth and strength to Beethoven's music.

The most famous of Beethoven's works are the nine symphonies. The fact that he wrote only nine, when compared with Haydn's output, shows how the symphony grew in Beethoven's hands. He worked on some of them, on and off, for years. There is a 'bigness' to the symphonies which has to do not so much with their actual length as with the variety and concentration of ideas which fills them.

As a young man, Beethoven was a fine pianist, and when his deafness put a stop to that side of his career, he

Left Chamber music was originally meant to be performed in a chamber, or room, and not in a concert hall. As now used, the term is applied to any music written for a small combination of instruments, with one instrument to a part. The picture shows a string quartet, two violins, viola and cello, which is the most important chamber music combination. The term chamber music was first used in English in 1603.

concentrated on writing music for the piano. Listening to his piano sonatas today it is hard to believe that the instrument he was writing for still looked and sounded rather like a harpsichord. It is almost as though he willed that instrument to grow into the modern grand piano, through the power of his own music.

The Romantic movement

A number of Beethoven's contemporaries, such as Ludwig (Louis) Spohr (1784-1859) and Johann Hummel (1778-1837), were very highly thought of when they were alive, but today they are largely forgotten. Muzio Clementi (1752-1832) only remains well known because piano students usually have to work their way through his exercises, which is not the happiest way to be remembered.

By contrast, Franz Schubert (1797-1828) was almost totally ignored both during his lifetime and for years after his death, while today he is recognised as one of the greatest of all composers.

Schubert wrote music which contains glorious melodies. Indeed, there have been few composers who could write tunes to compare with those of Schubert. It is not surprising, perhaps, that he also wrote so many songs, because of all forms of music nothing needs a good melody more than a song. Schubert wrote over six hundred songs and the best of them are without doubt among the finest ever written, with a truly amazing range of expression. With one or two exceptions, all these songs were written for solo voice with piano accompaniment. The accompaniment is usually as fine as the melody itself and for this reason is well worth listening to.

For his songs Schubert selected words from the work of German poets like Goethe and Heine. They are spoken of as Romantic poets, and Schubert, so far as his songs are concerned, is regarded as one of the first truly Romantic composers. The word romantic as used in the arts describes the opposite of classical. While classical music, painting and literature were much more concerned with *how* ideas and themes should be presented in terms of form and style, artists of the Romantic movement considered that what they had to say was more important than the way in which they said it. True classical music was free from any particular emotion. Romantic music is almost always concerned with such themes as love, joy or sorrow.

Franz Schubert (1797–1828) Austrian composer. Entered the royal chapel choir at Vienna in 1808. His first known composition dates from 1810. He composed at astonishing speed, particularly between the years 1813–16. His whole life was a struggle against poverty and disappointment. He revered Beethoven but was too modest ever to approach him. He created the art of lieder (German lyric songs) and was its greatest exponent. He died of typhus.

Above Berlioz, the greatest of French composers, loved to write music for large-scale forces of singers and musicians. His operas are massive, unwieldy affairs and are rarely performed. His symphonic music usually has a story to tell and he set to music several great plays by such authors as Shakespeare and Goethe. He was also an accomplished musical journalist and his memoirs are still widely read today.

Schubert called his songs by their German name of *lieder*. They amounted to a new musical form, and several important composers after him were also inspired to compose *lieder*. These included Schumann, Brahms, Strauss and Hugo Wolf (1860-1903).

The first of these, Robert Schumann (1810-56), was also a brilliant pianist – before he damaged one of his hands – and wrote some of the first, and best, Romantic music for the piano. One of his most popular works is *Carnaval*, a group of piano pieces which reflects the two contrasting sides of his character, the one dreamy and poetic, and the other bold and adventurous. Unhappily, the contrasts in Schumann's character developed into a mental disorder as he grew older. But his piano compositions, such as *Carnaval* and *Papillons* (Butterflies), are wonderfully fresh and full of romantic charm.

Another great composer of early Romantic music for the piano was Frédéric Chopin (1810-49). Though his mother was French and he lived for most of his life in France, Chopin was born and brought up in Poland, and he thought of himself as a Pole. The dances and melodies of Polish folk music figure largely in his compositions, especially his mazurkas and polonaises. Other musical forms which Chopin adapted to his own special style were the ballade, scherzo, waltz and nocturne. This last form he inherited from the Irish composer John Field (1782-1837). Because of the way Chopin brought out the piano's most expressive qualities he was sometimes known as the 'poet of the piano'.

The Hungarian Franz Liszt (1811-86) was more of a showman at the keyboard than a poet. During his long career the piano grew into the concert grand of today – a massive, sturdy instrument, capable of making music ring in people's ears. Liszt put it through its paces as no one else had done, and in the process made himself one of the star attractions of the age. As a young man he had striking good looks, and ladies are said to have fainted with emotion at the sight of him on the concert platform.

Liszt did have a deeper musical side to his character, though. One important thing he did was to transcribe

Beethoven's symphonies for the piano. This may seem a bit pointless today, when we have the radio and the gramophone to give us all the music we want, but in Liszt's own day there were no such things. Actual concert going was still confined to the rich, and most people had to make their own musical entertainment. Nearly every front room had a piano in it, and those who played reasonably well could thus get to know great pieces of music which they might otherwise never have heard.

Growth of the orchestra

It was not only the piano that Romantic composers were interested in. The orchestra, which had grown considerably during Beethoven's lifetime, offered them even greater opportunities for the treatment of romantic themes. These composers were especially interested in orchestral 'colour', that is, combining the instruments in new and unusual ways so as to produce descriptive effects, in much the same way as a painter mixes his paints to create just the right shade of colour in his painting.

In the past, composers had sometimes used the orchestra to describe scenes or events. Haydn had written a remarkable piece in his oratorio *The Creation* representing chaos. Beethoven had included a movement describing a thunderstorm in his *Pastoral* symphony. But one of the first composers to concentrate on using the orchestra to 'paint' a picture or capture the atmosphere of an occasion was Felix Mendelssohn-Bartholdy (1809-47). He did this in an overture he wrote for Shakespeare's play *A Midsummer Night's Dream.* The play is a fantasy involving fairies and other magical creatures, and the way Mendelssohn set the scene with his music was itself truly magical. He was only seventeen years old when he wrote it.

Another famous descriptive piece by Mendelssohn is his *Hebrides* overture, also known as 'Fingal's Cave'. This was inspired by a visit to the Western Isles of Scotland, and here the scene is of the sea surging round the entrance to the famous cave.

A more daring orchestrator than Mendelssohn was the Frenchman, Hector Berlioz (1803-69). He wrote a book on the subject, in which he listed many different combinations of instruments and described exactly what sound effects each would produce. In his own *Fantastic Symphony*, Berlioz conjures up the most thrilling impression of a witches' dance, and in another of his works, called *Harold in Italy*, he creates the impression of pilgrims walking along a road to the sound of a monastery bell.

Berlioz also wrote music on a very grand scale. In his *Grande Messe des Morts* (Mass for the Dead), he demanded brass bands, in addition to a large orchestra and chorus, and with these resources created the most startling effects. Many of Berlioz's experiments in orchestration were too advanced and revolutionary for the people of his day, and he found it difficult to get his music performed. But he paved the way for composers like Wagner, who were to build up the orchestra into the huge and elaborate ensemble we know today.

The Viennese school

Johannes Brahms (1833-97) was not at all like Berlioz. He tended to look back to the traditions of the past for inspiration. He was born and brought up in Hamburg, but settled in Vienna. Mozart, Beethoven and Schubert had all lived and worked in that city before him. Brahms saw himself as the latest member of this most distinguished line of composers whom we now speak of as belonging to the Viennese school. This made him feel a great weight of responsibility. He worked over a

Above In this picture Clara Schumann is seen at the piano, while her husband Robert stands before her. Clara was a brilliant pianist and after Robert's death in 1856 played on concert platforms all over Europe for more than thirty years. She died in 1896.

Frédéric Chopin (1810–49) Polish composer of French parentage. First played in public at the age of eight. He found fame easily in Vienna and later in Paris. He wrote very little for the orchestra and nearly all his works were composed for the piano, which he played brilliantly. He suffered all his life from consumption and eventually died of it in Paris.

Above Richard Wagner wrote his own epic stories for his big and powerful operas. Often these were founded on the great German myths of legendary heroes and gods. Wagner's portrait is shown here, while in the background is a scene from one of his most popular music dramas *The Flying Dutchman*

Johannes Brahms (1833–97) German musician. Received his early training from his father, a double-bass player in a Hamburg theatre. He was encouraged by Schumann to write music. Brahms devoted his life to composition and he excelled in every form except opera.

period of nearly twenty years on his first symphony, because he felt that people would compare it with Beethoven's last symphonic work, the *Choral* symphony, and he was afraid that his own symphony might not live up to such high standards.

Brahms never laboured over any of his other works to the same extent, but he was always an extremely careful worker, and a highly self-critical one. He probably destroyed more of his music than he allowed to be published. He wrote four big symphonies, two piano concertos, a violin concerto, a concerto for violin and cello, and a great number of smaller works. Most of these are what we might call serious, or even heavy, meaning that a great deal of thought and effort went into their creation, and that they need to be listened to with close attention if they are to be properly appreciated.

To this extent Brahms was very much the successor of Beethoven. But Brahms did not have Beethoven's inner fire and drive. Instead, his nature contained a much softer, more lyrical side. His second symphony is especially rich and mellow in character. He had just returned from holiday in Italy when he wrote it. Much of his piano music is almost as delicate and graceful as pieces by Schumann or Mendelssohn. Brahms always kept a firm grasp on his emotions, but he had a definite romantic side to his nature, despite his deep respect for the traditions of the past.

Richard Wagner

If Brahms kept a firm grip on his emotions, then his contemporary and fellow countryman, Richard Wagner (1813-83), squeezed every last drop from his own emotions in the creation of his music. Brahms, like Bach, never attempted to write an opera. Wagner wrote almost nothing but operas. He wrote probably the biggest and grandest operas that have ever been performed.

For centuries the German language had come to mean a great deal to the people of the different kingdoms and principalities of that country, as the one thing they shared in common. Mozart had used German in several of his operas, and in this connection also made use of a style called *singspiel*. In the Italian operas of his day everything was sung, including the passages of conversation which linked together the various arias and choruses. This style, going back to the days of Monteverdi, is known as recitative and aria. *Singspiel* – which means, literally, sing play – allowed the actual conversation to be spoken, as it would be in real life, and so added to the value of the language.

After Mozart, in the operatic field, came Carl Maria von Weber (1786-1826), who also used the German language in the form of *singspiel*. He wrote an opera called *Der Freischütz* (The Marksman) which has an exciting scene where all kinds of hair-raising magic and witchcraft are practised. Weber conjured up the scene brilliantly, and in doing so produced one of the first truly romantic operas.

Wagner was able to take over the development of German opera from these beginnings. He also wrote at a time when Germany was becoming a unified country. Wagner was inspired to combine music with the German language to the point where he believed he had created a new art form. To emphasise this he called his operas music-dramas.

Wagner's greatest work, in terms of size and complexity, is a cycle of four operas together called *Der Ring des Nibelungen* (The Ring of the Nibelungs), which is based upon Norse and Teutonic mythology. Wagner wrote the entire libretto himself, before he started composing the music. He also had a lot to do with the design and building of a special opera house at Bayreuth, in Bavaria, for performances of 'The Ring'. It was one of the biggest creative undertakings that anyone has ever attempted in the whole history of the theatre.

Yet, in the middle of it all, Wagner broke off the work to compose two other operas, which, in their different ways, are just as great as any part of 'The Ring'. One was *Tristan and Isolde*, and the other *The Mastersingers of Nuremberg*.

To obtain both the power and the effects he wanted Wagner enlarged the orchestra until it had reached the size of the modern symphony orchestra. He also demanded of each member of the orchestra standards of performance which previously only soloists had been expected to achieve. He developed a musical device called a *leitmotiv*, which was a theme or phrase intended to represent a particular character or idea. By the increasing use of the *leitmotiv* Wagner did away with the need for conventional arias, separated by stretches of conversation. Instead he was able to thread the music together into a vast and continuous tapestry of sound. Finally, Wagner revolutionised music by his use of harmony.

Above The interior of La Scala Opera House at Milan in Italy, built in 1778, perhaps the most famous operatic auditorium in the world.

Italian grand opera

Wagner's influence was so immense that we might think he dominated the operatic world during the second half of the 19th century, but this was not so. The Italians had a much older operatic tradition than the Germans, going back to the birth of opera.

In the early years of the 19th century, Gaetano Donizetti (1797-1848), Vincenzo Bellini (1801-35) and Gioacchino Rossini (1792-1868) all wrote operas of great charm and tunefulness. Rossini was particularly successful. He made a fortune out of his music but, after the completion of *William Tell* in 1829, wrote no more operas although he lived another forty years. He had already gone into a long

César Franck (1822–90) French composer. He settled in Paris in 1844 to teach music and compose. He is regarded as one of the greatest organ players and composers since Bach.

Above A scene from Act III of Puccini's opera *La Bohème* (1896) which has a strong claim to be the most popular opera ever written.

Giuseppe Verdi (1813–1901) Italian composer. His earliest lessons in music were from the organist of his parish church. Then he studied at Milan conservatory. Verdi had an exceptionally long career, from 1839 when *Oberto* was produced to *Falstaff* in 1893. Apart from his *Requiem* (1894) and a few other pieces all his music was written in the field of opera.

and happy retirement by the time Giuseppe Verdi (1813-1901) arrived.

Verdi found it very difficult to establish himself as a composer. In fact, he had almost given up hope of an operatic career, when his opera *Nabucco* was produced successfully in Rome. Other operas, notably *Rigoletto* and *Il Trovatore* (The Troubadour) helped to establish his reputation, and by the time he came to write *Aida* he was already famous. This opera, set in ancient Egypt, was written to celebrate the opening of the Suez Canal and first performed in Cairo in 1871. For such a world-famous occasion Verdi composed an appropriately grand opera, with huge settings and cast.

However, Verdi was too fine a musician to be content with something that was intended largely as a show-piece. His musical style was now fully developed, and towards the end of his long creative life he composed what most people consider to be his two greatest operas. In both cases he turned to Shakespeare for his inspiration. The first of these two operas was *Othello*. Then when he was nearly eighty years old, he wrote the comic opera *Falstaff*.

In these late operas, Verdi, like Wagner, paid more and more attention to the orchestra, and tended to treat the voice as just one more thread of sound to be woven into the whole musical fabric. His scoring, though, is lighter than Wagner's. He wanted a clear sound always to emerge from the orchestra, while Wagner was often more concerned with the sheer weight and body of orchestral sound.

To carry the Italian operatic tradition into the 20th century there was Giacomo Puccini (1858-1924). His use of the orchestra was even clearer and more refined than Verdi's. Puccini also had a wonderful gift for soaring melody and a great sense of theatre. Because of this, operas such as *La Bohème*, *Tosca* and *Madame Butterfly* remain very popular all over the world.

Strauss, Bruckner and Mahler

As Puccini followed in the footsteps of Verdi, so Richard Strauss (1864- 1949) followed Wagner as the next important German composer. Strauss wrote a number of operas, and the best-loved is *Der Rosenkavalier*, which has one of the richest sounding scores in all opera. It also contains a beautiful group of waltzes. Richard Strauss was not related to Johann Strauss (1825-99), who wrote such famous Viennese waltzes as *The Blue Danube* and *Tales From the Vienna Woods*. But the waltzes from *Der Rosenkavalier* are a splendid tribute to them and to the days, back in the 19th century, when Vienna was the gayest city in Europe.

Strauss also wrote a number of symphonic poems for the orchestra, including *Don Juan* and *Till Eulenspiegel.* Liszt had written symphonic poems before this, but Strauss made the symphonic poem really important. They are very romantic in character, because they tell a story in musical terms, and are therefore the exact opposite of the 'pure' music of the classical 18th century.

Wagner never wrote a symphony, but he did influence late 19th-century composers of symphonies. Anton Bruckner (1824-96) was a devout Roman Catholic, and in most of his symphonies he expressed his intense religious feelings. They are all long works, and the way Bruckner wrote for the orchestra often sounds very like Wagner.

Gustav Mahler (1860-1911), Jewish by birth, also became a Catholic. He was a deeply disturbed man, and all his anxiety and distress are poured into his nine massive symphonies. They are not in any way like the symphonies of Beethoven and Brahms. As in nearly all romantic works, emotion is much more important to them than structure and form.

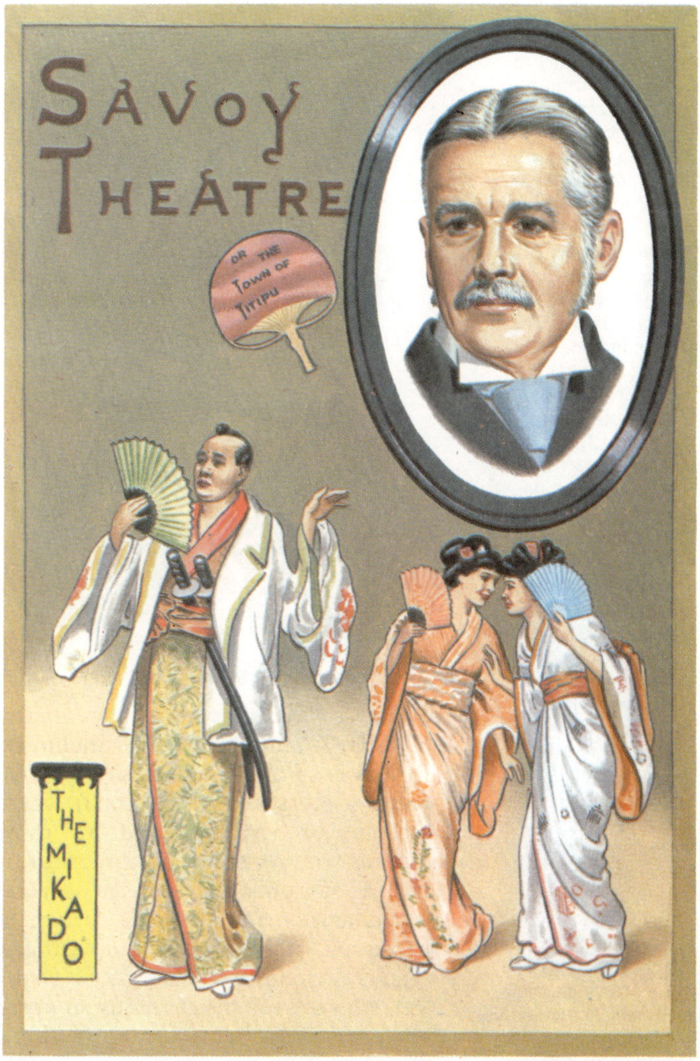

Above Between 1875 and 1896 a composer named Arthur Sullivan and a playwright W. S. Gilbert wrote the Savoy Operas, a series of brilliant and unique English comic operas, and so established one of the greatest theatrical partnerships of all time. Today the operas are known and loved in almost every country in the world. The illustration here is based on the cover of the programme used in 1885 at the first performance of *The Mikado*, one of the most popular operas.

Nationalism

Until the 19th century, composers had not really thought of themselves as German, French, Italian or English composers. As far as their music was concerned, they wrote in the style of their day, rather than in the style of this or that country. The idea that a composer might write music that stood for his particular country began at about the time of the Napoleonic Wars, when the armies of revolutionary France began to break up the old political order and new nations took shape on the map. As Italy struggled towards national unity, Verdi was looked upon not only as a great composer but as a national hero. Wagner was glorified by many as the creator of a new all-German art.

As other countries strove for national independence so they produced composers who wished to write music that belonged especially to their homeland. Chopin based a lot of his music on the folk dances of Poland. Later in the century Bedřich Smetana (1824-84) and Antonín Dvořak (1841-1904) did the same for their native Bohemia.

Even in the countries where there was no struggle for independence, composers felt inspired to write a 'national' kind of music. In Russia there had been no important composer before Mikhail Glinka (1804-57). He at once established a Russian style with his two operas *A Life for the Tsar* and *Russlan and Ludmilla*.

After him came a whole procession of talented Russian composers. Alexander Borodin (1833-87) was only a part-time musician – he was a chemist by profession – but his opera

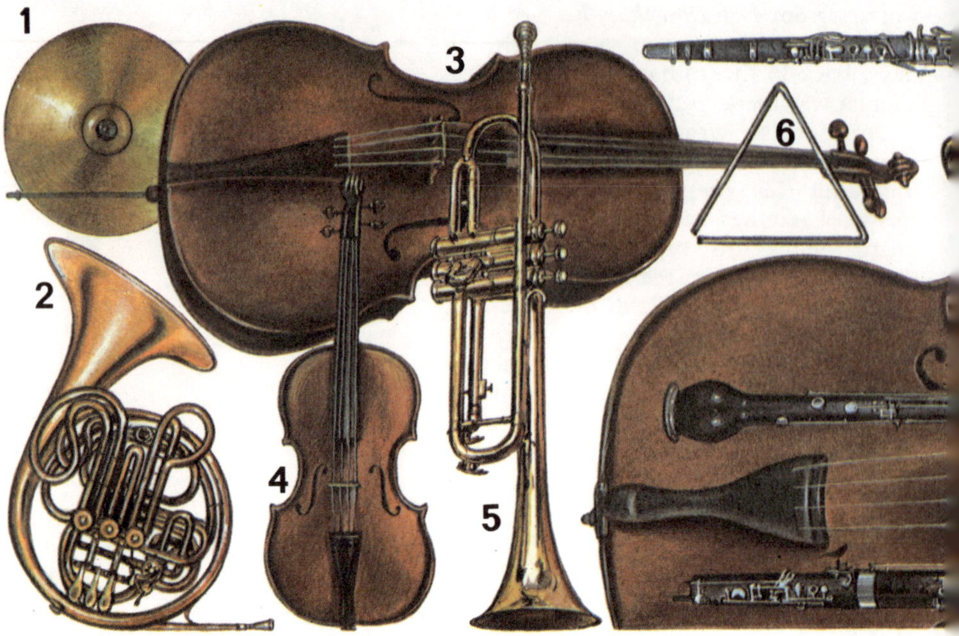

Right By Haydn's day the orchestra had achieved roughly the balance it has in a modern symphony orchestra, although in the 18th century the instruments were much cruder than they are now. Today's symphony orchestra is divided into four main groups: strings, woodwind, brass and percussion. The strings include the violin (14) – divided into first and second violins – the viola (4), the cello (3) and the double-bass (8). The woodwind includes the flute (12), the oboe (16), the clarinet (7) and the bassoon (11). The brass includes the trumpet (5), the trombone (9), the tuba (13) and the horn (2) – though sometimes the horns are regarded as a separate section. The percussion includes the cymbals (1), triangle (6) and timpani (15). There are many other instruments that are used occasionally in addition to the basic ones. These include the cor anglais (10), piccolo saxophone, harp and the many additional members of the percussion section, such as the bass and side drums, tambourine, bells, rattle and castanets.

Prince Igor contains some very exciting Russian-sounding music, including the famous Polovtsian Dances. Nikolai Rimsky-Korsakov (1844-1908) was a brilliant orchestrator, and his most famous work is the symphonic suite – like a symphonic poem in several movements – *Scheherazade,* which is based on stories from the *Arabian Nights.* Modest Mussorgsky (1839-81), who started his career as an army officer, was probably the most gifted of the Russian composers. His feeling for Russian folk music helped him to develop a most original style. He wrote an opera of great dramatic power, *Boris Godunov,* a group of piano pieces called *Pictures from an Exhibition,* and some very moving songs.

The most popular of all Russian composers was Peter Tchaikovsky (1840-93). There is an immediate feeling of excitement and drama to Tchaikovsky's music. His melodies stick in the mind, and all Tchaikovsky's best-loved works have at least one great tune to remember them by. Because of the wide appeal of his music, Tchaikovsky did much to popularise concert going during the closing years of the 19th century. He was himself in demand as a guest conductor, both in Europe and America, although he was an extremely shy man and hated appearing in public. Especially did he increase public interest in ballet with his scores for *The Sleeping Beauty, Swan Lake* and *The Nutcracker.*

In England the first composer to write music that was truly 'English' in character was Edward Elgar (1857-1934). He was also the first great English composer since Purcell. Elgar lived in Edwardian England, and he enjoyed the pageantry and splendour of London, then the capital city of the largest empire in the world. The patriotic hymn 'Land of Hope and Glory' uses a theme from one of his *Pomp and Circumstance* marches, though Elgar did not write the words, and did not like them. Elgar's real love was for the English countryside, in particular the region of the Malvern Hills in Worcestershire, where he was born. All his important orchestral works, including the *Enigma Variations,* expressed something of this deep love of England.

Other composers tried to get even closer to the 'soul' of England and English music by their study of English folk songs and dances. One of these was Ralph Vaughan Williams (1872-1958), who composed symphonies, operas, ballets and songs. Another was Gustav Holst (1874-1934), though his most popular composition, a thrilling orchestral suite called *The Planets,* does not sound at

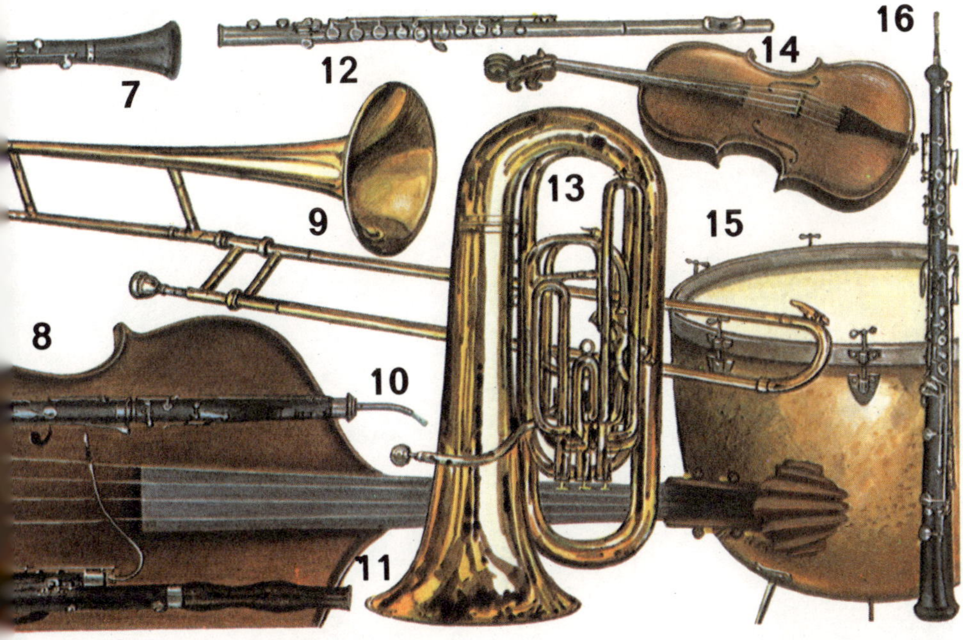

Peter Tchaikovsky (1840–93) Russian composer. Originally studied law but turned to a musical career in 1863. Studied at St Petersburg and first conducted in public in 1887. His operas are not widely known outside Russia but his six symphonies, symphonic poems and ballet music have made him one of the most popular composers of all time.

all like folk music. Frederick Delius (1862-1934) did not care much for England, and spent most of his life in France, but there is a very special 'English' sound to much of his music.

In Norway, Edvard Grieg (1843-1907) made a similar study of the folk music of his country. He then wrote what is probably the best-loved concerto of all, the Piano Concerto in A minor, and some attractive incidental music to *Peer Gynt*, a play by his fellow countryman, Henrik Ibsen.

Manuel de Falla (1876-1946) was Spanish, and he introduced the songs and dances of Spain into a number of operas and ballets. The famous 'Ritual Fire Dance' comes from his ballet *Love the Magician*.

New sounds

Claude Debussy (1862-1918) was the greatest French composer since Berlioz. Between the two there had been Georges Bizet (1838-75), who wrote the exciting opera *Carmen*, Charles Gounod (1818-93), Camille Saint-Saëns (1835-1921) and Gabriel Fauré (1845-1924). Debussy was a composer of true genius, who set music moving in an exciting new direction, just when people were getting tired of composers who could only imitate Wagner.

Debussy made a study of the old medieval modes, and also of Oriental music, and became fascinated with their harmonies and tonal scales. This study helped to form his particular musical 'language', which, far from being in any way old fashioned, was strikingly new. Debussy wrote music which created an impression of a scene. *Prélude à l'après-midi d'un faune* conjures up a hot, drowsy summer afternoon; *La Mer* (The Sea) produces the most subtle and exciting sounds to suggest the play of light on water and the feel of the wind and waves.

Debussy also wrote for the piano in an original way. Most of his piano pieces have descriptive titles, like *Jardins sous la pluie* (Gardens in the rain) or *Poissons d'or* (Gold fish) and none of them lasts very long – just long enough for Debussy to convey exactly the image he had in mind.

Maurice Ravel (1875-1937) also composed some wonderful impressionistic pieces for the piano. He was also a brilliant orchestrator and his score for the ballet *Daphnis and Chloe* is one of the most elaborate ever composed. Between them Debussy and Ravel created a French school of music that was one of the most important influences on the course of 20th-century music.

Quite unlike Debussy and Ravel, but almost as original in his own way, was Jean Sibelius (1865-1957). He started by writing patriotic pieces like *Finlandia*, at a time when his homeland,

Claude Debussy (1862–1918) French composer. Studied at the Paris Conservatory. He was most interested in music which suggested moods and scenes and explored the possibilities of new sounds. His music turned away from old classical and romantic traditions and it has been said of him that he broke the hold of German music on French composers.

Right Few composers in modern times have been able to express their music in terms that are completely personal and yet remain in close direct touch with a great mass of the listening public. Such is the gift of Benjamin Britten (1913–1976) whose operas and other compositions for the voice, in particular, have won both critical and popular acclaim not only in his native England but all over the world. In the background can be seen the Maltings, a converted barn in which concerts at the Aldeburgh Festival are held.

Igor Stravinsky (1882–1971) Russian composer. Studied music under Rimsky Korsakov. He first found fame through the music he wrote for the Diaghilev Ballet. He left Russia in 1914, settling first in Europe then in America. Stravinsky was an experimenter in music all his life and has probably had a greater influence on 20th-century music than any other composer.

Finland, was fighting to be independent of Russia. When he began writing symphonies his patriotism expressed itself at a deeper level. Sibelius loved the remote lakes and forests of his native land, and dark, cold sounds were often what he wanted from the orchestra. Instead of using the orchestra as most other composers had done since Wagner – to produce a dazzling and brilliant sound – Sibelius used the instruments very sparingly.

In Hungary, Béla Bartók (1881-1945) and Zoltán Kodály (1882-1967) made an intensive study of Magyar folk songs and dances. The Magyars were a race of people who came originally from Asia, and their music is sometimes very strange and wild to our ears. Bartók, especially, created out of this folk music a style which made him another of the most important composers of our century.

Bartók experimented with polytonality. This means writing a piece of music in which different instruments are playing in different keys at the same time, or, in the case of the piano, the left and right hands play in different keys. When some of Bartók's music was first published, few people understood or liked it, but today it has become more popular.

Leos Janácek (1854-1928) was born in Moravia - now a part of the Czech Republic - and his interest in folk art took him beyond music and dance to the actual sound of peasant speech. These speech sounds, and the sound of other things such as bird song, he translated into musical terms. Consequently he, too, produced some remarkable new sounds.

Atonality

Debussy and Bartók were two pioneers of 20th-century music. In different ways they broke away from the traditional system of scales and keys, but they did not invent an entirely new musical 'grammar'. This is what Arnold Schoenberg (1874-1951) set out to do. He developed what is called atonality. Other composers had come quite close to writing atonal music, that is, music not written in any particular key, but Schoenberg was the one to construct a completely new set of rules for its composition. Because atonal music remains so unfamiliar to most people's ears, it is widely thought to be ugly and lacking in feeling. But Schoenberg could write very emotional music in this way. His opera *Moses and Aaron* is full of deep feeling.

So, too, is much of the music of Alban Berg (1885-1935), who was a musical disciple of Schoenberg. Berg wrote a very dramatic and emotional opera called *Wozzeck,* which tells the story of a tormented, simple-minded soldier. This work also makes use of a device called *sprechgesang* – 'spoken song' – which requires the words of the opera to be delivered in a tone of voice between speech and song.

Another of Schoenberg's disciples, Anton Webern (1883-1945), also wrote atonal music in which every note had an important life of its own. Intervals of silence between the notes were also given great significance. Although such music can hardly be described as new any longer, it still sounds very advanced to most people.

On one side of Stravinsky are those composers who have not bothered much with atonality, but have still found something fresh to say using traditional methods. Paul Hindemith (1895-1963) in Germany and Francis Poulenc (1899-1963) in France have been two such composers. In England there have been Benjamin Britten and William Walton. Britten wrote a number of fine choral works and operas, notably *Peter Grimes,* that are performed all over the world. He was probably the leading operatic composer of recent years, but his talent was varied and exciting. He had a particular interest in working with children and writing music for them to perform.

Sergei Prokofiev (1891-1953) and Dimitri Shostakovich (1906-75) have been the two leading Soviet composers so far this century. Artists in the former U.S.S.R. were paid a salary by the State and expected to produce work which appealed to the people and gave them hope and confidence in the regime. Since atonal music does not have a very wide appeal it was frowned on by the government, so Prokofiev and Shostakovich kept to conventional methods of composition. But both managed to write highly original and exciting music.

Béla Bartók (1881–1945) Hungarian composer. He first appeared in public as a pianist at the age of ten. He became particularly interested in Hungarian folk music, which remained a great influence on his own composition. Although his music draws on an ancient tradition it is modern in its originality.

Music today

The late Igor Stravinsky was one of the foremost composers of this century. As a young man his genius was recognised by Sergei Diaghilev, who ran a famous ballet company. Diaghilev commissioned Stravinsky to write the music for three new ballets, *The Firebird*, *Petrouchka* and *The Rite of Spring*. Other composers who wrote music for the Diaghilev Ballet included Debussy, Ravel and de Falla, but none had written more brilliantly for the orchestra than the young Stravinsky. None had written more shockingly either. *The Rite of Spring* contained some passages of such deliberate harshness and discordancy that at the first performance in Paris in 1913 members of the audience shouted protests and the occasion ended in a public riot.

Stravinsky played a leading part in the development and progress of music over half a century, and we can think of many other 20th century composers in relation to him.

On the other side of Stravinsky are those composers who are generally thought of as belonging to the *avant-garde*, a French word meaning out in front. Much of the work done by *avant-garde* composers like Edgar Varèse (1885-1965), Pierre Boulez and Karlheinz Stockhausen is of great interest from an experimental point of view, although it is not understood by the majority of people.

Olivier Messiaen has gone much further along the road opened up earlier in the century by Debussy, and composed music which makes use of many strange and fascinating new harmonies. Other composers of our age, besides doing fresh work in the field of atonality, have become interested in entirely new ways of creating sound, for example, by the use of electronics. Some have even had music programmed by computers, which raises the question of whether or not it is truly creative work, and therefore true art.

Arnold Schoenberg (1874–1951) Austrian composer. Apart from a few early lessons he was self-taught. His particular form of musical expression began to show itself in 1907 with his *Chamber Symphony*. His music used the twelve notes of the chromatic scale and was in no fixed key. From 1933, when he was exiled from Germany, he lived in America.

Above Dancing in primitive societies is not an entertainment. Most dances have a purpose, with magical or religious meaning, so that a dance becomes a prayer for success in war or hunting or the gathering of crops.

Below This figure of a dancer is taken from a Greek vase painting of the 6th century, when the red-figure technique came into fashion.

Music and the dance

Dancing is the oldest of the arts. Early man danced before he added simple music to accompany his movements or singing to describe what he was doing. The urge to dance, or to express ourselves by the movement of our bodies, is so basic that it must have existed in men, and even in the ancestors of men, for tens of thousands of years. Today, when we say that we could 'jump for joy' or that we are 'hopping mad', we are still responding to an instinct that is more ancient than speech or music.

Dancing makes patterns in space and to have any real meaning requires a sense of rhythm: that is, bodily movement performed to some sort of regular beat or pulse. As in music, rhythm is one of the most important features of dancing.

Dancing is not just a matter of dance steps. Signs that have been carefully worked out and instinctive actions come into it as well. Signs have always been used by people to communicate with each other: a nod of the head means the same thing in most parts of the world. Some nations use gestures more than others. This is particularly true of people who live in Mediterranean countries, where the warm climate encourages outdoor life and a more expansive attitude to things.

Religion and magic

The dances of early man are linked to religion and magic. Dancing as entertainment has developed in most cultures from these same roots. Early man lived close to nature and his life was bound up with the earth, the sun and the moon, thunder and rain, and the animals that fed and clothed him. He danced to express his feelings about these things, and his need for help from whatever gods he worshipped. Before a tribe went hunting, the chief might lead an animal dance, with tribesmen pretending to be animals and acting out the events of a hunt. Even today, in remote parts of the world such dances are still performed, and they were often the subject of the early cave painters of palaeolithic times.

In these dances man stamped out rhythms with his feet, bent close to the ground for protection and painted his face or wore a mask. Masks were magical and gave power and were worn all over the world. Men and women usually danced separately and often for long periods. Sometimes, a trance-like state 'bewitched' dancers so that they could stab themselves or walk on hot coals without feeling pain. The climax of a dance was often an animal, or even a human, sacrifice.

Many dances were prayers – to banish evil spirits or to ask the gods for success in war. The thrilling war dances of African or Red Indian warriors are still sometimes performed, but usually in a ceremonial way to recall the old days of glory. There were also thanksgiving dances for a successful harvest and prayer dances for rain. Health dances were known as 'medicine dances' and were controlled by the medicine man. The world could be a terrifying place, and men and women danced to give themselves strength to survive in it.

Forms of dance

There have always been funeral dances, and not just among primitive people. The stately Spanish pavane was performed at funerals in Spain while the body lay in state awaiting burial. And two hundred years ago a Scottish widow was expected to dance beside her husband's corpse as a sign of affection. Man's play dances are now usually danced only by children – for fun. A typical example is the sailor's hornpipe. Courtship dances, too, are as old as mankind and their object has always been to allow men and women to get to know each other. Many of these forms of dancing played their part in shaping entertainment dances and, later, ballet. When dances were no longer danced just for the sake of the dancers but to please an audience, a form of theatre was born.

Dancing in the ancient world

European dance stems from the early Mediterranean civilisations. The Egyptians had trained professional dancers and acrobats over four thousand years ago. We know the Egyptians danced from the evidence of their paintings, and although none of their music has survived they certainly used small 'orchestras' to accompany the dancers. Dancing is mentioned in the Bible and it was the custom for religious dancing to be performed at important festivals.

Above Dancing in primitive tribes is more often than not performed by men. This is particularly so with hunting and war dances from which women are usually excluded, such as the one depicted here by a North American Indian tribe.

The Greeks loved dancing. Again there were strong links with religion and magic. The Greeks combined music, poetry and dancing into one entertainment, and as the chorus became more important in the drama so some of the conventional movements of theatrical dance grew up. We know from sculpture that they also enjoyed comic dancing. Dancing was an important part of Greek civilisation – one of the nine Muses (the mythological divinities who inspired artistic creation) was Terpsichore, the Muse of dancing.

At first the Romans admired dancing, but their other entertainments became so bloodthirsty that it declined in favour. For political reasons, conquered peoples were encouraged to

Above Asian peoples today, particularly in India, perform dances almost identical with those they did 2,000 years ago.

Above right The dances of the whole of South-East Asia are mostly based on ancient religious ceremonies.

Above The waltz took Europe by storm and became the most popular social dance in the early 19th century. This drawing was taken from an early book of instruction.

continue local dances. Christmas celebrations and May Day dances, which still survive in some parts of Europe, have a link with Roman times.

The Christian church rebelled against Roman cruelty and against all forms of secular entertainment. Although the Church was hostile to dancing, down the years the Christian civilisation 'borrowed' heathen dances and turned them into harmless pursuits. An English Morris dance stems from a prehistoric blood sacrifice! Until some time in the 12th century dancing played a part in church services, but it was eventually banished, never to reappear except in certain American sects like the Holy Rollers, a branch of the Negro Baptists.

Folk dancing

Many surviving European peasant, or folk, dances are very old. Peasant dancing varies a lot, and its national characteristics are today very clearly defined – the acrobatic agility of the Russian male dancer or the controlled abandon of the Spanish flamenco expert. About seventy years ago a new interest in folk songs and dances began, thanks to an Englishman, Cecil Sharp (1859-1924), who explored Britain and America noting down what he saw and heard. Now this interest has spread across the world, and local competitions keep national dancing vigorously alive.

In eastern temples and theatres dances had been deliberately preserved intact for centuries. Until recently little was known in the west of these ancient and beautiful styles of dance. Primitive African dances had been seen by Egyptian and Roman explorers, but there was no link with the east, apart from a few wandering gypsies, until the coming of the Moors.

Spanish dancing

Between 600 and the end of the 15th century, thousands of African Mohammedans, or Moors, settled in Europe. They brought their eastern dances with them. Moorish women could only dance for their families, but the men performed friendly, acrobatic and religious dances, eastern in style but with a shaking and jerking of the body, and snapping of the fingers, imported from Africa.

The Moors influenced Spanish music, architecture and dancing. Spanish dancing, so popular throughout the world, is Moorish with one important difference – Spanish women, not being Mohammedan, join in. Spanish dancing is noted for the tremendous concentration of the dancer, the bending of the spine, weaving hips and encircling arms, and the use of the eyes – and of veils and skirts. All this is eastern, but the beating of feet, the jumps and the castanets are southern European, and the rhythmic use of heel and foot is purely Spanish.

Classic Spanish dancing has several styles, all of which demand years of training. It is worlds away from

popular dancing elsewhere and suits the proud Spaniards to perfection.

Court dances

In the Middle Ages the courts of Europe did much to make dancing more graceful. New dances, based on peasant ones but with the rough steps and riotous behaviour left out, spread around Christendom as the rich noblemen travelled from country to country.

Court dances had two main functions – courtship and 'showing off'. Much use was made in the dances of cloaks, fans and handkerchiefs. As clothes were very splendid, dancing became a wonderful spectacle. In the 14th century the costume of the aristocracy, particularly of the ladies, was heavy and elaborate, with large head-dresses. This meant that dances tended to be rather sober affairs with stately processional movements.

As clothes became lighter, from Renaissance times onwards, dancing became more skilful. Courtiers took daily lessons. The steps were not difficult to learn, but to perform the dances with proper grace required training. By the 18th century those who danced such measures as the gavotte and minuet were highly accomplished and the dances themselves very beautiful to watch.

The waltz

In the 1770s dancing was revolutionised by the waltz. This was a more civilised version of an old German peasant dance, the *ländler*. At first, the new dance was regarded by many with horror, especially as it involved grasping a girl's waist, which had previously been very rare in dances. But the waltz conquered Europe in the 19th century and provided the link between the old and the new in dancing.

Other famous dances in the heyday of the waltz were the polka and the mazurka. 'Group' dances like the lancers and the quadrille were used chiefly as marches to change partners.

The last popular new dance invented in Europe was the riotous can-can, which began in France in the 1840s and involved dancers in doing such things as high kicks and the 'splits'. Since that time most new dances have come from America.

Above Dancing at court during the Middle Ages in Europe was largely a matter of 'showing off', not only to one's partner but to the whole assembly. The costumes of the time were elaborate and for this reason the dances tended to be slow and stately. This drawing is based on a 15th-century painting.

Above left Spanish dancing owes a lot of its character to the influence of the Moors, who moved into southern Europe from Africa during the long domination by Islamic peoples, which lasted from about the 7th to the 15th centuries.

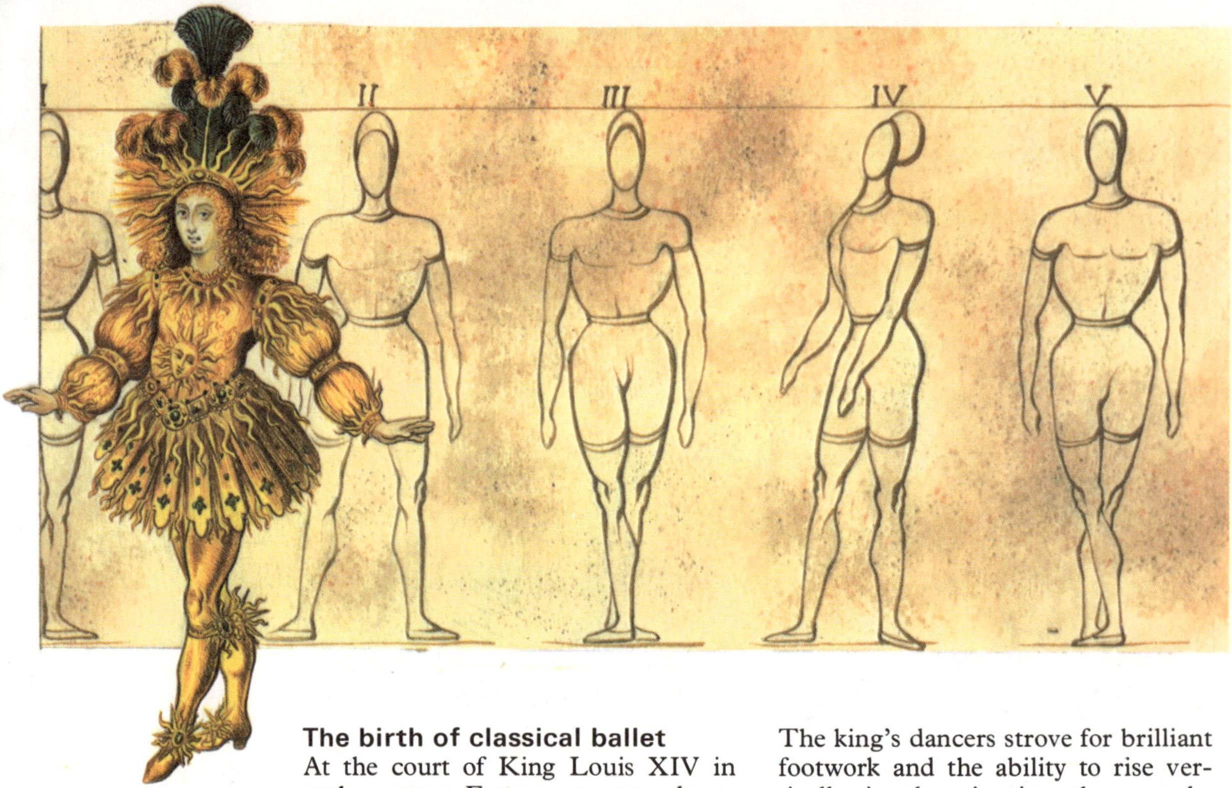

Above The classic five positions, on one of which each formal dance movement both begins and ends, were laid down in about 1700 by Beauchamps. Superimposed on an 18th-century drawing of the five positions is the figure of Louis XIV in a dance costume representing the sun.

Jean Noverre (1727–1810) French dancer and choreographer. Made his début as a dancer at 16. His reforms to the style of dancing have lasted until today. Garrick called him 'the Shakespeare of the dance'.

The birth of classical ballet

At the court of King Louis XIV in 17th-century France, country dance was transformed into a new style of dancing – the classical ballet. With few alterations it has stood the test of time for over three hundred years as one of the greatest art forms of mankind.

As classical ballet started at a court it is hardly surprising that its movements and postures are so noble and well-controlled, as a king's ought always to be. All the courtiers could dance, and modern ballet exercises are based on their movements.

Court 'ballets' actually began in Italy around 1400 and spread through Europe. They were really pageants consisting of parades and refined country dances. They were very expensive to mount and usually finished with a scene flattering the royal or lordly person in whose honour they were performed. The characters in the ballet were gods and heroes. Catherine de'Medici (1519-89) introduced similar displays to the court in Paris when she became wife of the French king, Henry II.

Louis XIV actually danced in the ballets at his court: he took daily lessons, as all modern dancers do. His dancing master, Charles Beauchamps (1636-1705), officially laid down the five basic positions of the feet in ballet which are still used today. The king's dancers strove for brilliant footwork and the ability to rise vertically in the air – in other words, elevation. Women were allowed to dance in the court ballets, but only started dancing publicly in 1681.

The early ballets had simple steps and the costumes of the dancers were heavy – the exact opposite of today's. Scenery was very splendid and wonderful 'transformation scenes' took place with the scenery changed by clever machinery. Some ballets went on for six hours! This became rather tiring for the dancers, who were, after all, only amateurs. So the dancing masters and their best pupils took over the most difficult dances. The profession of ballet dancer was born. By the 18th century, the performers – amateur and professional – wore masks. Their costumes were in the fashion of the day and not historically correct to the period of the ballet.

Louis XIV had founded the Royal Academy of Dance in 1661, and this, together with the popularity of ballet in France, is the reason why the language of ballet is French. The Paris *Opéra*, home of the Paris *Opéra* ballet staged its first ballet in 1671, two years after it opened as the *Académie d'Opéra*. From this time onwards, courts throughout Europe wanted their own opera and ballet companies.

In the 18th century, ballet was officially established in Denmark, Italy, Germany, Austria, Sweden and Russia, and flourished from time to time in Britain and elsewhere.

By now, ballet was becoming more athletic and more difficult, though dancers still had to make it look easy. Dancers were learning new patterns to make in the air and the importance of 'line' at all times, which means the outline of the body in action and repose. Pirouettes were being danced, a pirouette being a full turn of the body while balancing on the ball of the foot of one leg. Good dancers can turn continuously several times. The actual stories of ballets at this time were separate from the dances and were told in sign language.

Above Marie Camargo, from the painting by Lancret. Born in Brussels of a noble family she trained as a dancer in Paris and was an immediate success. The painting shows the shortened skirt which revealed her ankles and made possible new techniques of dancing.

Left In 1845 the choreographer Jules Perrot brought together the four leading dancers of the age, Carlotta Grisi, Marie Taglioni, Lucile Grahn and Fanny Cerrito, in a *Pas de Quatre* which was a high peak in the golden age of the romantic ballet. This drawing shows a modern version of the dance.

The first ballet stars

Some of the first ballet dancers are still remembered. Louis XIV's teacher, Beauchamps, is famous as the first great dancer and choreographer, which is the word used to describe the composer of the steps of a ballet. In 1716 a nine-year-old girl, Marie Sallé (1707-56), made a sensational debut in London and later became a leading French dancer and choreographer. She introduced sensible stories to ballet and lighter clothes. Ballet dancing at once became more natural.

The 18th century's most popular dancer was Marie Camargo (1710-70) who, unlike many women, was good at jumping. To make the most of this she raised her skirts a few centimetres above the instep to gain more freedom of movement, and thus made ballet history.

Another key figure was Jean Noverre (1727-1810), who demanded a sensible story, fewer 'star turns' which held up the action, better music, better acting, new steps, no stiff clothes and no masks. He devised the first five-act ballet to make a whole evening's entertainment, and made ballet more natural. But he was more honoured in Germany, Austria and Britain than in France. For a time he made the German town of Stuttgart the ballet capital of the world.

Another Frenchman, Jean Dauberval (1742-1806), invented comedy ballet. The story of his *La Fille Mal Gardée* (1789) is still used with great success by Britain's Royal Ballet and other international companies, though the steps and music are different. In the ballet ordinary people – even peasants – are heroes, and this was a revolutionary idea in the very year that the French Revolution broke out!

A year later, a Swedish dancer, Charles Didelot (1767-1836), made his debut in Paris. He taught in London, Paris and Russia, possibly introduced flesh-coloured tights for female dancers, and was the first to make dancers 'fly' on wires. He followed Noverre by improving costumes and plots.

Three famous 18th-century Italian dancers were Gaetano Vestris (1729-1808) and his son, Marie Auguste

Above The French painter Degas often visited the Paris Opéra to study and paint the dancers. Degas was attracted to ballet as a medium which expressed the movement of the human body, but most of his drawing was done in the rehearsal room. He was interested in the dancers' unusual attitudes as they waited or rested rather than in their graceful and conscious movements.

Vestris (1760-1842), and Salvatore Viganò (1769-1821). In 1812 Viganò became ballet master of the great La Scala theatre in Milan. Thanks to his influence Italy had its greatest ballet period at this time, which declined after his death.

The Romantic ballet

Ballet of the 18th century would seem unexciting and over simple for the audiences of today. Movements were restricted very much to steps on the ground. There were few leaps or rapid turns and women had not yet learned to dance on the points of their toes.

From the time of the French revolution until the battle of Waterloo in 1815, Europe was almost continuously at war. The Industrial Age, with all its noise and smoke, was beginning. As if to escape from this the arts became 'Romantic' and no art was more romantic than ballet during what came to be known as its golden age.

The first great dancer of this age was Marie Taglioni (1804-84), the first ballerina in the modern sense of the word, meaning the female dancer who plays the chief classical roles in a company. After the ballerina the other dancers are ranked in importance down to the members of the corps de ballet – the equivalent to an opera chorus. In the Russian Imperial Ballet during the 19th century this system of 'ranks' was as rigid and formal as that in an army command. Today, in the modern ballet company, this grading of talent continues and the names of some of the old ranks persist, such as the coryphée, who is somewhere between a member of the corps de ballet and the lowest grade of soloist – a sort of lance-corporal.

Taglioni was the supreme dancer of the 19th century. Her Italian father, Filippo, taught her and although nearly all the ballets he devised for her were worthless and long forgotten, the influence of her style remains – even to such small details as the traditional arrangement of the ballerina's hair, with centre parting and a bun at the back. She could float in the air more beautifully than any other dancer; she mounted her toes in poses and took a few steps on her points (although ballet shoes were not yet stiffened enough for real point work); she designed costumes and learned to make the most of her rather long and ungainly arms: and she conquered Europe. Her male partners are forgotten. The poor male dancer at this time was very much in the background and existed only to display the ballerina to an adoring public.

Taglioni's most celebrated performance was in *La Sylphide* in 1832, a ballet choreographed by her father which has been revived in a modern version. At this time ballet stars were the toast of all the towns in which they danced. They and their choreographers travelled Europe dancing and teaching.

The greatest teacher of the day was the Italian Carlo Blasis (1797-1878). His teaching methods were published

Marius Petipa (1819–1910) French choreographer and dancer. Was ballet master at the Maryinsky Theatre from 1867 until his death in 1910. His full-length ballets created a style for the classical works in the repertoire which have remained popular to this day.

Left A scene from a modern production of *Swan Lake*, which is still given in its entirety by companies all over the world.

in two great books *Treatise on the Dance* and *The Code of Terpsichore*, which are still the basis of modern classical ballet training. Ballet practice is the same all over the world, beginning with the deep knees bend and leg and feet exercises that Carlo Blasis laid down. However, certain nationalities have their own special skills, which first became evident at this time. By 1840, ballet was in many ways similar to today's, but less acrobatic, less well-acted and, because shoes were not yet stiffened enough, with little spectacular point dancing.

In this golden age of the 1840s many famous dancers appeared – the fiery Fanny Elssler (1810-84), who was a marvellous actress; the vivacious Fanny Cerrito (1817-1909); Carlotta Grisi (1819-99), for whom *Giselle* was created in 1841; the Dane, Lucile Grahn (1819-1907), called the 'Taglioni of the North'; and the first great American dancer, Augusta Maywood (1825-?), who danced mainly in Europe.

The male dancers of the day are only remembered if they were also great choreographers. Among them were Jean Coralli (1779-1854), who created *Giselle;* the ugly but brilliant Jules Perrot (1810-92), who was married to Grisi and excelled in mime – the use of face and body to convey feeling and dramatic action; and the great Danish dancer, August Bournonville (1805-79), whose works are still the mainstay of the Royal Danish Ballet.

Arthur Saint-Léon (1821-70) was a French dancer remembered mainly for his impossible behaviour – and for creating *Coppélia* (1870). Another Frenchman, Lucien Petipa (1815-98), was the first Albrecht in *Giselle*. He is remembered for catching Grisi in a jump from a high platform in *La Péri*, much to the audience's delight and astonishment. His brother, Marius (see above), could be called the father of Russian ballet. He was ballet master at St Petersburg from 1862 to 1910 and during those forty-eight years he produced fifty-four new ballets. These included such favourites as *The Sleeping Beauty* in 1890 and, with his assistant, Lev Ivanov (1834-1901), *Swan Lake* in 1895. He made long ballets with four or five acts fashionable and was a master of every department of the theatre.

Above Fanny Elssler, as depicted in the statuette by Barre which is now in the museum of the Paris Opéra.

Sergei Diaghilev (1872–1929) Russian impresario. He arranged exhibitions and concerts of Russian art and music in the west. First presented ballet in Paris in 1909. For 20 years he dominated the world of ballet during the most exciting period in the whole history of the art.

Above right The vivid and colourful settings for ballets like *Le Coq d'Or* were inspired by Russian peasant arts.

Above Isadora Duncan's visit to St Petersburg in 1905 had a great influence on the development of Russian ballet.

Isadora Duncan

During the second half of the 19th century ballet lost a lot of its appeal and became an empty display of acrobatic dancing and indifferent acting, with women playing men's parts. The exception was the Imperial Russian Ballet which maintained its standards without in any way developing new ideas or new talent. So far as the rest of the world was concerned, there was far more life to be found in the Negro minstrel shows in America, in can-cans in French cafés, and in the English music halls, than in the official temples of the dance.

Then an American woman, Isadora Duncan (1879-1927), transformed the ballet scene. She was not a trained dancer, but her influence on every country was immense. She discarded the traditional ballet costume for flowing draperies, and danced in bare feet simply, seriously and naturally. She was a sensation! It was not that she was a great dancer, or even that she created a new style of dancing, but wherever she went the old-style ballet seemed suddenly to be revealed for what it had become – unreal and in urgent need of change.

The Diaghilev Ballet

Isadora Duncan first danced in Russia in 1905. She was seen by Michael Fokine (1880-1942), a brilliant dancer who was to become the greatest choreographer in the history of dancing. He was already determined to change ballet from the shoddy thing it had become. He wanted more than a ballet which showed off only the brilliance of a ballerina. He wanted what Noverre had wanted – ballet to be great dramatic art.

Fokine sought to make all dancing full of meaning. Instead of routine gestures, he wanted the whole body to act. He wanted the male dancer to be important again, and the best music, costumes and scenery for ballet. His ideas were already thought out when he saw Duncan, but she inspired him because her dancing tried to express the whole range of human feeling.

Fortunately, a Russian impresario (organiser of entertainments) of genius, Sergei Diaghilev (1872-1929), was at hand to give Fokine the chance to realise his dreams. He had shown Russian paintings in Paris in 1907, and presented concerts of Russian music and opera in 1908. In 1909 came possibly the most exciting moment in ballet history: together with an opera company, Diaghilev brought part of the Russian ballet to Paris.

Fokine was the ballet master, and among the dancers were such immortals as Anna Pavlova (1881-1931),

Far left Anna Pavlova in *The Dying Swan* to the music of Saint-Saens. This was perhaps her most popular dance in every part of the world where she travelled with her own company.

Left One of the greatest partnerships ever formed in the history of ballet – Tamara Karsavina and Vaslav Nijinsky, seen here in the first performance of *Le Spectre de la Rose* in April 1911.

Tamara Karsavina and the supreme male dancer of all time, Vaslav Nijinsky (1890-1950). The opening night of the ballet has become legendary, driving the Parisian audience almost crazy with excitement. The season, and the seasons that followed it in 1910 and 1911, not only transformed ballet – the whole world of theatre was affected. Ballet had become a riot of dance, colour, scenery, costumes, music and lighting.

The particular highspots of these first seasons were Fokine's three wonderful ballets, *Scheherazade* to Rimsky-Korsakov's music, and *The Firebird* and *Petrouchka* with music by the young Stravinsky.

Diaghilev's company was as sensational a success in England as in France. Because of the First World War and the Russian revolution of 1917 it split up, but its stars, whether with Diaghilev's later *Ballets Russes* or elsewhere, spread the new style of ballet. Fokine fell out with Diaghilev in 1912 and worked with many companies, particularly in America. Nijinsky, who was as marvellous an actor as he was a dancer, became a legend in his own lifetime, immortal through his roles in *Petrouchka* and *Prélude à l'après-midi d'un faune*.

Anna Pavlova, after leaving Diaghilev, formed her own troupe. She is best remembered for her dancing in *The Dying Swan* to the music of Saint-Saëns, and in her day could spell-bind an audience as only a few great dancers, singers and actors in each generation can. She helped restore ballet's reputation in America and inspired many Americans to take up the art.

The supreme actress in Diaghilev's company was Tamara Karsavina, who created many of Fokine's great roles, including the Firebird. Her book, *Theatre Street,* is a ballet classic.

Two key figures in those first seasons were the artistic director, Alexandre Benois (1870-1960), and the painter Leon Bakst (1866-1924), whose designs did so much to revolutionise the 'look' of ballet and of the theatre as a whole. Bakst was particularly renowned for his use of bright colours.

Diaghilev's later stars included the great dancers and choreographers Leonide Massine (1896-1979) and Georges Balanchine (1904-83). Balanchine, who was less interested in acting than in exact, disciplined movements, had a tremendous influence in America. Massine achieved marvels in mass movements for dancers, and was famous for his 'symphonic' ballets danced to the music of Tchaikovsky, Brahms, Berlioz and Beethoven. When Diaghilev died in 1929, it was Massine

Michael Fokine (1880–1942) Russian choreographer. More than any other person he created modern ballet and led it away from the stylised artificial art it had become for him when, as a dancer, he had partnered Pavlova in St Petersburg. With such collaborators as Stravinsky, Bakst and Benois he led a ballet revolution.

Above There has been no more famous partnership in modern ballet than that between Margot Fonteyn and Rudolph Nureyev, seen in this photograph. Fonteyn's appearances with Nureyev, who left the Kirov Ballet to join the Royal Ballet, crowned her career as one of Britain's greatest ballerinas. Margot Fonteyn died in 1991 and Nureyev, in Paris, in January 1993.

who found new stars and brought many of Fokine's ballets to America for the first time.

Ballet today

Since the end of the First World War it has not been possible to point to any one country as the leading centre of ballet. The art flourishes all over the world, but particularly in Britain, the United States and Russia.

The impact of the Diaghilev Ballet in London directly inspired such dancers and choreographers as Alicia Markova, Marie Rambert and Ninette de Valois to form their own companies. The Sadler's Wells Ballet, with Ninette de Valois as its first director, became the Royal Ballet, which has appeared with such success all over the world. As well as producing the great English ballerina, Margot Fonteyn, it has given a home to dancers from other countries, such as Rudolf Nureyev, and provided choreographers and ballet masters for European and American theatres.

In the United States there are two leading companies, the New York City Ballet and the Ballet Theatre. Ballet has also developed in the American theatre through the great musical shows like *Oklahoma* and *West Side Story*, the dances for which were choreographed by such leading figures of the world of ballet as Agnes de Mille and Jerome Robbins.

In Russia ballet has been highly organised, ever since the days of the Russian Imperial Ballet at the Maryinsky Theatre in St. Petersburg. Much has changed in Russia, but the Kirov Ballet keeps up the Maryinsky tradition of quiet brilliance and disciplined perfection. At the famous Bolshoi Theatre, the accent is on vigour and athleticism. Even if the ballets produced in Russia still tend to be old-fashioned and, by today's standards, dramatically unconvincing, no one can deny that Russian dancers are probably the best-trained and most accomplished in the world.

The great traditions of classical ballet continue to be upheld by companies all over the world. In the old days there was no way of recording movements, and the details of a ballet had to be passed on from generation to generation in performance and rehearsal. The old ballets are now safer for posterity because reliable methods of writing down dance movements, called notation, have been devised. So that whatever happens to ballet in the future there is every chance that in 2041 theatregoers will be enjoying an authentic production of *Giselle* to celebrate its 200th birthday.

Index

The items in this index are arranged in strict alphabetical sequence according to the order of the consecutive letters of the whole entry, disregarding punctuation. Figures in bold type refer to illustrations.

Abacus **307**
Abraham 410
Absalom and Achitophel (Dryden) 359
Abstract painters 490
Abu Simbel **268**
Academy (Athens) 425–6, **425**
Academy of Art, French 469, 471, 481
Academy of Art, Royal 435, 475–6
Academy of Dance, Royal 522
Academy of Sciences (France), Royal 90
Acceleration 263–7, 279
Accordian 316, **316**
Accumulators 268
Achilles **343**
Acropolis, Athens **442–3**
Action painting 491
Act of Union (England and Ireland) 46
Acupuncture **320**
Adam, Robert 329
Adams' Universal microscope **251**
Adding machines 307–8, 316
Addison, Joseph 474
Adrian IV, pope 44
Advancement of Learning (Bacon) 355
Adventitious root **164**, 164–5
Aegisthus 344
Aeneas 347
Aeneid (Virgil) 347
Aeolian mode 495
Aerial photography 90
Aeroplanes **276–7**,**282–3**, **292–3**, 292–3, 316
Aeschylus 343–4
Aesculapius, see Asclepius
Aesop 342, 358
Aesthetics 421
Africa 82, 84, 86
Africa, map of **95**
African dance mask **388**
African elephant **234**
African iron sculpture **389**
Agamemnon 344
Agamemnon (Aeschylus) 343
Age of Bronze, The (Rodin) 483
Age of Reason, The 474–5, 503
Age of the earth 51–2
Agincourt, Battle of 45
Agni 401
Agricola (Bauer) Georg 62
Agricola, Julius 44
Agricola, Life of (Tacitus) 347
Agriculture in Britain 41–2
Ahab, Captain **367**
Ahriman 410
Ahura Mazda 410, **410**
Aida (Verdi) 512
Air pressure 77–8, 290
Air pump 253
Airships 292, **292**, 316
Air thermoscope **253**
Ajanta 446
Akbar the Great 446
Akhenaton 99, 394, 442
Akroyd-Stuart, Herbert 275
A la recherche du temps perdu (Proust) 371
Alaskan dance mask **390**
Albatross, Wandering **217**, 217
Albert, prince consort of England **34**
Alcaeus 343
Alchemists 252, **252**, 255
Alchemist, The (Jonson) 357
Alcohol 158, 179
Alcoholic drinks 179
Alcuin of York 448
Aldeburgh Festival **516**
Aldine Press 456, **456**
Aldrin, Edwin **129**, 132
Alexander, Cicely **484**
Alexander the Great 81, **81**, 320, 426, **443**, 443
Alexis of Thurii 344
Alfa Romeo car wheel **247**
Alfieri, Vittorio 358
Alfred (the Great), king of Wessex **13**, 44
Algae 151, 154–6, **155**
Algebra 316
Algol 124
Alhambra Palace **466**
Ali Baba **340**
Alice's Adventures in Wonderland (Carroll) **366**
Al-khowârizni 316
Ali (Mohammed's son-in-law) 420
Alleyn, Edward 378
Alligators 212–3
Alma, Battle of 46
Almayer's Folly (Conrad) 370
Al-Mutawakkil mosque **467**
Alpaca 233
Alpine plants **167**
Alps 59
Altar of Heaven, Peking **409**
Amalthea (satellite) 111
Amaterasu 409
Amati, Nicolo 500
Ambrose, St 495
Ambrosian chant 495
Amenhotep IV 394
American art 476
American continent 83
American literature 362, 366–7
American theatre 381
American War of Independence 46
Amino-acids 53
Ammeters 299
Ammon 189
Ammonites **57**, 189, 192–6, 201
Amoeba 183–5, 199
Amon-Re 394
Amos 411
Ampère, André Marie 295, 297
Ampere (unit of electrical current) 295
Amphibia, see Amphibians
Amphibians **187**, 191–2, 208, 210–12
Amphora, Greek **395**
Amritsar 420
Amsterdam **427**
Amundsen, Roald 86–7
An 391
Anaesthetics 316, 330–1, 334
Anatomy 320–2, 324
Anaximenes 422
Ancestor figures 440, **441**
Ancient religions 391
Ancient science 246
Anders, William 132
Andersen, Hans Christian 369
Andes 59–60
And Quiet Flows the Don (Sholokhov) 369
Andrew's Cross, St **14**
Andromeda (astronomy) 122–3, **123**, 125
Andromeda, Great Nebula in 122
Anemometer 316
Angelico, Fra **454**, **497**
Angiosperms 154, 160–2
Angkor Wat 452
Angler fishes 210
Angles 11, 44, 349
Anglesey 48
Anglo-Saxon cart wheel **247**
Anglo-Saxon Chronicle 351
Anglo-Saxon literature 350
Animalcules 183–4, **187**
Animal kingdom 184, 186–7
Animal reproduction 185
Animals 183–240
Animals, Classification of 186–7, **186–7**
Animals, First 53
Animals in Britain, Wild 48
Animal spirits (Galen) 322, 328
Ani papyrus **394**
Ankh **393**
Anna Karenina (Tolstoy) 368
Anne, queen of England **20**, 21
Annelida, see Annelids
Annelids **187**, 200
Anning, Mary **194**
Annuals 165, 173
Anouilh, Jean 370
Anselm, St 426
Answers, 371
Antarctica 87
Antarctic Ocean 72
Antares 127
Anteater 235
Antelopes 233
Anthrax 333
Anthropology 240, 336
Antibiotics 147, 158, 333
Antibodies (monoclonals) 334
Anticyclone 77
Antigone 344
Antiphanes of Athens 344
Antiseptics 316, 331–2
Ants 203, 205, 240
Anu 391
Apes **196–7**, 196–7, 237, **238–9**, 239
Apex' animals 185
Apollo (astronomy) 319, **395**, 396
Apollo 11 108, 129
Apollo spacecraft 132, *140*, 143
Apothecaries, Society of 323
Apothecary **323**
Appalachians 59
Appel, Karel 491
Apple 161, **163**, 177
Apsu 392
Aqualung 76–7, **77**
Aqueducts **284**, 444
Aquinas, St Thomas 417, **426**, 427
Arabian Camel **233**
Arabian Night's Entertainment **340**, 514
Arabic literature 341
Arabic medicine 322–3, 325
Arabic numerals 307
Arachnids 202, 206–7
Aramis 364
Arc de Triomphe, Paris **477**
Archaeopteryx **195**
Archilochus of Paros 343
Archimedes 245, 249, **249**, 290
Archimedes's screw **249**
Architecture 435–92
Arctic Fox **228**
Arctic Ocean 72
Arctic regions 87
Arecibo observatory radio telescope **125**
Arianna (Monteverdi) 499
Ariel (satellite) 111
Ariosto, Ludovico 354–5
Aristarchus of Samos 100
Aristophanes 344, 346
Aristotle 62, 100, 153, 245, 264–5, 320, 322, 335–6, 345, 347, **421**, 422, 426, **426**
Aristotle, Elements of 320
Arizona, meteorite craters 115
Ark of the Covenant 411
Arkwright, Richard **24**, 318
Arlecchino 376, **376**
Armada, Spanish 45
Armadillos **234**, 235
Armat, Thomas 318
Armillary sphere **103**
Armous, Milanese **457**
Armstrong, Neil 129, 132
Arnold, Matthew 367
Ars Armatoria (Ovid) 347
Ars antiqua 497
Arsinoitherium 196
Ars nova 497
Ars Poetica (Horace) 347
Art 435–92
Art, definitiion of 435
Artemis **395**
Artesian basin 68
Artesian wells 68, **69**
Arthropoda, see Arthropods
Arthropods 186, **187**, 202–7
Arthurian literature 351–3, 355, 367
Arthur, legendary king of England 44, 351, **351**, 353, 367
Artificial fibres 180
Artificial satellites **130**, 130–1
Artist's Studio, The (Courbet) **483**
Art Nouveau 481, 486, 488
Art Nouveau lorgnette **480**
Art Nouveau motif **486**
Art Workers Guild 479
Aschelminthes **187**
Asclepius 319, **319**
Asclepius, Temple to **319**
Asia 86
Asia, map of **92–3**
Asoka 404, 406, **407**
Assize of Clarendon 30–1
Assur 392
Assyrian gods 391–2
Asteroids **110**, 111, 114
Astley's circus 385
Astrolabe **126**, 316
Astrolabe, Mariner's 126
Astrology 101, 118
Astronauts 129–35, *135*
Astronaut's clothing *134*, 135
Astronauts, training of 134–5
Astronomical laboratory **136**
Astronomy 99–128
Astronomy, Early 100
Astrophel and Stella (Sidney) 355
As You Like It (Shakespeare) 356
Athena 344, 396–7, 443
Athos 364
Atlanta (Beardsley) **487**
Atlantic Ocean 72
Atlas 89
Atmospheric steam engine 271
Atolls 73
Atom bomb 314, **314**
Atomic bullets 312–3
Atomic clock 262
Atomic energy 268, 277, 306, 313–4
Atomic physics 256, 261
Atmoic power stations 268–9, 272, **312**, 314
Atomic radiation 311–2, 315
Atomic research 311–4
Atomic theory 250, 252–3, 256
Atmoic weapons 262, 283
Atomic weights 253–5
Atomists 423
Atom, Model of the 245–6, 253, 257, 270
Atoms 251–3, 255–7, 262, 311–3
Atoms, Electron structure of **256**
Atom, Splitting the 312–3
Aton 394
Atonality 516
At the Piano (Whistler) 484
Attis 398
Attwood, Thomas 26
Atum-Re 393
Augustan age, The 347
Augustine, St (354–430) 335
Augustine, St (d.604) 44, 494
Augustus 347, 398, 444
Auks 220
Aurelius, Marcus 321, 426
Aurelius, Marcus 321, 426
Aurora australis 105
Aurora borealis 105, **105**
Austen, Jane 41, 365
Australia 86
Australia, map of **98**
Australian native cat 225
Australopithecus 197, **197**, 240
Autogiro 316, **316**
Automation 308–10
Automobile engineers 274–5

Autumnal equinox 107
Avalokitesvara 406
Avatars 403
Averroës of Cordova 323
Aves, see Birds
Avicenna **322**, 323, 325
Avicenna, medical encyclopedia 323
Avogadro, Amedeo 253
Axe, Ceremonial **453**
Axel Heiberg Glacier 87
Axle 248
Aye-aye 238
Ayer, A. J. 432
Azores 82
Aztec art 460–1
Aztec gods 400, **400**
Aztec mosaic skull **400**
Aztecs 83, 100
Aztec sacrifices **400**

Babbage, calculating machine 308, **308**
Babbage, Charles 308, 316
Babbitt (Sinclair Lewis) 372
Babington, Anthony 45
Baboons 238, **238**
Babylonian civilisation 99
Babylonian gods 391
Bacchia (Euripides) 344
Bach, Carl Philipp Emanuel 503
Bach, Johann Christian 504
Bach, Johann Sebastian 432, **500**, 501–2, 504, 510–1
Bacon, Francis 355, 491
Bacon, Roger **258**, 317–8
Bacteria 151, 154, 157–8, 175, 326, 333
Bacteriology 331
Bactrian Camel **233**
Baden-Powell, 1st Baron **36**
Badger, Common 230
Badlands 67
Baekeland, Leo H. 316
Baffin Bay 84
Baffin, William 84
Bagpipes **496**
Bahamas 83
Baird, John Logie **302**, 303–4, 318
Bairnsfather, Bruce **26**
Bakelite 316
Bakst, Leon 527
Balaclava, Battle of 46
Balance spring 316
Balanchine, Georges 527
Balboa, Vasco Nunez de 83
Balcony, The (Manet) **484**
Baleen 236
Baleen whales 185
Balfour Declaration 47
Ballads 353
Ball bearings **278**
Ballet 522–8
Ballet Theatre of America 528
Balloons 292, **292**, 316
Ball-point pen 316, **316**
Balzac, Honoré de 364, **364**, 483
Banana plants **179**
Bank of England 46
Banks, Joseph **175**
Bannockburn, Battle of 11, 44
Banyan tree 165
Baptrism 415
Barbarian art 448
Barbarian literature 348
Barbed wire 316, **316**
Barbican, London **43**
Barbier de Séville, Le (Beaumarchais) 358
Barbizon painters 481–2
Bardeen, W. J. 304, 318
Bardi, Giovanni 499
Barium 313
Barley 147, 176, 179
Barnard, Christiaan 335
Barnum and Bailey 386
Barometer 316
Baroque art 468–71
Baroque music 500, 502–3
Baroque table **469**
Barrow's Goldeneye Duck **219**
Barry, Charles 480
Bartholomew Fair (Jonson) 357, **357**
Bartök, Béla 516, **517**

Basalt 65, 71
Bassoon **514–5**
Bathers, The (Seurat) **484**
Batholiths 71
Bathyscaphe **74**, 75
Bathysphere 316
Bats 236, **237**
Batteries, Electric 268
Battle of Britain 275, 303
Battleship Potemkin, The (Eisenstein) 384
Baudelaire, Charles 363
Bauhaus 481, 486, 488–9
Bayeux tapestry **13**, 449
Beagle, HMS 187, 234
Beardmore glacier 87
Beardsley, Aubrey 486–7
Bears 230
Beatrice 352, **426**
Beauchamps, Charles 522–3
Beaumarchais, Pierre 358
Beaumont, Francis 357
Beaver **226**, 227
Becker (Anouilth) 370
Becket, St Thomas **30**, 44, 353
Beckett, Samuel 370
Becquerel, Henri 255
Beebe, W. 310
Bees 203
Beethoven, Ludwig van **506**, 506–7, 509–10, 513, 527
Beetles 202–3, **202**
Being and Nothingness (Sartre) 432
Bel 391
Belemnites 57, 189, 195
Belenus 398
Bell, Alexander Graham 298, 318
Bellay, Joachim du 354
Bellini Giovanni **439**, 459, 462–3
Bellini, Vincerenzo 511
Belloc, Hilaire 371
Bell X–1 rocket aircraft **277**
Belshazzar **412**
Benedictines 416
Benedict, St 416
Bennett, Arnold 371
Ben Nevis 48
Benois, Alexandre 527
Bentham, Jeremy 429
Benz, Karl 274, 318
Benz three-wheeler car **274**
Beowulf 349–50, **349**
Berg, Alban 517
Berkeley, George 428, 476
Berlioz, Hector **508**, 509, 515, 527
Bernhardt, Sarah 382, **382**
Bernini, Giovanni 468–9, 472, 500
Beryllium **256**
Berzelius, Johan Jakob 62
Bessemer converter 288, **288**
Bessemer, Henry 288, **288**, 318
Betatrons 312
Betelgeuse 124, 127
Betterton, Thomas 379
Betty, William **380**, 381
Beverages 179
Beveridge Report 31–2
Beveridge, William **31**, 32
Beyle, Marie Henri (Stendhal) 364
Bhagavad Gita 403
Bhikkhus 405
Bible, The 45–6, 341, 355, 359, 375, 392, 410–11, 413, 415–6, 449–50, 519
Bichat, Marie 329
Bicycles **278**, 316
Biennials 164
'Big-Bang' evolutionary theory 127–8
Billingham ICI works **289**
Bill of Rights (1689) 21
Binary stars 124
Binary system 308
Biology 149, 243
Bio-physics 244
Bird of Paradise, Magnificent **224**
Birds **186–7**, 186–7, 196, 208, 216–24
Bird's nest orchid **157**
Birds of prey 185, **185**, 219
Biro, Georg 316
Birth of a Nation, The (D. W. Griffith) 384
Birth of Venus (Cabanel) 477

Biscoe, John 87
Bison 233
Bissell, Melville R, 316
Bitter Sweet (Coward) 385
Bizet, Georges 515
Black beetle, see Cockroach
Black Death 44, 324, 451
Blackfriars Theatre 377
Black Hole of Calcutta 46
Black Rhinoceros **233**
Black Swan, Australian **218**
Blake, Admiral 46
Blake, William 360, 368, 478
Blasis, Carlo 524–5
Bleeding (medicine) 320
Blenheim, Battle of 46
Blood, Circulation of the 325
Blood groups 334
Blood pressure 330
Blood transfusions 327, 334
Bluebells **154**, 154
Blue Danube, The (Johann Strauss) 512
Blue Nile 85
Blue Shark **210**, 210
Boadicea 44
Boar, Wild 234
Boat during a Flood (Sisley) **484**
Bobcat, Canadian 228
Boccacccio, Giovanni 352
Bode, Johann 115
Bode's law **115**
Bodhisattvas 405, **405**
Boeing B–17 *Flying Fortress* **292**
Boeing 747 (Jumbo Jet) **276**
Boeing *Super Fortress* **276**
Boer War 47
Bohème, La (Puccini) **512**
Bohr atom, The 257
Bohr, Niels 257, 313
Boiardo, Matteo 354
Boleyn, Anne 17
Bologna, Giovanni 462
Bologna medical school 323
Bolshoi Theatre 528
Bondi, Hermann 128
Bonnard, Pierre 488
Book of Hours **455**
Book of the Dead 395
Borelli, Gian 326
Boris Godunov (Mussorgsky) 514
Boris Godunov (Pushkin) 368
Borman, Frank 132
Borodin, Alexander 513
Bosch, Hieronymus 464–5
Boswell, James **361**
Bosworth Field, Battle of 45
Botany 149, 176
Botany Bay 85
Bothwell, Earl of 17
Bottegas 457
Botticelli, Sandro 457
Bottle-nosed Dolphin **237**
Boulez, Pierre 517
Boulton and Watt 271
Bournonville, August 525
Bow and arrow 248
Box camera 305
Boxer Rising (China) 47
Boyce, William 504
Boyle, Robert 252, 270, 428
Boyne, Battle of the 46
Boy Scouts **36**
Brachiopoda, see Brachiopods
Brachiopods **187**, 190
Bradley, F. H. 430, **430**
Brady, Mathew 489
Brahe, Tycho 101–2, **109**, 125, 127, 267
Brahmans 402
Brahms, Johannes 508–10, **510**, 513, 527
Brancusi, Constantin 492
Brandenburg concertos 502
Brandenburger, J. E. 316
Brandenburg, Margrave of 502
Brandt (Ibsen) 369
Brant, Isabella **471**
Braque, Georges 490
Brass instruments **514–5**
Brattain, John 304, 318
Braun, Wernher von 130
Breakspear, Nicholas, see Adrian IV
Brearley, Henry 318

Brecht, Bertolt 370
Breeder reactor 314
Brennan, Louis 317
Breton, André 373
Brewster, David 317
Bridges **286–7**
Bridgewater canal 39, **39**
Bridgewater, Duke of 39
Brighton, Royal Pavilion **22**
Brindley, James 39
Britain and European partners 42–3
Britain an official handbook (HMSO) 48
Britain in the 1980s 43
Britain, invasions of 44
Britannia tubular bridge 38
British Commonwealth 38, 41, 42
British Empire 38, 41
British Isles 48, 73
British Isles, map of **10**
British Museum 30
Britten, Benjamin **516**, 517
Broadcasting 47, 302–4, 385
Broadcasting House, London **46**
Bromeliaceae 178
Brontë, Anne 365
Brontë, Charlotte 365
Brontë, Emile 365
Brontosaurus 193
Bronze Age 247
Bronzino, Angelo 462
Brooke, Rupert 372
Brothers Karamazov, The (Dostoevsky) 368
Brown, John 328
Brown, Lancelot **475**
Browning, Robert 367
Bruant, Aristide **486**
Bruce, James 85
Bruckner, Anton 513
Bruegel, Peter 464–5
Brunel, Isambard Kingdom 40–1, **40**
Brunelleschi, Filippo 457
Bruno, Giordano 250
Brunonian theory of medicine 328
Brut (Layamon) 351
Bryophytes 154, 159
Buddha 404–4, **405**, 407, 446, 452
Buddhism 404–7, 409–10, 446, 452
Buddhist monks 405, 452
Buddhist temples 406
Buds, Lateral 170
Buds, Terminal 170
Buffalo 233
Buffalo Bill, see Cody, William F.
Bufonide, see Toads
Bugs 203–4
Building materials 285
Bunsen burner 316
Bunsen, Robert 316, 318
Bunyan, John 359, 365
Burbage, James 376
Burbage, Richard 356, 377–8
Burgundian composers 498
Burke, Robert **86**, 86
Burial at Ornans (Courbet) 483
Burial of Count Orgaz (El Greco) **468**
Burial rituals 387–8, 395
Burne-Jones, Edward 481
Burns, Richard 86, **87**
Buschmann 316, 318
Bust of a child (Klee) **488**
Butler, Edward 274, 318
Butler tricycle 274
Buttercup *(Ranunculus)*154, **154**
Butterflies 202, **202–3**
Buttes **51**, 67
Buzzard **185**
Byrd, Richard E. 87
Byrd, William 499
Byron, 6th Baron (George Gordon) 363, **363**, 478
Byzantine art **415**, 445

Cabanel, Alexandre 477
Cabot, John 83
Cactoblastis 148
Cactus 147, **148, 166**, 167–8, 174
Cade, Jack 45
Caecilians 211–2
Caernarvon Castle 11, **11**
Caesar, Julius 44, 259, 347

Caesium 262
Caesium clock 262, **262**
Cainozoic era 54–5
Cairo Museum 340
Cakes and Ale (Maugham) 372
Calais 45
Calais, Siege of 44
Calculator, Pocket 308
Calculating machine (Leibniz) **428**
Calculating machines 336
Calder, Alexander 492
Calder Hall atomic power station **312**, 314
Calderon, Pedro 354
Caledonian canal 38
Calendar 259
Calendar clock **259**
Calendar, Reformation of the 46
Calendar year 106
Calgary Herald, Canada 181
Calligraphy 452, **452**
Callisto (satellite) 111
Call of the Wild, The (London) 366
Calvin, John 417
Camargo, Marie 523, **523**
Cambrian period 54–7, **149**, 189
Cameleopard, see Giraffe
Camels 233, **233**
Camera, Box 305
Cameron, Julia Margaret 489
Camus, Albert 371
Canada 46

Canals in Britain 39–40
Canary islands 82
Canaveral, Cape **134–135**
Cancer (disease) 335
Cancer, Tropic of 103
Candide (Voltaire) 361
Candle clock **258**, 261
Canidae, see Dogs, Wolves and Jackals
Canis, see Dog
Cannery Row (Steinbeck) 372
Cano, Sebastian del 83
Canterbury Cathedral 9, 450
Canterbury Tales (Chaucer) **30**, 353, **353**
Cantoria, Florence Cathedral **498**
Canute, king of England 44
Canzoniere (Petrarch) 352
Cape Canaveral *136–7*
Cape Kennedy, see Cape Canaveral
Cape of Good Hope 82, 86
Cape Verde Islands 82
Capillaries 326
Capricorn, Tropic of 103
Caracal, Indian 228
Caractères (de la Buyère) 358
Car assembly plant 310, **310**
Caravaggio 409, 473
Carbohydrates 157
Carbolic acid 331
Carbon 52, 289, 296, 315
Carbon fibre 289
Carboniferous period 54–5, **149**, 191, **191**
Carew, Thomas 359
Caribou 232
Carlyle, Thomas **365**
Carmen (Bizet) 515
Carnaval (Schumann) 508
Carnivora, see Carnivores
Carnivores 228–31
Carolingian minuscule 448
Carothers, W. H. 318
Carpet sweeper 316
Carp family 208
Carracci, Annibale 469
Carrion flower **172**
Carroll, Lewis (Charles Dodgson) 366
Carrots 147, 151, 163, **164**, 164, 177
Cartogrphy 88–9
Cartwright, Edmund **24**, 317
Casa Milá (Gaudi) 486
Case-histories (medical) 323
Cash register 316
Cassini family 90
Cassiodorus 348
Caste 402–3
Castle of Otranto (Walpole) 362
Castle, The (Kafka)371
Catherine de' Medici 522
Catherine of Aragon 16–7
Cathode rays 300, 302–3
Catiline (Jonson) 357
Cato Street conspiracy 46, 47
Cato the Censor 346–7
Cattle 233
Cats 228
Catullus, Gaius Valerius 347
Caudata, see Newts and Salamanders
Cavalier poets **359**
Cavaliers 18
Cavendish laboratory 256
Cave paintings 198, 245, **387**, 387–8, 439
Caves 68–9
Caxton, printing trade mark **353**
Caxton, William 45, 353
Caymans 212
Cecil, Robert 18
Cecilia, St **455**
CEEFAX 304
Cellini, Benvenuto 462, 465
Cello **514–5**
Cellophane 316
Cells, Plant 149–51, **150**, 153, 158, 164, 169
Cell tissues 151
Celluloid 316
Celsus, Aulus Cornelius 321
Celtic design **12**
Celtic gods 398
Celtic jewellery 448
Celtic literature 349
Celts 11–12, 14
Celts, migration to Britain 44
Census, first in Britain 46

Cephalopod **189**, 189, 191, 201
Ceramic lamp **467**
Ceramic plate **467**
Cereals 176, 182
Ceres (asteroid) 114
Cernunnos 398, **399**
Cerrito, Fanny 523, 525
Cervantes, Miguel de 354
Cézanne, Paul 487
Chadwick, James 257, 311
Chaffee, Roger 132
Chagall, Marc 491
Chain, Ernst 333
Chain reaction 313
Chairing the Member (Hogarth) 475
Chalgrin, J. 477
Chalk 64–5
Chalk figures, Celtic **399**
Challenger, see Space Shuttle
Challenger Deep 74
Challenger, HMS **74**, 75
Chamberlain, Neville 47
Chamber music **507**
Chamber's Journal 372
Chamber symphony (Schoenberg) 517
Chameleon **215**
Chamois 234
Chancellor, Richard 83
Chandra-giri temple 406
Changeling, The (Middleton) 357
Channel Islands 9, 11, 13, 48
Chansons de geste 350
Chanson de Roland 350–1
Chaplin, Charlie 384, **384**
Chapman, George 355
Charcoal 179, 181
Charlemagne 448, **449**
Charles I of England 18–21, **19–20**, 46, 325, 359, 471–2, **472**, 474
Charles II of England 20, **20**, 42, 46, 329, 359, 378
Charles Edward Stewart, Prince 46
Charles V, king of Spain 72
Charles of Anjou 73
Charles the Great, see Charlemagne
Chartists 25–7, **27**, 46
Chartres Cathedral 450, **450**
Chartreuse de Parme, La (Stendhal) 364
Chaucer, Geoffrey 352–3, **353, 355**
Cheddar Gorge 66
Cheetah 229, **229**
Chekhov, Anton 368–9, **369**, 382–3
Chelonians 213
Chelsea pensioner **329**
Chelsea Royal Hospital **329**
Chemistry 243–4, 252, 255, 277, 289
Chemotherapy 333
Cherry Orchard, The (Chekhov) 369
Chesil Beach, Dorset 70
Chesterton, G.K. 371
Chevreul, Michel 485
Chewing gum 182
Childe Harold (Byron) 363
Child psychology 336
Children, employment of 32–4, **32**, 36
Chilean pine **161**
Chimpanzee **238**, 239–40
China 82
Chinchilla 227
Chinese art 452
Chinese literature 340–1
Chinese religion 408
Chinook 80
Chirico, Giorio de 490
Ch'iu Ying 453
Chlamydomonas 155–6, **155**, 158
Chlorine **256**
Chloroform 331
Chlorophyll **150**, 151–2, 155–7, 163, 184
Chloroplasts 151–2, 155, 169
Chocolate 179
Choephori (Aeschylus) 343
Cholera epidemic (1854) 329
Choleric man 320
Chopin, Frédéric 508, **509**, 513
Choral symphony (Beethoven) 506, 510
Chordata, see Vertebrates
Chrétien de Troyes 351
Christ Glorified in the Court of Heaven (Fra Angelico) **497**
Christian art, Early 445, 448
Christianity 410, 414–8
Chromosomes 151
Chronometer 260, 316
Church and the theatre 375
Churchill, Winston **15**, 47
Church of England 17, 37–8, 417
Church of South India 417
Church of the Nativity **415**
Cicero, Marcus Tullius 347
Cid, El (Rodrigo or Ruy Diaz) **350**
Cid, Le (Corneille) 358
Cid, Poema de Mio 350–1
Cierva, Juan de la 316
Cinderella 385
Cinema 305–6, 384–5, 489
Cinématographe (Lumière brothers) 305
Cinematography 316
Cinerama 385
Cinnabar 255
Circular motion 278
Circulation of the blood 325
Circus 385–6, **385**
Circus Maximus 385
Cirques 69
Citrus fruits 177
Civil War (England) 18–9, 21, 46, 357
Clarendon, Assize of 30–1
Clarinet **514–5**
Clarissa (Richardson) 361
Clark, William 85
Classical ballet 522
Classification of animals 186–7, **186–7**
Classification of plants 153–4
Claude, Georges 318
Claudel, Paul 373
Clavius 109
Clay 64
Clay map (Babylonian) **88**
Clemens, Samuel Langhorne (Mark Twain) 366, **367**
Clementi, Muzio 507
Clepsydra **259**
Clifton suspension bridge 40
Climate 76–7
Climbing plants 164, 166, 175
Clinging roots **164**
Clippies' on London buses **28**
Clive, Robert 46
Clocks **258–9**, 261–2, 316
Cloudbursts 78
Cloud chamber 312
Clouds 78, **78**
Clytemnestra 344
Coal 57, 64–5, 76, 268, 289
Coalbrookdale iron bridge **286**
Coalmine **65**
Cobra, Egyptian **214**
Cocaine 180, 331
Cocoa 179
Cockcroft, John **313**
Cockerell, C. S. 317
Cockroach 204
Cocteau, Jean 370
Code of Terpischore, The (Blasls) 525
Cody, William F. 386
Coelacanth **210**
Coelenterata, see Coelenterates
Coelenterates **187**, 199
Coffee 147, 179
Coleridge, Samuel Taylor 362–4
Colet, John 355
Colette 371
Collage 438
Collieries Act (Britain) 34
Collins, Wilkie 371
Colosseum (Rome) **444**
Colt, Samuel 318
Colubridae 215
Columba, St 44
Columbine 386
Columbus, Christopher 82, **82**, 126, 182, 498
Comédie-Française 378, 380, 382
Comédie Humaine (Balzac) 364
Comets 115
Command module (*Apollo* 11) **138–9**
Commedia dell'arte 358, 376, **376**, 378, 386
Commodus 346
Common Prayer, Book of 45
Commonwealth of Nations 38–9
Common Wild Rabbit **228**
Communications satellites 138–9
Communist Manifesto (Marx) 431
Compass, Mariner's **73**, 89
Compass, Ship's **87**
Compositae 177
Composite fruits 163
Compound microscope **151**
Computer drawing machine 308
Computers 308–9, 316
Conan Doyle, Arthur 372
Concertina 316
Concorde **282–3**
Condottiere **457**
Conductors (electrical) 294
Confucianism 408
Confucian Analects 408
Confucius 341, 408, **408**
Conglomerates 64
Congreve, William 359, 379
Conifers 160–1, **161**
Conrad, Joseph **370**
Conservation of energy 268
Constable, John 478–9
Constantine I 348, 416, **416**, 445
Constantine (the African) 323
Constellations 100, 118, 123
Constellations, northern sky **121**
Constellations, southern sky **120**
Constitutional monarchy 18
Contact lens 317
Continental drift 51, 58–9, **59**
Continental shelf, 73, **73**
Continental slope 73
Convair XFY-1 **292**
Conversion of St Paul, The (Caravaggio) **469**
Cooke, William 318
Cook, James 84–5, **86**, 87, 260
Cooper, Fenimore 362
Copernicus (moon crater) 109
Copernicus, Nicolas **100**, 101–3, 265
Copley, John Singleton 476
Coppélia (Delibes) 525
Copper, 65, **255**
Coptic church 393
Coq d'Or, Le (Rimsky-Korsakov) **526**
Coracle **290**
Coral islands 73
Coralli, Jean 525

Corals 64, 72, **187**, 189, 192, 194, 199
Coral snakes **215**
Cor anglais **514–5**
Cordoba mosque **418**
Corelli, Arcangelo 500, 503
Cork 180
Corneille, Pierre 358
Corn Laws (Britain) 46
Cornets, Peers' **23**
Corot, Jean 482
Corpuscles, Blood 326
Correlation of rocks 57
Cortés, Hernando 83, **83**, 400
Cortisone 333
Così fan tutte (Mozart) 505
Cosimo de Medici 456
Cosmic radiations 315
Cosmology 127
Cosmonauts 129, 133
Coster, see Laurens Janszoon
Cotopaxi 71
Cottages at Cordeville (Van Gogh) **487**
Cotton gin 317
Cotyledons **160**, 161
Coulomb, Charles Augustin 296
Coulomb (electrical charge) 296
Council houses 37
Counting machines 307–8
Count of Monte Cristo (Dumas) 364
Couperin, François 501
Courbet, Gustave 482–3, 485
Court dances 521, **521**
Court lady (T'ang period) **453**
Courtly love 350
Court of Criminal Appeal 31
Courtship dances 519
Cousin the Elder, Jean 465
Cousteau, Jacques 76–7
Covent Garden Opera House 381
Coward, Noel **385**
Cowper, William 360
Cowpox virus 330
Coypu 227
CPU, see Central processing unit
Crabbe, George 360
Crab Nebula 122, 125
Crabs **187**, 196, 202, 207
Cranach, Lucas 464
Crane, Stephen 366
Crayfish 207
Creation myths 392–3
Creation, The (Haydn) 509
Crécy, Battle of 44
Creek Indians 390
Creeping plants 167
Cremona 500
Creodonts 196
Cretaceous period 53–5, 149, 194–6
Cretan art 442
Crickets 204, **204**
Crime and Punishment (Dostoevsky) 368
Crimean War 46, 332–3
Crinoids 189
Cristofori, Bartolommeo 318, 500–1
Cristofori piano 501, **501**
Critique of Judgement (Kant) 429
Critique of Practical Reason (Kant) 429
Critique of Pure Reason (Kant) 429
Crocodile **212**, 212–3
Cro-Magnon man 198, **240**
Crompton, Samuel **24**, 318
Cromwell, Oliver 19, **19**, 21, 46, 327, 358–9
Cromwell, Richard 19
Crookes, William 256, 300
Cross-pollination 171–2
Crucible, The (Miller) 371
Cruciferae, see Crucifer family
Crucifer family 177, 182
Crucifixion (Grünewald) 463
Crusades 44
Crustaceans 202, 207, **207**
Crystallography 62
Crystal Palace, London **34**, 481
Crystal systems 62
Cubists 486–7, 490
Cuchulinn 349
Cuckoos 222
Cucurbitaceae 177
Cuff, Sergeant 372
Cugnot, Nicolas 272, 318
Cugnot, steam carriage **272**
Culloden, Battle of 46
Curie, Marie 255, 306, 311, 318, 333
Curie, Pierre 318, 333
Cuscus 225
Cuttings, Taking 164
Cuttlefish 201
Cuvilliés, François de 470
Cuzco 400
Cybele 398
Cybernetics 336
Cycads 160
Cyclone 78
Cyclopean masonry 284–5
Cyclops 285
Cyclotron 312
Cygnus (constellation) 101, 125
Cylinder seals **391**, 455
Cymbal **514–5**
Cymbeline (Shakespeare) 356
Cynognathus 192
Cyrano de Bergerac (Rostand) 370
Cyrus the Great 412, **413**

Dadaism 490
Dagda 398
Daguerre, Louis **304**, 305, 318, 489
Draguerreotype 304, 318
Daily Mail 371
Daily Mirror 371
Daimler, Gottlieb 274, 317
Daisy family 177
Dalai Lama 406
Dali, Salvador 335, 491
Dalton, John 252–3, **252**, 255–6
Dame aux camélias, La (Dumas) 370
Dance mask, African **388**
Dance mask, Alaskan **390**
Dance of Death, The 451, **451**, 464
Dance to the Music of Time (Poussin) **493**
Danes 13–4
Daniel 412
D'Annunzio, Gabriele 373
Dante Alighieri 353, **352**, 426
Daphne (Water flea) 207
Daphnis and Chloe (Ravel) 515
Darius the Median 412
Darkroom, Mobile 304
Darnley, Henry Stewart, Lord 17
D'Artagnan 364
Darwin, Charles 85, 187, **187**, 189, 193, 213, 234, 478
Das Kapital (Marx) 431
Dauberval, Jean 523
Daudet, Alphonse 364
Daumier, Honoré 482–3
D'Avenant, William 379
David 411, **411**
David Copperfield (Dickens) 365
David,Jacques Louis 477, **477**
David (Michelangelo) 459
Davison, Emily 27
Davy, Humphry 294, **295**, 317
Dead Sea Scrolls 413, **413**
Death of a Salesman (Miller) 371
Death of Marat (David) 477
Death of Ophelia, The (Millais) **481**
Deburau, Gaspard 386
Debussy, Claude 488, 515, **515**, 516–7
Decameron (Boccaccio) 352
Decapods 201
Decimal system 308
Decline and Fall of the Roman Empire (Gibbon) 346, 361
Deep sea fishes **210**
Deer 232
Deer, Red **48**
Defoe, Daniel 360
De Forest, Lee 302, 305
Degas, Edgar 484–5, 524
De Havilland *Comet* 4, **276**
Deimos (satellite) 111
Delacroix, Eugenè 478
Delius, Frederick 515
Delphi 396
Deltas **66**, 67
Deluge, The (Michelangelo) 459
De Medicine (Celsus) 321
Demeter 396–7
Democracy in Britain 15
Democritus 250, **422**, 423
Demoiselles d'Avignon, Les (Picasso)490
Dendera temple, Egypt, **101**
Dennis fire engine **274**
De Rerum Nature (Lucretius) 347
De revolutionibus orbium coelestium (Copernicus) 100, 103
Derain, André 487
Descartes, Rene 335, 357, 427, **427**, 428, 432, 468, 503
Desert plants 173–4, **174**
Deserts 70
Detective stories 366, 371–2, **372**
Dettingen, Battle of 46
Devonian period 54–5, 149, 190–1, **190**
Dew 78
Dewar, James 318
Dewey, John 432
Diaghilev Ballet 526–8
Diaghilev, Sergei 517, 526-7, **526**
Dialogues (Plato) 425
Diatoms 185
Diaz, Bartholomew 82
Dickens, Charles 365
Dickinson, Emily 373
Dicotyledons 154, 161, 163
Dictionary, Johnsons English 361
Didactic poetry 343
Didelot, Charles 523
Diderot, Denis 361
Dido and Aneas (Purcell) 500
Diesel engines 275, 317
Diesel locomotive **273**
Diesel, Rudolf 275, 317
Digital watches 261
Dinichthys 190
Dinosaur 183, 193–6, 213
Dinosaur eggs 56
Diode valve 302
Dione (satellite) 111
Dionysus 343, 374, 396
Diorite 64–5
Dioscorides 153
Diplodocus **192, 195**
Disciples, The 416
Discourse on Method (Descartes) 427
Discoveries and inventions 316
Discoveries 87
Diseases 325, 327–9, 331
Disney, Walt 384
Disraeli, Benjamin 26
Dissection 320–5
Dittersdorf, Karl von 504
Divers **77**, 216
Divina Commedia)Blake illustration) **478**
Divina Commedia (Dante) 352, 426
Divine Proportion 437
Divine right of kings 17
DNA molecule **246**
'Docking' in space 132, **132**, 279
Dodgson, Charles (Lewis Carroll) 366
Dodo **220**
Dogs 228–9
Doll's House, The (Ibsen) 369
Dolphins 236–7
Dome of the Rock **418**
Dome of the Rock, ceramic lamp **467**
Domesday Book 44
Domestic dogs **228**, 229
Dominicans 417
Dominic, St **426**
Domitian 346
Donald Duck 384
Donatello 457
Don Giovanni (Mozart) 505
Donizetti, Gaetano 511
Don Juan (Byron) 363
Don Juan (Richard Strauss) 513
Donne, John 358
Don Quixote (Cervantes) **354**, 360
Doppler, Christian 119, 282
Doppler effect 119, 122, 282
Dorian mode 495
'Dormitory' towns 41
Dostoevsky, Feodor 368
Double-base **514–5**
Dounreay 314
Dowland, John 499
Dragonflies 204
Dragonfly, Giant **191**
Draker *290*
Drake, Francis 45, **83**, 83
Drama 339–74
Dromedary, see Arabian Camel
Drugs 180–1, 325, 333–5
Druids 398–9
Drumlins 69
Drury Lane Theatre 379, **379–80**
Dryden, John 359, 363
Dry Fruits **163**, 163
Dr Zhivago (Pasternak) 369
Duccio di Buoninsegna 451
Duchamp, Marcel 490
Duchess of Malfi, The (Webster) 357
Duck-mole, see Platypus
Ducks 219
Du côté de Chez Swann (Proust) 371
Dufay, Charles François 294
Dufay, Guillaume 498
Dufy, Raoul 487
Dugong 236
Dumas *fils*, Alexandre 370
Dumas *père*, Alexandre 364
Dunbar, Battle of 44
Duncan, Isadore 526, **526**
Duncan, king of the Scots 44
Dunkirk, Evacuation of 47
Dunstable, John 498
Dupin, Aurore (George Sand) 364
Dürer, Albrecht 437, 439, 463–4, **463**, 466
Duse, Eleonore 382
Dutch painters 472
Duverney, Joseph 327
Dvořák, Antonin 513
Dyaus Pitar 401
Dyck, Anthony van 471–2, 475
Dyes 182
Dying Swan, The (Saint-Saëns) 527
Dykes 71
Dynamics 261, 263, 267, 276
Dynamite 317
Dynamo 317

Ea 391
Earth 105
Earth, atmosphere 107, **107**
Earth, circumference 246
Earth, core **58**, 58, 107
Earth, crust **58**, 58–61, 64, 72
Earth, diameter 107
Earth, mantle **58**, 58, 60–1, 72
Earth moving machines 269
Earth, orbit 106
Earth, origin of 51–3, **52**
Earthquakes 59, 60–1, **61**
Earth, structure of 58, **58**
Eastern theatre 383
East India Company 45
East Indies 83
Eastman, George 305
Echidna 225, 228
Echinodermata, see Echinoderms
Echinoderms **187**, 207
Eckhart, Meister 417
Eclipse of the moon **104**
Eclipse of the sun 100, 104, **104**
Eclogues (Virgil) 347
Ecole des femmes (Molière) 358
Ecology 173
Edda, Prose 349, 399
Edda, Poetic 348, 399
Edentates 235
Edgehill, Battle of 18
Edict of Milan 445
Edison, Thomas Alva 298–9, **299**, 305, 317–8, 384
Education Acts (Britain) 36–7, 46–7
Edward the Confessor 44
Edward the Elder 44
Edward I, king of England 11, 16, **20**, 44
Edward III, king of England **21**
Edward IV, king of England **21**, 45
Edward V, king of England **21**, 45
Edward VI, king of England **20**, 45
Edward VII, king of England **21**
Edward VIII, king of England **21**, 47
Edward II (Marlowe) 356

EEC, see European Economic Community
Eel 209
Egbert, king of Wessex 44, 48
Egypt 47
Egyptian art 442
Egyptian building methods **268**
Egyptian chariot wheel **247**
Egyptian dancing 519
Egyptian gods 393
Egyptian music 493
Egyptian scribe **340**
Egyptian temples 268, 442
Egyptian tomb painting **442**
Egyptian wall painting **393**
Egyptian warship **290**
Ehrlich, Paul 333
Eiffel, Gustave 480–1
Eiffel Tower, Paris **480**, 481
Einstein, Albert 105, **262**, 262, 313–4
Eisenstein, Sergi 384, 489
Either–Or (Kierkegaard) 431
Electra 344
Electrical energy 294–6
Electrical engineering 297
Electrical resistance 296
Electric batteries 268, 317
Electric blanket 317
Electric cell 295
Electric currents 256, 295
Electric flat iron 317
Electricity 256, 294–6
Electricity, Static 80
Electric lamp **298**, 299, 317
Electric light 298–9
Electric motor 317
Electric railway signal **296**
Electric telegraph **297**, 298
Electric trains **296**
Electric violin 298
Electromagnetic machine 317
Electromagnetism 297–8, 301–2
Electron, Controlling the 244, 294
Electron microscope **158**, 251, 317
Electronic clocks 261
Electronic 'eye' 302
Electronics 261
Electronics 246, 256–7, 262, 295–6, 300–2, 306, 311–2
Electrostatics 256, 294
Elegy in a Country Churchyard (Gray) 360
Elements, Aristotle's 264–5, 320
Elements, Chemical 252–5
Elements, Empedocles's **264**
Elements (Euclid) 244
Elements, Natural 118
Elements of Mechanics (Archimedes) 249
Elephants 234–5
Eleusian mysteries 396–7
Elgar, Edward 514
Eliot, George (Mary Ann Evans) 365–6
Eliot, T. S. 370, 373
Elizabeth I, queen of England **17**, 17–8, **20**, 45, 294, 356, 374, 465, 474, 498
Elizabeth II, queen of England **21**, 47–8
Elizabethan drama 355–7, **356–7**
Elizabethan theatres 376
Elk, European 232
Ellesmere manuscript **30, 353**
Ellipsoid 58, **59**
Elssler, Fanny 525, **525**
Eluard, Paul 373
Embalming 320, **321**
Embarkation for Cythera, The (Watteau) 471
Emerson, Ralph Waldo 366
Emma (Austen) 365
Empedocles 264, 320
Emperor Penguin **216**
Empiricists 428
Empiric school of medicine 320, 325
Encaustic painting 445
Endeavour 84
Energy 267–70
Engels, Friedrich **431**
England 9, 11–12, 14, 48
English art 474–5
English drama 359, 369
English language 13
Engligh literature 352–3, 355, 358–63, 365–7
English theatre 378–81
Enigma Variations (Elgar) 514
Enki 391
Enlil 391
Ennius 346
Enquiry (Hume) 429
Enume elish 392
Enzymes 153
Eocene period 54–5, 57, **149**, 196, 238
Eohippus 196, **196**
Epic poetry 342–3
Epicureans 426
Epicurus 426
Epidaurus, Temple to Asclepius **319**
Epidaurus, Theatre at 374
Epiphytes 159, 175
Epsilon Aurigae 127
Epstein, Jacob 492
Equilibrium 244, 284, 284–293
Equinoxes 106
Erasistratus 320, 325
Erasmus, Desiderius 355, 464, **464**
Eratosthenes 81, **246**
Erebus 87
Ernst, Max 490
Eroica symphony (Beethoven) 506
Eros (asteroid) 114
Erosion 51, 66, **66**, 69
Escorial, Madrid 468, **473**
Eskimo mask **440**
Eskmimos 390
Essais (Montaigne) 354
Essay Concerning Human Understanding (Locke) 428
Essay of Dramatic Poesy (Dryden) 359
Essays of Elia (Lamb) 362
Essenes 413
Essex, 2nd Earl of 45
Esterházy family 504
Ether 331
Ethics 421
Ethics (Spinoza) 428
Ethiopia 85
Etna 71
Etruscan art 444, **445**
Etruscan religion 398
Etruscan temples 444
Etruscan tomb painting **494**
Euceladus (satellite) 111
Euclid **244**
Eugene Onegin (Pushkin) 368
Euglena 199, **199**
Eumenides (Aeschylus) 343
Euripides 344, 362
Europa (satellite) 111
Europen Economic Community 42, 47
European gods 398
Europe, map of **91**
Eurypterids 190, **190**
Euthymides 443
Evangelical movement 417
Evans, Mary Ann, see Eliot, George
Evelyn, John 20
Evening News 371
Everest, Mount 86, 108
Everglades, USA 69
Everyman 353
Everyman in his Humour (Jonson) 357
Everyman out of his Humour (Jonson) 357
Evesham, Battle of 44
Evolution, Theory of 187
Executions of 3rd May, 1808, The (Goya) **476**
Existentialism 431
Exodus, The 410, 413
Expanding Universe, The 123
Experimental Researches on Electricity (Faraday) 294
Exploration 81
Exploration, maps **84–5**
Exploration, underwater 76–7
Explorer I *131*
Expressionist painters 487, 490, 492
Eyck, Jan van 454–5
Eyre, Edward John 85
Fables 342, 351, 358
Fables (La Fontaine) 358
Facts about Britain 48
Factory Acts (Britain) 34, 36, 46
Faerie Queen (Spenser) 355
Fair Maid of Perth, The (Scott) 365
Fairy tales 362–3, 369
Falkland Islands War 43, 47
Falla, Manel de 515, 517
Falling Water (Wright) 491
Falstaff (Verdi) 512
'Famille Rose' bottle **452**
Family of Darius before Alexander, The (Veronese) **463**
Fantastic symphony (Berlioz) 509
Faraday, Michael 256, **294**, 294 298, 301, 317–8
Faraday's laboratory **294**
Farmers, The first 389
Faroes 82
Faulkner, William 372
Fauré, Gabriel 515
Faust (Goethe) 362
Faustus, Dr (Marlowe) 356
Fauves, Les 487
Fawcett, P. H. 318
Fear and Trembling (Kierkegaard) 431
Feininger, Lyonel 488
Fermi, Enrico 313–4
Ferns 154, 159, **159**, 190
Ferns, fossils **57**
Fertilisers 182
Festival of Britain 47
Fetish 390
Feudal system 14, 44
Fibres 180
Fibrous root system 164, **164**
Fidelio (Beethoven) 506
Fielding, Henry 361, 368
Field, John 508
Field mouse 227
Field of the Cloth of Gold 45
Fighting Téméraire, The (Turner) **479**
Fille mal Gardée, La (Dauberval) 523
Fingal's Cave 71
Finlandia (Sibelius) 515
Finn 349
Finnegan's Wake (Joyce) 371
Fiords 70
Firebird, The (Stravinsky) 517, 527
Fire clock, Chinese **258**
Fire of London, Great 46, **326**, 474
Fire Salamander, European **211**
First artists, The 439
First Folio, Shakespeare 356
First World War 26–8, 47, **47**
Fir trees 154
Fisher, Alva J. 318
Fishes **186–7**, 186, 190, 192–4, 196, 208–10, **208–10**
Fish symbol (Christianity) 445
Fissipeda, see Dogs, Cats, Weasels and Bears
Fitch, John 318
Five pillars (Islam) 419
Five positions (ballet) **522**
'Fixed' stars 119
Flags (Great Britain) **14**
Flamboyant (architecutre) 454
Flamenco 520
Flamingo, Greater **218**
Flamsteed, John **124**
Flat-earth theories 99–100, **101**
Flatworms **187**, 200
Flaubert, Gustave 364
Fleas 205
Fleming, Alexander 318, 333, **333**
Fleming, John 302
Flemish painters 454, 464–5
Fleshy fruits 163, **163**
Fletcher, John 357
Fleurs du Mal, Les (Baudelaire) 363
Fliedner, Theodor 332
Flies 202, 204
Flodden Field, Battle of 45
Flooding 67
Floppy disks **309**
Florence **352**, 456–9
Florence Cathedral 457
Florentine painting 451, 457
Florey, Howard 333
Flotation, Principle of 290
Flower, Parts of a 170–1, **171**
Flowers, Structure of 170–1
Fluids 290
Flukes **187**, 200
Flute **514–5**
Flying Dutchman, The (Wagner) **510**
Flying fish 209
Flying foxes 236
Flying saucers 114
Flying shuttle 24, 317
Flying squirrel **227**
Fog 78
Föhn winds 80
Fokine, Michael 526–7, **527**
Fokker triplane **292**
Fokker tri-motor **292**
Folk dancing 520
Fontainebleau 465, **465**
Fontana di Trevi **468**
Fonteyn, Margot 528, **528**
Food chains 184–5
Food crops 147, 176
Food from the sea 75
Force 265–6
Ford, Henry 274, **310**
Ford Model T car, **274**, 310
Ford Motor Co. 310
Forests 148, 173
Forlanini, Enrico 317
Forrest, Edwin 382
Forrest, John 87
Forster, E.M. 371
Forsyte Saga, The (Galsworthy) 371
Forth Railway Bridge, Scotland **287**
Fortune Theatre 378
For Whom the Bell Tolls (Hemingway) 372
Fossils 53, **53**, 56–7, **57**, 187–9, **188**, 191, 194, 197
Foucault, Jean **106**, 317
Foucault pendulum **106**
Fountain Court, Hampton Court **475**
Fouquet, Jean 455
Four Noble Truths (Buddhism) 405
Foxes 229
Fox Indians 390
Fox, Samuel 318
Fracastoro, Girolamo 325
Fram 87
France, Anatole 365
Franciscane 414–5
Francis I, king of France 45, 462 465
Francis of Assisi, St 414, **426**
Francis, Sam 491
Franck, César **511**
Frankenstein (Mary Shelley) 362
Franklin, Benjamin **80**, 294, 317, 477
Frederick II, king of Germany 352
Freedom of speech 23
Frege, Gottlob 432
Freischutz, Der (Weber) 511
French art 465, 469–70, 476–7
French drama 358
French literature 351–4, 357–8, 361, 363–4
French theatre 378, 380–1
Frequency 263
Fresco 438, **451**
Freud, Sigmund **335**, 335–6
Friendly Societies 31
Friendship 7 (space capsule) 131, **131**
Friese-Greene, William 305, 384
Frigga 399
Fringe-fins 190
Frisch, Robert 313
Froebel, Friedrich 336
Frogs 186, 211, **211**
Frost, Robert 373
Fruits 163, 177–8
Fruits, Classification of 163
Fry, Elizabeth 33, **33**
Fuchs, Vivian 87
Fugue, The 501
Fuller, Richard Buckminster 285
Fumaroles 71–2
Funeral dances 519
Funerary barque **393**
Fungi 147, 154, **156–7**, 155–8, 175
Furniture beetle 203

Gabbro 64–5
Gabo, Naum 492
Gagarin, Yuri 131, **133**
Gainsborough, Thomas 475
Galapagos islands 187, 213
Galaxies, Moving 123
Galaxy, The 122–3, 125
Galen **321**, 321–2, 325, 328, 335
Galenus, Claudius, see Galen
Galilei, Galileo 101, 260–1, 263, **265**, 265–6, 305, 316, 318, 325, 468, 498–9
Galilei, Vincenzo 499
Galsworthy, John 371
Galvanic cell 295
Galvani, Luigi 295
Galvanised iron 295
Galvonometer 295
Gama, Vasco da 82, **82**
Game birds 220
Gamma rays **301**, 306
Ganymede (satellite) 111
Gaping Ghyll, Yorkshire 66
Gargantua (Rabelais) 354
Garnerin, André 318
Garrick, David 358, 379, **379**, 380
Garuda **401**
Gascoigne, William 317
Gases 251, 270, 290
Gas lighting 317
Gas, Natural 64–5, 76
Gassendi, Pierre 250
Gatling, Richard, 317
Gaudi, Antoni, 481, 486
Gauges, Railway **41**
Gauguin, Paul 486–8
Gautama, see Buddha
Gautier, Théophile 363
Gavials 212
Gawain and the Green Knight, Sir 351
Gazelles 233
Gecko 215
Geiger counter 311. **311**
Geissler, Heinrich 256–7
Geissler tube 256, **257**
Gellée, Claude 469, 474, 479
Gemini (spacecraft) **131**, 132
Gemstones 62–3
General Strike (Britain) 35–6, **36**, 47
Genes 151
Genet, Jean 370
Geodesic dome **285**
Geoffrey of Monmouth 351
Geological time scale chart **54–5**
Geometry theorem **423**
George I, king of England **21**, 22, 503
George II, king of England **21**, 22, 46, 502
George III, king of England **21**, 46, 125
George IV, king of England **21**, 22, 46
George V, king of England **21**, 28
George VI, king of England **21**
George, St 457
George, Stefan 373
George's Cross, St **14**
Georgics (Virgil) 347
'Georgium Sidus', see Uranus
Géricault Theodore 478
German art 463–4
German literature 362
German theatre 380–1
Gerusalemme Liberata (Tasso) 354
Geysers 71
G-force acceleration 133–4
Gharial (Indian) 212, **212**
Ghent altarpieces 455, **455**
Ghiberti, Lorenzo **457**
Ghirlandaio, Domenico 459
Giacometti, Alberto 492
Giant Panda **231**, 231
Giant's Causeway 71
Giant Tortoise **213**
Gibbon, Edward 346, **361**
Gibbons, Orlando 499
Giffard, Henri 292, 316
Giffard's airship **292**
Gide, André 371
Gilbert (the Englishman) 323
Gilbert, William 294–5
Gilbert, W. S. 513
Gilgamesh, Epic of **342**, 342, 350, 392
Gillette, King C. 318
Ginkgo tree 160
Giorgione 459, 462
Giotto di Bondone 451
Giraffe 234, **234**
Giselle (Coralli) 525
Giza, Pyramids of 269
Glaciers 66, 69–70
Gladstone, William 26, **26**, 47
Glass **300**, 442
Glass Menagerie, The (Williams) 370
Glencoe, Massacre of 46
Glendower, Owen 44
Glen, John 131, **132**
Glidden, Joseph F. 316, 318
Glinka, Mikhail 513
Globe Theatre **89**, 376, **377**, 384
Gloster E 28/39 276, **276**
Gloster *Meteor* 276, **276**
Gluck, Christoph Willibald 505
Gnat, see Mosquito
Gneiss 65
Gnu 65
Goats 234
Gobelins tapestry 470, 485
Gobi desert 86
Goddard, Robert Hutchings 130
Godwit **221**
Goes, Hugo van der 455
Goethe, Johann Wolfgang von 362–3, **363**, 380, 507
Gogh, Vincent van 439, 487, 490
Gogol, Nikolai 368
Gold ear-rings (Pre-Columbian) **461**
Golden bowl, The (James) 367
Golden Gate Bridge, San Francisco **287**
Golden Orioles **222**
Golden Pavilion, Kyoto **452**
Golden Section (or Mean) 437
Goldfish 208
Goldoni, Carlo 358
Gold pendant (Mixtec) **461**
Goldsmith, Oliver 361
Gold, Thomas 128
Goliath 411
Gordon, Bernard 323
Gordon, General 47
Gorges 66
Gorilla 239, **239**
Gorky, Maxim 368–9
Gospels, The 415
Gothic art 436, 449–51, **450**, 454–6, **496**
Gothic novels 361–2
Gouache paint 438
Goujon, Jean 465
Gounod, Charles 515
Gourds, Oranamental **176**, 177
Governor, Automatic 271
Govind Singh 420
Goya, Francisco 475–6, 478, 485
Graaf, R. de 327
Grafting (surgery) 334
Graf Zeppelin **292**
Graham, George 119
Grahame, Kenneth 372–3
Grahn, Lucile 523, 525
Gramineae 176
Grand Canyon **67**
Grande Messe des Morts (Berlioz) 509
Grand Testament (Villon) 353
Granite 64–5
Granth 420
Grapes 178–9, **179**
Graphic design **488**, 492
Graptolites 57, 189
Grass family 147, 176
Grasshoppers **204**, 204–5
Grave posts **389**
Gravitation 102, 266–7, 278
Gravity 107, **107**, 138
Gray, Stephen 294
Gray, Thomas 360
Great Auk **216**
Great Barrier Reef 74
Great Bear, see Ursa Major
Great Britain 9–11, 48
Great Britain (ship) 40
Great Council 15–6, 28–9
Great Crested Grebe **217**
Great Eastern **40**, 40–1
Great events in British history 44–7
Greater London 41
Great Exhibition (1851) **34**, 46, 479, 481
Great Fire of London 42, **326**
Great Red Spot, see Jupiter
Great Rift Valley 60
Great Train Robbery, The 384
Great Wave off Kanazawa, The (Hokusai) **453**
Great Western 40
Great Western Railway 40, 297
GWR diesel railcar **274**
Great Whin Sill 71
Grebes 216
Greco, El 468, **468**
Greek art, 442–3
Greek astronomy 100
Greek comic actor **344**
Greek dancing 519, **519**
Greek drama 339, **339**, 343–4
Greek gods 395
Greek literature 339, 342–5
Greek medicine 319–20, 322, 324
Greek modes 494–5
Greek mythology 395–6
Greek philosophy 245, 250, 422–3
Greek religion 395–6
Greek science 245, 249
Greek temples 443
Greek theatres 374, **374**
Green, Charles 292
'Green Revolution' 182
Greene, Graham 371
Greenland 82
Greenwich Hospital **42**
Greenwhich Mean Time 260–2
Greenwich observatory **124**, 260
Gregorian chant 494–5
Gregory of Tours 348
Gregory the Great 44, **494**, 495
Grendel 349
Grenfell, Julian 372
Greuze, Jean Baptiste 475
Grey, Lady Jane 21, 45
Grieg, Edward 515
Griffith, D. W. 384
Grimm, Brothers 362–3
Grisi, Carlotta 523, 525
Grissom, Virgil 132
Gropius, Walter 481, 488–9
Grünewald, Matthias 463
Guanaco 233
Guericke, Otto von 253
Guernica (Picasso) 490
Guggenheim Museum **489**
Guido d'Arezzo 496
Guillaume de Lorris 351
Guillaume de Machaut 497–8
Guillemot **221**
Gulf Stream 75, 78
Gulliver's Travels (Swift) 360, **361**
Gulls 220
Gundestrup bowl **399**
Gunpowder 317
Gunpowder plot 45, **45**
Gurney, Goldsworthy 272
Gurney steam carriage **272**
Gutenberg, Johannes 318, 455–6
Guthrum 44
Gwynne, Nell 379
Gymnosperms 154, 160–1
Gyro-compass 317
Gyroscope 317

Habeas Corpus Act 46
Hadley, John 318
Hadrian 44
Hadrian, Coins of **44**
Hadrian's Wall 44, 71
Hahn, Otto 313
Hahnemann, Samuel 329
Hail 78
Hales, Stephen 330
Half life of radioactive material 311, 315
Hallelujah Chorus 502
Hallenkirche 450
Haller, Albrecht von 328, **328**
Halley, Edmund, 115
Halley's Comet 115
Hals, Frans 472
Hamlet (Shakespeare) 356, 378, 380–1
Hamsters 226–7, **227**
Handel, George Frideric 502–4, **503**
Hanoverian kings 21
Hansa jet 32o HFB **277**
Hardie, James Keir **28**, 35
Hardy, Thomas 366
Hares 228
Hargreaves, James 24, 318
Harleian manuscript **30**
Harlequin 376, **376**, 386
Harlow New Town 42
Harmonic motion 279–81
Harmonograph **280**
Harmony 495
Harmony (Whistler) 484
Harmony in Grey and Green (Whistler) **484**
Harmsworth, Alfred, see Northcliffe, 1st Viscount
Harold in Italy (Berlioz) 509
Harold, king of England **13**, 44
Harris, Joel Chandler 366
Harrison, John 260–1, 316
Harrison's chronometers **260**
Harvey, William 325–6, **325**
Hastings, Battle of 13, 44, 115
Hastings, Warren 46
Hathaway, Anne 356
Haüy, René Just 62
Hawker Siddeley *Harrier* VTOL **276**
Hawthorne, Nathaniel 366
Haydn, Franz Josef 504–6, 509, 514
Hazlitt, William 381
Health Service, Britain 32, 37, 47
Hearst, William Randolph **371**
Heart of Midlothain, The (Scott) 365
Heart transplants 335
Heath, Edward 42–3
Heavens, The, map of **120–1**
Hebrides overture (Mendelssohn) 509
Hector **343**
Hedda Gabler (Ibsen) 369
Hedgehog 226, 228
Hegel, Friedrich 430–1, **430**
Heimskringla (Snorri Sturlason) 349
Heine, Heinrich 362, 507
Heinkel He 178, 317
Hel 399
Helium **256**
Helmont, Jean van 325
Hemicycle **258**
Hemingway, Ernest 373–3
Hemispheres 106
Henderson, Arthur 35
Hengist and Horsa 44, **45**
Henlein, Peter 262, 318
Henry, Joseph 298, 301, 317–8
Henry I, king of England **20**
Henry II, king of England **20**, 30–1, 44
Henry III, king of England **20**, 44
Henry IV, king of England **21**, 45
Henry V, king of England **21**, 45
Henry V (Shakespeare) 377
Henry VI, king of England **21**
Henry VII, king of England 16, **21**, 45, 454
Henry VIII, king of England **16**, 16–7, **21**, 31, 37, 45, 324, 355, 464
Henry II, king of France 522
Henry of Anjou, see Henry 11 of France
Henry of Portugal, Prince 82, **82**
Henry, prince of England 47
Hera 396
Heracles, see Hercules
Heraclitus 422–3
Herbert, George 358
Hercules 398
Hereward the Wake 44
Hermann und Dorothea (Goethe) 362
Hermes 396
Hero, device for opening doors **244**
Herodotus **344**, 345
Heron family 218
Hero of Alexandria 244
Hero of our Times, A (Lermontov) 368
Herophilus 320

Herring 209
Herring gull **221**
Herschel, Frederick (William) **125**
Herschel, John F. 317, 489
Herschel, telescope 125
Hertz (frequency measurement) 263
Hertz, Heinrich 263, 301
Hesoid 343
Hiawatha (Longfellow) 366
Hickok, Wild Bill 382
Highs, Thomas 318
Hill, Rowland 318
Hillary, Edmund 87, **87**
Hilliard, Alice **474**
Hilliard, Nicholas 474
Himalayas 59–60
Hindemith, Paul 517
Hindenburg 292, **292**
Hindu-Arabic numerals 307
Hindu art 446
Hindu gods **401**, 402–3
Hinduism 401–4, 410, 446
Hindu temples 403
Hipparchus 316
Hippocrates of Cos 319, 321–2, 335
Hippocratic Oath 319
Hippopotamus 234, **235**
Hiroshige 484
Hiroshima 314
Historia Coelestis Britannica (Flamsteed) 124
Historia Regum Britanniae (Monmouth) 351
History, Great events in British 44–7
History of Art among the Ancients (Winckelmann) 477
History of Plants (Theophrastus) 153
Hitler, Adolf 47, 130
Hoatzin **224**
Hobbes, Thomas 429
Hobby horse **278**
Hoff, Jacobs van't 289
Hofmannsthal, Hugo von 373
Hogarth, William 474–5
Hokusai 453, 484
Holbein, Hans 451, 462
Hollywood 384–5
Holmes, Sherlock 372, **372**
Holocene period 54–5
Hologram 307
Holst, Gustav 514
Holy Family, The (Raphael) **458**
Holy Lamb medallion **415**
Holy Roman Empire 449
Holy Trinity, The (Masaccio) 457
Homer 319, 339, 342–3, 355, 360
Hominidae 240
Homoeopathic method 329
Homo eructus see *Pithecanthropus*
Homo sapiens 198, 240, 388
Hong Kong 46
Hooded Merganser **219**
Hooke, Robert 151, 261, 287
Hooke, microscope **151**
Hoover Dam **68**
Hopkins, Gerard M. **368**
Horace 347
Hormones 333
Horn **514–5**
Horned Toad **211**
Horse **196**, 198, 231
Horsehead Nebula 122
Horsepower 279
Horses emerging from the sea (Delacroix) **478**
Horetails **159**, 190
Horus, 393, **393–4**, 395
Hospital, Chelsea Royal **329**
Houdon, Jean Antoine 470
House Martin **224**
House of Commons 14–7, **15**, 19, 22–4, 28, 48
House of Lords 14–5, 18–9, 22–4, 28–9, 48
Houses of Parliament, London 480
Hovercraft 293, **316**, 317
Howe, Elias 318
Hoyle, Fred 128
Hrothgar, king of Denmark 349
Huaca 400
Huastec culture 460
Hubble, Edwin 123
Hubert brothers 454
Hubris 396
Huckleberry Finn (Twain) 366–7
Hudson Bay 83
Hudson, Henry 83, **83**
Hugo, Victor 363–4, **483**
Huiracocha 400
Hui-tsung 452
Huitzilopochtli 400
Humboldt, Alexander von 85
Hume, David 428, 432
Hummel, Johann 507
Humming birds 222–3, **223**
Humoral school of medicine 328
Humours, Theory of (Hippocrates) 319–20
Hundred Years' War 44, 451
Hunter, Bronze (Nigeria) **441**
Hunterian collection (medicine) 329
Hunter, John 328, **329**, 330
Hunt, Holman 481
Hunting rituals 387–9
Hunt, Walter 318
Hurricanes 79, **79**
Hutton, James 51
Huxley, Aldous 371
Huxley, Thomas H. **193**
Huygens, Christiaan **260**, 261, 316
Hyades 124
Hyatt, J. W. and I, 316
Hydraulics 284
Hydrofoil **291**, 317
Hydrogen 253–5, **256**, 257, 262, 289
Hydrography **75**
Hydrophytes 173
Hydrostatics 249
Hyenas 229
Hygiene 330
Hyksos, The 410
Hyperion (satellite) 111
Hyperons 315
Hypodermic syringe 317
Hysteria 326

Iapitus (satellite) 111
Ibex 234
Ibsen, Henrik 369, **369**, 382–3, 515
Ice ages 69, 197–8
Icebergs 69
Iceland 82
Iceman Cometh, The (O'Neill) 370
Ichthyosaurs 193–6
ICI works, Billingham **289**
Idealism 430
Idealists 421
Idiot, The (Dostoevsky) 368
Idylls of the King (Tennyson) 367
Iffland, August 380
Igneous rocks 63, **64**, 71
Iguana 215
Iguanodon **192**, 195
Iliad (Homer) 342, **343**, 360
Illuminated manuscript 448, **497**
Immigrants to Britain 38–9
Immunology 329–31, 334
Impala 233
Imperial Russian Ballet 526, 528
Importance of Being Ernest, The (Wilde) 370
Impressionists, The 483, 485–7, 490
Impression, Sunrise (Monet) 485
Inca art 460–1
Inca gods 400
Incandescent electric lamp **298**, 299
Incarnation, The 416
Incas 83, 100, 248
Income Tax, Introduction 46
Incunabula 456
India 47, 82
Indian art 446
Indian literature 340–1
Indian Mutiny 46
Indian Ocean 72
Indra 401
Industrial Injuries Act 32
Industrial Relations Act, 1971 43
Industrial Revolution 24–5, **25**, 38, 261, 271, 367
Indus Valley civilisation 401
Inflorescence 169–70, **170**
Infra-red rays 77, 304
Ingres, Jean Auguste 477
Inoculation 327, 330
Inscriptions, Pyramid of **460**
Insect-eating plants **174–5**, 174–5
Insecticides 182
Insectivores 226–8
Insectivorous plants 174–5, **174–5**
Insects 186, **187**, 191, 202
Instruments, Musical 494, **514–5**
Insulators 294
Insulin 333
Insurance Act (Britain) 47
Insurance, National (Britain) 31–2
Intelligence tests 336
Interferons 333
Internal combustion engine 269, 274–5, 317
International Geophysical Year 87, 130
Interpretation of Dreams, The (Freud) 335
Interstellar material 122
Invasions Allied (1944) 47
Inventions and discoveries 316
Invertebrates 189–90, 200, 202, 207
Io (satellite) 11
Iona 44
Ionesco, Eugene 370
Ions 256
Iphigenie auf Tauris (Goethe) 362
Ireland, Northern 9, 11–13, 48
Ireland, Republic of 11–13, 48
Irish Home Rule 47
Irish literature 349
Iron Age 247
Iron bridge, Coalbrookdale **286**
Iron lungs 334
Iron sculpture, African **389**
Iroquois Indians 389
Irrigation 68
Irrigation, Artificial 248
Irving, Henry 382
Irving, Washington 362
Irwell aqueduct, River **39**
Isaiah 411–2
Isenheim altarpiece 463
Ishtar 391
Isis **393–4**, 395, 398
Islam 410, 418–20
Islamic art 446, 466–7
Islamic astronomy **126**
Islands 73, **73**
Isle of Man 11–13, 48
Isle of man railway **263**
Isle of Wight 48
Isnik ceramic plate **467**
Isotopes 315
Israelites 410–2, **411**, 415
Israili of Kairwan, Isaac 323
Italian art 468–9
Italian literature 352–4, 358
Italian opera 381, 511–2
Italian theatres 375–6, 381
Ivanov, Lev 525

Jackal 229
Jacobite rebellions 46
Jade ornament **440**
Jaguar 229
Jainism 407
Jain pillar **406**
Jain temples 407
Jaipur observatory **126**
James, Henry 366–7
James I (of England and VI of Scotland) 11, 17–8, **20**, 45, 325, 374, 377, 474
James II, king of England **20**, 20–1, 46
James IV, king of Scotland 45
James, William 432
Janáček, Leoš 516
Jane Eyre (Brontë) 365
Jansen, Zacharias 251, 317
Jansky, Karl 125, 318
Janszoon, Laurens 455
Janus (satellite) 111
Japanese art 452, 484–5
Jardins sous la pluie (Debussy) 515
Jazz Singer, The 306, 384
Jeans, James **110**
Jeffreys, Justice 46
Jehan, Shah 446–7
Jellyfish **187**, 189, **199**, 199
Jenner, Edward 318, 330, **330**
Jenneret, Charles Edouard, see Le Corbusier
Jerusalem 411–2, 414–5, 418
Jesuit observatory, Peking **127**
Jesuits 417
Jesus Christ 414–7, 419, 445
Jet engines 13, 276, 317
Jewellery 442, 448
Jewish festivals 413
Jewish National Home 47
Jew of Malta, The (Marlowe) 356
Jews, Expulsion of from England 44
Jina 407
Joan of Arc 45
Jodrell Bank radio telescope **124**
John the Baptist, St 414
John the Evangelist, St (Velasquez) **473**
John Gilpin, The Diverting History of (Cowper) 360
John, king of England **20**, 44, **45**
Johnson, Life of (Boswell) 361
Johnson, Samuel 361, **361**, 475
Johnson's English *Dictionary* 361
Joliot-Curie, Frederick 313
Jolson, Al 306
Jones, Inigo 42, 474
Jongleurs 350
Jonson, Ben 357–8, **357**
Joseph Andrews (Fielding) 361
Josquin des Prés 498
Joule, James 270
Joule (measurement of energy) 270
Journaism 371
Joyce, James 371
Judaism 410–2, 415, 418
Judson, W. L. 318
Julius II, pope 459
Jung 335
Jungle Books, The (Kipling) 366
Juno 397
Juno and the Paycock (O'Casey) 370
Juno (asteroid) 114
Jupiter 101, **110–1**, 111–4, **113**
Jupiter (Roman god) 397, 401
Jurassic period 54–7, **149**, 193
Jury service 30–1
Jutes 11, 44, 349
Juvenal 347, 360

Ka'abah 418–9, **419**
Kabuki plays **382**, 383
Kafka, Franz 371
Kaiserwerth 332–3
Kaleidoscope 317
Kali 403
Kandinsky, Vassily 488, 490
Kangaroos 225
Kant, Immanuel 335, 429–30, **429** 432
Karma 401–2, 405, 407
Karsavina, Tamara 527, **527**
Kay, John 24, 317
Kean, Edmund **380**, 381
Keaton, Buster 384
Keats, John 363
Kekule, Friedrich 289
Kells, Book of **348**, 448
Kemp, Will 378
Kendall, Larcum 260
Kennedy, Cape, see Canaveral, Cape
Kennedy, John 135
Kepler, Johann 101–2, **102**, 125, 267
'Key' animals 185
Keyboard instruments 500–1
Kharas, Little and Great 60
Khartoum, Fall of 47
Khnum 393
Kidnapped (Stevenson) 366
Kidney machines 334
Kidney transplants 334–5
Kierkegaard, Sören 431, **431**
Killer whale **236**
Kim (Kipling) **367**
Kinetic energy 268–70, 277
Kinetoscope 305
Kingfisher **222**
King Lear (Shakespeare) 356, 379
Kings and queens of England **20–1**
King's College, Cambridge **454**
Kipling, Rudyard 366–7
Kirchoff, Gustave 318
Kirov Ballet 528
Kitchener, 1st Earl 47

Kiwi 216, **216**
Klee, Paul 488, 491
Knitting machine 317
Koala 225, **225**
Koans 406
Koch, Robert 331
Kodály, Zoltán 516
Kodiak Bear **230**
Kokoschka, Oscar 491
Kola peninsula 61
Komarov, Vladimir 132
Komodo Dragon 215
Konarak, temple of **403**
Koran, The 341, 419
Kremer, Gerhard, see Gerhardus Mercator
Krill 183, 185, 236
Krishna 403
Krypton 313
Kudu 233
Kuiper's star 127
Kung-fu-tzu, see Confucius

Laboratory, Cavendish **254**
Laboratory, Marie Curie's **254**
Labour government, first in Britain 47
Labour Party in Britain 35, 47
Labours of Heracles **396**
Labrador 82
La Bruyère, Jean de 358
Ladybird 203
Laënnec, René 318, 330
La Fontaine, Jean de 358
Lagomorpha 228
Laika (dog space traveller) 131, **141**
Lakes 68
Lamaism 406
Lamarck, Jean **169**
Lambaréné 432
Lamb, Charles **362**
Lamb, Mary 362
Lamp, Incandescent electric **298**, 299
Lampreys 208
Lamp-shells **187**, 190–2
Lancaster, House of 20
Lancaster, aircraft **245**
Lanchester, Frederick 274
Lancret, Nicolas 523
Landing on the moon 129, **129**, 132, **140–1**
Landslides 66, 68
Langland, William 351
Language, Truth and Logic (Ayer) 432
Langur 238
Lao-Tzu 408, **408**
Laplace, Pierre 110, **112**, 270
La Réale 290
Large Magellanic Cloud 123
Lark, The (Anouilh) 370
La Rochefoucauld 357
Lascaux 198, **387**
Laser 306, **306**, 317
Last of the Mohicans (Fenimore Cooper) 362, **362**
Last Supper, The 415
Latex 181, **181**
Latimer, Hugh **37**, 45
Laud, William 46
Laughing Cavalier (Hais) 472
Laura 352, 355
Lavoisier, Antoine 252, 330
Law in Britain, The 29
Lawrence, D. H. 371
Lawrence, Ernest O. 312
Laws of motion 265–7, **266–7**, 278–9
Laws of Simultaneous Contrast of Colours, The (Chevreul) 485
Layamon 351
Leaf arrangement on stems **167**
Lef insects 205, **205**
League of Nations 47
Leaning tower of Pisa **449**
Leaning tower of Pisa, Galileo's experiments 265
Leaves 167–8, **168**
Leaves, classification of **168**
Le Corbusier 491
Leeches **187**, 200
Lee, Rev. William 317
Leeuwenhoek, Anton **158**, 326
Leeuwenhoek's microscope **158**
Légende des Siècles, La (Hugo) 363
Legend of Sleepy Hollow, The (Irving) 362
Leguminosae 176
Leibniz, Gottfried 270, 307–8, 427–8, **428**, 432
Leibniz's calculating machine **428**
Leichhardt, Ludwig 86
Lemaître, Abbé Georges 127
Lemming 227
Lemurs 237–8
Lenin (ship) **290**
Lenoir, Etienne 317
Le Nôtre, André 470
Leo I, pope 416
Leo X, pope 45
Leonardo da Vinci **250**, **324**, 436, 458–9, 465, 498
Leonardo, medical drawings **324**
Leonardo, scientific drawings **250**
Leoninus 496
Leopard 228–9
Lepois, Charles 326–7
Leptons 315
Lermontov, Mikhail 368
Letchworth 41
Le Sage, Alain René 361
Letters (Cicero) 347
Lever systems 248, **248**, 286
Leviathan (Hobbies) 429
Lewis, C. S. 372
Lewis, Meriwether 85
Lewis, Sinclair 372
Libra (constellation) **118**
Liddell, Alice 366
Lieder 508
Life after death 395
Life for the Tsar, A (Ginka) 513
Life in the Camp (Mir Sayyid Ali) **466**
Life on other planets 114
Life, Origin of 52–3
Life-support system in space 135
Lift 317
Lifting machines 248, **248**
Light 77
Light, Colours of 102, 118
Lighter-than-air craft 292, **292**
Lightning 80, 294, **295**
Lightning conductor 317
Light, Speed of 116
Light years 116
Liliaceae 177
Lily family 177
Limbourg brothers 455
Limestone 64, 66, 68
Limpet 201
Linacre, Thomas 324
Lincoln, Abraham 489
Lind, James 330
Lindsay, Nicholas Vachel 373
Linear accelerator 312
Linguistics 336
Linnaeus (Carl Linné) 153–4
Linoleum 317
Lion 228, **229**
Lion Court, Alhambra **466**
Lippershey, Hans **100**, 318
Lippi, Fra Filippo 457
Lipstick 182
Liquid-fuelled rocket 130, 136–7
Liquids 251–2, 270
Lister, Joseph 316, 331–2
Liszt, Franz 508–9, 513
Literary criticism 359
Literature 339–74
Little Auk **221**
Little dancer aged 14, The (Degas) **485**
Little Grebe 216, **217**
Little tern **221**
Liverpool and Manchester Railway **40**, 272
Liverworts 159, **159**
Living religions 401
Livingstone, David 86, **86**
Livius Andronicus 346
Livy 347
Lizards 212, 214–5
Llama 233
Lloyd George, David 27, **27**
Lobster 202, 207
Locke, John 428, **430**
Locking Piece (Moore) **492**
Locomotion No. 1 40, **272**
Locomotives, Steam 272, **272–3**, 279
Locomotive wheel, Model **247**
L'Octroi (Rousseau) **488**
Locust 297
Lodestone 297
Logarithmic tables 307
Logic 422, 426
Logical positivism 432
Logs, Transporting **180**
Lolita (Nabokov) 372
London Bridge 9, **18**
London, City of 41, 43
London, Greater 41
London, Jack 366
London, Tower of 9, **449**
Longfellow, Henry Wadsworth 366
Longitude and time 259–61
Loom, Power 317
Lord Chancellor of England **29**
Lorenzo de' Medici 250, 459
Loud, John 316
Loudspeaker 298–9
Louis XIII, king of France 469
Louis XIV, king of France 90, 378, 469–70, **469**, 500, 522–3, **522**
Louis Philippe, king of France **482**
Louvre, Paris 458, 483
Lovelace, Richard **359**
Lovell, James 132
Love the Magician (de Fella) 515
Lower Depths, The (Gorky) 369
Lower, Richard 327
Lucretius 347
Luddite riots 46
Ludwig II, king of Bavaria 479
Lully,Jean Baptiste 500
Lumière, Auguste 305, 384
Lumière, Louis, 305, 316, 384
Lunar module **129**, 132, **140–1**
Luna spacecraft 140
Luncheon of the Boating Party, The (Renoir) **485**
Lundström, J. E. 317
Lungfish 190–2, 210
Lunik spacecraft 140
Lurs **495**
Lute 499, **499**
Luther, Marting 417, **417**, 464, 468, 499
Luttrell, Geoffrey 497
Luttrell Psalter **496**
Luxembourg Palace 471
Lyceum (Athens) 426
Lydian mode 495
Lyell, Charles 51
Lynx, (constellation) 228
Lyra (constellation) 122
Lyrical Balads (Coleridge and Wordsworth) 362
Lyric poetry 343, 347
Lysippus 443

Macadamised roads **39**, 317
McAdam, John 39, 317
MacAlpine, Kenneth, king of Scotland 44
Macbeth, king of the Scots 44
Macbeth (Shakespear) 356, 379
McCormick, Cyrus H. 317
Machaon 319
Machiavelli, Niccolo 354–5,**355**
Machine-gun 317
Machines 286
Machines, Early 248–9
Mackenzie, Alexander 85
Mackenzie, Compton 371
Mackenzie River 85
Mackintosh, Charles Rennie 486
Macmillan, Kirkpatrick 316
Madame Bovary (Flaubert) 364
Madame Buttterfly (Puccini) 512
Madeira 82
Mademoiselle de Maupin (Gautier) 363
Madrigals 499
Mafeking, Relief of 47
Magdeburg experiment **253**
Magee, C. C. 318
Magellan, Ferdinand **72**, **82**, 83, 123
Magellanic Clouds 123
Magellan strait 72
Magna Carta 18, 44
Magnetic forces 297
Magnetic pole 107
Magnets 251
Magnifying glass 258
Magnitude of stars 118
Magritte, René 490
Mahavira, Vardhamana 407
Mahayana 406
Mahler, Gustave 513
Maidenhair tree 160
Maids of Honour, The (Velasquez) 473
Maiman, Theo 306, 317
Maimonides 323
Main Street (Lewis) 372
Mallard **219**
Mallarmé, Stéphane 364
Malory, Thomas 351, 353
Malpighi, Marcello 326
Malplaquet, Battle of 46
Malraux, André 371
Mamallapuram temple, **402–3**
Mammals 183, 186, **186–7**, 196–7, 208, 225–40
Mammoth Cave, USA 69
Mammoth fossils 56
Mammoth, Woolly 187–8, 198, **198**
Man 197–8, 237, 240
Mane 389–90, 400
Manatee **236**
Mandarin duck **219**
Mandrill 238
Manet, Edouard 484–5
Man explores his world 81
Mangrove trees 165, **165**
Man in space, First 131, **133**
Man-omade fibres 289
Mannerism 462, 465, 468
Mannheim school (music) 504
Mann, Thomas 371
Manon Lescaut (Prévost) 361
Man Pointing (Giacometti) **492**
Mansfield Park (Austen) 365
Man's life on earth, time scale 240
Manta Ray **210**
Mantegna, Andrea 457
Mantell, Dr and Mrs 195
Man travels in space 129
Mantua, Duke of 471, 499
Manutius, Aldus 456
Map, Africa **95**
Map, Antarctic exploration **84**
Map, areas of rainfall **76**
Map, areas of sunshine **77**
Map, Asia **92–3**
Map, Australia **98**
Map, Babylonia clay **88**
Map, British Isles **10**
Map, Europe **91**
Map, land in Cambrian times **55**
Map, land in Eocene times **55**
Map, land in Jurassic times **55**
Map, Mercator's **88**
Map, New Zealand **98**
Map, Nile delta **66**
Map, North America **96**
Map, Ordnance Survey **90**
Map, Roman roads **38**
Map, routes of world explorers **84–5**
Maps, earthwake and volcanic zones **61**
Maps, the heavens **120–1**
Maps, History of 88–9
Map, Sinai Peninsula **107**
Map, South America **97**
Map, South-East Asia **94**
Map, T-O **88**
Marble 65
Marchantia **159**
Marconi, Guglielmo 301, 318
Marduk 391–3, **392**
Mare, Walter de la 373
Margarine 317
Mariage de Figaro, Le (Beaumarcais) 358
Marianas Trench 75
Marine clock 261
Marine light, Automatic **315**
Mariner's compass **73**

Mariner spacecraft 112, 142
Marionettes 386
Marivaux, Pierre 358
Markhor 234
Markova, Alicia 528
Markus, Siegfried 274
Marlborough, Duke of 46, **47**
Marlowe, Christopher 355–6, **355**, 376, 378
Marmoset 238
Marram grass 164
Marriage of Figaro, The (Mozart) 505
Mars 110–4, **110–2**, 127, 397
Mars, spacecraft probes 141–2
Marston Moor, Battle of 18, 46
Marsupial mole 225
Marsupials 225–6
Martial 347
Marvell, Andrew 358
Marx, Karl **430**, 431
Maryinsky Theatre 525, 528
Mary I, queen of England 20, **20**, 37, 45
Mary II, queen of England **20**, 21, 46
Mary, queen of Scots **17**, 45
Masaccio 457
Masks, Theatrical 339, 374–5
Masques 378
Mass in B-minor (Bach) 502
Massine, Leonide 527
Master Builder, The (Ibsen) 369
Mastersingers of Nuremberg, The (Wagner) 380, 511
Mastodonsaurus **192**
Matches 317
Materialism 431
Materialists 421
Materia Medici (Dioscorides) 153
Matilda 44
Matisse, Henri **487**
Matter, The nature of 250–3
Maugham, Somerset **372**
Maune Loa 71
Maupassant, Guy de 364
Mauretania **290**
Mauriac, François 371
Maury, Matthew Fontaine 75
Mawson, Douglas 87
Maxims (La Rochefoucauld) 357
Maxwell, James Clerk 301
Maya culture 460
Mayer, Julius 270
Mayflower 46
Mayow, John 326
Maypole dances 398
Maywood, Augusta 525
Mécanique céleste (Laplace) 112
Mecca 418–20, 466
Mechanics 285–6
Mechanisation 309
Médée (Corneille) 358
Medical books 324–5
Medical encyclopedia (Avicenna) 323
Medical plants 147, 180
Medical school, Bologna 323
Medical school, Montpellier 323
Medical school, Salerno 323
Medical schools, Early 320
Medical schools, Middle Ages 323
Medical science 319–36
Medical services, Roman 321
Medicine 243, 319–36
Medicine man **320**
Medicine 180–1
Medieval dancing 521, **521**
Medieval music 496–7
Medina 418
Meditations (Descartes) 427
Medusa 462
Megaliths, Prehistoric **438**
Mège-Mouries, H, 317
Meitner, Lisa 313
'Melancholy man' 320
Melanesians 389
Méliès, Georges 384
Melville, Herman 366–7
Menai suspension bridge **38**
Menander 344
Mendeleyev, Dmitri 254
Mendel, Gregor **162**
Mendelian law of heredity 162
Mendelssohn-Bartholdy, Felix 509–10
Mercator, Gerhardus **88**, 89
Mercator's World Map **88**, 89
Merchant of Venice, The (Shakespeare) 356
Mercia 44
Mercury 110–2, **110–1**, **113**, 114
Mercury/Atlas ocket **133**
Mercury ore 255
Mercury spacecraft 131
Mer, La (Debussy) 515
Mérimée, Prosper 364
Mesas 67
Mesons 315
Mesophytes 173
Mesozoic era 54–5
Messerschmitt Me163B **276**
Messerschmitt Me262 **276**
Messiaen, Olivier 517
Messiah, The 413–4
Messiah (Handel) 502
Metallurgy 269, 288
Metals, Structure of 287–9
Metamorphic rocks 63, **64**, 65
Metamorphoses (Ovid) 347
Metamorphosis of Narcissus (Dali) **491**
Metaphysics (Aristotle) 426
Meteorites 115
Meteoroids 114
Meteorology 76
Meteors 114
Methodist Church 46, 417
Meung, Jean de 351
Mexico 83
Meyer, Lothar von 254
MGB Roadster **274**
Mice 226–7
Michelangelo 457, 459, **459**, 462, 465, 469, 478, 483, 498
Mickey Mouse 384
Microbes 331
Microchip 304, 308
Microcomputer 308
Micrometer 317
Microphone 297–9
Microscope 317, 326
Microscope, Adams' Universal **251**
Microscope, Compound **151**
Microscope, Electron **158**, 251
Microscope, Leeuwenhoek's **158**
Microscopic plants 155, **155**
Microscopic world, The 244, 250, 257
Middle C 281–2
Middleton, Thomas 357
Midsummer Night's Dream, A (Shakespear) 509
Migration of Butterflies 202
Migration of eels 209
Mikado, The (Gilbert and Sullivan) **513**
Milan Cathedral **436**, 450
Military Macaw **223**
Milky Way 122, 125
Mill 249
Millais, John Everett 481
Mille, Agnes de 528
Millepede 186, 202, 207
Miller, Arthur 370–1
Millet, Jean François 482–3
Mill, John Stuart 429, **429**
Milne, A. A. 372
Milton, John **358**, 359
Mimas (satellite) 111
Mime 386
Minaret **419**
Mineral deposits 63
Mineralogy 62
Minerals 61–3, **63**, 255
Minerals, crystal structures **63**
Minerals in the sea 76
Minerals, Uses of 65
Miners' safety lamp 317
Minerva **397**
Mini-minor **275**
Mining **62**
Mink 230
Minnesingers 497
Miocene period 54–5, 57, **149**, 197
Miracle plays 353, 375, **375**, 497
Miranda (satellite) 111
Miró, Joan 490
Mirror in the Chinese Taste **471**
Mir Sayyid Ali 446
Misanthrope, The (Bruegel) **464**
Misanthrope, Le (Molière) 358
Missile frigate **290**
Missionaries 417
Mistral 80
Mitchell, Thomas 86
Mites 202, 206–7
Mithraism 410
Mithras 44, 398
Mithras, Temple of (London) &
Mixtec culture 461
Moby Dick (Melville) 366, **367**
Model aircraft 245, **245**
Model parliament 16, 44
Models, Scientific 245–6, 261, 265
Modern architecture 491
Modern art 490
Modern drama 369–71
Modern music 515–7
Modern novel 371–2
Modern philosophy 426
Modern poetry 372–3
Modern sculpture 492
Modern theatre 382–3
Moeritherium 196
Mogul Empire 82
Mogul painting **447**, **466**
Mogul sword hilt **446**
Mohammed 341, 418–20, 466
Mohenjo-Daro 401
Mohenjo-Daro, dancing girl **446**
Mohole project **60**, 61
Mohorovicic, Andrija 61
Mohorovicic Discontinuity 61
Mohs, Friedrich 62
Mohs' scale 62
Mole 226
Molecules 252, 255, 289
Molière 346, 358, **358**, 378, 380, 500
Moll Flanders (Defoe) 361
Mollusca, see Molluscs
Molluscs 186, **187**, 189, 194, 199–201
Monadology (Leibniz) 428
Monads 428
Mona Lisa (Leonardo) **458**
Monarchy, Constitutional 18
Monarchy in England 48
Monasteries, Dissolution of the 45
Monasticism 416–7
Mondrian, Piet 490
Monet, Claude 484–5
Mongolia 82
Mongolian Wild Horse 231
Mongoli invasions 466
Mongoose **230**, 231
Monists 421
Monkey puzzle tree **161**
Monkeys 237–9
Monks, Buddhist 405
Monmouth, Duke of 46
Monocarpic perennials **164**
Monoclonals, see Antibodies
Monocotyledons 154, 161, 163
Monorail 317
Montague, Mary Wortley 330
Montaigne, Michel de 354–5
Monteverdi, Claudio 499, **499**, 500, 510
Montezuma 460
Montfort, Simon de 16, 28, 44
Montgolfier brothers 316
Montpellier, medical school 323
Mont St Michel **111**
Monument Valley, USA **51**
Moon, The 108, **108**, 111
Moon and Sixpence, The (Maugham) **372**
Moon craters 109
Moon, distance from the earth 108
Moon, eclipse of **104**
Moon, gravity on 108
Moon landing 129, **129**, 132, *140–1*
Moon, phases of **108**, 109
Moon probes 131, 139–41
Moon, seas 109
Moon, size 108
Moon, temperature 108–9
Moore, Henry 492
Moore, Sir John 46
Moorish dancing 520
Moose **232**
Moraine 69
Morality plays 353, 375, 497
More, Thomas 355, **355**, 464
Moreton Old Hall, Cheshire **465**
Morley, Thomas 499
Morphine 147, 180
Morris dancing 520
Morris, 'Sussex' chair **480**
Morris, Wandle chintz **480**
Morris, William 368, 479–80, 486, 488, 492
Morse code 298, 301, 317
Morse, Samuel F. B. 297–8, 317
Morse's signalling apparatus **298**
Morte d'Arthur (Malory) 351, 353
Mosaic 445
Mosasaur 195
Moses 410–1, **410**, 413
Moses and Aaron (Schoenberg) 517
Moses ben Maimon, see Maimonides
Moslems 418–20
Mosques 466, **467**
Mosquito 199, 202, 204
Moss animals **187**
Mosses 154, 159
Mother goddess figures **388**, 401, 440
Moths 202, **202–3**
Motion 244, 261, 263–83
Motor-car 318
Motor-cycle 318
Motor vehicles **274–5**
Moulton bicycle **278**
Mountain chains 59–60
Mountains, Block 60
Mountains, Erosion 51
Mountains, Folded 60, **60**
Mountains, Formation of 51, 59
Mount Vernon, Virginia **476**
Mourning becomes Electra (O'Neill) 370
Mouth-organ 318
Movable type 455–6
Moving pictures 305
Mozart, Wolfgang Amadeus 505–6, 509–11
Mucha, Alphonse 486
Mudskipper **190**
Muezzin **419**
Muktesvara temple **446**
Multi-stage rockets 137–8
Mummification 395
Munch, Edvard 486
Munich 47
Murders in the Rue Morgue, The (Poe) 366
Murdock, William 317
Murillo, Bartolomé 473
Mushrooms **156–7**
Music 493–517
Musical instruments 281
Musical instruments, Mechanical 310
Musical scale 281
Music and the dance 518
Music box, Mechanical **309**, 310
Music for the Royal Fireworks (Handel) 503
Music Hall 386
Musk Ox 234
Musk Rat 227
Mussels **187**, 200–1
Musset, Alfred de 363, 370
Mussorgsky, Modest 514
Mustard seedlings 161
Mystery plays 375, **375**
Myxomatosis 185

Nabokov, Vladimir 372
Nabucco (Verdi) 512
Naevius, Gnaeus 346
Nagasaki 314
Nakatsu-hime 408
Nammu 391
Nanak 420
Nanna 391
Nansen, Fridtjof 87, **87**
Napier, John 307
Napier's rods **307**
Napoleon I 46, 368, 465, 477, 506
Napoleon III 485
Napoleonic wars 368, **368–9**
Narnia (Lewis) 372

Narrow gauge locomotive **273**
Narwhal 237
NASA 142
Naseby, Battle of 18, 46
Nash, John 477
Nassau hot-air balloon **292**
National Gallery, London 363
National Health Service, Britain 32, 37, 47
National Insurance Scheme, Britain 31
Nationalism in music 513–4
National parks **183**
National Union of General Workers **35**
Natural Gas 64–5, 268
Natural History 147–240
Nature reserves **183**
Naval mutinies, English 46
Navigation 258, 260–1
Navigation craft, Automatic **310**
Neanderthal Man 198, **198, 340**, 387–8
Nebuchadnezzar 411
Nebulae 122
Nefertiti **442**
Negative (resinous) electricity 294
Nelson, Horatio **22**, 46, 290
Nematoda 200
Neo-classic art 476–7
Neolithic Man 389
Neon light 318
Nephthys **393**
Neptune 110–1, **110–1**, 113
Nereid (satellite) 111
Nero 445
Nervous system 326–8
Neumes 496
Neurology 335
Neutron bullets 312–3
Neutrons 257, 311–3, 315
Neutron star 125, 126
Newcomen steam engine **271**
Newcomen, Thomas 271, 318
Newfoundland 82
New Hebrides 84
Newlands, John 254
New Model Army 19, 46
New plants, Finding 182
Newspaper press **181**
Newspapers 371
Newt 186, 211–2
Newton, Isaac 102, 124, 265–7, **266**, 278, 297, 305, 428, 468
Newton's laws of motion 265–7, **266–7**, 278–9
Newton (unit of force) 266
New Towns Act 42
New York City Ballet 528
New York Journal 371
New Zealand 46, 73
New Zealand, map **98**
Niagara Falls 66
Niaux 388
Nièpce, Joseph N. 304–5, 318
Nietzsche, Friedrich 431, **431**
Nightingale, Florence **332**, 333
Night Watch, The (Rembrandt) 473
Nijinsky, Vaslav 527, **527**
Nile, Battle of 46
Nile delta, map **66**
Nile, source of 86
Nirvana 405
Nitrogen 153, 157–8, 174
Nitrogen cycle 158
Njala saga 349
Noah 341
Nobel, Alfred **314**, 317
Nocturne (Whistler) 484
Noh drama 382–3
Nordenskjöld, Nils 86
Norge **86**
Norman art **449**, 449
Norman conquest 11–3
Norman invasion of Britain **44**
Norman kings 20
Normans 12–4
Norsemen 44, 81
North American, map **96**
North American Bronco OV-10A **292**
North American X-15 **276**
Northanger Abbey (Austen) 365
North Atlantic Drift 75, 77
Northcliffe, 1st Viscount **371**
Northern hemisphere 106–7
Northern Ireland 9, 11–3, 48
Northern lights 105
Northern sky, map of **121**
North pole 87, 107
Notation 496–7
Nothosaurs 193
Notre Dame Cathedral, Chartres **450**
Notre Dame Cathedral, Paris **496**
Notre Dame Music School, Paris 496
Nova 124
Nova Scotia 83
Novel, The 360, 364–5, 371–2
Noverre, Jean **522**, 523, 526
Nuclear fission 313
Nuclear fusion 306, 314
Nuclear meson 315
Nuclear reactor 314–5
Nucleons 246, 315
Nucleus, Controlling the 244, 311–5
Numen 397
'Nuremberg Egg' **262**
Nureyev, Rudolf 528, **528**
Nursing services 332–3
Nutcracker, The (Tchaikovsky) 514
Nyasa, Lake 86
Nylon 289, 318

Oates, Titus 46
Oats 147, 176
Obelisks, method of erecting **284**
Oberon (satellite) 111
Oberth, Hermann 130
Oberto (Verdi) 512
Oboe **514–5**
Obsidian 64
O'Casey, Sean 370
Ocean currents 74
Ocean floor 73, **73**
Oceanography 72, 74–5
Oceans, The 72
Oceans, origin of 52–3, 72
Oceans, salt content 73
Ocean trenches 58, 60, 73
Octave law 254
Octopus, Common **200**, 201
Odin, see Wotan
Odysseus 343
Odyssey (Homer) 342–3, **343**, 346, 360
Oedipus 344
Oersted, Hans Christian 297–8
Offa, king of Mercia 44
Of Human Bondage (Maugham) 372
Ohain, H. von 317
Ohm, Georg Simon 296–7
Ohm's law 297
Ohm (unit of electrical resistance) 297
Oil 57, 64–5, 76, 268, 289, 438, 454
Oil crops 178
Okapi 234, **235**
Oklahoma 528
Old Curiosity Shop, The (Dickens) 365
Old Faithful (Yellowstone National Park) 72
Oldfield, Anne 380
Old Testament scenes **411**
Old Vic 384
Oligocene peiod 54–5, **149**, 197
Oliver Twist (Dickens) 365
Olympian gods 395–6
Olympus Mons 113
Omdurman, Battle of 47
O'Neill, Eugene 370
On Liberty (Mill) 429
Opera 381, 499–500, 517
Opéra, Paris 522, 524–5
Opie, John 380
Opossum, Virginian 226
Optical engineering 306
Oracles, The 396
Oral literature 340
Orang-utan 239, **239**
Orbiting satellites 138–9
Orchestral 'families' 504
Ordnance Survey 90, **90**
Ordovician period 54–5, 57, **149**, 189
Orenda 389
Oresteia (Aeschylus) 343–4
Orestes 344
Orfeo (Monteverdi) 499–500
Organic compounds 289
Organicism, school of medicine 327–8
Organum 498–7
Oriental art 452–3
Oriental cults in Rome 398
Origines (Cato) 346–7
Origin of Species, The (Darwin) 187
Orion (constellation) 122, 124
Orkneys 48, 82
Orlando Furioso (Ariosto) 354–5
Oriando Innamorato (Boiado) 354
Ormazd 410
Ornamental gourds **176**, 177
Orphée (Cocteau) 370
Orphic mysteries 396–7
Orrery **119**
Orrery, 4th Earl of 119
Orvieto Cathedral 450
Orwell, George 371
Oryx 233
Oscilloscope 280
Oseberg ship **83**
Osiris 393–5, 398
Osmunda regalis **159**
Ossian 349
Ostracoderms 190
Ostrich 216, **217**
Othello (Shakespeare) 356
Othello (Verdi) 512
Otis, Elisha 317
Otter **231**
Otto 4-stroke engine 274
Otto, Nikolaus 274
Oudenarde, Battle of 46
Oughtred, William 318
Ovid 347, 356
Owen, Richard **192**
Owen, Wilfrid 373
Owls 219–20
Oxygen 253–5, 288–9
Oxygen cycle **153**
Oyster **187**, 196, 201

Pacific Ocean 72, 83
Paddy fields **177**
Paeonies **147**
Pagodas 452
Pagodenburg, Schloss Nymphenburg **470**
Paine, Thomas 477
Painting 435–92
Painting, Methods of 438
Pakistan 47
Palaeocene period 54–5
Palaeomagnetism 59
Palaeontology 57, 187–8
Palaeozoic era 54–5, 160, 189
Palestine 47
Palestrina, Giovanni Pierluigi de 498–9, **498**
Palladian architecture 462–3, **463**, 474
Palladio, Andrea 462–3, 474
Palladium, London 386
Pallas (asteroid) 114
Palmae, see Palms
Palms 178
Palomar telescope, Mount **116**, 123
Pamela (Richardson) 361
Panama 83
Pandas 231
Pangolin 235
Panhard, René 274
Pankhurst, Christabel 27
Pankhurst, Emmeline 27
Pankhurst, Sylvia 27
Pantagruel (Rabelais) 354
Pantheon, Paris **106**
Pantomime 386
Panza, Sancho 354
Paper-cutting machine **302**
Paper-making machine 318
Papillons (Schumann) 508
Papin, Denis 270–1, 318
Papin's steam digester **271**
Paracelsus 325
Parachute 318
Paradise Lost (milton) 359
Paradoxes 423
Parallax **116**, 116–7
Paramecium 199
Parasites 152, 156–7, 175
Parasitic plants 152, 156–7, 175
Parazoa **187**
Paré, Ambroise 325
Parish councils (Britain) 47
Park Crescent, London **477**
Parkes, Alexander 316
Parking meter 318
Park, Mungo 85, **87**
Parliament in Britain 14–23, 26, 48
Parliament in Britain, State opening of **23**
Parmenides 423, 428
Parmigianino, Francesco 462
Parnassians 363–4
Parrots 222
Parsees 410
Parsons, Charles 272, 318
Parthenon **442–3**, 443
Parts of a flower 170–1, **171**
Pascal, Blaise 307, 316, 357, 429
Pascal's adding machine **307**
Pas de Quatre (Perrot) **523**
Pasmore, Victor 492
Passover 413
Pasternak, Boris 369
Pasteurisation **330**
Pasteur, Louis 289, 330–2
Pathfinder, The (Fenimore Cooper) 362
Patrick, St 349
Patrick's Cross, St *14*
Paul Revere's Ride (Longfellow) 366
Paul, Robert 384
Paul, St 415
Pavlova, Anna 526–7, **527**
Paxton, Joseph 34
Pea family 176
Pea fowl (peacock), Common **221**
Peary, Robert E. 87
Peasant's Revolt 44
Peccaries 234
Peel, Robert 33
Peenemünde 130
Peer Gynt (Grieg) 515
Peer Gynt (Ibsen) 369, 383
Peers' coronets **23**
Peirce, C. S. 432
Peking, Jesuit observatory **127**
Peking Man **197**
Peking Opera 383
Pelican, Common White **217**
Pelicans 217
Peloponnesian war 345
Pencil of Nature (Fox Talbot) 489
Pendulum 261, 265
Pendulum, Foucault's **106**
Penguins 216
Penicillin 147, 158, 318, 333, **333**
Penicillium notatum 333, **333**
Peninsular War 46
Pennines 60
Penny Black)postage stamp) 316
Penny farthing **2789**
Pensions Act (Britain) 47
Pentecost 413–4
People's Charter 26
Peppered Moth **186**, 187
Pepys's Collection, Cambridge **18**
Pepys, Samuel **359**
Perching Birds 223–4
Percussion 494, **514–5**
Perennials 165, 174
Perennials, Monocarpic **164**
Peri, Jacopo 499
Periodic Table 254, **254**, 257
Permian period 54–5, **149**, 191–2
Perotinus 496
Perpendicular (architecture) 454, **454**
Perpetual motion machines **268**, 269
Perrot, Jules 523, 525
Perseids, The 115
Persephone 397
Perseus **462**
Perseus (constellation) 124
Persian religion 410
Persius 347
Perspective in art 437, **437**
Persuasion (Austen) 365
Peru 83
Peste, La (Camus) 371
Peter Grimes (Britten) 517
Peterloo massacre 33, **33**, 46
Peter, St 414, 416

Petipa, Lucien 525
Petipa, Marius 525, **525**
Petit Testament (Villon) 353
Petrarch, Francesco 352, 355
Petrels 217
Petrol engines 269, 274–5
Petronius 347
Petrouchka (Stravinsky) 517, 527
Pharisees 413
Pharmacopoeia 325
Phidias 443
Philip II, king of Spain 45, 468, 473
Philip IV, king of Spain 473
Phillips, Thomas 363
Philosopher's stone 101, 252, 258
Philosophy 421–32
'Phlegmatic man' 320
Phobos (satellite) 111
Phoebe (satellite) 111
Phoenicians 11
Phonograph 299, **299**, 318
Phororhacos **192**
Photo-electric cell 303, 305-6
Photography 305, 318, 489
Photosynthesis 152, 155, 157, 161, 168–9, 171
Photo-transistor 304
Phylum, Animal 186, **187**
Physical Geography of the Sea, The (Maury) 75
Physicians 319
Physicians, Royal College of 324
Physics 243–4, 256–7, 277
Physics (Aristotle) 426
Physiology 322, 324
Piano 318
Piano, Cristofori 501, **501**
Picasso, Pablo 490
Piccard, Auguste 74–5
Piccard, Jacques 74–5
Picinotti 317
Pickford, Mary 384
Pickwick Papers, The (Dickens) 365
Pictures from an Exhibition (Mussorgsky) 514
Piero della Francesca 457
Piero de' Medici 459
Piers Plowman (Langland) 351
Pièta (Michelangelo) 459, **459**
Pigeons 221
Pigs 234
Pilgrimage of Grace, The 45
Pilgrim Fathers 46
Pilgrim's Progress (Bunyan) 359, **359**, 365
Pindar 343
Pine Marten 230
Pin-hole camera 305
Pioneer 10 and *11* **142**
Pipettes **300**
Pirandello, Luigi 370
Pisa Cathedral **449**
Pisa, Galileo's experiments 265
Pisa, Leaning tower of **449**
Pisano, Nicola 451
Pisces, see Fishes
Pi-Sheng 455
Piso, Carolus, see Lepois, Charles
Pissarro, Camille 484
Pitcher plants 175, **175**
Pithecanthropus **240**
Pitt (the Younger), William 46
Pizarro, Francisco 83, 400
Placoderms 190
Plague, Great 46, 324, **324**, 326
Plainsong 495, 497
Planck, Max 257
Planet, The (Locomotive) 40
Planetarium 119, 122
Planetary motion 101–2
Planetoids 114
Planets 103, 110–1
Planets, The (Holst) 514
Planets, Life on other 114
Planets, Motions of **266–7**
Planets, Rotation of 111
Planets, Satellites of 111
Planets, Statistics relating to 110–1
Plankton 207
Plant adaptations 173
Plantagenet kings 20
Plant cells 149–51, **150**, 153, 158, 164, 169
Plant classification 153–4
Plant ecology 173
Plant kingdom 153–4, 184
Plant reproduction 150, 156, 159
Plants 147–182
Plants, First 53
Plastic materials 289
Plastic surgery 334
Platanus tree **57**
Plateresque (architecture) 465, 468
Plate tectonics 58–60, **61**
Platyhelminthes **187**, 200
Plato 245, 345, 396, 421–2, 425–6, **425**
Platypus 225, **225**
Plautius, Aulus 44
Plautus, Titus Maccius 346
Play dances 519
Pléiade 354
Pleiades 124, 354
Pleistocene period 54–6, **149**
Plesiosaur **194–6**
Pleurococcus 155, **155**
Piny the Elder 321
Pliocene period **149**, 197
Plough (astronomy) **118**
Plugs (volcanoes) 71, **71**
Pluto (planet) 110–1, **111**, 114
Pluto (god) 386
Pneumatic tyre 318
Pnin (nabokov) 372
Pocket calculator 308
Podalirius 319
Poe, Edgar Allan 366
Poetaster, The (Jonson) 357
Poetics (Aristotle) 345, 347
Poetry, Nature of 339–40
Poissons d'Or (Debussy) 515
Poitiers, Battle of 44
Polar exploration 87
Polecat 230
Pole, North 59
Poles, The 107
Police, Metropolitan 33
Political philosophy 429
Pollination 160, 171–2, **172**
Pollock, Jackson 491
Polo, Maffeo 82
Polo, Marco 82, 318
Polo, Nicolo 82
Polynesians 389
Polyphonic music 496, 498
Polythene 318
Polytonality 516
Polyzoa **187**
Pomp and Circumstance marches (Elgar) 514
Pompano fish fossil **188**
Pompeii **71**
Pompey 375, 445
Pont du Gard, Nimes **284**
Ponte, Lorenzo da 505
Pontius Pilate 414
Pontormo, Jacopo 462
Poor Law Acts (Britain) 25, 32, 46
Pop art 492
Pope, Alexander 360, 363
Popocatepetl 71
Popular entertainment 384–6
Popular statistics (Britain) 48
Poquelin, Jean-Baptiste (Molière) 358, **358**, 378, 380
Porcupine 228
Porpoises 236–7
Portala, Tibet **407**
Porthos 364
Portolan chart **89**
Portrait of a young man with a hurdy gurdy (Watteau) **471**
Portuguese man-of-war 199, **199**
Poseidon 396
Positive (vitreous) electricity 294
Postage stamps 318
Post-Impressionism 486
Post Office, British 303
Potatoes 147, 152, 167, 177
Potato famine in Ireland 46
Potholes 66, **69**
Pottery 248
Potto 238
Poulenc, Francis 517
Pound, Ezra 373
Poussin, Nicolas 469, 492
Power 269
Power loom 24
Pragmatism 432
Praxiteles 443
Prayer dances 519
Praying mantis **204**, 205
Pre-Cambrian period 53–5, **149**, 189
Pre-Columbian art 460–1
Pre-literate societies 389–90
Prélude à l'après-midi d'un faune (Debussy) 515, 527
Pre-Raphaelites 367–8, 479–81, 484–6
Presbyterian Church of Scotland 37, 45, 417
Pre-Socratic philosophers 422–4
Press 249
Pressure cooker 270, **271**, 318
Prévost, Antoine-François 361
Prickly pear 147, **148**
Pride and Prejudice (Austen) 365
Priestley, Joseph **167**
Primates 237–40
Primitive art 440–1
Primitive dancing 518, **518**
Primitive medicine 319–20
Primitive religion 387–9
Prince Igor (Borodin) 514
Principe, Il (Machiavelli) 354
Principia Mathematica (Russell and Whitehead) 432
Principia (Newton) 266
Principles of Geology (Lyell) 51
Principles of Human Knowledge (Berkeley) 428
Printing 318, 455–6
Prints, Making 439
Prism **102**
Prison conditions 33
Prjevalsky, Nicholas 86
Probes into space 139–42
Proconsul **196**, 197
Prokofiev, Sergei 517
Prongbuck 233
Proportion in art 436, **436**
Prose, Nature of 339–40
Proslogion (St Anselm) 426
Protagoras 424
Protective clothing, atomic research **312**
Proteins 53, 157, 161
Protestant movement 37, 417
Protoceratops 195
Protons 256, 311–2, 315
Protoplasm 151, 153, 157
Protozoa **187**, 189, 199
Protozoans **188, 199**, 199
Proust, Marcel 371
Proxima Centaurii 116
Psycho-analysis 335–6
Psychological medicine 335
Psychology 335–6
Ptah 394
Pteranodon **192**, 195
Pteridophytes 154, 159
Pterodactyl 195–6
Ptolemy, Claudius 88–9, 100, 103, 118
Ptolemy's World Outline **89**
Puccini, Giacomo 512
Puck of Pook's Hill (Kipling) 366
Puffer fish **208**
Puffin **221**
Pugin, Augustus 480
Pulcinelle 376, **376**
Pulleys 248, **248**
Pulsars 125
Pulse-jet engine 276
Pulse rate 325
Puma 229
Pumice 64
Pump 249
Punch and Judy 358, 376, 386
Punch, Mr 376, **376**
Puppets 386
Purcell, Henry 500, 514
Puritan writers 359
Pushkin, Alexander 368
Pygmy Shrew **226**
Pyramids, Giza 269, 395
Pyramid Texts 395
Pyrenees 59, 388
Pythagoras 100, 423, 495
Python, Green **214**

Quantum theory 257
Quarantine regulations 330
Quartz crystal 261
Quartzite 65
Quasars 125–6
Queen Elizabeth II (ship) **290**
Queen mother head (Benin) **440**
Queen's House, Greenwich **474**
Quetzalcoatl 460, **460**, 466
Quimbaya gold mask **63**
Quinine 147, 180
Quirinus 397
Quiros, Pedro Fernandes de 84
Quixote, Don 354

Rabbits 185, **185**, 228
Rabelais, François 354
Raccoon, American 231
Rachel 381
Racine, Jean 358
Racing bicycle **278**
Radar 303, **303**, 318
Radiated Tortoise **213**
Radio 302–3, 385
Radioactive dating 51
Radioactive detection devices 311, 315
Radioactivity 255, 306, 311–2, 315
Radio astronomy 125
Radiography 333
Radioisotopes 315
Radiolocation 303
Radiosonde 80
Radio telescopes 102, 124–5, 318
Radiotherapy 333
Radio valve 305
Radio waves 301–2, **302**
Radio waves from space 125
Radium 255, 311, 315, 318, 333
Raft of the Medusa, The (Géricault) 478
Railways in Britain 40–1
Railway signal **296**
Rain 78
Rainbows 78–9
Rainfall, areas of (map) **76**
Rainhill Trials 272
Raising of Lazarus, The (Giotto **451**
Rake's Progress, The (Hogarth) 474
Raleigh, Walter 46
Ramadan 419
Rambert, Marie 528
Rameau, Jean Philippe 501
Ram-jet engine 276
Ramses I 393
Ramses III 290
Ranger spacecraft 140
Ranidae, see Frogs
Ransome, Arthur 372
Rape of the Lock, The (Pope) 360
Raphael 421, 458, 459, 462, 469, 481
Rasselas (Johnson) 361
Rationalists 427
Rats 226
Ravel, Maurice 515, 517
Raven **224**
Rays 210
Razor, Electric 318
Razor, Safety 318
Re 393–4
Reber, Grote 318
Rebirth 401–3, 405
Recuyell of the Historyes of Troye, The 353
Red Badge of Courage, The (Crane) 366
Red deer **48**
Red fox **228**
Red giants (stars) 126–7
Red House, Bexleyheath 480
Red Kangaroo 225, **225**
Red Planet, see Mars
Redwood tree **160**
Reformation, The 355, 357, 417, 464, 468
Reformation, Music of the 499
Reform Bills (Britain) 23, 25–6, 46–7
Refrigerator 270
Regulator, Speed 310
Reims Cathedral 450
Reindeer 232, **232**
Reis, Phillip 298, 318
Relative time 262

Relativity, Theory of 262, 313
Religio Medici (Browne) 359
Religion 387–420
Religion and dancing 518
Religious beliefs 37–8
Rembrandt van Rijn 472, **472**
Renaissance, The 456–9, 462–3
Renaissance literature 353–5, 358
Renaissance medicine 324
Renaissance music 498
Renoir, Pierre 485
Repertory theatres 384
Reproduction, Animal 185
Reproduction, Plant 150, 156, 159, 170
Reproductive system 330
Reptiles 186–7, 191–3, 195, 208, 212–6
Reptilia, see Reptiles
Republic, The (Plato) 425
Requiem (Verdi) 512
Research, scientific 243–4
Respiration (Human beings) 320, 322, 330
Respiration in plants 152, 169
Ressel, J. 318
Restoration, The 357
Restoration of the English monarchy 20
Retro-rockets 137, 141
Revolver 318, **318**
Reynard (Renart) 351
Reynolds, Joshua 475–6
Rhamphorhynchus **192**
Rhazes of Basra 323
Rhea (satellite) 111
Rhetoric (Aristotle) 345
Rhinoceros 232
Rhizoids 159
Rhizomes 159, 167
Ribera, José de 473
Rice 147, 176, **177**
Rice paddy fields **177**
Richard I, king of England **20,44**
Richard II, king of England **21**
Richard III, king of England **21**, 45
Richardson, Samuel 361, 368
Richelieu, Cardinal 364
Ridley, Nicholas 45
Rigoletto (Verdi) 512
Rig Veda 401
Rilke, Rainer Maria 373
Rimbaud, Arthur 364
Rimsky-Korsakov, Nikolai 514, 527
Ring des Nibelungen, Der (Wagner) 511
Ring Nebula 122
Rip Van Winkle (Irving) 362
Rite of Spring, The (Stravinsky) 517
Ritty, James 316
Rivers 66–7
River valley civilisations 249
Roads in Britain **38**, 39
Robbia, Luca Della 498
Robbins, Jerome 528
Robert I (the Bruce) **11**, 44
Robert, François 318
Robespierre 477
Robie House 491
Robinson Crusoe (Defoe) 361
Robinson, Dr 316
Rob Roy (Scott) 365
Rocket, The 272
Rocket engines 129–30, 136–7
Rocket into Interplanetary Space, The (Oberth) 130
Rocket, invention of 130
Rocket launching sites, USA **136–7**
Rocket, liquid-fuelled 130, 136–7
Rocket motors 266, 277
Rocket propulsion 130
Rockets 276
Rockets, multi-stage 137–8
Rockets, solid-propellant 137
Rockies 59
Rocks, correlation of 57
Rocks, formation of 58–9, 61
Rocks, igneous 63–4, **64**, 71
Rocks, metamorphic 63, **64**, 65
Rocks, sedimentary 64, **64**
Rocks, strata **56**
Rocks, uses of 65
Rococo art 469–71, 475–7
Rococo music 503
Rodents 226
Roderick Random (Smollett) 361
Rodin, Auguste 421, 483
Rodin, Charles 274
Rolls-Royce cars 275
Rolls-Royce Phantom II **275**
Roman art 444–5
Roman Catholic Church 37, 417
Romance in literature 351
Roman de la Rose (De Lorris and de Meung) 351–2
Roman de Renart 351
Roman drama 347
Roman Empire 44, 81, 285, 444–5, 448
Roman engineering 39, 284–5, 444
Romanesque art 449–50
Roman gods 397
Roman literature 346–8
Roman medical services 321
Roman medicine 321–2
Roman roads in Britain **38**, 39
Roman theatre **375**, 374–5
Romantic Ballet 524
Romantic movement in art 477–8
Romantic movement in music 507–8
Rome **346**, 347, 458–9
Romeo and Juliet (Shakespeare) 356
Roncevalles 351
Ronsard, Pierre de 354
Röntgen, Wilhelm 255, 300, 318, 333
Roosevelt, President 314
Root crops 147, 177
Roots, 163, **164**, 169, 173–5
Root tip **165**
Rosenkavalier, Der (Richard Strauss) 512–3
Roses, Wars of the 45
Rose Theatre 378
Rosse, Earl of 112
Rosse telescope 112
Rossetti, Christina 368
Rossetti, Dante Gabriel 367, 481, 484
Rossini, Gioacchimo 511
Ross, James Clark 87
Rostand, Edmond 370
'Rotten Boroughs' 24
Rouault, Georges 487, 490
Rouge et le Noir, Le (Standhal) 364
Roundheads 18
Roundworms **187**
Rousseau, Henri (Le Douanier) 488
Rousseau, Jean-Jacques 336, 361, 430, **430**, 477
Rousseau, Theodore 482
Rout of San Romano, The (Ucello) **456**
Rover safety bicycle **278**
Royal Academy of Art 435, 475–6
Royal Academy of Dance 522
Royal Academy of Sciences (France) 90
Royal Albert Bridge 40
Royal Ballet 528
Royal College of Physicians 324
Royal College of Surgeons **328**
Royal Danish Ballet 525
Royal Exchange 42
Royal fern **159**
Royal Institution 294–5, **294**, 303
Royal Mail coaches **39**
Royal Naval College **42**
Royal Pavillion, Brighton **22**
Royal Society of London 271
Royal Standard **14**
Royce, Henry 274
Rubber 181, **181**
Rubens, Peter Paul 439, 471–3, **471**
Runner bean seed **160**, 161
Running birds 216
Ruskin, John 481, 484
Rusland and Ludmilla (Pushkin) 368
Russell, Bertrand 432, **432**
Russian literature 368
Russian and Ludmilla (Glinka) 513
Rutaceae 177
Ruterford, Ernest **256**, 257, 311–3
Ruwenzori Mountains 86
Rye House Plot 46
Sable 230
Sachs, Hans 380
Sadducees 413
Sadler's Wells Ballet 528
Safety-pin 318
Sagas 349
Sago leaf painting **390**
Sagrada Familia **486**
St Edward's Crown **48**
St John the Baptist (Rodin) 483
St John the Evangelist on Patmos (Velasquez) **473**
St John Passion (Bach) 502
Saint-Léon, Arthur 525
St Mark's, Venice 415, **445**
St Matthew Passion (Bach) 502
St Paul's Cathedral, London 42
St Paul's Cathedral, London, Whispering gallery **281**
St Peter's Fields, Manchester 33
St Peter's, Rome 445, 459, 469
Saint-Saëns, Camille 515, 527
St Thomas's Hospital, London 333
Saladin 323
Salamanders 186, 191–2, 194, 211–2, **211**
Salamis, Battle of **345**
Salammbô (Flaubert) 364
Salerno medical school 323
Salientia, see Frogs and toads
Salisbury Cathedral 450
Salisbury Cathedral clock **261**
Salisbury Plain, 9, **9**
Sallé, Marie 523
Salmon family 208–9
Salomon J. P. 505
Salomon symphonies 505
Salon des Refusés 485
Salvini, Tommaso 382
Salyut I, 6 and 7 143
Samisen (Japanese instrument) **494**
Samoon 80
Sanchi, the Great Stupa **404**
Sandbars 70
Sandburg, Carl 373
Sand dunes 70
Sand, George (Aurore Dupin) 364
Sandglasses **259**, 261
Sandstone 64–5
San Francisco *Examiner* 371
'Sanguine man' 320
San Michele 457
Santa Maria Novella, Florence 457
Santa Sophia 445, 447
Sapotaceae family 182
Sappho 343
Saprophytes 156–6, 175
Satan 412
Satellites, Artificial **130**, 130–1, **139**
Satellites, Communications 138–9
Satellites in orbit 136–7, 138
Satellites, Weather 80, 139
Satire 343
Sartre, Jean-Paul 370–1, **431**, 431–2
Saturn **110–1**, 110–1, 113, **115**, 125, *142*
Saturn 5 rocket **129**, 132, **133**, 136, 137
Savannah, NS **315**
Savery, steam engine 271
Savery, Thomas 270
Savonarola, Girolamo 459
Savoy Operas **513**
Saxe-Coburg, House of 21
Saxe-Meiningen theatre company 382
Saxons 11–4, 44, 349
Scafell Pike 48
Scala La, Milan **511**
Scale in art 437
Scandinavian literature 348–9, 369
Scarlatti, Domenico 501
Scent of flowers 172
Scheherazade (Rimsky-Korsakov) 514, 527
Schick, Jacob 318
Schiller, Johann Friedrich von 362, 380
Schloss Neuschwanstein **479**
Schoenberg, Arnold 516–7, **517**
School of Athens (Raphael) **421**, 459
Schools, Founding of English 355
Schools in Britain **37**
Schopenhauer, Arthur 430, **430**
Schouwburg Theatre 378–9
Schubert, Franz **507**, 507–8
Schumann, Clara **509**
Schumann, Robert 508, **509**, 510
Schweitzer, Albert **432**
Schwitters, Kurt 490
Science 243–318
Science fiction **114**, 262, 372
Science Museum, London 272, 279
Scientific method 244
Scientific models 245–6, 261, 265
Scientific research 243
Scilly Isles 48
Scorpio (constellation) 101
Scorpions 186, **187**, 191, 202, 206
Scorpions, Sea **190**, 190–1
Scotland 9–13, 48
Scots Pine **161**
Scott Fitzgerald, F. 372
Scottish Highlands 59, 69
Scott, Robert Falcon **87**, 87
Scott, Walter 365
Scouts, Boy **36**
Screech owl **219**
Screw propeller 318
Scribe in ancient Egypt **340**
Scripts, examples of **341**
Scroll painting 452, **452**
Sculpture 435–92
Scurvy 330
Scutari hospital **332**
Sea, The 59, 69
Sea-anemones **187**, 199
Sea-cows 236
Sea-cucumber **187**, 189, 207
Seagull, The (Chekhov) 369
Sea horse **208**, 209
Sea-lily 190–2
Sea-lions 230, **231**
Seals 230
Seals, cylinder **391**
Seasons, The 106, 258
Seasons, The (Thomson) 360
Sea-squirts 208
Sea-urchin **57**, **187**, 189, 194–6, 199, **207**, 207
Seaweeds, see Algae
Second World War 38, 41, 43, 47, 314
Secretary Bird **217**
Sedgmoor, Battle of 46
Sedimentary rocks 64, **64**
Seed dispersal 162, **162**
Seed drill 318
Seeley, H. W. 317
Seismograph **61**, 60–1
Seismology 60
Sejanus (Jonson) 357
Self pollination 171
Semitic literature 340–1
Semitic peoples 341
Semmelweiss, Ignaz 332
Seneca 347
Sense and Sensibility (Austen) 365
Sequoia gigantea **160**
Serpent (instrument) **506**
Serval, African 228
Seth 395
Seurat, Georges 484–5
Severus 44
Sewing machine 318
Sextant 318
Seychelles 73
Seymouria 191
Shackleton, Ernest 87
Shadow clock **258**
Shaftesbury, 7th Earl of 33
Shakespeare, William 346, 348, 355–8, **356**, 376–9, 382, 509, 512
Shale 64
Shamans 390
Shamela (Fielding) 381
Sharp, Cecil 520
Sharks 210
Shaw, George Bernard **369**, 369–70, 382
Sheep 234
Sheet metal 289
Shelduck **219**
Shelley, Mary 362
Shelley, Percy Bysshe 363
Shellfish 189,195–6, 207
Shells 200–1, **201**

Shem 341
Sheridan, Richard Brinsley 369
She Stoops to Conquer (Goldsmith) 361
Shetlands 48, 81
Shield, Primitive **441**
Shiites 419–20
Shinto 409
Shinto priests **408**
Ship, how it floats 290
Ship, nuclear powered **315**
Ships **290–1**, 290–1
Shockley 318
Sholes 318
Sholokov, Mikhail 369
Shooting stars 114
Shore, John 280, 318
Short stories 368–9, 372
Shostakovitch, Dimitri 517
Shoveller **219**
Show boats, Mississippi **383**
Shrimp 202, 207
Shukongo-shin 404
Sibelius, Jean 515–6
Siddhartha, see Buddha
Siddons, Sarah 380
Sidereal day 106
Sidereal time 258–9
Sidereal year 106
Sidney, Sir Philip 355
Siemens telephone **299**
Siemens, William 317
Siena Cathedral 450
Sienese painting 451, 457
Sierra Nevada 60
Sight 327
Sikhism 420
Sikh religion 420
Sikh warriors **420**
Si le grain ne meurt (Gide) 371
Silent films 384
Silicon chip 304, **305**
Silurian period 54–5, 57, **149**, 189–90
Silver 65
Simmons Co. 317
Simnel, Lambert 45
Simonides of Ceos 343
Simple fruits 163
Simpson, James Young 316, 331
Simulator, space flight 141
Sinai, Mount 411, 413
Sinai Peninsula, map of **107**
Singer, Isaac 318
Singspiel 510
Sioux Indians 389–90
Sirius 118, 124
Sisley, Alfred 484
Sitar **495**
Siva 401, **401**, 403
Six Characters in Search of an Author (Pirandello) 370
Sklodowska, Marie, see Curie, Marie
Skunk, Striped 230
Sky divers 264, **264**
Skylab **135**, 143
Slate 65
Slave trade, Abolition of 46
Sleeping Beauty, The (Tchaikovsky) 514, 525
Slide rule 307, 318
Sloth 235
Slow Loris 238
Slugs 186, **200**, 201
Small Magellanic Cloud 123
Smallpox 330–1, 334
Smetana, Bedřich 513
Simbert, John 476
Smith, Adam 477
Smith, John 359
Smollett, Tobias 361
Snail 186, **187**, 189, 191, 200–1
Snakes 212, 214–5
Snorri Sturlason 349
Snow 78
Snowdon, Mount 48
Snowplough **79**
Snow Queen, The (Andersen) 369
Soane, John 329
Sobek 393
Social Contract, The (Roussea) 430
Social Democratic Party 43, 47
Social psychology 336
Society Islands 85
Society of Apothecaries 323
Sociology 336
Socrates 422, 424–5, **424**, 429
Soils 65
Solanaceae 177
Solanum family 177
Solar batteries 139
Solar day 106
Solar flares 104
Solar prominences 105
Solar system 52, **99**, 100–3, **103**, 246, 257
Solar time 258–9, 262
Solar year 106
Solid-propellant rockets 137
Solids 251–2, 270
Solid state electronics 304
Solomon 411
Solstices 106
Songs 507
Sophists 424
Sophocles 344
Sound barrier 283
Sound, speed of 282
Sound waves 280–3
South Africa 47
South America, map of **97**
South-East Asia, map of **94**
Southern hemisphere 106–7
Southern lights 105
Southern sky, map of **120**
South pole 87, 107
South Sea Bubble 46
Soutine, Chaim 490
Soyuz spacecraft 132, 143
Spacecraft, launching speeds **138**
Spacecraft probes 139–42
Spacecraft recovery 144
Spaceflight simulator 134
Spacelab 143, **143**
Space laboratories 143
Space Shuttle 143–4, **144**, 308
Space station (projected) 144
Spacesuits **134**, 135
Space travel 129–44, 244, 266–7, **266–7**, 279
Spanish art 465, 468, 473, 475–6
Spanish dancing 520, **521**
Spanish literature 351–2, 354
Spanish theatre 378
Spartali, Marie **489**
Spectacles 318
Spectator, The 474
Spectre de la Rose, Le (Weber) **527**
Spectroscope 118–9, 124, 318
Spectrum 77, 102, 118
Speed 278–9
Speke, John Hanning 86, **87**
Spencer, Lady Diana, see Wales, Princess of
Spencer, Edmund 355
Spermatophytes 154, 160
Sperry, Elmer A. 317
Sphagnum mosses 159
Spiders **187**, 202, 206, **206**
Spider's web **206**
Spina, Alexander de 318
Spinning frame 24, 318
Spinning jenny 24, **24**, 318
Spinning mule 24, 318
Spinoza, Barach 427–8
Spiny Anteater, see Echidna
Spirogyra 156
Spits 70
Splash-down techniques (spacecraft) 144, **144**
Splitting the atom 312–3
Spohr, Ludwig (Louis) 507
Sponges **187**, 190, 194
Sprechgesang 517
Springbok **232**, 233
Spring equinox 106
Springs, Hot 71–2
Sputnik 1 131
Sputnik 2 131
Sputnik 3 **130**
Squid 186, **187**, 189, 201
Squirrels 226
Stained glass **414**, 450, **450**
Stainless steel 318
Stalactites 68–9, **69**
Stalagmites 68–9, **69**
Stamitz, Johann 504
Standard, Battle of the 44
Stanislavsky, Constantin 383
Stanley, H. M. 86, **86**
Starch 152, 156, 161, 176
Star clusters 123
Star explosions 124
Starfish **187**, 189–21, 194–6, **207**, 207
Star-nosed Mole **227**
Stars, The 116
Stars, brightness 117–8
Stars, composition of 188
Stars, groups 122
Stars, magnitude 118
Stars, movement of 119
Stars, proper motion 118–9
Stars, variable 117, 124
State worship 409
Statics 249
Statistics 336
'Steady-State' theory 127–8
Steam carriage **272**
Steam engine 24, 270, **270**, 279, 318
Steam locomotives 272, **272–3**, 279, 318
Steam power 270–1
Steam rod carriage 318
Steam-ship 318
Steam tractor **24**
Steam turbine 272, 318
Steel 287–9
Steel converter 318
Steele, Richard 474
Stegosaurus **192**, 194
Steinbeck, John 372
Stem, The 165–7, 170, 173
Stendhal (Marie Henri Beyle) 364
Stephen, king of England **20**, 44
Stephen, St 415
Stephenson, George 38, 40, 272
Stephenson, Robert 272
Sterne, Laurence 361
Stethoscope 318
Stevenson, Robert Louis 366
Stevinus, Simon 265
Stewart, Prince Charles Edward 365
Stick Insects 205, **205**
Still Life with Fish (Braque) **490**
Stirling Bridge, Battle of 44
Stoat 230
Stockhausen, Karlheinz 517
Stockton and Darlington Railway 40, 272
Stoics 426
Stomata **152**, 169
Stone Age 247
Stone Age art 439
Stone head (Olmec) **461**
Stonehenge 9, **9**, 389
Stone of Destiny 44
Stoney, George 256
Storing food, plants 164, 169
Story in the Rocks 188
Stradivari, Antonio 500–1
Stradivari, violin **501**
Strafford, 1st Earl of 46
Strand Magazine 372
Strassman, Fritz 313
Strauss, Johann 512
Strauss, Richard 508, 512–3
Stravinsky, Igor **516**, 517, 527
Streetcar Named Desire, A (Williams) 370
Steptomycin 147, 158
Stress and strain 286
Stress patterns **289**
Strindberg, August 369
Strings, orchestral 494, **514–5**
Strip lighting 306
Stroboscope 263
Stroboscopic photography **263**, 265
Stromboli 71
Structural engineering 285
Structure of flowers 170–1, **171**
Structure of metals 287–9
Stuart, Gilbert 476
Stuart, John McDouall 86
Stubbs, George 482
Stupa **446**
Stupa, Sanchi **404**
Sturgeon, William 317
Subaru estate **274**
Submarine, control of 290
Suckling, John 359
Sudan 47
Suez Canal 46–7, 512
Suffrage Act, Women's 47
Suffrage (The right to vote) 25–7
Suffragettes 27–8, **27**
Sufism 419
Sugar 152–3, 177, 179, 181
Sugar cane 147, 153, 177, 181
Sullivan, Arthur **513**
Sulphur 255
Sumerian gods 391
Sumerians 99–100, 391
Summa Theologica (Aquinas) 427
Summer solstice 106
Sun, The 103–5
Sun, chromosphere 105
Sun, corona **104**
Sundials **258**, 261
Sun, distance from earth 103
Sun, eclipse of 100, 104
Sun, energy from 268
Sunflower 153, **178**, 178
Sun, heat from 77
Sunni 419
Sun, nuclear fuel 105
Sun, photosphere 103–4
Sunsets 77
Sunshine, areas of (map) **77**
Sun, size of 103
Sunspots 104, 105, **128**
Sun, temperature 105
Sun-worship 99
Supernova 122, 124–5
Supersonic aircraft 282–3
Supersonics 283
Surgeons 319
Surgeons, Royal College of **328**
Surgery 323, 325, 329–32
Surgical instruments 325, **331**
Surrealism 335, 490–1
Surrey, Earl of (Henry Howard) 355
Surrey Iron Railway 40
Surveying 90
Surveyor (spacecraft) 109, 140
Survival of the fittest 187
Surya 403
Surya temple **403**
Sutherland, Graham 491
Sutton Hoo treasure **448**
Swallows and Amazons (Ransome) 372
Swallow holes 66
Swamps 69
Swan, Joseph 299, 317
Swan Lake (Tchaikovsky) 514, **525**
Swans 219
Swan Theatre 376
Swedenborg, Emanuel **431**
Sweet Thursday (Steinbeck) 372
Sweyn, king of Denmark 44
Swift, Jonathan 360
Swifts 222–3
Swinton, Ernest 318
Sword of Orion 122
Sydenham, Thomas 327, **327**
Sydney Harbour Bridge **286**
Syllogism (diagram) **422**, 426
Sylphide, La 524
Symbiosis 175
Symbolists, The 364
Symington, William 318
Synchrotons 312
Synge, John Millington 370
Synthetic materials 289
System of Logic (Mill) 429

Tabernacles 413
Taboo 389
Tacitus 347
Tadpole 186, 191, 211–2
Taglioni, Filippo 524
Taglioni, Mrie 523–4
Tain Bo Cualnge (The Raiding of the Cattle of Cooley) 349
Taj Mahal, Agra **447**
Talbot, W. H. Fox 304–5, 489, **489**
Tales from the Vienna Woods (Johann Strauss) 512
Taliesin West (Wright) 491
'Talkies', The 384
Tallis, Thomas 499
Talmud 413

Tamburlaine (Marlowe) 356
Tammuz 391
Tanjore, temple **402**
Tank **316**, 318
Tannhäuser 497
Taoism 406, 408–9
Tao-Te-Ching 408
Tapeworms **187**
Tapir 231
Tap root 163–5
Tara brooch **448**
Tarantula 206
Tarsier 238
Tarsioids 196
Tartuffe (Molière) 358
Task, The (Cowper) 360
Tasman, Abel 84
Tasmania 84
Tasso, Torquato 354
Taurus 122, 124
Taxi, London Diesel **275**
Tchaikovsky, Peter 514, **515**, 527
Tea 147, **178**, 179
Telegraph, Electric 318
Telemann, George Philipp 503
Telephone 298–9, **299**, 318
Telescope 101–2, 318
Telescope, Herschel's 125
Telescope, Mount Palomar **116**, 123
Telescope, principle of **100**
Telescope, reflecting 102, **102**
Telescope, refracting 102, **102**, 265
Telescope, Rosse 112
Telescopes, Newton's **102**
Telescopes, Radio 102
Telescopes, Yerkes observatory **117**
Television 300, 302–4, 318, 385
Television camera **303**
Telford, Thomas **38**
Tell, William (Rossini) 511
Telstar 139
Tempera painting 438
Temperature 76–7
Temperature, Sea 75
Tempest, The (Shakespear) 356
Temples 392
Temple to Asclepius **319**
Ten Commandments 410
Tenniel, John 366
Tennyson, Alfred 367
Teotihuacan 460
Terence 346
Tereshkova, Valentina 131, **133**
Terminal velocity 264
Termite 202, 205, **205**, 240
Termite nest **205**
Terpsichore 519
Terrapins 214
Terror 87
Terylene 289
Tess of the D'Urbevilles (Hardy) 366
Test Act 37
Tethys (satellite) 111
Teutonic gods 399
Textile fringe (Peru) **461**
Texture in art 437
Thackeray, William Makepeace 365
Thales of Miletus 100, 422
Thallophytes 154–7
Thatcher, Margaret 43, 47
Theatre 374–84
Theatre and popular entertainment, The 374–86
Theatre Street (Karsavina) 527
Theogony (Hesiod) 343
Theophrastus 153, 358
Theory of Humours (Hippocrates) 319–20
Theory of the Earth (Hutton) 51
Theotocopoulos, Domenikos, see Greco, El
Theravada 406
Thermionic valve 302
Thermistor 304
Thermometer 318, 325
Thespians 374
Thespis 374
Thinker, The (Rodin) 421
Thirteen Clocks, The (Thurber) 372
Thompson, Robert 318
Thomson, Charles Wyville **74**, 75
Thomson, James 360
Thomson, J. J. 256–7, 300, 302, 311
Thor 399
Thoreau, Henry David 366
Thoth 393
Three Musketeers, The (Dumas) 364, **364**
Threepenny Opera, The (Brecht) 370
Three Tahitians (Gauguin) **487**
Through the Looking Glass (Carroll) 366
Thucydides 345
Thunder 80, 294
Thurber, James 372
Thyristor 304
Tiamat 392–3
Tibetan monasteries **407**
Ticks 207
Tidal waves, see Tsunami
Tides 74, 110
Tiffany, Louis 486
Tiger 228, **229**
Tiger, Chinese bronze **441**
Till Eulenspiegel (Richard Strauss) 513
Timber 179–80, **180–1**
Time 244, 258–62
Times, The 371, 477
Timpani **514–5**
Tin 65
Tinguely, Jean 492
Tintoretto 462, 468, 473
Tirthankaras 407
Titan 113
Titian 462, 468
Titov, Herman 131
Titus 444
Toads 186, 211
Toadstools **156–7**
Tobacco 182
Tolpuddle martyrs 34–5
Tolstoy, Leo 368
T-O maps **88**, 89
Tom Jones (Fielding) 361
Tompion, Thomas 262
Tom Sawyer (Twain) 366–7
Tom Thumb (Grimm) **363**
Tonic sol-fa 496
Tools of early man 243
Tornadoes 79
Torres, Luis Vaez de 84
Torres Strait 84
Torricelli, Evangelista 316
Tortoise 212–4
Tosca (Puccini) 512
Totemism 390
Totem pole **390**
Toucan **223**
Toulouse-Lautrec, Henri 486
Tower Bridge, London **286**
Tower of Babel 442
Tower of London 9, **449**
Town planning 43
Toy theatre **383**
Trachodon 195
Trade Unions 34–5
Trade winds 77
Trafalgar, Battle of 22
Trafalgar Square, London **28**, 68
Trajan 445
Trajan's column 445
Transformer, Electric 318
Transistor 304, 318
Transistorised telephone **299**
Transistor radio 304, **305**
Transmigration 401–2
Transparent Construction (Pasmore) **492**
Transplant surgery 334–5
Transportation **32**, 33, 35
Traps 248
Traveller's tree **166**
Travels in the Interior of Africa (Park) 85
Treasure Island (Stevenson) 366
Treatise (Hume) 429
Treatise on the Dance (Blasis) 525
Tree Frog, East African **211**
Très Riches Heures du Duc de Berry (Limbourg) **455**
Trevi fountains **468**
Trevithick, Richard **41**, 318
Trevithick steam locomotive **41**
Trial by battle 29, **29**
Trial by jury 30, **31**
Trial by ordeal 29
Trial, The (Kafka) 371
Triangle **514**
Triangulation 90
Triassic period 54–5, **149**, 192–3
Triassochelys 193
Triceratops **192**, 195
Trieste **74**, 75
Trilobites 57, 89, **189**, 192
Trinity, The 416
Triode valve 302
Tristram Shandy (Sterne) 361
Tristan and Isolde (Wagner) 511
Tristan da Cunha 71
Troilus and Cressida (Chaucer) 353
Trois Frères, cave 388
Trollope, Anthony 366
Trombone **514–5**
Tropical diseases 332
Tropic of Cancer 103
Tropic of Capricorn 103
Trotula 323
Troubadours 350, **351**, 352, 497
Trouvères 350
Trovatore, Il (Verdi) 512
Trumpet **514–5**
Tsetse Fly 199, 204
Tsiolkovsky, Konstantin 129
Tsunami 61, 75
Tuatara 212, **213**
Tuba **514–5**
Tudor kings 20–1
Tull, Jethro 318
Tumbelweed **173**
Tuning fork **280**, 281, 318
Turbine, Stream 272
Turbo-jet engine 276
Turbo-prop engine 276
Turgenev, Ivan 368
Turner, Joseph 435, 478–9
Turritella **53**
Turtles 193, 195, 199, 212–4
Twain, Mark (Samuel Langhorne, Clemens) 366, **367**
Twelfth Night (Shakespeare) 356
Twickenham, Pope's villa **360**
Twig gods (German) **399**
Two Gentlemen of Verona (Shakespeare) 356
Two Treatises on Government (Locke) 429
Tycho 109
Tyler, Wat 44
Tyndale, William 45, 355
Typewriter 318, **318**
Typhoons 79
Tyr 399
Tyrannosaurus **192**, 195

Uccello, Paolo 458–7
Ugly Duckling, The (Andersen) 369
Uintacyon **57**
Uintatherium 196, **197**
Ulfilas, Bishop 348
Ultrasonis 283
Ultra-violet light 306
Ultra-violet rays 77
Ulysses (Joyce) 371
Umayyad mosque, Cordoba **467**
Umbelliferae 177
Umbrella 318, **318**
Umbriel (satellite) 111
Uncle Remus (Harris) 366
Uncle Vanya (Chekhov) 369
Underwater exploration 76–7
Underwater 'house' **76**
Ungulates 231–4
Union Jack **14**, 46
Unité d'Habitation (Le Corbusier) 491
United Kingdom 9, 11–3, 46, 48
Universe, Origin of 127
Upanishads 401–2
Uraniborg **109**
Uranium 51–2, 235, 238, 255, 311–4
Uranus 110–1, **110–1**, 113–4, 125
Uranus spacecraft probes 142
Ur, cart wheel **247**
Urn Burial (Browne) 359
Ursa Major (constellation) 118
Ur, ziggrat of **392**
Uses of plants 176
Usher, James 51
Utilitarianism 429
Utrecht Psalter 448
Utu 391

Vaccination 318, 330–1
Vacuum 265
Vacuum electric discharge tube **300**
Vacuum flask 318
Valéry, Paul 373
Valois, Ninette de 528
Vanity Fair (Thackeray) 365
Varèse, Edgar 517
Variable stars 117, 124
Vase, Greek **395**
Vauxhall Gardens **502–3**
VDU, see Visual display unit
Vedanta 402
Vega 86
Vega, Lope de 354, 378
Vegetable spirits (Galen) 322
Veins on leaves 168
Velasquez, Diego 473, 484–5
Velocipede **278**
Velocity 278–9
Vendramin Family, The (Titian) **462**
Venezuela 83–4
Venice **435**, 458–9, 462
Venice, from the Canale Della Guidecca (Turner) **435**
Venice Preserv'd (play) **379**
Venus 101, **110–1**, 111–2, 114
Venus fly trap **174**
Venus of Willendorf figure **388**
Venus, spacecraft probes 141–2
Verdi, Giuseppe 512, **512**
Verein für Raumschiffart (VfR) 130
Verlaine, Paul 364
Vermeer, Jan 473
Verne, Jules 114
Veronese, Paolo 462–3
Verrocchio 250
Versailles, Palace of 470, **470**, 474
Versailles, Treaty of 46–7
Vertebrata, see Vertebrates
Vertebrates 186, **186–7**, 189, 191, 196, 202, 208–40
Vesalius, Andreas 324, **325**
Vespasian 445
Vespucci, Amerigo 83
Vesta (asteroid) 114, 397
Vestal Virgins **397**, 398
Vesta, Temple of **397**, 398
Vestris, Gaetano 523
Vestris, Marie Auguste 523–4
Vesuvius 71
Vibration 279–81
Vicar of Wakefield, The (Goldsmith) 361
Vickers Supermarine *Spitfire* **292**
Victoria Falls 86
Victoria, queen of England **21**, **34**, 46–7
Victoria (ship) **290**
Victory (ship) **290**
Vicuna 233
Video tape recorder 306
Vigano, Salvatore 524
Vigny, Alfred de 363–4
Viking Landers 1 and *2* 142
Viking longship **290**
Vikings 11–2
Villa Capra **463**
Villa Savoye **491**
Villon, François 353
Vinegar 158
Vineyards 178, **179**
Vinland map 82
Viol 498, 500
Viola **514–5**
Violin **514–5**
Violin, by Stradivari **501**
Viper **230**
Virchow, Rudolph 331
Virgil 347, **347**, 352, 359
Virginal **498**
Virginia 45
Virgo (constellation) **118**
Viruses 158, 333
Vishnu **401**, 403
Visible light 305
Visual Display Unit 308
Vitalist school of medicine 328–9
Vital spirits (Galen) 322, 330
Vitamins 176–7
Vita Nuova (Dante) 352

Vitruvius 436
Vivaldi, Antonio 500, 503
Vogelweide, Walther von der 497
Volcanoes 59, 60–1, **61**, 63, **70**, 71
Voles 226
Vollis Marineris 113
Volpone (Jonson) 357
Volta, Alessandro 295, 317
Voltaire **360**, 361, 380, 503
Volta's pile 295
Volt (electrical unit) 295–6
Voltmeters 299
Von Guericke's Magdeburg experiment **253**
Von Guericke's air thermoscope **253**
Voshkod 1 131
Voshkod 2 131–2
Vostok 1 131, **133**
Vostok 2 131
Votes for women 47
Voyager 1 and *2* 142
Voysey, C. F. 486
V-2 rocket 130, **130**

WAC Corporal 130
Wace, Robert 351
Waders 220
Wagner, Richard 380, 497, 509–13, **510**, 515–6
Wakan 389–90
Waldstein, Count 506
Wales 9, 11–13, 48
Wales, Prince of 43, 47
Wales, Princes of 11, 44
Wales, Princess of 43, 47
Walker, John 317
Walk in space 131–2, **131**
Wallace, Alfred Russel 85, 187, **189**
Wallace, William 11, 44
Wall painting, Egyptian **393**
Walpole, Sir Robert 46
Walrus 230, **230**
Walton, Ernest 313
Walton, Frederick 317
Walton, William 517
Waltz, The 512, **520**, 521
War and Peace (Tolstoy) 368, **368–9**
Warbeck, Perkin 45
War dances 519
Warner brothers 306
War of Independence, American 46
Warrior's Leavetaking, The 443
Wars of the Roses 45, 355
Warthog 234, **235**
Washing machine 318
Washington, George 470, 476
Wasps 203
Watches 261, **262**, 318
Water 251, 253
Water beneath the ground 68, **69**
Water clock **258–9**, 261
Water colour 438
Waterfalls 66
Water lilies 173, **173**
Waterloo, Battle of 33, 46
Water Music, The (handel) 503
Water plants 173
Water pollination 172
Water raising machine 270–1
Water Vole 227
Watson, Dr 372
Watson, Thomas A. 298
Watson-Watt, Robert 303, 318
Watteau, Antoine 470–1
Watt, James 24, 271–2, **279**, 310, 311, 318
Watt's 'sun and planet' engine **279**
Watt, unit of power 279
Waugh, Evelyn 371
Wavelengths **301**, 302
Waverley, Edward 365
Waverley (Scott) **365**
Waves 75, 280
Wealth of Nations (Smith) 477
Weasel family 230
Weather 76
Weather forecasting 80
Weather forecasting instruments **80**
Weather maps 78
Weather satellites 80, 139
Weaving 442
Webb, Philip 480
Weber, Carl Maria von 511
Webern, Anton 517
Webster, John 357
Wedmore, Treaty of 44
Weelkes, Thomas 499
Weightlessness 135, **135**
Weimar Court Theatre 380
Welfare State in Britain 28, 31–2
Wellington, Duke of 46
Wells 68
Wells, H. G. 372
Welwyn Garden City 42
Wembley Exhibition 47
Wesley brothers 46
Wesley, John **417**
Wessex, Kingdom of 44
West, Benjamin 476
Westerlies 77
Western music 494–6
Western Union Co. 299
West Indies 83
Westminster Abbey 454
West Side Story 528
Weyden, Rogier van der 455
Weyer, Johann 335
Whale, Blue 183–4, **184**, 226, 236–7
Whale, Sperm 183, 236
Whales 236–7
Whales, baleen 185
Wheat **176**
Wheatstone, Charles **297**, 316, 318
Wheatstone's five needle telegraph **297**
Wheel, The 247–8, **247**
Whispering gallery, St Paul's Cathedral **281**
Whistler, James McNeill 484–6
Whitby, Synod of 44
White Devil, The (Webster) 357
White dwarf (stars) 127
White, Edward **131**, 132
White Fang (London) 366
Whitehead, A. N. 432
White horse, Uffington **399**
Whitman, Walt 366, 488
Whitney, Eli 317
Whittier, John Greenleaf 366
Whittle, Frank 276, 317
Wilberforce, William 34
Wilbye, John 499
Wild Cats 228
Wildebeest 233
Wilde, Oscar 369
Wild life preservation **183**
Wild West shows 386
Wilhelm Meister (Goethe) 362
Wilhelm Tell (Schiller) 362
William I (the Conqueror), king of England **12**, 13–14, **20**, 44, 46, 115
William II, king of England **20**
William III, king of England **20**, 21
William IV, king of England **21**
William, prince of England 47
Williams, Ralph Vaughan 514
Williams, Tennessee 370
Willis, Thomas 327–8
Willoughby, Hugh 83
Wills, William 86, **86**
Winchester 44
Winchester Cathedral 496
Winckelmann, J. J. 477
Wind instruments 494, **514–15**
Wind in the Willows, The (Grahame) 372, **373**
Windlass 249
Wind pollination 172
Winds 70, 75, 79
Windsor, Duke of, see Edward VIII
Windsor Forest (Pope) 360
Windsor House of 21
Wine 178–9, **179**
Wings of a Dove, The (James) 367
Winnie the Pooh (Milne) 372
Winnower, The (Millet) 482
Winter solstice 106
Winter's Tale, The (Shakespeare) 356
Wireless messages, First 301
Wireless telegraphy 318
Witch-doctors 390
Wittgenstein, Ludwig 432
Wolhltemperierte Klavier, Das (Bach) 501
Wolf 229
Wolf, Hugo 508
Wolsey, Thomas 45, 355
Wolverine 230
Woman in space, First 131, **133**
Woman Weeping (Picasso) **490**
Wombat, Common **225**
Wood 179–80, **180–1**
Wood, Alexander 317
Wood-burning locomotive **273**
Woodcuts 439, 456
Woodland plants 148
Wood pulp 181
Wood Sawyers, The (Millet) **482**
Woodworm, see Furniture beetle
Woolf, Virginia 371
Woolly Mammoth 187–8, 198, **198**
Works and Days (Hesiod) 343
Wordsworth, William 362, 366
World as Will and Idea, The (Schopenhauer) 430
World Council of Churches 417
World in space, The 99
World of animals, The 183
World of art and architecture, The 435
World of literature and drama, The 339
World of music and the dance, The 493
World of plants, The 147
World of religion and philosophy, The 387
World of science and invention, The 243
World we live in, The 51
Worms **187**, 200, **200**
Wotan 399
Wozzeck (Berg) 517
Wracks (seaweed) 156
Wren, Christopher **42**, 327, 329, 474–5
Wright brothers 292, 316
Wright, Frank Lloyd 488–9, 491
Wuthering Heights (Brontë) 365
Wyatt, Thomas 355
Wycherley, William 359, 379
Wyclif, John 44
Wyndham, John 372

Xenophanes 396
Xenusion 189
Xerophytes 173–4
X-rays 255, 300–1, **301**, 306, 315, 333
X-ray tube 318

Yeast 156, 179
Yeats, William Butler 373
Yellow Book, The **487**
Yellow-necked Mouse 227
Yerkes observatory telescope **117**
Yeti, or Abominable snowman 238
Yggdrasil 399
Yoga 403
York, House of 20
Young, Thomas 301
Ysengrin 351

Zarathustra 410
Zealots 413
Zebra 231, **234**
Zen Buddhism 406
Zeno of Elea 423, **423**
Zeppelin, Ferdinand von 316
Zeppelins 292, **292–3**
Zeus 319, 395–7, 401
Ziggurats 392, **392**, 442
Zinc 65
Zionism 413
Zip fastener 318
Zodiac ceiling (Dendera) **101**
Zodiac, The 101, 118, 123
Zola, Emile 364, 366, 488
Zond spacecraft 132
Zoology 149
Zoraster, see Zarathustra
Zoroastrianism 409–10
Zulu War 47
Zworykin, Vladimir 302–3, 317

Acknowledgements

The publishers are grateful to the following:
Air Portraits, Birmingham, 245 top. Alte Pinakothek, Munich, 463 bottom, 471 right. Ampliacciones y Reproductiones Mas, Barcelona, 468 top. Antwerp Museum of Fine Arts, 439 left. Barber Institute of Fine Arts, University of Birmingham, 438 right, 471 left. Berner Kunstmuseum (Klee Foundation), 488 centre. British Leyland 310 top. Cathedral of St Bavon, Ghent, 455 left. Church of Santo Tome, Toledo, 468 top. Courtauld Institute Galleries, London 488 top. Mike Davis, London, 525 top. John R Freeman & Co. Ltd., London, 493. Gernsheim Collection, University of Texas, 489 top right. Girauldon, Paris, 455, 476 top. Glasgow Art Gallery & Museum, 439 centre. Glaxo Laboratories Ltd., Greenford, 333. Hamlyn Group, 12, 13, 450 right, 469 top right, 492 centre. Hotel Lauzun, Paris, 469 top right. Peter Jackson, London, 502. Edward James Foundation, 491 top. Kupferstichkabinett, Berlin, 438 centre. Lords Gallery, London, 439 right. Louvre, Paris, 458 left, 464 top, 472 top, 483 top, 484 top right, 484 centre, 484 bottom, 487 top right, 524 Mander & Mitchenson Theatre Collection, London, 379, 388 top. Musées des Arts Decoratifs, Paris, 480 bottom right. Musée Bayeux, 12, 13. Musée des Beaux Arts, Nantes, 523. Musée Condé, Chantilly, 455 right. Musée de l'Impressionnisme, Paris. 484 centre. Musée Jacquemart André, Paris, 438 left. Museo Nacional del Prado, Madrid, 476 top. Musée Toulouse Lautrec, Albi, 486 top. National Aeronautics & Space Administration, Washington D.C. 107 centre, 129 left, 131, 135 top, 135 bottom, 142 bottom, 144. National Gallery, London, 456, 462, 463 centre, 472 bottom, 473 top, 479, 497 top. National Gallery of Scotland, Edinburgh, 487 top left. Victor Pasmore, 492 centre, Sir Roland Penrose Collection, London, 490 left, Phillips Collection, Washington D.C., 478 top, 485 top, Photograph on a Kodak Film, 263. Picturepoint Ltd., London, 108, 144 bottom, Peter Roberts, London, 245 bottom. Royal Photographic Society, London, 489 bottom right. Scala, Florence, 451 top, 458 left, 459 top, 464 top right, 469 top left. Sloane Museum, London, 475 top. Tate Gallery, London, 478 bottom, 481, 482 top right, 484 top left, 485 bottom, 490 right, 491 top. Board of Trinity College, Dublin, 348. Victoria and Albert Museum, London, 435, 474 bottom, 480 bottom centre, 482 top left. Wallace Collection, London, 493. Reg Wilson, London, 528.